For She...
Wel...
o...

JEWISH TRAVEL GUIDE 2001

International Edition

Published in association with
the *Jewish Chronicle*, London

Editor
MICHAEL ZAIDNER

VALLENTINE MITCHELL
LONDON • PORTLAND, OR

First published in 2001 in Great Britain by
VALLENTINE MITCHELL & CO. LTD.
Newbury House, 900 Eastern Avenue
London IG2 7HH

and in the United States of America by
VALLENTINE MITCHELL
c/o ISBS,
5824 N.E. Hassalo Street
Portland, Oregon 97213-3644

ISBN 0 85303 414 1
ISSN 0075 3750

Printed in Great Britain by
Creative Print and Design (Wales), Ebbw Vale

Contents

Index to Advertisers

Editor's Note

The *Jewish Travel Guide 2001* has again been updated in order to ensure that the Jewish traveller is supplied with the most accurate information we are able to obtain. This year the layout has been improved in order to include even more information but still remain clear and legible to the reader.

As in previous years, each establishment listed in the Guide was sent a form containing the information held about it within our database. Any changes or errors that were notified to us were then incorporated in this new edition. One major problem, however, is that establishments can close down and we are not notified. Establishment that have not replied for a number of years are deleted unless, of course, we receive confirmation from some other source that they still exist.

A number of correspondents keep us in touch with certain important locations and we are always pleased to receive communications from readers of useful information which will help us to improve the guide.

Nevertheless, circumstances do continue to change and no responsibility can be accepted for any errors or omissions, or for any kashrut and other claims made by establishments listed in this guide.

Again, as in previous years, we must remind all readers that establishments may close down or cease to be kosher. It is therefore in the interest of travellers to consider checking by phone before arranging a particular visit. Nowhere is this more important than in central and eastern Europe where such changes can be particularly rapid.

Additionally, please be aware that telephone area codes are being constantly revised throughout the world. We have, of course, endeavoured to keep up to date with all such changes.

Following requests, the listing of Kosher fish has been greatly enlarged and is now listed on pages 385 to 388.

Finally, the editor wishes to thank Kim Knight for all her hard work and dedication to this project and to thank Barbara Kirby for her valuable assistance.

As in previous years, we have endeavoured to provide interesting as well as practical information for each location.

MICHAEL ZAIDNER
December 2000

Publisher's Note

WE NEED YOUR ASSISTANCE TO KEEP THIS GUIDE UP TO DATE

The editor and the publishers have made every effort to ensure that this guide is as accurate and up to date as possible.

As in previous years, an update forms is included the back of this book for those who become aware of additions they would like to be considered for inclusion. In addition, we would wish to be notified of any errors that may have occurred in the preparation of this book.

All information may be sent to us in London by post to our address

Newbury House
900 Eastern Avenue
London IG2 7HH

or by fax to 020 8599 0984. (Please note in this connection that handwritten items are not always legible when sent by fax.) Additionally, it may be sent by Email to jtg@vmbooks.com or to our website: www.vmbooks.com

Potential advertisers or those who wish to sell copies of the *Jewish Travel Guide* may also use any of the above means to contact us with their requirements.

Details of *The Jewish Year Book* and all other Vallentine Mitchell publications are also available on our website.

Albania

There have been Jews living on the territory now known as Albania since Roman times and there are remains in Dardania (in the north of the country) of an ancient synagogue. The community was re-established by Jews from Iberia escaping the Spanish Inquisition in the fifteenth and early sixteenth centuries.

The number of Jews in Albania never increased significantly, and, in 1930, there were only 204 Jews in the country. However, this number was soon augmented by refugees escaping the Nazis. The local population was not, on the whole, hostile to the Jews and helped most of them to hide during the war when Italy, and then Germany, occupied the country.

The strict communist regime which followed the war led to the isolation of the Jewish community until the fall of communism. In 1991, almost the entire community, about 300, was airlifted to Israel. The few Jews who remained in Albania live in the capital, Tirana.

The Albanian-Israel Friendship Society will be happy to provide any further information.

GMT + 1 hour
Country calling code (355)
Total Population 3,420,000
Jewish Population Under 100
Emergency Telephone (Police - 24445) (Fire - 23333) (Ambulance - 22235)
Electricity Voltage 220

Tirana

Contact Information
Albanian-Israel Friendship Society
Rruga 'Barrikatave' 226   (42) 22611

Algeria

Jews first settled in Algeria soon after the start of the diaspora following the destruction of the Second Temple. A later influx occurred when Jews were escaping from Visigothic Spain.

In the twelfth and thirteenth centuries, Islamic conversion was forced on the Jews. Many Jews, however, crossed the Mediterranean from Spain during the time of the Inquisition, and these included some famous scholars. In 1830 the French occupied the country and, in due course, granted the Jews French citizenship.

Algerian Jews suffered anti-semitism from both the local Muslim population and the wartime Vichy government. After the Allied landings in 1942, the anti-Jewish laws were slowly lifted. In the late 1950s, 130,000 Jews lived in Algeria, but after the civil war, which led to independence from France in 1962, most of the community moved to France, with some to Israel, leaving very few behind. The present-day community, centred in Algiers, has a synagogue but no resident rabbi.

GMT + 1 hour
Country calling code (213)
Electricity voltage 110/220
Total Population 28,566,000
Jewish Population Under 100

Algiers

Representative Organisations
Association Consistoriale Israélite d'Alger
6 rue Hassena Ahmed   (2) 62-85-72

Synagogues
6 rue Hassena Ahmed   (2) 62-85-72

Blida

Representative Organisations
Consistoire d'Algerie
29 rue des Martyrs   (3) 49-26-57

Andorra

Andorra, which is governed by two co-princes: the Bishop of Urgel in Spain and the President of France, does not have a Jewish history.

There are currently however around 15 Jewish families.

A synagogue was established in 1997 in Escaldes and is the first in Andorra's 1,100-year history.

While its liturgy leans towards Sephardism it is also influenced by its Ashkenazi members. There is a community centre in Escaldes.

GMT + 1 hour	Total Population 64,000
Country calling code (376)	Jewish Population Under 100
Emergency Telephone (Police - 825 225) (Fire and Ambulance - 118)	

Contact Information
Dr David ben-Chayil or Dr David Bezold
Francesco B.P. 244, Andorra la Vella
                                        333 567
                    Email: bezold@andorra.ad
For visits to the synagogue contact Isaac Benisty
Telephone 860 758

The first Jewish arrivals (Conversos, or 'secret Jews') came in the sixteenth and seventeenth centuries from Portugal and Spain. They assimilated quickly. A more significant Jewish immigration occurred in the middle of the nineteenth century, from western Europe, and at the end of the nineteenth century many Jews arrived from eastern Europe, taking advantage of the 'open-door' policy towards immigrants. The new arrivals set up some Jewish agricultural settlements, under the auspices of the Alliance Israelita Universelle, and on the whole mixed with the local population.

The largest Jewish community is in Buenos Aires, with smaller communities in provincial centres. There are also some Jewish families remaining in the Jewish agricultural colonies, with Moiseville, Rivera and General Roca being the three most important.

There are Jewish newspapers, restaurants and other institutions. The Delegation of Argentine Jewish Associations (DAIA) represents all Jewish organisations at a political level.

GMT - 3 hours	Total Population 34,995,000
Country calling code (54)	Jewish Population 300,000
Emergency Telephone (Police - 101) (Fire - 100) (Ambulance - 107)	
Electricity voltage 226	

Bahia Blanca

Contact Information
Beit Jabad Bahia Blanca
C.C. 405 8000   (291) 36582

Buenos Aires

The first recorded Jewish event in Buenos Aires was a wedding in 1860. Around 220,000 Jews live in Buenos Aires. There are fifty or so synagogues in the city and kosher food is widely available. The most interesting synagogues for visitors are in Once although fewer Jews live there now.

Bakeries
Confitería Aielet
Aranguren 2911, Flores   (11) 637-5419
Confitería Ganz
Paso 752, Once   (11) 961-6918

Argentina

Confitería Helueni
Tucumán 2620, Once   (11) 961-0541
Confitería Mari Jalabe
Bogota 3228, Flores   (11) 612-6991
Panadería Malena
Av. Pueyrredón 880, Once   (11) 962-6290

Booksellers
Ediciones del Seminario Rabínico Latinoamericano
José Hernandez 1750, Belgrano 1426 (11) 4783-2009
Fax: (11) 4781-4056
Email: srlatino@uole.com
Kehot Lubavitch Sudamericana
San Luis 3281 1186   (11) 865-0625
Fax: (11) 865-0625
Email: kehot@iname.com
Web site: www.kehot-lubavitch.com.ar
Librería Editorial Sigal
Av. Corrientes 2854 1193
(11) 861-9501; 865-7208; 962-1131
Fax: (11) 962-7931; 865-7208
Email: lib-sigal@cybergal.com
Web site: www. libreria-sigal.com

Contact Information
Asociacion Shuva Israel
Paso 557, Once   (11) 962-6255
Beit Jabad Belgrano
O'Higgins 2358, Belgrano 1428   (11) 781-3848
Beit Jabad Villa Crespo
Serrano 69   (11) 855-9822
Chabad Lubavitch Argentina
Agüero 1164, Flores 1425   (11) 963-1221
Congregacion Israelita de la Republica Argentina
Libertad 785, Centro
(11) 4372-2474/4371-8929/4374-7955/4372-0014
Fax: (11) 4372-2474
The total number of synagogues in Buenos Aires where
there is a minyan at least Friday night and Shabbat
morning exceeds fifty. Call any of the above numbers
to locate the synagogue nearest you.
Jabad Lubavich La Plata
Calle 50 No. 463 1900   (11) 25-8304
Kehot Lubavich
S. Luis 3281 1186   (11) 865-0629

Embassy
Embassy of Israel
Avenida de Mayo 701-10° 1084   (11) 4345-6207/08
Fax: (11) 4345-6207
Email: cidipal@israel-embassy.org.ar

Groceries
Almacén Behar
Campana 347, Flores   (11) 613-2033
Almacén Shalom
San Luis 2513, Once   (11) 962-3685

Autoservicio Ezra
Ecuador 619, Once   (11) 963-7062
Autoservicio Siman Tov
Helguera 474, Flores   (11) 611-4746
Azulay, Helguera 507, Flores
Battías, Paso 706, Once
Kahal Jaredim
Argerich 386, Flores   (11) 612-4590
Kaler, San Luis 2810, Once
Kol Bo Brandsen
Brandsen 1389, Barracas
Kol Bo I, Ecuador 855, Once   (11) 961-3838
Kol Bo II, Viamonte 2537, Once   (11) 961-2012
Kosher Delights
La Pampa 2547, Belgrano   (11) 788-3150
La Esquina Casher
Aranguren 2999, Flores   (11) 637-3706
La Quesería, Viamonte 2438, Once   (11) 961-3171
La Tzorja, Ecuador 673, Once   (11) 961-1096
Yehuda Kosher Foods
Moldes 2452, Belgrano   (11) 637-1465

Kashrut Information
The Central Rabbinate of the Vaad Hakehillot
Ecuador 1110, Once   (11) 961-2944
The Orthodox Ashkenazi Chief Rabbi of Argentina is
Rabbi Shlomo Benhamu Anidjar.

Libraries
Sociedad Hebraica Argentino
Sarmiento 2233   (11) 952-5570
Also has art gallery.
YIVO Library, Pasteur 633, Third floor   (11) 45-2474

Media

Newspapers
Comunidades
Die Presse
Kesher Kehilari

La Voz Judia
Mundo Israelita

Nueva Sion

Mikvaot
Helguera 270, Once   (11) 612-0410
Moldes 2431, Belgrano   (11) 4786-8046
Email: ajdut@netcomputer.com.ar

Museums
Museo Judio de Buenos Aires
Libertad 769   (11) 372-2474;0014
Fax: (11) 372-2474
Email: adaszko@mail.retina.ar.
Hours: Tuesday and Thursday 4pm to 7pm.

Argentina

Representative Organisations

AMIA (Central Ashkenazi community)
Pasteur 633   (11) 953-9777; 953-2862
The community centre has now been reopened
following the terror bomb attack in 1994
Asociacion Israelita Sefaradi Argentina (AISA)
Paso 493   (11) 952-4707
DAIA (Political representative body of Argentine Jewry)
Pasteur 633, Fifth floor   (11) 953-5380; 953-5394
Vaad Hakehillot
Pasteur 633, Second floor   (11) 953-9777; 953-2862

Restaurants

Confiterie Helueni
Tucuman 2620, Once   (11) 961-0541

Dairy

Soultani Café
San Luis 2601, Once   (11) 961-3913

Meat

Al Galope, Tucumán 2633, Once   (11) 963-6888
McDonald's, Shopping Abasto, (Corrientes and
Anchorena), Once
Supervision: Rav Oppenheimer - Ajdut Israel.
There are two McDonalds. Only one is kosher.

Synagogues

Ashkenazi Orthodox

Baron Hirsh, Billinghurst 664   (11) 862-2624
Bet Rajel, Ecuador 522   (11) 862-2701
Brit Abraham, Antezana 145   (11) 855-6567
Etz Jaim, Julian Alvarez 745   (11) 772-5324
Sinagoga Israelita Lituana
Jose Evaristo Uriburu 348   (11) 952-7968
Torah Vaaboda
Julian Alvarez 667   (11) 854-0462
Zijron le David
Azcuenaga 736   (11) 953-0200

Conservative

Beit Hilel, Araoz 2854, Palermo   (11) 804-2286
Colegio Wolfson, Comunidad Or-El
Amenabar 2972   (11) 544-5461
Comunidad Bet El
Sucre 3338   (11) 552-2365
Dor Jadash, Murillo 649, Villa Crespo (11) 854-4467
Nueva Comunidad Israelita
Arcos 2319   (11) 781-0281
Or Jadash, Varela 850, Flores   (11) 612-1171
Templo la Paz (Chalom)
Olleros 2876   (11) 552-6730

German Orthodox

Ajdut Yisroel
Moldes 2449   (11) 4783-2831
                      Fax: (11) 4781-6725
              Email: ajdut@netcomputer.com.ar

Progressive

Benei Tikva, Vidal 2049   (11) 795-0380

Reform

Templo Emanu-El
Tronador 1455   (11) 552-4343
                              Fax: (11) 4555-4004
              Email: kol_emanuel@name.com

Sephardi Orthodox

Aderet Eliahu
Ruy Diaz de Guzman 647   (11) 302-9306
Agudat Dodim, Avellaneda 2874   (11) 611-0056
Bajurim Tiferet Israeil
Helguera 611   (11) 611-3376
Comunidad Sefaradi de Buenos Aires
Camargo 870   (11) 4855-9645
                              Fax: (11) 4855-9377
              Email: acisba@continuidad.ar
Etz Jaim, Carlos Calvo 1164   (11) 302-6290
Jaike Grimberg
Campana 460   (11) 672-2347
Kehal Jaredim
Helguera 270, Once   (11) 612-0410
Od Yosef Jai, Tucuman 3326   (11) 963-2349
Or Misraj, Ciudad de la Paz 2555 (11) 784-5945
Shaare Sion, Helguera 453   (11) 4637-5897
                              Fax: (11) 4637-1301
              Email: editorial@shaaresion.org.ar
              Web site: www.shaaresion.org.ar
Shaare Tefila
Paso 733   (11) 962-2865
Shalom, Olleros 2876   (11) 552-2720
Shuba Israel, Ecuador 627   (11) 862-0562
Sinagoga Rabino Zeev Gringberg
Canalejas 3047   (11) 611-3366
Sucath David, Paso 724   (11) 962-1091
                              Fax: (11) 962-1264
              Email: perspect@satlink.com
              Web site: www.judaicasite.com
Yeshurun, Republica de la India 3035 (11) 802-9310
Yesod Hadat, Lavalle 2449   (11) 961-1615

Concordia

Contact Information

Beit Jabad Concordia
Entre Rios 212 3200   (45) 21-1934
                              Fax: (45) 21-7898

Cordoba

Contact Information
Jabad Lubavitch Cordoba
Sucre 1380, Barrio Cofico 5000   (351) 71-0223

Groceries
Almacén, Sucre 1378, Barrio Cofico 5000
(351) 71-0223

Rosario

Contact Information
Beit Jabad Rosario
S. Lorenzo 1882 P.A. 2000   (341) 25-2899

Groceries
La Granja Kasher
Montevideo 1833   (341) 49-6210

Tucuman

Contact Information
Beit Jabad Tucuman
Lamadrid 752 4000   (381) 248892
Fax: (381) 248893
Email: jabadtucuman@amet.com.ar

Groceries
Almacén y Carnicería
9 de Julio 625   (381) 31-0227
Beit Jabad Tucuman
Lamadrid 752 4000   (381) 248892
Fax: (381) 248893
Email: jabadtucuman@amet.com.ar

Australia

The first Jews in Australia arrived with the first convict ships from the United Kingdom in 1788 and regular, organised worship started in the 1820s. The first free Jewish settler arrived with her husband, a deported convict, in 1816. The community grew in the nineteenth century, with the first synagogue being established in the mid-1840s. Events such as the Australian gold rush and pogroms in eastern Europe were catalysts for more Jewish immigration.

The Jewish contribution to Australian life has been prominent, with the commander of the ANZAC forces in the First World War being a practising Jew, Sir John Monash. The twentieth century saw some 7,000 Jewish refugees from Nazi Europe settling in Australia, and the community contains the largest percentage of Holocaust survivors in the world. They are a major influence on the present community, which is expanding and comparatively religious. There have also been two Jewish governors-general.

The community is led by the Executive Council of Australian Jewry. Seventy-five per cent of primary and fifty-five per cent of secondary Jewish school children attend Jewish schools and there is a low level of inter-marriage. Melbourne has the largest community (42,000), with 35,000 in Sydney. There are Jewish newspapers, radio programmes of Jewish interest and museums on Jewish themes.

GMT + 7 to 10 hrs	Total Population 18,287,000
Country calling code (61)	Jewish Population 100,000
Emergency Telephone (Police, Fire and Ambulance - 000)	Electricity voltage 240/250

Australian Capital Territory

Canberra

Embassy
Embassy of Israel
6 Turrana Street, Yarralumla 2600   (262) 73-1309
Fax: (262) 73-4279
Email: israel.aust@embassy.net.au

Synagogues
The A.C.T. Jewish Community Synagogue
National Jewish Memorial Centre, cnr Canberra Ave &
National Circuit, Forrest 2603   (262) 951-052
Fax: (262) 958-608
Postal address: POB 3105, Manuka 2603

Australia/New South Wales

New South Wales

Newcastle

Synagogues
122 Tyrrell Street 2300   (49) 26-2820
Contact: Dr L.E. Fredman, 123 Dawson St, Cooks Hill, 2300 N.S.W.

Sydney

The first Jewish convict settlers were generally illiterate in both English and Hebrew, and there was no Jewish organisation until a Chevrah Kadishe was formed in 1817.

Most of Sydney's Jews are now settled outside the city in two suburban areas: the eastern suburbs including Bondi and the North Shore.

Bakeries
Carmel Cake Shop
14 O'Brien Street, Bondi
Supervision: NSW Kashrut Authority.

Booksellers
Gold's World of Judaica
9 O'Brien Street, Bondi 2026   (2) 9300-0495
Fax: (2) 9389-7345
Email: goldsyd@matra.com.au
Shalom Gift and Book Shop
323 Pacific Highway, Lindfield 2070   (2) 9416-7076
Fax: (2) 9416-7076

Butchers
Eilat, 173 Bondi Road, Bondi   (2) 9387-8881
Supervision: NSW Kashrut Authority.
Hadassa, 17 O'Brien Street, Bondi   (2) 9365-4904
Fax: (2) 9130-4760
Supervision: NSW Kashrut Authority.

Embassy
Consul General of Israel
37 York Street, Level 6 2000   (2) 9264-7933
Fax: (2) 9290-2259
Email: israsyd@acon.com.au

Hospitals
Wolper Jewish Hospital
8 Trelawney Street, Woollahra   (2) 9328-6077

Kashrut Information
Kosher Consumer Association
(2) 9337-6657
Fax: (2) 9371-0348

NSW Kashrut Authority
PO Box 7206, Bondi Beach 2026   (2) 9365-2933
Fax: (2) 9365-0933
Email: rabbig@ka.org.au
Web site: www.ka.org.au

Media

Newspapers
Australian Jewish News
146 Darlinghurst Road, Darlinghurst 2010
(2) 9360-5100
Fax: (2) 9332-4207

Mikvaot
117 Glenayr Avenue, Bondi   (2) 9130-2509

Museums
Sydney Jewish Museum
148 Darlinghurst Road, Darlinghurst 2010
(2) 9360-7999
Fax: (2) 9331-4245
Email: sydjmus@tmx.mhs.oz.au
Kosher restaurant (Dairy) on site.

Religious Organisations
Sydney Beth Din
166 Castlereagh Street, NSW 2000   (2) 9267-2477
Fax: (2) 9264-8871
Email: admin@greatsynagogue.org.au

Representative Organisations
Executive Council of Australian Jewry
146 Darlinghurst Road, Second floor,
Darlinghurst 2010   (2) 9360-5415
Fax: (2) 9360-5416
Email: ecaj@tig.com.au

Restaurants

Dairy

Toovya the Milkman
379 Old South Head Road, North Bondi 2026
(2) 9130-4016
Supervision: NSW Kashrut Authority.
Not Cholov Yisrael. Vegetarian and vegan food. Eat in or take away. Delivery to eastern suburbs, including to hotel room. Hours: Sunday to Thursday, 5 pm to 10 pm; Saturday, after Shabbat to midnight. Nearest metro: 387 bus from Bondi junction to the door.
Toovya's Kosher Pizza
379 Old South Head Road, N. Bondi   (2) 9130-4016
Supervision: NSW Kashrut Authority.

Yabba, 50 Mitchell St, N Bondi 2026   (2) 9365-0600

Meat

Beaches Kosher Restaurant
11 O'Brien Street 2026   (2) 9365-5544
NSW Kashrut Authority
Café Maccabee
Corner Darlinghurst and Burton Street, Darlinghurst
Lewis' Continental Kitchen
2 Curlewis Street, Bondi 2026   (2) 9365-5421
Fax: (2) 9300-0037
Email: lewis@acon.com.au
Web site: www.acon.com.au/lewis
Supervision: NSW Kashrut Authority Inc..
Glatt kosher. Sunday to Friday.
Savion Restaurant
38 Wairoa Ave   (2) 9130-6357
Supervision: NSW Kashrut Authority.
The Pie Factory
Hall Street, Bondi Beach   (2) 9130-6743
Fax: (2) 91306742
Supervision: NSW Kashrut Authority.
Also take away.
Tibby's Continental Restaurant
Cnr. Campbell Parade & Francis Street
(2) 9130-5051
Supervision: NSW Kashrut Authority.
Tibby's Kosher Restaurant at Jaffa
61-67 Hall Street, Bondi Beach 2026   (2) 9130-5051
Supervision: NSW Kashrut Authority.
Open Saturday to Thursday for dinner. Continental,
Chinese, Sephardi and Israeli food. Glatt kosher.

Synagogues
Adath Yisroel
243 Old South Head Road, Bondi   (2) 9300-9447
Central Synagogue
15 Bon-Accord Avenue, Bondi Junction
(2) 9389-5622
Coogee Synagogue
121 Brook Street, Coogee   (2) 9315-8291
Cremorne & District
12a Yeo Street, Neutral Bay   (2) 9908-1853
Fax: (2) 9908-1852
Great Synagogue
166 Castlereagh Street   (2) 9267-2477
Fax: (2) 9264-8871
Email: admin@greatsynagogue.org.au
Houses the Rabbi L.A. Falk Memorial Library and the
A.M. Rosenblum Jewish Museum.
Illawarra Synagogue
502 Railway Parade, Allawah   (2) 9587-5643
Email: georgefoster1@compuserve.com

Kehillat Masada
9-15 Link Road, St Ives 2075   (2) 9988-4417
Fax: (2) 9449-3897
Email: kmasada@one.net.au
Maroubra Synagogue (K.M.H.C.)
635 Anzac Parade, Maroubra 2035   (2) 9344-6095
Fax: (2) 9344-4298
Email: maroubrasyn@bigpond.com
Mizrachi, 339 Old South Head Road, Bondi
(2) 9130-7221
Fax: (2) 9130-7221
Email: mizrachisydney@bigpond.com
Postal address: Bondi Mizrachi Synagogue, 101/60
Blair Street, North Bondi, NSW 2026
North Shore Synagogue
15 Treatts Road, Lindfield   (2) 9416-3710
Fax: (2) 9416-7659
Paramatta Synagogue
116 Victoria Road, Paramatta   (2) 9683-5381
Sephardi Synagogue
40-42 Fletcher Street, Bondi Junction   (2) 9389-3355
Fax: (2) 9369-2143
Shearit Yisrael
146 Darlinghurst Road, Darlinghurst 2010
(2) 9365-8770
South Head & District Synagogue
666 Old South Head Road, Rose Bay   (2) 9371-7300
Fax: (2) 9371-7416
Email: admin@southhead.org
Strathfield & District Synagogue
19 Florence Street, Strathfield 2135   (2) 9642-3550
Fax: (2) 9642-4803
Western Suburbs Synagogue
20 Georgina Street, Newtown
Yeshiva 36 Flood Street, Bondi   (2) 9387-3822
Fax: (2) 9389-7652

Conservative
Temple Emanuel
7 Ocean Street, Woollahra 2025   (2) 9328-7833
Fax: (2) 9327-8715
Email: info@emanuel.org.au
Web site: www.emanuel.org.au
"Look forward to welcoming visitors from abroad".

Liberal
North Shore Temple Emanuel
28 Chatswood Avenue, Chatswood 2067
(2) 9419-7011
Fax: (2) 9413-1474
Email: nste@nste.org.au

Sefardim
Beth Yosef, Ground Floor, 243 Old South Head Road,
Bondi

Australia/New South Wales

Tour information

(2) 9328-7604

For information about tours of Jewish Sydney, contact the Great Synagogue at the number listed above or Karl Maehrischel at this number.

Queensland
Brisbane

Bakeries
Brumby's Bakery
408 Milton Road, Auchenflower 4066   (7) 3371-8744

Community Organisations
Jewish Communal Centre
2 Moxom Road, Burbank 4156   (7) 3349-9749

Mikvaot
Queensland Mikvah
46 Bunya Street, Greenslopes 4120   (7) 3848-5886

Religious Organisations
Brisbane Chevra Kadisha
242 Kingsford Smith Drive, Hamilton 4007
(7) 3262-6564
The number listed is Mr Philips' home number.
Chabad House of Queensland
43 Cedar Street, Greenslopes 4120   (7) 3848-5886
Fax: (7) 3848-5886
Email: kthomas@onenet.au

Synagogues
Brisbane Hebrew Congregation
98 Margaret Street 4000   (7) 3229-3412
South Brisbane Hebrew Congregation
46 Burya Street, Greenslopes 4120
(7) 3397-9025
Fax: (7) 3397-9025
Temple Shalom
13 Koolatah Street, Camp Hill 4152   (7) 3398-8843

Gold Coast

Bakeries
Goldstein's Bakery
509 Olsen Avenue, Ashmore City 4214
(7) 5539-3133
Fax: (7) 5597-1064
Supervision: Rabbi Gurevitch, Gold Coast Hebrew Congregation.
Under the umbrella of the NSW Kashrut Authority. Challah and kosher breads available at 14 stores along the Gold Coast, including Surfers Paradise shop (Tel) 5531-5808

Community Organisations
Association of Jewish Organisations
31 Ranock Avenue, Benown Waters 4217
(7) 5597-2222

Synagogues
Gold Coast Hebrew Congregation
34 Hamilton Avenue, Surfers Paradise 4215
(7) 5570-1851
Temple Shalom
25 Via Roma Drive, Isle of Capri 4217
(7) 5570-1716

South Australia
Adelaide

Bakeries
Bagel Boys
134 Goodwood Road 5034   (8) 8271-0818
Open 7 days.
Bakers Delight
Frewville Shopping Centre, Glen Osmond Road

Groceries
Kosher Imports
c/o Hebrew Congregation, 13 Flemington Street, Glenside 5065   (8) 9532-9994
Judaica and Kosher products available.

Synagogues

Orthodox

Adelaide Hebrew Congregation
13 Flemington Street, Glenside 5065   (8) 8338-2922
Fax: (8) 8379-0142
Mikva on premises. Mailing address: PO Box 320, Glenside 5065.

Progressive

Beit Shalom
41 Hackney Road, Hackney 5069   (8) 8362-8281
Fax: (8) 8362-4406
Email: bshalom@senet.com.au
Web site: www.user.senet.com.au/~bshalom
Mailing address: P.O.Box 47, Stepney 5069

Tasmania
Hobart

Contact Information
Jewish Centre
Chabad House, 93 Lord Street, Sandy Bay 7005
(3) 6223-7116
Fax: (3) 6223-7116
Contact in advance for Shabbat meals and Mikveh.

Synagogues

Progressive

Hobart Hebrew Congregation
PO Box 128B, Hobart 7000   (3) 6234-4720
Email: heards@bigpond.com
The oldest synagogue in Australia, having been consecrated 4 July 1845. Open 9.30 am and one Friday per month 6.15 pm. Other days by arrangement.

Launceston

Contact Information

Chabad House of Tasmania
5 Brisbane Street, Launceston 7250   (3) 6334-0705
For all enquiries please call or fax the Hon. Manager Mr Gershon Goldsteen at (3)6344 9960 or email him at: hydronav@tassie.net.au

Synagogues

PO Box 66, St John Street 7250   (3) 6343-1143
The synagogue in St John Street is the second oldest in Australia, founded in 1846.

Victoria

Ballarat

Synagogues

211 Drumond Street North 3350   (353) 32-6330

Melbourne

With 42,000 Jews, Melbourne has the largest Jewish community in the country, and the largest Jewish school in the world (the Mount Scopus).

Bakeries

Big K Kosher Bakery
316 Carlisle Street,, Balaclava 3183   (3) 9527-4582
Supervision: Rabbi A.Z. Beck, Adass Israel.

Glicks Cakes and Bagels
330a Carlisle Street, Balaclava 3183   (3) 9527-2198
Supervision: Melbourne Kashrut.

Greenfield Cakes
7 Willow Street, Elsternwick   (3) 9528-4261
Supervision: Rabbi A.Z. Beck, Adass Israel.
At same location is King David Kosher Meals on Wheels (Refuah), hospital meals, airline and TV dinners.

Haymishe Bakery
320 Carlisle Street, Shop 4, Balaclava 3183   (3) 9527-7116
Supervision: Rabbi A.Z. Beck, Adass Israel.

Kosher Delight Bakery
75 Glen Eira Road, Ripponlea   (3) 9532-9994
Supervision: Rabbi A.Z. Beck, Adass Israel.

Lowy's Cakes & Catering
59 Gordon Street, Elsternwick   (3) 9530-0246
Supervision: Rabbi A.Z. Beck, Adass Israel.

Meal-Mart
251 Inkerman Street, St Kilda 3182   (3) 9525-5077
Fax: (3) 9525-4230
Supervision: Rabbi A.Z. Beck, Adass Israel.
Pies, salads, pre-cooked and frozen foods.

Booksellers

Golds Book & Gift Company
3 - 13 William Street, Balaclava 3183   (3) 9527-8775
Fax: (3) 9527-6434
Email: info@golds.com.au
Web site: www.golds.com.au

Butchers

Continental Kosher Butchers
155 Glenferrie Road, Malvern 3144   (3) 9509-9822
Fax: (3) 9509-9099
Supervision: Rabbi J.S. Cohen and Rabbi M. Gutnick, Melbourne Kashrut..

Melbourne Kosher Butchers
251 Inkerman Street, East St Kilda 3182
(3) 9525-5077
Fax: (3) 9525-4230
Supervision: Rabbi A.Z. Beck, Adass Israel.
Sell other kosher products as well. Hours: Monday, 10 am to 5:30 pm; Tuesday to Thursday, 7 am to 5:30 pm; Friday, 7 am to 3 pm. Winter 2pm.

Solomon Kosher Butchers
140-144 Glen Eira Road, Elsternwick 3185
(3) 9532-8855
Fax: (3) 9532-8896
Supervision: Rabbi Y.D. Groner, Agudas Chabad Kashrut Committee.
Hours: Monday to Thursday, 7 am to 5:30 pm; Friday, 7 am to 3 pm.

Yumi's Kosher Seafoods
29 Glen Eira Road, Ripponlea 3183   (3) 9523-6444
Fax: (3) 9532-8189
Supervision: Rabbi A.Z. Beck, Adass Israel.
Suppliers of kosher quality fresh fish.

Caterers

Kosher Meals on Wheels
572 Inkeman Street, Caulfield 3162   (3) 9527-5525
Supervision: Rabbi A.Z. Beck, Adass Israel.

Chocolate Shops

Kosher

Alpha Kosher Chocolates
17 William Street, Balaclava   (3) 9527-2453
Australia's only kosher chocolate factory. Hand made chocolates of export quality. Visitors welcome. Open Sunday mornings.

Australia/Victoria

Contact Information

Mizrachi Hospitality Committee
81 Balaclava Road, Caulfield 3161   (3) 9525-9833
Fax: (3) 9527-5665
Mailing address: P.O.Box 2247. Caulfield Junction.
VIC 3161.

Delicatessens

E.S. Delicatessen
74 Kooyong Road, Caulfield 3161   (3) 9576-0804
Supervision: Melbourne Kashrut.

Eshel Take-Away Foods & Catering
59 Glen Eira Road, Ripponlea 3161   (3) 9532-8309
Fax: (3) 9532-8089
Supervision: Rabbi A.Z. Beck, Adass Israel.

Groceries

Benedikt Imports
40 Pakington Street, St Kilda 3182   (3) 9534-8192
Importers of kosher foods and wines.

Dainty Foods (Kravsz)
62 Glen Eira Road, Ripponlea 3183   (3) 9523-8463
Grocers/Importers

Gefen Liquor Store
144 Chapel Street, Balaclava 3183   (3) 9531-5032
Fax: (3) 9525-7388
Hours: Monday to Thursday, 9 am to 5 pm; Friday, 9
am to 4 pm. Public transport access: #3 tram to corner
of Carlisle and Chapel Streets or Sandringham line
train to Balaclava Station.

Milecki's Balaclava Health Food
277 Carlisle Street, Balaclava 3183   (3) 9527-3350
Open every day except Shabbat and all Jewish
holidays. Hours: 9 am to 9 pm. Close to rail station
and on tram line.

Rishon Foods Party Ltd.
23 Williams Street, Balaclava 3183   (3) 9527-5142
Singers, 57 Kooyong Road, Caulfield 3162
(3) 9509-2387
Fax: (3) 9509-2387

Tempo Kosher Supermarket
391 Inkerman Street, St Kilda 3183   (3) 9527-5021
Manufacturers of a range of kosher foods, including
cheese, butter and juice drinks.

Hospitals

Masada Hospital
26 Balaclava Road, East St Kilda
Supervision: Rabbi A.Z. Beck, Adass Israel.
Kosher kitchen only.

Hotels

Kimberley Gardens
441 Inkerman Street, Balaclava 3183   (3) 9526-3888
Fax: (3) 9525-9691
Strictly Glatt kosher.

Judaica

The Antique Silver Co.
253 Carlisle Street, Balaclava 3183   (3) 9525-8480
Fax: (3) 9525-8479
Large selection of Judaica and ritual objects.

Libraries

Kadimah Jewish Cultural Centre & National Library
7 Selwyn Street, Elsternwick 3185   (3) 9523-9817
Hours: 9.30am-2.30pm

Makor Library
306 Hawthorn Road, South Cantfield 3162
(3) 9272-5611
Fax: (3) 9272-5629
Email: jlibrary@vicnet.net.au
Web site: www.vicnet.net.au/~jlibrary

Media

Newspapers

Jewish News, PO Box 1000, South Cantfield
Publish weekly newspaper.
Yidishe Gesheften
(3) 9532-7323
Fax: (3) 9523-0106
Jewish advertising monthly.

Mikvaot

Caulfield Mikva
9 Furneaux Grove, East St Kilda 3183
(3) 9528-1116/9525-8585
Lubavitch Mikva
38 Empress Road, East St Kilda 3183   (3) 9527-7555
Fax: (3) 9525-8838
Email: ktrubin@wavenet.net.au

Museums

Jewish Holocaust Centre
13 Selwyn Street, Elsternwick 3185   (3) 9528-1985
Fax: (3) 9528-3758
Email: hc@sprint.com.au
Hours: Mon-Fri 10.00am-2pm. Sun 11.00-3pm
Jewish Museum of Australia
26 Alma Road, St Kilda 3182   (3) 9543-0083
Fax: (3) 9543-0844

Religious Organisations

Orthodox

Council of Orthodox Synagogues of Victoria
c/o Jetset House, 5 Queens Road 3000
(3) 9828-8000

Australia/Victoria

Melbourne Beth Din
Synagogue Chambers, 572 Inkerman Road, North
Caulfield 3161 (3) 9527-8337
Fax: (3) 9527-8072
Orthodox Rabbinate of Australia
ISB on Accord Avenue, Bondi Junction 2022
(2) 9389-5622
Fax: (2) 9389-5418
Rabbinical Council of Victoria
c/o Honorary Secretary, Rabbi Mordechai Gutnick, 7
Meadow St, East St Kilda 3183 (3) 9525-9542
Fax: (3) 9525-9546

Progressive

Victorian Union for Progressive Judaism
78 Alma Road, St Kilda 3182 (3) 9510-1488
Fax: (3) 9521-1229
Email: Eampbeth@starnet.com.au

Representative Organisations
Jewish Community Council of Victoria Inc.
306 Hawthorn Road, South Cantfield 3162
(3) 9272-5566
Fax: (3) 9272-5560
Email: jccv@netspace.net.au
Head body of Melbourne Jewish community.

Restaurants

Meat

Kosher Express
263-265 Carlisle St, Balaclava (3) 9527-9911
Fax: (3) 9527-9922
Supervision: Mehadrin Melbourne.
Lamzini's, 219 Carlisle Street, St. Kilda (3) 9527-1283
Supervision: Melbourne Kashrut.

Synagogues
Kollel Beth Hatalmud
362a Carlisle Street, East St Kilda 3183
(3) 9527-6156
Fax: (3) 9527-8034
Email: kbt@blaze.net.au

Independent

Bet Hatikva Synagogue
233 Nepean Highway, Gardenvale 3185
(3) 9576-9755

Liberal

Bentleigh Progressive Synagogue
549 Centre Road 3204 (3) 9563-9208
Fax: (3) 9557-9880
Email: suzpol@techno.net.au
Leo Baeck Centre
33 Harp Road, East Kew 3102 (3) 9819-7160

Temple Beth Israel
P O Box 128, St Kilda 3182 (3) 9510-1488
Fax: (3) 9521-1229
Email: tempbeth@starnet.com.au
Web site: www.starnet.com.au/tempbeth

Orthodox
Brighton Hebrew Congregation
132-136 Marriage Road, East Brighton 3187
(3) 9592-9179
Office hours: Tuesday, Thursday, Friday 9am-12pm.
PO Box 202 Bentleigh 3204. Visitors welcome.
Burwood Hebrew Congregation
38 Harrison Avenue 3125 (3) 9808-3120
Caulfield Hebrew Congregation
572 Inkerman Road, Caulfield 3161 (3) 9525-9492
Fax: (3) 9527-8463
Email: chcmelb@ozemail.com.au
Chabad House
Duver Heights (3) 9387-3822
Elwood Talmud Torah Congregation
39 Dickens Street, Elwood 3184 (3) 9531-1547
Kew Synagogue
53 Walpole Street, Kew 3101 (3) 9853-9243
Fax: (3) 9853-1354
Melbourne Hebrew Congregation
Cnr. Toorak & St Kilda Roads, S. Yarra 3141
(3) 9866-2255
Fax: (3) 9866-2022
Email: mhc@bigpond.com
Mizrachi, 81 Balaclava Road, Caulfield 3161
(3) 9525-9833
Fax: (3) 9527-5665
Communication: P O Box 2247, Caulfield Junction,
VIC 3161
Moorabbin & District Synagogue
960 Nepean Highway, Moorabbin 3189
(3) 9553-3845
North Eastern Malvern Chabad
Glenferrie Road, Malvern
Sephardic Synagogue Congregation Rambam
90 Hotham Street, East Street, East St Kilda 3183
(3) 9527-3285
South Caulfield Synagogue
47 Leopold Street, South Cantfield 3162
(3) 9578-5922
St Kilda Hebrew Congregation Inc.
12 Charnwood Grove, St Kilda 3182 (3) 9537-1433
Fax: (3) 9525-3759
Web site: www.stkildashule.org.au
Yeshiva Shule
92 Hotham Street, East St Kilda 3183 (3) 9522-8222
Fax: (3) 9522-8266

Australia/Victoria

Tourist Sites
North Eastern Jewish War Memorial Centre Inc.
6 High Street, Doncaster 3108   (3) 9816-3516
Fax: (3) 9857-4430
Email: nejc@one.au

Western Australia
Perth

Delicatessens
Aviv Catering
The Jewish Centre, 61 Woodrow Avenue, Yokinea
6060   (8) 9276-6030
Fax: (8) 9276-6030
Supervision: Kashrut Authority of Western Australia.
Open 10am-2pm

Representative Organisations
Council of Western Australian Jewry
J.P. PO Box 763, Morley 6062

Synagogues
Jewish Community Centre of W.A.
Woodrow Avenue, Mt Yokine 6060   (8) 9276-8572
Fax: (8) 9276-8330
Email: peter@lennys.com.au
Northern Suburbs Congregation
4 Vernon Street, Noranda 6062   (8) 9275-5932
Perth Hebrew Congregation
Freedman Road, Menora 6050   (8) 9271-0539
Email: phc@theperthshule.asn.au
Web site: www.theperthshule.asn.au

Liberal
Temple David
34 Clifton Crescent, Mt Lawley 6050   (8) 9271-1485

Lubavitch
Chabad House
396 Alexander Drive, Dianella 6062   (8) 9275-4912

Austria

The arrival of Jews in this area of Europe (probably with the Romans) was more than a 1,000 years ago. The community was expelled from Austria between 1420 and 1421, but Jews were allowed to return in 1451. The Jews were granted their own quarter of Vienna in 1624, but were expelled again in 1670. The economy declined after the expulsion, and so they were asked to return.

It was not until 1782 that the situation became more stable when Joseph II began lifting the anti-Jewish decrees that his mother, Maria Theresa, had imposed on her Jewish subjects. The Jews received equal rights in 1848 and, in 1867, legal and other prohibitions were lifted.

Anti-semitism did continue, however, and many influential anti-semitic publications were available in Vienna and were keenly read by many people, including the young Adolf Hitler. After the First World War, Austria lost its empire (which included Czech lands and Galicia, which had a very large Jewish community), and the Jewish population fell accordingly. At the time of the Nazi take-over in 1938, 200,000 Jews lived in the country. Some 70,000 were killed in the Holocaust, the rest having escaped or hidden.

Today there are several synagogues in Vienna. The city has an active ultra-orthodox community and kosher food is available.

GMT + 1 hour	Total Population 8,102,000
Country calling code (43)	Jewish Population 10,000
Emergency Telephone (Police - 133) (Fire - 122) (Ambulance - 144)	Electricity voltage 220

Baden

Cemeteries
Jewish Cemetery
Halsriegelstrasse 30   (2252) 85405
Contains some 3,000 graves.
Keys to be obtained at Tourist Information Centre, tel. 2252-4453157.

Synagogues
Grabengasse 14   (2236) 26383 or (2252)-45705
Services are held Shabbat mornings from May to September. Contact Dr. Grossinger any time except Shabbos/holidays. Kosher catering possible. Event room (for 50 persons). Baden is R. Naftali Carlebach's last kehillah in Europe and the site of his distinguished sons R. Shlomo's z'tzal and R. Eliyahu Chaim's z'l Barmitzvah.

Edlach

Monument
A memorial to Dr Theodor Herzl, erected by the Viennese Jewish community, can be seen in the garden of the local sanatorium, where the founder of the Zionist movement died in 1904.

Eisenstadt

Cemeteries
Old Cemetery
The old cemetery, closed around 1875, contains the grave of Rav Meir Eisenstaat (Maharam Esh), who died in 1744. To this day it is the scene of pilgrimages, particularly on the anniversary of his death. Keys to the cemetery are with the porter of the local hospital, which adjoins the old cemetery.

Museums
Austrian Jewish Museum
Unterbergstrasse 6   (2682) 65145
Fax: (2682) 65145; 65144
Email: info@oejudmus.or.at
The museum now also comprises the restored private synagogue of Samson Wertheimer, Habsburg court Jew and Chief Rabbi of Hungary (1658–1724). The museum is open daily except Monday from 10 am to 5 pm. The Eruv Arch, spanning Unterbergstrasse, is at the end near the Esterhazy Palace. The road chain was used in former times to prevent vehicular traffic on Shabbat and Yom Tov.

Graz

Community Organisations
Community Centre
Synagogenplatz 1   (512) 712 4684

Innsbruck

Community Organisations
Community Centre
Sillgassse 15   (512) 586-892

Kobersdorf

The synagogue is currently being rebuilt.

Cemeteries
Jewish Cemetery
Waldgasse
The keys of the cemetery on the Lampelberg are with Mr Piniel, Waldgasse 25 (one of the two houses to the left of the cemetery) and Mr Grässing, Haydngasse 4.

Linz

Community Organisations
Community Centre
Bethlehemstrasse 26   (732) 779-805

Salzburg

The Salzburg community dates back to 803 when Archbishop Arno summoned a Jewish doctor to set up a practice in the town.

Community Organisations
Community Centre
Lasserstrasse 8 5020   (662) 875-665
Community synagogue and mikva are to be found at the same address.

Vienna

Vienna was in the past the most important centre for Central European Jews. From 180,000 Jews in the 1930s, there are about 1,000 Jews (mainly elderly) in Vienna today. Professor Freud's clinic is a popular attraction, and the Jewish Museum of Vienna gives much information on the history of the Jews.

Bakeries
Engländer
Hollandstrasse 10 1020   (1) 214-5617
Supervision: Rabbi Abraham Yonah Schwartz.

Bed & Breakfasts
Pension Lichtenstein
Grosse Schiffgasse 19 1020   (1) 216-8498
Fax: (1) 214-7690
Web site: www.pension-lichtenstein.at
The pension consists of 'suites' (sleeping area, living area, kitchenette and bathroom). The stove can be used as a hot plate for Shabbat. It is within walking distance of the old Jewish quarter of Vienna in one direction, and 5-20 minutes from some small synagogues, kosher bakery in the other direction. Visits should be coordinated in advance as there is no front desk reception; the key is kept in the owner's office around the block. Recommended for families and couples interested in self-catering.

Booksellers
Chabad-Simcha-Center
Hollandstrasse 10 1020   (1) 216-2924
Chai Vienna
Praterstrasse 40 1020   (1) 216-4621
Fax: (1) 216-4621

Austria

Butchers

B. Ainhorn
Stadtgutgasse 7 1020   (1) 214-5621
Supervision: Rabbi David Grunfeld.
Also supplies "Fast Food".

Rebenwurzel
Grose Mohrengasse 19 1010   (1) 216-6640
Supervision: Rabbi Chaim Stern.

Sephardi Butcher
Volkertmarkt 1020   (1) 214-9650

Cemeteries

Floridsdorfer Cemetery
Ruthnergasse 28 1210
Those wishing to visit must first obtain a permit from
the community centre.

Rossauer Cemetery
Seegasse 9 1090
This is the oldest Jewish cemetery in Vienna, dating
from the sixteenth century. It has now been restored
after being devastated by the Nazis and is open daily
from 8 am to 3 pm. Access is via the front entrance of
the municipal home for the aged at Seegasse 9-11, but
a permit must first be obtained from the community
centre.

Vienna Central Cemetery
Simmeringer Haupstr.244 A-1110
     (1) 531 04 904, 767 6252
The Jewish section (the only one still in use) is at Gate 4
and there is an older Jewish part at Gate 1.

Währinger Cemetery
Semperstrasse 64a 1180
Those wishing to visit must first obtain a permit from
the community centre.

Contact Information

Jewish Community Centre
Seitenstettengasse 4   (1) 531 04104
     Fax: (1) 531 04108
     Email: office@ikg-wien.at

Jewish Welcome Service Vienna
Stephansplatz 10 1010   (1) 533-2730
     Fax: (1) 533-4098
     Email: jewish.welcome@verkehrsbuero.at
     Web site: www.jewish.welcome.at
Open: Monday to Friday 9.00am to 5.30pm.

Documentation Centres

Documentation Centre of Austrian Resistance
Old City Hall, Wipplingerstrasse 8 1010
     (1) 534-3601 779
     Fax: (1) 534-3699 01771
     Email: docarch@ns.adis.at
     Web site: www.doew.at
Hours of opening: Monday to Thursday 9 am to 5 pm.

**Documentation Centre of Union of Jewish Victims of the
Nazis**
Salztorgasse 6 A-1010   (1) 533-9131
     Fax: (1) 535-0397

Embassy

Embassy of Israel
Anton-Frankgasse 20 1180   (1) 476-460

Groceries

Gross-Import-Wien
Nicklegasse 1, Wien A-1020   (1) 214-0607
     Fax: (1) 214-7690
Koscherland, Kleine Sperlgasse 7   (1) 212-8169
Kosher Supermarket & Shutnes Laboratory
Hollandstrasse 7 1020   (1) 269-9675
Supervision: Rabbi Abraham Yonah Schwartz.
Ohel Moshe
Hollandstrasse 10 A-1020   (1) 216-9675
Supervision: Rabbi Abraham Yonah Schwartz.
Rafael Malkov
Tempelgasse 6, Ferdinandstrasse 2 A-1020
     (1) 214-8394
Vinothek Gross
Taborstrasse 15 1020   (1) 212-6299

Hotels

Hotel Stefanie
12 Tabor Strasse 1020   (1) 211-500
     Fax: (1) 211-50160
     Email: stefanie@schick-hotels.com
Four star hotel with kosher breakfast on request.

Media

Newspaper

Die Gemeinde   (1) 531 04 271
     Fax: (1) 531 04 279
Monthly.

Mikvaot

Agudas Yisroel
Tempelgasse 3 1020   (1) 214-9973
Machsike Haddas
Fleischmarkt 22 1010   (1) 512-5262

Museums

Jewish Museum of the City of Vienna
Dorotheergasse 11 A-1010   (1) 535-0431
     Fax: (1) 535-0424
Hours: Sunday to Friday, 10 am to 6 pm; Thursday, 10
am to 8 pm. Cafeteria and bookshop on site. The
cafeteria is not under supervision.

Austria

Sigmund Freud Museum
Berggasse 19 1090
(1) 319-1596
Fax: (1) 317-0279
Email: freud-museum@t0.or.at
Web site: www.freud-museum.at
Hours: 9.00am to 5.00pm, July to September 9am - 6pm

Restaurants
Kosher Restaurant
Seitenstettengasse 4 A-1010
(1) 535-2530

Snack Bar
Berl Ainhorn Koscher Fleisch und Imbiss
Gross Stadtgutgasse 7 1020
(1) 214-5621

Sites
Mauthausen Memorial Site
(1) 723-82269
Fax: (1) 723 83696
Those wishing to visit the site should contact the Jewish Welcome Service.
Seitenstettengasse Synagogue
Seitenstettengasse 4 1010
(1) 531-040
Fax: (1) 531-04108
Email: office@ikg-wien.at
Web site: www.ikg-wien.at
Built in 1824-26 and partly destroyed during the Nazi period, this beautiful synagogue was restored by the community in 1988. For information about guided tours, contact the Community Centre offices.

Synagogues
Orthodox
Agudas Yeshurun
Riemergasse 9 1010
Agudas Yisroel
Grünangergasse 1 1010 (1) 512-8331
Agudas Yisroel
Tempelgasse 3 1020 (1) 214 9262
Machsike Haddas
Große Mohreng. 19 A-1020 (1) 216 0679
Misrachi, Judenplatz 8 1010 (1) 535-4153
Ohel Moshe
Lilienbrunngasse 19 1020 (1) 216-8864
Rambam Syn. im Maimonides Zentrum
Bauernfeldgasse 4 A-1190
Sephardi Centre
Tempelgasse 7 1020 (1) 214 3097
Shomre Haddas
Glasergasse 17 1090
Thora Etz Chayim
Grosse Schiffgasse 8 1020 (1) 214 5016

Progressive
Or Chadasch
Rosentalgasse 5-7/4/3 1140
(1) 967 1329
Fax: (1) 914 5245

Azerbaijan

Azerbaijan

Azerbaijan has a remarkable Jewish history, which can be better explored now that the country is independent from the Soviet Union. The Tats (mountain Jews) believe that their ancestors arrived in Azerbaijan at the time of Nebuchadnezzar. They lived in several mountain villages, and adopted the customs of their non-Jewish neighbours. They spoke a north Iranian language, known as Judeo-Tat, to which they had added some Hebrew words. The Soviets clamped down on their way of life after 1928, changing the alphabet of their language from Hebrew to Latin and then, in 1938, to Cyrillic. Some of their synagogues were also closed down. Zionist feeling is high, with almost 30,000 emigrating to Israel since 1989.

The other strand in Azerbaijan's Jewish population are the Ashkenazis who arrived in the nineteenth century from Poland and other countries to the west.

The community has some 10–15 organisations in Baku, the capital, including Zionist and youth groups. The largest synagogue in Baku is the Tat synagogue, but there are also Ashkenazi and Georgian synagogues. Synagogues are found in other towns.

GMT + 5 hours	Total Population 7,570,000
Country calling code (994)	Jewish Population 20,000

Baku

Embassy
Embassy of Israel
Stroiteley Prospect 1

Synagogues
Mountain Jews
Dmitrova Street 39 370014   (12) 892-232-8867

Ashkenazi
Pervomoskaya Street 271   (12) 892-294-1571

Kuba

Synagogues
46 Kolkhoznaya Street

Do you eat fish out?

If so, there is a comprehensive list of kosher fish listed alphabetically by country on pages 385 to 388 which you should find useful on your travels.

Luis de Torres, the official interpreter for Columbus, was the first Jew in the Bahamas, as well as being one of the first Europeans there. He was a Converso, a 'secret Jew' who officially had converted to Catholicism, but who practised Judaism in private. The British arrived in 1620, and eventually gained control of the islands. Although there was a Jewish attorney-general and chief justice in the islands in the eighteenth century, few Jews settled there until the twentieth century, coming from eastern Europe and the UK after the First World War, and settling in Nassau, the capital.

There are approximately 100 Jewish residents in the Bahamas. However it is estimated that about 350,000 Jews visit the Islands each year as tourists. There are Reform Congregations in Nassau and Freeport. Freeport has a synagogue named after Luis De Torres. Both cities have Jewish cemeteries, that in Nassau being more historic.

GMT - 5 hours	Total Population 284,000
Country calling code (1242)	Jewish Population 200
Emergency Telephone (Police, Fire and Ambulance - 919)	Electricity voltage 120

Freeport

Embassy
Consul General of Israel

362-4421

Synagogues
Freeport Hebrew Congregation

373-4025
Fax: 373-2130
Email: hurst100@yahoo.com
Are pleased to welcome tourists, and offer a licensed
Marriage Registrar.The President of the Congregation
can be reached at 373-4025
Luis de Torres Synagogue
East Sunrise Highway, PO Box F-41761   373-2008
Services are held regularly

Nassau

Synagogue

Progressive

Bahamas Jewish Congregation
P O B CB-11002   363-2305

Jewish history in Barbados starts in 1628, a year after the British first settled there. Jewish settlers came from Brazil, Surinam, England and Germany, and were mainly Sephardi. The first synagogue was established in Bridgetown (the capital) in 1654. Early settlers were engaged in cultivating sugar and coffee.

The Jewish population was well treated, and Barbados was the first British possession in which Jews were granted full political emancipation. Despite a largely favourable climate, the community suffered losses from hurricanes, which destroyed sugar plantations, and the Jewish population fell to 70 by 1848. In 1925, no Jews remained, but a new influx (30 families escaping Nazism) came shortly after.

The synagogue was restored in 1987, and postage stamps were produced which commemorated its restoration. The Jewish population remains small, but it was a group of Barbadian Jews who founded the Caribbean Jewish Congress. The Jewish cemetery, one of the oldest in the Americas, is now back in use.

GMT - 4 hours	Total Population 265,000
Country calling code (1246)	Jewish Population Under 100
Electricity voltage 110	

Barbados

Community Organisations

Barbados Jewish Community

PO Box 651, Bridgetown   (809) 427-0703
                             Fax: (809) 436-8807

Caribbean Jewish Congress

PO Box 1331, Bridgetown   (809) 436-8163

Synagogue Restoration Project

PO Box 256, Bridgetown   (809) 432-0840

Local inquiries to Henry Altman, Little Mallows, Sandy Lane, St. James. Tel: 432-6462

Synagogues

Barbados Synagogue

Synagogue Lane

Services are held Friday evenings at 7 pm at 'True Blue', Rockley New Road, Christ Church, during the summer, and at the synagogue in winter.

Belarus

For the adventurous traveller, who has a keen interest in Jewish history, Belarus (also known as White Russia) makes an interesting and unusual destination. Situated in the western side of the former Soviet Union, this largely flat country borders Poland asnd Lithuania to the west, Ukraine to the south and Russia to the east. Belarus finally achieved independence in 1991, and within its present borders are many towns and villages of Jewish interest, such as Minsk, Pinsk and Grodno. One of the most famous villages in Belarus is Lubavitch, a hamlet in the far east of the country, near the Russian border, where the world-wide Lubavitch movement had its origins.

The majority of this region's Jews died in the Holocaust and although emigration to Israel is high, the community is slowly rebuilding itself after decades of Soviet control. Americans and Israelis are contributing rabbis to help in this revival, and Jewish schools have been set up. Yiddish is used far more here than in other parts of the former USSR.

GMT + 2 hours	Total Population 10,264,000
Country calling code (375)	Jewish Population 60,000
Emergency Telephone (Police, Fire and Ambulance - 03)	Electricity voltage 220

Baranovichi

Synagogues

39 Svobodnaya St.

Bobruisk

Synagogues

Engels St.

Borisov

Synagogues

Trud St.

Brest

Synagogues

Narodnaya St.

Gomel

Synagogues

13 Sennaya St.

Minsk

Embassy

Embassy of Israel

Partizanski Prospekt 6A 220002   (172) 304-444

Synagogue

Progressive

Association of Progressive Jewish Congregations in Belarus

Per K Chyornogo 4, apt 18, Simcha 220012
                                  (172) 846-089
                             Fax: (172) 662-928
                      Email: simcha@open.by

Synagogues

22 Kropotkin St.   (172) 558-270
Kommunisticheskaya St.

Moghilev

Synagogues

1 2nd Krutoy La.

Orsha

Synagogues

Nogrin St.

Rechitsa

Synagogues

120 Lunacharsky St.

Belgium

Jewish settlement in the area now Belgium dates back to the thirteenth century, and suffered a similar fate to other medieval European Jewish communities – taking the blame for the Black Death and suffering expulsions. The Sephardim were the first to resettle in Belgium, mainly in Antwerp. After independence in 1830, conditions for the Jews improved and more Jews began to settle there. The diamond centre of Antwerp later developed rapidly, attracting many Jews from eastern Europe.

By 1939, the Jewish population had grown to 100,000, a large proportion of them being refugees hoping to escape to America. Some succeeded, but many became trapped after the German invasion. Some 25,000 Belgian Jews were deported and killed in the Holocaust. A national monument stands in Anderlecht in Brussels to their memory, listing the names of the victims.

The present Jewish population includes a large Chassidic community in Antwerp, where there are some 30 synagogues. There are also more than ten synagogues in Brussels. There are Jewish schools in Antwerp and Brussels, and Jewish newspapers.

GMT + 1 hour	Total Population 10,160,000
Country calling code (32)	Jewish Population 40,000
Emergency Telephone (Police - 101) (Fire and Ambulance - 101)	Electricity voltage 220

Antwerp

Seen by some as 'the last shtetl in Europe', Antwerp is a well-known Hassidic centre. Antwerp's Jewish population (15,000) has one of the highest numbers of Ultra-Orthodox in the Diaspora. Served by 30 synagogues (many of them small shtiebels), there are also kosher restaurants and food shops.

Bakeries

Gottesfeld, Mercatorstraat 20	(3) 230-0003
Kleinblatt, Provinciestraat 206	
	(3) 233-7513; 226-0018
	Fax: (3) 232-0920
Steinmetz, Lange Kievitstraat 64	(3) 234-0947

Booksellers

I. Menczer, Simonstraat 40	(3) 232-3026
N. Seletsky, Lange Kievitstraat 70	(3) 232-6966
	Fax: (3) 226-9446
Stauber, Van Leriusstraat 3	(3) 231-8031

Butchers

Berkowitz, Isabellalei 9	(3) 218-5111
Farkas, Lange Kievitstraat 66	(3) 232-1385
Fruchter, Simonstraat 22	(3) 233-1811; 1557
	Fax: (3) 231-3903
Kosher King, Lange Kievitstraat 40	(3) 233-6749

Kosher King, Isabellalei 7	(3) 239-4189
Mandelovics, Isabellalei 96	(3) 218-4779
Moszkowitz, Lange Kievitstraat 47	(3) 232-6349
	Fax: (3) 226-0471

Contact Information

Machsike Hadass (Israelitische Orthodoxe Gemeente)	
Jacob Jacobsstraat 22	(3) 233-5567
Shomre Hadass (Israelitische Gemeente)	
Terliststraat 35 2018	(3) 232-0187
	Fax: (3) 226-3123
Email: shomre-hadas@net4all.be	
Web site: www.members.net4all.be/shomre-hadas	

Delicatessens

Weingarten, Lange Kievitstraat 124	(3) 233-2828

Groceries

Col-Bo, Jacob Jacobsstraat 40	(3) 234-1212
Grosz-Modern, Terliststraat 28	(3) 232-4626
Herzl & Gold, Korte Kievitstraat 38	(3) 232-2365
Stark, Mercatorstraat 24	(3) 230-2520
Super Discount	
Belgielei 104-108	(3) 239-0666
Superette Lamoriniere	
199 Lamboriniere Straat	(3) 239-3110
	Fax: (3) 281-3205

Belgium

Media

Newspapers

Belgisch Israelitisch Weekblad
Pelikaanstraat 106-108 2018   (3) 233-7094
     Fax: (3) 233-4810

Mikvaot

Machsike Hadass
Steenbokstraat 22   (3) 239-7588
Shomre Hadass
Van Diepenbeeckstraat 42   (3) 239-0965

Museums

Plantin-Moretus Museum
Vrijdagmarkt (nr Groenplaats)   (3) 233-0688
Open daily (except Monday). Contains examples of early Jewish printing, such as the famous Polyglot Bible.

Restaurants

Blue Lagoon, Lange Herentalsestraat 70
     (3) 226-0114
Supervision: Machsike Hadass.
Also sell chocolates, contact R Suchowolski on 230-2871 or fax: 281-1702. Five minutes from Central station..
Garden of Eden
Plantin En Moretuslei 10 2018   (3) 281-4281
     Fax: (3) 700-4034
Open: 12pm-2pm and 6pm-10pm.

Dairy

USA Pizza, 118a Isabellalei   (3) 281-2300
Supervision: Machzikey Hadas.
Take away option.

Meat

Hoffy's, Lange Kievitstraat 52   (3) 234-3535
     Fax: (3) 226-0282
     Email: hoffys@pandora.be
Jacob, Lange Kievitstraat 49   (3) 233-1124

Synagogues

Orthodox

Hoofd synagoog
Oostenstraat 43   (3) 239-3038
Machsike Hadass
Jacob Jacobsstraat 22 22-2018
     (3) 233-5567/232-0021
     Fax: (3) 233-8797

Tour Information

Toerisme Antwerpen
Grote Markt 15 2000   (3) 232-0103
     Fax: (3) 231-1937
     Email: toerisme@antwerpen.be
     Web site: www.dma.be

Arlon

Synagogues

Rue St Jean   (63) 217-985
Established 1863. The secretary, J.C. Jacob, can be reached at 11 rue des Martyrs, 6700. A monument has been erected in the new Jewish cemetery to the memory of the Jews of Arlon deported and massacred by the Nazis.

Brussels

The capital of Belgian is less well endowed with kosher facilities than Antwerp, although there are 23,000 Jews living in the city. The headquarters of the European Union of Jewish Students is based there. The Anderlecht area has a monument to the Belgian Holocaust victims and a memorial to Jews who fought in the Belgian Resistance.

Bakeries

Bornstein, 62 rue de Suéde, St Gilles   (2) 537-1679

Booksellers

Colbo, 121 rue du Brabant   (2) 217-2620
Menorah, 12 Ave. J. Voldens 1060   (2) 537-5073

Butchers

Lanxner, 121 rue de Brabant 1030   (2) 217-2620
Supervision: Rabbinate of the Jewish Orthodox Community of Brussels.
Grocery: Jewish specialities, also Delicatessen. Hours: Sun, Mon, Fri 8.30am to 13.00pm. Tues 8.30am to 18.00pm. Wed-Thurs 8.30am to 19.30pm.

Community Organisations

Centre Communautaire Laic Juif
Yitzhak Rabin Center, 52 rue Hotel des Monnaies
     (2) 543-0270
     Fax: (2) 543-0271
     Email: info@cclj.be

Contact Information

Beth Chabad, 87 Ave du Roi   (2) 537-1158

Embassy

Embassy of Israel
40 Avenue de l'Observatoire 1180   (2) 373-5500

Groceries

Hod Taim, Boulevard Jamar 51   (2) 527-1832

Media

Newspapers

Centrale, 91 Av. Henri Jaspar   (2) 538-8036
Monthly

Fax de Jerusalem
68 Ave Ducpétiaux   (2) 538-5673
Fax: (2) 534-0236
Email: alyabelgique@skynet.be
Weekly
Kehilatenou, 2 rue Joseph Dupont   (2) 512-4334
Monthly
Regards, 52 rue Hotel des Monnaies   (2) 538-4908
Fax: (2) 537-5565
Fortnightly

Mikvaot
Machsike Hadass
67a rue de la Clinique   (2) 537-1439

Museums
Jewish Museum
74 Ave de Stalingrad 1000   (2) 512-1963
Fax: (2) 513-4859
Email: info@mjb.jmb.org
Hours: Mon-Thurs 12.00 - 5.00 pm. Sunday 10.00
am to 1.00 pm. Closed Friday, Saturday and Jewish
holidays.

Religious Organisations
Communaute Israelite de Bruxelles
2 Rue Joseph Dupont 1000   (2) 512-4334
Fax: (2) 512-9237
Machsike Hadass (Communauté Israélite Orthodoxe de Bruxelles)
67a rue de la Clinique   (2) 524-1486; 521-1289
Yechiva de Bruxelles
50 Ave Brugmann 1190   (2) 347 2143

Restaurants
Chez Gilles
Rue de la Clinique 21 1070   (2) 522-1828
Supervision: (O).
Open from 9am - 5 pm.

Meat

Athenee Maimonide
Boulevard Poincarte 67   (2) 523-6336

Sites
National Monument to the Jewish Martyrs of Belgium
corner rue Emile Carpentier and rue Goujons, Square
of the Jewish Martyrs, Anderlecht
This monument commemorates the Jews of Belgium
who were deported to concentration camps and killed
by the Nazis during the Second World War. The names
of all 23,838 are engraved on the monument.

Synagogues
32 Rue de la Regence 1000   (2) 512-4334
Fax: (2) 512-9237

Communaute Israelite de Bruxelles
2 Rue Joseph Dupont 1000   (2) 512-4334
Fax: (2) 512-9237

Liberal

Communaute Israelite Liberal de Belgique - Beth Hillel
Avenue de Kersbeek 96 1190   (2) 332-2528
Fax: (2) 376-7219
Email: cilb@skynet.be

Orthodox

Adath Israel
126 rue Rogier, Scharbeek, Schaerbeek (2) 241-1664
Ahavat Reim
73 rue de ThySt Gilles   (2) 648-3837
Beth Hamidrash
rue du Chapeau, Anderlecht, Anderlecht
(2) 524-1486
Beth Itshak
115 Ave du Roi 1060   (2) 538-3374; 520-1359
Communaute Israelite de Bruxelles
Rue de la Regence 32 1000   (2) 512-4334
Fax: (2) 512-9237
Maale, 11 Ave Messidor 1180   (2) 344-6094
Or Hahayim
77 rue P. Decoster 1190   (2) 344-2342

Sephardi

Communauté Sepharade de Bruxelles
47 rue du Pavillon 1030   (2) 215-0525
Fax: (2) 215-0242

Charleroi
Community Organisations
Community Centre
56 rue Pige-au-Croly

Ghent
Contact Information
Jacques Bloch
Veldstraat 60   (9) 225-7085
Email: jbloch@compaqnet.be
The treasurer of the community will be happy to meet
English-speaking visitors. As the community is a very
small one, there is no permanent synagogue. Services
are held on the High Holy Days.

Knokke
Synagogues
30 Van Bunnenlaan   (50) 61-0372

Belgium

Liège

Community Organisations
Community Centre
12 Quai Marcellis 4020

Museums
Musee Serge Kruglanski
19 rue L. Fredericq 4020   (43) 438-043
         Fax: (43) 226-0234

Synagogues
19 rue L. Frédéricq 4020   (41) 436-106

Mons

Contact Information
SHAPE 7010   (65) 445-808; 444-809
Nearby, at Casteau, the International Chapel of
NATO's Supreme Headquarters Allied Powers Europe,
includes a small Jewish community, established 1951,
that holds regular services. Call for further information.

Ostend

Hotels
Hotel Royal Astor
Hertsstraat 15   (59) 803-773
Open for Sukkot

Synagogues
Van Maastrichtplein 3
Services during July and August. Inquiries to Mrs.
Liliane Wulfowicz, Parklaan 21, B-8400 (59) 802-405.

Waterloo

Synagogues
Communaute Israelite de Waterloo et du Brabant Sud
(CIWABS)
140 Avenue Belle-Vue, 1410 Waterloo
     (2) 354 6789
Regular Services Shabbat and Festivals; English
speaking visitors very welcome

Bermuda

Jews have lived in Bermuda since the seventeenth century, but the first formal congregation was
not established until the twentieth century.

The resident Jewish population is very small, but the transient population (of tourists largely from
the USA, Britain and Canada) is much greater. High holy-day services are normally held at the US
Naval Air Station Chapel. Friday services are held, usually monthly, at the Unity Foundation, 75
Reid Street, Hamilton.

GMT - 4 hours	Total Population 64,000
Country calling code (1)	Jewish Population Under 100
Emergency Telephone (Police - 112) (Fire - 113) (Ambulance -115)	Electricty voltage 110

Ferry Reach

Contact Information
Diana Lynn
17 Biological Lane GE01   (441) 297-2267
         Fax: (441) 297-8143
         Email: dlynn@bbsr.edu

Hamilton

Community Organisations
Jewish Community of Bermuda
PO Box HM 1793 HM HX   (441) 291-1785

The history of the Jews of Bolivia dates back to the Spanish colonial period. Conversos (converts to Christianity who practised Judaism in secret) came with the Spaniards in the seventeenth century.

The main influx of Jews occurred in 1905, with immigrants from eastern Europe, but the number entering Bolivia was much smaller than that to other South American countries. In 1933 there were only some 30 Jewish families. At the end of the decade, however, there was a small increase in Jewish immigration as German and Austrian Jews fled from Europe. Ironically, the Jewish community did not grow very much, even though the government granted every Jew an entry visa.

Many Jews started to leave Bolivia in the 1950s because of political instability and the apparent lack of educational opportunities. The present-day community has a central organisation known as the Circulo Israelita de Bolivia.

GMT - 4 hours	Total Population 7,593,000
Country calling code (591)	Jewish Population 400
Electricity voltage 110/220	

Cochabamba

Representative Organisations
Asociacion Israelita de Cochabamba
PO Box 349, Calle Valdivieso

Synagogues
Calle Junin y Calle Colombia, Casilla 349

La Paz

Synagogues
Circulo Israelita de Bolivia
Casilla 1545, Calle Landaeta 346, PO Box 1545
(2) 32-5925
Fax: (2) 34-2738
Representative body of Bolivian Jewry. All La Paz organisations are affiliated to it. Service Shabbat morning only.

Comunidad Israelita Synagogue
Calle Canada Stronguest 1846, PO Box 2198
Affiliated to the Circulo. Friday evening services are held here.

Tour information
Centro Shalom
Calle Canada Stronguest 1846

Santa Cruz

Community Organisations
Centro Cruceño
PO Box 469

Representative Organisations
WIZO, Castilla 3409

Have you any information for us?

Any comments you may have on this guide are always welcomed. Please do get in touch if you have any relevant information which you may feel will be of use to other travellers.
Details on how to do this are on page vi.
Additionally forms are available at the back of the book.

Bosnia-Hercegovina

Sephardi Jews were the first to arrive in the area, in the late sixteenth century. They established a Jewish quarter in Sarajevo, and this was home for poorer Jews until the Austrians conquered the land in 1878. It was the Turks, however, who emancipated the Jews in the nineteenth century when Bosnia-Hercegovina was under Ottoman rule.

When Bosnia-Hercegovina became part of the newly formed Yugoslavia, after the First Word War, the community maintained its Sephardi heritage and joined the all-Yugoslav Federation of Jewish Religious Communities. The Jewish population numbered 14,000 in 1941. This number dropped sharply after the Germans conquered Yugoslavia.

After the war the survivors were joined by many who had decided to return. The Sephardi and Ashkenazi communities became unified. La Benevolencija, founded 100 years ago, is a humanitarian organisation which supported the plight of the community and became well known in the early 1990s at the time of the civil war. After the Yugoslav civil war, many made aliyah to Israel, reducing the community still further.

GMT + 1 hour	Total Population 3,524,000
Country calling code (387)	Jewish Population 600
Emergency Telephone (Police - 664 211) (Fire - 93) (Ambulance - 94)	Electricity voltage 220

Sarajevo

Cemeteries
Kovacici
This historic Jewish cemetery is in town. Not far from the centre of town, on a hill called Vraca, there is a monument with the names of the 7,000 Jews from the area who fell victim to the Nazis.

Community Organisations
Sarajevo Jewish Community "La Benevolencija"
Hamdije Kresevljakovica 83 7100   (33) 663-472
Fax: (33) 663-473

Museums
Jewish Museum
Mulamustafe Baseskije Street
This historic museum, placed in the oldest synagogue in Sarajevo, with priceless relics dating back to the expulsion from Spain, is temporarily closed to the public.
Novi Hram
This gallery is also located in a former synagogue. The president of the community will gladly show visitors around.

Synagogues
Synagogue and Community Centre
Hamdije Kresevljakovica 59   (33) 663-472
Fax: (33) 663-473
Email: la_bene@soros.org.ba

The first Jewish settlers in Brazil came with the Portuguese in 1500. They were mainly Conversos, escaping persecution in Portugal, and worked on the sugar plantations. The huge area which is called Brazil today was in the process of being conquered by the Dutch and the Portuguese. The Portuguese gained the upper hand in 1654, and there was much anti-Jewish persecution. Many fled and some went on to found the first Jewish community in New York, then known as New Amsterdam. A seventeenth-century mikveh was discovered in 2000 in the basement of the Tsur Israel Synagogue in Recife.

With Brazilian independence in 1822, conditions became more favourable for Jews and many came from north Africa and Europe. The majority of Jews in Brazil today, however, originate from the immigration of east European Jews in the early twentieth century. From about 6,000 Jews in 1914, the community grew to 30,000 in 1930. After 1937 Brazil refused to allow Jewish immigrants into the country, but some limited immigration managed to continue despite the restrictions.

A central organisation was established in 1951 (the CONIB), and this includes 200 various Jewish organisations. Brazilian Jews live in an atmosphere of tolerance and prosperity, and assimilation is prominent.

There are synagogues in all the major cities.

GMT - 3 to - 5 hrs   Total Population 157,872,000
Country calling code (55)   Jewish Population 130,000
Emergency Telephone (Police - 147) (Fire - 193) (Ambulance - 192)   Electricity voltage 220/100

Amazonas

Manaus

Community Organisations
Grupo Kadima, Rua Ramos Ferreira 596

Bahia

Salvador

Synagogues
Rua Alvaro Tiberio 60   (71) 3-4283
Community centre and Zionist organisation are at the same address.

Brasilia

Embassy
Embassy of Israel
Av. das Nacoes Sul, Lote 38
                        (61) 244-7675/244-7875
                        Fax: (61) 244-6129

Synagogues
ACIB, Entrequadras Norte 305-306, Lote A
                        (61) 23-2984
Community centre is at the same address.

Minas Gerais

Belo Horizonte

Contact Information
Lojinha do Beit Chabad
Av. Serzedelo Corrêa 276   (91) 241-2250

Mikvaot
Rua Rio Grande do Norte 477   (91) 221-0690

Representative Organisations
Associação Israelita Brasileira
Rua Rio Grande do Norte 477   (91) 221-0690
Uniao Israelita de Belo Horizonte
Rua Pernambuco 326   (91) 224-6013

Synagogue
Congregacao Israelita Mineira
Rua Rio Grande do Norte 477   (31) 224-2129
                        Fax: (31) 224-2129
                        Email: cim@pib.com.br
Av. Leonardo Malchez 630, Centro

Brazil/Para

Para

Belém

Community Organisations
Community Centre
Travessa Dr. Moraes 37

Contact Information
Lojinha do Beit Chabad
Av. Serzedelo Corrêa 276   (91) 241-2250

Synagogues
Eshel Avraham
Travessa Campos Sales 733
Shaar Hashamaim
Rua Alcipreste Manoel Theodoro 842

Parana

Curitiba

Community Club and Jewish Federation
Centro Israelita do Parana
Rua Mateus Leme 1431 80530   (41) 338-7575
                           Fax: (41) 338-7922

Synagogues

Orthodox

Francisco Frischmann
Rua Cruz Machado 126   (41) 224-5218
                           Fax: (41) 224-8172

Pernambuco

Recife

Community Organisations
Community Centre
Rua da Gloria 215

Synagogues
Rua Martins Junior 29

Rio de Janeiro

The old Jewish area is situated around Rua Alfandega. The country's first Ashkenazi Synagogue (Grande Templo Israelite) is an imposing building which was renovated in 1986.

Community Organisations
Confederacao Israelita de Brazil (Conib)
Avenida Nilo Pecanha 50   (21) 240-0034
                           Fax: (21) 240-2717

Tours of Jewish Interest
Michel Mekler
Av. Graca Aranha 81/608Centro 20030
                           (21) 220-8817
Web site: www.orbita.starmedia.com/via/~caritur

Campos

Community Organisations
Community Centre
Rua 13 de Maio 52

Greater Rio de Janeiro

Butchers
Frigorifico
Rua Ronald Carvalho 265
Copacabana 22021-020
                           (21) 295-7341
Supervision: Rav Stauber.

Cultural institution
ASA - Associacao Sholem Aleichem
Rua Sao Clemente 155
Botafogo 22260   (21) 539-7740
                           Fax: (21) 266-1980
Email: asakinderland@uol.com.br
The institition is dedicated to promote cultural events (seminars, debates, video exhibitions, etc.).

Embassy
Consul General of Israel
Av. Copacabana 680   (21) 255-5432

Groceries
Kosher House
Rua Anita Garibaldi 37 lj. A, Copacabana
                           (21) 255-3891

Mikvaot
Kehilat Yaakov
Rua Capelao Alvares da Silva 15
Copacabana 22041

Museums
Museu Judaico do Rio de Janeiro
Rua Mexico
90 sala 110, Andar 20031-141   (21) 240-1598
                           Fax: (21) 240-1598

Religious Organisations
Chevre Kedishe
Rua Barao de Iguatemi 306   (21) 502-9933
                           Fax: (21) 502-3215

Representative Organisations
Organizaco Israelita do Estado do Rio de Janeiro
Rua Tenente Possolo 8

Rabinado do Rio de Janeiro
Rua Pompeu Loureiro 40

Fax: (21) 236-0249

Restaurants
Cafeteria no Rabinato
Rua Pompeu Loureiro 40 Copacabana

(21) 236-0249
Hours: 10am to 5pm Sunday to Thursday.

Kosher House
Rua Anita Garibaldi 371, Copacabana

Synagogues

Liberal

Associacão Religiosa Israelita
Rua General Severiano 170
Botafogo 22290

(21) 226-9666; 237-9283

Orthodox

Agudat Israel
Rua Nascimento Silva 109, Ipanema 22421

(21) 267-5567

Grande Templo Israelita
Rua Tenente Possolo 8, Centro 20230

(21) 232-3656

Kehilat Yaakov
Rua Capelao Alvares da Silva
Copacabana 22041

Niteroi

Community Organisations
Centro Israelita
Rua Visconde do Uruguai 255, 24030

Sociedade Hebraica
Rua Alvares de Azevedo 185, Icarai 24220

Petropolis

Religious Organisations
Machane Israel Yeshiva
Rua Duarte de Silveira 1246 25600   (242) 45-4952

Synagogues
Sinagoga Israelita Brasileira
Rua Aureliano Coutinho 48 25600

Rio Grande do Sul

Erechim

Synagogues
Av. Pedro Pinto de Souza 131

Passo Fundo

Synagogues
Rua General Osório 1049

Pelotas

Synagogues
Rua Santos Dumont 303

Porto Alegre

Butchers
Kosher Butcher
Rua Fernandes Vieira 518   (51) 250-441

Cultural Organisations
**Instituto Cultural Judaico Marc Chagall - Projeto
Memoria**
Rua Dom Pedro II, 1220/sala 216   (51) 343-5748

Mikvaot
Rua Francisco Ferrer 170

Museums
Museu Judaico
Rua João Telles 329   (51) 226-0379

Religious Organisations
City Rabbinate
Rua Henrique Dias 73   (51) 219-649

Synagogues

Liberal

SIBRA, Mariante 772   (51) 331-8133
Services on Shabbat only.

Orthodox

Beit Chabad, Rua Felipe Camarão 748

(51) 330-7078
Daily services.
Centro Israelita Porto Alegrense
Rua Henrique Dias 73   (51) 228-1935
Daily services.
Linath Ha-Tzedek
Rua Bento Figueredo 55   (51) 332-1065
Daily services.
Poilisher Farband
Rua João Telles 329   (51) 226-0379
Daily services.
União Israelita Porto Algrense
Rua Dr Barros Cassal 750   (51) 311-6515
Fax: (51) 311-5886
Daily services.

Sephardi

Centro Hebraico Riograndense
Rua Cel. Machado 1008
Services on Shabbat only.

Brazil/Sao Paulo

Sao Paulo

Campinas

Synagogues
Beth Yacob Campinas
Rua Barreto Leme 1203   (19) 231-4908
    Fax: (19) 442-171

Guaruja

Synagogues
Beit Yaacov
Av. Leomil 628   (13) 387-2033
Neve Itzhak
Av. Leomil 950   (13) 386-3167

Mogi Das Cruzes

Community Organisations
Jewish Society
Rua Dep. Deodato Wertheimer 421   (11) 469-2505

San. Jose dos Campos

Synagogues
Beit Chabad, Rua Republica do Ira 91
    (11) 3064-6322

Santo Andre

Synagogues
Beit Chabad, Rua 11 de Junho 172   (11) 449-1568

Santos

Community Organisations
Club, Rua Cons. Neblas 254   (132) 32-9016

Synagogues
Beit Sion, Rua Borges 264
Sinagoga Beit Jacob
Rua Campos Sales 137

São Caetano do Sul

Synagogues
Sociedade Religiosa S. Caetano do Sul
Rua Para 67   (11) 442-3514

São Paulo

Bakeries
Buffet Mazal Tov
Rua Peixoto Gomide 1724   (11) 883-7614
    Fax: (11) 3064-5208

Matok Bakery, Rua P. João Manoel 709
    (11) 3064-6668
Supervision: Rabbi I. Dichi.
Matok Bakery, Al. Barros 921   (11) 66-7514
Supervision: Rabbi I. Dichi.

Booksellers
Livraria Sêfer
Alameda Barros, 893 01232-001   (11) 3826-1366
    Fax: (11) 3826-4508
    Email: sefer@sefer.com.br
    Web site: www.sefer.com.br
Bookseller and Judaica

Butchers
Casa de Carnes Casher
Rua Fortunato 241   (11) 221-2240
Under supervision of Rabbi Elyahu B. Valt.
Mehadrin, Rua S. Vicente de Paulo   (11) 67-9090
Under supervision of Rabbi M.A. Iliovitz.
Mehadrin, Rua Prates 689   (11) 228-1771
Under supervision of Rabbi M.A. Iliovitz.

Embassy
Consul General of Israel
Rua Luis Coelho 308, 7th Floor
    (11) 257-2111; 257-2814

Groceries
All Kosher, Rua Albuquerque Lins 1170
    (11) 825-1131
Amazonas, Rua Amazonas 91   (11) 229-1336
Chazak, Rua Haddock Lobo 1002   (11) 3068-9093
Chazak, Rua Afonsa Pena 348a   (11) 229-5607
Dom Bosco, Rua Guarani 114   (11) 228-6105
Mazal Tov, Rua Peixoto Gomide 1724   (11) 883-7614
    Fax: (11) 3064-5208
Sta. Luzia, Al. Lorena 1471   (11) 883-5844
Look for kosher section.
Zilanna, Rua Itambé 506   (11) 257-8671

Media

Magazines

Morasha Magazine
Rua Dr Veiga Filho 547, Higienopolis 01229-000
    (11) 3662-2154
    Fax: (11) 3030-5630
    Email: morasha@uol.com.br
    Web site: www.morasha.com

Newspapers

O Hebreu
Rua Cunha Gago 158 05421-000   (11) 3819-1616
    Fax: (11) 3819-1616
    Email: ohebrew@ohebrew.com.br
    Web site: www.communidadejudaica.com/ohebrew
Monthly.

Resenha Judaica
Rua Antonio Carlos 582/5   (11) 255-8794
Weekly.
Tribuna Judaica
Rua Tanabi 299 05002-010
    (11) 3871-3234/3873-3020/3862-9074
    Fax: (11) 3871-3234
    Email: tjudaica@uol.com.br
Weekly.

Mikvaot
Micre Taharat Menachem - Perdizes
Rua Dr. Manoel Maria Tourinho 261   (11) 3865-0615
By appointment only.
Congregacao Mekor Haim
Rua Sao Vicente de Paulo 276 01229-0101
    (11) 3826-7699
    Fax: (11) 3666-6960
    Email: revista_nascente@hotmail.com

Orthodox

Beit Yaacov Synagogue
Rua Dr Veiga Filho 547, Higienopolis 01229-000
    (11) 3662-2154
    Fax: (11) 3662-2154
    Email: morasha@uol.com.br
Congregacao Monte Sinai
Rua Piaui 624, Higienopolis 01241-000
    (11) 3824-9229
    Fax: (11) 3824-9229
    Email: cmsinai@sanet.com.br

Religious Organisations
Centro Judaico Religioso de Sao Paulo
    (11) 220-5642
Office hours: 9 am to 1 pm weekdays.
Comunidade Israelita Ortodoxa de Sao Paulo
Kehilat Hacharedim, Rua Haddock Lobo 1091
    (11) 282-1562; 852-9710
This Community centre has two synagogues.

Restaurants
Hebraica Kosher Restaurant
Rua Hungria 1000
    (11) 815-6788; 815-6980; 818-8831
    Fax: (11) 815-6980
Supervision: Rabbi Elyahu B. Valt.
Buffet Mosaico inside the Hebraica São Paulo club.
Closed Mondays, open Saturday night 1 1/2 hours
after Shabbat.

Kosher Center
Rua Corrèa de Melo 68 01123-020   (11) 223-1175
    Fax: (11) 223-3721
Supervision: Rabbi M.A. Iliovitch Shlita of Kehal
Hachareidim.
Restaurant and Bakery. Hours: Sun 9.00am-4.00pm.
Mon-Thurs 8.00am-6.00pm. Fri 7.30am-3.00pm
Restaurant Beit Chinuch
Rua P. João Manoel 727   (11) 280-5111
    Fax: (11) 280-4553
    Email: lavne@uninet.com.br
Phone for directions and times.

Dairy
Kosher Pizza, Rua padre Joao Manoel 881
    (11) 3064-9022

Meat
Bero, Rua Pelxoto Gomide 2020   (11) 3086-2808
Reservations are preferred

Synagogues
Beit Chabad Perdizes
Rua Dr. Manoel Maria Tourinho 261   (11) 3865-0615
By appointment only.
Congregacao Mekor Haim
Rua Sao Vicente de Paulo 276 01229-010
    (11) 3826-7699
    Fax: (11) 3666-6960
    Email: revista_nascente@hotmail.com

Hasidic
Kehal Chassidim
Rua Mamore 597   (11) 224-0278

Hungarian
Adas Yereim, Rua Talmud Tora 86   (11) 282-1562;
852-9710

Liberal
Congregacao Israelita Paulista
Rua Antonio Carlos 653   (11) 256-7811
    Fax: (11) 257-1446
    Email: scrtgeral@dialdata.com.br
    Web site: www.cip.sp.com.br

Orthodox
Beit Chabad Central
Rua Chabad 60 01417-030   (11) 3060-9777
    Fax: (11) 3060-9778
    Email: esther@chabad.org.br
    Web site: www.chabad.org.br

Brazil / Sao Paolo

Progressive
Comunidade Shalom
Rua Coronel Joaquim Ferreira Lobo 195 04544-150
(11) 829-1477
Fax: (11) 828-9177
Beit Itzchak
Rua Haddock Lobo 1279 (11) 881-3804
Fax: (11) 881-3064, 0302
Beit Yaacov
Rua Dr Veiga Filho 547, Higienopolis 01229-000
(11) 3662-2154
Fax: (11) 3662-2154
Email: morasha@uol.com.br
Kehal Machzikei Hadat
Rua Padre Joao Manuel 727 (11) 280-5111
Sinagoga Israelita Paulista – Beit Chabad
Rua Augusta 259 01305-000 (11) 258-7173
Sephardi

Templo Israelita Brasileiro Ohel Yaacov
Rua Abolicao 457 (11) 606-9982
Fax: (11) 227-6793

Travel Agencies
Carmel Tur, Rua Xavier de Toledo 121/10
(11) 257-2244
Sharontur, Rua de Graca 235 (11) 223-8388
Email: dsmaletz@ibm.net
Open: 8.00am-6.00pm. Closed Shabat (Saturday) & Sunday. International & domestic tickets. Car rental, exchange, hotel reservations. Languages spoken: English, Hebrew, Spanish. Contact person: Mr. Dov Smaletz
Vertice, Rua Sao Bento 545/10 (11) 3115-1960
Fax: (11) 3068-0325

Sorocaba

Synagogues
Community Centre
Rua Dom Pedro II 56 (11) 31-3168

Bulgaria

Dating back to the Byzantine conquest, the community in Bulgaria was established by Greek Jews in Serdica (Sofia, the capital). The Jewish community grew when the Bulgarian state was founded in 681. Czar Ivan Alexander (1331–71) had a Jewish wife (who converted to Christianity).

The community has included eminent rabbinic commentators, such as Rabbi Dosa Ajevani and Joseph Caro, the codifier of the Shulchan Aruch, who escaped to Bulgaria after the expulsion from Spain. The various Jewish groups joined to form a unified Sephardi community in the late seventeenth century.

About 50,000 Jews lived in Bulgaria in 1939. Despite much pressure from the Nazis, the government and general population refused to allow Jews to be deported. Only Jews from Macedonia and Thrace, occupied by Bulgaria, were deported. Despite being saved, most of the community emigrated to Israel after the war. The 10 per cent who remained were then under the control of the communists and had little contact with the outside world.

Since the fall of communism, the community has been reconstituted and now has synagogues in Sofia and Plovdiv. The community is ageing, although 100 children attend a Sunday school run by the Shalom Organisation, the central Jewish organisation for Bulgaria.

GMT + 2 hours	Total Population 8,366,000
Country calling code (359)	Jewish Population 3,000
Emergency Telephone (Police - 166) (Fire - 160) (Ambulance - 150)	Electricity voltage 220

Pazardjik

Community Organisations
Community Centre
Asson Zlatarov St. 26 (34) 28-364

Plovdiv

Libraries
Library and House of Culture
Vladimir Zaimov St. 20 (32) 761-376

Synagogues
Tsar Kalojan St. 15
In the courtyard of a large apartment complex.

Rousse

Synagogues
Community Centre
Ivan Vazov Sq. 4 (82) 270-540

Sofia

About half of Bulgarian Jewry lives in Sofia. The Great Synagogue of 1878 ranks among the largest of Sephardi synagogues.

Cemeteries

Jewish Cemetery
Orlandovtzi suburb
Take a tram (Nos. 2, 10 or 14) to the last stop for this large Jewish cemetery.

Community Organisations

Social & Cultural Organisation of Bulgarian Jews
Shalom, Alexander Stambolisky St. 50   (2) 870-163
Publishes a periodical 'Evreiski Vesti' and a yearbook. It also maintains a museum devoted to 'The Rescue of Bulgarian Jews, 1941-1944'. At the same address are the offices of El Al, the Joint and the Jewish Agency.

Embassy

Embassy of Israel
1 Bulgaria Sq. NDK, 7th floor   (2) 951-5029
                                       Fax: (2) 952-1101

Religious Organisations

Central Jewish Religious Council
Ekzarh Josef St. 16   (2) 831-273
                                       Fax: (2) 835-085

Synagogues

Ekzarh Josef St. 16   (2) 831-273
                                       Fax: (2) 835-085
Adjacent to the synagogue is a museum dedicated to the history of Bulgarian Jewry.

Canada / Alberta

The Jewish settlement of Canada began with the British expansion into Canada. In 1760, the Shearith Israel synagogue was founded in Montreal and in 1832 Jews received full civil rights. In the 1850s the community began to spread from Montreal to Toronto and Hamilton.

The community grew throughout the early twentieth century, from 16,000 in 1900 to 126,000 in 1921. After the Second World War, Jewish immigration increased and by 1961 the population was 260,000.

The headquarters of the Canadian Jewish Congress is in Montreal. This is the main national organisation for Canadian Jewry, and the community is provided with a full range of services, with Jewish schools, yeshivot, newspapers and the unique (in the Americas) Montreal Jewish Library. There are also several kosher restaurants.

GMT - 3 to 8 hours

Country calling code (1)

Emergency Telephone (Police, Fire and Ambulance - 911)

In remote areas, calls have to be made via the operator.

Total Population 29,784,000

Jewish Population 360,000

Electricity voltage 110

Alberta

Calgary

Bakeries

Susan's Kosher Bakery
131, 2515 - 90th Avenue SW   (403) 238-5300
                                    Fax: (403) 238-3023
Supervision: Calgary Kosher.
Hours of operation: Sunday 10 am to 2 pm, Tuesday to Thursday 9 am to 6 pm, Friday 8 am to 4 pm (winter 8 am to 2 pm). Closed Mondays and Shabbat.

Delicatessens

Schaier's Meat & Kosher Deli
2515 90th Av. S.W.   (403) 251-2552
Wolf's Kosher World & Deli
42 180-94th Av. S.E   (403) 253-3354
Hours: Sunday to Thursday, 10 am to 8 pm; Friday, 10 am to 2 pm.

Media

Newspapers

Jewish Free Press
8411 Elbow Dr. SW T2V 1K8   (403) 252-9423
                                    Fax: (403) 255-5640
                          Email: jewishfp@cadvision.com

Religious Organisations
Calgary Rabbinical Council
                                    (403) 253-8600
                                    Fax: (403) 253-7915

Representative Organisations
B'nai Brith Canada
Western Region, 10655 Southport Rd S.W., Suite 1400
T2W 4Y1   (403) 225-5256
                                    Fax: (403) 278-0176

Calgary Jewish Community Council
1607 90th Av. S.W.   (403) 253-8600
                                    Fax: (403) 253-7915
                          Email: cjcc@jewish-calgary.com
                          Web site: www.jewish-calgary.com
The Council issues a booklet 'Keeping Kosher in Calgary'.

Restaurants
Karen's Cafe, Calgary Jewish Centre, 1607 90th Av.
S.W.   (403) 255-5311
Hours:Monday to Thursday, 10 am to 7 pm; Friday, 10 am to 1 pm. Closed on Sunday

Synagogues
Westridge Community Synagogue
502 Wolf Willow Road   (403) 489-6602

Conservative

Beth Tzedec
1325 Glenmore Trail S.W. T2Y 4Y8   (403) 252-8319
                          Email: info@bethtzedec.ab.ca

Orthodox

Congregation House of Jacob-Mikveh Israel
1613-92nd Av., Jerusalem Rd. SW T2V 5C9
                                    (403) 259-3230
                                    Fax: (403) 259-3240
                          Email: hojmi@cadvision.com
                          Web site: www.cadivision.com/hojmi

Reform
Temple B'nai Tikvah
Calgary Jewish Centre, 1607 90th Av. S.W. T2V 4V7
(403) 252-1654
Fax: (403) 252-1709
Email: temple@cadvision.com

Edmonton
Media

Newspapers

Edmonton Jewish Life
10342 107th Street T5J 1K2   (780) 488-7276
Fax: (780) 487-4342
Email: ejlife@powersurfr.com
Edmonton Jewish News
#330, 10036 Jasper Ave T5J 2W2   (780) 421-7966
Fax: (780) 424-3951

Representative Organisations
Edmonton Jewish Federation
7200 156th St. T5R 1X3   (780) 487-0585
Fax: (780) 481-1854
Email: edjfed@netcom.ca
Contact Gayle Tallman, Exec. Director, for additional
information.

Restaurants

Dairy

King David Pizza
West Edmonton Mall   (780) 486-9020

Synagogues

Othodox

Beth Israel
131 Wolf Willow Road T5T 1T1   (780) 482-2840
Fax: (780) 482-2470
Email: edbeth@telusplanet.net

Reform

Beth Shalom
11916 Jasper Av. T5K 0N9   (780) 488-6333
Fax: (780) 488-6259
Email: bshalom2@telusplanet.net
Temple Beth Ora
7200 156th St. T5R 1X3   (780) 487-4817
Fax: (780) 481-1854
Email: bethora@planet.eon.net

Canada / British Columbia

Lethbridge
Synagogues

Orthodox

Beth Israel
914 15th Street South T1J 3A5   (403) 327-8621

British Columbia
Kelowna
Synagogues

Traditional

Beth Shalom Sanctuary
OJCC, 102-1 North Glenmore Road V1V 2E2
(250) 862-2305
Fax: (250) 862-2365
Email: ojc@cnx.net
Shabbat services last Saturday of the month, 9:30 am.

Richmond
Bakeries
Garden City Bakery
#360-9100 Blundell Road   (604) 244-7888
Supervision: Orthodox Rabbinical Council of British
Columbia.

Kashrut Information
Orthodox Rabbinical Council of British Columbia
8080 Francis Road V6Y 1A4   (604) 275-0042
Fax: (604) 277-2225
Email: bckosher@direct.ca
Kashrut Director, Rabbi A. Feigelstock; Kashrut
Administrator, Rabbi Levy Teitlebaum.

Synagogues

Conservative

Beth Tikvah
9711 Geal Road V7E 1R4   (604) 271-6262
Friday, 8 pm; Shabbat, 9:30 am. Wheelchair access.

Orthodox

Eitz Chaim
8080 Frances Road V6Y 1A4   (604) 275-0007
Fax: (604) 277-2225
Daily, 7 am and sunset; Shabbat, 9 am and sunset;
Sunday, 9 am. Wheelchair access.

Surrey – White Rock
Community Organisations
White Rock/South Surrey Jewish Community Centre
PO Box 75186 V4A   (604) 541-9995
Monthly Shabbat services. Wheelchair access.

Canada / British Columbia

Synagogues

Hasidic

The Centre for Judaism of the Lower Fraser Valley
2351 128th Street   (604) 541-4111
                                        Email: shfy@aol.com
Weekly Shabbat services.   Wheelchair access.

Vancouver

Bed & Breakfasts
Shulamit Mass
5434 Manson Street V5Z 3H1   (604) 266-8965

Bed and Breakfasts
Mrs Levin's Kosher Bed & Breakfast
Apt 101, 2772 Spruce V6H 2R2   (604) 738-2457

Cafeterias

Dairy

Cafe Sabra Too (Jewish Community Centre)
950 West 41st Avenue V5Z 2N7   (604) 257-5111
Supervision: Orthodox Rabbinical Council of British
Columbia.
Fresh kosher cookies, muffins, falafel, salads and more
items. Take-out, eat-in and catering. Dairy, pareve
(meat is take-out only). Hours: Monday to Thursday,
8:30 am to 8 pm; Friday, 8:30 am to 2 pm; Sunday,
10 am to 6:30 pm.

Community Organisations
Jewish Community Centre of Greater Vancouver
950 West 41st Avenue V5Z 2N7   (604) 257-5111
                                Fax: (604) 257-5119
                        Email: library@intergate.bc.ca
                        Web site: www.jccgv.com

Contact Information
Jewish Federation of Greater Vancouver
950 West 41st Avenue, Suite 200 V5Z 2N7
                                    (604) 257-5100
                                Fax: (604) 257-5119
            Email: shalom_vancouver@ultranet.ca
                Web site: www.shalomvancouver.org
Executive Director Daniella Givon

Shalom Vancouver
950 West 41st Avenue V5Z 2N7   (604) 257-5111
                                Fax: (604) 257-5119
            Email: shalom_vancouver@ultranet.ca
                Web site: www.shalomvancouver.org
Jewish Information Referral & Welcome Service for
newcomers and visitors. Publishes a 'Guide to Jewish
life in British Columbia'. Hours: Monday to Friday 10
am to 2 pm.

Media

Newspapers

Western Jewish Bulletin
301, 68 East 2nd Avenue V5T 1B1   (604) 689-1520
                                Fax: (604) 689-1525

Restaurants

Dairy

Chagall's @ JCC (Chagalls)
950 West 41st Avenue   (604) 263-7507
                                Fax: (604) 263-7507
Supervision: British Columbia Kosher Council.
Deliveries to Hotels - Pareve available on request.
Dairy, cafeteria style café and restaurant.

Sabra Kosher Bakery, Restaurant and Grocery
3844 Oak Street V6H 2M5   (604) 733-4912
                                Fax: (604) 733-4911
Supervision: Orthodox Rabbinical Council of British
Columbia.
Fresh kosher cookies, muffins, falafel, salads and more
items. Take-out, eat-in and catering. Dairy, pareve
(meat is take-out only). Hours: Monday to Thursday,
8:30 am to 8 pm; Friday, 8:30 am to 2 pm; Sunday,
10 am to 6:30 pm.

Surat Sweet
1938 West 4th Avenue   (604) 733-7363
Indian vegetarian - Gujarati style

Meat

Omnitsky Kosher B.C.
5866 Cambie Street   (604) 321-1818
                                Fax: (604) 321-1817
                    Email: erappaport@home.com
                    Web site: www.escape.ca
Supervision: Orthodox Rabbinical Council of British
Columbia.
Fresh meats, poultry. Manufacturers of all beef
delicatessen products under B.C.K.

Synagogoes

Orthodox

Torat Hayim Community (participatory)
483 Eastcot Road   (604) 922-5062
Fax: (604) 984-4168
Shabbat: 10.30 am followed by Kiddush

Synagogues

Conservative

Beth Israel
4350 Oak Street V6H 2N4   (604) 731-4161
Daily, 8 am (public holidays, 9 am) and 6 pm; Friday,
8:15 pm; Shabbat, 9:15 am and 6 pm; Sunday, 9 am
and 6 pm. Wheelchair access.

Congregation Har El
North Shore Jewish Community Centre,
1305 Taylor Way, West Vancouver V7T 2Y7
(604) 925-6488
Fax: (604) 922-8245
Executive Director: Sheila Milstein. Friday, 7 pm;
Shabbat, 10 am (Seasonal). Visitors welcome.

Hasidic

Chabad Richmond
200-4775 Blundell Road
Email: chabad@axionet.com
Chabad-Lubavitch
5435 Baillie Street V5Z 3M6   (604) 266-1313
Fax: (604) 263-7934
Email: chabadbc@axionet.com
Daily, 7 am and sunset; Shabbat, 10 am; Sunday, 9
am. Wheelchair access.

Jewish Renewal

Or Shalom
710 East 10th Avenue V5T 2A7   (604) 872-1614
Fax: (604) 872-4406
Email: orshalom@telus.net
Web site: www.orshalom.bc.ca
Family Kabbalat Shabbat and potluck dinner monthly;
Shabbat 10 am. Wheelchair access.

Orthodox

Louis Brier Home
1055 West 41st Avenue V6M 1W9
(604) 261-9376
Daily mincha, 4:30 pm; Friday, 4:15 pm; Shabbat, 9
am. Wheelchair access.

Schara Tzedeck
3476 Oak Street V6H 2L8   (604) 736-7607
Monday and Thursday, 7 am; Tuesday, Wednesday
and Friday, 7:15 am; weekdays, sunset; Friday, 7:30
pm; Shabbat, 9 am and half hour before sunset;
Sunday, 8:30 am.

Reform

Temple Sholom
7190 Oak Street V6P 3Z9   (604) 266-7190
Monday and Wednesday, 7:15 am; Friday, 8:15 pm;
Shabbat, 10 am.

Sephardi Orthodox

Beth Hamidrash
3231 Heather Street V5Z 3K4
(604) 872-4222; 873-2371
Daily, 7 am; Shabbat, 9 am; Sunday and public
holidays, 8:30 am; Friday, 5 pm; Shabbat, sunset.

Traditional

Burquest Jewish Community
720 6th St., PO Box 187, New Westminster BC V3L
3C5   (604) 526-7235
Fax: (604) 291-3496
Email: info@burquest.org
Web site: www.burquest.org
Oneg Shabbat services second Friday of each month, 8
pm. Wheelchair access.
Shaarey Tefilah
785 West 16th Avenue   (604) 873-2700
Friday evening, call for time; Shabbat and Sunday, 9
am. Wheelchair access.

Victoria

Community Organisations
Victoria Jewish Community Centre
3636 Shelbourne Street   (250) 477-7184
Fax: (250) 477-6283

Synagogues

Conservative

Emanu-El
1461 Blanshard V8W 2J3   (250) 382-0615
Thursday, 7 am; Shabbat, 9 am. Wheelchair access.

Manitoba

Winnipeg

Bakeries
City Bread
238 Dufferin Avenue R2W 2X6   (204) 586-8409
Goodies' Bake Shop
2 Donald Street R3L 0K5   (204) 489-5526

Canada / Manitoba

Gunn's
247 Selkirk Avenue R2W 2L5   (204) 586-6150

Butchers
Omnitsky's
1428 Main Street R2W 3V4   (204) 586-8271
Tuxedo Quality Foods
1853 Grant Avenue R3N 1Z2   (204) 987-3830
Frozen only

Communal Organisations
Asper Jewish Community Campus
C300 - 123 Doncaster Street R3N 1B2
    (204) 477-7400
    Fax: (204) 477-7405
    Email: info@jewishwinnipeg.org
    Web site: www.jewishwinnipeg.org
Home to Winnipeg Jewish Theatre, Canadian Jewish
Congress and Jewish Heritage Centre

Groceries
Bathurst Street Market
1570 Main Street R2W 5J8   (204) 338-4911

Media

Newspapers

Jewish Post & News
113 Hutchings Street R2X 2V4   (204) 694-3332
    Fax: (204) 694-3916
Jewish Radio Hour Weekly – Sundays, at 1:30 pm.
Channel 11.

Mikvaot
Community Mikvah
123 Doncaster Street R3N 2B1   (204) 477-7445
Mikva Chabad-Lubavitch
455 Hartford Avenue R2V 0W9   (204) 339-4761
    Fax: (204) 586-0487
    Email: aaltein@mbnet.mb.ca
Mailing address: 2095 Sinclair Street, Wpg.MB R2V
3K2.

Restaurants
Bathurst Downstairs Deli
1570 Main Steet R2W 5J8   (204) 338-4911
Nosh-A-Rye Café
123 Doncaster Street R3B 2K1   (204) 477-7418
    Fax: (204) 477-7507

Synagogues

Egalitarian Conservative

Beth Israel
1007 Sinclair Street R2V 3J5   (204) 582-2353
Congregation Shaarey Zedek
561 Wellington Crescent R3M 0A6   (204) 452-3711

Orthodox
Chevra Mishnayes
700 Jefferson Avenue R2V OP6   (204) 338-8503
Lubavitch Centre
2095 Sinclair Street R2V 3K2   (204) 339-8737

New Brunswick
Fredericton

Synagogues
Sgoolai Israel
Westmorland Street E3B 3L7   (506) 454-9698
    Fax: (506) 452-8889
    Email: samuels@unb.ca
For information on availability of kosher food, call
Rabbi Yochanan Samuels: (506) 454-2717

Moncton

Synagogues
Tiferes Israel
56 Steadman Street E1C 8L9   (506) 858-0258
    Fax: (506) 858-0259
    Email: tifisrl@nbnet.nb.ca
Mikva on premises.

St John

Museums
Saint John Jewish Historical Museum
29 Wellington Row E2L 3H4   (506) 633-1833
    Fax: (506) 642-9926
    Email: sjjhm@nbnet.nb.ca
May-mid Octoberr 10am to 4pm Monday to Friday.
Also, during July and August, Sunday 1pm to 4pm or
by appointment. This is the only Jewish museum in the
Atlantic Provinces of Canada. There are eight display
areas as well as library and archives. Guided tours
available.

Synagogues

Conservative

Shaarei Zedek
76 Carleton Street E2L 2Z4   (506) 657-4790
Community centre on premises.

Newfoundland

St John's

Synagogues
Hebrew Congregation of Newfoundland & Labrador (Beth El)
Elizabeth and Downing Avenues A1C 5L4
(709) 737-6548
Fax: (709) 737-6995
Email: mpaul@mun.ca
Mailing address: P O Box 724, St. John's A1C 5L4, NF, Canada

Nova Scotia

Glace Bay

Synagogues

Orthodox
1 Prince Street B1A 3C8   (902) 849-8605

Halifax

Community Organisations
Atlantic Jewish Council
5670 Spring Garden Road, Suite 508 B3J 1H6
(902) 422-7491
Fax: (902) 425-3722
Email: jgoldberg@theajc.ns.ca
Web site: www.theajc.ns.ca
Covers Nova Scotia, New Brunswick, Price Edward Island, Newfoundland and Halifax. Also at this address: Canadian Jewish Congress, Atlantic Region, Canadian Zionist Federation, United Jewish Appeal Appeal, Canadian Young Judea, Hadassah, Jewish National Fund, Atlantic Provinces Jewish Student Federation, Camp Kadimah, Regional Chaplaincy.

Media

Newspapers

Shalom Magazine
5675 Spring Garden Road, Suite 800, Halifax, NS B3J 1H1
(902) 422-7491
Fax: (902) 425-3722
Email: jgoldberg@theajc.ns.ca

Synagogues

Conservative

Shaar Shalom
1981 Oxford Street B3H 4A4   (902) 423-5848

Orthodox
Beth Israel
1480 Oxford Street B3H 3Y8   (902) 422-1301
Mikva on premises.

Sydney

Synagogues

Conservative

Temple Sons of Israel
P.O. Box 311, Whitney Avenue B1P 6H2
(902) 564-4650

Yarmouth

Contact Information
R & V Indiq
13 Parade Street B5A 3A5
Will be happy to provide details of the local Jewish Community.

Ontario

Belleville

Synagogues

Conservative

Sons of Jacob
211 Victoria Avenue K8N 2C2   (613) 962-1433

Brantford

Synagogues

Orthodox

Beth David
50 Waterloo Street N3T 3R8   (519) 752-8950

Chatham

Synagogues

Conservative

Children of Jacob
29 Water Street N7M 3H4   (519) 352-3544

Cornwall

Synagogues
Beth-El
321 Amelia Street K6H 3P4   (613) 932-6373

Canada / Ontario

Guelph

Synagogues

Traditional

Beth Isaiah
47 Surrey Street W. N1H 3R5   (519) 836-4338
                                     Email: cgdk@aol.com
Full line of Kosher products at Ultra-519-763-3827.

Hamilton

Butchers
Hamilton Kosher Meats
889 King Street West L8S 1K5

Delicatessens
Westdale Deli
893 King Street West L8S 1K5   (905) 529-2605
                                      Fax: (905) 529-2605

Media

Newspapers

Hamilton Jewish News
P.O. Box 7528
Ancaster L9G 3N6   (905) 648-0605
                                     Fax: (905) 648-8388

Representative Organisations
Hamilton Jewish Federation
1030 Lower Lions Club Road
P.O. Box 7258, Ancaster L9G 3N6   (905) 648-0605
                                     Fax: (905) 648-8350
                        Email: hamujajf@interlynx.net

Synagogues

Conservative

Beth Jacob
375 Aberdeen Avenue L8P 2R7   (905) 522-1351

Orthodox

Adas Israel
125 Cline Avenue S. L8S 1X2   (905) 528-0039
                                     Fax: (905) 528-7497

Reform

Anshe Sholom
215 Cline Avenue N. L8S 4A1   (905) 528-0121
                                     Fax: (905) 528-2994

Kingston

Community Organisations
B'nai B'rith Hillel Foundation
26 Barrie Street   (613) 542-1120

Synagogues

Orthodox

Beth Israel
116 Centre Street K7L 4E6   (613) 542-5012
                        Email: bethisrael@kingston.net

Reform

Temple Iyr Hamelech
331 Union Street West K7L 2R3   (613) 789-7022

Kitchener

Synagogues
Temple Shalom
116 Queen Street North N2H 2H7   (519) 743-0401

Traditional

Beth Jacob
161 Stirling Avenue South N2G 3N8   (519) 743-8422

London

Community Organisations
Jewish Community Council
536 Huron Street N5Y 4J5   (519) 673-3310
                                Email: ljf@icis.on.ca
There are no kosher establishments, but kosher frozen
meat, prepared foods and select groceries are
available at the local A&P, IGA North London market,
and Loblaws Stores. Communal inquiries to Executive
Director at the above number.

Media

Newspapers

London Jewish Community News
536 Huron Street N5Y 4J5   (519) 673-3310
                                     Fax: (519) 673-1161
                        Email: susan.merskey@sympatico.ca

Synagogues

Conservative

Congregation Or Shalom
534 Huron Street N5Y 4J5   (519) 438-3081
                                     Fax: (519) 439-2994

Orthodox

Congregation Beth Tefilah
1210 Adelaide Street North N5Y 4T6   (519) 433-7081
                                     Fax: (519) 433-0616
                        Email: beth_tefilah@canada.com
                        Web site: www.execulink.com/~cbt/
Mikva on premises.

Canada / Ontario

Reform

Temple Israel
651 Windermere Road N5X 2P1   (519) 858-4400
Fax: (519) 858-2070
Email: jwitts@julian.uwo.ca

Mississauga

Synagogues
Solel Congregation
2399 Folkway Drive L5L 2M6   (905) 820-5915
Fax: (905) 820-1956

Niagara Falls

Synagogues

Conservative

B'nai Jacob
5328 Ferry Street L2G 1R7   (416) 354-3934

North Bay

Synagogues
Orthodox

Sons of Jacob
302 McIntyre Street West P1B 2Z1   (705) 497-9288
Fax: (705) 497-9812
Email: martyb19@hotmail.com
Friday evening services.

Oakville

Synagogues

Reform

Shaarei-Beth El
186 Morrison Road L6J 4J4   (905) 849-6000
Fax: (905) 849-1134
Email: sbe@idirect.com
Web site: www.webhome.idirect.com/~sbe

Oshawa

Synagogues

Orthodox

Beth Zion
144 King Street East L1H 1B6   (905) 723-2353

Ottawa

Ottawa is the capital of Canada and its fourth largest city. The first Jewish settler came in 1858 when Ottawa was still known as Bytown. Ottawa has always been strongly traditional and has a growing community presently numbering around 13,000.

Butchers
United Kosher Meat & Deli Ltd
378 Richmond Road   (613) 722-6556
Kosher meals and sandwiches available on weekdays.

Religious Organisations
Vaad Ha'ir (Jewish Community Council)
151 Chapel Street K1N 7Y2   (613) 232-7306
Fax: (613) 563-4593
Vaad Hakashruth located here for all kashrut information.

Synagogues
Conservatives

Agudath Israel
1400 Coldrey Avenue K12 7P9   (613) 728-3501

Reform
Temple Israel
1301 Prince of Wales K2C 1N2   (613) 224-1802

Orthodox

Beth Shalom Congregation
151 Chapel Street K1N 7Y2   (613) 789-3501
Beth Shalom West
15 Chartwell Avenue K2G 4K3   (613) 723-1800
Machzikei Hadas
2310 Virginia Drive K1H 6S2   (613) 521-9700

Representative Organisations
Canadian Jewish Congress National Office
100 Sparks Street, Suite 650 K1P 5B7
(613) 233-8703
Fax: (613) 233-8748
Email: canadianjewishcongress@cjc.ca
Web site: www.cjc.ca
Publishes the National Synagogue Directory. Contact to find out information on synagogues in the city to which you are travelling.

Restaurants

Dairy

Rideau Bakery
384 Rideau Street   (613) 789-1019
Supervision: Ottawa Va'ad HaKashrut.
A light lunch sandwich counter in down-town Ottawa.
Viva Pizza, 1726 Carling Avenue   (613) 722-6645

Owen Sound

Synagogues

Conservative

Beth Ezekiel
3531 Bay Shore Road N4K 5N3   (519) 376-8774

Canada / Ontario

Pembroke

Synagogues
Beth Israel
322 William Street K8A 1P3   (613) 732-7811

Peterborough

Synagogues
Conservative

Beth Israel, Waller Street   (705) 745-8398

Richmond Hill

Synagogues
Beth Rayim
9711 Bayview Avenue L4C 9X7   (905) 770-7639
The Country Shul
Carville Road and Bathurst Street   (905) 770-4191

St Catharine's

Community Organisations
Community Centre
Newman Memorial Building   (416) 685-6767

Synagogues
Reform

Temple Tikvah
83 Church Street, PO Box 484 L2R 3C7
          (416) 682-4191

Traditional

B'nai Israel
190 Church Street L2R 4C4   (416) 685-6767
          Fax: (416) 685-3100

Sudbury

Synagogues
Orthodox

Shaar Hashomayim
158 John Street P3E 1P4   (705) 673-0831

Thornhill

Booksellers
Israel's Judaica Centre
441 Clark Avenue West L47 6W7   (905) 881-1010
          Fax: (905) 881-1016
          Email: contact@israelsjudaica.com
          Web site: www.israel.judaica.com
Also sells gifts.
Matana Judaica
248 Steeles Avenue West, #6 L4J 1A1
          (905) 731-6543
          Fax: (905) 882-6196
Also sells gifts.

Delicatessens
Marky's Delicatessen North
7330 Yonge Street L4J 1V8   (905) 731-4800
Wok'n'Deli
441 Clarke Avenue West L4J 6W7   (905) 882-0809

Restaurants
Dairy

My Zaidy's Pizza
441 Clark Avenue West L4J 6W8   (905) 731-3029

Meat

Miami Grill, 441 Clark Avenue   (905) 709-0096
Supervision: COR.
Taste of Tikvah
7700 Bathurst Street   (905) 771-0699
Supervision: COR.

Thunder Bay

Synagogues
Orthodox

Shaarey Shomayim
627 Gray Street P7E 2E4   (905) 622-4867

Toronto

There have been one and a half centuries of organised Jewish life in Toronto since its start in 1849. The Jewish population increased significantly during the 1980s, and now Toronto is home to almost half of Canada's Jews. There is a good range of Jewish facilities in the city.

Bakeries
Bagels Galore
First Canadian Place M5X 1E1   (905) 363-4233
Carmel Bakery
3856 Bathurst Street   (905) 633-5315
Dairy Treats Bakery
3522 Bathurst Street   (905) 787-0309
Richman's Bakery
4119 Bathurst Street   (905) 636-9710

Booksellers
Israel's Judaica Centre
897 Eglinton Avenue West M6C 2C1
          (905) 256-2858
          Email: contact@israelsjudaica.com
          Web site: www.israel.judaica.com
Negev Importing Co Ltd
3509 Bathurst Street M6A 2C5   (905) 781-9356
Toll free: 1-888-618-9356
          Fax: (905) 781-0071
          Email: negev_imp@hotmail.com

Canada / Ontario

Community Organisations

Bernard Betel (Senior Centre)
1003 Steeles Avenue West M2R 3T6   (416) 225-2112
Fax: (416) 225-2097
Email: betelctr@idirect.com
Centre operates Conservative Synagogue - has two
Sephardil congregations on site - Beth Yosef and
Tehillat Yerushalayim.

Jewish Federation of Greater Toronto
4600 Bathurst Street
North York M2R 3V2   (905) 635-2883
Fax: (905) 635-9565
Email: office@ujafed.org

Contact Information

Jewish Information Service
4588 Bathurst Street
Suite 345, Willowdale M2R 1W6   (905) 635-5600
Fax: (905) 636-5813
Email: webmaven@jewishtoronot.net
Web site: www.jewishtoronto.net
Publishes a Jewish Community of Services Directory for
Greater Toronto, as well as other Jewish publications.

Cultural Organisations

Silverman Heritage Museum
Baycrest Centre for Geriatric Care, 3560 Bathurst Street
M6A 2E1   (905) 785-2500 Ext.2802
One of the few judaica museums in Canada it has an
active exhibit program.

Delicatessens

Marky's Delicatessen
280 Wilson Avenue, Downsview   (905) 638-1081
Mati's Fallafel House
3430 Bathurst Street M6A 1C2   (905) 783-9505
Sells dairy products only.

Embassy

Consul General of Israel
180 Bloor Street West, Suite 700 M5S 2V6
(905) 640-8500
Fax: (905) 640-8555
Email: hasbara@idirect.com
Israel Government Tourist Office: 964-3784

Gift shop

Miriam's, 3007 Bathurst Street
(416) 781-8261/265-7427
Fax: (416) 781-8261
Email: leslier@surfen.net

Media

Newspapers

Canadian Jewish News
10 Gateway Blvd
Suite 420, Don Mills M3C 3A1
(905) 422-2331
Fax: (905) 422-3790

Jewish Tribune
15 Hove Street
Downsview M3H 4Y8,   (905) 633-6227
Fax: (905) 630-2159

Memorials

Holocaust Education & Memorial Centre
4600 Bathurst Street
Willowdale M2R 3V2   (905) 635-2883

Religious Organisations

JEP/Ohr Somayach Centre
2939 Bathurst Street M6B 2B2   (905) 785-5899
Has a minyan.
Kashruth Council
4600 Bathurst Street, Ste 240 M2R 3V2
(905) 635-9550
Fax: (905) 635-8760
All enquiries about kashrut here.

Restaurants

Chicken Nest
3038 Bathurst Street M6B 4K2   (905) 787-6378
Hakerem
3030 Bathurst Street
Willowdale MB6 3B6   (416) 787-6504
Fax: (416) 787-6504

Dairy

Dairy Treats Cafe
3522 Bathurst Street M6A 2C6   (905) 787-0309
King David Pizza
3020 Bathurst Street M6B 2B6   (905) 781-1326
Milk'n Honey
3457 Bathurst Street
Downsview M6A 2C5   (905) 789-7651
Fax: (905) 789-4788

Pizza Tova, 3020 Bathurst Street   (905) 781-1326
Supervision: COR.
Tov Li Pizza
5972 Bathurst Street
Willowdale M2R 1Z1,   (905) 650-9800

Canada / Ontario

Meat

King Solomon's Table
3705 Chesswood Drive
Downsview M3J 2P6   (905) 630-0666
                               Fax: (905) 630-4585
Open Monday to Thursday 12.00 noon to 10.00pm.
Sunday 4.00pm to 10.00pm. Closed Friday and
Saturday. Open Saturday night in the winter. Kashrut:
COR.

Marky's Delicatessen
6233 Bathurst Street, (just South of Steel)
                                    (905) 227-0707
Supervision: Kashruth Council of Toronto.

Windsor

Community Organisations
Jewish Community Council
1641 Ouellette Avenue N8X 1K9   (519) 973-1772

Media

Periodicals
Windsor Jewish Community Bulletin

                               Fax: (519) 973-1774

Synagogues

Orthodox

Shaar Hashomayim
115 Giles Blvd East N9A 4C1   (519) 256-3123
                               Fax: (519) 256-3124

Shaarey Zedek
610 Giles Blvd East N9A 4E2   (519) 252-1594

Reform

Congregation Beth-El
2525 Mark Avenue N9E 2W2   (519) 969-2422

Quebec
Montreal

1760 saw the arrival of the first Jews in Montreal:
civilians attached to the British army. In the 1920s
and 1930s the Boulevard St-Laurent was
equivalent to London's East End or New York's
Lower East Side. There are now just over 100,000
Jews in the city. Twenty per cent of them are North
African Sephardim.

Bakeries

Biscuit Adar, 5458 Westminister   (514) 484-1198
Supervision: Vaad Hair.
Kosher Cookies
Boulangerie-Adir
6795 Darligton   (514) 342-1991
Supervision: Vaad Hair.
Cite Cashere, 4747 Van Horne   (514) 733-2838
Supervision: Vaad Hair.
Delice Cashere
4655 Van Horne   (514) 733-5010
Supervision: Vaad Hair.
Katzberg Home Bread and Cake Delivery
5355 Jeanne Mance   (514) 273-4042
Supervision: Vaad Hair.
Kleins Kosher Bakery
5540 Hutchison   (514) 274-4633
Supervision: Vaad Hair.
Kosher Quality Bakery
5855 Victoria   (514) 731-7883
                               Fax: (514) 731-0205
Supervision: Vaad Hair.
Hours: Sunday - Wednesday 6am to 9pm. Thursday
6am to 10pm. Friday 6am winter 2pm or summer
4pm.
La Biscuit Adar
1204 Beaumont   (514) 343-0272
Supervision: Vaad Hair.
Montreal Kosher
7005 Victoria   (514) 739-3651
Supervision: Vaad Hair.
Montreal Kosher
2135 St. Louis, St. Laurent   (514) 747-5116
Supervision: Vaad Hair.
Montreal Kosher
2865 Van Horne, Wilderton Shopping Centre
                                    (514) 739-3651
Supervision: Vaad Hair.
New Homemade Kosher Bakery
6915 Querbes   (514) 270-5567
Supervision: Vaad Hair.
New Homemade Kosher Bakery
6685 Victoria   (514) 733-4141
Supervision: Vaad Hair.
New Homemade Kosher Bakery
6795 Darlington   (514) 342-1991
Supervision: Vaad Hair.
New Homemade Kosher Bakery
5638 Westminister   (514) 486-2024
Supervision: Vaad Hair.
New Homemade Kosher Bakery
1085 Bernard W.   (514) 276-2105
Supervision: Vaad Hair.

Canada / Quebec

Patisserie Chez Ma Souer
5095 Queen Mary   (514) 737-2272
Supervision: Vaad Hair.
Pita Royal, 5897 Van Horne   (514) 488-9414
Supervision: Vaad Hair.
Renfels Bakery
2800 Bates   (514) 733-5538
Supervision: Vaad Hair.

Booksellers
Kotel Book & Gift Store
6414 Victoria Avenue H3W 2S6   (514) 739-4142
Fax: (514) 739-7330
Rodal's Hebrew Book Store & Gift Shop
4689 Van Horne Avenue H3W 1H8   (514) 733-1876
Fax: (514) 733-2373
Email: rodals@ican.net
Victoria Gift Shop
5875 Victoria Avenue H3W 2R6   (514) 738-1414

Community Organisations
Federation CJA
5151 ch, de la Côte Ste-Catherine H3W 1M6
(514) 735-3541
Operates the Jewish Information and Referral Service (JIRS), Tel: 737-2221.
Jewish Community Council of Montreal
6333 Decarie, Suite 100 H3W 3E1   (514) 739-6363
Fax: (514) 739-7024
Email: semanuel@generation.net
Visitors requiring additional information about kosher establishments should contact the Vaad Ha'ir at the above numbers. Also apply to them for a list of kosher butchers, bakeries and caterers.

Consulate General
Consul General of Israel
1155 Boulevard Rene Levesque Ouest, Suite 2620 H3B 4S5   (514) 940-8500
Fax: (514) 940-8555
Email: cgisrmtl@videotron.net
Web site: www.israelca.org

Libraries
Jewish Public Library
5151 Côte Ste-Catherine Road H3W 1M6
(514) 345-2627
Fax: (514) 345-6477
Email: c-stern@hotmail.com

Media
Newspapers
Canadian Jewish News
6900 Decarie Blvd, #341 H3X 2T8   (514) 735-2612

Restaurants
Dairy
Bistrot Casa Linga
5095 Queen Mary H3W 1X4   (514) 737-2272
Cummings Jewish Centre for Seniors Cafeteria
5700 Westbury Avenue H3W 3E8   (514) 342-1234
Fax: (514) 739-6899
Email: info@cummings-senior-centre.org
Supervision:
Exodus
5395 Queen Mary   (514) 483-6610
Supervision: Vaad Hair.
Foxy's
5987A Victoria Avenue   (514) 739-8777
Supervision: Vaad Hair.
Pizza Pita
5710 Victoria Avenue   (514) 731-7482
Supervision: Vaad Hair.
Pizza, pita and a variety of Milchig dishes. Open 9.30am-11.30pm daily, Saturday night until 2.30am.
Tatty's Pizza
6540 Darlington   (514) 734-8289
Supervision: Vaad Hair.

Meat
Chez Babys
Cote St. Luc Road
Supervision: Montreal Sephardic Vaad.
El Morocco II
3450 Drummond Street   (514) 844-6888; 844-0203
Fax: (514) 844-1204
Email: elmorocco@spring.ca
Supervision: Vaad Hair.
Open for lunch and dinner until 10 pm. Located downtown near hotels and boutiques.
Ernie's & Ellie's Place
6900 Decarie Blvd H3X 2T8   (514) 344-4444
Fax: (514) 344-0001
Supervision: Vaad Hair.

Synagogues
Canadian Jewish Congress National Headquarters
Samuel Bronfman House, 1590 Docteur Penfield Avenue H3G 1C5   (514) 931-7531
Fax: (514) 931-0548
Email: mikec@cjc.ca
Contact to find out which of the many synagogues in Montreal is nearest .

Quebec City
Cemeteries
Beth Israel Ohev Sholom
Boulevard Rene Levesque, Sainte-Foy
(418) 658-6677
This is an official monument and historic site - 5 miles from the old center.

Canada/Quebec

Synagogues

Orthodox

Beth Israel Ohev Shalom
1251 Place de Merici G1R 1Y2   (418) 688-3277

Ste. Agathe-des-Monts

A resort in the Laurentian Mountains known as the "Catskills" of Montreal where members of the Montreal community spend their summer months.

Synagogues
House of Israel Congregation
31 Albert Street J8C 1Z6   (819) 326-4320
                                         Fax: (819) 326-8558
                      Web site: www.houseofisrael.org

Saskatchewan

Moose Jaw

Synagogues

Conservative

Moose Jaw Hebrew Congregation
937 Henry Street S6H 3H1   (306) 692-1644

Regina

Synagogues

Orthodox

Beth Jacob
4715 McTavish Street S4S 6H2   (306) 757-8643
                                        Fax: (306) 352-3499

Reform

Temple Beth Tikvah
Box 33048, Cathedral Post Office S4T 7X2
                                        (306) 761-2218

Saskatoon

Synagogues

Conservative

Agudas Israel
715 McKinnon Avenue S7H 6H2   (306) 343-7023
                                        Fax: (306) 343-1244
             Email: jewishcommunity@sk.sympatico.ca
Will be pleased to welcome visitors.

Cayman Islands

In addition to a very small permanent Jewish community there are a number of Jews who spend part of the year on the Islands.

GMT - 5 hours	Total Population 32,000
Country calling code (1345)	Jewish Population Under 100
Emergency Telephone (Police - 911) (Ambulance - 555)	Electricity voltage 110

Grand Cayman

Contact Information
Harvey DeSouza
P.O. Box 72, Grand Cayman   949-7739

The original Jewish settlers in Chile were Conversos. Rodrigo de Organos, a Converso, was the first European to enter the country in 1535. The Inquisition, however, curtailed the growth of the community.

The first legal Jewish immigration, albeit small, occurred only after Chile's independence in 1810. In 1914 the Jewish community numbered some 500, but this increased in the late 1930s with those refugees from Nazism who were able to avoid the strict immigration laws. Anti-semitism, however, also grew, and the Comite Representativo was formed to respond to it.

There is an umbrella organisation and a large Zionist body in Chile. B'nai B'rith and WIZO also function in Chile. Most of the community is not religious, but some keep Kosher and there are several synagogues in Santiago (the capital) and a few kosher shops. There are two Jewish schools and several Jewish newspapers are published.

GMT - 4 hours	Total Population 14,375,000
Country calling code (56)	Jewish Population 15,000
Emergency Telephone (Police - 133) (Fire - 132) (Ambulance - 131)	Electricity voltage 220

Arica

Community Organisations
Sociedad Israelita
Dr Herzl, Casilla 501

Iquique

Community Organisations
Comunidad Israelita
Playa Ligade 3263, Playa Brava

La Serena

Community Organisations
Community Centre
Cordovez 652

Rancagua

Community Organisations
Comunidad Israelita
Casilla 890

Santiago

The majority of Chilean Jews live in Santiago. The city has a couple of notable features in connection with its Jewish community – the Circulo Israelita Synagogue has an interesting stained glass design in its interior, and the 'Bomba Israel' is a fire service, manned by volunteers who include a few rabbis. Two of their fire engines carry the Chilean and Israeli flags.

Embassy
Embassy of Israel
San Sebastian 2812, Casilla 1224   (2) 246-1570

Representative Organisations
Communal Headquarters (Comite Representativo de las Entidades Judias de Chile)
Miguel Claro 196   (2) 235-8669

Restaurants

Meat

Kosher Deli, Americo Vespucio Sur 1301
(2) 251-3145
Fax: (2) 251-3190
Supervision: Jabad.

Synagogues

Ashkenazi

Comunidad Israelita de Santiago
Serrano 214-218

German

Sociedad Cultural Israelita B'ne Jisroel
Portugal 810

Hungarian

Maze, Pedro Bannen 0166   (2) 274-2536

Orthodox

Bicur Joilim, Av. Matte 624
Jabad Lubavitch
Gloria 62, Las Condes   (2) 228-2240
Jafets Jayim, Miguel Claro 196

Sephardi

Maguen David, Av. R. Lyon 812

Chile

Temuco

Community Organisations
Comunidad Israelita
General Cruz 355

Valdivia

Community Organisations
Community Centre
Arauco 136 E.

Valparaiso

Community Organisations
Comunidad Israelita
Alvarez 490, Vina del Mar   (32) 680-373

China

Jews have been in China since the twelfth century. There was an established, thriving community in Kaifeng for some 700 years until it finally lost its identity.

During the 1930s refugees from Germany fled to Shanghai and other cities. However, the community subsequently migrated and until the last year or so there was no Jewish life in the country. This has now changed.

Also included here is Hong Kong, previously listed as a separate entity, but, since July 1997, again a region of China.

GMT + 8 hours	Total Population 1,218,709,000
Country calling code (86) (Hong Kong 852)	Jewish Population 2,500
Emergency Telephone (Police - 110) (Fire - 119)	Electricity voltage 220/240

Beijing

Embassy
Embassy of Israel
1 Jianguo Menwai Da Jia 100004 (10) 6505-2970/1/2
Fax: 6505-0328

Hong Kong

Although there were some Jewish merchants trading out of Hong Kong over the centuries, the first permanent community consisted of Jews who came from Baghdad in the early nineteenth century. The first synagogue was not established until 1901, the early settlers preferring to organise communal events from their homes. The majority of the community were Sephardi, but Nazi persecution led to more Ashkenazi settlers arriving in Hong Kong, via Shanghai. Since the Second World War many Chinese Jews have emigrated through Hong Kong to Australia and the USA, although some have remained in Hong Kong. Following the reversion to Chinese control in mid-1997, the Jewish community is still thriving, and the mood is optimistic.

The Jews have contributed greatly to the building of the infrastructure of Hong Kong and, since the 1960s, many Western Jews, attracted by the success of this major financial centre, have made their homes there. The first communal hall was founded in 1905, but a new, multi-purpose complex (the Jewish Community Centre) has recently been opened, which is one of the most luxurious in the world. This centre includes everything from a library and a strictly kosher restaurant to a swimming pool and sauna.

Cemeteries
The Jewish Cemetery
Located in Happy Valley   2589-2621
Fax: 2548-4200

Community Organisations
Hong Kong Jewish Community Centre
One Robinson Place, 70 Robinson Road, Mid-Levels
2801-5440
Fax: 2877-0917
Web site: www.jcc.org.hk
Two kosher restaurants under full-time Mashgiach supervision Meals on Shabbat, take-away and delivery service available. There is also a kosher supermarket, library, swimming pool, gymnasium and leisure facilities and a full programme of activities and classes. Visitors are welcome.

Cultural Organisations

The Jewish Historical Society of Hong Kong

2807-9400
Fax: 2887-5235

Publishes monographs on subjects of Sino-Judaic interest and maintains an archive. Information from Mrs Judith Green.

Embassy

Consul General of Israel

Room 701 Admiralty Centre, Tower 2, 18 Harcourt Street
2529-6091
Fax: 2865-0220
Email: isrcons@asiaonline.net

Restaurants

Shalom Grill

2/F Fortune House, 61 Connaught Road, Central
2851-6218; 2851-6300
Fax: 2851-7482
Email: darvick@darvick.com.hk

Glatt kosher . Friday night , Saturday and weekday open. Sunday-Thursday Lunch 12.30-2.30pm. Dinner 6.30-9.30pm. Friday 12.30-2.30pm.

Synagogues

Orthodox

Lubavitch in the Far East (Chabad)

1A Kennedy Heights, Mid-Levels

2523-9770
Fax: 2845-2772
Email: chabadhk@netvigator.com

Shul at the Furama Hotel, Room 601. Daily Shacharit at 7:15 and Mincha-Ma'ariv ten minutes before sunset. Shabbat services are followed by Shabbat meals. Due to its popularity and limited space, meals have to be reserved and paid for in advance. Visitors to Hong Kong may book rooms at the Furama Hotel at discounted rates through the Chabad office.

Ohel Leah Synagogue

70 Robinson Road, Mid-Levels

2589-2621
Fax: 2548-4200
Web site: www.hkjew.com

Built in 1902 and carefully restored in 1998, the orthodox Ohel Leah Synagogue known by some as the "crown jewel" of Asian Jewry still remains the region's most vibrant centre of Jewish religious activity. Classes, daily services, a Beth Din, and a mikveh operate on premises. Adjacent to a world class glatt kosher Jewish Community Center with dairy and meat restaurants. Gourmet catered shabbat meals - Friday eve is by reservation and shabbat community kiddush luncheon is complimentary following services. Book nearby hotels at discounted rates through the synagogue office.

Zion Congregation

21 Chatham Road, Kowloon   2366-6364
Corner of Mody Road (opposite to Kowloon Shangri-La Hotel)

Sephardi

Beit Midrash Shuva Israel and Community Centre

2/F Fortune house, 61 Connaught Road, Central
2851-6218; 2851-6300
Fax: 2851-7482
Email: darvick@darvick.com.hk

Friday night , Saturday and weekday services are held.

Kaifeng

Museum

Kaifeng Museum

The Kaifeng Museum documents the ancient history of Kaifeng Jewry. The most significant artifact is a 15th century etched stone with inscriptions describing Kaifeng's Jewish history and customs from the times of Abraham.

China

Shanghai

Synagogues
Jewish Community of Shanghai
1277 Beijing Xi Lu 20th floor 200040
(21) 6289-9903

Fax: (21) 6289-9957
Email: sjcchina@usa.net
Web site: www.chinajewish.org
A Jewish community has been established in Shangai -
the first Jewish community here for 50 years
Shabbat services are held in the Portman Ritz Hotel.

Colombia

The first Jews in Colombia were Conversos, as was common in South America. However, they were soon discovered by the Inquisition which was established in Colombia.

The next influx of Jews came in the nineteenth century, and then a mass immigration from eastern Europe and the Middle East occurred after 1918. Jews were banned from entering after 1939, but this restriction was eased after 1950.

The present community is a mix of Ashkenazi and Sephardi elements, each having their own communual organisations. There are also youth and Zionist organisations. There is a central organisation for Colombian Jewry in Bogota (the capital). WIZO and B'nai B'rith are represented. There are also Jewish schools and synagogues, and Jewish publications and radio programmes.

GMT - 5 hours
Country calling code (57)
Emergency Telephone (Police - 112) (Fire - 119) (Ambulance - 132)

Total Population 35,652,000
Jewish Population 5,650
Electricity 110/120

Baranquilla

Community Organisations
Centro Israelita Filantropico
Carrera 43, No 85-95, Apartado Aereo 2537
(53) 342-310; 351-197
Comunidad Hebrea Sefaradita
Carrera 55, No 74-71, Apartado Aereo 51351
(53) 340-054; 340-050

Bogota

Embassy
Embassy of Israel
Calle 35, No 7-25, Edificio Caxdax
(1) 245-6603; 245-6712

Media
Monthly
Menorah, Apartado Aereo 9081

Religious Organisations
Union Rabinica Colombiana
Tranversal 29, No 126-31   (1) 274-9069; 218-2500

Synagogues
Congregacion Adath Israel
Carrera 7a, No 94-20   (1) 257-1660; 257-1680
Fax: (1) 623-2237

Mikva on premises.

Ashkenazi
Centro Israelita de Bogota
Transversal 29, No 126-31   (1) 274-9069
Kosher meals available by prior arrangement with
Rabbi Goldschmidt, 218-2500.

German
Asociacion Israelita Montefiore
Carrera 20, No 37-54   (1) 245-5264

Orthodox
Comunidad Hebrea Sefaradi
Calle 79, No 9-66   (1) 256-2629; 249-0372
Mikva on premises.
Jabad House, Calle 92, No 10, Apt. 405
Rabbi's Tel:(1)257-4920

Cali

Representative Organisations
Union Federal Hebrea
Apartado Aereo 8918   (2) 443-1814
Fax: (2) 444-5544
An umbrella organisation co-ordinating all Jewish activities in Cali.

Synagogues

Ashkenazi
Sociedad Hebrea de Socoros
Av. 9a Norte # 10-15, Apartado Aereo 011652
(2) 668-8518
Fax: (2) 668-8521

Costa Rica

German
Union Cultural Israelita
Apartado Aereo 5552

(2) 668-9830
Fax: (2) 661-6857

Sephardi
Centro Israelita de Beneficiencia
Calle 44a, Av. 5a Norte Esquina, Apartado Aereo 77

(2) 664-1379
Fax: (2) 665-5419

Medellin

Community Organisations
Union Israelita de Beneficencia
Carrera 43B, No 15-150, Apartado Aereo 4702

Costa Rica

The first Jews arrived in Costa Rica in the nineteenth century, from nearby islands in the Caribbean, such as Jamaica. The next wave of immigrants came from eastern Europe in the 1920s. Thereafter Costa Rica did not welcome new Jewish immigrants, and passed laws against foreign merchants and foreign land ownership. However, the Jewish community in Costa Rica established a communual organisation in 1930, which includes WIZO, B'nai B'rith and other groups. There is a monthly newsletter, and a synagogue in San Jose. Most Jewish children attend the Haim Weizmann School, which has both primary and secondary classes.

It is interesting to note that the Costa Rican embassy in Israel is in Jerusalem, and not Tel Aviv, where most other embassies are situated.

GMT - 6 hours
Country calling code (506)
Emergency Telephone (Police, Fire and Ambulance 911)

Total Population 3,400,000
Jewish Population 2,500
Electricity voltage 110/220

San Jose

Contact Information
Centro Israelita Sionista de Costa Rica
Calle 22 y 22, Apdo 1473-1000

233-9222
Fax: 233-9321

Embassy
Embassy of Israel
Edificio Centro Colon, Piso 11, P.O.Box 5147-1000

221-60-11/221-64-44
Fax: 257-0867
Email: embofisr@sol.racsa.co.cr

Groceries
Little Israel Pita Rica
Frente a Shell, Pavas

290-2083
Fax: 296-4802

The only kosher bakery and mini-market in Costa Rica.

Hotels
Barcelo San Jose Palacio
Apdo 458-1150

220-2034; 220-2035
Fax: 220-2036
Email: Palacio@sol.racsa.co.cr

Hotel has separated kosher kitchen and its key in the mashgiach's (Rabbi Levkovitz) hands. The hotel is about a half hour walk to the synagogue.

Camino Real, Prospero Fernandezy, Camino Real Boulevard

289-7000
Fax: 289-8930
Email: caminoreal@ticonet.co.cr

Hotel has new separated kosher kitchen, with the key in the mashgiach's (Rabbi Levkovitz) hands.

Melia Confort Corobici
PO Box 2443-1000

232-8122
Fax: 231-5834
Email: melia.confort.corobici@solmelia.com

There is no separate kosher kitchen, but it is fairly close to the Orthodox synagogue. The hotel has two separate storage rooms for Kosher cookware.

Synagogues
Shaarei Zion

Croatia

Jews were in the land now known as Croatia before the Croats themselves. The Croats arrived in the seventh century, the Jews some centuries before with the Romans: there are remains of a third-century Jewish cemetery in Solin (near Split).

The first Jewish communites were involved in trade with Italy across the Adriatic Sea, and also in trade along the River Danube. Their success was brief, however, and they were expelled in 1456, only returning more than 300 years later. At that time the Hapsburgs ruled Croatia, and Joseph II allowed the Jews to return. The area became part of the newly formed Yugoslavia after the First World War, and the Jewish community became part of the Federation of Jewish Communities in Yugoslavia.

The Croatian Jews suffered greatly under the German occupation in the Second World War when the local Ustashe (Croatian Fascists) assisted the Germans. Despite their efforts, some Jews survived and even decided to rebuild their community when peace returned.

Today, after the civil war, there are synagogues in towns across the country. There are some Hebrew classes and newsletters are published. There are also many places of historical interest, such as Ulicia Zudioska (Jewish Street) in Dubrovnik.

GMT + 1 hour	Total Population 4,775,000
Country calling code (385)	Jewish Population 2,000
Emergency Telephone (Police - 92) (Fire - 93) (Ambulance - 94)	Electricity voltage 220

Dubrovnik

Synagogues
Zudioska Street 3

Zudioska means 'Street of the Jews'. This is the second oldest synagogue in Europe and is located in a very narrow street off the main street – the Stradun or Placa. The Jewish community office is in the same building. Zudiosla Street is the third turning on the right from the town clock tower. There are about 30 Jews in the city. Tourists help to make up a minyan in the synagogue on Friday night and High Holy Days.

Osijek

Community Organisations
Brace Radica Street 13   (31) 211-407

     Fax: (31) 211-407

The community building contains objects from the synagogue that was destroyed during the Second World War. The community numbers about 150 members and has two cemeteries. No regular services are held. A former building of the pre-war synagogue in Cvjetkova Street is a Pentecostal church today. There is a plaque at the site of the destroyed synagogue in Zupanijska Street.

Rijeka

Synagogues
Filipovieva ul. 9, PO Box 65 51000

     (51) 425-156/336-032

The community numbers about 60. Services are held in the well maintained synagogue on Jewish holidays.

Split

Community Organisations
Zidovski Prolaz 1   (21) 45-672

The synagogue at Split is one of the few in Yugoslavia to have survived the wartime occupation. The Jewish community numbers about 200. There is a Jewish cemetery, established in 1578. More information from the community offices at the above number.

Zagreb

Booksellers
Voice of the Jewish Communities of Croatia

Email: jcz@oleh.srce.hr

Community Organisations
Jewish Community of Zagreb
Palmoticeva Street 16, PO Box 986   (1) 434-619
Fax: (1) 434-638
Email: jcz@public.stce.hr
Before the war Zagreb had 11,000 Jews. There are now only about 1,500, but they remain very active in Jewish communal life. Services are held in the community building on Friday evenings and holidays.

Monuments
Central Synagogue
Praska Street 7
There is a plaque on the spot of this pre-war synagogue.

Mirogoj Cemetery

There is an impressive monument in this cemetery to the Jewish victims of the Second World War.

Cuba

Until 1898, there was only a tiny Jewish population on the island. With the end of Spanish colonial rule in that year, Jews from nearby areas, such as Jamaica and Florida, and Jewish veterans of the Spanish–American War began to settle in Cuba. A congregation was established in 1904. Later, Turkish Sephardim formed their own synagogue. The community was then augmented by immigrants from eastern Europe who had decided to stay in Cuba, which was being used as a transit camp for those seeking to enter America. A central committee was established for all Jewish groups in the 1930s. Cuba clamped down on immigration at that time, and the story of the German ship St Louis (full of Jewish refugees), which was refused entry into Cuba, is well known.

About 12,000 Jews lived on the island in 1952. Havana had by far the largest community, and 75 per cent of the Cuban community was Ashkenazi. Although the Cuban revolution did not target Jews, religious affiliations were initially discouraged and many Jews emigrated (as did many non-Jews). The remaining community has synagogues, and a Sunday school. Kosher food and Judaica are imported, mainly from Canada and Panama. Cuba broke off diplomatic relations with Israel in 1973, although in 1998/99 a number of Jews were allowed to emigrate to Israel.

GMT - 5 hours
Country calling code (53)
Emergency Telephone (Police - 82 0116) (Fire - 81 1115) (Ambulance 404 551)
Electricity voltage 110/220

Total Population 11,117,000
Jewish Population 1,300

Havana

Synagogues

Conservative

Patronado de la Casa de la Comunidad Hebrea de Cuba
Calle 13 e I, Vedado   (7) 32-8953
Modern community centre as well.

Orthodox

Hadath Israel
Calle Picota 52, Habana Vieja   (7) 61-3495

Reform

The United Hebrew Congregation
Av. de los Presidentes 502
The Jewish cemetery is at Guanabacoa.

Cyprus

Cyprus

During the Roman Empire, Jewish merchants made their home on Cyprus. However, after a revolt which destroyed the town of Salamis, they were expelled. In medieval times, small Jewish communities were established in Nicosia, Limassol and other towns but the community was never large.

It is interesting to note that Cyprus was seen as a possible 'Jewish Homeland' by the early Zionists. Agricultural settlements were established at the end of the nineteenth century, but they were not successful. Herzl himself tried to persuade the British government to allow Jewish rule over Cyprus in 1902, but met with failure.

Some German Jews managed to escape to Cyprus in the early 1930s. After the war, many Holocaust survivors who had tried to enter Palestine illegally were deported to special camps on the island. Some 50,000 European Jews were held there. Since the establishment of the state of Israel, the Jewish community on the island has become small, and the Israeli embassy has served as a centre for community activities.

GMT + 2 hours	Total Population 767,000
Country calling code (357)	Jewish Population Under 100
Emergency Telephone (Police, Fire and Ambulance - 112)	Electricity voltage 240

Nicosia

Community Organisations
Committee of the Jewish Community of Cyprus
PO Box 24784 1303   (2) 694758
                    Fax: (2) 662077
        Email: amiyes@spidernet.com.cy
Contact Mrs Z. Yeshurun for information.

Embassy
Embassy of Israel
4 Grypari Street   (2) 664195
                            Fax: (2) 666338
            Email: israel@cytanet.com.cy

Have you any information for us?

Any comments you may have on this guide are always welcomed. Please do get in touch if you have any relevant information which you may feel will be of use to other travellers.
Details on how to do this are on page vi.
Additionally forms are available at the back of the book.

Czech Republic

Prague, the capital of this small central European country, has become a major tourist attraction. It is one of the few cities actively to promote its Jewish heritage, which dates from early medieval times. The oldest (still functioning) synagogue in Europe is there (the Altneuschul), as well as other interesting Jewish sites.

After the arrival of the first Jews in the country, in the tenth century, they suffered similar tragedies to those of other medieval Jewish communities – forced baptism by the Crusaders and expulsions, together with some tolerance. Full emancipation was reached in 1867 under the Hapsburgs. The celebrated Jewish writer, Franz Kafka, lived in Prague and did not neglect his Judaism, unlike many other Czech Jews who assimilated and intermarried.

The German occupation led to 85 per cent of the community (80,000 people) perishing in the Holocaust. Further difficulties were faced in the communist period after the war, but since the 1989 'Velvet Revolution', Judaism is being rediscovered. The community (mostly elderly) has several synagogues around the country, a kindergarten and a journal, and there are kosher restaurants in the old Jewish quarter in Prague.

GMT + 1 hour
Country calling code (420)
Emergency Telephone (Police - 158) (Fire - 150) (Ambulance - 155)

Total Population 10,316,000
Jewish Population 6,000
Electricity voltage 220

Boskovice

Museum
Medieval Ghetto

(501) 454601; 452077
Fax: (501) 452077
Email: museum@mas.cz
17th-century Jewish town, synagogue and cemetery.

Brno

Community Organisations
Community Centre
Kpt. Jarose 3 (5) 21-5710
The community president can be reached at 77-3233.

Synagogues
Skorepka 13

Holesov

Museums
Schach Synagogue
Dating from 1650, this synagogue is now a museum. Open in the mornings. At other times the curator will show visitors around, if contacted. The old cemetery is close by.

Karlovy Vary (In German Carlsbad)

Once a very popular spa town. The beautiful synagogue, destroyed on Kristallnacht, is recorded by a plaque on the wall of the Bristol Hotel.

Synagogues
Community Centre
Masaryka 39
Services, Friday evening and Shabbat morning.

Liberec

Synagogues
Community Centre
Matousova 21
Reichenberg 46001 (48) 510-3340
Each weekday 9-11 a.m.

Mikulov

Sites
Nikolsburg
Only one synagogue, still being restored, remains of the many which flourished here when the town was the spiritual capital of Moravian Jewry and the seat of the Chief Rabbis of Moravia. The cemetery contains the graves of famous rabbis.

Czech Republic

Olomouc

Synagogues
Community Centre
Komenskeho 7   (68) 522-3119

Ostrava

Synagogues
Community Centre
Ceskobratrska 17   (69) 611-2389

Pilsen

Synagogues
Community Centre
Smetanovy Sady 5, Pilsen   (19) 723-5749
Services Friday evenings. The Great Synagogue is now closed.

Prague

Most of the Jews in the Czech Republic live in Prague, which has had a thousand year history of Jewish settlement. The impact of the Jews in Prague has been great - the Golem has entered Prague folklore, and the Altneushul is the oldest functioning synagogue in Europe. The Jewish Quarter in the old town contains many historical sites.

Terezin is some forty miles from Prague and is easily visited. On the way is the town of Lidice, destroyed in June 1942 by the Nazis in retaliation for the assassination of Reinhard Heydrich.

Cemeteries
Old Jewish Cemetery
The oldest cemetery in Europe, containing the graves of such famous rabbis & scholars as Avigdor Karo (died 1439), Yehuda Low ben Bezalel (1609), David Gans (1613) & David Oppenheim (1736).

Contact Information
Jewish Town Hall
Maislova 18 1
Houses the Federation of Jewish Communities in the Czech Republic as well as the Shalom restaurant.

Embassy
Embassy of Israel   (2) 333-25109
Badeniho Street 2 7   (2) 333-20092

Hotels
President Hotel
Namesti Curieovych 100 116-88   (2) 231-4812
Fax: (2) 231-8247
A few minutes walk from the old Jewish quarter.

Judaica art and souvenirs
Precious Legacy
Maiselova 16, Prague 1, Josefov   (2) 232-1951
Fax: (2) 232-0398, 472-1068
Email: legacy_tours@oasanet.cz

Museums
Jewish Museum in Prague
Jachymova 3   (2) 2481-0099
Fax: (2) 231-0681
Reservation centre, tel: 42 2 231-7191. Fax:42 2 231-7181

Restaurants
Golan, Na Prikope 10 1   (2) 242-31501
Fax: (2) 242-31502
Supervision: Chief Rabbi of the Czech Republic. Also caters for groups.
Jerusalem, Brehova 5 1   (2) 232-4729
Fax: (2) 232-4729
Sells a few groceries. Boxed lunches and Shabbat meals can be ordered.

Meat
King Solomon, Siroka 8, Prague 1   (2) 248-18752
Fax: (2) 786-4664
Web site: www.kosher.cz

Synagogues
Altneuschul, Cervena ul.7 1   (2) 231-0909
Jubilee Synagogue
Jerusalemska 7

Tours
Precious Legacy Tours
Maiselova 16, Prague 1, Josefov   (2) 232-0398
Fax: (2) 472-1068
Email: legacy_tours@oasanet.cz
Web site: www.legacytours.cz

Heritage Tours   (2) 472-1068
Jewish Town Hall
Maislova 18 1
With Hebrew clock.
Wittmann Tours
Manesova 8, 120 00 Praha 2   (2) 2225-2472
Fax: (2) 2225-2472
Email: sylvie@wittmann-tours.com
Web site: www.wittmann.tours.com

Travel Agencies
Matana Travel Agency of the Jewish Community of Prague
Maiselova 15 11000   (2) 232-1954
Fax: (2) 232-1049
Email: matana@ms.qnet.cz
Web site: www.tours.cz/matana/

Teplice

Synagogues
Community Centre
Lipova 25
Teplitz-Schönau   (417) 26-580

Terezin

Museums
Theresienstadt
There is a new museum in the town dedicated to the
Jews who were deported from Theresienstadt to
Auschwitz. There is also a cemetery in which 11,250
individual and 217 mass graves and the crematorium
are placed.

Usti Nad Labem

Community Organisations
Community Centre
Moskevska 26,Aussig   (47) 520-8082

Denmark

Denmark

Jews were allowed to settle in Denmark in 1622, earlier than in any other Scandinavian country. Thereafter, the community grew, with immigration largely from Germany. The Danish king allowed the foundation of the unified Jewish community of Copenhagen in 1684, and the Jews were granted full citizenship in 1849.

In the early part of the twentieth century many refugees arrived from eastern Europe, and Denmark welcomed refugees from Nazi Germany. When the Germans conquered Denmark and ordered the Jews to be handed over, the Danish resistance managed to save 7,200 (90 per cent of the community) by arranging boats to take them to neutral Sweden. Some Jews did however stay behind and were taken to the transit ghetto of Theresienstadt (Terezin), where many died.

After the war, most of the Jews returned, and there is now a central Jewish organisation based in Copenhagen. There are also old-age homes, synagogues and a mikva. WIZO and B'nai B'rith are also represented. Kosher food is available.

GMT + 1 hour	Total Population 5,237,000
Country calling code (45)	Jewish Population 9,000
Emergency Telephone (Police, Fire and Ambulance - 112)	Electricity voltage 220

Copenhagen

With a Jewish population of almost 9,000, the vast majority of Danish Jews live in the capital. The Community Centre contains most of the offices of the Jewish community, and three old age homes are jointly run with the Copenhagen Municipality. The Great Synagogue and the cemetery dating from 1693 are interesting sites.

Bakeries
Mrs Heimann   3332-9443

Butchers
Kosher Delikatesse
87 Lyngbyvej 2100   3918-5777
Fax: 3918-5390

Community Organisations
Jewish Community Centre
Ny Kongensgade 6 1472   3312-8868
Fax: 3312-3357

Embassy
Embassy of Israel
Lundevangsvej 4, Hellerup 2900   3962-6288
Fax: 3962-1938
Email: israel@pip.dknet.dk

Groceries
I. A. Samson
Roerholmsgade 3 1352   3313-0077
Fax: 3314-8277
Kosher grocery, provisions and delicatessen.

Mikvaot
12 Krystalgade 1172   3393-7662; 3332-9443

Jewish Community Centre
Ny Kongensgade 6 1472   3312-8868
Fax: 3312-3357

Synagogues
Orthodox
12 Krystalgade 1172   3929-9520
Fax: 3229-2517
Daily and Shabbat services.
Machsike Hadass
Ole suhrsgade 12 1354   3315-3117
Web site: www.samsonkosher.dk
Daily and Shabbat services.

Hornbaek

A resort and seaside town where many members of the Copenhagen community spend the summer months, or weekends. It is the area of the coast from which the Jewish community escaped in 1943.

Hotels
Hotel Villa Strand
Kystvej 12 3100   2176-8680
Fax: 3316-1850

Synagogues
Granavenget 8   4220-0731
Open from Shavuot to Succot.

Dominican Republic

Dominican Republic

Jewish settlement in the Dominican Republic is comparatively late – the oldest Jewish grave dates back to 1826. Descended from central European Jews, the community was not religious and many married Christians. The President Francisco Henriquez y Carvajal (1916) traced his ancestry back to the early Jewish settlers.

In 1938 the republic decided to accept refugees from Nazism (one of the very few countries of the world that did so freely), and even provided areas where they could settle. As a result, there were 1,000 Jews living there in 1943. This number declined as, once again, the Jewish community assimilated and married the local non-Jewish population. Despite this, many non-Jewish husbands, wives and children take part in Jewish events.

Two synagogues and a rabbi who divides his time between them are features of Jewish life. There is also a Sunday school in Santo Domingo and a bi-monthly magazine is produced. There is a small Jewish museum in Sosua.

GMT - 4 hours	Total Population 7,961,000
Country calling code (1)	Jewish Population 250
Emergency Telephone (Police, Fire and Ambulance - 999)	Electricity voltage 220/240

Santo Domingo

Embassy
Embassy of Israel
Av. Pedro Henriquez Urena 80 1404
                            (809) 542-1635; 542-1548

Representative Organisations
Consejo Dominicano de Mujeres Hebreas
PO Box 2189   (809) 535-6042
                        Fax: (809) 688-2058

Synagogues
Centro Israelita de la Republica Dominicana
Av. Ciudad de Sarasota 21   (809) 535-6042
                    Email: lalo@codetel.net.do

Sosua

Contact Information
Felix G. Koch
                            (809) 571-2284
Welcomes all Jewish visitors.

Ecuador

Ecuador

As in most Latin American countries Conversos comprised the earliest Jewish settlers in Ecuador. It was not until 1904 that East European Jews began to arrive, and numbers increased further following the Nazi take-over in Germany, as Ecuador granted refuge to more Jews than other neighbouring countries. About 3,000 Jews entered Ecuador in the 1930s. The Jewish population peaked in 1950 at 4,000, but this number declined owing to emigration. In recent years, some Jews have moved to Ecuador from elsewhere in South America.

A synagogue and other organisations such as WIZO and B'nai B'rith are based in Quito. There are no Jewish schools, but children do have access to Jewish education.

GMT - 5 hours

Country calling code (593)

Emergency Telephone (Police - 101) (Fire - 102) (Ambulance - 131)

Total Population 11,700,000

Jewish Population 1,000

Electricity voltage 110/120

Guayaquil

Synagogues
Community Centre
cnr. Calle Paradiso & El Bosque

Quito

Community Organisations
Communidad Judia Del Ecuador
Calle Roberto Andrade, OE3 580 y Jaime, Roldos
Urbanizacion Einstein (Carcelen)   (2) 828-452
Fax: (2) 828-452
Email: aiq@uio.satnet

Embassy
Embassy of Israel
Av. Eloy Alfaro 969, Casilla 2463
(2) 547-322 & 548-431

Egypt

For more than two thousand years there has been a virtually continuous Jewish presence in the vicinity of Cairo and an even more ancient Jewish presence in Egypt is recounted in the Bible. After the exodus Jews returned to Egypt during the time of Alexander the Great and at that time the Ben Ezra synagogue was built. The Bible was translated into Greek during that period. In the first century CE, the Jewish presence declined but a renaissance occurred with Moses Maimonides's arrival in Egypt in the twelfth century. Most of his books were written in Cairo and his yeshiva still exists in the Jewish quarter. From then on, the Jewish community expanded and flourished, especially with the arrival of refugees from pogroms and during the First and Second World Wars.

Before 1948 there were about 70,000 Jews in Egypt. The 1956 Suez War and the 1967 Six Day war encouraged Jewish emigration. At present, the community is small but the Jewish heritage, mostly synagogues classified as antiquities, represent an inestimable treasure worth visiting – as, for example, the recently restored Ben Ezra synagogue, home of the world-famous Genizah of some 400,000 documents (the majority of which are now in Cambridge, England).

GMT + 2 hours	Total Population 60,896,000
Country calling code (20)	Jewish Population 200
Emergency Telephone Electricity voltage 220	

Alexandria

Synagogues
Eliahu Hanavi
69 Nebi Daniel Street, Ramla Station
(3) 492-3974; 597-4438

Cairo

Cairo, has had a long and important Jewish history. The community has however declined in line with the rest of Egyptian Jewry. However, there are a number of interesting sites, such as the recently restored Ben Ezra Synagogue, where the Cairo Genizah used to be located.

Community Organisations
13 Rue Sabyl El Khazindar, Abbassieh
(2) 824-613 & 824-885
Web site: www.geocities.com

Embassy
Embassy of Israel
6 Ibn Malek St., Gizeh
(2) 3610528
Fax: (2) 3610414
Email: isremcai@mail.rite.com

Synagogues
Ben-Ezra
6 Harett il-Sitt Barbara, Mari Girges, Old Cairo
(2) 847-695

Meir Enaim, 55 No.13 Street, Maadi
Under the supervision of the Jewish Community of Cairo and can be visited on request.
Shaarei Hashamayim
17 Adli Pasha Street
Downtown Cairo
(2) 749-025
Services are held on holidays. There is an interesting library across from the synagogue, which is only accessible with a key. Ask the guards.

The Jewish connection to El Salvador is not a strong one. It is believed that some Portuguese Conversos crossed the country a few hundred years ago. After that, some Sephardis from France moved to Chaluchuapa. Other Jews came from Europe, but in smaller numbers than those settling in other Latin American countries. There were only 370 Jews in 1976, a number reduced during the civil war, when many emigrated. Some returned however when the war was over.

An official community was set up in 1944 and a synagogue was opened in 1950. WIZO is present, and there is also a Zionist Organisation.

El Salvador is one of the few countries to have an embassy in Jerusalem, rather than Tel Aviv.

GMT - 6 hours
Country calling code (503)
Emergency Telephone (Police, Fire, Ambulance - 123)

Total Population 5,897,000
Jewish Population 120
Electricity voltage 110

San Salvador

Embassy
Colonia Escalon
85 Av. Norte, No 619   238-770; 239-221

Synagogues
Conservative
23 Blvd. del Hipodromo 626, Colonia San Benito
237-366

Friday evening services only.
Comunidad Israelita de El Salvador
Boulevard del Hipodromo 626, # 1 Colonia San
Benito, PO Box 06-182   263-8074
                                    Fax: 264-5499
Services Friday, Shabbat Morning and Holydays

Despite being the only country officially declared 'Judenrein' (free of Jews) at the Wannsee conference in 1942, there is a Jewish community here today. The community has always been small, and is believed to have begun in the fourteenth century. However, most Jews arrived in the nineteenth century, when Czar Alexander II allowed certain groups of Jews into the area.

By 1939, the community had grown to 4,500 and was free from restraints. After the Soviet and Nazi occupations in the Second World War the Jews returned, mainly from the Soviet Union. Now that Estonia is independent, the Jewish community is able to practise freely.

Communual organisations include a WIZO and a Union of Jewish Students, and there is a close tie with the Finnish community across the Baltic Sea. There is one synagogue in Tallinn (the capital), rebuilt after the war, but most Jews are not religious and there are few young people in the community. However, a newspaper appears every month and there is a radio programme, 'Shalom Aleichem', broadcast monthly.

GMT + 2 hours
Country calling code (372)
Emergency Telephone (Police - 02 or 002) (Fire - 01 or 001) (Ambulance - 03 or 003)
Electricity voltage 220

Total Population 1,471,000
Jewish Population 2,500

Tallinn

Community Organisations
Jewish Community of Estonia
Karu Street 16, PO Box 3576 10507   (2) 62-3034
                              Fax: (2) 62-3034
                              Email: ciljal@icom.ll
Publishes a monthly, called 'Hashaher', in Estonian and

operates a radio programme on Radio 4 (Thurs., 22:15-23:00). Information on vegetarian restaurants available.

Synagogues
9 Magdalena Street, PO Box 3576 EE0090
                                    (2) 55-7154

Ethiopia

Ethiopia

The Falashas (Ge'ez for 'stranger', applied to the Ethiopian Jews) of Ethiopia became known world-wide in the early 1980s, when many were airlifted to Israel. The origins of the Beta Israel, as they call themselves, are unclear and little is known for certain. Historians have concluded that they may have become Jewish as early as the second or third century. The Jewish Ethiopians followed the Torah, but did not have access to the rabbinic commentaries, as they were cut off from the outside Jewish world. Ethiopian history even records Jewish kings, as Judaism influenced the medieval Ethiopian Zague dynasty to such an extent that some of its rulers converted, or at least followed some Judaism. The kingdom fell in 1617 and many Jews then converted to Christianity, the prevailing religion.

As the area became known to the West through nineteenth-century explorers, some Western Jews set up schools in the country. The Jewish population was believed to have been about 50,000 in 1934. After the establishment of Israel, more interest was taken in the Ethiopian community and the Ethiopian civil war was the catalyst for Operation Moses, when 10,000 people were airlifted to Israel in 1984–85. A further 15,000 left for Israel in 1991.

GMT + 3 hours	Total Population 56,713,000
Country calling code (251)	Jewish Population 500
Electricity voltage 220	

Addis Ababa

Community Organisations
PO Box 50   (1) 111-725 & 446-471

Do you eat fish out?

If so, there is a comprehensive list of kosher fish listed alphabetically by country on pages 385 to 388 which you should find useful on your travels.

Finland

When Henry Marks, at the age of 20, moved to Fiji from Australia in 1881, he was the first recorded Jew on the island. Over the years, he developed a successful business across the region, and was later knighted.

Indian and other Jews later moved to Fiji but did not organise any official community. In recent years the Fiji Jewish Association has been created. The Israeli embassy organises an annual seder.

GMT + 12 hours	Total Population 802,000
Country calling code (679)	Jewish Population Under 100
Emergency Telephone (Police, Fire, Ambulance - 000)	Electricity voltage 240

Representative Organisations
Fiji Jewish Association
PO Box 882, Suva   387-980
                                          Fax: 387-946
                              Email: contex@is.com.fj

When Finland was occupied by Russia in the nineteenth century, many Jewish conscripts in the Russian army settled in Finland after their discharge. They were still subject to several restrictions, but these ended after Finland's independence in 1917. In addition to these 'Cantonists', as they were known, immigrants came to Finland from eastern Europe. Finland proved a safe haven, as the government refused to hand over Finnish Jews to the Nazis, despite being allied to Germany in its war with Soviet Russia.

The community is keen to preserve a sense of Jewish identity among the young generation, who are encouraged to experience Jewish life in Israel. The community is also keen to help other Jews in the newly independent Baltic states across the sea to the south of the country. There is a central body for Jewish Communities, and kosher food is available. There are also a school and synagogues.

GMT + 2 hours	Total Population 5,132,000
Country calling code (358)	Jewish Population 1,200
Emergency Telephone (Police - 10022) (Fire and Ambulance - 112)	Electricity voltage 220

Helsinki

Embassy
Embassy of Israel
Vironkatu 5A 00170   (9) 135-6177
                                       Fax: (9) 135-6959
                       Email: postmaster@ilemb.pp.fi

Restaurants
Community Centre
Malminkatu 26   (9) 692-1297; 694-1302
                                       Fax: (9) 694-8916
                                   Email: hjc@hjc.pp.fi
Kosher meals available. Telephone 694-1297 or 685-4584 to arrange.
Kosher Deli, Malminkatu 24   (9) 685-4584
                                       Fax: (9) 694-8916
                          Email: kosher.deli@hjc.pp.fi
Hours: Tuesday to Wednesday, 1 pm to 5 pm;
Thursday, 9 am to 5 pm; Friday, 9 am to 2 pm.

Synagogues

Orthodox

Jewish Community Synagogue
Malminkatu 26 00100   (9) 586-0310
                                       Fax: (9) 694-8916
                                   Email: jc@hjc.pp.fi
Services Monday and Thursday morning, 7:45 am, other weekdays 8 am; Friday evening, 7 pm (summer), 5 pm (winter); Shabbat and Sunday mornings, 9 am.

Turku

Synagogues
Brahenkatu 17   (2) 231-2557
                                       Fax: (2) 233-4689
The secretary is always pleased to meet visitors.

France

France

France now boasts the largest Jewish community in Europe. The Jewish connection with France is a long one: it dates back over 1,000 years as there is evidence of Jewish settlement in several towns in the first few centuries of the Jewish diaspora. The community grew in early medieval times, and contributed to the economy of the region. Two great Jewish commentators, Rashi and Rabenu Tam, both lived in France. However, French Jewry suffered both from the Crusaders and from other anti-semitic outbursts in the medieval period.

Napoleon heralded the emancipation of French Jewry and, as his armies conquered Europe, the emancipation of other communities began. Despite this, incidents such as the Dreyfus Affair highlighted the fact that anti-semitism was not yet dead. The worst case of anti-Semitism in France occurred under the German occupation, when some 70,000 Jews were deported from the community of 300,000. After the war, France became a centre for Jewish immigration, beginning with 80,000 from eastern Europe, and then many thousands from North Africa, which eventually swelled the Jewish population to nearly 700,000.

The community is well served with organisations. Paris has 380,000 Jews alone, more than in the whole of the UK. There are many kosher restaurants, synagogues in many towns throughout the country, newspapers, radio programmes and schools in several cities. In Carpentras and Cavaillon there are two synagogues which are considered to be national monuments.

GMT + 1 hour	Total Population 58,392,000
Country calling code (33)	Jewish Population 700,000
Emergency Telephone (Police - 17) (Fire - 18) (Ambulance - 15)	Electricity voltage 220

Agen

Synagogues
52 rue Montesquieu 47000   05.53.66.24.20

Aix-en-Provence

Butchers
Zouaghi
7 rue Sevigné 13100   04.42.59.93.94
Supervision: Grand Rabbinate of Marseille.

Synagogues
3 bis rue de Jerusalem 13100   04.42.26.69.39

Aix-les-Bains

Butchers
Berdah, 29 Av. de Tresserve 73100   04.79.61.44.11
Eurocach
Av. d'Italie 73100

Hotels

Kosher

Auberge de La Baye
Chemin du Tir-Aux-Pigeons 73100   04.79.35.69.42
Strictly kosher. Tennis courts and swimming pool.

Mikvaot
Pavillon Salvador
rue du President Roosevelt 73100   04.79.35.38.08

Synagogues
Rue Paul Bonna 73100   04.79.35.28.08
Mikva on Premises

Amiens

Synagogues
38 rue du Port d'Amont 8000

Angers

Synagogues
12 rue Valdemaine 49100

Annecy

Synagogues
18 rue de Narvik 74000   04.50.67.69.37

Annemasse

Butchers
Yarden, 59 rue de la Liberation, Gaillard 74240
          04.50.92.64.05

Antibes-Juan-les-Pins

Butchers
Boulangerie Nouvelle
Le Kineret 25, av. D l'Esterel 06160   04.92.93.16.01
         Fax: 04.93.88.14.76
Berreche
12 av. Courbet 06160   04.93.67.16.77

Restaurants
Maxime
6 Bd de la Pinede   04.92.93.99.40
L'Alhambra
12 bis, Avenue de l'Esterel   04.93.67.65.17
Le Relais de Belleville
47 Avenue Guy de Maupassant 06160
Supervised

Synagogues
Villa La Monada, Chemin des Sables 06600
           04.93.61.59.34

Arcachon

Synagogues
Cours Desbey
Open July & August only

Avignon

Butchers
Chelly, 1-5 rue Chapeau Rouge 84000
           04.90.82.47.50
Supervision: Grand Rabbinate of Marseille.
Eden, 25 rue Ninon Vallin 84000   04.90.85.99.95
Bensoussan
25 rue Ninon Vallin 84000   04.90.85.99.95
Supervision: Grand Rabbinate of Marseille.

Mikvaot
           04.90.86.30.30
Mme Cohen Zardi

Synagogues
2 Place de Jerusalem 84000   04.90.85.21.24
         Fax: 04.90.85.21.24

Bar-le-Duc

Synagogues
7 Quai Carnot

Bayonne

Synagogues
35 rue Maubec 64100   05.59.55.03.95

Beauvais

Synagogues
Rue Jules Isaac 60000   03.44.05.46.90

Belfort

Community Organisations
27 rue Strolz 90000   03.84.28.55.41
Publishes 'Notre Communaute' (quarterly)

Synagogues
6 rue de l'As-de-Carreau 90000   03.84.28.55.41
         Fax: 03.84.28.55.41

Benfeld

Community Organisations
6 rue du Grand Rempart 67230

Synagogues
7a rue de la Dime 67230   08.88.74.47.11

Besancon

Butchers
M. Croppet, 18 rue des Granges   03.81.83.35.93
Thursdays Only

Community Organisations
10 rue Grosjean 25000   03.81.80.82.82

Synagogues
23c Quai de Strasbourg 25000

Beziers

Synagogues
19 Place Pierre-Semard 34500   04.67.28.75.98
Operates a Kosher Food Store

Biarritz

Synagogues
Rue Pellot 64200
July August and Yom Kippur

Bischeim-Schiltigheim

Synagogues
9 Place de la Synagogue 67800   02.38.33.02.87

Bitche

Synagogues
28 rue de Sarreguemines 57230
Services, Rosh Hashana & Yom Kippur

Bordeaux

Community Organisations
15 Pl. Charles-Gruet 33000   05.56.52.62.69

Mikvaot
213 rue Ste. Catherine 33000   05.56.91.79.39

France

Restaurants
Mazal Tov, 137 cours Victor Hugo   05.56.52.37.03

Synagogues
8 rue du Grand-Rabbin-Joseph-Cohen 33000
   05.56.91.79.39

Boulay

Synagogues
Rue du Pressoir 57220   03.87.79.28.34

Boulogne-sur-Mer

Synagogues
63 rue Charles Butor

Bouzonville

Synagogues
Rue des Benedictins 57320

Brest

Synagogues
40 rue de la Republic 29200
Services, Friday, 7.30pm.

Caen

Butchers
Boucherie Marcel
19 and 26 Rue de l'Engannerie 14000
   02.31.86.16.25

Synagogues
46 Av. de la Liberation 14000   02.31.43.60.54

Cagnes-sur-Mer

Synagogues
5 rue des Capucines 06800

Caluire- et- Cuire

Synagogues
107 Av. Fleming 69300   04.78.23.12.37

Cannes

Butcher
Cannes Casher
9 rue Marceau   04.93.39.85.08
Chez Sylvie
15 rue Mal Joffre   04.93.39.57.92

Community Centres
20 Boulevard d'Alsace   04.93.38.16.54
   Fax: 04.93.68.92.81

Groceries
La Emounah, 32 rue de Momont
Near the main synagogue.

Mikvaot
20 Boulevard d'Alsace   04.93.99.79.03
Contact: Mme Annie Rebibo

Restaurants
Dairy

Pizza Dick
7 bis , rue de Mimont 06400   04.92.59.10.82
Meat

Le Tovel
3 rue du Dr Gerard Monod 06400   04.93.39.36.25

Synagogues
Chabad Lubavitch
20 Rue Commandant Vidal 06400   04.92.98.67.51
Sephardi
20 Boulevard d'Alsace   04.93.38.16.54
   Fax: 04.93.68.92.81

Carpentras

Services are held on festivals in the ancient synagogue in the Place de la Mairie, 84200, classed as a national monument. Built in 1367 and rebuilt in 1741, it is worth a visit. Hours 10-12; 3-5. Inquiries to 04.90.63.39.97.

Synagogues
   04.90.63.39.97

Cavaillon

The remains of the old synagogue, built in 1774, are regarded as a French historical monument. The Musées et Patrimoine de Cavaillon organise tours. Contact 52 Place de Castil-Blaze, 84300.
   04.90.76.00.34
   Fax: 04.90.71.47.06

Synagogues
   04.90.76.00.34
   Fax: 04.90.71.47.06

Tours of Jewish Interest
Musees de Patrimoine de Cavaillon
52 Place de Castil-Blaze 84300   04.90.76.00.37
   Fax: 04.90.71.47.06

Chalon-sur-Saone

Synagogues
10 rue Germiny 71100

Chalons-sur-Marne

Synagogues
21 rue Lochet 51000

Chambery

Synagogues
44 rue St-Real
Services, Friday, 7pm and festivals.

Chateauroux

Contact Information
Michel Touati
3 Allee Emile Zola, Montierchaume, Deols 36130
02.54.26.05.47

Clermont-Ferrand

Synagogues
6 rue Blatin   04.73.93.36.59

Colmar

Community Centres
3 rue de la Cigogne 6800   03.89.41.38.29
                                    Fax: 03.89.41.12.96
Kosher food can be purchased in the community centre
on Wednesdays and Thursdays. Kosher restaurant;
Wednesday noon during the school period.

Synagogues
3 rue de la Cigogne 68000   03.89.41.38.29
                                    Fax: 03.89.41.12.96

Compiegne

Synagogues
4 rue du Dr.-Charles-Nicolle 60200

Deauville

Synagogues
14 rue Castor 14800   02.31.81.27.06

Restaurant
King J.J.
23 Rue Gambetta   01 31.87.46.48

Dieuze

Synagogues
Av. Foch 57260

Dijon

Butchers
Albert Levy
25 Srue de la Manutention 21000   03.80.30.14.42

Synagogues
5 rue de la Synagogue   03.80.66.46.47
Mikva on premises.

Dunkerque

Synagogues
19 rue Jean-Bart 59140

Elbeuf

Synagogues
29 rue Gremont 76500   02.35.77.09.11

Epernay

Synagogues
2 rue Placet 51200   03.26.55.24.44
Services, Yom Kippur only.

Epinal

Synagogues
Rue Charlet 88000   03.29.82.25.23

Evian-les-Bains

Synagogues
Adjacent to 1 av. des Grottes, 74500 04.50.75.15.63

Eze-Village

Hotels
Hotel les Terrases d'Eze
Route de la Turbie 06360   04.92.41.55.55
                                    Fax: 04.92.41.55.10

Faulquemont-Crehange

Synagogues
Place de l'Hotel de Ville 57380
Services, festivals & High Holydays only.

France

Forbach

Synagogues
98 Av. St.-Remy 57600   03.87.85.25.57

Frejus

Synagogues
98 Villa Ariane, rue du Progres, Frejus-Plage 83600
                                        04.94.52.06.87

Grasse

Synagogues
82 Route de Nice 06130   04.93.36.05.33

Grenoble

Butchers
C. Cohen
19 rue Turenne 38000   04.76.46.48.14

Groceries
Aux Delices du Soleil
49 rue Thiers   04.76.46.19.60
Ghnassia, 15 place Gustave Rivet   04.76.87.80.90
David France, 4 ave de Vizille   04.76.70.49.15

Media
Radio
Radion Kol Hashalom
4 rue des Bains 38000   04.76.87.21.22

Religious Organisations
Rabbinate
4 rue des Bains 38000   04.76.47.63.72

Synagogues
Synagogue and Community Centre
4 rue des Bains 38000   04.76.46.15.14
Rachi
11 rue André Maginot 38000   04.76.87.02.80
                                   Fax: 04.76.87.27.14
                         Email: rabbin38@aol.com
Mikva at same address.
Beit Habad
10 rue Lazare Carnot 38000   04.76.43.38.58

Grosbliederstroff

Synagogues
6 rue des Fermes 57520

Hagondange

Synagogues
Rue Henri-Hoffmann 57300

Haguenau

Mikvaot
7 rue Neuve

Synagogues
3 rue du Grand-Rabbin-Joseph-Bloch 67500
                                        03.88.73.38.30

Hyeres

Synagogues
Chemin de la Ritorte 83400   04.94.65.31.97

Ingwiller

Synagogues
Cours du Chateau 67340

Insming

Synagogues
Rue de la Synagogue 57670

Izieu

Museums
The Izieu Children's Home
01300
            recording 04.79.87.20.00; booking 04.79.87.20.08
                              Fax: 04.79.87.25.01
                              Email: izieu@alma.fr
                        Web site: www.izieu.alma.fr
The Izieu Children's Memorial Museum is dedicated to
the memory of 44 children and their guardians, taken
away on April 6 1944 by the Gestapo under the
command of Klaus Barbie. The Museum's mission is to
defend dignity, justice and to contribute to the fight
against all forms of intolerance. Two buildings can be
visited: The House takes the visitors back to the
everyday life of the children's home, the Barn presents
the historical background through permanent and
temporary exhibitions. Meetings, conferences and
discussions are organized throughout the year.

La Ciotat

Synagogues
1 Square de Verdun 13600   04.42.71.92.56
Services, Friday 7pm (Winter), 7.30pm (Summer).
Saturday 9am.

La Rochelle

Contact Information
Pierre Guedj
19 rue Bastion d'Evangile 17000   05.46.67.38.91

La Seyne-sur-Mer

Butchers
Elie Benamou
17 rue Baptistin-Paul 83500   04.94.94.38.60

Synagogues
5 rue Chevalier-de-la-Barre 83500   04.94.94.40.28

Le Havre

Synagogues
38 rue Victor-Hugo 76600   02.35.21.14.59

Le Mans

Synagogues
4-6 Blvd. Paixhans 72000   02.43.86.00.96

Libourne

Synagogues
33 rue Lamothe 33500

Lille

Groceries

Monoprix
Shopping Centre Euralille, rue du Molinel 59000

Synagogues
5 rue Auguste-Angellier 59000
                    03.20.30.69.86 or 03.20.85.27.37
Mikva on premises.

Limoges

Synagogues
25-27 rue Pierre-Leroux 87000   05.55.77.47.26

Lorient

Synagogues
18 rue de la Patrie 56100
Services, Friday nights, festivals & Holy-days only.

Luneville

Synagogues
5 rue Castara 54300

Lyons

Media
Le Bulletin
13 Quai Tilsitt 69002   04.78.37.13.43
                                Fax: 04.78.38.26.57
                              Email: acil@free.fr

La Voix Sepharade
317 rue Duguesclin 69007   04.78.58.18.74

Hachaar, 18 rue St. Mathieu 69008   04.78.00.72.50
CIV News
4 rue Malherbe, Villeurbanne 69100   04.78.84.04.32
Radio Judaica Lyon (R.J.L.)
POB 7063 69341   04.78.03.99.20
FM 94.5

Mikvaot
Chaare Tsedek (N. African)
18 rue St.-Mathieu 69008   04.78.00.72.50
Rav Hida (N. African)
La Sauvegarde, La Duchere 69009   04.78.35.14.44
Orah Haim
17 rue Albert-Thomas, St.-Fons 69190
                                     04.78.67.39.78

Organisations
Beth Din, 34 rue d'Armenie, 3e   04.78.62.97.63
                                Fax: 04.78.95.09.47
Consistoire Israelite de Lyon
13 Quai Tilsitt 69002   04.78.37.13.43
                                Fax: 04.78.38.26.57
                              Email: acil@free.fr
Regional Chief Rabbi
13 Quai Tilsitt 69002   04.78.37.13.43
                                Fax: 04.78.38.26.57
Consistoire Israelite Sepharade de Lyon
Yaacov Molho Community Centre, 317
Rue Duguesclin 69007   04.78.58.18.74
                                Fax: 04.78.58.17.49

Restaurants
Le Grillon d'Or
20 rue Terme 69001   04.78.27.33.09
Happy to prepare a meal to go.
Le Jardin d'Eden
14 rue Jean Jaures
Villeurbanne 69002   04.72.33.85.65

Dairy
Lippo
9 Rue Michel Servet
Villeurbanne 69100   04.78.84.15.00

Pizza Cach
13 Rue d'Inkerman
Villeurbanne 69100   04.72.74.44.98

Le Pinocchio
5 Rue A. Boutin
Villeurbanne 69100   04.78.68.62.95

Prestopizza
61 Rue Greuze
Villeurbanne 69100   04.78.68.08.41

France

Meat

Lippmann Henry
4 Rue Tony Tollet Villeurbanne   4.78.42.49.82
                                   Fax: 4.78.42.93.52
Supervision: Yon Beth Din.

Mac David
28 Rue Michel Servet
Villeurbanne 69100   04.78.03.31.62

La Palmeraie
27 Rue des charmettes
Villeurbanne 69100   04.78.24.37.03

Croq Sandwiches
32 Crs Emile-Zola
Villeurbanne 69100   04.78.84.16.07

Synagogues

Orthodox

Grande Synagogue
13 qui Tilsitt   04.78.37.13.43
                                   Fax: 04.78.38.26.57
                                   Email: acil@free.fr

Sephardi

Neveh Chalom
13 rue Duguesclin 69007   04.78.58.18.54
                                   Fax: 04.78.58.17.49

Macon

Synagogues
32 rue des Minimes 71000

Marignane

Synagogues
9 rue Pilote-Larbonne 13700

Marseilles

Bakeries
Erets, 205 rue de Rome 13005   04.91.92.88.73
Supervision: Grand Rabbinate of Marseille.
Avyel Cash
28 rue St Suffren 13006   04.91.87.95.25
Supervision: Grand Rabbinate of Marseille.
Cacher Food
31 blvd Barry 13013   04.91.70.13.43
Supervision: Grand Rabbinate of Marseille.
Le Parve
72 av. Alphonse Daudet 13013   04.91.66.95.16
Supervision: Grand Rabbinate of Marseille.
L'Entremets
206 avenue de la Rose 13013   04.91.70.72.19
Supervision: Grand Rabbinate of Marseille.

Atteia et Fils
19 Place Guillardet 13013   04.91.66.33.28
Supervision: Grand Rabbinate of Marseille.

Butchers
Zennou Raphael
20 marché Capucin 13001   04.91.54.02.54
Supervision: Grand Rabbinate of Marseille.
Attias, 3 rue Halles Delacroix 13001   04.91.54.02.96
Supervision: Grand Rabbinate of Marseille.
Dayan, 4 rue de la Glace 13001   04.91.54.03.70
Supervision: Grand Rabbinate of Marseille.
Ayad, 8 cours Belsunce 13001   04.91.90.73.40
Supervision: Grand Rabbinate of Marseille.
Guedj, 6 cours Julien 13006   04.91.48.44.24
Supervision: Grand Rabbinate of Marseille.
Dav Cacher
46 rue Negresco 13008   04.91.23.32.96
Supervision: Grand Rabbinate of Marseille.
Zouaghi, 2 blvd Latil 13008   04.91.80.01.20
Supervision: Grand Rabbinate of Marseille.
Chez David
9 blvd G. Ganay 13009   04.91.75.04.56
Supervision: Grand Rabbinate of Marseille.
Jamap, 13 place Mignard 13009   04.91.71.11.70
Supervision: Grand Rabbinate of Marseille.
Raphael Cash
299 avenue de Mazargues 13009   04.91.76.44.13
Supervision: Grand Rabbinate of Marseille.
Yad Kel, 143 blvd Paul Claudel 13010
                                   04.91.75.03.57
Supervision: Grand Rabbinate of Marseille.
King Cacher
25 rue F. Mauriac 13010   04.91.80.00.01
Supervision: Grand Rabbinate of Marseille.
Eric Hadjedj
2 place Migranier 13010   04.91.35.10.27
Supervision: Grand Rabbinate of Marseille.
Sebane, 59 rue Alphonse Daudet 13013
                                   04.91.66.98.76
Supervision: Grand Rabbinate of Marseille.

Embassy
Consul General of Israel   04.91.53.39.87
146 rue Paradis 13006   04.91.53.39.94

Groceries
Av bon gout
28 rue St Suffren 13006   04.91.37.95.25
Emmanuel
93 avenue Clot Bey 13008   04.91.77.46.08
Raphael Cash
299 avenue de Mazargues 13009   04.91.76.44.13
King Kasher
25 rue François Mauriac 13010   04.91.80.00.01
Les Délices d'Eden
Ctre Cial residénce Bellevue 13010 04.91.75.03.57

Delicash
94 blvd Barry 13013   04.91.06.39.04

Religious Organisations
Consistoire de Marseille
117 rue de Breteuil 13006
04.91.37.49.64; 04.91.81.13.57
Fax: 04.91.53.98.72

Restaurants

Meat

Nathania
17 rue du Village 13006   04.91.42.05.31
Supervision: Grand Rabbinate of Marseille.
Erets, 205, rue de Rome 13006   04.91.92.88.73
Supervision: Grand Rabbinate of Marseille.

Melun
Synagogues
Cnr. rues Branly & Michelet 77000   01.64.52.00.05

Menton
Synagogues
Centre Altyner, 106 Cours du Centenaire
04.93.35.28.29

Merlebach
Synagogues
19 rue St.-Nicolas 57800

Metz
Butchers
Claude Sebbag
22 rue Mangin 57000   03.87.63.33.50
Supervision: Chief Rabbi of Moselle.

Groceries
Galaries Lafayette
4 rue Winston Churchill 57000   03.87.38.60.60
Atac
23 rue de 20e Corps Américain 57000

Religious Organisations
Rabbi Bruno Fizon
27/29 en Jurve   03.87.36.43.82

Synagogues
Adass Yechouroun
41 rue de Rabbin Elie-Bloch 57000

Main Synagogue and Community Centre
39 rue du Rabbin Elie-Bloch 57000
03.87.75.04.44
This street was renamed from rue de l'Arsenal, in memory of a youth movement rabbi deported and killed by the Nazis during the Second World War.

Montauban
Synagogues
14 rue Ste.-Claire 82000   05.63.03.01.37

Montbeliard
Synagogues
Rue de la Synagogue 25200

Montpellier
Butchers
Eretz, 41 rue de Lunaret 34000   04.67.72.67.94

Community Organisations
Centre Communautaire et Cultural Juif
560 blvd. d'Antigone 34000   04.67.15.08.76

Synagogues
Mazal Tov
18 rue Ferdinand-Fabre 34000   04.67.79.09.82
Ben-Zakai
7 rue General-Laffon 34000   04.67.92.92.07

Mulhouse
Synagogues
2 rue des Rabbins 68100   03.89.66.21.22
Fax: 03.89.56.63.49
Mikva on premises. The old cemetery is also worth a visit.

Nancy
Community Organisations
19 Blvd. Joffre 54000   03.83.32.10.67

Museums
The Musee Historique Lorrain
64 Grand rue 54000
The museum has an important collection of sifrei Torah, prayer books and other ritual objects.

Restaurants
Restaurante Universitaire
19 Blvd. Joffre 54000   03.83.32.10.67
Open weekdays at noon.

Synagogues
17 Blvd. Joffre 54000   03.83.32.10.67

France

Nantes

Synagogues
5 Impasse Copernic 44000   02.40.73.48.92
Mikva on premises.

Nice

Booksellers
Librairie Tanya
25 rue Pertinax 06000   04.93.80.21.74
                          Fax: 04.93.13.87.90
           Email: librairie.tanya@wanadoo.fr

Kashrut Information
                                04.93.85.82.06
A list of kosher butchers and bakers can be obtained
from the Chief Rabbi.

Mikvaot
22 rue Michelet 06100   04.93.51.89.80

Religious Organisations
Regional Chief Rabbinate of Nice, Cote d'Azur and
Corsica
1 rue Voltaire 06000   04.93.85.82.06
Centre Consistorial and Synagogue
22 rue Michelet 06100   04.93.51.89.80
Publishes an annual calendar and guide to Nice and
district.

Restaurants

Dairy

Le Leviathan, 1 ave Georges Clemenceau
                                04.93.87.22.64
Le cheme Chamayime
22 rue Rossini 06000   04.93.88.47.01
Supervision: Rabbanut of Nice and Lubavitch.

Meat

Le Richone, 26 rue Pertinax   04.93.13.82.69
                          Fax: 04.93.88.81.95
Supervision: Rabbanut of Nice.
Kinerth, 37bis, av.Georges Clemenceau
                                04.93.87.56.36
Supervision: Rabbanut of Nice.

Synagogues
Main Synagogue
7 rue Gustave-Deloye 06000   04.93.92.11.38

Nimes

Community Organisations
5 rue d'Angouleme 30000   04.66.26.19.51

Synagogues
40 rue Roussy 30000   04.66.29.51.81
Mikva on premises.

Obernai

Synagogues
Rue de Selestat 67210

Orleans

Synagogues
14 rue Robert-de-Courtenay, (to the left of the
Cathedral) 45000
Information on services to be had from M Attali, tel:
02-38621662.

Paris

The city of Paris is divided into districts
(arrondissements) designated by the last two digits
of the postcode. In the categories below,
establishments are listed in numerical order
according to the postcode (that is, -01, -02, -03
and so on).

The historic centre of Paris Jewish life is found in
the Marais area (4th arrondissement) although a
Synagogue stood on Ile de la Cite before Notre
Dame. Another more central area is that around
rue Richer (9th arrondissement) which although
not historic as such has many kosher restaurants of
varying styles and prices.

A most important new site to be visited is the
new Musee d'art et d'histoire du Judaisme which
opened in December 1998.

Bakeries
Korcarz, 29 rue des Rosiers 75004   01.42.77.39.47
                          Fax: 01.48.58.28.44
Supervision: Beth Din of Paris/Chief Rabbi Mordechai
Rottenberg.
Mezel, 1 rue Ferdinand Duval 75004
                                01.42.78.25.01
Supervision: Beth Din of Paris.
Les Ailes
34 rue Richer 75009   01.47.70.62.53
Supervision: Beth Din of Paris.
Douieb, 11 bis rue Geoffroy Marie 75009
                                01.47.70.86.09
Supervision: Beth Din of Paris.
Zazou, 20 rue du Fbg Montmartre 75009
                                01.47.70.81.32
Supervision: Beth Din of Paris.
Korcarz, 25 rue de Trévise 75009   01.42.46.83.33
Supervision: Beth Din of Paris/Chief Rabbi Mordechai
Rottenberg.
Golan, 10 rue Geoffroy Marie 75009
                                01.48.00.94.71
Supervision: Beth Din of Paris.
Dahan, 7 rue Maillard 75011   01.43.79.43.55
Supervision: Beth Din of Paris.

Nathan de Belleville
67 blvd de Belleville 75011   01.43.57.24.60
Supervision: Beth Din of Paris.
Mendez, 3 Ter rue de la Présent. 75011
    01.43.57.02.03
Supervision: Beth Din of Paris.
Charles Tr. Patissier
10 rue Corentin Cariou 75019   01.47.97.51.83
Supervision: Beth Din of Paris.
Aux Delices de Maxime
69 rue de Crimée 75019   01.40.36.44.76
Supervision: Beth Din of Paris.
Medayo, 71 rue de Meaux 75019   01.40.03.04.20
Supervision: Beth Din of Paris.
Contini, 116 avenue Simon Bolivar 75019
    01.42.00.70.80
Supervision: Beth Din of Paris.
Mat'amim
17 rue de Crimée 75019   01.42.40.89.11
Supervision: Beth Din of Paris.
Le Relais Sucre
135 rue Manin 75019   01.42.41.20.98
Supervision: Beth Din of Paris.
Kadoche
2 avenue Corentin Cariou 75019
    01.40.37.00.14
Supervision: Beth Din of Paris.
Eliyor
21 rue Bisson 75020   01.43.49.12.66
Supervision: Beth Din of Paris.
Zazou
8 rue Rouvet 75020   01.40.36.67.61
Supervision: Beth Din of Paris.
Lilo
20 rue Desnoyer 75020   01.47.97.63.20
Supervision: Beth Din of Paris.
Nani
104 blvd de Belleville 75020   01.47.97.38.05
Supervision: Beth Din of Paris.

Butchers
Tordjemann
40 rue St Paul 75004   01.42.72.93.22
Saada
17 rue des Rosiers 75004   01.42.77.76.22
Adolphe
14 rue Richer 75009   01.48.24.86.33
La Charolaise Richer
51 rue Richer 75009   01.47.70.01.57
Berbeche
46 Rue Richer 75009   01.47.70.50.58
Chez Andre
7 Rue Geoffroy Marie 75009   01.47.70.49.03
Charlot
33 Rue Richer 75009   01.45.23.10.34
La Rose Blanche
43 rue Richer 75009   01.48.24.84.65
Chez Jacques
19 rue Bouchardon 75010   01.42.06.76.13
Maurice Zirah
91 rue de la Roquette 75011   01.43.79.62.53
Chez Lucien
180 rue de Charonne 75011   01.43.70.59.29

Chez Halak B. Y.
51 rue Richard Lenoir 75011   01.43.48.62.26
Chez Andre
69 bld de Belleville 75011   01.43.57.80.38
Chez Jojo
20 rue Louis Bonnet 75011   01.43.55.10.29
J V Temim
2 rue de Dr Goujon 75012   01.43.45.78.77
Boucherie Guy
266 rue de Charenton 75012   01.43.44.60.90
Berbeche
6 rue du Moulinet 75013   01.45.80.89.10
Berbeche
5 rue Vandrezanne 75013   01.45.88.86.50
Boucherie Claude
174 rue Lecourbe 75015   01.48.28.02.00
Kassab
88 bd Murat 75016   01.40.71.07.34
Sarl Gm Levy
83 rue de Lonchamp 75016   01.45.53.04.24
Ste Delicatess
209 av de Versailles 75016   01.44.40.07.59
E spaces Courses Elles
177 rue de Courcelles 75017   01.47.63.36.26
Berbeche
39 rue Jouffroy 75017   01.44.40.07.59
Krief
104 rue Legendre 75017   01.46.27.15.57
Emsalem
17 Quai de la Gironde 75019
    01.40.36.56.64
Berbeche
15/17 rue Henri Ribiere 75019   01.42.08.06.06
Andre-Manin
135 rue Manin 75019   01.42.38.00.43
A Viandes Cacheres
6 av Corentin Cariou 75019   01.40.36.02.41
Even Shapir
15 rue de Crimee 75019   01.42.02.43.00
Chez Meyer
16 rue Menadier 75019   01.42.45.22.09
Hayof
1 rue Edouard Pailleron 75019
    01.42.45.72.22
Emsalem
18 rue Corentin Cariou 75019
    01.40.36.56.64
Boucherie Smadja
90 bd de Belleville 75020   01.46.36.25.36
Henrino
122 bd de Belleville 75020   01.47.97.24.52

Embassy
Embassy of Israel
3 rue Rabelais 75008   01.40.76.55.00
    Fax: 01.40.76.55.55
    Email: info@amb-israel.fr

Groceries
Francois
45 rue Richer 75009   01.47.70.17.43

France / Paris

Doueib, 11 bis rue Geoffroy Marie 75009
01.47.70.86.09
Le Haim, 6 rue Paulin Enfert 75013   01.44.24.53.34
Chekel, 14 av de Villiers 75017   01.48.88.94.97
Supervision: Beth Din of Paris.
Also sell delicatessen and sandwiches. Hours: 9 am to
8 pm. Nearest Metro: Villiers. Near Champs-
Elysées/Opéra.
Compt Pdts Alimentaires
111 av de Villiers 75017   01.42.27.16.91
Chochana
54 Av Secretan 75019

Hotels
Hotel Touring
21 rue Buffault 75009   01.48.78.09.16
Fax: 01.48.78.27.74
Email: infos@hotel-touring.fr
Web site: www.hotel-touring.fr

Pavillon De Paris
7 rue de Parme 75009   01.55.31.60.00
Fax: 01.55.31.60.01
Email: mail@pavillondeparis.com
Web site: www.pavillondeparis.com

Hôtel Aida Opéra
17 rue du Conservatoire 75009   01.45.23.11.11
Fax: 01.47.70.38.73
Email: comotel@easyhet.fr
Supervision: Beth Din of Paris..
Kosher breakfast.
Hotel Geoffroy-Marie Opera
12 Rue Geoffroy-Marie 75009   01.47.70.11.85
Fax: 01.42.46.09.36
Supervision: Beth Din of Paris.
Breakfast only
L'Hotel de Mericourt
50 rue de la Folie Mericourt 75011   01.43.38.73.63
Fax: 01.43.38.66.13
Situated in an area with many Kosher facilities.

Library
Library Judaica of the Seminaire Israelite de France
9 rue Vauquelin 75005   01.47.07.22.94
Visit only by appointment

Mikvaot
176 rue du Temple 75003   01.42.71.89.28
The mikvah is located in the centre of Paris, near Place
de la République, at the rear of the building. The staff
is English speaking.
19-21 rue Galvani 75017   01.45.74.52.80

Mayan Hai Source de Vie Haya Mouchka
2-4 rue Tristan Tzara 75018
01.40.38.18.29; 01.46.36.11.09
1 rue des Annelets 75019   01.44.84.05.36
For men and women. Telephone is an answer machine for women only.

Mikve Haya Mouchka
25 rue Riquet 75019   01 40.36.40.92
Fax: 01 40.36.88.90
75 rue Julien-Lacroix 75020
01.46.36.39.20; 01.46.36.30.10
For men and women.

Museums

Musée d'art et d'histoire de Judaisme
Hotel de Saint-Aignan, 71 rue de Temple 75003
01.53.01.86.60
Fax: 01.42.72.97.47
Open Monday to Friday from 11.00 to 18.00 and Sunday from 10.00 to 18.00.

Religious Organisations

Communauté Israélite Orthodoxe de Paris
10 rue Pavée 75004   01.42.77.81.51
Fax: 01.48.87.26.29

Restaurants

Contini, 42 rue des Rosiers 75004   01.48.04.78.32
Supervision: Beth Din of Paris.
Adolphe, 14 rue Richer 75009   01.47.70.91.25
Supervision: Beth Din of Paris.
Brasserie du Belvedere
109 avenue de Villiers 75017   01 47.64.96.55
Supervision: Beth-Din Paris.
Supervision: Rev. Rottenberg.
La Mere Lachaise
78 bd Menilmontant 75020   01.47.97.61.60

Dairy

Panini Folie
11 rue du Ponceau 75002   01.42.33.14.55
Supervision: Beth Din of Paris.
Contini, 42 rue des Rosiers 75004   01.48.04.78.32
Supervision: Beth Din of Paris.
Hamman Café
4 rue des Rosiers 75004   01.42.78.04.46
Supervision: Beth Din of Paris.
Cine Citta Café
7 rue d'Aguesseau 75008   01.42.68.05.03
Supervision: Beth Din of Paris.
Maestro Pizza
19 rue d'Anjou 75008   01.47.42.15.60
Supervision: Beth Din of Paris.

France / Paris

Casa Rina
18 Faubourg Monmartre 75009   01.45.23.02.22
Supervision: Beth Din of Paris.
King Salomon
46 rue Richer 75009   01.42.46.31.22
Supervision: Beth Din of Paris.
Le Bistrot Blanc
52 rue Blanche 75009   01.42.85.05.30
Supervision: Paris Beth Din.
Cine Citta Café
58 rue Richer 75009   01.42.46.09.65
Supervision: Beth Din of Paris.
Dizengoff Café
27 rue Richer 75009   01.47.70.81.97
Supervision: Beth Din of Paris.
Open from 8.00 am (breakfast) to 11.00 pm
Le New's
56 avenue de la République 75011   01.43.38.63.18
Supervision: Beth Din of Paris.
Coktail Café
82 avenue Parmentier 75011   01.43.57.19.94
Supervision: Beth Din of Paris.
Gin Fizz
157 boulevard Serrurier 75019   01.42.00.51.28
Supervision: Beth Din of Paris.

Pizza Curial
44 rue Curial 75019   01.40.37.15.00
Supervision: Beth Din of Paris.

Meat

Darjeeling
1 bis, rue des Colonels Renard 75017
   01.45.72.09.32
Web site: www.darjeeling-ontable.com
Juliette
12/14 rue Duphot 75001   01.42.60.18.05
   Fax: 01.42.60.18.98
Supervision: Beth Din of Paris.
La Petite Famille
32 rue des Rosiers 75003   01.42.77.00.50
Supervision: Beth Din of Paris.
Micky's Deli
23 bis rue des Rosiers 75004   01.48.04.79.31
Supervision: Chief Rabbi Mordechai Rottenberg.
Yahalom, 22 rue des Rosiers 75004
   01.42.77.12.35
Supervision: Chief Rabbi Mordechai Rottenberg.
Chez Gaby
50 rue Broca 75005   01.43.31.04.14
Supervision: Beth Din of Paris.

KOSHER RESTAURANT
UNDER THE CONTROL OF THE BETH DIN

JULIETTE

An elegant and gastronomical restaurant of great French tradition

12/14, rue Duphot, Dans la Cour
75001 **PARIS**
Tel. 00.33.1.42.60.18.05/18.10

Centre Edmond Fleg
8 bis, rue de l'Eperon 75006　01.46.33.43.31
Supervision: Beth Din of Paris.
Sivane
36 rue de Berry 75008　01.49.53.01.21
Supervision: Beth Din of Paris.
Mao Tsur
10 rue Geoffroy Marie 75009　01.47.70.62.53
Fax: 01.47.70.27.76
Supervision: Beth Din of Paris.
Zazou Burger
19 rue du Fbg Montmartre 75009　01.40.22.08.33
Supervision: Beth Din of Paris.
Yankees Cafe
31 rue du Fbg Montmartre 75009　01.42.46.52.46
Supervision: Beth Din of Paris.
Synagogue Beth El
4 rue Saulnier 75009　01.45.23.34.89
Supervision: Beth Din of Paris.
Shabbat meals by arrangement
Snack Quick Delight
24 rue Richer 75009　01.45.23.05.12
Supervision: Beth Din of Paris.
Douieb
11 bis rue Geoffroy-Marie 75009
01.47.70.86.09
Supervision: Beth Din of Paris.
Le Gros Ventre
7/9 rue Montyon 75009　01.48.24.25.34
Supervision: Beth Din of Paris.
Georges de Tunis
42 rue Richer 75009　01.47.70.24.64
Supervision: Beth Din of Paris.
Berbeche Burger
47 rue Richer 75009　01.47.70.81.22
Supervision: Beth Din of Paris.
Centre Communautaire de Paris
5 rue Rochechouart 75009　01.49.95.95.92
Supervision: Beth Din of Paris.
Chez David
11 rue Montyon 75009　01.44.83.01.24
Supervision: Beth Din of Paris.
Les Ailes
34 rue Richer 75009　01.47.70.62.53
Supervision: Beth Din of Paris.
Les Cantiques
16 rue Beaurepaire 75010　01.42.40.64.21
Supervision: Beth Din of Paris.
Deliver.
Cash Food
63 rue des Vinaigriers 75010　01.42.03.95.75
Supervision: Beth Din of Paris.
Dolly's Food
9 rue Cité Riverain 75010　01.48.03.08.40
Supervision: Beth Din of Paris.

Le Cabourg
102 boulevard Voltaire 75011　01.47.00.71.43
Supervision: Beth Din of Paris.
Hours: 12 pm to 2:30 pm and 7 pm to 11 pm.
Le Lotus de Nissan
39 rue Amelot 75011　01.43.55.80.42
Supervision: Beth Din of Paris.
Le Manahattan
231 boulevard Voltaire 75011　01.43.56.03.30
Supervision: Beth Din of Paris.
Yung Pana
115 Boulevard Voltaire 75011　01.43.79.20.48
Supervision: Beth Din of Paris.
La Libanaise
13 rue des Sablons 75016　01.45.05.10.35
Supervision: Beth Din of Paris.
Fradji, 42 rue Poncelet 75017　01.47.54.91.40
Supervision: Beth Din of Paris.
Nini, 24 rue Saussier-Leroy 75017　01.46.22.28.93
Supervision: Beth Din of Paris.
Brasserie du Belvedere
109 av de Villiers 75017　01.47.64.96.55
Supervision: Beth Din of Paris.
Alelouya
36 Bd Barbes 75018　01.42.52.88.50
Supervision: Beth Din of Paris.
La Muraille de Chine
44 rue d'Hautpoul 75019　01.42.01.20.30
Supervision: Beth Din of Paris.
Mille Delices
52 avenue Secrétan 75019　01.40.18.32.32
Supervision: Beth Din of Paris.
Lumieres de Belleville
102 boulevard de Belleville 75020　01.47.97.51.83
Supervision: Beth Din of Paris.
Le Petit Pelleport
135 rue Pelleport 75020　01.40.33.13.17
Supervision: Beth Din of Paris.
Auberge de Belleville
110 boulevard de Belleville 75020　01.43.15.02.59
Supervision: Beth Din of Paris.
Chez François
5 rue Ramponeau 75020　01.47.97.40.06
Supervision: Beth Din of Paris.
Chez Jeannot
112 boulevard de Belleville 75020　01.47.97.35.06
Supervision: Beth Din of Paris.
Chez Rene et Gabin
92 boulevard de Belleville 75020　01.43.58.78.14
Supervision: Beth Din of Paris.
Elygel, 116 boulevard de Belleville 75020
01.47.97.09.73
Supervision: Beth Din of Paris.

France / Paris

Synagogues

Liberal

Union Liberale Israelite de France
24 rue Copernic, XV1   01.47.04.37.27

Masorti

Communaute Juive Massorti de Paris
8 Rue George Bernard Shaw (off Rue Dupleix) 75015
01.45.67.97.96
Fax: 01.45.56.89.79
Email: RuzieDr@aol.com
Web site: www.jtsa.edu/synagogues/adathsfr/
The Paris Jewish Masorti (Conservative) Community.
Services Friday night 6.30pm. Shabbat morning 10am
festivals and Rosh Chodesh.

Orthodox

Netzach Israël Ohel Mordehai
5 rue Sainte-Anastase 75003
Groupe Rabbi Yehiel de Paris
25 rue Michel-Leconte 75003   01.42.78.89.17
Synagogue Tephilat Israël Frank-Forter
24 rue du Bourg-Tibourg 75004   01.46.24.48.94
Name?
14 place des Vosges 75004   01.48.87.79.45
Fax: 01.48.87.57.58
Synagogue des Tournelles
21 bis rue des Tournelles 75004
01.42.74.32.65; 01.42.74.32.80
Fax: 01.40.29.90.27
Email: david-halim@septodont.fr
Fondation Roger Fleishmann
18 rue des Ecouffes 75004   01.48.87.97.86
Agoudas Hakehilos Instit Yad Mordekhai
10 rue Pavée 75004   01.48.87.21.54
Fax: 01.48.87.21.59
Oratoire Mahziké Adath Mouvement Loubavitch
17 rue des Rosiers 75004
Adath Yechouroun
25 rue des Rosiers 75004   01.44.59.82.36
Centre Rachi
30 boulevard du Port-Royal 75005   01.43.31.98.20
Séminaire Israélite de France
9 rue Vauquelin 75005   01.47.07.21.22
Fax: 01.43.37.75.92

Centre Edmond Fleg
8 bis rue de l'Epéron 75006   01.46.33.43.31
Houses the Union des Centres Communautaires (UCC),
which can be contacted via the same telephone
number. Their fax number is 01.43.25.86.19.
Tikваténou, the Jewish youth movement of the
Consistoire, is also located here, Tel: 01.46.33.43.24;
Fax: 01.43.25.20.59.
E.E.I.F.
27 avenue de Ségur 75007   01.47.83.60.33
Hékhal Moché
218-220 rue du Faubourg St-Honoré 75008
01.45.61.20.25
Located behind the Golden Tulip Hotel .
Siège du Beth Loubavitch
8 rue Lamartine 75009   01.45.26.87.60
Fax: 01.45.26.24.37
Kollel Rav Lévy
37 boulevard de Strasbourg 75009
Grande Synagogue de Paris
44 rue de la Victoire 75009
01.40.82.26.26 ext. 2773 or 01.45.26.95.36
Fax: 01.45.26.95.36
Email: grandesynaparis@col.fr
Web site: www.col.fr/grande-synagogue-paris
Beth-Israël
4 rue Saulnier 75009   01.45.23.34.89
Tiferet Yaacob
71 rue de Dunkerque 75009   01.42.81.32.17;
01.42.49.65.12
Adass Yereim
10 rue Cadet 75009
01.42.46.36.47 or 01.48.74.51.78
Fax: 01.48.74.35.35
Nussach Ashkenez
Synagogue Berit Chalom
18 rue Saint-Lazare 75009
01.48.78.45.32; 01.48.78.38.80

Beth-El, 3 bis rue Saulnier 75009   01.47.70.09.23
Fax: 01.45.23.15.75
Rachi Chull
6 rue Ambroise-Thomas 75009   01.48.24.86.95
UNAT La Fraternelle
13-15 rue des Petites-Ecuries 75010   01.42.46.65.02
Beth-Eliaou
192 rue Saint-Martin 75010   01.40.38.47.53
Fax: 01.40.36.41.95

A.U.J.
130 rue du Faubourg Saint-Martin 75010
01.40.05.98.34
9 rue Guy-Patin 75010   01.42.85.12.74
4 rue Martel 75010

Rav Pealim (Braslav)
49 boulevard de la Villette 75010   01.42.41.55.44
Synagogue Don Isaac Abravanel
84-86 rue de la Roquette 75011   01.47.00.75.95
Ora Vesimha
37 rue des Trois-Bornes 75011   01.43.57.49.84
Adath Israël
36 rue Basfroi 75011   01.43.67.89.20
Ets Haim
18 rue Basfroi 75011   01.43.48.82.42
Ozar Hatorath Shoul
40 rue de l'Orillon 75011   01.43.38.73.40
    Fax: 01.43.38.36.45
Chivtei Israel
12-14 Cité Moynet 75012   01.43.43.50.12
    Fax: 01.43.47.36.78
    Email: ravatlan@club-internet.fr
Oratoire de la Fondation Rothschild (Maison de Retraite)
76 rue de Picpus 75012   01.43.44.72.98
    Fax: 01.43.44.71.39
Névé Chalom
29 rue Sibué 75012   01.43.42.07.70
    Fax: 01.43.48.44.50
Avoth Ouvanim
59 avenue d'Ivry 75013   01.45.82.80.73
    01.45.85.94.39
Merkaz Beth Myriam
19 rue Domrémy 75013   01.45.86.83.99
    Fax: 01.45.86.83.99
Beith Chalom
25 villa d'Alésia 75014   01.45.45.38.71
    Fax: 01.43.37.58.49
6 bis villa d'Alésia 75014   01.45.40.82.35
    Fax: 01.45.40.72.89
223 rue Vercingétorix 75014   01.45.45.50.51
Ohel Mordekhai
13 rue Fondary 75015   01.40.59.96.56

23 bis rue Dufrénoy 75016   01.45.04.94.00;
01.45.04.66.73
Ohel Avraham
31 rue Montevideo 75016   01.45.05.66.73
    Fax: 01.40.72.83.76
Centre Rambam
19-21 rue Galvani 75017   01.45.74.52.80
Beth Hamidrach Lamed
67 rue Bayen 75017   01.45.74.52.80
Synagogue ACIP
42 rue des Saules 75018   01.46.06.71.39
Synagogue de Montmartre
13 rue Sainte-Isaure 75018   01.42.64.48.34

Beth Loubavitch
25 rue Riquet 75019   01.40.36.93.90
    Fax: 01.40.36.60.15
Ohr Tora
15 rue Riquet 75019
    01.40.38.23.36; 01.40.36.42.23
Beth Chalom
11-13 rue Curial 75019   01.40.37.65.16;
01.40.37.12.54
Synagogue Michkenot Israel
6 rue Jean-Nohain 75019   01.48.03.25.59
    Fax: 01.42.00.26.87
Ohr Yossef
44-48 Quai de la Marne 75019   01.42.45.74.20
    Fax: 01.40.18.10.74
Chaare Tora
1 rue Henri-Turot 75019   01.42.06.41.12
    Fax: 01.42.06.95.47
Beth Loubavitch
53 rue Compans 75019   01.42.02.20.35
Rabbi David ou Moché
45 rue de Belleville 75019   01.40.18.30.63
    Fax: 01.40.18.30.62
Heder Loubavitch
25 rue des Solitaires 75019   01.42.02.98.95
    Fax: 01.42.02.04.62
Kollel Ysmah Moché
36 rue des Annelets 75019   01.43.63.73.94
Pah'ad David
11 rue du Plateau 75019   01.42.46.47.03
    Fax: 01.42.46.47.56
Collel Hamabit
7 rue Rouvet 75019   01.40.38.13.59
Ohaley Yaacov
11 rue Henri-Murger 75019   01.42.49.25.00

Ohr Chimchon Raphaël
5 passage Dagorno 75020   01.46.59.39.02
    Fax: 01.46.59.14.99
Maor Athora
16 rue Ramponeau 75020   01.47.97.69.42
Beth Loubavitch
93 rue des Orteaux 75020   01.40.24.10.60
Synagogue Michkan-Yaacov
118 boulevard de Belleville 75020   01.43.49.39.59
Synagogue Achkenaze & Sephardi
49 rue Pali Kao 75020   01.46.36.30.10
Beth Loubavitch
47 rue Ramponeau 75020   01.43.66.93.00

France / Paris

Synagogue Bet Yaacov Yossef
5 square des Cardeurs, 43 rue Saint-Blaise 75020
01.43.56.03.11

Paris Suburbs

Alfortville

Butchers
Tiness, 12 Etienne Dollet 94140   01.49.77.95.79

Antony

Butchers
A.B.C., 96 av de la Division Leclerc 92160
01.46.66.13.43

Synagogues

Orthodox

Community Centre and Synagogue
1 rue Sdérot, Angle 1, Rue Barthélémy 92160
01.46.66.19.17

Asnieres

Mikvaot
82 rue du R.P. Christian-Gilbert 92600
01.47.99.26.59

Synagogues

Orthodox
73 bis rue des Bas 92600   01.47.99.32.55

Athis-Mons

Synagogues
55 rue des Coquelicots 92100   01.69.38.14.29

Aulnay-Sous-Bois

Synagogues
80 rue Maximilien Robespierre 93600
01.48.69.66.93

Bagneux

Bakeries
Princiane
1 rue de l'Egalité, Parc de Garlande 92220
01.47.35.90.77
Fax: 01.47.35.93.67
Email: princiane@princiane.com
Supervision: Beth Din of Paris. Orthodox Union..

Butchers
Isaac, 188 av Aristide Briand 92220   01.45.47.00.21

Bagnolet

Bakeries
Sonesta, 27 rue Adélaide Lahaye 93000
01.43.64.92.93
Fax: 01.43.60.51.26
Supervision: Beth Din of Paris.

Bobigny

Restaurants
Le Simane Tov
22-24 rue Henri Barbusse 93000   01.48.43.79.00
Supervision: Beth Din of Paris.

Bondy

Synagogues

Orthodox

Maison Communautaire
28 avenue de la Villageoise 93140   01.48.47.50.79

Boulogne

Bakeries
Ariel, 143 avenue J.B. Clément 92100
01.46.04.24.42
Supervision: Beth Din of Paris.

Groceries
Ednale, 28 rue Georges Sorel 92100   01.46.03.83.37

Synagogues

Orthodox
43 rue des Abondances 92100   01.46.03.90.63
Fax: 01.46.03.90.63

Bussiere

Mikvaot
Domaines de Melicourt 77750
01.60.22.54.85; 01.60.22.53.01

Champigny-Sur-Marne

Synagogues

Orthodox

Synagogue Beth-David
25 avenue du général-de Gaulle 94500
01.48.85.72.29

Charenton

Butchers
Mazel Tov
14 rue Victor Hugo 94220   01.43.68.41.23

Chelles

Synagogues

Orthodox

14 rue des Anémones 77500   01.60.20.92.93

Choisy-le-Roi

Butchers
Chez Ilane
131 Marechal de Lattre de Tassigny 94600
    01.48.52.27.74

Mikvaot
28 avenue de Newbum 94600
    01.48.53.43.70; 01.48.92.68.68

Synagogues

Orthodox

28 avenue de Newburn 94600   01.48.53.48.27

Clichy-sur-Seine

Synagogues
26 rue de Mozart (Espace Clichy) 92210
    01.47.39.02.43

Créteil

Bakeries
Caprices et Delices
5 rue Edouard Manet 94000   01.43.39.20.20
Supervision: Beth Din of Paris.
La Nougatine
20 Esplanade des Abîmes 94000   01.49.56.98.56
Supervision: Beth Din of Paris.
Tov 'Mie
25 rue du Dr Paul Casalis 94000   01.48.99.00.39
Supervision: Beth Din of Paris.
Les Jasmins de Tunis
C.C. Kennedy 94000   01.43.77.50.66
Supervision: Beth Din of Paris.
Quick Chaud
26 allée Parmentier 94000   01.48.99.08.30
Supervision: Beth Din of Paris.

Butchers
Boucherie Patrick
2 rue Edouard Manet 94000   01.43.39.29.64

La Charolaise Julien
Cte Commercial Kennedy, Loge 13 rue Gabriel Peri
94000   01.43.39.20.43

Mikvaot
Rue du 8 Mai 1945 94000
    01.43.77.01.70; 01.43.77.19.68

Restaurants

Meat

Prumo Cacher
17, allee du Commerce 94000   01.49.80.04.25
Supervision: Beth Din of Paris.

Synagogues

Orthodox

Community Centre
rue du 8 Mai 1945 94051
    01.43.77.01.70; 01.43.39.05.20
    Fax: 01.43.99.03.60

Enghien

Mikvaot
47 rue de Malleville 95880   01.34.17.37.11

Synagogues

Orthodox

47 rue de Malleville 95880   01.34.12.42.34

Epinay

Butchers
Chalom, 90 av Joffre 93800   01.48.41.50.64

Fontainebleau

Synagogues

Orthodox

38 rue Paul Seramy 77300   01.64.22.68.48

Fontenay-Aux-Roses

Synagogues
Centre Moise Meniane
17 avenue Paul-Langevin 92660   01.46.60.75.94

Fontenay-s/Bois

Mikvaot
Haya Mossia
177 rue des Moulins 94120
    01.48.77.53.90; 01.48.76.83.84

France / Paris Suburbs

Garges-Les-Gonesse

Butchers
Chez Harry
1 rue J B Corot 95140   01.39.86.53.81
Boucherie Berbeche
C C Pal de la Dame Blanche 95140   01.39.86.42.06

Mikvaot
15 rue Corot 95140   01.39.86.75.64

Synagogues

Orthodox

Maison Communautaire Chaare Ra'hamim
14 rue Corot 95140   01.39.86.75.64

Issy-Les-Moulineaux

Synagogues
72 boulevard Gallieni 92130   01.46.48.34.49

La Courneuve

Synagogues
13 rue Saint-Just 93120   01.48.36.75.59

La Garenne-Colombes

Synagogues
Synagogue and Community Centre of Courbevoie / La
Garenne-Colombes
13 rue L.M. Nordmann 92250   01.47.69.92.17

La Varenne St-Hilaire

Synagogues
10 bis avenue du chateau 4210   01.42.83.28.75

Le Blanc Mesnil

Synagogues
65 rue Maxime-Gorki 93150   01.48.65.58.98

Le Chesnay

Mikvaot
39 rue de Versailles 78150
          01.39.54.05.65; 01.39.07.19.19

Le Kremlin-Bicetre

Synagogues

Orthodox

41-45 rue J.F. Kennedy 94270   01.46.72.73.64

Le Perreux Nogent

Synagogues
Synagogue-Nogent/Le Perreux/Bry-Sur-Marne
165 bis avenue du Gal-de Gaulle 94170
          01.48.72.88.65

Le Raincy

Mikvaot
67 boulevard du Midi 93340   01.43.81.06.61

Synagogues

Orthodox

Maison Communautaire
19 allée Chatrian 93340   01.43.02.06.11

Le Vesinet

Mikvaot
29 rue Henri Cloppet 78110
          01.30.53.10.45; 01.30.71.12.26

Synagogues

Orthodox

Maison Communautaire
29 rue Henri-Cloppet 78110   01.30.53.10.45

Les Lilas

Butchers
Boucherie Des Lilas
6 rue de la Republique 93260   01.43.63.89.15

Levallois

Restaurants
Delicates Eden
102 rue Rivay 92300   01.42.70.97.06
Supervision: Beth Din of Paris.

Maisons-Alfort

Mikvaot
92-94 rue Victor-Hugo 94700   01.43.78.95.69

Massy

Mikvaot
Allée Marcel-Cerdan 91300   01.42.37.48.24

Synagogues

Orthodox

Allée Marcel-Cerdan 91300   01.69.20.94.21

Meaux

Synagogues
11 rue P. Barennes 77100   01.64.34.76.58

Meudon-La-Foret

Mikvaot
Rue de la Synagogue 92360
01.46.32.64.82; 01.46.01.01.32

Synagogues

Orthodox

Maison Communautaire
rue de la Synagogue 92360   01.48.53.48.27

Montreuil

Bakeries
Nat Cacher
21 rue Gabriel Péri 93100   01.48.58.05.25
Supervision: Beth Din of Paris.
Korcarz, 134 bis rue de Stalingrad 93100
01.48.58.33.45
Supervision: Beth Din of Paris/Chief Rabbi Mordechai
Rottenberg.
Le Relais Sucre
62 rue des Roches 93100   01.48.70.22.60
Supervision: Beth Din of Paris.

Butchers
Boucherie Andre
64 rue des Roches 93100   01.48.57.57.17
Andre Volailles
62 rue des Roches 93100   01.48.57.57.17

Montrouge

Butchers
Boucherie Vivo
2 rue Camille Pelletan 92120   01.47.35.23.06

Mikvaot
Ismah-Israel
90 rue Gabriel-Péri 92120   01.42.53.08.54

Synagogues

Orthodox

Centre Communautaire Regional Malakoff-Montrouge
90 rue Gabriel-Péri 92120   01.46.32.64.82
Fax: 01.46.56.20.49

Neuilly

Butchers
Neuilly Cacher
2/6 rue de Chartres 92200   01.47.45.06.06

Groceries
King David
14 rue Paul- Chatrousse 92200   01.47.45.18.19

Synagogues

Orthodox

12 rue Ancelle 92200   01.47.47.78.76
Fax: 01.47.47.54.79

Neuilly sur Seine

Restaurants

Meat

King David
14 rue Paul-Chatrousse 92200   01.47.45.18.19
Supervision: Beth Din of Paris.
Deliver. Hours: 8 am to 10 pm.

Noisy-Le Sec

Synagogues

Orthodox

Beth Gabriel
2 rue de la Pierre Feuillère 93130   01.48.46.71.79

Pantin

Bakeries
Crousty Cash
27 avenue Anatole France 93100   01.48.40.89.74
Supervision: Beth Din of Paris.

Butchers
Levy Baroukh
5/7 rue Anatole France 93500   01.48.91.02.14

Restaurants
Chez Jacquy
24 rue du Pré-Saint-Gervais 93500   01.48.10.94.24
Supervision: Beth Din of Paris.

Pavillons

Butchers
Societe Brami
36 av Victor Hugo 93320   01.48.47.15.76

Ris-Orangis

Synagogues

Orthodox

1 rue Jean-Moulin 91130   01.69.43.07.83

Roissy-En-Brie

Mikvaot
Rue Paul-Cézanne, C.Cial Bois Montmartre 77680
01.60.28.34.65; 01.60.29.09.44

France / Paris Suburbs

Synagogues

Orthodox

Maison Communautaire
1 rue Paul-Cézanne, Centre Commercial Bois
Montmartre 77680   01.60.28.36.38

Rosny-Sous-Bois

Synagogues
62-64 rue Lavoisier 93110   01.48.54.04.11
Fax: 01.69.43.07.83

Rueil-Malmaison

Synagogues
6 rue René-Cassin 92500   01.47.08.32.62

Saint-Denis

Synagogues
51 boulevard Marcel-Sembat, (à côté de la
Gendarmerie) 93200   01.48.20.30.87

Saint-Leu-La-Foret

Mikvaot
2 rue Jules Vernes 95320
01.39.95.96.90; 01.34.14.24.15

Saint-Ouen-L'Aumône

Synagogues

Orthodox

Maison Communautaire
9 rue de Chennevières 95310   01.30.37.71.41

Sarcelles

Bakeries
Zazou
C.C. les Flanades 95200   01.34.19.08.11
Supervision: Beth Din of Paris.
Oh Delices
71 avenue Paul Valéry 95200   01.39.92.41.12
Supervision: Beth Din of Paris.
Louis D'or
90 avenue Paul Valéry 95200   01.39.90.25.45
Supervision: Beth Din of Paris.
Natania
34 blvd Albert Camus 95200
01.39.90.11.78
Supervision: Beth Din of Paris.

Butchers
Boucherie Du Coin
60 bd Albert Camus 95200   01.39.90.53.02
Hazout
5 Av Paul Valery 95200   01.39.90.72.95

Mikvaot
Mayanot Rachel
14 avenue Ch.-Péguy 95200   01.39.90.40.17

Restaurants
Berbeche Burger
13 avenue Edouard-Branly 95200   01.34.19.12.02
Supervision: Beth Din of Paris.

Dairy
Marina, 103 avenue Paul-Valéry 95200
01.34.19.23.51
Supervision: Beth Din of Paris.

Synagogues

Orthodox

Maison Communautaire
74 avenue Paul-Valéry 95200   01.39.90.59.59
Mikva on premises.

Sartrouville

Synagogues
Synagogue Rabbi Shimon bar Yohai et Rabbi Meir Baal
Hannes
1 rue de Stalingrad 78500   01.39.15.22.57

Savigny-Sur-Orge

Mikvaot
1 avenue de L'Armée-Leclerc 91600
01.69.24.48.25; 01.69.96.30.90

Sevran

Mikvaot
25 bis du Dr Roux 93270   01.43.84.25.40
Mikva Kelim.

Synagogues

Orthodox
Synagogue Mayan-Thora
25 bis rue du Dr. Roux, BP. 111 93270
01.43.84.25.40

St-Brice-Sous Foret

Synagogues
Centre Communautaire Ohel Avraham
10 rue Pasteur 95350   01.39.94.96.10

Stains

Synagogues

8 rue Lamartine (face n°2), Clos St-Lazare 93240
01.48.21.04.12
Provisional address: 8 avenue Louis Bordes (Ancien
Conservatoire Municipal).

Thiais

Community Organisations
Community Centre Choisy-Orly-Thiais
Voie du Four, 128 avenue du Marechal de Lattre de
Tassigny 94320   01.48.92.68.68
Fax: 01.48.92.72.82

Trappes

Synagogues

Orthodox

7 rue du Port-Royal 78190   01.30.62.40.43

Villiers-Sur-Marne

Synagogues
30 rue Léon-Douer, B.P. 15 94350   01.49.30.01.47
Fax: 01.49.30.85.40

Versailles

Synagogues
10 rue Albert-Joly 78000   02.39.07.19.19
Fax: 02.39.50.96.34
Mikva on premises.

Villejuif

Bakeries
Eden Eclair
30 rue Marcel Gromesnil 94800   01.47.26.42.96
Supervision: Beth Din of Paris.

Villeneuve-La-Garenne

Mikvaot
42-44 rue du Fond-de-la Noue 92390
01.47.94.89.98

Synagogues

Orthodox

Maison Communautaire
44 rue du Fond-de-la-Noue 92390   01.47.94.89.98

Villiers-Le Bel

Mikvaot
1 rue Léon Blum 95400
01.39.94.45.51; 01.34.19.64.48

Synagogues

Orthodox

1 rue Léon-Blum 95400
01.39.94.30.49; 01.39.94.94.89

Vincennes

Butchers
Boucherie Hayache
146 Av de Paris 94300   01.43.28.16.04
Boucherie Des Levy
32 rue Raymond du Temple 94300   01.43.74.94.18

Synagogues

Orthodox

Synagogue Sepharade
30 rue Céline-Robert 94300   01.47.55.65.07
Synagogue Achkenaze
30 rue Céline-Robert 94300   01.43.28.82.83

Vitry

Synagogues
133-135 avenue Rouget-de-l'Isle 94400
01.46.80.76.54; 01.45.73.06.58
Fax: 01.45.73.94.01

Yerres

Mikvaot
Beth Rivkah
43/49 rue R. Poincare 91330
01.69.49.62.74; 01.69.49.62.62
Fax: 01.69.79.27.70
Email: beth-rivkah@wanados.fr

Pau

Synagogues
8 rue des Trois-Freres-Bernadac 64000
05.59.62.37.85

Perigueuex

Synagogues
13 rue Paul-Louis-Courrier 24000   05.53.53.22.52

Perpignan

Butchers
Gilbert Sabbah
3 rue P.-Rameil 66000   04.68.35.41.23
Fax: 04.68.51.09.83

France

Cemeteries
Rivesaltes
66000
Near the camp from which thousands of Jews were deported to Auschwitz.
Haut Vernet
66000

Synagogues
54 rue Arago 66000

Phalsbourg

Synagogues
16 rue Alexandre-Weill 57370

Poitiers

Synagogues
1 rue Guynemer 86000

Reims

Memorials
War Memorial, Blvd. General Leclerc
With an urn containing ashes from a number of Nazi death camps.

Synagogues
49 rue Clovis 51100   03.26.47.68.47

Rennes

Community Organisations
32 rue de la Marbaudais 35000   02.99.63.57.18
Services held. Telephone for times.

Roanne

Synagogues
9 rue Beaulieu 42300   04.77.71.51.56

Rouen

Synagogues
55 rue des Bons-Enfants 76100   02.35.71.01.44
The Jewish Youth Club can provide board residence for student travellers and holiday-makers.

Saint-Avold

Cemeteries
The American Military Cemetary
Containing the graves of many Jewish soldiers who fell in the Second World War.

Synagogues
Pl. du Marche 57500   03.87.91.16.16

Saint-Die

Synagogues
Rue de l'Eveche 88100
Services, festivals and Holy-days only.

Saint-Etienne

Synagogues
34 rue d'Arcole 42000   04.77.33.56.31

Saint-Fons

Synagogues
17 Av. Albert-Thomas 69190   04.78.67.39.78

Saint-Germain

Synagogues

Liberal

Kehilat Gesher (Franco-American)
10 rue de Pologne 78100   01.39.21.97.19
Email: rabbenutom@compuserve.com

Saint-Laurent-du-Var

Synagogues
Villa 'Le Petit Clos', 35 Av. des Oliviers 06700

Saint-Louis

Cemeteries
The Hegenheim Cemetary

This cemetary dates from 1673.

Community Organisations
19 rue du Temple 68300   03.89.70.00.48
Kosher products available.

Synagogues
Rue de la Synagogue 68300
3 rue de General Cassagnou 68300

Saint-Quentin

Synagogues
11 ter Blvd. Henri-Martin   03.23.08.30.72

Sarrebourg

Synagogues
12 rue du Sauvage

Sarreguemines

Synagogues
Rue Georges-V 57200   03.87.98.81.40
Mikva on premises.

Saverne

Synagogues
Rue du 19 Novembre 67700

Sedan-Charleville

Synagogues
6 Av. de Verdun 08200

Selestat

Synagogues
4 rue Ste.-Barbe 67600

Sens

Synagogues
14 rue de la Grande-Juiverie 89100   03.86.95.16.65

Strasbourg

With a Jewish population of 16,000, this city, contested by France and Germany throughout history, currently has an important Jewish community, with several kosher restuarants, butchers and even a kosher vineyard.

Bakeries
Crousty Cash
4 rue Sellénick 67000   03.88.35.68.21

Booksellers
Librairie du Cedrat
15 rue de Bitche 67000   03.88.37.32.37
                                Fax: 03.88.35.63.11
                        Email: nfraenckel@aol.com
Also Judaica Antiquities
Librairie Du Cedrat
19 rue du Marechal-Foch 67000   03.88.36.38.39
                                Fax: 03.88.37.96.60

Butchers
Buchinger
63 rue du Faubourg de Pierre 67000 03.88.32.85.03
Buchinger
13 rue Wimpheling 67000   03.88.61.06.98
David, 20 rue Sellenick 67000   03.88.36.75.01

Groceries
Yarden, 3 rue Finkmatt 67000   03.88.22.49.76
Yarden, 13 Blvd. de la Marne 67000
        03.88.60.10.10/Office 03.88.60.51.96
                                Fax: 03.88.61.71.11

Media
Newspapers
Echos-Unir
1a rue du Grand-Rabbin-Rene-Hirschler 67000
03.88.14.46.50
                                Fax: 03.88.24.26.69
Monthly publication.
Mikvaot
7, rue Turenne
1a rue du Grand-Rabbin-Rene-Hirschler 67000
                                03.88.14.46.68

Museums
Musee Alsacien
23, quai Alsacien   03.88.35.55.36
Has a section on Jewish Art
Musee Judeo-Alsacien
62a, Grand'Rue, Bouxwiller 67330   03.88.70.97.17
Religious Organisations
Regional Chief Rabbi
5 rue du General-de-Castelnau 67000
                                03.88.32.38.97
                                Fax: 03.88.25.05.65
Consistoire Israelite du Bas-Rhin
23 rue Sellenick 67000   03.88.25.05.75
                                Fax: 03.88.25.12.75
                        Email: cibr1@libertysurf.fr

Restaurants
Autre Part
60. Bld Clemenceau   03.88.37.10.02
Dizengoff Café
68, bld. Clemenceau   03.88.36.74.88
Le King
28 rue Sellenick 67000   03.88.52.17.71
Restaurant Universitaire
ORT-Laure Weil, 11 rue Sellenick 67000
                                03.88.76.74.76
                                Fax: 03.88.76.74.74
                Email: ort.strasbourg@ort.asso.fr
Meat
Massada, 7, rue Baldung Grien   03.88.35.43.43
Synagogues
There are in all more than 15 synagogues in Strasbourg; the following are among the largest and oldest.

Esplanade
17, rue de Nicosie 67000
Synagogue de la Paix
1a rue du Grand-Rabbin-Rene-Hirschler 67000
                                03.88.14.46.50
                                Fax: 03.88.24.26.69
                        Email: cis@media-net.fr

Ets Hayim
7, rue Turenne 67000

France

Ashkenazi
Adath Israel
7 rue Sellenick 67000

Vineyards
Kosher
Goxwiller, R. Koenig, 35 rue Principale 67000
03.88.95.51.93

Tarbes

Synagogues
Cite Rothschild
6 rue du Pradeau 65000

Thionville

Synagogues
31 Av. Clemenceau 57100   03.82.54.47.89
Fax: 03.82.53.03.76

Toul

Synagogues
Rue de la Halle 54200

Toulon

Butchers
Fenech, 15 avenue Colbert 83000   04.94.92.70.39
Supervision: Grand Rabbinate of Marseille.
Abecassis
8 rue Vincent Courdouan 83000   04.94.97.39.86
Supervision: Grand Rabbinate of Marseille.

Synagogues
Av. Lazare Carnot 83050   04.94.92.61.05
Mikva on premises.

Toulouse

Butchers
Maalem
7 rue des Chalets 31000   05.61.63.77.39
Lasry
8 rue Matabiau 31000   05.61.62.65.28
Ghenassia
9 bd Larrament 31000   05.61.42.05.81
Cacherout Diffusion
37 Blvd. Carnot 31000   05.61.23.07.59

Community Organisations
Community Centre
2 Place Riquet 31000   05.61.23.36.54

Groceries
Novogel
14 rue Edmund Guyaux 31200
05.61.57.03.19

Mikvaot
15 rue Francisque Sarcey 31000   05.61.48.89.84

Religious Organisations
Grand Rabbinat du Toulouse et des Pays de la Garonne - A.C.I.T.
2 Place Riquet 31000   05.62.73.46.46
Fax: 05.62.73.46.47

Religious Orgnisations
Regional Chief Rabbi
17 rue Calvert 31500   05.61.21.51.14

Restaurants
Le Kotel
9 rue Clemence Isaure 31000   05.61.29.03.04
Community Centre
2 Place Riquet 31000   05.62.73.56.56

Synagogues
Chaare Emeth
35 rue Rembrandt 31000   05.61.40.03.88

Ashkenazi
Adat Yechouroun
3 rue Jules-Chalande 31000   05.61.62.60.41

Sephardi
Palaprat
2 rue Palaprat 31000   05.61.21.69.56

Tours

Community Organisations
Community Centre
6 rue Chalmel 37000   02.47.05.59.07

Synagogues
37 rue Parmentier 37000   02.47.05.56.95

Troyes

Memorials
A statue of Rashi was unveiled at the Troyes cemetery in 1990.

Mikvaot
1 rue Brunneval   03.25.73.34.44

Synagogues
5 rue Brunneval

Valence

Synagogues
1 Place du Colombier 26000   04.75.43.34.43

Valenciennes

Synagogues
36 rue de l'Intendance 59300   03.27.29.11.07

France / Other Departments

Venissieux

Synagogues
12 Av. de la Division-Leclerc 69200   04.78.70.69.85

Verdun

Synagogues
Impasse des Jacobins 55100

Vichy

Synagogues
2 bis rue du Marechal Foch 03200

Vittel

Synagogues
Rue Croix-Pierrot 88800   03.29.08.10.87
Open in July and August only.

Wasselonne

Synagogues
Rue des Bains 67310

Other Departments

Corsica

Contact Information
Jo Michel Reis
La Grande Corniche, Routes des Sanguinaires, Ajaccio
9521-5752
There are between ten and fifteen families in the town.

Synagogues
3 rue du Castagno Bastia 20200
Services Shabbat morning and festivals.

Guadeloupe

Synagogues
Bas du Fort, Gosier, Lot 1   (590) 90.99.09
The synagogue, community centre and
restaurant/kosher store are all located here.

La Réunion

Contact Information
Leon Benhamou
(262) 29.05.45

Hotels

Kosher

Hotel Astoria
16 rue Juliette Dodu
St. Denis 97400   (262) 20.05.58
Fax: (262) 41.26.30

Synagogues
Communauté Juive de la Réunion
8 rue de l'Est, St Denis 97400   (262) 23.78.33
High Holy Day services and communal seder held here.

Martinique

Synagogues
Kenafe Haarets
12 Anse Gouraud
Fort-de-France 97233   (596) 61.71.36
A community centre is also located here which supplies
kosher food.

Georgia

Georgia

Georgia has had a very long history of Jewish settlement, dating back to two centuries before the destruction of the Second Temple, if the archaeological findings are correct. These earliest Jewish communities may have descended from the Babylonian exiles.

Many Jewish organisations operate in the country, some of which are academic, such as the 'Georgian Jewish Society for Natural Science and Technology'. The Georgian Jews are also well informed about their religion, which is not usual in a former Soviet republic.

Synagogues are found in major towns, there is a school in Tbilisi (the capital) and there are some newsletters. It is worth noting that the non-Jewish population has traditionally been far less anti-Semitic than the populations of some other ex-Soviet republics.

GMT + 4 hours	Total Population 5,361,000
Country calling code (995)	Jewish Population 17,000
Emergency Telephone (Police - 02) (Fire - 01) (Ambulance - 03)	Electricity voltage 220

Akhaltsikhe

Synagogues
109 Guramishvili Street

Batumi

Synagogues
6 9th March Street

Gori

Synagogues
Chelyuskin Street

Kutaisi

Synagogues
12 Gapanove Street
Near the main Square .

Onni

Synagogues
Baazova Street

Poti

Synagogues
23 Ninoshivili
Tskhakaya Street

Sukhumi

Synagogues
56 Karl Marx Street

Surami

Synagogues
Internatsionalaya Street

Tbilisi

Organisations
Jews of Georgia Assoc.
Tsarity Tamari Street 8 380012   (32) 234-1057

Synagogues
45-47 Leselidze Street

Ashkenazi
65 Kozhevenny Lane

Sephardi
Leselidze Street

Tshkinvali

Synagogues
Isapov Street

Tskhakaya

Synagogues
Mir Street

Vani

Synagogues
4 Kaikavadze Street

It may be a surprise to many that Germany comes immediately after France and the UK in the population table of Western European Jews. German Jews have contributed much to the culture of European Jews in general since their arrival in what is now Germany in the fourth century. The massive Jewish presence in Poland and other east European states stemmed from German Jews escaping persecution in the late Middle Ages. They took the early Medieval German language with them, which formed Yiddish, the old lingua franca of European Jews.

The Jews who stayed behind in Germany contributed much towards Jewish and German culture, with the Reform movement starting in nineteenth-century Germany, and Heine and Mendelssohn contributing to German poetry and music respectively. The Enlightenment and modern orthodoxy also began in Germany.

The rise of Nazism destroyed the belief that the German Jews were more German than Jewish. Many managed to escape before 1939, but 180,000 were killed in the Holocaust (of the 503,000 who lived in Germany when Hitler came to power). Following the events of 1933–45, it seems incredible that any Jew should want to live in Germany again. However, the community began to re-form, mainly immigrants from eastern Europe, especially Russia. Now there are again Jewish shops in Berlin, and kosher food is once more available. There are many old synagogues which have been restored, and several concentration camps have been kept as monuments to history. There is also a great interest in Jewish matters among some of the non-Jewish young generation.

GMT + 1 hour	Total Population 81,891,000
Country calling code (49)	Jewish Population 75,000
Emergency Telephone (Police - 110) (Fire and Ambulance - 112	Electricity voltage 220

Aachen

Representative Organisations
Bundesverband Jüdischer Studenten in Deutschland
Oppenhoffallee 50 (241) 75998

Alsenz

Sites
Synagogue, Kirchberg 1 (636) 23149
Fax: (636) 23149
Restored 18th century synagogue.

Amberg

Community Organisations
Community Centre
Salzgasse 5 (962) 113140

Andernach

Mikvaot
Rhine Valley
This Rhine Valley town contains an early 14th century mikva. Key obtainable from tourist office.

Annweiler

Tourist Sites
(623) 53333
The oldest cemetery in the Palatinate dating from 16th century.

Augsburg

Community Organisations
Community Centre
Halderstr. 8 (821) 517985
There is a Jewish museum in the restored Liberal synagogue.

Bad Kissingen

Hotels
Eden Park
Rosenstrasse 5-7 97688 (971) 717-200
Fax: (971) 717-272
There is a restaurant on the premises that serves kosher food and traditional meals.

Germany

Bad Kreuznach

Community Organisations
Community Centre
Gymnasialstr. 11   (671) 26991

Bad Nauheim

Hotels
Accadia
Lindenstr. 15/Frankfurterstr. 22   (6032) 39068

Restaurants
Judische Gemeinde
Karlstr. 34   (6032) 5605 or 0171-9509084
                     Fax: (6032) 5605
In the Jewish Community Centre. Entry for restaurant
from Friedenstr.

Synagogues
Judische Gemeinde
Karlstr. 34   (6032) 5605; 0171-9509084
                     Fax: (6032) 5605
Synagogue is in the Jewish Community Centre.

Baden-Baden

Synagogues
Werderstr. 2 76530   (722) 139-1021
                Fax: (722) 139-1024

Bamberg

Community Organisations
Community Centre
Willy-Lessing-Str. 7   (951) 23267

Bayreuth

Community Organisations
Community Centre
Munzgasse 2   (921) 65407

Berlin

Jewish life is beginning to grow again in Berlin,
formerly an important centre for German Jewry.
There are many sites which testify to the tragedy
that befell the community before and during the
war, such as the ruined Oranienburgerstrasse
Synagogue, which has been turned into a Jewish
centre. The site of the Wannsee Conference, to the
south-west of the city (where the Holocaust was
officially planned), has been turned into a
museum.

Bed & Breakfasts
Guestrooms
Tucholskystrasse 40Mitte 10117   (30) 281-3135
                  Fax: (30) 281-3122
           Web site: www.adassjisroel.de
Synagogue and Kosher restaurant in the house.

Booksellers
Literaturhandlung
Joachimstaler-Str. 13 10719   (30) 882-4250
                  Fax: (30) 885-4713

Literaturhandlung
Fürstenstr. 17, München, Munich 80333
                (30) 89-2800135
             Fax: (30) 89-281601
   Email: literaturhandlung@t-online.de

Butcher
Kosher Butcher
Goethestr. 61 10625
The butcher sells wine, sweets and other things.
Opening hours: 10 am to 5 pm (Friday untill 2 pm
only)

Cemeteries
Adass Jisroel
Wittlicherstrasse 2
Weissensee 13088   (30) 925-1724
Established in in 1880, this historic cemetery is used to
this very day. Rabbi Esriel Hildesheimer, Rabbi Prof.
David Zvi Hoffmann, Rabbi Eliahu Kaplan and many
other wise and pious Jews are buried here.

Community Centre
Ignatz Bubis-Gemeindezentrum
Tucholskystrasse 40Mitte 10117   (30) 281-3135
                  Fax: (30) 281-3122
        Email: jg.ffm@t-online.de
Supervision: Rabbinate of Adass Jisroel.
Open daily, except Shabbat, from 11 am to 10 pm.
Closes Friday two hours before Shabbat.

Community Organisations
Community Centre
Fasanenstr. 79-80, off the Kurfurstendamm
                (30) 88028-250
             Fax: (30) 88028-250
This has been built on the site of a famous synagogue,
destroyed by the Nazis

Germany

Judischer Kulturverein (Jewish Cultural Center)
Oranienburgerstr. 26, Berlin-Mitte 10117
(30) 282-6669; 285-98052
Fax: (30) 285-98053
Email: jkv.berlin@t-online.de
Hours: Monday-Thursday 11am to 5pm, Friday 11am
to 2pm and 1 hour before evening and Sunday events.
Friday for Kiddush 6-9 pm. (Summer 7 pm) (entrance
around the corner)

Embassy
Embassy of Israel
Auguste-Viktoria Strasse 74-78 14193
(30) 89045-500
Fax: (30) 89045-222
Email: botschaft@israel.de
Web site: www.israel.de

Groceries
Kachol Laven
Passauer Str.4 10789 (30) 217-7506
Kolbo
Auguststrasse 77-78Mitte 10117 (30) 281-3135
In addition to kosher food and wines, sifrei kodesh as
well as general literature about Jewish subjects can be
obtained here.

Grocery
Schalom Koschere Lebensmittel (Kosher shop)
Wielandstr. 43 10625
Opening hours: 10 am to 5 pm (Friday until 3 pm
only in the winter).

Kashrut Information
Judische Gemeinde zu Berlin
Joachimstaler Str 13 10719 (30) 88020-0
Fax: (30) 88028-150
Rabbinate of Adass Jisroel
Tucholskystrasse 40Mitte 10117 (30) 281-3135
Fax: (30) 281-3122

Libraries
Jewish Community
Fassenstrasse 79 10623
Jewish Library
Oranienburger Str. 28 10117 (30) 880-28-427/429

Media
Magazine
Judisches Berlin
Fasanen Str. 79 10623 (30) 88028-260;88028-269
Fax: (30) 88028-266
Email: jued.berlin@jg-berlin.org
Monthly

Magazines
Judische Korrespondenz
Oranienburgerstr. 26, Berlin-Mitte 10117
(30) 282-6669; 285-98052
Fax: (30) 285-98053
Email: jkv.berlin@t-online.de
Monthly.

Newspapers
Allgemeine Judische Wochenzeitung
Postfach 04 03 69, Tucholskystrasse 9 10117
(30) 2844 5650
Fax: (30) 2844 5699
Email: ajw@Juedische-Presse.de
Fortnightly.
Hadshot Adass Jisroel
Tucholsky str. 40 10117 (30) 281-3135
Published by Adass Jisroel and obtainable through their
offices (see above for number).

Museum
Jewish Museum
Lindenstrasse 9-14 10969 (30) 2599 3456
Fax: (30) 2599 3400
Email: n.bodermann@jmberlin.de
Web site: www.jmberlin.de
The building is now open and well worth visiting. The
official opening is however not until 9 September 2001.

Religious Organisations
Zentralrat der Juden in Deutschland
Tucholskystr. 9, Berlin 10117 (30) 284-4560
Fax: (30) 284-45613
Email: zentralratdjuden@aol.com

Restaurants
Café Oren
Oranienburger Str. 28 10117 (30) 282-8228;
Fax: (30) 285-99313
Rimon
Oranienburgerstr. 26, Berlin-Mitte 10117 (30) 283-8403-2
Hours: Daily 10 am to 12 pm

Meat
Restaurant Arche Noah
Fasanenstr. 79-80 10623 (30) 88-26138
Shabbat reservations and payment have to be arranged
before beginning of Shabbat. The restaurant is located
in the first floor of the community building. Opening
hours: Daily 12 noon to 3.30 pm and 6.30 pm to
10.30pm.

Synagogues
Liberal
Pestalozzistr. 14, 1000 10625 (30) 313-8411

Germany

Orthodox

Adass Jisroel
Joachimtaler Strasse 13Mitte 16719
Daily minyan
Adass Jisroel
Tucholskystrasse 40Mitte 10117   (30) 281-3135
                              Fax: (30) 281-3122
                   Web site: www.adassjisroel.de
Established 1869. Rabbinate, Kashrut supervision and
mohel can all be reached at this number. Near its
community centre, there is a guest house, a kosher
restaurant and a shop which sells kosher products.

Tourist Information
Staatliches Israelisches Verkehrsbureau
Stollbergstrasse 6 15   (30) 883-6759
                              Fax: (30) 882-4093

Bochum

Synagogues
Alte Wittener Str. 18 44803   (234) 361563
                              Fax: (234) 360187

Bonn/Bad Godesberg

Synagogues
Templestr. 2-4, cnr. Adenauer Allee 53113
                                      (228) 213560
                              Fax: (228) 2618366

Braunschweig

Community Organisations
Community Centre
Steinstr. 4   (531) 45536

Museums
Braunschweigisches Landesmuseum
Abt. Judisches Museum, Burgplatz 1 D-38100
                                      (531) 1215-0
                              Fax: (531) 1215-2607
                   Email: derda@landesmuseum-bs.de
                   Web site: www.landesmuseum-bs.de
Founded in 1746, this museum was formerly the oldest
Jewish museum in the world. It was re-opened in 1987
under the auspices of the Braunschweigisches
Landesmuseum. Hours Tues.-Sun: 10am to 5pm;
Thurs. 10am to 8pm.

Bremen

Synagogues
Schwachauser Heerstr. 117   (421) 498-5104
                              Fax: (421) 498-4944

Celle

Synagogues
Im Kreise 24 29221
Formerly a beautiful synagogue it now houses travelling
exhibits on various themes of Jewish history and of
Jewish life in Celle where a community started between
1671 and 1691. There are now enough Jews in the
town to form a minyan.

Chemnitz
Community Organisations
Community Centre
Stollberger Str. 28   (371) 32862

Coblenz
Community Organisations
Community Centre
Schlachthof Str. 5   (261) 42223

Cologne
Hotels
Leonet, Rubensstr. 33   (221) 236016

Restaurants

Meat
Community Centre
Roonstr 50, 50674   (221) 240-4440
                              Fax: (221) 240-4440
Phone in advance. Glatt kosher.

Synagogues
Roonstr. 50,, Köln 50674   (221) 921-5600
                              Fax: (221) 921-5609
                   Email: synagoge-koeln@netcologne.de
                              Web site: www.sgk.de
Daily services. There are a youth centre, Jewish
museum and library at the same address.

Darmstadt
Community Organisations
Community Centre
Wilhelm-Glassing-Str. 26   (6151) 128897

Dortmund

Representative Organisations
Landesverband der Judischen Gemeinden von
Westfalen
Prinz-Friedrich-Karl-Str. 12 44135   (231) 528495
Fax: (231) 5860372
Email: lvjuedwest@aol.com

Synagogues
Prinz-Friedrich-Karl-Str. 9 44135   (231) 528497

Dresden

Representative Organisations
Landesverband Sachsen der Judischen Gemeinden
Bautzner Str 20 01099   (351) 804-5491;802-2739
Fax: (351) 804-1445
A memorial to the six million Jews killed in the
holocaust stands on the site of the Dresden Synagogue,
burnt down by the Nazis in November 1938.

Synagogues
Fiedlerstr. 3   (351) 693317

Dusseldorf

Hotels
Gildors Hotel
Collenbachstr. 51   (211) 488005
Israeli owned.

Synagogues
Zietenstr. 50   (211) 469120
Fax: (211) 485156

Emmendingen

Synagogues
Lenzhausle am Schlossplatz   (764) 157-1989

Erfurt

Community Organisations
Community Centre
Juri-Gagarin-Ring 16   (361) 24964

Essen

Community Organisations
Community Centre
Sedanstr. 46   (201) 273413
Fax: (201) 287112

Essingen

Cemeteries
Largest cemetary in the Palatinate, where Anne Frank's
ancestors are buried, 16th Century. Key at the Mayor's
Office.

Frankfurt-Am-Main

Butchers
Aviv Butchery & Deli
Hanauer Landstr. 50   (69) 433013
Fax: (69) 446084

Community Organisations
Community Centre
Westendstr. 43   (69) 74 07 21
Fax: (69) 746874
Email: jg.ffm@t-online.de
This community produces a magazine, "Judische
Gemeinde-Zeitung Frankfurt".

Hotels
Luxor Hotel, Am Allerheiligentor 2-4
(69) 293067 / 69
Fax: (69) 287766
This hotel, which is under Jewish management, is within
walking distance of the Freiherr-vom-Stein-Str.
synagogue.

Mikvaot
Judische Gemeinde
Westendstr 43 D-60325   (69) 740721
Fax: (69) 746874

Museums
Jewish Museum
Untermainkai 14-15, 60311   (69) 212-35000
Fax: (69) 212-30705
Email: info@juedischesmuseum.de
Web site: www.juedischesmuseum.de
Sunday, Tuesday to Saturday 10.00 am-5.00 pm.
Wednesday 10.00am-8.00pm. Closed Monday.

Representative Organisations
Zentralwohlfahrtsstelle der Juden in Deutschland
Hebelstrasse 6 60318   (69) 94 43 71-15
Fax: (69) 49 48 17

Restaurants
Sohar's, Savignystrasse 66 60325   (69) 75 23 41
Fax: (69) 741 0116
Supervision: Rabbi Menachem Halevi Klein, Frankfurt
Rabbinate.
Hours: Tuesday to Thursday and Sunday, 12 pm to 8
pm; Friday, 12 pm to Shabbat; Shabbat, 1:30 pm to 4
pm; Monday, closed. Special arrangements can be
made by phone. Friday and Shabbat meals must be
ordered in advance. Provide party service, airline
catering and delivery to hotels. Fifteen minute walk
from synagogue, fair centre and main train station.

Germany

Synagogues
Baumweg 5-7   (69) 439381
Beth Hamidrash West End
Altkanigstr. 27   (69) 723805
Westend Synagogue
Freiherr-vom-Stein-Str. 30   (69) 726263
This is the city's main synagogue.

Tourist Information
Tourismus-und Congress GmbH
Kaiserstrabe 56   (69) 2123-8800
Fax: (69) 2123-7880 - Reservat

Freiburg

Community Organisations
Community Centre
Engels Strasse   (761) 383096
Fax: (761) 382332
Services: Erev Shabbat in Summer 1930h in Winter 1830h. Shabbat morning 9.30am. Kosher Kiddush after services.

Friedberg/Hessen

Tourist Sites
Judengasse 20
The ancient mikva, built in 1260 is located here. The town council has issued a special explanatory leaflet about it, and it is now scheduled as a historical monument of medieval architecture.

Fulda

Community Organisations
Community Centre
von Schildeckstr. 13   (66) 170252
Fax: (66) 147465
Services every Friday 6.30pm, every Shabat 9.00am

Furth

Community Organisations
Community Centre
Blumenstr. 31   (91) 177-0879

Tourist Sites
Julienstr. 2
There is a beautifully restored synagogue as well as a historic mikva.

Gelsenkirchen

Community Organisations
Community Centre
Von-der-Recke-Str. 9   (20) 923143 & 206628

Hagen

Community Organisations
Community Centre
Potthofstr. 16   (2331) 711-3289

Halle/Saale

Community Organisations
Community Centre
Grosse Markerstr. 13   (345) 26963

Hamburg

Community Organisations
Community Centre
Schaferkampsallee 27 20357   (40) 440-9440
Fax: (40) 410-8430

Synagogues
Hohe Weide 34 20253   (40) 440-9440
Mikvah on premises.

Hanover

Community Organisations
Community Centre
Haecklstr. 10 810472

Synagogues
Haecklstr. 10 810472

Heidelberg

Restaurants
College Restaurant
Theaterstr.9   (6221) 168-767
Kosher meals available (by arrangement & in advance - it is not open all year round) Mon.-Fri at college restaurant, 100 yards from College of Jewish Studies situated at Friederichstrasse 9.

Herford

Community Organisations
Community Centre
Keplerweg 11   (52) 212039

Hildesheim

Synagogues
Jewish Community in Hildesheim
Postfach 10 07 07
Hildesheim, Lower Saxony D31135   (512) 1704962
Fax: (512) 1704964
Rabbi Dr. Walter Homolka is responsible for all Lower Saxony.

Germany

Hof/Saale

Community Organisations
Community Centre
An Wiesengrund 20　　　　　　(92) 815-3249

Ichenhausen

Museums
Museum of Jewish History
Located in the fine baroque synagogue, not far from Ulm.

Ingenheim

Tourist Sites
Klingenerstr. 20
16th century cemetery can be visited. Key obtained from Klingenerstr. 20

Kaiserslautern

Community Organisations
Community Centre
Basteigasse 4　　　　　　　　(63) 169720

Karlsruhe

Community Organisations
Community Centre
Knielinger Allee 11　　　　　　(72) 172035

Kassel

Community Organisations
Community Centre
Bremer Str. 9　　　　　　　　(56) 112960

Konstanz

Community Organisations
Community Centre
Sigismundstr. 19　　　　　　　(75) 312-3077

Krefeld

Community Organisations
Community Centre
Wiedstr. 17b　　　　　　　　(21) 512-0648

Landau

Synagogues
Frank-Loebsches Haus, Kaufhausgasse 9 D-76829
　　　　　　　　　　　　　(6341) 86472
　　　　　　　　　Fax: (6341) 13294
　　　　Email: sabine.haas.landau.de

Leipzig

Community Organisations
Community Centre
Lahrstr. 10　　　　　　　　　(341) 291028

Lubeck

Synagogues
Synagogue & Community Centre
St Annen Str. 11 23552　　　　(451) 798-2182
　　　　　Fax: (451) 0451-798-2182
Supervised through the Hamburg community.

Magdeburg

Community Organisations
Community Centre
Graperstr. 1a　　　　　　　　(391) 52665

Mainz

Community Organisations
Community Centre
Forsterstr. 2 55118　　　　　　(6131) 613990
　　　　　　　Fax: (6131) 611767

Tourist Sites
Untere Zahlbacherstr. 11
The key to the 12th century Jewish cemetery can be obtained at the 'new' Jewish cemetery.

Mannheim

Community Organisations
Community Centre
F 3-4　　　　　　　　　　　(621) 153974

Marburg/Lahn

Community Organisations
Community Centre
Unterer Eichweg 17　　　　　(642) 132881

Michelstadt

Tourist Site
Michelstadt
The town has an old synagogue which is now a museum of both Judaism and Jewish history. It is open every day in the summer except Saturday.

Minden

Community Organisations
Community Centre
Kampstr. 6　　　　　　　　　(57) 123437

Germany

Monchengladbach

Synagogues
Community Centre
Albertusstr. 54 41363
(216) 123879
Fax: (216) 114639

Monsey

Community Organisations
Community Centre
Klosterstr. 8-9
(25) 144909

Mulheim/Oberhausen

Community Organisations
Community Centre
Kampstr. 7
(20) 835191

Munich

Community Organisations
Community Centre
Reichenbachstr. 27
(89) 202-4000

Meat/Groceries
Danel Feinkost
Pilgersheimerstrabe 44 81543
(89) 669-888
Fax: (89) 669-820
Email: danel@t-online.de
Danel Feinkost
Viktualien-Markt, Westenriederstrabe 9 80331
(89) 2280-0258

Museums
Judisches Museum Munchen
Maximilian Str. 36

Restaurants
Community Centre
(89) 202 38252
Run by the community centre at Reichenbachstrasse.
Hours: 12pm - 2.30pm; 6pm - 9pm. Shabbat meals
must be ordered by Friday noon. Closed Sunday;
August.

Synagogues
Reichenbachstr. 27
(89) 202-4000
Fax: (89) 201-4604
Mikva on premises.
Possartstr. 15
(89) 474-440
Mikva on premises.
Schwabing Synagogue
Georgenstr. 71
(89) 271-5322
Fri. evenings and Sabbath mornings only.

Liberal
Beth Shalom
(89) 8980-9373
Fax: (89) 8980-9374
Email: obeth.shalom@hagalil.com
Please ask for address and timetable.

Neustadt/Rheinpfalz

Community Organisations
Community Centre
Ludwigstr. 20
(63) 212652

Odenbach

Tourist Sites
(67) 532745
There is a historic synagogue with baroque paintings in
this small village near Bad Kreuznach.

Offenbach

Community Organisations
Community Centre
Kaiserstr. 109 63065
(69) 820036
Fax: (69) 820026

Osnabruck

Community Organisations
Community Centre
In der Barlage, 41 49078
(54) 148420
Fax: (54) 143-4701
Kashrut information or visitors who wish to eat Kosher
on Shabbat; please contact Rabbi Marc Sterm at Tel:
49 541-48553. Address same as the Jewish
Congregation.

Synagogues

Orthodox
Jewish Congregation Synagogue
In der Barlage, 41 49078
(54) 148420
Fax: (54) 143-4701

Tourist Sites
The Feiix-Nussbaum-Haus Museum
Lotter Str 2
About 20 minutes walk from the congregation

Paderborn

Community Organisations
Community Centre
Pipinstr. 32
(52) 512-2596

Potsdam

Community Organisations
Potsdam Community Centre
Heinrich-Mann-Allee 103 Haus 16
(331) 872018

Regensberg

Community Organisations
Community Centre
Am Brixener Hof 2   (94) 157093; 21819

Rulzheim

The key to the early 19th century synagogue in this village near Karlsruhe is obtainable from the town hall.

Saarbrucken

Community Organisations
Community Centre
Lortzing Str. 8 66111   (68) 135152

Synagogues
Synagogengemeinde Saar
Lortzingstr 8 66111   (681) 910-380
                                    Fax: (681) 910-38-13

Schwerin/Mecklenburg

Community Organisations
Judische Gemeinde zu Schwerin
Schlachterstr. 3-5   (38) 555-07345

Speyer

Tourist Sites
                                    (62) 353332
This town contains the oldest (11th c.) mikva in Germany, Judenbadgasse. To visit it, obtain the key from the desk at the Hotel Trutzpfuff, in Webergasse, just around the corner, or contact Prof. Stein at the Historical Museum. There are some early 19th c. village synagogues in the wine-growing region of the Palatinate.

Straubing

Community Organisations
Community Centre
Wittelsbacherstr. 2 94315   (94) 211387

Stuttgart

Religious Organisations
Israelitische Religionsgemeinschaft Wurttembergs
Hospitalstr. 36 70174   (711) 228360
                                    Fax: (711) 2283618

Restaurants

Meat

Schalom Kosher Restaurant
Hospitalstrasse 36 70174   (711) 294752
Supervision: Orthodox Rav of the Stuttgart community. Open during morning hours through to about 7.00pm except Mondays (when its closed). Located on the premises of the Stuttgart Jewish community centre

Sulzburg

There is a beautifully restored early 19th century synagogue here, some 20 miles from Freiburg. Keys are obtainable from the Mayor's office.

Trier

Community Organisations
Community Centre
Kaiserstr. 25   (65) 140530; 33295

Veitschochleim

Located a few miles from Wurzburg is the town of Veitshochheim, which reconsecrated a pre-World War II Synagogue and opened a Jewish Museum in March 1994. Originally built in 1730, the Synagogue was the community centre for local Jews, who had lived in the area for nearly three hundred years, from 1644 to 1942, when the last Jews were deported from Veitshochheim to the Nazi concentration camps.

In 1986 the stone fragments of the original interior, including the Bima and the Ahron Hakodesch, were discovered beneath the floor, where they had been buried in 1940. This find prompted local officials to transform the Synagogue back to its original function and splendour, using photographs from the 1920s as a guide.

Wachenheim

A large 16th century cemetery. Key available from the Town Hall. First records of registration of Jews date from the year 831.

Wiesbaden

Restaurants
Communal Offices
Friedrichstr. 31-33   (611) 933303-0
                                    Fax: (611) 933303-9

Synagogues
Friedrichstr. 33   (6121) 301870; 301282

Germany

Worms

The original Rashi Synagogue, built in the 11th century and the oldest Jewish place of worship in Europe, was destroyed by the Nazis in 1938. After the Second World War, it was reconstructed and was reconsecrated in 1961. The building also contains a 12th century mikva and a Jewish musuem. There is also an ancient Jewish cemetery.

Wuppertal

Community Organisations
Community Centre
Friedrich-Ebert-Str. 73   (202) 300233

Wurzburg

There are old Jewish cemeteries in Wurzburg, Heidingsfeld and Hochberg.

Community Organisations
Community Centre
Valentin-Becker-Str. 11 97072   (93) 151190
                             Fax: (93) 118184
Also guest rooms for tourists. Kosher meals available.

Mikvaot
Community Centre
Valentin-Becker-Str. 11 97072   (93) 151190
                             Fax: (93) 118184
Appointments to be made.

Museums
The Synagogue and Museum of Jewish Culture
Thungershelmer Strabe 17, D- 97209
                         (931) 9802-764
            Fax: (931) 9802-766
    Email: museum@veitschoechheim.de
       Web site: www.veitshoechheim.de
Recently restored.

Synagogues
Community Centre
Valentin-Becker-Str. 11 97072   (93) 151190
                             Fax: (93) 118184

Tourist Sites
There are old Jewish cemeteries in Wurzburg, Heidingsfeld and Hochberg.

Gibraltar

The first Jewish people in Gibraltar were Sephardi, who had crossed over the border from Spain before the Inquisition began in the fourteenth century. Many more followed in the ensuing centuries.

When Britain took possession, Jews were banned, but later they were allowed in as traders and finally, in 1749, they were granted full permission to live there. The community began to flourish and the Jewish population, which now also included many North African Jews, rose to 2,000.

At the end of the Second World War, some of the community returned after being evacuated to Britain. There are now fairly good Jewish facilities, namely four synagogues and newsletters. Gibraltar has had a Jewish prime minister and a Jewish mayor.

GMT + 1 hour

Country calling code (350)

Emergency Telephone (Police, Fire, Ambulance 999)

Total Population 28,000

Jewish Population 600

Electricity voltage 220/240

Bakeries
J. Amar
47 Line Wall Road 73516

Butchers
A. Edery
26 John Mackintosh Sqaure 75168
Fax: 42529

Community Organisations
Managing Board of Jewish Community
10 Bomb House Lane 72606
Fax: 40487

Contact Information
Solomon Levy M.B.E. J.P
3 Convent Place, PO Box 190
77789; 42818, 78047 (home)
Fax: 42527
Email: slevy@gibnet.gi
The president of the Jewish community is happy to provide information for Jewish travellers.

Cultural Organisations
Jewish Social & Cultural Club
7 Bomb House Lane 79636
Email: asuissa@gibnet.gi
Mailing address: Avner Suissa, 20 Lime Tree Lodge, Montagu Gardens, Gibraltar.

Delicatessens
Uncle Sam's Deli
62 Irish Town 51236; 51226
Fax: 42516
Email: dabamick@gibnet.gi.com
Provides kosher groceries and wine. Catering and takeaway service. Full glatt Kosher service. Fully licensed.

Embassy
Consul General of Israel
Marina View, Glacis Road, PO Box 141 77244

Groceries
I&D Abudarham
32 Cornwall's Lane 216 78506
Fax: 73249
Email: djabudar@gibnet.gi
Kosher wines, meats & poultry.

Hotels
The Rock Hotel
The hotel has kosher facilities (meat and dairy) and can cater for pre-booked groups of 10 or more. Kosher take-away food can also be delivery to a room.

Judaica
A.Cohen, 3 Convent Place, PO Box 190 52734
Email: sofergib@prontomail.com
Supplier of Mezuzot ,Tephilim and Shaatnez

Mikvaot
12 Bomb House Lane 77658 & 73090
Fax: 72359

Restaurants
Jewish Club
Open daily from 10 am to 11 pm, except Shabbat, but arrangements can be made with this restaurant owner for Shabbat meals.
Leanse Restaurant
7 Bomb House Lane 41751
Kosher.

Synagogues
Abudarham
20 Parliament Lane 78506 78047
Fax: 42527

Gibralter

Etz Hayim
Irish Town 75955
Nefusot Yehuda
65 Line Wall Road 73037

Shaar Hashamayim
19 Engineer Lane 78069   74030
                                            Fax: 74029
Enquiries: Joseph de M. Benyunes P.O.Box 1474

Greece

After the Hellenistic occupation of Israel (the Jewish revolt during this occupation is commemorated in the festival of Hanukah), some Jews were led into slavery in Greece, beginning the first recorded Jewish presence in the country. The next significant Jewish immigration occurred after the Inquisition, when many Spanish Jews moved to Salonika, which was a flourishing Jewish centre until the German occupation in the Second World War.

By the early 1940s, the Jewish population had grown to over 70,000, with 45,000 living in Salonika. With typical thoroughness, the Nazis deported not only the Jews from the Greek mainland, but also many communities from the Greek islands, including Crete. A local rabbi was a key member of the Greek resistance in the north of the country, and many local Christians did protect their Jewish neighbours in Athens. After the war, many of the survivors emigrated to Israel.

Today, there are Sephardi synagogues in Greece and, in Athens, a community centre and a Jewish museum. There are Jewish publications and a library in the community centre. In Aegina, Corfu and other Greek islands, ancient synagogues may be visited.

GMT + 2 hours   Total Population 10,490,000
Country calling code (30)   Jewish Population 5,000
Emergency Telephone (Police - 100) (Fire - 199) (Ambulance - 166)   Electricity voltage 220

Athens

Almost 3,000 Jews live in Athens. The community has access to a centre, containing a library and the opportunity to have a kosher meal. The Jewish museum in the centre of the city details the rise and tragic fall of Greek Jewry.

Kosher meals are served at the Athens Jewish Cultural Centre upon request (contact Mrs Rachel Sasson, tel. 01-21 13 371 – Delivery at the Hotels of Athens can also be arranged).

Embassy
Embassy of Israel
Marathonodromou Street 1, Paleo Psychico, POB
65140 15452   (1) 671-9530

Museums
Jewish Museum of Greece
39 Nikis Str 10557   (1) 322-5582
                                    Fax: (1) 323-1577
Open daily from 10am to 2pm except Saturday

Representative Organisations
Central Board of the Jewish Communities of Greece
36 Voulis Street 10557   (1) 324-4315-18
                                    Fax: (1) 331-3852
                            Email: hhkis@hellasnet.gr
                            Web site: www..kis.gr

Restaurants
Jewish Community Centre
8 Melidoni Street 10553   (1) 325-2875
                                    Fax: (1) 322-0761

Synagogues
Sephardi
Beth Shalom
5 Melidoni Street 10553   (1) 325-2773; 2823; 2875
                                    Fax: (1) 322-0761

Chalkis

Community Organisations
Community Centre
35 Kotsou Street 34100   (221) 80690

Kashrut Information
Community Centre
                                          (221) 27297

Synagogues
36 Kotsou Street
This synagogue has been rebuilt and renewed many times on its original foundations.Tombstone inscriptions in the cemetery go back more than fifteen centuries. Only open on High Holidays.

Corfu

Community Organisations
Community Centre
5 Riz. Voulephton St. 49100   (661) 45650
     Fax: (661) 43791

Tourist Sites
Velissariou St.   (661) 38802
There was an ancient synagogue and cemetery here, destroyed by the Nazis.

Ioannina

Community Organisations
18 Josef Eliyia St. 45221   (651) 25195
Contact: John Kalef-Ezra on 32390

Larissa

Synagogues
Community Centre
29 Kentavron St. 41222   (41) 532 965

Rhodes

Synagogues
Khal Shalom Kadosh
1 Simmiou St.
Dodecanese Islands   (241) 29406
The Synagogue belongs to the Jewish Community of Rhodes which counts 38 members. It was built around 1577 in the medieval City of Rhodes which used to be the Old Jewish Quarter. A photographic museum is functioning next to the Synagogue.The Synagogue is on the World Monuments Fund list of 100 most endangered sites. Tourists wishing to visit these sites should contact: Jewish Community of Rhodes, No 5 Polydorou Str, Old City. Telephone (0030) 241-22364 or Fax (0030) 241-73039

Salonika

At the turn of the 20th century Salonika, then part of the Ottoman Empire, had a Jewish majority. The official day off was Saturday.

Cultural Organisations
The Israelite Fraternity House
24 Vassileos Irakliou St.   (31) 221030
Yad le Zikaron
24 Vassileos Irakliou St.   (31) 275701

Libraries
The Centre for Historical Studies of Salonika Jews
24 Vassiléos Irakliou St., 1st Floor   (31) 223231
     Fax: (31) 229069

Synagogues
Monastirioton
35 Sygrou Str. 54630   (31) 524968

Trikkala

Synagogues
15 Athanassiou Diakou St
Yad Lezicaron
24 Vassileos Irakliou Str.   (31) 223231

Verria

Synagogues
15 Athanassiou Diakou Str.
Situated in the ancient Jewish quarter.

Volos

Community Organisations
Xenophontos & Moisseos Streets 38333
     (421) 25302
     Fax: (421) 25302

Kashrut Information
20 Parodos Kondulaki
Small Jewish communities are to be found in Cavala & Carditsa. In Hania, the former capital of the island of Crete, there is an old synagogue in the former Jewish quarter.

Synagogues
Xenophontos & Moisseos Streets
Open primarily on High Holidays.

Tourist Sites
Holocaust Monument
Riga Ferreou Square

Guatemala

Conversos were the first recorded Jews in the country, but, a few centuries later, the next Jewish immigration occurred with the arrival of German Jews in 1848. Later, some east European Jews arrived, but Guatemala was not keen to accept refugees from Nazism and, as a result, passed some laws which, although not mentioning Jews directly, were aimed against Jewish refugees.

Even though these laws were in place, in 1939 there were 800 Jews in Guatemala. After the war, an Ashkenazi community centre was built in 1965, but despite accepting some Jewish Cuban refugees, the community is shrinking owing to assimilation and intermarriage.

Most Jews live in Guatemala City, and others in Quetzaltenango and San Marcos. WIZO and B'nai B'rith are both represented, and there is a Jewish school and kindergarten.

GMT - 6 hours	Total Population 10,928,000
Country calling code (502)	Jewish Population 1,500
Emergency Telephone (Police 120) (Fire 122) (Ambulance 125)	Electricity voltage 110

Guatemala City

Communal Organisation
Communidad Judia Guatemalteca
Apartado Postal 502   (2) 311-975
                               Fax: (2) 325-683

Embassy
Embassy of Israel
13 Av. 14-07, Zona 10   (2) 371305

Synagogues

Ashkenazi
Centro Hebreo
Ta Av. 13-51 Zona 9   (2) 367643

Sephardi
Maguen David, 7a Av. 3-80, Zona 2   (2) 232-0932

Do you eat fish out?

If so, there is a comprehensive list of kosher fish listed alphabetically by country on pages 385 to 388 which you should find useful on your travels.

Haiti

Christopher Columbus brought the first Jew to Haiti – his interpreter, Luis de Torres, a Converso who had been baptised before the voyage. Thereafter more Jews settled but the community was destroyed in an anti-European revolt of Toussaint L'Ouverture in 1804. A hundred or so years later, Jews from the Middle East and some refugees from the Nazis settled in Haiti but many subsequently emigrated to Israel.

The remaining community has benefited from the help of the Israeli embassy, and services are held in the embassy or at a private address. There is no central Jewish organisation, and the community is too small to support other Jewish facilities.

GMT - 5 hours
Country calling code (509)
Emergency Telephone (Police - 114) (Ambulance - 118)

Total Population 7,041,000
Jewish Population Under 100
Electricity voltage 110

Port au Prince

Contact Information
Religious services are held at the home of the Honorary Consul, Mr Gilbert Bigio.

Honduras

During the Spanish colonial period, some Conversos did live in Honduras, but it was only in the nineteenth century that any significant Jewish immigration occurred. In the early twentieth century, refugees from Nazism followed a handful of immigrants from eastern Europe. Honduras was one of the small number of countries to aid refugees from Nazism, and many Jews owe their lives to the help of Honduran Consulates which issued visas in wartime Europe.

Tegucigalpa (the capital) contains the largest Jewish population, but the only synagogue in the country is in San Pedro Sula (services are held in private homes in Tegucigalpa). There is also a Sunday school and WIZO branch.

GMT - 6 hours
Country calling code (504)
Emergency Telephone (Police - 119) (Fire - 198) (Ambulance - 37 8654)
Electricity voltage 110/220

Total Population 5,666,000
Jewish Population Under 100

San Pedro Sula

Contact Information
530157
Services Friday and Shabbat at synagogue and community centre.

Embassy
Embassy of Israel
Palmira Building, 5th Floor   324232; 325176

Tegucigalpa

Contact Information
315908
Services usually held in private homes. Contact secretary at above number.

Hungary

Hungary

There were Jews living in Hungary in Roman times, even before the arrival of the Magyars (ancestors of the present-day Hungarians). The Jews suffered during the Middle Ages, when there was some anti-semitism, but conditions improved under Austro-Hungarian rule, and Judaism was recognised as being on a legal par with Christianity in 1896.

Hungary lost a considerable amount of territory after the First World War, and as a result many of its original Jewish communities (such as Szatmar) found themselves within other countries. Anti-semitism reached a peak in March 1944, when, during the German occupation, most Jewish communities began to be transported to Auschwitz. A number of those who were deported survived when Auschwitz was liberated by the Red Army in January 1945.

After the war, Hungary had the largest Jewish community in central Europe. Inevitably, the community dwindled through emigration (especially after the 1956 uprising) and assimilation. Communism in Hungary was far more lenient than in other Warsaw Pact countries, and synagogues were allowed to operate. Since 1989, religious interest has increased, and the government has recently renovated the Dohány Synagogue, the second biggest synagogue in the world and the largest in Europe. The Jewish population is still the largest in the region, although most are not religious.

GMT + 1 hour	Total Population 10,201,000
Country calling code (36)	Jewish Population 80,000
Emergency Telephone (Police - 107) (Fire - 105) (Ambulance - 104)	Electricity voltage 220

Budapest

Once known in the nineteenth century as 'Judapest', this city contains the majority of Hungarian Jews. There are several functioning synagogues, from orthodox to 'neolog' (Hungarian reform). The recently restored Dohány synagogue was built to accommodate 3,000 in prayer.

Bakeries
Dob utca 20
Kacinczy utca 28
Opening hours are variable.

Embassy
Embassy of Israel
Fullank Utca 8, II 1026

Groceries
Koser Bott, Nyar utcal   (1) 322-9276
Kosher products, bread etc.
The Orthodox Central Synagogue
VII, Kazinczy utca 27
Kosher milk and cheese are available here three mornings a week.

Hotels
Kosher
King's Hotel
Nagydiofa u. 25-27, Budapest VII 1072
                                  (1) 352-7675
                           Fax: (1) 352-7675
Strictly kosher hotel and restaurant.

Media
Newspapers
Uj Elet (New Life)
Central Board Hotel

Mikvaot
VII Kazinczy utca 16

Museums
Hungarian Jewish Museum and Archives
Dohany u.2 1077   (1) 343-6756
                           Fax: (1) 343-6756
              Email: bpjewmus@mail.c3.hu
         Web site: www.c3.hu/~bpjewmus

Organisations
Central Board of the Federation of Jewish Communities in Hungary
VII, Sip utca 12   (1) 342-1355
                           Fax: (1) 342-1790
              Email: bzsh@mail.matav.hu

Hungary

The Central Rabbinical Council
VII, Sip utca 12   (1) 142-1180
Rabbi Schweitzer is Chief Rabbi of Hungary and
Director of the Rabbinical Seminary.

Restaurants
Central Kitchen & Food Distribution
IX, Pava utca 9-11

Meat
King's Hotel
Nagydiofa Utca 25-27   (1) 352-7675
Supervision: Orthodox   Community.

Synagogues
Dohany Street Synagogue
VII Dohany Utca 4-6
Built in 1859, it is the largest in Europe and the second
largest in the world. In its grounds lie buried Hungarian
Jewish victims of the Nazis. There is also a
commemorative plaque to Hanna Senesh, the Jewish
girl parachutist who was captured and tortured before
being shot by the Nazis. A plaque commemorating
Theodor Herzl, the founder of Zionism, is in the Jewish
Museum.
Heroes Synagogue
VII Wesselenyi utca 5

Orthodox
The Orthodox Central Synagogue
VII, Kazinczy utca 27   (1) 132-4331

Tourist Information
Jewish Information Service
                          (1) 166-5165
                    Fax: (1) 166-5165

Tours of Jewish Interest
Chosen Tours   (1) 185-9499
                    Fax: (1) 166-5165
Tours of Jewish sites are provided by Chosen Tours by
telephone arrangement.

Sopron

Museums
The Old Synagogue Museum
Uj utca 22-24 H-9400   (99) 311327
                    Fax: (99) 311347
          Email: smuzeum@mail.c3.hu
A department of the Sopron Museum. Medieval
Synagogue restored as a museum in 1976. Open from
1 May to 1 October, daily between 9am and 5pm.
Closed Tuesdays

Synagogues
Orthodox
Jewish Orthodox
Tomolom utca 22 H-9400   (99) 313558

Tourist Sites
Uj utca 11
A second medieval Synagogue which formerly housed
the Museum is undergoing restoration. The ruins of the
1891 synagogue, out of use since 1956, can be seen
at Pap-ret H-9400.
The Neologue Cemetery
Dating from the 19th c. There is a memorial wall
dedicated to the 1,600 local victims of the Holocaust.

India

India

The Jewish population of India can be divided into three components: the Cochin Jews, the Bene Israel and the Baghdadi Jews. The Cochin Jews are based in the south of India in Kerala. This community can be further divided into Black (believing themselves to be the original settlers) and White (of European or Middle Eastern origin). Most of the community has emigrated, but there is still a synagogue in Cochin which is a major tourist attraction.

The Bene Israel believe they are descended from Jewish survivors of a ship wrecked on its voyage from ancient Israel. They follow only certain Jewish practices, such as kosher food and shabbat, and also adhere to certain Muslim and Hindu beliefs – for example, they abstain from eating beef. In the eighteenth century, they settled in Bombay and now form the largest group of Indian Jews.

Baghdadi Jews – immigrants from Iraq and the other Middle Eastern countries – arrived in India in the late eighteenth century, and followed British Colonial rather than local custom. Many emigrated to Israel in the 1950s and 1960s.

During the Indo-Pakistan war of 1972, the leading Indian military figure was General Samuels. In 1999 Lt. Gen J. F. R. Jacob was appointed Governor of Punjab State.

There is a central Council of Indian Jewry, based in Mumbai, where most of the Indian Jews live. Kosher food is available, and there are three Jewish schools in the city. Relations with Israel have recently improved and it is now a major trade partner.

GMT + 5.5 hours	Total Population 1,000,000,000
Country calling code (91)	Jewish Population 6,000
Electricity voltage 220	

Cochin

Contact Information
Inquiries, Princess Street, Fort   (484) 24228; 24988

Synagogues
Chennamangalam
Jew Street, Chennamangalam
Built in 1614 and restored in 1916, this synagogue has been declared a historical monument by the Government of India. A few yards away is a small concrete pillar into which is inset the tombstone of Sara Bat-Israel, dated 5336 (1576).
Paradesi
Jew Town, Mattancherry 2
The only Cochin synagogue that is still functioning. Built in 1568.

Khamasa

Synagogues
Magen Abraham
Bukhara Mohalla, opp. Parsi Agiari 380001
                    (79) 535-5224

Kolkata

Representative Organisations
Jewish Association of Calcutta
1&2 Old Court House Corner   (33) 224861
General inquiries to this telephone number.

Synagogues
Bethel Synagogue
26/1 Pollack Street
Magen David Synagogue
109a Peplabi Rash, Bihari Bose Road, 1, (formerly Canning Street)
Neveh Shalome Synagogue
9 Jackson Lane, 1

Mumbai

Mumbai is home to the majority of the remaining Indian Jews. There are three Jewish schools, and the Council of Indian Jewry is in the city. Thane, some 22 miles away, is where much of the community now lives.

Embassy
Consul General of Israel
50 Kailash, G. Deshmukh Marg, 26   (22) 386-2793

Kosher Food

ORT India
68 Worli Hill Estate, PO Box 6571 400018
(22) 496-2350; 8423; 8457
Fax: (22) 496-2350; 491-3203
Email: ortbbay@bom5.vsnl.net.in
Web site: www.ortindia.com
The Jewish Education Resource Centre provides kosher food from its Bakery and Kitchen to all travellers. ORT India also arranges conducted tours to places of Jewish interest in Mumbai and to ancient synagogues in the Konkan region of Maharashtra State.

Synagogues

Beth El Synagogue
Rewdanda, Allibag Tehsil, Raigad
Beth El Synagogue
Mirchi Galli, Mahatma Gandhi Road, Panvel 410206
Beth Ha-Elohim Syn
Penn
Etz Haeem Prayer Hall
2nd Lane, Umerkhadi 400009   (22) 377-0193
Gate of Mercy (Shaar Harahamim)
254 Samuel Street, Nr Masjid Railway Station 400003
(22) 345-2991
This is the oldest Bene Israel synagogue in India, established in 1796 and known as the Samaji Hasaji Synagogue or Juni Masjid until 1896 when its name was changed to Shaar Harahamim.
Hessed-El Synagogue
Poynad, Alibag Tehsil
Knesseth Eliahu Synagogue
V.B.Ghandi Road (Forbes Street), Fort 400001
(22) 283-1502
Freddie Sofer welcomes visitors to join him for lunch after Shabbat service.
Kurla Bene Israel Prayer Hall
275 S. G. Barve Road (C.S.T. Road), Kurla, West
Bombay 400070   (22) 514-5014
Magen Aboth Synagogue
Alibag
Magen David Synagogue
J.J.Nagpada, Byculla 400008   (22) 300-6675
Magen Hassidim Synagogue
8 Mohammaed Shahid Marg, (formerly Moreland Road), Agripada 400011   (22) 309-2493
Rodef Shalom Synagogue
Sussex Road, Byculla 400027
Shaar Hashamaim Synagogue
Tembi Naka, opp. Civil Hospital, Thane 400601
(22) 853-4817
Shaare Rason Synagogue
90 Tantanpura Street, 3rd Road, Don Tad, Israel Mohalla, Khadak 400009
Shahar Hatephilla Synagogue
Mhasla

Tifereth Israel Synagogue
92 K. K. Marg, Jacob Circle 400011   (22) 305-3713

Tour Information

Tov Tours & Travels (India)
96 Penso Villa, 1st Floor, Dadar 400028
(22) 022-445-0134
Fax: (22) 022-437-1700
Tours of Jewish India

Tours of Jewish Interest

ORT India
68 Worli Hill Estate, PO Box 6571 400018
(22) 496-2350; 8423
Fax: (22) 364-7308
Email: jhirad@giasbm01.vsnl.net.in
The Travel and Tourism Department arranges tours in Bombay & Raighad District.

New Delhi

Synagogues

Judah Hyam Synagogue
A/7 Nirman Vihar, Patparganj 110092
(11) 224-3136
The Judah Hyam Annexe houses a library and centre for Jewish and inter-faith studies.
Judah Hyam Synagogue
2 Humayun Road 110003   (11) 463-5500

Pune

Synagogues

Ohel David Synagogue
9 Dr Ambedekar Road 411001   (206) 132048
Email: oheldavid@ip.eth.net
Succath Shelomo
93 Rasta Peth 411011
Inquiries to Hon. Sec. 247/1 Rasta Peth, Trupti Apt., Pune 411011 or Dr S. B. David 9 Bund Garden Road, Pune 411001

Thane

Kashrut Information

Pearl Farm
A/1 Dhobi Alley, Sulabha, Thane, Maharashtra 400601   (22) 536-0539
Kosher goat meat and fish.

Iran

Iran

Iran, formerly known as Persia, has an ancient connection with Jews. The first Jewish communities in Persia date from First Temple times. King Cyrus, the Persian king who conquered Babylon, allowed the Jews to return to Israel from their exile. Not all returned, however, and some settled in Persia. The Persian community grew over time, suffering oppression after the Islamic conversion in 642. Certain segments of the Jewish community also grew in wealth in early medieval times.

In the twentieth century, there was a brief period of hope for the Jews in Iran when the country became more Western oriented after 1925. However, the 1979 revolution quashed the hope for a more tolerant Iran, and many thousands of Jews decided to emigrate. Association with Zionism became a capital offence and a number of Jews have been executed since 1979. The Jews are seen as dhimmi, 'subordinates' to Islam, and as such are allowed some religious practices, but are so closely watched that maintaining a Jewish life is difficult. The tombs of Esther and Mordechai (from the Purim story) are in Hamadan, south-west of the capital Tehran. Iran currently has the largest Jewish community in the Middle East outside Israel.

Kosher food has become expensive and is difficult to obtain.

GMT + 3.5 hours	Total Population 62,231,000
Country calling code (98)	Jewish Population 25,000
Electricity voltage 220	

Isfahan

Synagogues
Shah Abass Street

Tehran

Synagogues
Haim, Gavamossaltaneh Street

Meshedi
Kakh Shomali Avenue, opp. Abrishami School

The Iraqi
Anatole France Street

Tourist Sites
Jewish Quarter of Tehran, Mahalleh, off Sirus Avenue

Irish Republic

The first report of Jews in Ireland records that in 1079 'five Jews came over the sea'. The small community was expelled in 1290, along with the Jews from the rest of the British Isles. The community slowly grew again after Jews were allowed to return and a few Marranos settled in Dublin. There was never a strong community, however, and only in 1822 did a significant influx of Jews occur when immigrants came from England and eastern Europe.

Immigration continued and large numbers arrived from the Russian Empire after 1881. Some settled in Ireland intentionally but others believed that they had landed in America, deceived by their boat captains. In 1901, the community was 3,800 strong. The highest figure for the Jewish population of Ireland has been estimated at 8,000. Robert Briscoe (1894-1969) who played an important role in the struggle for Irish independence was twice Lord Mayor of Dublin.

Currently, most Jews live in Dublin. There is a kosher butcher and several synagogues in Dublin, but the community is shrinking.

GMT + 0 hours	Total Population 3,559,000
Country calling code (353)	Jewish Population 1,000
Emergency Telephone (Police, Fire , Ambulance 999)	Electricity voltage 220

Cork

Synagogues
10 South Terrace

(21) 870413
Fax: (21) 876537
Email: rosehill@iol.ie

Services: For information contact Fred Rosehill 870413.

Dublin

The centre of Irish Jewry, Dublin's position on the east coast meant that many Jews settled there in the flight from Eastern Europe in the nineteenth century. The Jewish Museum in Dublin, opened by the then President of Israel, Irish-born Chaim Herzog, in 1985 during a state visit to Ireland, gives much information on the town's Jewish history.

Dublin was also the home of possibly the world's most famous fictional Jew, Leopold Bloom of James Joyce's 'Ulysses'.

Bakeries
Deli Boutique
Orwell road, Rathgar 6

(1) 496-7612
Fax: (1) 496-6783

Hemmingway's Deli
Ballsbridge Terrace 4
Rowan's Deli
Main Street, Rathfarnham 14

Butchers
B. Erlich, 35 Lower Clanbrassil Street 8   (1) 454-2252
Fax: (1) 490-6609

Supervision: Board of Shechita.

Embassy
Embassy of Israel
Carrisbrook House, 122 Pembroke Road, Ballsbridge,
Ballsbridge 4

(1) 668-0303
Fax: (1) 668-0418
Email: info@embisrael.iol.ie

Mikvaot

(1) 490-5348

Museums
Irish Jewish Museum
3-4 Walworth Road 8

(1) 490-1857
Fax: (1) 490-1857

Open Tuesday, Thursday and Sunday. May to September 11 am to 3.30 pm; October to April 10.30 am to 2.30 pm.
Group visits by arrangement. (1) 490-1857.

Religious Organisations
Board of Shechita
1 Zion Road 6

(1) 492-3751
Email: irishcom@iol.ie

The Chief Rabbinate of Ireland
Herzog House, 1 Zion Road 6

(1) 492-3751
Fax: (1) 492-4680
Email: irishcom@iol.ie

Synagogues

Machzikei Hadass
Rathmore Villas, Rear of 77 Terenure Road North 6W

(1) 492-3751
Email: machadass@jerusalemail.com
Web site:
www.jpostmail.com/jpost/users/machadass

Terenure Hebrew Congregation
Rathfarnham Road, Terenure, Terenure 6
The Jewish Home of Ireland
Denmark Hill, Leinster Road West, Rathmines, Dublin 6

(1) 497-6258
Fax: (1) 497-2018
Email: thejewishhomeofirl@tinet.ie

Services are held Friday evening at start of Sabbath and Sabbath morning.

Progressive

7 Leicester Avenue, Rathgar, Po Box 3059 6

(1) 490-7605
Email: djpc@ulps.org

Friday evening at 8.15pm, first Sabbath in the month and Festivals at 10.30am

"COME AND VISIT US"
You have an open invitation from the hundreds of girls at the
GENERAL ISRAEL ORPHANS' HOME FOR GIRLS

בית היתומות הכללי

**HAMEIRI BLVD., WEINGARTEN SQ., KIRYAT MOSHE
P.O. BOX 207, JERUSALEM 91000**

(A short walk from the Central Bus Station)

Your visit will bring joy to our children, and they will inspire you.

Please write or call for transportation.
Tel: 523291 and 523292.

General Information

Israel, the Promised Land of the Bible, is today a modern, thriving, bustling and vibrant country. For centuries, the sites of many of the most stirring events in the history of mankind lay dormant beneath shifting sands and crumbling terraces, until the land was reclaimed by the People of Israel returning from exile. In today's Israel, cities, towns and villages, fertile farms and green forests, sophisticated industries and well-developed commercial enterprises have replaced barren hillsides, swamps and desert wilderness.

Climate

Israel enjoys long, warm, dry summers (April–October) and generally mild winters (November–March), with somewhat drier, cooler weather in hilly regions, such as Jerusalem and Safed. Rainfall is relatively heavy in the north and centre of the country with much less in the northern Negev and almost negligible amounts in the southern areas. Regional conditions vary considerably, with humid summers and mild winters on the coast; dry summers and moderately cold winters in the hill regions; hot, dry summers and pleasant winters in the Jordan Valley; and year-round semi-desert conditions in the Negev.

Languages

Hebrew, the language of the Bible, and Arabic are the official languages of Israel. Hebrew, Arabic and English are compulsory subjects at school. French, Spanish, German, Yiddish, Russian, Polish and Hungarian are widely spoken. Local and international newspapers and periodicals in a number of languages are readily available. All street and most commercial signs are in Hebrew and English and often in Arabic.

Passports and Visas

Every visitor to Israel must hold a valid passport; stateless persons require a valid travel document with a return visa to the country of issue. Visitors may remain in Israel for up to three months from the date of arrival, subject to the terms of the visa issued. Visitors who intend to work in Israel must apply to the Ministry of the Interior for a special visa (B/1).

Electrical Appliances

The electric current in Israel is 220 volts AC, single phase, 50 Hertz. Most Israeli sockets are of the three-pronged variety but many can accept some European two-pronged plugs as well. Electric shavers, travelling irons and other small appliances may require adapters and/or transformers which can be purchased in Israel.

Health Regulations

There are no vaccination requirements for visitors entering Israel.

Pets: Dogs or cats accompanying visitors must be over four months old, inoculated against rabies and bear a valid official veterinary health certificate from the country of origin.

Accommodation

Kashrut

In Israel, kosher means under official rabbinical supervision. Most hotels (but not all) do adhere. Kosher restaurants, hotels and youth hostels are by law required to display a kashrut certificate.

Hotels

Israel has over 300 hotels, offering a wide choice of accommodation to suit all tastes, purposes and budgets, ranging from small, simple facilities to five-star luxury establishments, with prices varying according to grade and season. Hotel rates are quoted in US dollars and do not include

Israel

the 15% service charge.

Kibbutz Hotels

The kibbutz (collective settlement) is an Israeli social experience, in which all property is collectively owned and members receive no salaries but are provided with housing, education for their children, medical services, social amenities and all other necessities. Most of the 280 kibbutzim throughout Israel are essentially agricultural settlements but many are moving to a more industrially orientated economy.

Several kibbutzim, mostly in northern and central Israel have established hotels on their premises providing visitors with a close view of this world-renowned lifestyle. They offer guests the opportunity of a relaxed, informal holiday in delightful rural surroundings. Some present special evening programmes about the kibbutz experience.

For further information and a special tour of Israel's kibbutzim and kibbutz hotels, contact any Israel Government Tourist Office (IGTO), or the tourist information offices (TIO) in Israel, or Kibbutz Hotels, I Smolinskin St., Tel Aviv. Tel.: 03-5278085 Fax: 03-5230527.

Youth Hostels

The Israel Youth Hostels Association (IYHA), affiliated with the International Youth Hostels Association, operates some 30 youth hostels throughout the country for guests of all ages. All offer dormitory accommodation and most also provide meals and self-service kitchen facilities. Some hostels also provide family accommodation for parents accompanied by at least one child. Individual reservations should be booked directly at specific hostels and group reservations with the IYHA.

The IYHA also arranges individual 14, 21 or 28 day package tours, called 'Israel on the Youth Hostel Trail'. These include nights in any of 25 hostels with breakfast and dinner, unlimited bus travel, a half-day guided tour, free admission to National Parks, a map and other informative material.

For further information, contact the Israel Youth Hostels Association, I Shazar Street, 91060 Jerusalem, Tel: 02-6558400, Fax: 02-6558401.

Currency and Bank Information

The currency of Israel is the New Israeli Sheqel (NIS) (plural sheqalim). Each sheqel is divided into 100 agorot (singular agora). Bank notes circulate in denominations of NIS 200, 100, 50 and 20 sheqels and coins in denominations of 5 sheqels, 10 sheqels, 1 sheqel and 50 and 10 agorot. One may bring an unlimited amount of local and foreign currency into Israel in cash, travellers' cheques, letters of credit, or State of Israel Bonds. Foreign currency may be exchanged at any bank and at many hotels.

Most banks are open from Sunday to Thursday from 08:30 to 12:00, and from 16:00 to 18:00 on Sunday, Tuesday and Thursday. On the eve of major Jewish holidays, banks are open from 08:30 to 12:00. Bank branches in major hotels usually offer convenient additional banking hours.

Shopping

Colourful oriental markets and bazaars may be found in the old city of Jerusalem and in several other towns and villages. The unique variety of goods available includes handmade items of olive wood, mother-of-pearl, leather and straw, as well as hand-blown glass and exotic clothing. In all cities and towns there are shopping malls which are open from 08:00 until 22:00. There are duty-free shops at Ben Gurion, Eilat and Ovda International Airports.

Opening Hours:

Most shops are open daily, Sunday to Thursday, from 9:00 to 19:00, although some close for a mid-day break between 13:00 and 16:00. On Fridays and the eve of major Jewish holidays, shops close early in the afternoon. Some Muslim-owned establishments are closed on Fridays and some Christian shops on Sundays

Radio and Television

Radio programmes are broadcast daily in English, Arabic, French, Yiddish, Russian and other languages. There are three daily news programmes in English and French. Many programmes shown on Israeli TV are in English with Hebrew, Arabic and Russian subtitles.

The Israel Broadcasting Authority news in English is screened nightly on the first TV channel at 18:15.

Facilities for the handicapped

Many hotels and public institutions in Israel (including Ben Gurion International Airport) provide ramps, specially equipped lavatories, telephones and other conveniences for the handicapped.

Milbat, the Advisory Centre for the Disabled at Sheba Medical Center in Tel Aviv (Tel: 03-5303739), will be pleased to answer visitors' questions.

The Yad Sarah Organization with branches located throughout Israel provides wheelchairs, crutches and other medical equipment on loan, free of charge (a small deposit is requested). For more specific information, contact the organization's main office in Jerusalem, Tel: 02-624 4242.

Travellers to Israel, especially those with specific medical/paramedical needs, can turn to Traveller Hotline operated by Ezer Mizion, the Israel Health Support Fund. This volunteer organization provides all paramedical information and needs free of charge to the traveller, via the International Office (02-537 8070) and Travellers Hotline (02-500 211). Transport and other arrangements can be organized prior to arrival and special inquiries/needs can be seen to while in Israel.

Organized Tours

Numerous organized tours, mostly in air-conditioned buses or minibuses, are conducted by licensed tour operators. Itineraries and prices are determined in accordance with the Ministry of Tourism guidelines to ensure a full sightseeing programme in maximum comfort. Half-day, full-day and longer tours are available, some combining air with road travel. Tours depart regularly from major cities as well as from popular resort areas during the peak season. All organized tours are accompanied by experienced, licensed multilingual guides identified by an official emblem bearing the words 'Licensed Tourist Guide'.

Smaller groups may hire a licensed driver-guide and a special touring limousine or minibus, identified by the red Ministry of Tourism emblem.

Full details of itineraries, prices and schedules are available at travel agencies, tour companies, I.G.T.Os and T.I.Os.

Major public institutions and organizations such as WIZO, Hadassah, universities and the Knesset (Parliament) conduct guided tours of their facilities. Walking tours of the larger cities are arranged by the municipalities.

Visitors should be aware that certain tourist sites such as the Tomb of the Patriachs and Jericho are now within the boundaries of the Palestinian Authority.

They should consult the local tourist offices in Israel concerning travel to those areas.

When visiting religious sites take care to be modestly dressed.

Buses

Buses are the most popular means of urban and inter-city transport throughout Israel. The Egged Bus Cooperative operates nearly all inter-city bus lines and also provides urban services in most cities and towns. (The greater Tel Aviv area is serviced by the Dan Cooperative and independent

Israel

bus companies operate in Beer Sheva and Nazareth.) Fares are reasonably priced and service is regular. Most bus lines do not operate on the Sabbath (Friday evening to Saturday evening) and on Jewish holidays. Students are eligible for discount fares on inter-urban bus routes on presentation of an International Student Card. Special monthly tickets are available for Dan and Egged urban bus lines. Overseas visitors can purchase 'Israbus' passes valid on all Egged bus lines for periods of 7,14, 21 and 30 days. Tickets can be obtained at any Egged bus station.

Traffic Regulations

A valid International Driving Licence is recognised and preferred, although a valid national driving licence is also accepted, provided it has been issued by a country maintaining diplomatic relations with Israel and recognising an Israeli driving licence.

Traffic travels on the right and overtakes on the left. Drivers coming from the right have priority, unless indicated otherwise on the road signs, which are international. Distances on road signs are always given in kilometres (1 km is equal to 0.621 miles).

The speed limit is 50 km (approx. 31 miles) per hour in built-up areas; 80–90 km (approx. 50–56 miles) per hour on open roads.

Special Programmes For Tourists

Plant a Tree With Your Own Hands

Tree-planting centres have been established by the Jewish National Fund at several locations throughout Israel. For a nominal contribution, visitors may plant trees and receive a certificate and pin to mark the event. For further information, contact the Jewish National Fund, P.O.Box 283,91002 Jerusalem, Tel: 02-6707402 Fax: 02-62411781 or 96 Hayarkon Street, 63432 Tel Aviv, Tel: 03-5234367 Fax: 03-5246084.

GMT + 2 hours	Total Population 5,481,000
Country calling code (972)	Jewish Population 4,700,000

Emergency Telephone (Police - 100) (Fire - 102) (Ambulance - 101)

Afula

Restaurants

| La Cabania, Ha'atzmaut Square | (6) 659-1638 |
| San Remo, 4 Ha'atzmaut Square | (6) 652-2458 |

Akko

Hotels

Palm Beach

| P.O. Box 2192 24101 | (4) 981-5815 |
| | Fax: (4) 991-0434 |

Supervision: Kashrut by local Rabbi.
Hotel, Restaurant and Convention Centre

Kosher

Palm Beach Club Hotel

Sea Shore 2410	(4) 987-7777
	Fax: (4) 9910434
	Email: palmbech@netvision.net.il

Museums

Akko Municipal Museum
Old City

Restaurants

Vegetarian

Amirei Hagalil
Akko-Safed Road, nr. Moshav Amirim 20115
(4) 698-9815/6

Tourist Information

| Eljazar Street, opposite Mosque | (4) 177-022-7764; |
| 999-1764 | |

Youth Hostels

Acre Youth Hostel

| | (4) 991-1982 |
| | Fax: (4) 991-1982 |

Arad

Hotels

Kosher

| Arad, 6 Hapalmach Street | (7) 995-7040 |
| | Fax: (7) 995-7272 |

Margoa, Mo'av Street, POB 20 89100   (7) 995-1222
Fax: (7) 995-7778
Email: margoa@mail.inter.net.il
Supervision: Kushrut: Rabbinat Arad.
Nof Arad
Moav Street   (7) 995-7056
Fax: (7) 995-4053

Youth Hostels
Blau-Weis   (7) 995-7150
This organisation is located in the centre of town.

Ashdod

Hotels

Kosher

Miami
12 Nordau Street   (8) 852-2085
Fax: (8) 856-0573

Tourist Information
4 Haim Moshe Shapira Street, Rova Daled
(8) 864-0485/090

Avihail

Museums
Bet Hagedudim (History of Jewish Brigade W.W.I)
988-22212
Fax: 986-21619

B'nei Berak

Hotels
Wiznitz
16 Damesek Elizier Street   (3) 777-1413

Restaurants
Dairy
Capit
34 Rabbi Akiv St.   (3) 579-6927

Beersheba

Hotels

Kosher

Desert Inn
Tuviyahu Av.Beersheba   (7) 642-4922
Fax: (7) 641-2722

Museums
Man in the Desert Museum

Situated 5 miles north-east of the city.
Negev Museum
Ha'atzmaut Street, cnr of Herzl Street

Tours of Jewish Interest
Bedouin Market
The market is held every Thursday but it has been
affected negatively by tourism and modernization.
Permanent Bedouin encampments can be seen south of
town.

Bet Shean

Museums
Bet Shean Museum
1 Dalet Street

Caesarea

Hotels

Kosher

Dan Caesarea Golf Hotel
P.O.Box 1120 30600   (6) 626-9111
Fax: (6) 626-9122
Email: caesarea@danhotels.com
Web site: www.danhotels.com

Restaurants
Caesarean Self Service
Paz Petrol Station   (6) 633-4609

Dan

Museums

Natural History and Archeology

Bet Ussishkin
12245   (6) 694-1704
Fax: (6) 690-2755
Email: ussishkin@kibutzdan.co.il

Dead Sea
Ein Bokek

Hotels

Kosher

Caesar Premier
(7) 668-9666
Fax: (7) 652-0303
The Caesar Resort Hotel on the shores of the Dead Sea
introduces the latest in design and comfort. Contact the
Caesar Group sales office in Tel Aviv for information,
Tel: (03) 696-8383; Fax: (03) 696-9896.
Crown Plaza   (7) 659-1919
Hod   (7) 658-4644
Hyatt Regency
(7) 659-1234

Israel

Nirvana   (7) 658-4626
Radisson Moriah Plaza

    (7) 659-1591

Degania Alef

Museums
Bet Gordon

Eilat

Hotels

Kosher

Ambassador
Rte. 90 (Eilat-Taba Road) 88000   (7) 638-2222
    Fax: (7) 638-2200

Americana Eilat
PO Box 27
North Beach 88000   (7) 633-3777
    Fax: (7) 633-4174
    Email: info@americanahotel.co.il
    Web site: www.americanahotel.co.il

Caesar
North BeachNorth Beach   (7) 630-5555
    Fax: (7) 633-3497

Club-In Villa Resort
Rte. 90 (Eilat-Taba Road)
Box 1505 Coral Beach 88000

    (7) 633-4555
    Fax: (7) 633-4519

Dalia
North Beach   (7) 633-4004
    Fax: (7) 633-4072

Dan Eilat
Promenade North Beach   (7) 636-2222
    Fax: (7) 636-2333

Edomit, New Tourist Center   (7) 637-9511
    Fax: (7) 637-9738

Howard Johnson Plaza Neptune
North Beach   (7) 636-9369
    Fax: (7) 633-4389

King Solomon's Palace
Promenade
North Beach   (7) 633-3444
    Fax: (7) 633-4189

Marina Club
North Beach   (7) 633-4191
    Fax: (7) 633-4206

Orchid
Rte. 90 (Eilat-Taba Road), Box 994 88000
    (7) 636-0360
    Fax: (7) 637-5323

Princess
Rte. 90 (Eilat-Taba Road), Box 2323 88000
    (7) 636-5555
    Fax: (7) 637-6333

Radisson Moriah Plaza
Promenade, Box 135   (7) 636-1111
    Fax: (7) 633-4158

Radisson Moriah Plaza
Promenade North Beach   (7) 636-1111
    Fax: (7) 633-4158

Red Rock
North Beach 88102   (7) 637-3171
    Fax: (7) 637-1705

Royal Beach
North Beach   (7) 636-8888
    Fax: (7) 636-8811

Museums
Museum of Modern Art
Hativat Hanegev Street

Restaurants
Café Royal
King Solomon's Palace Hotel North Beach
    (7) 667-6111
Chinese Restaurant
Shulamit Gardens Hotel North Beach   (7) 667-7515
Dolphin Baguette
Tourist Centre
Egged
Central Bus Station   (7) 667-5161
El Morocco
Tourist Centre
Golden Lagoon
New Lagoona Hotel North Beach   (7) 667-2176
Halleluyah
Building 9, Tourist Centre   (7) 667-5752
Off the Wharf
King Solomon's Palace Hotel North Beach
    (7) 667-9111

Dairy

La Trattoria, Radisson Moriah Plaza Hotel,
North Beach   (7) 636-1111

Meat

El Gaucho, Arrava Road. (Rte. 90)
    (7) 633-1549

Tours of Jewish Interest
Orionia   (7) 667-2902
Pirate   (7) 667-6549

Youth Hostels
Eilat   (7) 637-0088

Ein Harod

Museums
Bet Sturman & Art Institute

Israel

Galilee

Hotels
Kosher

Ayelet Hashahar
Upper Galilee Katzrin 12200   (6) 693-2611
Fax: (6) 693-4777

Hacienda
Ma'alot   (4) 957-9000
Fax: (4) 997-4404

Rakefet
Mishgav
Western Galilee   (6) 980-0403
Fax: (6) 980-0317

Restaurants
Lev Hagolan
30 Dror. Street Katzrin   (6) 961-6643
Orcha
Commercial CentreKatzrin   (6) 696-1440

Youth Hostels
Karei Deshe (Tabgha)
Yoram   (6) 672-0601
Fax: (6) 672-4818

11 miles north of Tiberias

Golan Heights

Leisure
Hamat Gader
The Golan Heights rise steeply fron the Sea of Galilee to the Mount Avital plateau. The Hamat Gader were thought to be the nicest spa baths in the whole Roman world, according to the Byzantine empress Eudocia. There are impressive ruins including the extensive Roman and Byzantine spa, which served as a grand bathing resort for six centuries, and an ancient synagogue. Four mineral springs and a freshwater spring emerge at Hamat Gader and so it is used today as a modern bathhouse. There is also an alligator farm where dozens of alligators and crocodiles can be seen lazing around.

Restaurants
Hamat Gader Restaurant
Hamat Gader   (6) 675-1039

Gush Etzion

Jewish History
Gush Etzion Bloc
The bloc has just celebrated its thirtieth anniversary of Jewish renewal. There are a few historial sites to see here.

Museums
Gush Etzion Museum
Kfar Etzion   (2) 993-5160 & 993-8308
Fax: (2) 993-3067
Email: audvske@kfar-etzion.co.il
Sound and Light show, reservation required.

Restaurants
Cravings Café
Dekel Shopping Center, Efrat   (2) 993-3188
Pizzeria Efrat
Te'ena Shopping Center, Efrat   (2) 993-1630

Meat
The Oak Tree Restaurant
Judaica Center, Gush Etzion Junction   (2) 993-4370
Fax: (2) 993-4949
Email: judaica1@netvision.net.il
Available for groups and events.

Tours of Jewish Interest
Gush Etzion Judaica Center
Gush Etzion Junction
(2) 993-4040; Tourism Dept. 993-8388
Fax: (2) 993-4949
Email: judaica1@netvision.net.ill
Web site: www.judaica.org.il
There is a wide range selection of Judaica items displayed here and at Kfar Etzion together with an audio visual show that movingly describes the history of the Gush. Kosher restaurant on premises.

Hadera

Museums
The Khan Museum
74 Hagiborim Street, POB 3232 38131
(6) 632-2330; 632-4562
Fax: (6) 634-5776
Hours: Sunday to Thursday, 8 am to 1 pm; Friday, 9 am to 12 pm; Sunday and Tuesday, 4 pm to 6 pm.

Haifa
Hotels
Kosher

Dan Carmel
87 Hanassi Avenue   (4) 830-6306
Fax: (4) 838-7504

Dan Panorama
107 Hanassi Avenue   (4) 835-2222
Fax: (4) 835-2235
Email: danhtls@danhotels.co.il

Dvir
124 Yafe Nof Street   (4) 838-9131
Fax: (4) 838-1068

Nof
101 Hanasi Avenue   (4) 835-4311
Fax: (4) 838-8810
Email: s1@actcom.co.il

Israel

Shulamit
15 Kiryat Sefer Street 34676   (4) 834-2811
                                      Fax: (4) 825-5206

Museums

Bet Pinchas Biological Insititute
124 Hatishbi Street   (4) 837-2886; 837-2390
                             Fax: (4) 837-7019
                             Email: biolinst@netvision.net.il
Includes nature museum, zoo and botanical garden.
Entrance via Gan Ha'em. Hours: Sunday to Thursday,
winter, 8 am to 4 pm, July to August, 8 am to 7 pm;
Friday and holiday eves, 8 am to 2 pm; Saturday, 9
am to 5 pm; winter, 9 am to 4 pm.

Dagon Grain Museum
Plumer Square   (4) 866-4221
                       Fax: (4) 866-4211
Free admission. Tours Sunday to Friday, 10:30 am.

Israel Oil Industry Museum
Shemen Factory, 7 Tovim Street, POB 136 31000
                       (4) 865-4237
                       Fax: (4) 862-5872

Israel Railways Museum
Haifa East Railway Station   (4) 856-4293
                                    Fax: (4) 856-4310

Mane Katz Museum
89 Yafe-Nof Street 34641   (4) 838-3482
                                  Fax: (4) 836-2985

Moshe Shtekelis Museum of Pre-History
124 Hatishbi Street, Entrance from Gan Ha'em

Museum of Clandestine Immigration & Navy Museum
204 Allenby Road 35472   (4) 853-6249
                                Fax: (4) 851-2958
Open: Sunday-Thursday 08.30 am - 16.00 pm.

Museum of Haifa
26 Shabbtai Levi Street   (4) 852-3255
Includes museums of Ancient Art, Modern Art and
Music & Ethnology. Hours: Sunday, Monday,
Wednesday, Thursday, 10 am to 4 pm; Tuesday, 4 pm
to 7 pm; Friday and holidays, 10 am to 1 pm;
Saturday, 10 am to 2 pm.

**The Israel National Museum of Science, Planning and
Technology.**
The Historic Technion Building, Balfur Street, Hadar Ha
carmel   (4) 862-8111
                Fax: (4) 867-9104
                Email: museum@mustsee.org.il
                Web site: www.mustsee.org.il

The National Maritime Museum
198 Allenby Road   (4) 853-6622
                          Fax: (4) 853-9286
Hours: Sunday, Monday, Wednesday, Thursday, 10 am
to 4 pm; Tuesday, 4 pm to 7 pm; Friday and holidays,
10 am to 1 pm; Saturday, 10 am to 2 pm.

Tikotin Museum of Japanese Art
89 Hanassi Avenue, Mount Carmel   (4) 838-3554
                                         Fax: (4) 837-9824
Hours: Monday, Wednesday, Thursday, 10 am to 5
pm; Tuesday, 10 am to 2 pm and 5 pm to 8 pm;
Friday and holiday eves, 10 am to 1 pm; Saturday, 10
am to 2 pm.

Archaeology and Art
Reuben & Edith Hecht Museum
Haifa University 31905   (4) 825-7773
                               Fax: (4) 824-0724
                               Email: mushecht@research.haifa.ac.il
                               Web site: www.mushecht.haifa.ac.il
Hours: Sunday, Monday, Wednesday, Thursday, 10 am
to 4 pm; Tuesday, 10 am to 7 pm; Friday, 10 am to 1
pm; Saturday, 10 am to 2 pm. Admission free. Kosher
Restaurant.

Restaurants

Banker's Tavern
2 Habankim Street   (4) 852-8439
Lunch only. Closed Shabbat.

Ben Ezra
71 Hazayit Street   (4) 884-2273

Egged
Central Bus Station   (4) 851-5221
Self-service

Gan Rimon
10 Habroshim Street   (4) 838-1392
Lunch only.

Ha'atzmaut
63 Derech Ha'atzmaut   (4) 852-3829

Hamber Burger
61 Herzl Street   (4) 866-6739

Hamidrachov
10 Nordau Street   (4) 866-2050

Paznon
Hof Carmel   (4) 853-8181

Rondo
Dan Carmel Hotel, 87 Hanassi Blvd.   (4) 838-6211

Technion
Neve Shaanan   (4) 823-3011
Self service. Lunch only.

The Chinese Restaurant of Nof
Nof Hotel, 101 Hanassi Blvd.   (4) 838-8731

The Second Floor
119 Hanassi Blvd.   (4) 838-2020

Tsemed Hemed
Herbert Samuel Square   (4) 824-2205

Dairy
Milky Pinky (Milk Bar)
29 Haneviim Street   (4) 866-4166

Meat
Mac David
131 Hanassi Boulevard   (4) 838-3684
Mac David
1 Balfour Street

Tourist Information
106 Sderot Hanassi   (4) 837-4010
What's on in Haifa
                            (4) 864-0840

Israel

Tours of Jewish Interest
(4) 867-4342
Mt Carmel, Druse villages, Kibbutz Ben Oren and Ein Hod artists' colony: Suns, Mons, Tues, Thurs, Sats, 9:30am.

(4) 867-4342
Bahai shrine and gardens, Druse villages, Muchraka, the Moslem village of Kabair, the Carmelite monastery and Elijah's cave, Weds, 9:30am.

Youth Hostels
Carmel   (4) 853-1944
Fax: (4) 853-2516
Shlomi, Hanita Forest   (4) 980-8975

Hanita
Museums
Tower & Stockade Period Museum

Haon
Holiday Villages
Kibbutz Haon, Jordan Valley   (6) 675-7555/6

Hazorea
Museums
Wilfrid Israel House of Oriental Art

Herzlia
Hotels
Kosher

Dan Accadia, Herzliya on Sea   (9) 959-7070
Fax: (9) 959-7092
Email: danhtls@danhotels.co.il
Tadmor, 38 Basel Street   (9) 952-5000
Fax: (9) 957-5124
Email: hotel@tadmor.co.il
The Sharon
Herzlia on Sea 46748   (9) 952-5777
Fax: (9) 956-8741
Email: hasharon@netvision.net.il
Web site: www.sharon.co.il

Restaurants
Dona Flor
22 Hagalim Blvd.
Herzlia Pituach   (9) 950-9669

Tadmor Hotel School
38 Basel Street 46660   (9) 952-5050
Fax: (9) 957-5124
Email: hotel@tadmor.co.il

Tourist Information
English Speaking Residents Association
PO Box 3132 46104   (9) 950-8371
Fax: (9) 954-3781
Email: esra@trendline.co.il

Jaffa
Museums
The Antiquities Museum of Tel Aviv-Jaffa
10 Mifratz Shlomo Street, Old Jaffa 68038
(3) 682-5375
Fax: (3) 681-3624
Part of Eretz Museum Tel Aviv. Opening hours: Sunday-Thursday 09.00-13.00.

Tours of Jewish Interest
Tel Aviv-Yafo Tourism Association
Ramat Gan
Walk takes 2.5 hours, starting at Clock Square near Yefet Street, in the centre of Jaffa. Free.

Jerusalem
Accommodation Information
Good Morning Jerusalem
9 Coresh Street 94146   (2) 623-3459
Fax: (2) 625-9330
Email: gmjer@netvision.net.il
Web site: www.accommodation.co.il
Lists rooms and apartments available for tourists.

Bed & Breakfasts
Kosher

A Little House in the Colony
4/a Lloyd George Street
German Colony 93110   (2) 563-7641
Fax: (2) 563-7645
Email: melonit@netvision.net.il
16 rooms, air-conditioning, Israeli breakfast, cafeteria, small garden.

B&B Le Sixteen
16 Midbar Sinai Street
Givat Hamivtar 97805   (2) 532-8008
Fax: (2) 581-9159
Email: le16@le16-bnb.co.il
Web site: www.le16-bnb.co.il
Member of the Jerusalem Home Accommodation Association. Can provide guest studios with kosher dairy kitchenettes.

Contact Information
Jeff Seidel's Jewish Student Information Centre
5 Bet-El, Jewish Quarter, Old City   (2) 628-2634
Fax: (2) 628-8338
Email: jseidel@netmedia.net.il
Web site: www.jeffseidel.com

Israel

Jewish Student Information Centre
Hebrew University Off-Campus Center, 5/4 Etzel Street,
French Hill   (2) 581-4939
Email: jseidel@netmedia.net.il

Guest Houses

Bet Shmuel
6 Shamma Street 94101   (2) 620-3473; 620-3465
Fax: (2) 620-3467
Single and family guest rooms with a capacity of 240
beds; conference facilities and banquet services;
restaurant and coffee shop; international culture and
education centre with central location.

Holiday Villages
Youth Recreation Centre Holiday Village
Yefei Nof
Jerusalem Forest   (2) 641-6060

Hotels

Kosher

Ariel Hotel Jerusalem
31 Hebron Road   (2) 568-9999
Fax: (2) 673-4066
Email: info@arieljrm.co.il
Reservations available also through Utell International.
Kashruth under the Jerusalem Rabbinate. Walking
distance from Old City.
Caesar, 208 Jaffa Road   (2) 500-5656
Fax: (2) 538-2802
Email: caesarjm@netvision.net.il
Supervision: Jerusalem Rabbinate.
150 comfortably furnished rooms.
Central, 6 Pines Street   (2) 538-4111
Fax: (2) 5381-480
Four Points
4 Vilnai Street 96110   (2) 655-8888
Fax: (2) 651-2266
Supervision: Jerusalem Rabbinate.
The hotel is located in the prestigious hotel area at the
entrance to the city and is within walking distance of the
Israel Museum and the Knesset.
Hyatt Regency Jerusalem
32 Lehi Street   (2) 533-1234
Fax: (2) 581-5947
Email: hyattjrs@trendline.co.il
Web site: www.hyattjer.co.il
Jerusalem Hilton
7 King David Street 94101   (2) 621-1111
Fax: (2) 621-1000
Jerusalem Tower
23 Hillel Street   (2) 620-9209
Fax: (2) 625-2167
Email: jthotels@inisrael.com

King David
23 King David Street 94101   (2) 620-8888
Fax: (2) 620-8882
Email: kingdavid@danhotels.com
King Solomon
32 King David Street   (2) 569-5555
Fax: (2) 624-1174
Email: solhotel@netvision.net.il
Laromme
Liberty Bell Park, 3 Jabotinsky Street 92145
(2) 675-6666
Fax: (2) 675-6777
Email: hotel@laromme-hotel.co.il
Lev Yerushalayim
18 King George Street   (2) 530-0333
Fax: (2) 623-2432
Menorah
44 Jaffa Road   (2) 622-3122
Fax: (2) 625-0707
Mount Zion
17 Hebron Road   (2) 568-9555
Fax: (2) 673-1425
Email: hotel@mountzion.co.il
Supervision: Jerusalem Rabbinate.
Palatin, 4 Agripas Street   (2) 623-1141
Fax: (2) 625-9323
Radisson Moriah Plaza Jerusalem
39 Keren Hayessod Street 94188   (2) 569-5695
Fax: (2) 623-2411
Supervision: Jerusalem Rabbinate.
Reich
1 Hagai StreetBet Hakerem   (2) 652-3121
Fax: (2) 652-3120
Renaissance Jerusalem Hotel
Ruppin Bridge, at Herz Blvd 91033   (2) 659-9999
Fax: (2) 651-1824
Email: renjhot@netvision.net.il
Glatt Kosher. Contact: Eli Velter
Sheraton Jerusalem Plaza
47 King George Street   (2) 629-8666
Fax: (2) 623-1667
Supervision: Jerusalem Rabbinate, Kosher Lamehadrin.
Windmill, 3 Mendele Street   (2) 566-3111
Fax: (2) 561-0964

Museums
Ammunition Hill Memorial & Museum, Ramat Eshkol
(2) 582-8442

Israel

Bible Lands Museum Jerusalem
25 Granot Street, POB 4670 91046   (2) 561-1066
                                    Fax: (2) 563-8228
                    Email: biblelnd@netvision.net.il
                    Web site: www.blmj.org
The home of one of the most important collections of ancient artifacts displaying rare works of art from the dawn of civilisation to the Byzantine period. Gift shop, special exhibitions,weekly lectures and concerts. Hours: Sunday, Monday, Tuesday, Thursday, 9:30 am to 5:30 pm; Wednesday, April to October, 9:30 am to 9:30 pm, November to March, 1:30 pm to 9:30 pm; Friday and holiday eves, 9:30 am to 2 pm; Saturday and holidays, 11 am to 3 pm. Daily guided tours. Kosher restaurant.

G.U.Y.'s Gallery
12 Hebron Road 92261   (2) 672-5111
                        Fax: (2) 672-5166
Judaica, Israeli art, Archaeology
Herzl Museum, Herzl Blvd., Mount Herzl
Isaac Kaplan Old Yishuv Court Museum
6 Or Hachaim Street, POB 1604 91016
                        (2) 627-6319
                        Fax: (2) 628-4636
The museum is located in the heart of the Jewish Quarter in the Old City of Jerusalem in a sixteenth-century building. It displays Ashkenazi and Sephardic life styles from the beginning of the nineteenth century. Hours: Sunday to Thursday, 9 am to 2 pm.

Israel Museum, Hakirya
Includes Bezalel National Museum, Samuel Bronfman Biblical & Archaeological Museum, Shrine of the Book & the Rockefeller Museum in East Jerusalem.
L.A. Mayer Museum for Islamic Art
2 Hapalmach Street, P O Box 4088 91040
                        (2) 566-1291/2
                        Fax: (2) 561-9802
Museum of Musical Instruments
Rubin Academy of Music, 7 Smolenskin Street
Museum of Natural History
6 Mohilever Street
Museum of the History of Jerusalem
Tower of David, Jaffa Gate   (2) 628-3273
Nahon Museum of Italian Jewish Art
27 Hillel Street 94581   (2) 624-1610
                          Fax: (2) 625-3840
This special museum collects and preserves objects pertaining to the life of the Jews in Italy from the Middle Ages to the present day. The main attraction is the ancient synagogue of Conegliano Veneto, a township some 60 km from Venice. Hours: Sunday, Tuesday, Wednesday, 9 am to 5 pm, Monday, 9 am to 2 pm, Thursday, Friday 9 am to 1 pm. For guided tours contact the numbers above.

S.Y. Agnon's House
16 Klausner Street Talpiot 93388   (2) 671-6498
                                    Fax: (2) 673-8285
Hours: Sunday to Thursday, 9 am to 1 pm.
Shocken Insititute
6 Balfour Street
Siebenberg House of Archaeological Museum
6 Hagittit Street
Jewish Quarter   (2) 628-2341
The Sir Isaac & Lady Wolfson Museum
Hechal Shlomo, 58 King George Street   (2) 624-7908
                                        Fax: (2) 623-1810
Tourjeman Post Museum
1 Hel Hahandassa Street   (2) 628-1278
Yad Vashem, The Holocaust Martyrs' and Heroes' Remembrance Authority
Har Hazikaron, PO Box 3477 91034   (2) 644-3400
                                    Fax: (2) 644-3443
                    Email: info@yad-vashem.org.il
                    Web site: www.yadvashem.org.il

Organisations
Ezer Mizion "Help from Zion"
25 Yirmiyahu St., Romena 94467   (2) 537-8070
                                  Fax: (2) 538-3315
                    Email: ezer_m@netvision.net.il
Uri Ezrachi - International Office
Travelers Aid of Israel
PO Box 2828   (2) 582-0126
               Fax: (2) 532-2094
        Email: wolfilaw@netvision.net.il
Legal counselling, social and human services, immigrant assistance, interest free loans, stranded travelers, medical assistance, crime victim assistance, homelessness, emergency assistance.
Yad Sarah
P.R. Department, Kiryat Weinbergl Blvd. 95141
               (2) 644-4242
        Email: infor@yadsarah.org.il
        Web site: www.yadsarah.org.il
Yad Sarah home care organization lends, free against a returnable deposit, regular and high-tech medical rehab. equipment. Visitors in wheelchairs can use the Yad Sarah special transportation vans, at a low fee. By pre-arrangement you can have the van and driver waiting at Ben Gurion airport. Minimum two weeks notice please for this service. Yad Sarah has 85 branches in Israel.

Israel

Religious Organisations
Israel Council of Young Israel
Heichal Shlomo Building, 58 King George Street 91371
(2) 623-1631
Fax: (2) 623-1363
Email: young-il@internet-zahav.net
Mailing address: P O B 7306, 91072 Jerusalem, Israel.
Office hours: Sunday through Thursday 9.00 am to 3.00 pm.

Restaurants
Casa Italiana
6 Yoel Salamon Street
Clafouti
2 Hasoreg Street   (2) 624-4491
Dagrill
21 King George Street   (2) 622-2922
Feferberg's
53 Jaffa Road   (2) 625-4841
Ye Olde English Tea Room
68 Jaffa Road   (2) 537-6595

Dairy
Bagel Nash
14 Ben-Yehuda Street   (2) 622-5027
Besograyim
45 Ussishkin Street   (2) 624-5353
Dagim Beni
1 Mesilat Yesharim Street   (2) 622-2403
Daglicatesse, 1 Rachel Imenu   (2) 563-2657
La Pasta
16 Rivlin Street   (2) 622-7687
Mamma Mia
38 King George Street 94262   (2) 624-8080
Fax: (2) 623-3336
Supervision: Jerusalem Rabbinate.
Located in the centre of town in an old (1899) restored building. Air conditioned. Hours: Sunday to Thursday, 12 pm to midnight, Friday 12 pm to 4 pm; Saturday, from the end of Shabbat.
Of Course!, Zion Confederation House,
Emile Botta Street   (2) 624-5206
Off The Square
8 Ramban Street
Supervision: Jerusalem Rabbinate, Kosher Lamehadrin.
Poire et Pomme
The Khan Theatre, 2 Remez Square   (2) 671-9602
Primus
3 Yavetz Street   (2) 624-6565
Rimon
4 Lunz Street   (2) 622-2772
Theatre Lounge
Jerusalem Theatre, 20 Marcus Street   (2) 566-9351
Zeze
11 Bezalel Street   (2) 623-1761

Meat
Burger Ranch
3 Lunz Street   (2) 622-5935
Burger Ranch
18 Shlomzion Hamalka Street
(2) 622-2392
El Gaucho
22 Rivlin Street   (2) 622-6665

El Marrakesh
4 King David Street   (2) 622-7577
El Morocco
43 Yirmiyahu Street, Centre One
(2) 500-1670
Fax: (2) 538-3496
Supervision: Rabbi Meir Kruyzer.
Marvad Haksamim
16 King George Street
Norman's Steak 'n Burger
27 Emek Refaim Street   (2) 566-6603
Fax: (2) 673-1768
Email: rmjb@netvision.net.il
Web site: www.normans.co.il
Supervision: Jerusalem Rabbinate.
Pampa
3 Rehov Yosef Rivlin   (2) 623-1455
Shaul's Shwarma Centre
14 Ben-Yehuda Street   (2) 622-5027
Shemesh
21 Ben-Yehuda Street   (2) 622-2418
Shipodei Hagefen
74 Agrippas Street   (2) 622-2367
Yemenite Step
12 Yoel Salamon Street   (2) 624-0477
Yo-si Peking
5 Shimon Ben-Shetach Street
(2) 622-6893

Pizzerias
Pizzeria Rimini
7 Paran StreetRamat Eshkol
Pizzeria Rimini
15 King George Street   (2) 622-6505
Pizzeria Rimini
43 Jaffa Road   (2) 622-5534
Pizzeria Trevi
8 Leib Yaffe Street   (2) 672-4136

Vegetarian
Village Green
10 Ben-Yehuda Street

Vegetarian (K)
Village Green
10 Ben Yehuda Street   (2) 625-2007
Fax: (2) 625-7972
Also catering and takeaway.
Village Green
33 Jaffa Street   (2) 625-3065
Fax: (2) 625 3062
Take away
Village Green
Jaffa Street 33   (2) 625-1464
Fax: (2) 623-1980
Also catering and takeaway.

Synagogues
Two synagogues of interest among many are
Great Synagogue
60 King George Street

Ashkenazi

Yeshurun, 44 King George Street   (2) 624-3942
Fax: (2) 622-4528
Email: netypjer@netvision.net.il

Tourist Information
ISSTA, 5 Eliashar Street   (2) 622-5258
Ministry of Tourism
24 King George Street   (2) 675-4811
The Israel Youth Hostels Association
Convention Hall Building, P.O.B. 1075 91060
(2) 655-8400
Tourism Coordinator with the Palestinian Authority
Israel Ministry of Tourism, PO Box 1018,
Jerusalem 91009   (2) 675-4903
Fax: (2) 624-0571

Tours of Jewish Interest
American Peylim Student Union
10 Shoarim Street   (2) 653-2131
Free tours of Jewish Quarter and free accommodation,
in the hostel quarters.
Knesset (Parliament)
(2) 654-4111
Sunday & Thursday 8.30am and 2.30pm
**Society for the Protection of Nature in Israel: Israeli
Nature Trails**
13 Helen Hamalka Street   (2) 624-4605
Fax: (2) 625-4953
Email: spnijeru@inter.net.il

Youth Hostels
Bet Bernstein
1 Keren Hayesod Street   (2) 625-8286
80 rooms.
Davidka, 67 HaNevi'im Street, PO Box 37110
(2) 538-4555
Fax: (2) 538-8790
75 rooms. 4-6 bedded.
Ein Karem   (2) 641-6282
97 rooms. 10 minutes from the Louise Waterman-Wise
Hotel in Bayit Vegan
Jerusalem Forest
(2) 675-2911
140 rooms.
Moreshet Yahadut
(2) 628-8611
Old city. 75 rooms.
The Israel Youth Hostels Association
Convention Hall Building, POB 1075, Jerusalem 91060
(2) 655-8400

Youth Travel Bureau
POB 6001, Jerusalem 91060   (2) 655-8432
There are 31 youth hostels in Israel for students, youth
groups and adults, which are supervised by the Israel
Youth Hostels Association (a member of the
International Youth Hostels Federation). All hostels offer
the standard facilities of dormitories, kosher dining
rooms, etc. Most hostels also have a guest house
section, with double and family rooms and private
facilities. Most are air-conditioned.

Katzrin
Restaurants
Lev Hagolan
30 Dror Street   (2) 961-6643
Orcha
Commercial Centre   (2) 696-1440

Kfar Etzion
Museums

Gush Etzion Museum

Kfar Giladi
Museums
Bet Hashomer

Kfar Vitkin
Youth Hostels
Emer Hefer   (9) 866-6032
25 miles north of Tel Aviv.

Kibbutz Harduf
Restaurants
Vegetarian Organic
Vegetarian Organic Restaurant
17930   (4) 950-1104
Fax: (4) 986-6835

Kibbutz Yotvata
Leisure
Biblical Wildlife Reserve Hai Bar Arava
The reserve is situated 37 miles north of Eilat.
Biologoists have settled every breed of animal that is
mentioned in the Bible. Animals include herds of
Somalian wild asses, oryx antelope, ibex, ostriches,
desert foxes, lynx, hyenas and the last desert leopard in
the Negev, living out her days on the reserve. Guided
tours start at 9 and 10.30 am, noon and 1.30pm.

Restaurants
Dairy
Dairy Restaurant
(7) 635-7449

Israel

Korazim

Holiday Villages
Amnon Bay Recreation Centre
(6) 693-4431
Vered Hagalil Guest Farm
(6) 693-5785
Fax: (6) 693-4964
Email: vered@veredhagalil.co.il

Lod

Tourist Information
Ministry of Tourism
Ben Gurion International Airport   (3) 971-1485

Lohamei Hagetaot

Museums
Ghetto Fighters' House, Holocaust & Resistance
Museum
D.N. Western Gallilee 25220   (4) 995-8080
Fax: (4) 995-8007
Email: simstein@gfh.org.il
Web site: www.gfh.org.il
Hours: Sunday-Thursday 9.00am-4.00pm. Friday
9.00am-1.00pm. Saturday and holidays 10.00am-
5.00pm. Kosher dining room and cafeteria

Maagan

Holiday Villages
Maagan Holiday Village
Sea of Galilee 15160   (6) 665-4400
Fax: (6) 665-4455
Email: maaganhv@netvision.net.il

Maayan Harod

Youth Hostels
Hankin   (6) 658-1660
7 miles east of Afula.

Mahanayim

Tourist Information
Zomet Mahanayim   (6) 693-5016

Moshav Shoresh

Hotels

Kosher

Shoresh Holiday Complex
Harey Yehuda   (2) 533-8338
Fax: (2) 534-0262
Email: info@shoresh.co.il
Web site: www.shoresh.co.il

Naharia

Leisure
Rosh Hanikra
Rosh Hanikra is situated 4 miles north of Naharia, on
the Lebanese border, and has an extensive system of
caves which the sea has washed out of the soft chalk.
There is also a lookout point with an adjacent
restaurant which reveals a panorama of the coast.

Museums
Naharia Municipal Museum
Hagaaton Boulevard

Restaurants
Cafe Tsafon, 10 Gaaton Blvd.   (4) 992-2567

Tourist Information
Israel Camping Union
P.O.B. 53   (4) 992-5392

Nahariya

Hotels

Kosher

Carlton
23 Ha'agaaton Blvd   (4) 992-2211
Fax: (4) 982-3771
Rosenblatt
59 Weizmann Street   (4) 992-0069
Fax: (4) 992-8121

Nazareth

Restaurants
Iberia
Rassco Centre, Nazareth Elite   (6) 655-6314
Nof Nazareth
23 Hacarmel Street, Nazareth Elite
(6) 655-4366

Negev

Museums
Dimona Municipal Museum

Man in the Desert Museum
Beersheba
5 miles north-east of the city.
Negev Museum
Ha'atzmaut Street, Cnr. of Herzl Street, Beersheba
Ramon Crater   (7) 88691

Restaurants
Bulgarian
112 Keren Kayemet StreetBeersheba   (7) 623-8504

Youth Hostels
Bet Noam
Mitzpeh Ramon   (7) 658-8433
Fax: (7) 658-8074

Israel

Bet Sara
Ein Gedi (7) 658-4165
1.5 miles north of Kibbutz Ein Gedi on Dead Sea.
Blau-Weiss
Arad (7) 995-7150
Centre of town.
Hevel Katif: Hadarom
(7) 684-7597
Fax: (7) 684-7680
For more detailed information, apply either to the Israel Youth Hostels Assoc. or to the nearest Israel Government Tourist Office.
Isaac H. Taylor
Masada (7) 658-4349
28 miles from Arad.

Netanya
Holiday Villages
Kosher
Green Beach Holiday Village
(9) 865-6166
Fax: (9) 835-0075

Hotels
Arches, 4 Remez Street 42271 (9) 860-9860
Fax: (9) 860-9866
Email: arches-hotel@correy.com
Galei Hasharon
42 Ussishkin Street 42273 (9) 834-1946
Fax: (9) 833-8128
Galil
26 Nice Blvd. (9) 862-4455
Fax: (9) 862-4456
Ginot Yam
9 David Hamelech Street (9) 834-1007
Fax: (9) 861-5722
Goldar
1 Usishkin Street (9) 833-8188
Fax: (9) 862-0680
Email: order@goldar.co.il
Supervision: Rabbinate of Netanya.
Grand Yahalom
15 Gad Machnes Street (9) 862-4888
Fax: (9) 862-4890
Green Beach
PO Box 230 (9) 865-6166
Fax: (9) 835-0075
Jeremy
11 Gad Machnes Street (9) 862-2651
Fax: (9) 862-2651
King Koresh
6 Harav Kook Street (9) 861-3555
Fax: (9) 861-3444
King Solomon
18 Hamaapilim Street (9) 833-8444
Fax: (9) 861-1397
MacDavid
7a Ha'atzmaut Street (9) 861-8711
Margoa
9 Gad Machnes Street (9) 862-4434

Maxim
8 King David Street (9) 862-1062
Fax: (9) 862-0190
Metropol Grand
17 Gad Machnes Street (9) 862-4777
Fax: (9) 861-1556
Orly
20 Hamaapilim Street (9) 833-3091
Fax: (9) 862-5453
Palace
33 Gad Machnes Street (9) 862-0222
Fax: (9) 862-0224
Opposite the beach, near town center.
Park
7 David Hamelech Street (9) 862-3344
Fax: (9) 862-4029
Residence
18 Gad Machnes Street (9) 862-3777
Fax: (9) 862-3711
The Seasons
1 Nice Boulevard (9) 860-1555
Fax: (9) 862-3022
Email: seasons@netmedia.net.il
Supervision: Rabbinate of Netanya.
Buses nearby.
Museums
Netanya Museum of Biology & Archaeology

Synagogues
Congregation Agudath Achim
45 Jabotinsky Street
New Synagogue of Netanya
7 MacDonald Street (9) 861-4591
Ohel Shem Civic Auditorium
Cultural Centre, 4 Raziel Street (9) 833-6688
Young Israel Congregation of North Netanya
39 Shlomo Hamelech Street (9) 862-1856
Tourist Information
Kikar ha'Atzmaut (9) 882-7286

Neve Zohar
Museums
Bet Hayotser, Dead Sea area

Petach Tikva
Museums
Bet Yad Labanim
30 Arlosov Street

Qatzrin
Museums
Golan Archaeological Museum
(6) 696-1350
Fax: (6) 696-9637

Ra'anana
Restaurants
Dana, 198 Achuza (9) 790-1452
Lady D
158 Achuza (9) 791-6517

Israel

Limosa
5 Eliazar Jaffe (9) 790-3407
Pica Aduma
87 Achuza (9) 791-0508

Ramat Gan

Museums
Bet Emmanuel Museum
18 Chilbat Zion Street
Pierre Gildesgame Maccabi Sports Museum
Kfar Hamaccabiah (3) 671-5871
Fax: (3) 574-6565
Email: lod@netvision.net.il

Ramat Hanegev

Tourist Information
Zomet Mashabay Sadeh (7) 655-7314

Ramat Yohanan

Youth Hostels
Yehuda Hatzair
(4) 844-2976
Fax: (4) 844-2976

11 miles north-east of Haifa.

Rehovot

Restaurants
Rehovot Chinese Restaurant
202 Herzl Street (8) 947-1616

Rosh Hanikra

Youth Hostels
Rosh Hanikra (4) 998-2516
Near the grottos.

Rosh Pina

Youth Hostels
Hovevei Hateva
(6) 693-7086

16 miles north of Tiberias

Safed

Hotels
Kosher

David
Mount Canaan (6) 692-0062
Nof Hagalil
Mount Canaan (6) 692-1595
Pisgah
Mount Canaan (6) 692-0105
Rimon Inn
Artists Colony (6) 692-0665/6
Ron
Hativat Yiftah Street (6) 697-2590

Museums
Bet Hameiri Institute(History & Heritage of Safed)

Israel Bible Museum Israel Bible Museum
Citadel Hill, POB 4706 (6) 699-9972
Near Ron Hotel
Museum of Printing Art
Artists' Colony (6) 692-3022
Tourist Information
50 Jerusalem Street (6) 692-0961/633
Youth Hostels
Bet Benyamin (6) 692-1086
Fax: (6) 697-3514
In southern part of town.

Tel Aviv

Accommodation Information
Kibbutz Hotels Chain: Head Office
1 Smolanskin Street, P.O.B. 3193 61031
(3) 524-6161
Fax: (3) 527-8088
Email: batya@kibbutz.co.il
Web site: www.kibbutz.co.il

Contact Information
Jewish Student Information Centre
Tel Aviv University Off-Campus Center, 82/10 Levanon Street, Ramat Aviv
Email: jseidel@netmedia.net.il

Hotels
Kosher

Adiv
5 Mendele Street (3) 522-9141
Ambassador
56 Herbert Samuel Street (3) 510-3993
Fax: (3) 517-6308
Armon Hayarkon
268 Hayarkon Street (3) 605-5271
Fax: (3) 605-8485
Avia
Ben Gurion Intl. Airport Area (3) 539-3333
Fax: (3) 539-3319
Basel
156 Hayarkon Street (3) 520-7711
Fax: (3) 527-0005
Bell
12 Allenby Street (3) 517-7011
Fax: (3) 517-4352
Carlton Tel Aviv
10 Eliezer Peri Street (3) 520-1818
Fax: (3) 527-1043
Email: request@carlton.co.il
City
9 Mapu Street (3) 524-6253
Fax: (3) 524-6250
Dan Panorama
Charles Clore Park (3) 519-0190
Dan Tel Aviv
99 Hayarkon Street (3) 520-2525
Fax: (3) 524-9755
Email: dantelaviv@danhotels.com
Deborah
87 Ben-Yehuda Street (3) 544-822
Fax: (3) 517-1777

Grand Beach, 250 Hayarkon Street   (3) 543-3333
Fax: (3) 546-6589
Email: reservation@grandbeach.co.il
Web site: www.grandbeach.co.il
Synagogue on premises.
Howard Johnson - Shalom
216 Hayarkon Street   (3) 524-3277
Fax: (3) 523-5895
Email: h_shlom@netvision.net.il
Maxim, 86 Hayarkon Street, P.O.B. 3442 63903
(3) 517-3721/5
Fax: (3) 517-3726
Metropolitan
11-15 Trumpeldor Street 63803   (3) 519-2727
Fax: (3) 517-2626
Email: reserve@metrotlv.co.il
Web site: www.hotelmetropolitan.co.il
Ramat Aviv
151 Namir Road   (3) 699-0777
Fax: (3) 699-0997
Renaissance Tel Aviv
121 Hayarkon Street 63453   (3) 521-5555
Fax: (3) 521-5588
Email: reserv@renaissance-tlv.co.il
Sheraton Moriah
155 Hayarkon Street   (3) 521-6666
Fax: (3) 527-1065
Email: shermor@inter.net.il
Sheraton Tel Aviv Hotel & Towers
115 Hayarkon Street   (3) 521-1111
Fax: (3) 523-3322
Email: shtelviv@netvision.net.il
Tal
287 Hayarkon Street   (3) 542-5500
Fax: (3) 542-5501
Tel Aviv Hilton
Independence Park 63405   (3) 520-2222
Fax: (3) 527-2711
Email: fom_tel-aviv@hilton.com
Yamit Park Plaza
79 Hayarkon Street   (3) 517-7111
Fax: (3) 517-4719
Email: yamit@netvision.net.il

Museums

Bet Bialik, 22 Bialik Street   (3) 525-3403
Fax: (3) 525-4530
Bet Eliahu-Hahagana
23 Rothschild Blvd. 65122   (3) 560-8624
Fax: (3) 566-6131
Bible Center (Beth Tanach)
16 Rothschild Boulevard 66881   (3) 517-7760
Fax: (3) 510-7661
Eretz Israel Museum
2 Haim Levanon Street 69975   (3) 641-5244
Fax: (3) 641-2408

Haaretz Museums
17 Ben-Gurion Boulevard
Includes eight smaller museums at Ramat Aviv, as well
as the Israel Theatre Museum.
Helena Rubenstein Pavilion for Contemporary Art
6 Tarsat Blvd   (3) 528-7196
Web site: www.tamuseum.co.il
Jabotinsky Institute
38 King George Street   (3) 528-7320
Fax: (3) 528-5587
Email: jabo@actcom.co.il
Web site: www.jabotinsky.org
Hours: Sunday to Thursday, 8 am to 4 pm.
Museum of the Jewish Diaspora (Beth Hatefutsoth)
Klausner Street, Ramat Aviv   (3) 646-2020
Fax: (3) 646-2134
Email: bhwebmaster@bh.org.il
Web site: www.bh.org.il
Tel Aviv History Museum
27 Bialik Street
Tel Aviv Museum of Art
27 Shaul Hamelech Boulevard 64283   (3) 696-1297
Fax: (3) 695-8099
Web site: www.tamuseum.co.il
Hours: Monday and Wednesday 10 am - 4 pm,
Tuesday and Thursday 10 am to 10 pm , Friday
10am to 2 pm and Saturday, 10 am to 4 pm Public
transport: buses 9, 11 18, 28, 70, 82, 90, 91, 111.
Parking facilities.

Restaurants
Hamakom
1 Lilienbaum Street   (3) 510-1823
Shaul's Inn
11 Elyashiv Street, Kerem Hatemanim
(3) 517-3303
Fax: (3) 517-7619
Supervision: Chief Rabbinate of Tel Aviv.
Oriental and Yemenite food. Popular and exclusive
sections. Hours: 12 pm to 12 am.

Dairy
Hungarian Blintzes
35 Yirmiyahu Street   (3) 605-0674
Meat
Olive Leaf, Sheraton Tel Aviv Hotel and Towers,
115 Hayarkon Street   (3) 521-1111
Fax: (3) 523-3322
Web site: www.sheraton-telaviv.com
Prestigious restaurant. Innovative cuisine with
Mediterranean flavours.

Synagogues
Bilu
122 Rothschild Blvd.
Great
314 Dizengoff Street
Ihud Shivat Zion
86 Ben-Yehuda Street
Central European rite.

Israel

Tiferet Zvi, Hermann Hacohen Street

Ashkenazi

Main Synagogue
110 Allenby Road

Progressive

Kedem, 20 Carlebach Street

Sephardi

Ohel Mis'ad, 5 Shadal Street

Tourist Information
Shop # 6108, 6th Floor, New Central Bus Station
(3) 639-5660
Fax: (3) 639-5659
ISSTA, 109 Ben Yehuda Street
The Ministry of Tourism
6 Wilson Street, Tel Aviv   (3) 556-2339
The Ministry of Tourism publishes a guide called 'The
Best of Israel', detailing shops participating in the VAT
refund scheme and recommended restaurants.

Travel Agencies
Interom Tourism Ltd.
(3) 924-6425
Fax: (3) 579-1720

Tiberias

Hotels

Kosher

Ariston
19 Herzl Blvd.   (6) 679-0244
Fax: (6) 672-2002
Astoria
13 Ohel Ya'akov Street   (6) 672-2351
Fax: (6) 672-5108
Caesar
103 The Promenade   (6) 672-7272
Fax: (6) 679-1013
Carmel Jordan River
Habanim Street   (6) 671-4444
Fax: (6) 672 2111
Gai Beach
Derech Hamerchatzaot   (6) 670-0700
Fax: (6) 679-2766
Galei Kinnereth
1 Kaplan Street   (6) 672-8888
Fax: (6) 679-0260
Golan
14 Achad Ha'am Street   (6) 679-1901
Fax: (6) 672-1905

Kinar
N.E. Sea of Galilee   (6) 673-8888
Fax: (6) 673-8811
Email: kinarmamag@kinar.co.il
Lavi Kibbutz Hotel
Lower Galilee 15267   (6) 679-9450
Fax: (6) 679-9399
Email: lavi@lavi.co.il
Web site: www.lavi.co.il
Glatt Kosher, Shomer Shabbat.
Pagoda
Lido Beach, PO Box 253 14102
(6) 672-5513
Fax: (6) 672-5518
Email: liz@kinneret.co.il
Open Sunday to Thursday 12.30-11.30pm. Saturday -
opens for dinner only.
Quiet Beach
Gedud Barak Street   (6) 679-0125
Fax: (6) 679-0261
Tzameret Inn
Plus 2000 Street   (6) 679-4951
Fax: (6) 673-2444
Washington
13 Zeidel Street   (6) 679-1861
Fax: (6) 672-1860

Museums
Tiberias Hot Springs Lehmann Museum
Hammat Tiberias National Park

Tourist Information
HaBanim Street, The Archaeological Park
(3) 672-5666

Youth Hostels
Taiber   (6) 675-0050
Fax: (6) 675-1628
2.5 miles south of Tiberias.

Zichron Ya'achov

Museums
Nili Museum & Aaronson House
40 Hameyasdim Street

Tours of Jewish Interest
American P'eylim Student Union
10 Shoarim Street   (6) 653-2131
Free tours of Jewish Quarter and free accommodation,
in the hostel quarters.
Jerusalem Youth Centre
9 Shonei Halachot Street   (6) 628-5623
Free accommodation.

Italy has an ancient connection with the Jews, and was home to one of the earliest Diaspora communities. Before the Roman invasion of ancient Israel, Judah Maccabee had a representative in Rome, and one of the reasons for the invasion was the Romans' desire to access the salt supply from the Dead Sea. There were Jewish communities in Italy after the destruction of the Second Temple, as Italy was the trading hub of the Roman empire. After Christianity became the official religion in 313, restrictions began to be placed on the Jewish population, forcing the community to migrate from town to town across the country.

In the medieval period, there was a brief flourishing of learning, but the Spanish conquered southern Italy in the fifteenth century, expelling the Jews from Sicily, Sardinia and, eventually, Naples. The first-ever ghetto was established in Venice in 1516. Conquest by Napoleon led to the emancipation of Italian Jewry, and full equal rights were granted in 1870.

Ironically, the Italian Fascist party contained some Jewish members, as Mussolini was not anti-semitic and, even under pressure from Hitler, did not instigate any major anti-semitic policy. The situation changed after Germany's occupation of the north in 1943. Eventually, almost 8,000 Italian Jews were killed in Auschwitz, although the local population hid many of those who survived.

Today there is a central organisation which provides services for Italian Jews. B'nai B'rith and WIZO are represented, and there are kosher restaurants in Rome, Milan and other towns. There are also Jewish schools.

GMT + 1 hour	Total Population 57,226,000
Country calling code (39)	Jewish Population 35,000
Emergency Telephone (Police - 112) (Fire - 115) (Ambulance - 116)	Electricity voltage 220

Ancona

Community Organisations
Community Offices
Via Fanti 2 bis   (071) 202638

Mikvaot
Via Astagno

Asti

Museums
Via Ottolenghi 8Torino

                    (0141) 539281

Synagogues
Via Ottolenghi 8Torino

Bologna

Cafeterias
Comunita Ebraica Bologna
Via Gombruti 9 40123   (051) 232-066
                              Fax: (051) 229-474
Supervision: Rav Moshe Saadoun.
Lunch Sunday to Friday; dinner Friday; closed mid-July and August.

Community Organisations
Comunita Ebraica Bologna
Via Gombruti 9 40123
                (051) 232-066 & 227-931 (office of Rabbi)
                              Fax: (051) 229-474
                    Email: comebrbol@libero.it
        Web site: www.menorah.it/ceb/indice.htm

Mikvaot
Mikveh Chaya Mushkah
Via Oreste Regnoli 17/1   (051) 623-0316

Synagogues
Via Mario Finzi

Italy

Casale Monferrato

Synagogues
Community Offices
Vicolo Salomone Olper 44   (0142) 71807
Fax: (0142) 454814
Email: qqcasale@mail.dex-net.com
Web site: www.menorah.it/qqcasale/indice.htm

The synagogue, built in 1595 is one of the most interesting in North Italy. It also contains a Jewish museum. Casale-Monferrato is on the Turin–Milan road, and can be reached by turning off it about 13 miles beyond Chivasso. Casale may also be reached with tollway A26 (exit Casale north or south, whichever comes first). It is better to make advance appointments for visiting either the Synagogue or Museum.

Cuneo

Synagogue and Communal Office
Via Mondovi   (0171) 692-007

A beautiful synagogue; parts dating from 15th century. Services are now only held on Yom Kippur. In 1799 a special Purim was established after the Synagogue was saved from destruction by a shell.

Ferrara

Community Organisations
Community of Ferrara
Via Mazzini 95 44100   (0532) 24 70 04
Fax: (0532) 24 70 04

Mikvaot
Via Mazzini 95   (0532) 24 70 04

Museums
Jewish Museum of Ferrara
Via Mazzini 95 44100   (0532) 21 02 28
Fax: (0532) 21 02 28
Email: museoebraico@comune.fe.it
Web site: www.comune.fe.it/museoebraico

Guided tours in English on Sunday to Thursday 10 am 11am 12 am. Closed on Fridays and Saturdays.

Synagogues
Via Mazzini 95   (0532) 24 70 33

Florence

Bakeries
Forno dei Ciompi
Piazza dei Ciompi   (055) 241-256
Kosher Bakery
Forno dei Ciompi, Piazza, Dei Ciompi

Butchers
Bruno Falsettini
Mercato Coperto di S., Ambrogio   (055) 248-0740
8 am to 10 am, Book in advance
Gionvannino, Via dei Macci 106   (055) 248-0734
7.30 am to 1.00 pm - Book in advance.

Community Organisations
Community Offices
Via L.C. Farini 4 50121   (055) 245252
Fax: (055) 241811
Email: comebrfi@fol.it
Web site: www.fol.it/sinagoga

Community Office and Mikvah: Via L. C. Farini 4 - 50121 Florence; From Sunday to Friday from 9.30 am to 12.30 pm (Sunday closed in July and August)

Mikvaot
Via L.C. Farini 4 50121   (055) 245252
Fax: (055) 241811
Email: comebrfi@fol.it
Web site: www.fol.it/sinagoga

Museums
Jewish Museum
Via L.C. Farini 4 50121   (055) 245252
Fax: (055) 241811
Email: comebrfi@fol.it
Web site: www.fol.it/sinagoga

There is also a religious and artistic souvenir shop. Open Sunday - Thursday 10am to 1pm. Groups are kindly requested to book in advance. For further information and booking, please contact the Community offices.

Restaurants
Ruth's
Via Farini 2/A   (055) 248-0888
Bookings required for Shabbat meals and groups. Take away.

Synagogues

Orthodox

Via De Banchi   (055) 212-474
After the service there is a public Kiddush. For the
timetable of services ask in the Community Office.
Via L.C. Farini, 4 50121   (055) 245252
Fax: (055) 241811
Email: comebrfi@fol.it
Web site: www.fol.it/sinagoga
After service public Kiddush. Services on Shabbat and
holidays, not daily. The Synagogue is open for tourists
from Sunday to Thursday from 10.00 am to 1.00 pm
and from 2.00 pm to 4.00 pm., (summer from 10.00
am to 1.00 pm and 2.00 pm to 5.00 pm) on Friday
only in the morning.

Genoa

Community Organisations
Community Offices
Via Bertora 6 16122

Synagogues
Synagogue and Community Offices
Via Bertora 6 16122   (010) 839-1513
Fax: (010) 846-1006
Email: comgenova@tin.it
Every Friday and Shabbat morning.

Gorizia

Synagogues
Via Ascoli 19, Gradicia, Gradicia   (03831) 532115

Leghorn

Butchers
Corucci
Banco 25, Mercato Centrale, Livorno, Livorno
(0586) 884596

Mikvaot
Community Offices
Piazza Benamozegh 1, Livorno
(0586) 896290

Museums
Jewish Museum
via Micali 21, Livorno   (0586) 893361
Visits only by appointment.

Synagogues
Community Offices
Piazza Benamozegh 1, Livorno   (0586) 896290
Fax: (0586) 896290

Mantua

Synagogues
Community Offices
Via G. Govi 11, Mantova   (0379) 321490

Merano

Museums
Jewish Museum
Via Schiller 14   (0473) 236127
Fax: (0473) 237520
Hours: Tuesday and Wednesday 3-6pm. Thursday 9-
12am. Friday 3-5pm.

Synagogues
Community Offices
Via Schiller 14   (0473) 236127

Milan

Home of the second largest community in Italy
(10,000). The Ambrosiana Museum (Piazza Pio XI)
contains a number of Hebrew books, manuscripts
and other Judaica.

Community Organisations
Community Offices
Sally Mayer 2   (02) 483-02806
Fax: (02) 483-04660

Documentation Centres
Contemporary Jewish Documentation Centre
Via Eupili 8   (02) 316338
Fax: (02) 336-02728

Groceries
Eretz, Largo Scalabrini 5   (02) 423-6891
Fax: (02) 423-4753
Hours: 9 am to 7:30 pm. Buses, 50, 95, 13, 61,
subway 1 (red), stop, Bande-Nere.

Mikvaot
Central Synagogue
Via Guastalla 19   (02) 551-2101

Italy

Restaurants

Eshel Isroel, Via Benvenuto Cellini 2   (02) 545-5076
Supervision: Rav G. H. Garelik.
Open weekdays
Pizzeria Carmel
viale San Gimignano 10   (02) 416368
Fax: (02) 48512145
Supervision: Rav S. Behor.
Hours: 12 pm to 2:30 pm and 5:30 pm to 10:30 pm.
Nearest public transport: buses 58, 61, 50, 95, subway 1.

Meat

Re Salomone, Via Washington, 9   (02) 469-4643
Fax: (02) 43318049
Email: resalomone@tiscalinet.it
International Meat restaurant with Mediterranean,
Italian and Oriental food and take-away
Rey Solomon
Calle Washington 9   (02) 469-4643

Synagogues
Beth Shelomo
Galleria Vittorio Emanuele, (Via Ugo Foscolo 3.) 20121
(02) 8646-6118
Fax: (02) 2901-9561
Email: fweb.shlomo@bethshlomo.it
Web site: www.bethshlomo.it
Services are held on Friday evening, Shabbat, Sunday
morning and Holy days.
Central Synagogue
Via Guastalla 19   (02) 551-2101
Merkos L'Inyonei Chinuch
Via Carlo Poerio 35 20129   (02) 295-31213
New Home for Aged
Via Leone XIII   (02) 498-2604
Services on Sabbaths and festivals. Kosher food
available upon reservation
New Synagogue
Via Eupili 8
Service on Sabbaths and festivals

Lubavitch
Ohel Yacob, Via Benvenuto Cellini 2   (02) 545-5076

Orthodox Sephardi
Via Guastalla 19   (02) 551-2029
Fax: (02) 551-92699
Rabbi Dr Laras is the Chief Rabbi

Persian
Angelo Donati Beth Hamidrash
Via Sally Mayer 4-6

Tourist Information
Uffizio Nazionale Israeliano del Turismo
Via Podgora 12/b 20122   (027) 602-1051
Fax: (027) 760-124-77

Modena

Butchers
Macelleria Duomo
Mercato Coperto (Covered Market), Stand 25
(059) 217269

Synagogues
Community Offices
Piazza Mazzini 26   (059) 223978

Naples

Synagogues
Community Offices
Via Cappella Vecchia 31, Napoli, Napoli
(081) 764-3480
Email: c.l.na@virgilio.it

Ostia Antica

Here can be found the partially restored excavated
remains of a first-century synagogue built on the
site of another one which stood there 300 years
earlier. This is the oldest synagogue in Europe.
Ostia Antica is near Leonardo da Vinci
International Airport and about 40 minutes by train
from Rome (Termini or Pyramid stations). To reach
the synagogue, cross the footbridge on leaving the
station. The entrance to the excavations is straight
ahead.

Padua

Mikvaot
Via S. Martino e Solferino 9, Padova, Padova
(049) 871-9501

Synagogues
Community Offices
Via S. Martino e Solferino 9, Padova, Padova
(049) 875-1106

Parma
Synagogues
Community Offices
Vicolo Cervi 4

Perugia
Synagogues
P. della Republica 77   (075) 21250

Pesaro

The remains of an old synagogue, built in the second half of the 16th century, is currently being restored by the town council. It is unusual as the Bimah is built on columns one storey above floor level. Pesaro is also the birth place of Rossini.

Pisa

Synagogues
Community Offices
Via Palestro 24   (050) 542580
Services are held on festivals and Holy-days. During the week the resident beadle will be glad to show visitors round the synagogue, which is famed for its beauty. It is very near the Teatro Verdi.

Riccione

Hotels
Vienna Touring Hotel
                                                  (054) 160-1245
In the summer, kosher food is obtainable. Provides vegetarian food and particularly welcomes Jewish guests.

Rome

About half of Italian Jewry (some 15,000) live in Rome. As there has been such a long period of Jewish settlement, a Nusach Italki (Italian prayer ritual) has developed, which is practised in some synagogues in the town. Kosher restuarants and kosher food are available. Titus' Arch, depicting the destruction of Jerusalem by the Romans, is in the city, and Jews were forbidden to walk under it. The ghetto of Rome is behind the Great Synagogue. A visit worth considering is to the ancient Jewish burial sites along the Appian Way. Check about tour arrangements with the Jewish Community offices, 580-3667.

Bakeries
Limentani Settimio
Via Portico d'Ottavia 1

Bed & Breakfasts
Pension Carmel
via Goffredo Mameli 11 00153   (06) 580-9921
                                     Fax: (06) 581-8853
             Email: reservation@hotelcarmel.it
Kosher pension situated in the old district of Trastevere, ten minutes from the main synagogue.

Butchers
Massari
Piazza Bologna 11   (06) 429120
Sion Ben David
Via Filippo Turati 110   (06) 733358
Terracina
Via Portico d'Ottavia 1b   (06) 654-1364

Embassy
Embassy of Israel
Via Michelle Mercati 14 00197   (06) 322-1541
Embassy of Israel to The Holy See
Via M. Mercati 12 00197   (06) 3619-8690
                                     Fax: (06) 3619-8626

Groceries
Sabra, Via S. Ambrogio 6

Media

Newspapers
Shalom, Lungotevere Cenci 1
                            (06) 574-5036/574-2006
                                     Fax: (06) 574-2253
               Email: shalom.mensile@flashnet.it
               Web site: www.litos.it/shalom
Monthly.

Mikvaot
Lungotevere Cenci (Tempio) 9

Museums
The Jewish Museum
Lungotevere Cenci 9
The main synagogue building contains a permanent exhibition covering the 2,000-year history of the Italian Jewish community. Another link with this long history is the Rome Ghetto almost adjoining. It can be reached by taking buses 44, 56, 60 or 75, near the neighbouring Ponte Garibaldi. It is a maze of narrow alleys dating from Imperial Roman times, within which, until 1847, all Roman Jews were confined under curfew. A striking monument has been erected to the memory of 335 Jewish and Christian citizens of Rome who were massacred in 1944 by the Nazis in the Fosse Ardeatine. It lies just outside the Porta San Paolo, a few yards from the main synagogue.

Religious Organisations
The Italian Rabbinical Council
Headquarters, Lungotevere Sanzio 9
                            (06) 580-3667; 580-3670

Representative Organisations
Unione Comunita Ebraiche Italiane (Union of Italian Jewish Communities)
Lungotevere Sanzio 9   (06) 580-3667; 580-3670
                                     Fax: (06) 589-9569
Information on Italian Jewry, its monuments and history may be obtained from here.

Italy

Restaurants
La Taverna Del Ghetto
8, Via Portico, D'Ottavia   (06) 6880-9771
Supervision: Orthodox Chief Rabbi of Rome.
Simcha Labi
Via Imperia 2, CAP 00161
Supervision: Chabad Rabbi.

Meat
Oriental Foods Kosher
Via Livorno, 8-10   (06) 440-4840
                                       Fax: (06) 440-4840

Pizzerias
Zi Fenizia
via Santa Maria del Pianto 64-65 00186
                                            (06) 689-6976
Kashrut certificate is for meat - they do not use any
cheeses in their pizzas.

Synagogues
Orthodox
The Great Synagogue
Lungotevere Cenci (Tempio) 9   (06) 684-0061
                                      Fax: (06) 684-00684
                                    Email: rohacer@tin.it
                                Website: www.litos.it.org

Orthodox Ashkenazi
Via Balbo 33

Tours
Guides
G. Palombo
Via val Maggia 7
                                  (06) 810-3716; 993-2074
Ruben E. Popper
12 Via dei Levii   (06) 761-0901
                                      Fax: (06) 761-0901
Telephone number is afternoons only.

Senigallia
Synagogues
Via dei Commercianti

Siena
Synagogues
Vicolo delle Scotte 14   (0577) 284647
The committee has issued a brochure in English, giving
the history of the community which dates back to
medieval times. The Synagogue dates from 1750.
Services are held on the Sabbath and High Holy-days.
Further information from Burroni Bernardi, Via del
Porrione. M. Savini, via Salicotta 23. Tel: 283140 (close
to the synagogue)

Spezia
Synagogues
Via 20 Settembre 165

Trieste
Community Organisations
Community Offices
Via San Francesco 19   (040) 371466
                                      Fax: (040) 371226
Chief Rabbi: Rav Dr. Avraham Umberto Piperno. Tel:
3722681

Synagogues
Via Donizetti 2   (040) 631898

Tour Information
Smile Service
via Martiri della Liberta' 17 34134   (040) 372-8464
                                     Fax: (040) 372-6630
This service agency organises tours around the Jewish
sites of Friuli Venezia-Giulia.

Turin
Booksellers
Biblioteca "E. Artom"
P.tta Primo Levi 12Torino 10125   (011) 669-9097
Libreria Claudiana
Via Principe Toncmaso 1Torino 10125
                                         (011) 669-2458

Community Organisations
Community Centre
P.tta Primo Levi 12Torino 10125   (011) 658-585

Groceries
Panetteria Bertino
Via B. Galliari 14Torino 10125   (011) 669-9527

Mikvaot
P.tta Primo Levi 12Torino 10125   (011) 658-585

Restaurants
Salomon e Augusto Segre - Jewish rest home
Via B. Galliari 13Torino 10125   (011) 658-585
Only by reservation

Synagogues
P.tta Primo Levi 12Torino 10125   (011) 658-585
Daily 6.50 am and sunset; Shabbat 9 am and half an
hour before sunset (winter) or 6.30 pm (summer); on
Shabbat (in winter) between Minchah and Maariv a
Seudat Shelishit is held.

Urbino

Synagogues
Via Stretta

Venice

Jews settled in Venice early in the tenth century and became an important factor in the economic life of the city. In 1516 however the authorities banished the Jews to the Ghetto Nuovo (new foundry) district so establishing the first Ghetto. The high walls surrounding the area still exist.

The 14th-century Jewish cemetery (the second oldest in Europe after the one in Worms) has recently been restored and was reopened in 1999 for guided tours (for details call the Jewish Museum).

Community Organisations
Community Offices
Cannaregio
Ghetto Nuovo 2899-30121

(041) 715-012
Fax: (041) 524-1862

Gift Shop
David's
Ghetto Nuovo 2880
Jewish articles & religious appurtenances are available from here.

Mordehai Fusetti
Ghetto Nuovo, Ghetto Vecchio 1219   (041) 714024
Jewish articles & religious appurtenances are available from here.

Guest Houses
Jewish Rest Home
Cannaregio 30121
Ghetto Nuovo 2874

(041) 716002
Fax: (041) 714394

Kosher meals and accommodation can be had here. Early booking is advised.

Hotels
Buon Pesce, S. Nicolo 50.   (041) 760533
Open Apr. to Oct. Danieli (tel) 26480

Libraries
Jewish Library and Archives "Renato Maestro"
30121 Venice
Cannaregio, Ghetto Nuovo 2899   (041) 718833
Fax: (041) 5241862
Email: renatomaestro@libero.it

Mikvaot
Jewish Rest Home
Ghetto Nuovo 2874   (041) 715118

Museums
Jewish Museum
Cannaregio
Ghetto Nuovo 2902/B   (041) 715-359
Fax: (041) 723-007

Jewish Museum (Open Sunday through Friday from 10.00am to 4.30pm from October to May and from 10.00am to 7.00pm from June to September). Closed on Saturdays and Jewish holidays. Guided visits to the Synagogues in English start every hour from the Jewish Museum. Sandwiches and drinks are available.

Restaurants

Meat

Gam-Gam
Cannaregio 1122
Old Jewish Ghetto   (041) 715-284
Supervision: Rabbi G. Garelick - Lubavitch, R. Della Rocca - Jewish Community of Venice.
Glatt Kosher. Shabbat arrangements available. Open lunch and dinner.

Synagogues
Chabad
Cannaregio
Ghetto Nuovo 2915   (041) 716214

Schola Levantina
Ghetto Vecchio 1228   (041) 715-012
Shabbath services are held during winter. Friday about one hour before sunset and Saturday at 9.00am; on Saturday at 3.45pm (later in spring and summer). Tefillah Mincha and Seuda Shelishit.

Schola Spagnola
Ghetto Vecchio 1146   (041) 715-012
Shabbath services are held during summer. Friday about one hour before sunset and Saturday at 9.00am; on Saturday at 3.45pm (later in spring and summer). Tefillah Mincha and Seuda Shelishit.

Vercelli

Community Organisations
Community Offices
Via Oldoni 20

Synagogues
Via Foa 70

Verona

Community Organisations
Community Centre
Via Portici 3   (045) 800-7112
Fax: (045) 596627
Email: comebraica@libero.it

Italy

Synagogues
Via Portici 3

Viareggio

Contact Information
Mr Sananes, via Pacinotti 172/B   (0584) 961-025
Private office: Tirreno Tour, 26 Viale Carducci, Tel:
30777, during daytime.

Sardina

There is no Sardinian Jewish community today, but
the island is of more than passing Jewish interest.
In 19 C.E. the Emperor Tiberius exiled Jews to
Sardinia. There was a synagogue at Cagliari, the
island's capital, at least as early as 599, for in that
year a convert led a riot against it. Sardinia
eventually came under Aragonese rule, and when
the edict of expulsion of the Jews from Spain was
issued in 1492, the Jews of the island had to leave.
Since then there has been no community.

Sicily

Although there are very few Jews in Sicily today,
there is a long and varied history of Jewish
settlement on the island stretching back to at least
the sixth century and possibly – according to some
scholars – to the first or second centuries.

By the late Middle Ages, the community
numbered 40,000. In 1282, Sicily came under
Spanish rule. A century or so later, there was a
wave of massacres of Jews, and another in 1474.
These culminated in the introduction of the
Inquisition in 1479, and the expulsion of the Jews
in 1492.

During the time of Spanish colonisation, Jamaica witnessed many Conversos arriving from Portugal. After the British took over in 1655, many of these could again openly practise Judaism. Soon, other Jews, mainly Sephardim, followed from Brazil and other nearby countries. The community received full equality in 1831 (before a similar step was taken in England).

The Jews played an important role in Jamaican life, and in 1849 the House of Asembly did not meet on Yom Kippur! However, assimilation and intermarriage took their toll and in 1921 the Ashkenazi and Sephardi synagogues combined. There is now only one synagogue on the island, but there are remains of old synagogues in Kingston, Port Royal and other towns.

Community life includes WIZO, B'nai B'rith, and a school (the Hillel Academy). The community lost members after the Cuban revolution, because many feared a similar revolution in Jamaica. However, this was not the case.

GMT - 5 hours	Total Population 2,505,000
Country calling code (1)	Jewish Population 300
Emergency Telephone (Police - 119) (Fire - 110) (Ambulance - 110)	Electricity voltage 110

Kingston

Synagogues
Shaare Shalom
Duke Street & Charles Street   (876) 927-7948
Fax: (876) 978-6240
Services, Friday, 5:30 pm (all year), Shabbat, 10 am; festivals, 9 am all year round.

Japan

After Japan became open to Western ideas and Westerners in the mid-nineteenth century, a trickle of Jewish immigrants from the Russian Empire, the UK and the USA began to make their homes there. Many were escaping anti-semitism and by 1918 there were several thousand in the country.

Individual Japanese, despite being allied to Nazi Germany, did not adopt the anti-semitic attitude of the Nazis, and the Japanese consul in Kovno Lithuania even helped the Mir Yeshivah escape from occupied Europe in 1940.

The post-war American occupation of the country brought many Jewish servicemen, and the community was also augmented by Jews escaping unrest in China. In recent years, there have been some Jewish gaijin, or 'foreign workers'.

In Tokyo there is a synagogue, which provides meals on shabbat, a Sunday school, and offices for the Executive Board of the Jewish Community of Japan, which is the central body.

GMT + 9 hours	Total Population 125,162,000
Country calling code (81)	Jewish Population 2,000
Emergency Telephone (Police - 110) (Fire and Ambulance - 119)	Electricity voltage 110

Hiroshima

Tourist Sites
Holocaust Education Centre
866 Nakatsuhara, Miyuki, Fukuyama 720
(849) 558001
Fax: (849) 558001
Email: hecjpn@urban.ne.jp
Web site: www.urban.ne.jp/home/hecjpn/
Open Tuesday, Wednesday, Friday and Saturday,
10:30 am to 4:30 pm.

Kobe

Synagogues

Orthodox Sephardic

Ohel Shelomoh (Jewish Community of Kansai)
4-12-12 Kitano-cho, Chuo-ku, Port PO Box 339 651-
0191 (78) 221-7236; 231-6633
Fax: (78) 242-7254
Email: j.yohay@seifu.ac.jp

Nagasaki

Now there are no known Jews living in Nagasaki. As a centre of foreign trade in the mid 19th century it had a community. The old Jewish cemetery is located at Sakamoto Gaijin Bochi. The site of the first synagogue in Japan is Umegasaki Machi.

Okinawa

While there is no native Jewish community on Okinawa, there are normally 200-300 Jews serving with the US military on the island. Regular services are conducted by the Jewish chaplain at Camp Smedley D. Butler, and visitors are welcome.

Tokyo

Community Organisations
Beth David Synagogue
8-8 Hiroo, 3-chome, Shibuya-ku 150 (3) 3400-2559
Fax: (3) 3400-1827
Email: jccmanager@gol.com
Web site: www.jccjapan.co.jp

Embassy
Embassy of Israel
3 Niban-cho, Chiyodaku (3) 3264-0911

Restaurants
Japan Jewish Community Center
8-8 Hiroo, 3-chome, Shibuya-ku 150 (3) 3400-2559
Fax: (3) 3400-1827
Email: jcc@crisscross.com
They sell prepared foods and kosher wine, as well as serve meals on Friday evening and Shabbat. Reservation strongly recommended

Synagogues
Beth David Synagogue
8-8 Hiroo, 3-chome, Shibuya-ku 150 (3) 3400-2559
Fax: (3) 3400-1827
Services are held Friday evening at 6:30 pm (7 pm during summer); Shabbat morning, 9:30 am; and on Holy-days and festivals. Advance notification requested. Mikvah on premises.

Kenya

Kazakhstan

Essentially this community began when the Soviets rescued several thousand Jews at the time of the Nazi invasion of the Soviet Union in 1941. Others joined after the war. The community is mainly based in Almaty, the former capital, and also in Chimkent. Some 2,000 Bukharan and Tat Jews also live in the country.

The central organisation is the Mitzvah Association, which heads various Jewish groups. It even has a chair on the All-Peoples Assembly of Kazakhstan. There is a high rate of emigration to Israel. There are synagogues in Almaty and Chimkent.

GMT + 6 hours
Country calling code (7)
Emergency Telephone (Police, Fire and Ambulance - 03)

Total Population 17,155,000
Jewish Population 15,000
Electricity voltage 220

Almaty

Community Centre
e 206 (raimbeka) Tashkentskaya Street 480061
(3272) 439-358
Fax: (3272) 507-770
Email: synagogues@chabad.kz
Also includes a kosher butcher and store and Mikva.

Synagogues
e206 (raimbeka) Tashkentskaya Street 480061
(3272) 439-358
Fax: (3272) 507-770
Email: synagogues@chabad.kz

Astana

Synagogues
Prospect Republic 11 apt. 3   (3172) 286-923
Email: astanasynagogues@chabad.kz

Chimkent

Synagogues

Sephardi

Svobody Street, 47th Lane

Kenya

Kenya could have been the site of the first Jewish state for two thousand years as this offer was made to the Zionists in 1903. It was, however, rejected in 1905. There were some Jews living in Kenya at that time, and a synagogue was built in 1912. Many more Jews came here after the war as Holocaust survivors, and recently some Israelis have worked on a short-term basis in the country. Kenya was an ally to Israel in its rescue of the Jews from Entebbe in Uganda. Jews have contributed much to the hotel industry and professional life of the country.

Regular services are held every Saturday in the Nairobi Hebrew Congregation, and there is a Community Centre next to the synagogue. The centre, the Vermont Memorial Hall offers educational and social events.

GMT + 3 hours
Country calling code (254)
Emergency Telephone (Police, Fire and Ambulance 999)

Total Population 29,137,000
Jewish Population 400
Electricity voltage 220/240

Nairobi

Community Organisations
Community Centre
Vermont Memorial Hall
Open Mon., Tues., Fri 9am to 1pm; Wed 2.30pm to 5.30pm; Services Friday evening at 6.30pm; Sat

morning at 8am. All Festivals. Kosher chickens available.

Synagogues
Nairobi Hebrew Congregation
cnr. University Way & Uhuru Highway, PO Box 40990
(2) 222770, 219703

Krgyzstan

This central Asian ex-Soviet republic has only a short history of Jewish settlement. The community originated from migrants after the Russian Revolution and evacuees from the German advance into the Soviet Union in the Second World War. As a result, community members are almost all Russian speakers and are assimilated into the Russian minority of the country.

Before the collapse of the Soviet Union, there was no organised community. Following 1991, there is a synagogue in Bishkek (the capital), where there is also a Jewish library and an Aish HaTorah centre. The main umbrella group is the Menorah Society of Jewish Culture.

GMT + 5 hours	Total Population 4,512000
Country calling code (996)	Jewish Population 4,500
Emergency Telephone (Police, Fire and Ambulance - 03)	

Bishkek

Synagogues
193 Karpinsky Street

The Jews in the medieval principalities of Courland and Livonia represent the earliest Jewish settlement in Latvia. Tombstones from the fourteenth century have been found. After the Russian take-over, Jews were only allowed to live in the area if they were considered 'useful', or had lived there before the Russians took control, because the area was outside the 'Pale of Settlement' that the Russian Empire had designated for the Jews.

The Jews contributed much to Latvia's development, but this was never recognised by the government, which tried to restrict their influence in business matters. Religious Jewish life was also strong. When the Nazis invaded Latvia, 90 per cent of the 85,000 Jews were systematically murdered by them and their Latvian collaborators.

The bulk of today's community originates from immigration into Latvia after the war, although 3,000 Holocaust survivors did return to Latvia. Before the collapse of communism, there was much Jewish dissident activity. There is a Jewish school and a Jewish hospital. There are some Holocaust memorial sites, in Riga (the capital), and also in the Bierkernieki Forest, where 46,000 Holocaust victims were shot.

GMT + 2 hours	Total Population 2,490,000
Country calling code (371)	Jewish Population 15,000
Emergency Telephone (Police - 02) (Fire - 01) (Ambulance - 03)	Electricity voltage 220

Daugavpils

Community Organisations
Jewish Community
Saules Street 47

Fax: (54) 8254-24658

Synagogues
Suvorov Street
Gogol Street

Liepaja

Community Organisations
Jewish Community
Kungu Street 21   (34) 25336

Rezhitsa

Synagogues
Kaleru Street

Riga

Cultural Organisations
Latvian Society for Jewish culture
Skolas 6 LV1322   (2) 289-580
Fax: (2) 821-494

Embassy
Embassy of Israel
Elizabetes Street 2 LV1340

Synagogues
6/8 Peitavas Street, L.V. 1050   721-0827
Fax: 722-1793
Hot kosher meals may be ordered in advance. Also has a Mikveh.

Lithuania

The history of Lithuania Jewry is as old as the state of Lithuania itself. There were Jews in the country in the fourteenth century, when Grand Duke Gedeyminus founded the state. The community eventually grew, and produced many famous yeshivas and great commentators, such as the Vilna Gaon. The community began to emigrate (particularly to South Africa) at the beginning of the nineteenth century; even so in 1941 there were still 160,000 Jews in the country. Ninety-five per cent of these were murdered in the Holocaust, by the local population as well as the Nazis.

The remaining post-war community included some who had hidden or had managed to survive by other means and some Jews from other parts of the Soviet Union. Interestingly, the Lithuanian Soviet Socialist Republic was more tolerant of Jewish activity than some of the neighbouring republics, such as Latvia. Now that Lithuania is independent, Jewish life is free once again.

The Lubavitch movement is present, and there are synagogues in Vilnius (known to many as Vilna), the capital, and Kaunas. There is also a school and it is possible to study Yiddish. There are tours available to show the old Jewish life in Lithuania. The grave of the Vilna Gaon can be visited, as well as Paneriai, otherwise known as Ponary, where thousands of Jews were shot during the Holocaust.

GMT + 2 hours	Total Population 3,707,000
Country calling code (370)	Jewish Population 6,000
Emergency Telephone (Police - 02) (Fire - 01) (Ambulance - 03)	Electricity voltage 220

Druskininkai

Community Organisations
Jewish Community
9/15 Sporto Street   () 54590

Kaunas

Community Organisations
Jewish Community
26 B Gedimino Street   (7) 203717
Fax: (7) 7201135
Hours of opening: Sunday to Thursday 3-6pm

Synagogues
11 Ozheshkienes Street

Klaipeda

Community Organisations
Jewish Community
3 Ziedu Skersqatvis   (6) 93758

Panevezys

Community Organisations
Jewish Community
6/22 Sodu Street 5300   (54) 68848

Shiauliai

Community Organisations
Jewish Community
24 Vyshinskio   (1) 26795

Lithuania

Vilnius

Otherwise known as Vilna, this town used to be known as the 'Jerusalem of Lithuania'. There was a very important Jewish community in the town before the Holocaust. The town still has the largest community of Lithuanian Jews, and there are many sites of historical interest, including the Vilna Gaon's grave and the State Jewish Museum.

Bakeries
Matzah Bakery
39 Pylimo Street   (2) 61-2523

Community Organisations
Jewish Community of Lithuania
Pylimo St. 4 2001   (2) 61-3003
                                      Fax: (2) 22-7915
                            Email: jewishcom@post.5ci.lt
                          Web site: www.litvakai.mch.mii.lt
Opening hours: Monday to Friday 10 a.m. 6.00 p.m.

Cultural Organisations
The Israel Centre of Cultures and Art in Lithuania
4 Pylimo, 2nd Floor 2001   (2) 61-1736 or 652139

Museums
The Vilna Gaon Jewish State Museum
Pylimo 4, LT 2001   (2) 62-0730
                                      Fax: (2) 22-7083
                            Email: jmuseum@puni.osf.lt
Holocaust exhibition and Museum administration, Pamenkalnio 12, The Tarbut School, Exhibitions and seat of Jewish Community. Opening hoursL Monday to Thursday 9 am to 5 pm and Friday 9 am to 4 pm.

Synagogues
Main Synagogue (Choral Synagogue)
39 Pylimo Street   (2) 61-2523

Luxembourg

The small community in Luxembourg faced massacres and expulsions during medieval times and Jews only began to resettle here several hundred years later. Napoleon heralded the rebirth of the community when he annexed Luxembourg, and by 1823 a synagogue had been built, but the community remained small, although in 1899, another synagogue was built.

Later many refugees from the Nazis arrived in the country, bringing the number of Jews to nearly 4,000. After the Nazi take-over, 750 Luxembourg Jews were killed, but many others were saved by the local population.

The present community is generally prosperous and assimilated. The Consistoire Israelite, established by Napoleon, is recognised by the government as the representative of the community, and is also financed by the government. The orthodox synagogue is situated fairly centrally in Luxembourg City.

GMT + 1 hour	Total Population 415,000
Country calling code (352)	Jewish Population 600
Emergency Telephone (Police - 113) (Fire and Ambulance - 112)	Electricity voltage 220

Esch-Sur-Alzette

Synagogues
52 rue de Canal
Minyan services held on Friday evenings.

Luxembourg City

Communal Organisation
Consistoire Israelite de Luxembourg
45 Av. Monterey 2018   452914
                                      Fax: 473772

Embassy
Consul General of Israel
38 BD Napoleon 1er L-2210   446-557
                                      Fax: 453-676

Groceries
Calon
rue de Reins 3

Kashrut Information
34 rue Alphonse munchen 2172   452366

Synagogues
45 Av. Monterery   452914
                                      Fax: 250430

Malaysia

At the southern end of the former Yugoslavia, this new country has an ancient Jewish heritage dating back to Roman times. The Jews took advantage of the area's favourable commercial position, lying between Turkey and Western Europe, and the remains of a synagogue at Stobei dating back to the second and third centuries is evidence of a once-thriving Jewish community.

Iberian Jews escaping the Inquisition settled in the area, and brought with them Sephardi customs and the Ladino language (based on Spanish). The fate of the 8,000 Macedonian Jews under Bulgarian occupation during the Second World War is in stark contrast to the fate of the Bulgarian Jews - the Macedonian Jews were deported to their deaths, yet the Bulgarian Jews were saved by the defiance of the king and the people. Only ten per cent of the Macedonian community survived, of whom many have emigrated to Israel.

Today's community is mainly based in the capital Skopje, but there are no synagogues and there is little access to Jewish life. However, the community does have contact with Jews in Serbia and Greece.

GMT + 1 hour	Total Population 1,968,000
Country calling code (389)	Jewish Population 100
Emergency Telephone (Police - 92) (Fire - 93) (Ambulance - 94)	Electricity voltage 220

Skopje

Community Organisations
Community Offices
Borka Talevski Street 24   (91) 237-543

Malaysia

Malaysia is a Muslim state, and the Jewish population is tiny, barely into double figures. There is, however, a Jewish cemetery on the island of Penang, in Georgetown in Jalan Yahudi (Jewish Street). The cemetery is looked after by Selvaraj Sundram a Hindu. Decades ago the then vibrant Jewish community hired his great grand father to look after the site. His family has done so since; funds now being provided by an anonymous German. The Jews who today live on Penang originate from refugees from Russia. There was a synagogue, but it is now closed.

GMT + 8 hour	Total Population 10,359,000
Country calling code (60)	Jewish Population under100
Emergency Telephone (Police , Fire, Ambulance 999)	Electricity voltage 220

Malta

Malta

There is evidence of an ancient Jewish community on Malta, as archaeologists have discovered remains from 2,000 years ago. Malta fell into Arab hands in the early Middle Ages, when there were still a few Jews on the island. The island then changed to Sicilian hands and, in 1492, the Jews were expelled.

Between the sixteenth and eighteenth centuries, the island was used as a prison for Jewish captives of the Knights of St. John. They were held for ransom, but managed to find time to build a synagogue. The synagogue in Spur Street Valetta, opened in 1912, was demolished in 1995 as part of a redevelopment scheme.

GMT + 1 hour	Total Population 373,000
Country calling code (356)	Jewish Population under 100
Emergency Telephone (Police 191, Ambulance 196, Fire 199)	Electricity voltage 240

Birkirkara

Communal Organisation
P O Box 4   445924

Conversos were the first Jews in the country, and some achieved high positions in early Spanish colonial Mexico. As the Inquisition was still functioning here some 200 years after the sixteenth century, the number of Jewish immigrants was small. When Mexico became independent of Spain, Jews gradually began to enter the country, coming from German and other European communities.

It was during the twentieth century that most Jewish immigrants entered Mexico. There were both Ashkenazis and Sephardis, and they settled throughout the country. The communities grew on a parallel level, rather than together, with two languages, Yiddish and Ladino.

The current community is largely middle class and all the various groups come under the Comite Central Israelita. There are numerous synagogues and there are also kosher restaurants. The community is well equipped with Jewish schools and yeshivas.

GMT - 6 to 8 hours	Total Population 92,720,000
Country calling code (52)	Jewish Population 50,000
Emergency Telephone (Police, Fire and Ambulance 080)	Electricity voltage 110

Acapulco

Hotels
The Hyatt Regency
Costera Miguel Aleman 1 39869   (74) 69-1234
                                       Fax: (74) 84-3087
                              Email: hyatta@netmex.com
The hotel has a synagogue and a mikve.

Restaurants
The Hyatt Regency
Costera Miguel Aleman 1 39869   (74) 69-1234
                                       Fax: (74) 84-3087
                              Email: hyatta@netmex.com
Open only during the high season (generally Nov/Dec to March/April).

Cuernavaca

Synagogues
Madero 404   (73) 186-846
At the home for the elderly

Guadalajara

Community Organisations
Comunidad Israelita de Guadalajara
Juan Palomar y Arias 651   (36) 416-463
     Fax: (36) 427-168
Includes kosher restaurant, mikve and two synagogues. Phone in advance.

Mexico City

In 1550 it has been said there were more crypto-Jews in Mexico City than Roman Catholics. There are now 50,000 Jews, the vast majority of Mexican Jewry. With 23 synagogues, kosher restuarants and Jewish schools, the city is well equipped with Jewish facilities. Polanco is a Jewish area in the city with some synagogues. The first synagogue, dating from 1912, is in the downtown area.

Butchers
Fuente de Templanza 17, Tecamachalco
Mehadrin.
Carniceria Sary
Santa Ana 64, Tecamachalco
Mehadrin.
Pollos Mugrabi
Platon 133, Polanco
Mehadrin.

Embassy
Embassy of Israel
Sierra Madre 215, PO Box 11000 10   (5) 201-1500
     Fax: (5) 201-1555

Groceries
Casa Amig
Horacio 1719, Col. Polanco
     (5) 540-1455
Super Teca Kosher
Acuezunco 15, San Miguel
     (5) 905-589-9823, 9860 or 3225

Media

Newspapers
CDI, Centro Deportivo, Plaza de toros of Cuatro
Caminos   (5) 557-3000
Spanish weekly.
Di Shtime, Pedro Moreno 149   (5) 546-1720
Yiddish weekly.
Foro de Vida Judia en el Mundo
Aviacion Commercial 16, Col. Polanco 15700
     (5) 571-1114

Spanish monthly.
Kesher
Leibnitz 13-10, Colonia Anzures CP 11590
     (5) 203-0446
     Fax: (5) 203-9084
     Email: info@kesher.org.mx
Spanish bi weekly. Mailing address: Ap. Postal 41-969, Lomas de Chapultepec. CP 11001
La Voz de la Kehila
Acapulco 70, 2nd Floor   (5) 211-0501
Spanish monthly.

Mikvaot
Banos Campeche 58   (5) 574-2204
Platon 413   (5) 520-9569
Av. de los Bosques 53, Tecamachalco   (5) 589-5530
Bernard Shaw 110, Polanco   (5) 203-9964
Tevila Cuernavaca
Priv. de Antinea 4, Col. Delicias
     (5) 15 08 41; 18 16 55

Museums
The Holocaust Museum
Acapulco 70, Col Condesa   (5) 211-051

Organisations
Comunidad Monte Sinai
Tennyson 134, Polanco   (5) 280-6369
     Fax: (5) 281-3969
T.O.V.
Fuente de Concordia 73, Col. Tecamachalco
     (5) 589-8756
     Fax: (5) 589-9101
     Email: isaacb@mail.internet.com.mx
     Web site: www.tovnet.com

Religious Organisations
Comite Central
     (5) 520-9393; 540-7376
Comunidad Maguen David

     Email: mdavid@ort.org.mx
Contact for any religious questions.
Jerusalem de Mexico
Anatore France 359, Local C, Polanco   (5) 531-2269

Restaurants

Meat

Aladinos
Ingenieros Militares 255   (5) 395-2959
     Fax: (5) 395-9219
Hilarios
Cofre de Perote 244-B   (5) 540-0453
Jewish Sport Center
Manuel Avila Camacho   (5) 557-3000
Supervision: Rab. David E. Tabachnik.

Mexico

Restaurant Pini
Ejercito Nacional 458d
Supervision: Maguen David.

Sinai
Izazaga (between 5 de febrero and 20 de noviembre,
Near Pino Suarez   (5) 709-4906
Supervision: Maguen David.

Synagogues
Agudas Achim
Montes de Oca 32, Condesa 06140   (5) 553-6430
Bet Midrash Tecamachalco
Fuente de Marcela 23, Col. Tecamachalco
     (5) 251-8454
Beth Moshe
Tennyson No 134, Col. Polanco 11560
     (5) 280-6369 ;6375
     Fax: (5) 281-3969
     Email: monsinai@ort.org.mx
Beth Yehoshua
Fuente de San Sulpicio No. 16, Col. Tecamachalco
53950   (5) 294-8617
Bircas Shumel
Plinio 311, Polanco   (5) 280-2769
Cuernavaca
Prolongacion Antinea Lote 2, Delicias
Eliahu Elfasi
Fuente de Templanza 13, Col. Tecamachalco
     (5) 294-9388
Shabbat services only.
Jajam Elfasi, Fuente Del Pescador 168, Col.
Tecamachalco
Shabbat services only.
Kolel Aram Zoba
Sofocles 346, Col. Polanco   (5) 280-2669; 4886;
Kolel Maor Abraham
Lafontaine 344, Col. Polanco   (5) 545-2482
Midrash Latorah
Cerrada de Los Morales 8, Col. Polanco 11510
     (5) 280-0875; 280-3526
     Fax: (5) 280-5978
Rabbi Asher Zrihen, formerly of London, will be happy
to welcome and assist visitors.
Nidche Israel
Acapulco 70, Condesa   (5) 211-0575
Or Damesek, Seneca 343   (5) 280-6281
Ramat Shalom
Fuente del Pescador 35, Tecamachalco
     (5) 251-3854
Shaare Shalom
Av. de Los Bosques 53, Tecamachalco   (5) 251-0973
Shuba Israel
Edgar Alan Poe 43, Col. Polanco
     (5) 545-8061 & 280-1036

Conservative
Bet El
Horacio 1722, Polanco los Morales
     (5) 281-2592
     Fax: (5) 281-2467
     Email: comunidad.betel@bigfoot.com
Beth Israel
Virreyes 1140, Lomas   (5) 520-8515
English speaking.

Orthodox
Beth Itzhak, Eujenio Sue 20, Polence

Sephardi
Maguen David
Bernard Shaw 110, Polanco
     (5) 203-9964
Sephardi Synagogue
Monterey 359   (5) 564-1197;1367

Monterrey
Community Organisations
Centro Israelita de Monterrey
Canada 207, Nuevo León   (83) 461-128
Includes a Synagogue and Mikva.

Tijuana
Contact Information
JCC Chabad House
Centro Social Israelita de Baja California
Av. 16 Septiembre, Baja California 3000
     (66) 862-692; 862-693
     Fax: (66) 341-532
     Email: chabadtj@telnor.net
Synagogue and Mikva on premises.

Synagogues
Tijuanua Hebrew Congregation
Amado Nervo 207
Baja California

Monaco

Moldova

Moldova used to be a Soviet Republic bordering Romania to the west and the Ukraine to the east. When the Jews first entered what is now Moldova, the area was known as Bessarabia, and was on an important trade route between Turkey and Poland. By the time of Russian rule in 1812, there was a permanent Jewish community. The Russians included the area in the 'Pale of Settlement', which held the majority of the Jews of their empire. By the end of the nineteenth century, there were over 200,000 Jews in the region. However, the twentieth century started with the infamous progrom in the capital Kishinev (Chisinev), where 49 Jews were killed and much damage was done to Jewish property. Emigration began to increase. The area fell under Romanian control between 1918 and 1940, but the community continued to lead a normal life until the Second World War, when many thousands of the pre-war community of over 250,000 were killed during the German occupation.

After the war, some survivors continued to live in Moldova, and Jews from other parts of the Soviet Union joined them. There is an umbrella society for Moldovan Jews, and there are synagogues and schools. The Lubavitch movement is active in building up religious life.

GMT + 2 hours
Country calling code (373)
Electricity voltage 220

Total Population 4,450,000
Jewish Population 30,000

Chisinau

Most of Moldova's Jews live in Chisinau (some 15,000 people). This city was the scene for two notorious progroms in 1903 and 1905.

Religious Organisations
Yeshiva of Chisinau
Sciusev 5 277001
(2) 274-362
Fax: (2) 274-331
Email: agudath@yeshiva.mldnet.com
Aside from Jewish studies, a mikva and kosher food can be found on premises.

Synagogues
Yakimovsky per. 8 277000
(2) 221-215

Teleneshty

Synagogues
4 28th June Street

Tiraspol

Contact Information
336-495
Fax: 322-208
Details of the Jewish Community from Dr Vaisman.

Monaco

Some French Jews lived in Monaco before 1939, and the government issued them with false papers during the war, thus saving them from the Nazis. This tiny country has also attracted retired people from France, North Africa and the UK.

There is an official Jewish body, the Association Culturelle Israelite de Monaco, and there is a synagogue, a school and a kosher food shop. Half of the total Jewish population are Ashkenazi and the other half are Sephardi, and 60 per cent of the community is retired.

GMT + 1 hour
Country calling code (377)
Emergency Telephone (Police - 17) Fire and Ambulance - 18)

Total Population 30,500
Jewish Population 1,000
Electricity voltage 220

Monaco

Monte Carlo

Communal Organisation
Association Culturelle Israelite de Monaco
15 Av. de la Costa   9330-1646

Synagogues
15 Av. de la Costa, opp. Balmoral Hotel MC 98000
                                             9330-1646
Services, Friday even. at 6.30pm and Sat. morning at
8.45am and Sat. afternoon at 5.30pm

Morocco

There were Jews in Morocco before it became a Roman province. Since the first century, the Jewish population settled in Morocco has increased steadily owing to several waves of immigration from Spain and Portugal following the expulsion of Jews by the Inquisition in 1492.

Under Moslem rule, the Jews experienced climate of tolerance although they have suffered some persecution. During the Vichy period during the Second World War, Sultan Mohammed V protected the community. Almost 250,000 Jews have emigrated to Israel, Canada, France, Spain and Latin America, but they maintain strong links with the Kingdom.

Since ancient times, the Jewish community has succeeded in cohabiting harmoniously with the Berber and then with the Arab community. Today the present Jewish population is a living community, playing a significant role in Moroccan society – although they have declined in number.

GMT + 0 hours
Country calling code (212)
Emergency Telephone (Police and Ambulance - 19) (Fire - 15)

Total Population 26,736,000
Jewish Population 7,000
Electricity voltage 110/170

Agadir

Mikvaot
Av. Moulay Abdallah, cnr. rue de la Foire   (8) 842339

Organisations
Community Offices
Imm. Arsalane Av. Hassan II   (8) 840091
                                  Fax: (8) 822268

Synagogues
Av. Moulay Abdallah, cnr. rue de la Foire   (8) 842339

Casablanca

Mikvaot
32 rue Officier de Paix Thomas   (2) 276688

Organisations
Community Offices
rue Abbou Abdallah al Mahassibi
                          (2) 270976 & 222861
                                  Fax: (2) 266953

Restaurants
Americano
7 Place d'Aknoul
Aux Bon Delices
261 Blvd. Ziraoui, opp. Lycee Lyautey

Synagogues
Benisty
13 rue Ferhat Achad
Bennaroche
24 rue Lusitania
Em Habanim
14 rue Lusitania
Hazan
rue Roger Farache
Ne'im Zemiroth
29 rue Jean-Jacques Rousseau
Temple Beth El
61 rue Jaber ben Hayane

El Jadida

Organisations
Community Offices
PO Box 59

Essaouira (formerly Mogador)

Organisations
Community Offices
2 rue Ziri Ben Atyah

Synagogues
2 rue Ziri Ben Atyah

Fez

Hotels
La Boutique, rue de Beyrouth
Mrs Mamane will be pleased to assist all Jewish visitors.

Mikvaot
Talmud Torah
rue Dominique Bouchery

Organisations
Community Offices
rue Dominique Bouchery

Restaurants
Meat

Centre Maimonide
24 rue Zerktouni, (adjacent to Hotel Splendide)
(5) 620-593
Fax: (5) 659-412
Supervision: Local Rabbanut.

Synagogues
Beth El
rue de Beyrouth
Sadoun
ruelle 1, blvd. Mohammed V.
Talmud Torah
rue Dominique Bouchery

Kenitra

Mikvaot
58 rue Sallah Eddine

Organisations
Community Offices
58 rue Sallah Eddine

Synagogues
rue de Lyon

Marrakech

Mikvaot
Boulevard Zerktouni (Gueliz)
(4) 448-754
Fax: (4) 438-676

Contact: Mme Kadoch

Organisations
Community Offices
PO Box 515
(4) 448754

Restaurants
El Borj
(4) 43 16 46

Le Sepharade, 31 Lotissement Hassania, Gueliz
(4) 43 98 09

Synagogues
Beth-el
Boulevard Zerktouni (Gueliz)
(4) 448-754
Fax: (4) 438-676
Bittoun
Medina, Rue Arset Laamach, Touareg
In course of renovation.
Rabbi Pinhas Ha Cohen
Medina Rue Arset, Laamach
(4) 389-798
Salat Laazama
Rue Talmud Torah, Mellah, Hay Essalam (4) 403-798

Meknes

Mikvaot
5 rue de Ghana
(5) 21968 or 22549
Tourists will be assisted if telephoning 24 hours in advance of their requests.

Synagogues
5 rue de Ghana
(5) 21968 or 22549

Oujda

Organisations
Community Offices
Texaco Maroc, 36 Blvd. Hassan Loukili

Rabat

Mikvaot
3 rue Moulay Ismail

Organisations
Community Offices
1 rue Boussouni

Restaurants
Cercle de l'Alliance
3 rue Mellila
(7) 72 76 79
The Menora
Villa 5, Rue Er Riyad
(7) 26 01 03

Synagogues
3 rue Moulay Ismail

Safi

Synagogues
Beth El, rue de R'bat
Mursiand
rue de R'bat

Tangier

Hotels
El Minzah (140)
85 rue de la Liberte
(9) 935-885
Fax: (9) 934-546

La Grande Villa de France
rue de Belgique

Morocco

Les Almohade (150)
Av. des F. A. R.
Rambrant, Av. Pasteur   (9) 378-7071
Rif, Av. d'Espagne

Mikvaot
Shaar Raphael
27 Blvd. Pasteur   (9) 231304

Organisations
Community Centre
1 rue de la Liberte   (9) 31633 or 21024

Synagogues
Shaar Raphael
27 Blvd. Pasteur   (9) 231304
Temple Nahon
rue Moses Nahon

Tourist Sites
rue des Synagogues, off rue Siaghines
There are a number of synagogues in the old part of
the town in this street.

Tetuan

Organisations
Community Offices
16 rue Moulay Abbas

Synagogues
Benoualid
The old Mellah
Pintada
The old Mellah
Yagdil Torah
Adj. Community Centre

Mozambique

The small community in Mozambique originally consisted of South African Jews who were forced out of South Africa by President Kruger for supporting the British at the beginning of the twentieth century. The synagogue was opened in 1926, and there is a cemetery in Alto Maha. The biggest Jewish community is in Maputo.

GMT + 2 hours	Total Population 17,878,000
Country calling code (258)	Jewish Population Under 100
Emergency Telephone (Police - 119) (Fire - 198) (Ambulance - 117)	Electricity voltage 220

Maputo

Organisations
Jewish Community of Mozambique

Av. Tomas Nduda 235, PO Box 235   (1) 494413
Email: xero_servicos@mail.garp.co.mz

Myanmar (formerly Burma)

The first Jews came to Myanmar in the early eighteenth century from Iraq and other Middle Eastern countries. A synagogue was built in 1896, and the Jewish population swelled to 2,000 before 1939, but most of these fled to Britain and India before the Japanese invasion in the Second World War. In the first years of the twentieth century Rangoon and Bassein both had Jewish mayors. Not many returned after the war (only a few hundred), and the community began to decline through intermarriage and conversion. The handful of remaining Jews are elderly and services are held only on the High Holy Days when a minyan is made up with help from the Israeli embassy.

There is also a tribe of Jews in the north of the country (the Karens), who have their own prayer houses and who believe that they are descended from the tribe of Menashe.

GMT + 6.5 hours	Total Population 45,922,000
Country calling code (95)	Jewish Population Under 100
Emergency Telephone In Yangon only (Police - 199) (Fire - 191) (Ambulance - 192)	
Electricity voltage 220/230	

Yangon (formerly Rangoon)

Embassy
Embassy of Israel
49 Pyay Road   (1) 222-290; 222-709; 222-201
                      Fax: (1) 222-463
Email: emisrael@datserco.com.mm

Synagogues
Musmeah Yeshua
85 26th Street   (1) 75062

Namibia

Namibian Jewry began at the time when the country was a German colony, before the First World War. The cemetery at Swakopmund dates from that settlement. Keetmanschoop also had a congregation, but this no longer exists. The Windhoek synagogue is still in use, and was founded in 1924. Services are held on shabbat and festivals.

South Africa provides some help for the community, such as a cantor on festivals, and the Cape Board of Jewish Education assists with Hebrew education. From approximately 100 Jewish families in the 1920s and 1930s, the number has dwindled.

GMT + 2 hours
Total Population 1,709,000

Country calling code (264)
Jewish Population Under 100

Emergency Telephone (Police - 1011) (Fire - 2032270) (Ambulance - 2032276)

Electricity voltage 220/240

Windhoek

Synagogues
Cnr. Tal & Post Streets, PO Box 563

Nepal

Nepal has no Jewish history. It is however well visited by Israeli and other young Jewish tourists. Each year a large seder is organised by the Lubavitch movement. In 2000 approximately 1,000 attended at the Radisson Hotel

GMT + 5.45 hours
Total Population 20,892,000

Country calling code (977)
Jewish Population Under 100

Kathmandu

Embassy
Embassy of Israel   (1) 411 811
Bishramalaya House   Fax (1) 413 920
Lazimpat St   Email kathmandu@israel.org
G.P.O. Box 371

Netherlands

Netherlands

Although some historians believe that the first Jews in Holland lived there during Roman times, documentary evidence goes back only to the twelfth century. The contemporary settlement occurred when Portuguese Marranos found refuge from the Inquisition in Holland. Religious freedom was advocated in the early seventeenth century and Jews contributed much to the Netherlands' 'golden age' of prosperity and power.

By the time of Napoleon, the community had grown to 10,000 (the largest in western Europe), mainly by incoming Jewish traders from eastern Europe. The Jews were emancipated in 1796, but the community began to decline slowly during the nineteenth century. Of the 140,000 Jews (including 30,000 German Jewish refugees) in Holland in 1939, the Germans transported 100,000 to various death camps in Poland, but the local Dutch population tended to behave sympathetically towards their Jewish neighbours, hiding many. Anne Frank and her family are the most famous of the hidden Jews from Holland. Amsterdam witnessed a strike in February 1941, called as a protest against the Jewish deportations.

Today, there are three Jewish councils in the Netherlands, representing the Ashkenazi, Reform and Orthodox communities. There are many synagogues in Amsterdam, as well as synagogues in other towns. There are kosher restaurants in Amsterdam, which also has many historical sites – Anne Frank House, the Portuguese Synagogue, still lit by candlelight, and the Resistance Museum

GMT + 1 hour	Total Population 15,575,000
Country calling code (31)	Jewish Population 30,000
Emergency Telephone (Police, Fire and Ambulance - 112)	Electricity voltage 220

Amersfoort

Synagogues
Drieringensteeg 2   (33) 720943

Amsterdam

The first Jews were said to have come to the city in 1598. It soon became the centre of the Marrano diaspora. The Jewish Historical Museum and the Anne Frank house are essential visits. The Rijksmuseum contains a number of paintings of Jewish interest including 'The Jewish Bride' by Rembrandt.

Bakeries
Maasstraat 16   (20) 662-4827
Gouden Graan
Olympiaplein 148   (20) 664-3667
Supervision: Amsterdam Jewish Community.
Theeboom
Bolestein 45-47   (20) 642-7003
Supervision: Amsterdam Jewish Community.
Hours: Sunday - Friday 9.00 - 1700, closed on Tuesday. Trams: 12, 25.

Booksellers
Joachimsthal's Boekhandel
Van Leijenberghlaan 116 1082 DB   (20) 442-0762
Fax: (20) 404-1843
Email: jachims@xsyall.nl
Open Sunday to Thursday 9.30 am. to 6 pm. Friday 9.30 am. to 5 pm.
Livraria Montezinos & Ets Haim Library
Mr. Visserplein 3
Open for research only Mon.-Thurs. 9am to 12.30pm
Samech Books
Gunterstein 69   (20) 642-1424
Fax: (20) 642-1424
Email: samech@dds.nl.

Butchers
Marcus, Rituel
Scheldestr. 63   (20) 664-0036
Supervision: Amsterdam Jewish Community.
Marcus, Rituel
Ferd. Bolstraat.44   (20) 671-9881
Fax: (20) 642-6532
Supervision: Amsterdam Jewish Community.

Chocolate Shops

Chocolate shop Bonbon Jeannette
Hall Central Station Amsterdam, Stationsplein 15 1012
AB   (20) 421-5194
                                      Fax: (20) 421-5194
Their bitter and dairy chocolates and bonbons are
kosher and are sanctioned by the Chief Rabbinate for
the Netherlands. Open daily, 8 am to 9 pm.

Chocolate shop Bonbon Jeannette
Europaplein 87 1078 GZ   (20) 664-9638
                                      Fax: (20) 675-6543
Their bitter and dairy chocolates and bonbons are
kosher and are sanctioned by the Chief Rabbinate for
the Netherlands. Hours: Monday to Friday, 9 am to 6
pm; Sunday, 9 am to 5 pm; closed Mondays in July
and August. Nearest means of public transport: tram 4
and buses 15, 71, 220 and 315.

Delicatessens

Mouwes Koshere Delicatessan
Kastelenstraat 261 1082   (20) 661-0180

Hotels

Golden Tulip Amsterdam Centre
Stadhouderskade 7 1054 ES   (20) 685-1351
                                      Fax: (20) 685-1611
                      Email: info@gtacentre.goldentulip.nl

Hotel Doria
Damstraat 3 1012   (20) 638-8826
                                      Fax: (20) 638-8726
                              Email: doria@euronet.nl
Kosher breakfast

Hotel la Richelle
Holbeinstr 41   (20) 671-7971
                                      Fax: (20) 671-0541
Kosher breakfast on request

Libraries

Bibliothecha Rosenthaliana
Singel 423
A fine collection of Judaica and Hebraicai is in the
university library.

Media

Newspapers

Nieuw Israelietisch Weekblad
Rapenburgerstr. 109 1011 VL   (20) 627-6275
                                      Fax: (20) 624-2519
                              Email: niw@xs4all.nl
                        Web site: www.xs4all.nl/~niw

Mikvaot

Mr. Visserplein 3   (20) 625-6222
Heinzestr. 3   (20) 662-0178/671-9393

Museums

Anne Frank House
Prinsengracht 263   (20) 556-7100
                                      Fax: (20) 620-7999
                        Web site: www.annefrank.nl
The original hiding place of Anne Frank, where she
wrote her diary. Open daily from 9am to 7pm (April
1st to September 1st daily from 9am to 9pm. January
1st and December 25th 12 noon to 5pm). Last entry 30
minutes before closing time.

Jewish Historical Museum
Jonas Daniël Meÿerplein 2-4 1011 RH
                                            (20) 626-9945
                                      Fax: (20) 624-1721
                              Email: info@jhm.nl
                              Web site: www.jhm.nl
Housed in a complex of 4 former synagogues.
Sandwich shop serving kosher food.. Open daily from
11am to 5pm. Group visits by arrangement.

Netherlands

The Resistance Museum
Plantage Kerklaan 61   (20) 620-2535
       Fax: (20) 620-2960
       Email: info@verzetsmuseum.org
       Web site: www.verzetsmuseum.org
Open all year except Mondays, January 1st, April 30th
and December 25th. Permanent Exhibition: From 10
May 1940 to 5 May 1945, the Netherlands were
occupied by Nazi Germany. Almost every Dutch
person was affected by the consequences of the
occupation.

Religious Organisations
Ashkenazi Community Offices/Community Center
van der Boechorststr. 26, PO Box 7967 1008 AD
       (020) 646-0046
       Fax: (020) 646-4357
       Email: info@nihs.nl
       Web site: www.nihs.nl

Restaurants
Mrs B. Hertzberger
Plantage Westermanlaan 9 1018 DK
       (20) 623-4684
5 minutes from Portuguese Synagogue. Friday night
and Shabbat meals only. Reservation in advance. Also
lunchboxes for groups.
Museum Café
Jewish Historical Museum, Jonas Daniel Meijerplein 2-4
       (20) 626-9945
       Fax: (20) 624-1721
Hours 11am to 5pm daily
Nasj Viel Restaurant
Jewish Youth Center, De Lairessestraat 13, (near
Concertgebouw) 1071   (20) 676-7622
       Fax: (20) 673-5215
       Email: info@nasjviel.nl
Supervision: Amsterdam Rabbinate.
Open: Sunday - Thursday 6.00pm - 10.00pm. (kitchen
closes at 9.00pm) Groups can be accommodated -
reserve in advance.
Sandwichshop Sal. Meijer
Scheldestraat 45 1078 GG   (20) 673-1313
       Fax: (20) 642-9020
Supervision: Amsterdam Jewish Community.

Kosher

Meat
Jerusalem of Gold
Jodenbreestraat 148 1011 NS   (020) 6250923
       Fax: (020) 6415854
       Web site: www.jerusalemofgold.homepage.com
Supervision: Amsterdam Jewish Community.
Hours: noon to 10pm daily

Nasj view, Carmel
Amstelveensewag 224 1075 XT   (20) 675-7636
Supervision: Amsterdam Jewish Community.
Hours: 12 pm to 11:30 pm, Sunday to Thursday. Cater
Shabbat meals for groups if ordered in advance.
Transport: trams 6, 16, bus 15, 63, 170, 171, 172.
Shabbes - Tisch
Brendele Hertzberger, Plantage Westermanlaan 9 1018 DK
       (20) 623-4684
Supervision: Rabbinate of The Netherlands.
5 minutes from Portuguese Synagogue. Friday night
and Shabbath only. Reservations in advance

Vegetarian
Bolhoed, Prinsengacht 60-62   (20) 626-1803
Hours: 12 pm to 10 pm daily. Serve organic vegetarian
and vegan food.

Snack Bars
Vlaams Friteshuis (Vleminckx)
Voetboog Str.33, (alleyway off Spui)
       (020) 624-6075
This vendor sells only fries (chips), cooked in vegetable
oil. A variety of sauces are available. The chips are
served in a paper cone.

Synagogues
Buitenveldert
van der Boechorststr. 26, PO Box 7967 1008 AD
       (20) 646-0046
Contact hours daily 9am to 5pm.
Kehilas Ja'Akow (E. Europe)
Lekstr. 61
Kehilas Ja'Akow (E. Europe)
Gerrit van der Veenstraat 26 1077 ED
       (20) 676-3602
Nidche Jisroel Jechanes
Nieuwe Kerkstr 149   (20) 676-6400
       Fax: (20) 672-2973
Shabbat service at 9.30 hours.
The Portuguese Synagogue
Mr. Visserplein 3   (20) 624-5351
       Fax: (20) 625-4680
This synagogue has been completely restored and is
open from Sunday - Friday from 10 am to 4 pm.

Ashkenazi
Ashkenazi Rabbinate of Amsterdam
van der Boechorststr. 26, PO Box 7967
       (20) 646-0046
       Fax: (20) 646-4357
       Email: rabbinaat@nihs.nl
Contact hours Monday and 2 to 6 pm.

Netherlands

Beth Shalom Home for Aged
Kastelenstraat 80, Amsterdam 1083   (20) 661-1516
Fax: (20) 661-2517
Monday, Thursday, Rosh Chodesh, Chol Hamo'eed,
Chanuka and Purim morning; Shabbat and Yomtov
evening, morning, afternoon and evening. Open to the
general public, meals can be arranged.
General Hospital Amstelveen (C.I.Z.)
Laan van de Helende Meesters 8, Amstelveen
(20) 347-4747
Fax: (20) 347-4917
Email: role@zha.nl.
The synagogue is a part of the 'Jewish Wing' of the
General Hospital. Services: Saturday and Festival
mornings. Open to the general public.

Liberal

Jacob Soetendorpstr. 8 1079   (20) 642-3562
Fax: (20) 442-0337
Email: ljgadam@xs4all.nl
Web site: www.xs4all.nl/~ljg

Houses the Judith Druk Library and the Centre for
Jewish Studies.

Orthodox
Gerard Dou Synagogue
Gerard Doustr. 238   (20) 675-0932
Fax: (20) 867-1626
Email: gd_sjoel@joods.nl
Web site: www.joods.nl/gd_sjoel
Services: Saturday and Festival mornings
Raw Aron Schuster Sjoel
Jacob Obrechtplein
Daily services

Sephardi
Portuguese Synagogue & Community Centre
Texelstr. 82   (20) 624-5351

Tourist Sites
Portuguese Jewish Cemetery
7 Kerkstraat, Ouderkerk aan de Amstel 1191
(20) 496-3498
Fax: (20) 496-5496
Email: bethaim@wxs.nl
Established 1614. One of the oldest Sephardic
Cemeteries still in use in Europe. Menasseh ben Israel
is buried here, as are the parents of the philosopher
Spinoza. 10 kilometres south-east of Amsterdam.

Arnhem

Synagogues
Pastoorstr. 17a   (26) 442-5154

Liberal
Liberaal Joodse Gemeente Arnhem
Veluws Hof 24, Ermelo 3852 JJ   (341) 557-860
Email: elisjewa@hetnet.nl

Breda

Synagogues
School Straat

Bussum

Synagogues
Kromme Englaan 1a   (35) 691-4882

Delft

Synagogues
Beth Studentiem
Hillel House, Jewish Students Centre, Technical
University, Koornmarkt 9   (15) 212-0300

Eindhoven

Religious Organisations
Synagogue Inquiries
(40) 241-2710

Synagogues
H. Casimirstr. 23   (40) 751-1253

Enschede

Synagogues
Prinsestr. 16
(53) 432-3479; 435-3336; 435-1293; 434-4788
Fax: (53) 430-9725
Email: jmhartog@a1.nl

Liberal
Liberal Congregation Inquiries
Haaksbergen   (53) 435-1330

Groningen

Synagogues
Postbus 550 9700 AN   (50) 312-3151

Haarlem

Synagogues
Kenaupark 7   (23) 332-6899; 324-2051

Hilversum

Synagogues
Synagogue, Laanstr. 30   (35) 621-2044
Inter-Provincial Chief Rabbinate also based at this
address. Rabbi's J. S. Jacobs, S. Evers and A. L. Heintz
Tel: 035-623-9238

Leiden

Organisations
Jewish Students Centre
Levendaal 8   (71) 513-0382

Synagogues
Levendaal 14-16 2311 JL   (71) 512-5793
Fax: (71) 512-5793

Maastricht

Synagogues
Capucijnengang 2
Est. 1840

Rotterdam

Synagogues
Joodse Gemeente Rotterdam
A B N Davidsplein 2   (10) 466-9765
Fax: (10) 467-5713
Mikva on premises.

Liberal
Molenhoek Hillegersberg   (20) 644-2619
Inquiries to Secretary on 010-461-3211

The Hague

Delicatessens
Jacobs
Haverkamp 220   (70) 347-4980

Embassy
Embassy of Israel
Buitenhof 47 2513 AH

Synagogues
Corn. Houtmanstraat 11, Bezuidenhout 2593 RD
(70) 347-0222
Fax: (70) 347-9002
Email: raabinaat-haag@zonnet.nl
Mikva on premises, appointments should be made
24hrs in advance by telephoning 350-7621
Beis Jisroel
Doorniksestraat 152 2587 AZ   (70) 358-6363
Fax: (70) 347-9002

Liberal
Liberal Synagogue
Prinsessegracht 26   (70) 365-6893
Fax: (70) 360-3883

Tourist Sites
Spinoza House
Paviljoensgracht
Spinoza House is of special interest, as is the 18th c.
Portuguese Synagogue in the Prinsessegracht, which is
now used by the Liberal congregation.

Tulburg

Synagogues
Liberal Synagogue Brabant
(70) 365-6893
Inquiries to 013-467-5566

Utrecht

Bakeries
De Tarwebol, Zadelstr. 19   (30) 231-4887

Synagogues
Springweg 164 3511 VZ   (30) 231-4742
Fax: (30) 272-2091
Email: heintz@globalxs.nl

Liberal
Liberal Synagogue
(20) 644-2619
Inquiries to 030-603-9343

Zwolle

Synagogues
Samuel Hirschstr. 8, Postbox 1468 8001
(38) 211412

Netherlands Antilles

The first Jew in Aruba, then a part of Netherland Antilles, was Moses Salomo Maduro (1753).

A Samuel Cohen served as an interpreter to the Dutch army which captured Curaçao from the Spaniards in 1634. A congregation was founded in 1651. The Jews of Curaçao enjoyed excellent relations with the Dutch West India Company who owned the island until the end of the eighteenth century.

The Sephardi synagogue established in 1732 is the oldest synagogue building in continuous use in the western hemisphere. It has sand its floor covering because the synagogue is modelled on the Tabernacle used in the Sinai desert during the 40 years of wandering. It is also a reminder of the days of the Marranos when sand was used to muffle sounds.

Curaçao also has the oldest existing Jewish cemetery in the western hemisphere.

GMT - 4 hours	Total Population 207,000
Country calling code (599)	Jewish Population 400
Emergency Telephone (Police - 114) (Ambulance - 112)	Electricity voltage 110/220

Curaçao

Embassy
Consul General of Israel
Blauwduifweg 5, Willemstad   (9) 736-5068
Fax: (9) 737-0707
Email: midalya@ibm.net

Kashrut Information
There is no kosher restaurant in Curacao.However many Kosher items may be purchased at the "food store" of the Congregation Shaarei Tsedek.

Museums
Jewish Cultural Historical Museum
Hanchi di Snoa 29, PO Box 322   (9) 461-1633
Fax: (9) 465-4141
Opening hours: Monday to Friday 9.00 to 11.45am and 2.30 to 4.45pm. If there is a cruise ship in port also on Sundays from 9am to noon. Closed on Shabbaths and Holidays. On permanent display are a great many ritual, ceremonial and cultural objects, many of which date back to the 17th and 18th centuries and are still in use by adjacent congregation Mikve Israel-Emanuel (founded 1651, oldest in the Hemisphere).

Synagogues

Ashkenazi Orthodox

Congregation Shaarei Tsedek
Leliweg 1a, PO Box 498   (9) 737-5738
Fax: (9) 736-9546

Sephardi, Reconstructionist

United Congregation Mikve'Israel Emanuel
Hanchi di Snoa 29, PO Box 322   (9) 461-1067
Fax: (9) 465-4141
Email: info@snoa.com
Sabbath services are Friday at 6.30pm (second Friday in the month is a family service), Saturday at 10am. Holy-day services at same times.

New Zealand

New Zealand Jewry is almost as old as the European presence in the country. The year 1829 marks the beginning of Jewish settlement, and Jews played a prominent role in the development of the country in the nineteenth century, especially in trading with Australia and Britain. Auckland Jewish community was founded in 1841, followed by Wellington in 1843. There was also a Jewish Prime Minister, Sir Julius Vogel, in the nineteenth century.

British Jews emigrated to New Zealand in the twentieth century, but New Zealand restricted immigration from Nazi Europe.

Today the community has six synagogues, four on the North Island and two on the South Island. Auckland and Wellington have Jewish day schools, WIZO and B'nai B'rith are both present, and the 'Kosher Kiwi Guide' is published in Auckland. There has been recent Jewish immigration from South Africa.

GMT + 12 hours	Total Population 3,602,000
Country calling code (64)	Jewish Population 5,000
Emergency Telephone (Police, Fire, Ambulance - 111)	Electricity voltage 230

Auckland

Bakeries
Manhattan Bagels

(9) 309-9098

Representative Organisations
Auckland Jewish Council
80 Webb St, Wellington

(4) 384-4229

Fax: (4) 384-4229

Has a small shop selling kosher food.

Synagogues

Orthodox

Auckland Hebrew Congregation
108 Greys Avenue, PO Box 68-224

(9) 373-2908

Fax: (9) 303-2147

New Zealands largest selection of kosher goods. Open Wednesday to Friday 8.30 am to 3.30pm. Sundays 9.00am to 11.00am

Progressive

Beth Shalom Synagogue
180 Manukau Road, Epsom 3

(9) 524-4139

Fax: (9) 524-7075

Email: bshalom@ihug.co.nz

Christchurch

Representative Organisations
Christchurch Jewish Council

(3) 358-8769

Synagogues
406 Durham Street

(3) 365-7412

Dunedin

Synagogues
Progressive Congregation
cnr. George & Dundas Streets

Wellington

Community Organisations
Wellington Jewish Community Centre
80 Webb Street

(4) 384-5081

Fax: (4) 384-5081

Email: bethel@ihug.co.nz

There are no kosher restaurants in Wellington. Visitors who want kosher meals & kosher food should contact the centre office of the Community Centre or the Kosher Co-op, on 384-3136.

Delicatessens
Dixon Street Delicatessen

(4) 384-2436

Fax: (4) 384-8692

Not fully kosher but provides kosher challahs and various American & Israeli kosher foods.

Embassy
Embassy of Israel
Level 13, 111 The Terrace, Equinox House, P O Box 2171

(4) 472-2368

Fax: (4) 499-0632

Email: israel-ask@israel.org.nz

Web site: www.webnz.co.nz/israel

New Zealand

Groceries

Kosher Co-op, 80 Webb Street   (4) 384-3136
Open on Wednesday, Friday and Sunday for kosher
meats,cheese and imported products. Shabbat
hospitality can be arranged with adequate notification.

Media

Newspapers

New Zealand Jewish Chronicle
PO Box 27-156   (4) 934-6077
Fax: (4) 934-6079
Email: mike@rifkov.co.nz
Monthly newspaper of local, Israeli and Jewish News

Mikvaot

Wellington Jewish Community Centre
80 Webb Street   (4) 384-5081
Fax: (4) 384-5081
Email: bethel@ihug.co.nz

Representative Organisations

Wellington Regional Jewish Council
54 Central Terrace 5   (4) 475-7622
Email: zwartz@actrix.gen.nz

Synagogues

Orthodox

Beth-El Synagogue
80 Webb Street   (4) 384-5081
Fax: (4) 384-5081
Email: bethel@ihug.co.nz

Progressive

Temple Sinai, 147 Ghuznee Street   (4) 385-0720
Fax: (4) 385-0572
Email: temple@actrix.gen.nz

Norway

The only way Jews could enter Norway before the nineteenth century was with a 'Letter of Protection', as Danish control limited the amount of Jewish entry. The situation changed in the 1840s, when a Norwegian liberal poet, Henrik Wergeland, argued for the admission of Jews into the country, and the parliament eventually agreed. There were only some 650 Jews in the country after emancipation in 1891, mainly in Oslo and Trondheim. By 1920, the community numbered 1,457 and by the time of the Nazi invasion there were 1,800. Despite attempts by the Norwegian resistance to smuggle Jews to Sweden, 760 Jews were transported to Auschwitz, although 930 were able to reach Sweden. The Jewish survivors were joined after the war by Displaced Persons, especially invited by the Norwegian government.

The current situation forbids shechita, but there are no other restrictions on Jewish life. There is a synagogue in Oslo, and a kosher food shop. B'nai B'rith and WIZO are present, and there is also a Jewish magazine. An old-age home was built in 1988. Trondheim, in the north of the country, has the northernmost synagogue in world.

GMT + 1 hour	Total Population 4,348,000
Country calling code (47)	Jewish Population 1,500
Emergency Telephone (Police - 112) (Fire - 110) (Ambulance - 113)	Electricity voltage 220

Oslo

Oslo is the major centre of Norwegian Jewry, with 900 Jews living in the capital. The Resistance Museum is of interest as is the Wergeland Monument in the Var Frisler Cemetery.

Embassy

Embassy of Israel
Drammensveien 82c, Oslo 0244   2244-7924
Fax: 2256-2183
Email: israel@online.no

Restaurants

Kosher Food Centre
Waldemar Thranesgt. 0171   2260-9166
Supervision: Rabbi Michael Melchior.
There are no kosher hotels or restaurants in Oslo but there is the Kosher Food Centre. Open 4 pm to 6 pm Tuesday and Thursday, and 12 pm to 2 pm on Friday. Closed Shabbat.

Vegetarian

Frisksport Vegeta Vertshus
Munkedamsveien 3b 0161   2283-4020; 2283-4232
Fax: 6690-0162
Email: arewr@online.no
Hours: 11 am to 11 pm, 7 days a week. Large salad
and hot dish buffet all day. Lacto-ovo-vegetarian food.

Synagogues
Bergstien 13-15 0172   2269-6570
Fax: 2246-6604
Email: kontor@dmt.oslo.no

Tourist Sites
Ostre Gravlund Cemetary
There is a Jewish war memorial erected here.

Trondheim

Synagogues
Ark. Christiesgt. 1   7352-6568 or 4752-2030
Fax: 7353-1108
Email: palkom@online.no
The Worlds northernmost synagogue. The synagogue
also has a Museum

Panama

There were some Jews, most of them pretending to be Christians, who came to Panama during colonial times. Panama was an important crossroads for trade and, as a result, many Jews passed through the country on their journeys in the region.

In 1849, immigrant Sephardic Jews in Panama founded in the Hebrew Benevolent Society, the first Jewish congregation in the Isthmus. They from the pious congregation of Netherland Antilles (Curaçao) to settle in Panama. This congregation disappeared in a few years.

Jews from Saint-Thomas (Virgin Islands) and Curaçao founded in 1876 the Kol Shearith Israel Synagogue in Panama City, and in 1890 the Kahal Hakadosh Yangacob in Colon.

By the end of the First World War, a number of Middle Eastern Jews had settled in the country and founded the Israelite Benevolent Society Shevet Ahim. During the years of the Second World War, immigrants from Europe arrived at Panama, establishing Beth-El, the only Ashkenazi community in the country. The majority of Jewish community is Sephardi (around 80 percent).

There have been two Jewish presidents in Panama, the only country apart from Israel of course where this has happened.

GMT - 5 hours	Total Population 2,677,000
Country calling code (507)	Jewish Population 7,000
Emergency Telephone (Police - 104) (Fire - 103)	Electricity voltage 120

Panama City

Bakeries
Pita Pan, Plaza Bal Harbour, Paitilla   264-2786

Meat

Ricuras de Esther
Calle 48, Urb. Marbella   265-7190
Supervision: Shevet Ahim.

Butchers
Shalom Kosher
Plaza Bal Harbour, Paitilla   264-4411

Super Kosher
Calle San Sebastian, Paitilla   263-5254
Supervision: Shevet Ahim Rabinate.
Also Kosher supermarket, bakery and restaurant.
Open from 8.30am to 8.30 pm Sunday to Thursday.
Friday until 4.30pm

Chocolate Shops
Candies Bazaar
Via Argentina, 155 L-2   269-4857
Chocolatier, Calle 53,, Urb. Marbella   264-4712
La Bonbonniere
Calle Juan XXIII, Paitilla   264-5704

Panama

Embassy
Embassy of Israel
Edificio Grobman, Calle Manuel Maria Icaza,
5th Floor 5   264-8257

Mikvaot
Beneficiencia Israelita Beth El
Calle 58E,, Urb. Obarrio   223-3383
Sociedad Israelita Shevet Ahim
Calle 44-27   225-5990
                                    Fax: 227-1268

Organisations
Consejo Central Comunitario Hebreo de Panama
P O Box 3309 4   263-8411
                                    Fax: 264-7936
Jewish Centre: Centro Cultural Hebreo De beneficiencia
Calle 50 Final, PO Box 7166, 5 5   226-0455
                                    Fax: 226-0869
(K) Restaurant open daily for lunch and supper. Closed Saturdays.

Pizzeria
Pizzeria Italiana
Centro Cultural Hebreo de Beneficiencia, Calle 50
Final   226-0455
                                    Fax: 226-0869

Restaurants
Restaurante Don Jacobo
Centro Cultural Hebreo de Beneficiencia, Calle 50
Final   226-0455
                                    Fax: 226-0869
Open daily for lunch and supper

Dairy
Pita Pan, Plaza Bal Harbour, Paitilla   264-2786

Meat
Shalom Kosher
Plaza Bal Harbour, Paitilla   264-4411

Synagogues

Ashkenazi
Beneficiencia Israelita Beth El
Calle 58E, Urb. Obarrio   223-3383
Mikva on premises

Orthodox Sephardi
Ahavat Sion, Calle Juan XXIII, Paitilla   265-1891
Daily Services. Mikva for women on premises.
Sociedad Israelita Shevet Ahim
Calle 44-27   225-5990
                                    Fax: 227-1268
Daily services.

Reform
Kol Shearith Israel
Av. Cuba 34-16 5   225-4100

Paraguay

Jewish settlement in this land-locked country came late for this area of South America. The few who came over from Western Europe at the end of the nineteenth century rapidly assimilated into the general population. The first synagogue was founded early in the twentieth century by Sephardis from Palestine, Turkey and Greece. Ashkenazis arrived in the 1920s and 1930s from eastern Europe and some 15,000 came to the country to escape Nazism, intending to move on into Argentina. Some of these settled in Paraguay.

Paraguay, in more recent times, has accepted Jews from Argentina who were fleeing from the military regime.

Today there are three synagogues, a Jewish school and a Jewish museum in Asuncion. There is a high rate of intermarriage, but children of mixed marriages may receive a Jewish education.

GMT - 5 hours
Country calling code (507)
Emergency Telephone (Police, Fire, Ambulance - 00)

Total Population 4,960,000
Jewish Population 1,200
Electricity voltage 220

Peru

Asuncion

Embassy
Embassy of Israel
Calle Yegros No. 437 C/25 de Mayo, Edificio San
Rafael, Piso 8, PO Box 1212
(21) 495-097; 496-043; 496-044
Fax: (21) 496-355

Organisations
Consejo Representativo Israelita de Paraguay
General Diaz, 657, PO Box 756   (21) 441-744
Fax: (21) 448-289

Synagogues
General Diaz, 657

Peru

The original Jews in Peru arrived with the first Europeans, as many Marranos were leaders in the Spanish army which invaded the country in 1532. After the Inquisition was set up in 1570, the Jews were persecuted, and many were burned alive. After 1870, groups of Jews came over from Europe, but tended to disappear into the general population. In 1880, a group of North African Jews settled in Iquitos and worked in the rubber industry. More Jewish immigration occurred after the First World War, and later Nazi refugees entered the country. By the end of the Second World War the Jewish population had reached 6,000, but this subsequently declined.

Almost all of the present Jewish population are Ashkenazi. Two Jewish newspapers are produced and most Jewish children go to the Colegio Leon Pinelo school, which is well known for its high standards. There is a cemetery at Iquitos built by the nineteenth-century community. The community is shrinking owing to intermarriage and assimilation.

GMT - 5 hours
Country calling code (51)
Emergency Telephone (Police - 105) (Fire -116) (Ambulance - 470 5000)   Electricity voltage 220

Total Population 23,944,000
Jewish Population 3,000

Lima

Caterers
Salon Majestic
Av. Bolivar 965, Pueblo Libre, 21   (2) 463-0031
Fax: (2) 461-8912
Supervision: Chief Rabbi Abraham Benhamu and Rabbi Efraim Zik.
Catering for special groups and parties by prior arrangement only.

Embassy
Embassy of Israel
Natalio Sanchez 125 6to Piso, Santa Beatriz 1
(2) 433-4431
Fax: (2) 433-8925

Groceries
Minimarket Kasher
Av. Gral. Juan A. Pezet 1472, San Isidro, 27
(1) 264-2187
Fax: (1) 264-2187
Email: ssaplet@com.petu
Supervision: Rabbi Zik.
Pharmax
Kosher items available.

Santa Isabel
Kosher items available.
Wong
Kosher items available.

Hotels
Hostal Regina
Av. 2 de Mayo 1421, San Isidro, 27
(2) 441-2541; 442-8870
Fax: (2) 421-2044
Only a short walk to the Centro Sharon Synagogue
Hotel Libertador
Los Eucaliptos 550, San Isidro, 27   (2) 421-6680
Fax: (2) 442-3011
Only a short walk to the Centro Sharon Synagogue

Kashrut Information
Chief Rabbi   (2) 442-4505
Fax: (2) 442-8147
Email: abenhamu@mail.mba-sil.edu.pe
Rabbi Benhamu is the Chief Rabbi of Peru.
Rabbinate Rabbi Efraim Zik
Av. de Mayo 1815, San Isidro 27   (2) 214697
Email: efraimzik@hotmail.com
There is no kosher restaurant in Lima. Visitors who want kosher meals should contact the Mini Market Koshet, Tel: 511 2642187 at Av. Pezet 1472, San Isidro..

Peru

Media

Newspapers

J.T.A. - Publicationes Memora S. A.
Psje. Malvas 135, Brena, 5   (2) 425-0850
       Fax: (2) 442-0534
Daily publication.
Shofar, Enrique Barron 1145, Santa Beatriz 1
       (2) 471-1331
       Fax: (2) 471-1331
Monthly.

Mikvaot

Union Israelita
Ave. Gral. Juan A. Pezet 1472, San Isidro, 27
       (2) 264-2187
Sociedad Israelita Sefardi; Beit Jabad

Museums

Museum of the Inquisition
Junin 548, Lima 1   (2) 427-0365
Dungeon and torture chamber of the headquarters of the Inquisition for all Spanish South America from 1570 to 1820. On the right side of the Plaza Bolivar

Organisations

Asociacion Judia de beneficencia y Culto de 1870
Libertad 375, Miraflores 18
       (1) 445-1089 or 445-5148
       Fax: (1) 445-1089
       Email: guillob@mailtv.ole.com

Synagogues

Conservative

Asociacion Judia de Beneficiencia y Culto de 1870
Jose Galvez 282, Miraflores 18
       (2) 445-1089 or 445-5148
       Fax: (2) 445-1089
       Email: fambrons@junin.itete.com.pe

Orthodox

Beit Jabad, Salverry 3095, San Isidro, 27
       (1) 264-6060
       Fax: (1) 264-5499
       Email: chabadperu@unired.net.pe
       Web site: www.lp.edu.pe/jabad
Synagogues, mikva, Kosher food.
Centro Social y Cultural Sharon
Av. 2 de Mayo 1815, San Isidro, 27   (2) 440-0290
       Fax: (2) 421-3684
Sociedad de beneficencia Israelita Sefardi
Enrique Villar 581, Santa Beatriz, 1
       (2) 442-4505 or 471-7230
       Fax: (2) 422-8147
Union Israelita del Peru
Av. Dos de Mayo 1815, San Isidro 27   (1) 421-3688
       Fax: (1) 421-3684
Services are held at the Centro Sharon

Tourist Sites

Pilatos House
Ancash 390, Lima 1
17th c. private mansion, now used by the National Institute of Culture. On the 2nd floor was the synagogue of the Marrano Jews.

Philippines Republic

Conversos who came with the Spanish in the sixteenth century were the first Jewish presence in the region. In the late nineteenth century, western European Jews came to trade in the area, and after the Americans occupied the country in 1898, more Jews arrived from a variety of places, including the USA and the Middle East. The first synagogue was built in 1924. The Philippines accepted refugees from Nazism, but the Japanese occupied the islands during the war and the Jewish population was interned. After the war many of the community emigrated. However, a new synagogue opened in 1983, and services are also held in the US Air Force bases around the country.

GMT + 8 hours
Country calling code (63)
Electricity voltage 220

Total Population 71,750,000
Jewish Population 200

Manila

Embassy
Embassy of Israel
Trafalgar Plaza 23rd Floor
105 H.V. dela Costa Street, Salcedo Village, Makati
City, Metro Manils 1200   (2) 892-5329/30/31/34
              Fax: (2) 894-1027
      Email: israelembphl@netasia.net
Postal address: POB 1697 MCPO, Makati Metro,
Manila 1299

Mikvaot
Jewish Association of the Philippines (Beth Yaacov Synagogue)
H. V. de la Costa Street, Salcedo Village, Makati, Metro
Manila 1200   (2) 815-0263, 0265
              Fax: (2) 818-9990
Kosher requirements By arrangement.

Synagogues
Jewish Association of the Philippines (Beth Yaacov Synagogue)
H. V. de la Costa Street, Salcedo Village, Makati, Metro
Manila 1200   (2) 815-0263, 0265
              Fax: (2) 818-9990
Services; Fri at 6.30pm, Sat at 9.30am

Poland

After just five years of German occupation in the Second World War, the thousand-year-old Jewish settlement in Poland, one of the largest Jewish communities in the world, had been almost totally eradicated.

Jews came to Poland, in order to escape anti-semitism in Germany, in the early Middle Ages. They were initially welcomed by the rulers, and the Jews became greatly involved in the economy of the country.

Before the Second World War most Jews lived in the east and south of the country, under Russian and Austrian domination respectively until 1918. After 1918, Poland became an independent country once more, with over 3,000,000 Jews (300,000 in Warsaw.) The community continued to flourish before 1939, with Yiddish being the main language of the Jews. The community was destroyed in stages during the war, as Poland became the centre for the Nazi's destruction of European Jewry. After the war, the borders shifted again, and the 100,000 or so survivors mostly tried to emigrate. The few who remained endured several progroms even after the events of the Holocaust.

Today the community is comparatively small, and most of the members are elderly, but there is a functioning synagogue in Warsaw and many Jewish historical sites are scattered throughout the country. The Polish Tourist Board publishes information about the Jewish heritage in Poland.

GMT + 1 hour   Total Population 38,731,000
Country calling code (48)   Jewish Population 8,000
Emergency Telephone (Police - 997) (Fire - 998) (Ambulance - 999)   Electricity voltage 220

Bialystok

Although there are only a few Jews living here now, before the Second World War it was more than 60 per cent Jewish, giving it the then highest concentration of Jews in any city in the world.

It is possible to visit the sites of a number of buildings of great Jewish interest.

Cemeteries
Wschodnis Street

Historic Sites
Synagogue, Branickego Street

Bielsko-Biala

Organisations
Elzbieta Wajs, Ul Mickiewicza 26 43-300   (2) 22438

Bytom

Organisations
Ul Smolenia 4 41902   (3) 813510

Poland

Cracow

Booksellers
Jarden, 2 Szeroka Street, Miodowa 41   (12) 217166

Cultural Festival
Jewish Culture Festival

(12) 429-2573
Email: office@jewishfestival.art.pl
The eleventh annual Jewish Culture Festival will be held in Summer 2001

Galleries
Hadar
13 Florianska Street   (12) 218992

Organisations
Judaica Foundation
Ul Rabina Meiselsa 17   (12) 423-5595
Fax: (12) 423-5034
Email: uwrussek@cyf-kr.edu.pl
Zwiakzek Wyznania Mojzeszowego
Ul Skawinska 2   (12) 662347

Restaurants

Meat

Na Kazimierzu
ul. Szeroka 39 31-053   (12) 229-644
Fax: (12) 219-909
Billed as the 'only kosher restaurant in Cracow and the south of Poland'. Hours: 12 pm to 12 am everyday. Traditional Shabbat courses are available on Shabbat.

Synagogues
Eizik Synagogue
18 Kupa Street   602 350 671 (Mobile)
Contact Sasha Pecaric
Remuh, Ul Szeroka 40

Gliwice

Contact Information
Ul Dolnych Walow 9 44100   (32) 314797

Katowice

Contact Information
Ul Mlynska 13 40098   (32) 537742

Legnica

Contact Information
Ul Chojnowska 37 59220   (76) 22730

Lodz

Organisations
Jewish Chabad

(42) 331221, 336825
Jewish Congregation
Zachodnia 78   (42) 335156

Lublin

Once a major Jewish town in eastern Europe, Lublin today has fewer than a hundred Jews. Prewar Lublin was a centre for Torah study, and a large yeshivah was built only a few years before the Second World War, and is now used as a college. Majdanek Concentration Camp lies within the city's boundary, clearly visible from a major road leading south east. There is a particularly moving memorial in the camp, consisting of the ashes from the camp's crematoria.

Contact Information
Ul Lubartowska 10 20080   (81) 22353

Rzeszow

Synagogues
ul. Bonicza, edge of Pl. Ofiara Getta

Szczecin

Contact Information
Ul Niemcewicza 2 71553   (91) 221674

Warsaw

Before the war, Warsaw had approximately 300,000 Jews. Now there are only a couple of thousand, mostly elderly. There are many sites which can be visited, such as surving fragments of the Ghetto walls and "A memorial Route to the struggle and Martyrdom of the Jews 1940-1943" known as "Memory Lane". The old Jewish cemetery, untouched by the Nazis, is very imposing, and is still in use. The Warsaw Ghetto fighters are included in the inscription to Tomb of the Unknown Soldier in the centre of the city.

Embassy
Embassy of Israel
Ul I Kryzwickiego 24

Mikvaot
Nozyk Synagogue
6 Twarda Street

(22) 620-43-24 (ext 121) 620-06-76
Fax: (22) 620-10-37
Email: varshe@kehillah.jewish.org.pl
Contact Rachel Bookstein, tel: 620 34 96.

Portugal

Monument
Monument to the Ghetto Heroes
Zamenhofa
Erected in 1948 this monument symbolises the heroic Ghetto defiance of the 1943 uprising.

Organisations
The Jewish Historical Institute
3/5 Tlomackie Street 00090   (22) 827-9221
                                     Fax: (22) 827-8372
                            Email: zihinb@ikp.atm.com.pl
This establishment has a remarkable collection of Judaica. It includes a library of documents on the manuscripts stolen by the Germans from all over Europe.

Restaurants
Menora
Plac Grzybowski 2   (22) 203754
Nove Miasto Ecological Restaurant
Rynek Nowego Miasta 13/15   (22) 831-4379
                                     Fax: (22) 831-4379
                     Web site: www.novemiasto.waw.pl
Panorama
Al Witsoa 31   (22) 642-0666

Salad Bar
Ul Tamka 37   (22) 635-8463

Synagogues
Nozyk Synagogue, Jewish Community of Warsaw, Union of Jewish Communities in Poland.
6 Twarda Street 00-950   (22) 6204324
                                     Fax: (22) 6201037
                   Email: varshe@kehillah.jewish.org.pl
The synagogue was renovated in 1977-83 and is well worth a visit..

Theatre
Jewish National Theatre
Plac Grzybowski 12/16
Performances are given in Yiddish

Tours of Jewish Interest
Shalom Tours   (22) 220-3037
                                     Fax: (22) 220-0559

Wrocklaw

Museums
Historical Museum
Slezna Street 37   (71) 678236

Portugal

Portuguese Jewry had a parallel history to Spanish Jewry until the twelfth century, when the country emerged from Spain's shadow, and Jews worked with the Portuguese kings in developing the country. However, they were heavily taxed and had to live in special areas, although they were free to practise their religion as they pleased. As a result, the community flourished.

Persecution began during the period of the Black Death, and the Church was a key instigator of the riots which broke out against the Jews. After the Inquisition in neighbouring Spain, many Jews fled to Portugal, but were expelled in 1496. Many Jews converted in order to remain in the country and help with the economy. These became the Portuguese 'Conversos' and some of their descendants are converting back to Judaism today.

Over the last century and a half, Jews have begun to re-enter the country, and many others have used it as an escape route to America. Most of the community are Sephardi, and there is a Sephardi synagogue in Lisbon. There is also a central Jewish organisation which is a unifying force for Jews in the country.

GMT + 0 hours
Country calling code (351)
Emergency Telephone (Police, Fire and Ambulance - 115)

Total Population 9,927,000
Jewish Population 900
Electricity voltage 220

Algarve

Community Organisations
Jewish Community of Algarve
Rua Juoice Biker 11-5°., Portimão 8500-701
                                     (282) 416-710
                                     Fax: (282) 416-515

Belmonte

Organisations
Jewish Community of Belmonte
Apt. 18, Bairo de Santa Maina, 6250 Belmonte
                                     (275) 912465
                                     Fax: (275) 912465

Portugal

Faro

Museums
Faro Jewish Cemetery and Museum
(282) 416-710
Fax: (282) 416-515
Only remaining vestige of the first post-Inquisition Jewish presence in Algarve. Open weekday mornings from 9:30 am to 12:30 pm. Situated opposite entrance to Faro Hospital. Enquiries to Ralf Pinto, Jewish Community of Algarve.

Lisbon

The Plaza Rossio, not far from the Royal Palace, housed the Inquisition. The building itself was destroyed in 1755 and the National Theatre of Dona Inana was erected in its place. There is a street in the Olfama, Lisbon's oldest district, Call Rua de Judiaria.

Community Organisations
Communal Offices
Rua Alexandre Herculano 59 1250
(21) 385-8604
Fax: (21) 388-4304

Embassy
Embassy of Israel
Rua Antonio Enes 16-4 1020-025
(21) 355-3640
Fax: (21) 355-3658
Email: israemb@mail.telepac.pt

Jewish Tours
Jewish Heritage Tours
Avenida 5 de Outubro, 321 1649-015
(217) 919-954
Fax: (217) 919-959
Email: fit.lisboa@space.pt
Web site: www.jewisheritage.pt
Tours to explore Jewish Ancestral Roots in Portugal and to meet the descendants of the conversos, the 'secret' Jews.

Kosher Meals
Mrs R. Assor, Rua Rodrigo da Fonseca 38.1'D
(21) 386-0396
Fax: (21) 395-3725
Email: iassor@mail.telepac.pt
Kosher meals and delicatessen are obtainable if prior notice is given. For kosher meats, contact the communal offices.

Organisations
Jewish Club & Centre
Rua Rosa Araujo 10
(21) 572041

Synagogues
Jewish Community
Rua Alexandre Herculano 59 1250
(21) 385-8604
Fax: (21) 388-4304
Email: cilisboa@mail.telepac.nl
10.00 am until 5 pm except Friday. Tours for visitors (until 1pm). For groups please book in advance.

Ashkenazi

Avenida Elias Garcia
100-1'-1050

Oporto

Synagogues
Rua Guerra Junqueiro 340

The Jewish community in Puerto Rico is just 100 years old, with the first Jews arriving in 1898 after the beginning of American rule. During the Second World War, many Jewish American servicemen went to the island, along with refugees from Nazism. A Jewish Community Centre dates from the early war years. After the war the community grew with an influx of Cuban and American Jews.

San Juan, the capital, has the largest Jewish population, and there are two synagogues.There is also a Hebrew school, held in the community centre. The first Chief Justice of Puerto Rico was Jewish.

GMT - 4 hours	Total Population 3,736,000
Country calling code (1)	Jewish Population 3,000
Emergency Telephone (Police - 343 2020) (Fire 343 2330)	Electricity voltage 120

San Juan-Santurce

Community Centre and Synagogue
Shaare Zedeck
903 Ponce de Leon Av., Santurce 00907
(787) 724-4157

Synagogues

Reform

Temple Beth Shalom
San Jorge Av. & Loiza St., Santurce 00907

Romania

Romanian Jewry began at the time the Romans gave the country its name and language. In the fifteenth century, community life had begun to be organised, and settlement had spread to the town of Iasi and some Moldavian towns. Jews were welcomed from Poland and other east European countries, despite the opposition of the Church. Over the years, the community grew in size with further immigration, but emigration became the dominant factor after 1878, when the Treaty of Berlin, which demanded equal rights for Jews, was not implemented in Romania. Following Romania's acquisition of the large area of Transylvania from Hungary after 1918, the Jewish population increased once more. The Jews were finally emancipated, but harsh discriminatory decrees were passed in 1937, and Romania's alliance with Nazi Germany during the war led to 385,000 of the 800,000 Romanian Jews being killed in the Holocaust.

It is ironic that Romanian Jewry was able to function relatively normally under the harsh Ceausescu regime. He was the only Warsaw Pact leader not to sever relations with Israel in 1967, and he allowed Jewish practices to continue, even permitting the then Chief Rabbi, Dr Moses Rosen, to have a seat in the parliament. This freedom also tolerated emigration to Israel, which was seen by Ceausescu as advantageous to Romania. Post-1989, the community still has its central body, the Federation of Jewish Communities, and there are kosher cafeterias in several cities. The community is ageing, but many synagogues are still functioning, and there are also Jewish newspapers and a Yiddish theatre. The Choral Synagogue in Bucharest is of particular interest to visitors.

GMT + 2 hours	Total Population 22,650,000
Country calling code (40)	Jewish Population 14,000
Emergency Telephone (Police - 955) (Fire - 981) (Ambulance - 961)	Electricity voltage 220

Arad

Hotels
Hotel Astoria
Revolutiei 79-81   (57) 281-990
Hotel Parc
Bd. Dragulina 25   (57) 280-820

Organisations
Community Offices
10 Tribunal Dobra Street   (57) 281310
Home for the Aged
22, 7 Episcopei Street

Restaurants
Ritual
22, 7 Episcopei Street   (57) 280731

Romania

Synagogues
Muzeul Judetean
Piata George Enescu 1   (57) 280114
Neologa
10 Tribunal Dobra Street

Orthodox
12 Cozia Street

Bacau

Organisations
Community Offices
11 Alexandru cel Bun Street   (34) 134714

Restaurants
11 Alexandru cel Bun Street

Synagogues
Avram A. Rosen Synagogue
31 V. Alecsandri Street
Cerealistilor
29 Stefan cel Mare Street

Borsec

Hotels

Kosher

Transylvania Hotel
c/o Interom Tours   972-3924-6425
     Fax: 972-3579-1720

Synagogues
c/o Interom Tours   (972) 3924-6425
     Fax: (972) 3579-1720

Botosani

Mikvaot
67 7 Aprilie Street

Organisations
Community Offices
220 Calea Nationala   (31) 0315-14659

Restaurants
69 7 Aprilie Street   (31) 0315-15917

Synagogues
Great
1a Marchian Street
Mare
18 Muzicantilor Street
Yiddish
10 Gh. Dimitrov Street

Brasov

Organisations
Community Offices
27 Poarta Schei Street   (68) 143532

Restaurants
27 Poarta Schei Street   (68) 144440

Synagogues
27 Poarta Schei Street

Travel Agents
International Tourism and Trade
Jozef Bem Str. 2, 4000 Sf. Gheorghe   (67) 316375
     Fax: (67) 351551
     Email: it&t@phamors.ro

Bucharest

Community Organisations
Federation of Jewish Communities of Romania
Str. Sf. Vineri 9-11, Sector 3   (1) 313-2538
     Fax: (1) 312-0869
     Email: asiran@pcnet.ro
Kosher supervision on 11 restaurants in the main
Jewish communities of Romania.

Documentation Centres
Romanian Jewish History Research Centre
12 Juliu Barasch Street   (1) 323-7246

Embassy
Embassy of Israel
6 Burghelea Street   (1) 613-2634/5/6

Mikvaot
5 Negustori Street

Museums
Museum of the Jewish Community in Romania
3 Mamoulari Street   (1) 615-0837
Hours: Wednesday and Sunday, 9 am to 1 pm.

Religious Organisations
Chief Rabbi of Romania
Strada Sf. Vineri 9   (1) 613-2538
     Fax: (1) 312-0869

Representative Organisations
Federation of Romanian Jewish Communities
24 Popa Rusu Street   (1) 211-8080
The Federation publishes a bi-monthly, 'Revista
Realitatea Evreiasca'.

Restaurants
Jewish Community
18 Popa Soare Street   (1) 322-0398
This restaurant is operated by the Jewish Community.

Synagogues
Choral Temple
Strada Sf. Vineri 9   (1) 147-257
Credinta
48 Vasile Toneanu Street
Ieshua Tova
9 Nikos Beloiannis Street   (1) 659-5675
Near the Lido and Ambassador hotels.

Sephardi
Great Synagogue
9-11 Vasile Adamache Street   (1) 615-0846

Theatres
Jewish State Theatre
15 Iuliu Barasch Str., Sector 3 74212
                                    (1) 323-4530;4035
                                    Fax: (1) 323-2746
                                    Email: tes@dnt.ro
                                    Web site: www.tes.ro

Cluj Napoca
Mikvaot
16 David Fransisc Street

Organisations
Community Offices
25 Tipografiei Street   (64) 11667

Restaurants
5-7 Paris Street   (64) 11026

Synagogues
Beth Hamidrash Ohel Moshe
16 David Fransisc Street
Sas Hevra
13 Croitorilor Street
Templul Deportatilor
21 Horea Street

Constanta
Organisations
Jewish Community Office and Cultural Club
3 Sarmisagetuza Street   (41) 611598

Synagogues
Great Temple
2 C. A. Rosetti Street
Small
3 Sarmisagetuza Street

Dorohoi
Organisations
Community Office
95 Spiru Haret Street   (31) 611797

Restaurants
14-18 Dumitru Furtuna Street

Synagogues
Great, 4 Piata Unirii Street

Galati
Organisations
Community Office
9 Dornei Street   (36) 413662

Restaurants
9 Dornei Street   (36) 413662
Synagogues
Meseriasilor, 11 Dornei Street

Iasi (Jassy)
Mikvaot
15 Elena Doamna Street

Organisations
Community Office
15 Elena Doamna Street   (32) 114414
Restaurants
15 Elena Doamna Street   (32) 1117883
Synagogues
Great
7 Sinagogilor Street
Schor
5 Sf. Constantin Street

Oradea
Mikvaot
5 Mihai Viteazu Street

Organisations
Community Office
4 Mihai Viteazu Street   (59) 134843

Restaurants
5 Mihai Viteazu Street   (59) 131383

Synagogues
Great
4 Mihai Viteazu Street
Neolog
22 Independentei Street

Piatra Neamt
Organisations
Community Office
7 Petru Rares Street   (33) 623815

Synagogues
Leipziger, 12 Meteorului Street
Old Baal Shem Tov
7 Meteorului Street
Old historical monument.

Radauti
Organisations
Community Office
11 Aleea Primaverii, Block 14, Apt.1 (30) 461333

Synagogues
Great
2, 1 Mai Street
Vijnitzer
49 Libertatii Street

Romania

Satu Mare

Organisations
Community Office
4 Decebal Street   (61) 743783

Synagogues
Great, 4 Decebal Street

Sighet

Organisations
Community Office
8 Basarabia Street   (62) 511652

Synagogues
Great, 8 Basarabia Street

Suceava

Organisations
Community Office
8 Armeneasca Street   (30) 213084

Synagogues
Gah Chavre, 4 Dimitrie Onciu Street

Timisoara

Mikvaot
55 Resita Street

Organisations
Community Office
5 Gh. Lazar Street   (56) 132813

Restaurants
10 Marasesti Street   (56) 136924

Synagogues
Cetate
6 Marasesti Street
Fabric
2 Splaiul Coloniei
Iosefin
55 Resita Street

Tirgu Mures

Organisations
Community Office
10 Brailei Street   (65) 115001

Synagogues
21 Aurel Filimon Street

Tushnad

Hotels
Kosher

Olt Hotel
c/o Interom Tours   972-3924-6425
                        Fax: 972-3579-1720

Vatra Dornei

Organisations
Community Office
54 M Eminescu Street   (30) 371957

Synagogues
Vijnitzer, 14 Luceafarul Street

Russia

In early Russian history, Jews were not allowed to settle, and the few who did were later expelled by various Czars. After 1772, Russia acquired a large area of Poland, in which lived a large number of Jews. There were still restrictions against the Jews, and eventually they were allowed to settle only in the 'Pale of Settlement', an area in the west of the Russian Empire. 2,000,000 Jews emigrated from the Empire between 1881 and 1914, escaping anti-semitism.

Jews were only allowed into Russia itself in the mid nineteenth-century, and by 1890 there were 35,000 Jews in Moscow. Most were expelled the following year. The community grew after the Second World War, drawing Jewish immigration from Belarus and Ukraine to cities such as Moscow and Leningrad. Birobidzhan was a failed experiment to give the Jews their own 'Autonomous District', and those who moved there (in the far east, near China) soon moved away. Under communism, the country was restricted in both religious practices and emigration to Israel, but since 1991 there has been a revival in Jewish learning. There are synagogues functioning in many cities, and there are now 100 Jewish schools. The major threat is still from anti-semitic right-wing groups, who are unfortunately increasing their activity.

GMT + 2 to 12 hours	Total Population 148,126,000
Country calling code (7)	Jewish Population 550,000
Emergency Telephone (Police - 02) (Fire - 01) (Ambulance - 03)	Electricity voltage 220

Astrakhan

Synagogues
30 Babushkin Street

Birobidjan

Birobidjan was created in 1934 as a Jewish homeland in the wilds of Siberia. It was not a success and was effectively terminated in the 1940s. There has, however, now been a resurgence of interest in what was known as the Jewish Autonomous District.

Synagogues
9 Chapaev Street, Khabarovsk Krai

Bryansk

Synagogues
82 Lermontov Street

Lubavitch
Synagogue of Bryansk
27a Uritskovo Street 241000   (0832) 445-515

Derbent

Synagogues
94 Tagi-Zade Street

Lubavitch

Jewish Community of Derbent
23 Kandelaky Street 368600   (8724) 021-731

Ekaterinburg

Synagogues
14 Kuibyshev Street, (formerly Sverdlovsk)
18/2 Kirov Street, (formerly Sverdlovsk)

Irkutsk

Synagogues
17 Karl Liebknecht Street

Kazan

The capital of Tatarstan, an autonomous Russian republic, has 10,000 Jews an Ort school and its own Jewish newspaper.

Synagogues

Lubavitch

Synagogue of Kazan
15 Profsouznaya Street 420111   (8432) 329-743

Kostrama

Synagogues
Synagogue of Kostrama
16a Sennoi Peroulok 156026   (0942) 514-388

Krasnoyarsk

Synagogues
Synagogue of Krasnoyarsk
65 Surikova Street 660049   (3912) 223-615
Fax: (3912) 440-137
Email: jckras@hotmail.com

Kursk

Synagogues
3 Bolshevitskaya Street

Makhachkala

Synagogues
111 Yermoshkin Street

Moscow

Some 200,000 Jews now live in Moscow, and since the collapse of the USSR in 1991 the community has experienced a revival. The Choral Synagogue on Arkhipova Street, which was built in 1891 and was used during the Soviet regime, is again the focus of Jewish religious life. The Lubavitch movement has its own centre, and there has been an upsurge of interest in Jewish education.

Contact Information
Rabbi Pinchas Goldschmidt
Chief Rabbi of Moscow   (95) 923-4788; 924-2424

Embassy
Embassy of Israel
Bolshaya Ordinka 56   (95) 230-6777
Fax: (95) 238-1346

Museums
Poliakoff Synagogue
Bolshaya Brennaya 6

Restaurants

Meat

King David Club
Bolshoi Spasoglinishchevsky per. (Arkhipova St)
6, door code 77   (95) 925-4601
Fax: (95) 924-4243
Email: ail@ail.msk.ru
Supervision: Rabbi Pinchas Goldschmidt, Chief Rabbi of Moscow.
This kosher food centre serves as a glatt kosher restaurant and a mini hotel. Catering services are available as are lunchboxes.

Russia

Na Monmartre, Vetoshny per., 9   (95) 725-4797
Supervision: Rabbi Berl Lazar.
On the 5th floor of a modern shopping center

Synagogues
2nd Korenyovsky Lane, Moscow Oblast
Moscow Choral Synagogue
Bolshoi Spasoglinishchevsky per. (Arkhipova St) 10
                                 (95) 924-2424
Poliakoff Synagogue
Chabad Center, Bolshaya Brennaya 6   (95) 202-7696
                                Fax: (95) 202-7645

Lubavitch
Chabad Lubavitch
4 Novoushevsky Peroulok 103055   (95) 218-0001
                                Fax: (95) 219-9707
                            Email: lazar@glasnet.ru
Chabad Lubavitch Synagogue
6 Balshaya Bronya Street. 103104   (95) 202-4530
                                Fax: (95) 291-6483
Darkei Shalom Synagogue
1 Novovladikinsky Peroulok 103055   (95) 903-0782
                                Fax: (95) 903-2218

Nalchik

Synagogues
73 Rabochaya Street, cnr. Osetinskaya

Nizhny Novgorod

Synagogues

Lubavitch
Nizhny Novgorod Synagogue
5a Gruzinskaya Street 603000   (8312) 336-345
                                Fax: (8312) 303-759

Novosibirsk

Synagogues
23 Luchezarnaya Street

Lubavitch
Synagogue of Novosibirsk
14 Kominististheskaya   (3832) 210-698

Penza

Synagogues
15 Krasnaya Street

Perm

Synagogues
Kuibyshev Street
Pushkin Street

Rostov-na-Donu

Synagogues

Lubavitch
Synagogue of Rostov-na-Dou
18 Gazetny Peroulok 344007   (8632) 624-759
                                Fax: (8632) 624-119

Sachkhere

Synagogues
145 Sovetskaya Street
105 Tsereteli Street

Samara

Synagogues
3 Chapaev Street

Lubavitch
Jewish Community Center of Samara Synagogue
84B Chapaevskaya St 443099   (8462) 334-064
                                Fax: (8462) 320-242
                            Email: samara@fjc.ru
The community center has a mikvah, and a kosher
lemihadrin kitchen

Saratov

Synagogues
Posadskov Street
2 Kirpichnaya Street

Lubavitch
Synagogue of Saratov
208 Posadskovo Street 410005   (8452) 249-592

St Petersburg

With 100,000 Jews, St Petersburg is witnessing a
similar Jewish revival to Moscow. There are
opportunities to pray, learn and eat kosher – this
was not the case (in general) before 1991 in the
then USSR. Americans and Israelis are the main
motivators behind the revival, but St Petersburg
Jewry is also eager to learn about religion, now
that there is the freedom to do so.

Mikvaot
2 Lermontovsky Prospekt   (812) 113-8974

Representative Organisations
St Petersburg Jewish Association
Ryleev St, 29-31, a/b 103   (812) 272-4113

Restaurants
Dining Room at Shamir School
Ligovskiy Prospekt 161-8   (812) 116-1003

Synagogues
The Grand Choral Synagogue of St. Petersburg
2 Lermontovsky Prospekt 190121   (812) 114-4428
Fax: (812) 113-6209
Email: pewzner@synagogue.spb.su
This is the second street past the Mariinsky Opera &
Ballet Theatre.

Tour Information
Zekher Avoteinu
Jewish Tourist and Genealogical Agency, Pr.
Netakkustiv 6-57 195027   (812) 536-3843
Fax: (812) 175-1229
Email: zekhera@hotmail.com
Web site: www.zekheravoteinu.virtualave.net/index.htm
The centre carries out a tour programme combining
Jewish and general sightseeing in Russia and the
former Pale of Jewish Settlement. It also undertakes
genealogical research for families whose ancestors
were from the Russian Empire. Representative in USA:
6801 19th Avenue, 4C, Brooklyn, NY 11204, USA.
Tel: 1 718 236 6037.

Tshelyabinsk
Synagogues
Lubavitch
Synagogue of Tshelyabinsk
PO Box 16187 454091   (3512) 333-618
Fax: (3512) 303-759

Tula
Synagogues
15 Veresaevskaya Street

Vladikavkaz (formerly Ordzhonikidze)
Synagogues
Revolutsiya Street, (formerly Ordzhonikidze)

Yekatrinburg
Synagogues
Lubavitch
Yekatrinburg Synagogue
118/93 Shekmana Street 620144   (3432) 236-440
Fax: (3432) 293-054

Singapore

As Singapore developed into an important south-east Asian trading centre in the mid-nineteenth century, some Jewish traders from India and Iraq set up a community there in 1841. A synagogue was built in 1878, and another in 1904. By the time of the Japanese occupation in the Second World War, the community had grown to 5,000, and included some eastern European Jews. The Japanese imprisoned the community and took their property. After the war, emigration to Australia and the USA reduced numbers, but in recent years Israelis who work in the country and other Jews have moved in. Ninety per cent of the community are Sephardi.

David Marshall, who had been a POW in Japan, returned to Singapore and in 1955 became Chief Minister.

One of the two synagogues is used regularly, and there is a mikva and a newsletter. The Sir Manasseh Meyer Community Centre is the hub of Jewish life. The Jewish community today is small and professional.

GMT + 8 hours	Total Population 3,045,000
Country calling code (65)	Jewish Population 300
Emergency Telephone (Police, Fire, Ambulance 999)	Electricity voltage 220/240

Contact Information
Rabbi Abergel
Email: mordehai@singnet.com.sg
Contact for more detailed information on the
community and availability of kosher products.

Embassy
Embassy of Israel
58 Dalvey Road S-1025   235-0966
Fax: 733-7008

Singapore

Representative Organisations

Jewish Welfare Board
Robinson Road, PO Box 474

Synagogues

Orthodox

Chesed-El
2 Oxley Rise S-0923   732-8832
Services, Monday only, Shacharit and Mincha/Maariv.

Maghain Aboth Synagogue
24/26 Waterloo Street 187950   337-2189
Fax: 336-2127
Email: jewishwb@singnet.com.sg

Daily and Shabbat services are held, except for Monday when services are held at Chesed-El Synagogue, 2 Oxley Rise, at 7:30 a.m. Because Singapore has equatorial times, Mincha/Maariv falls between 6:30 and 6:45 p.m. throughout the year. Shacharit: weekdays, 7:30 a.m., Shabbat 09:00 a.m. Every Shabbat lunch is served for the community. Breakfast is currently served every morning after services. Mikvah is available for use. For details please contact (65) 737 9112 Rabbi Mordechai Abergel. There are kosher meat, cheeses, wine and other grocery items on sale at the synagogue.

Slovakia

Slovakia has passed through the control of various countries over the centuries, finally gaining independence after the peaceful splitting of Czechoslovakia in 1992. Before 1918 the region was part of Hungary and many in southern Slovakia, near the Hungarian border, still speak Hungarian.

In 1939, the Jewish population in the Slovak area of Czechoslovakia numbered 150,000 but the Hungarians occupied the south of the country, and assisted the Germans in deporting Jews to Auschwitz and other camps. Many survivors emigrated after the war, but some remained, and are now rediscovering their Jewish heritage. Since independence, B'nai B'rith and Maccabi have been established, but anti-semitism has re-emerged. There are kosher restaurants in Bratislava and Kosice, and Jewish education is beginning once more.

GMT + 1 hour

Country calling code (421)

Emergency Telephone (Police -158) (Fire - 150) (Ambulance - 155)

Total Population 5,350,000
Jewish Population 6,000
Electricity voltage 220

Bratislava

Known in German as Pressburg, Bratislava was a key centre of Judaism when Slovakia was under Hungarian rule before the First World War. Bratislava was especially famous for the number of Jewish scholars living there, including the Chatam Sofer. The preserved underground tomb of the Chatam Sofer and other rabbis is now a place of pilgrimage.

Bed & Breakfasts

Chez David
Zamocka 13
Pressburg 81101
(7) 544-13 824; 544-16 943
Fax: (7) 544-12 642
Supervision: Rabbi Baruch Myers, the Jewish Religious Community.

Kosher food is obtainable here as well. (Open for lunch only.)

Mikvaot

Zamocka 13
Pressburg 81101
(7) 544-13 824; 544-13 943
Fax: (7) 531-642

Museums

The Museum of Jewish Culture
Zidovska Street
Bratislava, Pressburg 81101
(7) 59349142/3/4
Fax: (7) 59349145

Contact person: Prof. PhDr. Pavol Mest'an Dr. Sc

Underground Mausoleum
Pressburg
Contains the graves of 18 famous rabbis, including the Chatam Sofer. The key is available from the community offices.

Slovakia

Representative Organisations
Central Union of Jewish Religious Communities in the Slovak Republic
Kozia ul. 21, Bratislava 81447
(7) 5441-2167; 5441-8357
Fax: (7) 5441-1106
Email: uzzno@netax.sk

Restaurants
Chez David
Zamocka 13
Pressburg 81101
(7) 544-13 824; 544-16 943
Fax: (7) 544-12 642
Supervision: Rabbi Baruch Myers, the Jewish Religious Community.

Synagogues
Heydukova 11-13, Pressburg
Services held Mon. Thurs. - Sat.

Galanta
Mikvaot
Partizanska 907

Synagogues
Partizanska 907
Daily services held.

Kosice
Restaurants
Community Centre
Zvonarska Ul 5, Kaschau 04001
(95) 622-1047

Synagogues
Puskinova Ul 3, Kaschau
Beth Hamidrash
Zvonarska Ul 5, Kaschau
Daily services held.

Piestany
Cemeteries
Old Cemetery
Janosikova Ul 606

Synagogues
Hviezdoslavova 59
Shabbat and festival services held.

Presov
Community Organisations
Community Centre
Sverthova 32
(91) 31271
Fax: (91) 31271
Synagogue and museum on premises.

Trnava
Monuments
Monument to Deportees
Halenarska Ul 32
In the courtyard of the former synagogue.

Synagogues
Kapitulska Ul 7

Do you eat fish out?

If so, there is a comprehensive list of kosher fish listed alphabetically by country on pages 385 to 388 which you should find useful on your travels.

Slovenia

Maribor was the centre for medieval Jewish life in what is now Slovenia. Expulsion followed after the Austrian occupation in the late Middle Ages, but in 1867 the Jews in the Austrian empire were emancipated and some returned to Solvenia. The community was never large. During the Second World War the members of the small Jewish community either escaped to Italy, fought with the Yugoslav partisans, or were deported.

There is a Jewish Community of Slovenia, connected to the Croatian community, but none of the synagogues in this small country is functioning at present. There is one synagogue in Maribor that is classed as an historic monument and dates from the Middle Ages. There are also some sites from medieval times such as the cemeteries in Ljubljana (the capital) and Murska Sobota.

GMT + 1 hour	Total Population 1,942,000
Country calling code (386)	Jewish Population Under 100
Emergency Telephone (Police - 113) (Fire - 112) (Ambulance - 94)	Electricity voltage 220

Ljubljana

Community Organisations
Jewish Community of Slovenia and Ljubljana
PO Box 37 1101   (61) 221-836, 170-2320
                              Email: jss@siol.net

Jewish Community of Slovenia and Ljubljana
PO Box 37 1101   (61) 221-836, 170-2320
                              Email: jss@siol.net
Synagogue   (61) 315-884

Although some believe that Jews were present in the country at around the time of the first European settlement in the area (the seventeenth century), the community only really began in the nineteenth century, when religious freedom was granted. In 1836 the explorer Nathaniel Isaacs published 'Travels and Adventures on Eastern Africa', an important contemporary account of Zulu life and customs.

The year 1841 saw the first Hebrew Congregation in Cape Town, and the discovery of diamonds in the Transvaal later in the century prompted a wave of Jewish immigration.

The main immigration of Jews into South Africa occurred at the end of the nineteenth century, when many thousands left eastern Europe, the majority from Lithuania (40,000 had arrived by 1910). Although the country did not accept refugees from the Nazis, about 8,000 Jews managed to enter the country after their escape from Europe.

Today the community is affluent and has good relations with the government. There is a South African Board of Deputies, and many international Jewish associations are present in the country. There are kosher hotels and restaurants, and Jewish museums. Kosher wine is produced at the Zaandwijk Winery.

GMT + 2 hours	Total Population 41,734,000
Country calling code (27)	Jewish Population 106,000
Emergency Telephone (Police - 1011) (Fire - 1022) (Ambulance - 10222)	
Electricity voltage 220/250	

South Africa

Cape Province
Cape Town

Cape Ventures

Tailormade kosher travel and touring requirements co-ordinated for both individuals and groups within South Africa.

Tel/Fax (21) 439 8787
Mobile: (0) 450 7078
email: cape@mweb.co.za

Bed & Breakfasts
Kosher
Dinah's Guest House
6 Molteno Road
Oranjezicht 8001 (21) 241-568
Fax: (21) 241-598
Email: dinas@grm.co.za
Web site: www.tourcape.co.za
Supervision: Cape Beth Din.
SA Tourism Board accredited kosher guest house. Walking distance to Gardens Synagogue (Orthodox), close to city centre, with 'meet and greet' facility from airport.

Butchers
Claremont Kosher Butchers and Deli
150 Main Road
Corner Oliver Sea Point, Capetown, Claremont 7800
(21) 7132-2120
Fax: (21) 713-2123
Email: adlercaz@hixnet.co.za
Supervision: Cape Beth Din.
Can deliver to your door.

Pick 'N Pay
Constantia (21) 794-5690
Supervision: Cape Beth Din.
Pick 'N Pay
Sea Point 8001 (21) 438-2049
Supervision: Cape Beth Din.
Also bakery.

Pick 'N Pay
Claremont (21) 683-2900
Supervision: Cape Beth Din.
Shoprite
Rondebosch (21) 689-4563
Supervision: Cape Beth Din.

Delicatessens
Goldies
64 Regent Road Sea Point 8001 (21) 434-1116
Supervision: Cape Beth Din.
Sit-down deli and take-away. Meat and pareve. Hours: Sunday to Thursday, 7 am to 8 pm; Friday, to 5 pm.

Reingold's Deli & Butchery
Plumstead (21) 762-8093
Supervision: Cape Beth Din.

Hotels
Kosher
Cape Sun, Strand Street (21) 238-844
Supervision: Cape Beth Din.
Only serves breakfast.

Libraries
Jacob Gitlin Library
Albow Centre, 88 Hatfield Street 8001
(21) 462-5088
Fax: (21) 465-8671
Email: gitlib@netactive.co.za

Mikvaot
Arthur's Road Sea Point (21) 434-3148; 439-8787

Museums
Cape Town Holocaust Centre
88 Hatfield
St Gardens, Sea Point 8001 (21) 462-553
Fax: (21) 462-554
Email: ctholocaust@mweb.co.za
Web site: www.museums.org.za/ctholocaust

South African Jewish Museum
84 Hatfield Street, Gardens (21) 465-1546
Fax: (21) 465-0284
Email: lee@sajewishmuseum.co.za
Open Sunday - Friday. Shop and Kosher café.

Religious Organisations
Union of Orthodox Synagogues Cape Council
191 Buitenkant Street 8001 (21) 461-6310
Fax: (21) 461-8320
Email: uoscape@iafrica.com
Beth Din located at same address and phone number.

Representative Organisations
South African Jewish Board of Deputies Cape Council
Leeusig House, 3rd floor, 4 Leeuwen Street 8001
21) 423-2420
Fax: (21) 423-2775
Email: sajbodcc@iafrica.com

Restaurant
Avron's Place Restaurant & Grill
307 Main Road (21) 439-7610
Fax: (21) 439-7599
Email: almeleh@netactive.co.za

Kaplan Student Canteen
University of Cape Town (21) 650-2688
Supervision: Cape Beth Din.
Lunches, take-away and orders. Meat and pareve. Open Monday to Friday. Closed December/January for varsity holidays and during summer vacation.

South Africa

Synagogues

Temple Israel
5 Salisbury Road Wynberg   (21) 762-1745
                                  Fax: (21) 797-8309
                          Email: templeis@iafrica.com

Orthodox

Camps Bay
Chilworth Road Camps Bay   (21) 438-8082
                                  Fax: (21) 438-8082
                      Email: cbhc@netactive.co.za

Cape Town Hebrew Congregation
84 Hatfield Street, Gardens   (21) 465-1405
                                  Fax: (21) 461-7659
                        Email: cthc@mweb.co.za

Claremont Hebrew Congregation
Grove Avenue (at Morris Rd)
P.O. Box 23035, Claremont 7735
                                  (21) 671-9007
                                  Fax: (21) 683-3011
                      Email: clarshul@iafrica.com

Constantia
Old Rendal Road
Constantia 7806

Green & Sea Point Hebrew Congregation
10 Marais Road, Sea Point   (21) 439-7543
                                  Fax: (21) 434-3760
                      Email: gspheb@mweb.co.za

Milnerton
29 Fitzpatrick Road
Cambridge Estate 7441   (21) 697-1913
                                  Fax: (21) 461-8320

Muizenberg
Camp Road, Muizenberg   (21) 788-1488
Schoonder Street Shul
10 Yeoville Road, Vredehoek   (21) 452-239
                                  Fax: (21) 461-1510

Wynberg Hebrew Congregation
5 Mortimer Road Wynberg 7800   (21) 797-5029
                                  Fax: (21) 761-4669

Reform

Temple Israel
Salisbury Road Wynberg   (21) 797-3362
Temple Israel
Upper Portswood Road, Green Point   (21) 434-9721
                                  Fax: (21) 434-2400

East London

Synagogues

Orthodox

Shar Hashomayim
Lukin Road

Reform

Belgravia Crescent

Kimberley

Synagogues

United Hebrew Institutions
20 Synagogue Street 8301   (531) 825-652

Oudtshoorn

Synagogues

United Hebrew Institutions
291 Buitenkant Street   (443) 223-068
There is a Jewish section in the C.P. Nel Museum.

Paarl

Synagogues

New Breda Street   (2211) 24087
Community centre and Talmud Torah at same address.

Port Elizabeth

Museums

Jewish Pioneers' Memorial Museum
Raleigh Streetr cnr Edward Street   (41) 335-197
                                  Fax: (41) 335-197
Open between 10 am and noon every Sunday. The
Museum has a ramp for disabled access via
wheelchairs. It is also a National Monument. For
further information visitors may phone Dr Sam
Abrahams (41) 5833671

Synagogues

Orthodox

Port Elizabeth Hebrew Congregation United Synagogue
55 Roosevelt Street
Glendinningvale 6001   (41) 331-332
                                  Fax: (41) 333-293

Progressive

Temple Israel
Upper Dickens Street   (41) 336-642

Hotels

Kosher

Belmont Hotel
3 Holmfirth Road
Sea Point 8005   (21) 439-1155
                                  Fax: (21) 434-9451

Supervision: Cape Beth Din.

Free State

Bloemfontein

Religious Organisations
United Hebrew Institutions
Community Centre, 1 Dickie Clark Street,
PO Box 1152 9300   (51) 436-2207
                                      Fax: (51) 436-6447
Mornings.

Representative Organisations
O.F.S. & Northern Cape Zionist Council
Community Centre, 2 Fairview, PO Box 564 9300
                                           (51) 480-817
                                      Fax: (51) 480-104

Synagogues
Orthodox
United Hebrew Synagogue
16 Waverley Road   (51) 436-7609
                                      Fax: (51) 436-6447

Gauteng

Benoni

Religious Organisations
United Hebrew Institutions
32 Park Street   (11) 845-2850

Brakpan

Religious Organisations
United Hebrew Institutions
11 Heidelberg Road, Parkdene   (11) 744-4822

Germiston

Religious Organisations
United Hebrew Institutions
President Street   (11) 825-2202

Johannesburg

It is appropriate that the largest city in South Africa should have the largest Jewish community in the country. About 60% of the country's Jews live there (a community of some 60,000) and the headquarters of many of South African Jewry's institutions are housed there. There are approximately thirty synagogues in the city.

Bakeries
Friends Bakery
Ridge Road, Glenhazel   440-5094/5

Booksellers
Chabad House Books
Fairmount Shopping Centre, George Street, Fairmount
                                           (11) 485-1957
                                      Fax: (11) 648-1139

Ohr Someyach Books
2 Syleslyn Place
15 Northfield Avenue, Glenhazel 2192
                                            11) 887-1437
                                      Fax: (11) 887-7092
                                 Email: ohr@netactive.co.za

Butchers
Bolbrand Poultry Shoppe
74-76 George Avenue
Sandringham 2192   (11) 640-4080; 640-4170
Supervision: Beth Din.

Checkers
Emmerentia, Balfour Park 2196
                                           (11) 880-6962
Supervision: Beth Din.
Gardens Kosher
Braides Avenue 2052   (11) 483-3357
                                      Fax: (11) 728-3660
Supervision: Beth Din.
Kinneret Butchery
Saveways, Fairmount Shopping Centre, Sandringham
                                           (11) 640-6592
Supervision: Beth Din.
Maxi Discount Kosher Butcher
74 George Avenue
Sandringham 2192   (11) 485-1485; 485-1486
                                      Fax: (11) 485-2991
Supervision: Beth Din.

Pick 'N Pay
Gallo Manor
Supervision: Beth Din.
Rishon Butchery
Balfour Park Shopping Centre
Atholl Road, Balfour Park 2090
                                           (11) 786-5396
Supervision: Beth Din.
Yumpolski's
5 Durham Street, Raedene 2192   (1) 485-1045
                                       Fax: (1) 485-1082
Supervision: Beth Din.

Community Organisations
Chabad House
27 Aintree Avenue, Savoy Estate, Yeoville 2090
                                           (11) 440-6600
                                      Fax: (11) 440-6601
                               Email: chabad@netactive.co.za

South Africa

Delicatessens & Bakeries

Feigel's Kosher Delicatessan
Shop 3
Queens Place, Kingswood Road, Glenhazel 2192
(11) 887-1364
Supervision: Beth Din.

Feigel's Kosher Delicatessan
Bramley Gardens Shopping Centre, shop 1, 280
Corlett Drive   (11) 887-9505/6
Supervision: Beth Din.
Hours: Friday, 7:30 am to 4:30 pm; Sunday, 8 am to 1
pm; Monday to Thursday, 10 am to 5 pm.

Kosher King
74 George Avenue, Sandringham   (11) 640-6234
Supervision: Beth Din.
Hours: Monday to Thursday, 8:30 am to 5 pm; Friday,
8 am to 3 pm; Sunday, 9 am to 1 pm.

Mamale's Deli
Shop No 38
Morning Glen Shopping Centre, Bowling Avenue, Gallo
Corner Avenue, Gallo Manor 2052   (11) 804-2068
Supervision: Beth Din.

Neil's Bakery
Fairmount Shopping Centre, 10 Bradfield Drive,
Fairmount   (11) 640-2686
Supervision: Beth Din.
Hours: Monday to Thursday, 7:30 am to 5 pm; Friday,
to 2:30 pm; Sunday, to 1 pm.

Pick 'N Pay
cnr. Grant Avenue & 6th Street Norwood
(11) 483-3357
Supervision: Beth Din.
Closed on Shabbat and Yom Tov.

Saveways Spar Supermarket
Fairmount Shopping Centre
cnr. Livingston St & Sandler Avenue, Fairmount 2192
(11) 640-6592; 3056
Supervision: Beth Din.
Hours: Monday to Thursday, 8 am to 6 pm; Sunday
and public holidays, 8 am to 1 pm.

Shirley's Bakery & Deli
442 Louis Botha Avenue
Highlands North 2192   (11) 640-2629
Supervision: Beth Din.

Shoshana's Bakery
1 Glenstar Centre, Kingswood Avenue, Glenhazel
(11) 885-1039
Supervision: Beth Din.

Shula's
42 Kenmere Road, cnr. Hunter Street, Yeoville
(11) 487-1072
Supervision: Beth Din.

The Pie Works
Shop 35 Greenhill Road
Emmerentia 2195   (11) 486-1502
Fax: (11) 486-0580
Supervision: Beth Din.
Hours: weekdays, 8 am to 5 pm; Friday, to 4 pm;
Sunday, to 2 pm.

The Pie Works
74 George Avenue
Sea Point, Sandringham 2192   (11) 485-2447
Supervision: Beth Din.
Hours: weekdays, 8 am to 5 pm; Friday, to 4 pm;
Sunday, to 2 pm.

Hotels

Courtleigh Hotel
38 Harrow Road, Berea 2198   (11) 487-1577
Fax: (11) 648-6743
Email: kosher@global.co.za
Supervision: Beth Din.

Libraries

Kollel Library
22 Muller Street, Yeoville 2198   (11) 648-1175

Media

Magazines

Jewish Affairs
Building 1, Anerley Office Park, 7 Anerley Road,
Parktown   (11) 486-1434
Fax: (11) 646-4940
Email: sajbod@iafrica.com
Quarterly journal of the South African Jewish Board of
Deputies.

Jewish Heritage
PO Box 3 7179
Birnham Park 2015   (11) 880-1830

Jewish Tradition
PO Box 46559, Orange Grove, 2119 Johannesburg
(11) 648-9136
Fax: (11) 648-4014
Email: isaacrez@yebo.co.za
Publication of the Union of Orthodox Synagogues of
South Africa.

South African Jewish Observer
PO Box 29189
Sandringham 2131   (11) 640-4420
Fax: (11) 640-4442
Publication of the Mizrachi organisation of South Africa.

The South African Jewish Times
Publico House, 30 Andries Street, Wynberg
(11) 887-6500
Fax: (11) 440-5364

South Africa

Mikvaot
Goldberg Centre, 24 Raleigh Street, Yeoville
(11) 648-9136
Beth Harer (Glenhazel Area Hebrew Congregation)
PO Box 28836
Sandringham, Glenhazel 2131   (11) 640-5061

Religious Organisations
The Southern African Union for Progressive Judaism
357 Louis Botha Avenue
Highlands North   (11) 640-6614

Union of Orthodox Synagogues of South Africa
Goldberg Centre, 24 Raleigh Street, Yeoville
(11) 648-9136
Fax: (11) 648-4014
The Office of the Chief Rabbi as well as the Beth Din
are located here. Beth Din fax: 648-2325.

Restaurants
D.J.'s Take Away
Balfour Park Shopping Centre
Shop No. 121, Balfour Park 2090   (11) 440-1792
Supervision: Beth Din.

Haifa Haktanah
576 Louis Botha Avenue, Gresswold   (11) 887-1059
Supervision: Beth Din.
Hours: Monday to Thursday, 10 am to 10 pm; Friday, t
4 pm; Motzei Shabbat, 1 hour after Shabbat till late.
The Only Kosher Nandos
27 Aintree Avenue Savoy   885-1496

Dairy
Brazillian
2 Brazilia in the Balfour Park shopping centre
Supervision: Beth Din - JHB.
Michelo's
3 Dunottar Street, (off Louis Botha Ave)
(11) 485-4626
Supervision: Beth Din - JHB.
Shula's
173 Oxford Road, Rosebank 2196   (11) 880-6969
Fax: (11) 880-6605
Supervision: Beth Din.
Hours: Sunday to Thursday, 7 am to 11 pm; Friday, to
4 pm; Motzei Shabbat to 1 am.

Meat
Marc Chagall, Balfour Park Shopping Center
(11) 728-3000
Supervision: Beth Din - JHB.
Nandos Savoy, 27 Aintree Ave   (11) 885-1496
Supervision: Beth Din - JHB.

On The Square
Mutual Square, Rosebank 2196   (11) 880-4153
Supervision: Beth Din.
Hours: Sunday to Thursday, 10 am to 3 pm; 6 pm to
10 pm; Motzei Shabbat, 1 hour after Shabbat to 12
am.

Synagogues
There are more than 50 synagogues in Johannesburg.
Contact the appropriate Religious Organisation for
details.

Tour Information
Celafrica Tours
PO Box 357
Highlands North 2037   (11) 887-5262
Fax: (11) 885-3097
Email: celpro@hixnet.co.za
Web site: www.celafrica.com
The company specialises in kosher tours to southern
Africa, for people needing kosher food and Shabbat
arrangements.

Krugersdorp

Religious Organisations
United Hebrew Institutions
Cilliers Street, Monument, PO Box 1008 1740
(11) 954-1367
Fax: (11) 953-4905

Pretoria

Embassy
Israel Embassy & Consulate-General
3rd Floor, Dashing Centre, 339 Hilda Street, Hatfield
(12) 421-2227

Groceries
One Stop Superliner
217 Bronkhorst Street, Baileys Muckleneuk,
Brooklyn 0181   (12) 463-211

Kashrut Information
Pretoria Council of BOD
(012) 344-2372
Fax: (012) 344-2059

Museums
Sammy Marks Museum
Swartkoppies Hall   (12) 803-6158
Fax: (12) 803-5308
Email: nchm@nchm.co.za

South Africa

Restaurants
JAFFA Old Age Home
42 Mackie Street, Baileys Muckleneuk 0181
(12) 346-2006
Fax: (12) 346-2008
Email: jaffa@smartnet.co.za
Hotel as well. Prior booking necessary. Kosher catering, resident mashgiach.

Synagogues
Adath Israel
441 Sibelius Street, Lukasrand 0181   (12) 344-1511
Fax: (12) 343-0287

Progressive

Temple Menorah
315 Bronkhorst Street, New Muckleneuk, PO Box 1497
(12) 467-296

Springs

Religious Organisations
United Hebrew Institutions
Charterland Avenue, Selcourt 1559   818-2572

KwaZulu-Natal

Durban

Butchers
Pick 'N Pay
Musgrave Centre, Berea 4001   (31) 214-208
Bakery as well.

Community Organisations
Durban Jewish Club
44 Old Fort Road 4001   (31) 337-2581
Fax: (31) 337-9600
Email: velna@eastcoast.co.za
Mailing address: P.O.Box 10797, Marine Parade 4056.

Representative Organisations
Council of KwaZulu-Natal Jewry
44 Old Fort Road 4001   (31) 337-2581
Fax: (31) 337-9600
Email: velna@eastcoast.co.za
Mailing address: P.O.Box 10797, Marine Parade, 4056

Synagogues

Orthodox

Durban Hebrew Congregation
cnr. Essenwood & Silverton Roads, PO Box 50044,
Musgrave Road 4062   (31) 214-755
Fax: (31) 211-964

Progressive

Durban Progressive Jewish Congregation
369 Ridge Road   (31) 286-105
Fax: (31) 292-429

Umhlanga

Contact Information
Chabad of Umhlanga
POBox 474 4320   (31) 562-487
Fax: (31) 561-5845
Open all hours. Regular minyanim especially Shabbat and Yomim Tovim. Ladies' Mikvah 20 minutes away. Kosher hospitality. For kosher tours in Southern Africa contact Shlomo on the above numbers.

South Korea

Before the Korean War (1950-53) there were a handful of Jews in the country who had escaped from Russia. During the Korean War a larger community came to South Korea – US army soldiers. There is still an American detachment based in the country, and among them are some Jews. They have been joined by individuals coming to the country to work. Services are held at the US army base in Seoul, and the US army have their own Jewish chaplain in the country.

GMT + 9 hours	Total Population 45,314,000
Country calling code (82)	Jewish Population 150
Emergency Telephone (Police - 112) (Fire and Ambulance - 119)	Electricity voltage 110/220

Seoul

Synagogues
South Post Chapel
Building 3702, Youngsan Military Reservation
(2) 793-3728

Fax: (2) 796-3805
Civilians welcome to participate in all Jewish activities, inc. kosher le-Pesach sedarim, meals and services.

Spain has an ancient connection with the Jews, and the term 'Sephardi' originates from the Hebrew word for Spain. Beginning in Roman times, the Jews have suffered the usual cycle of acceptance and persecution, with a 'golden age' under the Islamic Moorish occupation, which began in 711. Great Jewish figures arose in the Spanish community, such as Ibn Ezra and the Ramban. However, the situation changed when the Christians gained the upper hand, and blood libels began. In 1492, almost 100 years after a particularly violent period of persecution, the Jews were expelled from Spain. Many thousands were baptised but practised Judaism in secret (the Marranos), and many were caught and burnt at the stake.

Jewish life began again in the nineteenth century. The Inquisition ended in 1834 and by 1868 Spain had promulgated religious tolerance. Synagogues could be built after 1909, and Spain accepted many thousands of Jewish refugees before and during the Second World War.Angel Sanz-Briz alone helped to save thousands of Hungarian Jews by issuing 'letters of protection' and entry visas.

There has been a recent immigration from North Africa, and the community today has a central body, synagogues in several towns (including Torremolinos and Malaga). Rambam's synagogue in Cordoba can be visited, and there are several other old synagogues in the country.

GMT + 1 hour
Country calling code (34)
Emergency Telephone (Police - 092 or 091) (Fire - 080) (Ambulance - 092)
Electricity voltage 220

Total Population 39,270,000
Jewish Population 14,000

Alicante

Organisations
Communidad Israelita
Apdo. 189, Playa de San Juan 03540 (96) 515-1572

Synagogues
Vila Carlota, 15 Urb Montivoli, Villajoyosa

Avila

The Mosen Rubi Church, cnr. Calle Bracamonte and Calle Lopez Nunez, was originally a synagogue, built in 1462.

Barcelona

The ancient community of the city lived in the area of the Calle (from the Hebrew Kahall) and the cemetery was in Montjuic (Mountain of the Jews). Most of the original tombstones are now in the Provincial Archaeological Museum.

Butchers
Carniceria, Porvenir 24 (93) 200-3375
Supervision: Barcelona Rabanut.

Elias Shoshanna
35 calle Viriato (91) 446-7847
Supervision: Harav ben Dahan, rabbi of the community.

Mikvaot
Calle de l'Avenir 24 08071 (93) 200-6148, 8513

Organisations
Communidad Israelita de Barcelona
Margenat 103 08071 (93) 211-9116
Community Centre
Calle de l'Avenir 24 08071 (93) 200-6148 or 8513

Restaurants
Vegetarian

Self Naturista
Carrer de Santa Anna 11-17 08002 (93) 318 23 88
Fax: (93) 318 26 84

Synagogues
Calle Avenir 24 08021 (93) 200-6148, 8513
The first synagogue to be built in Spain since the Inquisition.

Spain

Tour Information
Communitat Jueva Atid De Catalunya
Castanyer 27, baixos 08022   (93) 417-3704
                            Fax: (93) 417-3704
                    Email: atid@arquired.es
                 Web site: www.atid.freeservers.com

Travel Agencies
Jewish Travel Agency
Viajes Moravia, Consejo de Ciento 380
                            (93) 246-0300

Bembibre
The synagogue here was converted into a church.

Benidorm
Kashrut Information
                            (96) 522-9360

Besalu
The Juderia, one of the oldest in Catalonia, is by the River Fluviá. A mikva was recently discovered there.

Burgos
During the 13th century Burgos was the largest Jewish community in North Castile. The Juderia was in the area of the Calle Fernan Gonzalez.

Caceres
Essential Information
Between the 13th and 15th century, Jewish life flourished here, and in 1479 there were 130 families, making up one-quarter of the town's population. Part of the Juderia still exists. The San Antonio Church on the outskirts of the town is a 13th-century former synagogue.

Ceuta
Kashrut Information
Calle Sargento Coriat 8

Synagogues
Calle Sargento Coriat 8

Cordoba
Tourist Sites
Calle de los Judios 20
This is an ancient synagogue (declared as a monument). Near by, a statue of Maimonides has been erected in the Plazuela de Maimonides. The entrance to the ancient Juderia is near the Almodovar Gate.

El Escorial
Libraries
San Lorenzo Monastery
The library of San Lorenzo Monastery contains a magnificent collection of medieval Hebrew Bibles and illuminated manuscripts. On the walls of the Patio of Kings, in the Palace of Philip II, are sculpted effigies of the six Kings of Judah.

Estella
The Jewish community here was one of the most important in the kingdom of Navarre. The Santa Maria de Jus Castillo Church was once a synagogue.

Girona
The Jewish quarter of Girona, known as the Call, is located in the heart of the old town. Its main street exists today, and is known as Carrer de la Força. The Jewish Quarter of Girona is one of the best-preserved to be found in Europe today.

During the Middle Ages, the Jewish community of Girona achieved considerable importance. It was there that the most important Cabbala school in Western Europe was developed, largely under the guidance of Rabbi Mossé ben Nahman, or Ramban, perhaps its best-known representative.

The Bonastruc ça Porta Centre houses the Museum of Catalan-Jewish Culture and the Nahmanides Institute for Jewish Studies, on the site where the 15th-century synagogue was located.

In the municipal archives there is an important collection of fragments of Hebrew manuscripts dating from the 13th and 14th centuries. The Archaeological Museum contains more than 20 medieval gravestones with Hebrew inscriptions found in the old Jewish cemetery.

Spain

Organisations

Patronat Municipal Call De Girona

c/ Sant Llorenc s/n 17004

(972) 21 67 61

Fax: (972) 21 67 61

Email: callgirona@grn.es

Web site: www.ajuntament.gi/el-call

The Catalan Museum of Jewish Culture. Temporary exhibitions on Jewish subjects. Guided tours.

Granada

The Juderia ran from the Corral del Carlon to Torres Bermejas.

Hervas

This village in the Gredos Mountains, 150 miles west of Madrid, has a well-preserved Juderia, declared a national monument. Its main street has been renamed Calle de la Amistad Judeo Cristiana.

Madrid

About 3,500 Jews live in Madrid. A new synagogue was completed in 1968, and there is a community centre providing kosher food. The Prado has a number of paintings of Jewish interest.

Delicatessens
Department Store
El Corte Ingles, Castellana

Spain

Embassy
Embassy of Israel
Calle Velasquez 150, 7th Floor 28002
(91) 411-1357

Gift Shops
Kewn Shop, Sefarad II
Silva 8 28013 (91) 547-0722
Email: sefaradgalleries@bravored.com
Jewish religious articles.
Sefarad Handicrafts
Gran Via 54 (91) 548-2577, 547-6142
Fax: (91) 548-2577
Email: sefaradgalleries@bravored.com
Jewish religious articles.

Libraries
Calle Balmes 3 (91) 445-9843, 9835

Mikvaot
Calle Balmes 3 (91) 445-9843, 9835

Museums
Museo Arquelogico
Calle de Serrano 13
See casts of Hebrew inscriptions from medieval
buildings.

Organisations
Community Centre
Calle Balmes 3 (91) 591-3131
Fax: (91) 594-1517
Email: cimsecretaria@teleline.es

Restaurants
Community Centre
Calles Balmes 3 (91) 591-3131
Fax: (91) 594-1517
Email: cimsecretaria@teleline.es
For groups only.

Synagogues
Calle Balmes 3 (91) 591-3131
Fax: (91) 594-1517
Email: cimadrid@teleline.es
The capital's first synagogue since the expulsion of Jews
in 1492 was opened in December 1968. The building
also houses the Community Centre, as well as mikvah,
library, classrooms, an assembly hall and the office of
the community. Nearest underground station: Metro
Iglesias.
Congregacion Bet El
Castello 77 28006 (91) 519-3227
Fax: (91) 662-3730
Email: betel_es@hotmail.com
Web site: www.members.xoom.com/betelspain/

Tourist Information
Ogicina Nacional Israeli de Turismo
Gran via 69, Ofic 801 28013 (91) 559-7903
Fax: (91) 542-6511

Malaga

Butchers
Carmiceria Kosher
Calle Somera 14 29001 (95) 260-4201

Mikvaot
Calle Somera 12 29001

Synagogues
Alameda Principal, 47,20.B 29001

Tourist Sites
There is a statue of the 11th-century Hebrew poet,
Shlomo Ibn-Gabirol, a native of Malaga, in the
gardens outside the Alcazaba Castle, in the heart of
the city.

Marbella

Bakeries
La Tahona (95) 282-2781

Groceries
Hipercor
El Corte Ingles, Puerto Banus
Joelle Kanner
(95) 277-4074
Kosher poultry and wine.

Media
Publications
Edificio Marbella 2000
Paseo Maritima
Focus, PO Box 145 29600
Community Journal

Mikvaot
Beth El, 21 Calle Jazmines, Urbanizacion
El Real, Km. 184
(95) 277-4074, 0757 or 282-4983

Organisations
Community Centre
Paseo Maritima

Synagogues

Beth El, Urbanizacion El Real, Km 184, Jazmines 21
(95) 277-4074, 282-4983 or 282-6649
Email: ikanner@vnet.es
About 2 miles from the town centre to the east.
Services: Friday eve. (winter) 7.00pm, (summer)
8.30pm; Shabbat morn. & all festivals 10am. Kosher
food on request, cal mobil: Sylvia: 646 759 073,
Michel: 610 916 170. Mikveh on premises.

Melilla

Kashrut Information

Calle General Mola 19 North Africa

Synagogues

Barrio Poligono
There are nine other synagogues in the Barrio
Poligono. These are open on festivals and High Holy-
days only.

Isaac Benarroch
Calle Marina 7 North Africa
Jacob Almonznino
Calle Luis de Sotomayor 4 North Africa
Salama
Calle Alfonso XII 6 North Africa
Solinquinos
Calle O'Donnell
North Africa

Yamin Benarroch
Calle Lopez Moreno 8 North Africa

Montblanc

The Jewish quarter was in the Santa Clara district,
where the church was once a synagogue.

Santiago de Compostela

The cathedral has 24 statues of Biblical prophets
framed in the so-called 'Holy Door'.

Segovia

The Alcazar contains the 16-century 'Tower of the
Jews'. Calle de la Juderia Vieja and Calle de la
Juderia Nueva are the sites of the medieval Jewish
quarters, where the former synagogue now houses
the Corpus Christi Convent.

Seville

The old synagogue, now the church of Los
Venerables Sacerdotes, is in the Barrio de Santa
Cruz. Seville Cathedral preserves in its treasures
two keys to the city presented to Ferdinand III by the
Jews. The Columbus Archives (Archives of the
Indies), 3 Queipo de Llano Av., preserve the
account books of Luis de Santangel, financier to
King Ferdinand and Queen Isabella. Arco &
Torreon of the Juderia, in the old Calle de la
Juderia, was the gate connecting the Alcazar and
the Jewish quarter. There is a Jewish cemetery in
part of the city's Christian burial ground in the
Macarena district.

Synagogue

Communidad Israelita de Sevilla
Calle Bustos Tavera 8

Tarazona

The Juderia is near the bishop's palace. It is
situated between the Conde and the Rue Alta.

Tarragona

Tarragona Cathedral, Calle de Escribanias Viejas.
This has in its cloister a seventh-century stone
inscribed in Latin and Hebrew. Some very old coins
are preserved in the Provincial Archaeological
Museum. The gate to the medieval Juderia still
stands at the entrance to Calle de Talavera.

Toledo

Though it now has no established community,
Toledo is the historical centre of Spanish Judaism.
Well worth a visit are two ancient former
synagogues. One is the El Transito (in Calle de
Samuel Levi), founded by Samuel Levi, the
treasurer of King Pedro I, in the 14th century. It has
been turned by the Spanish Government into a
museum of Sephardi culture. The other, now the
Church of Santa Maria la Blanca, is the oldest
Jewish monument in Toledo, having been built in
the 13th century. It stands in a quiet garden in what
was once the heart of the Juderia, not far from the
edge of the Tagus River. Also of interest is the
house of Samuel Levi, in which El Greco, the
famous painter, lived. The house is now a museum
of his works.

The Plaza de la Juderia, half-way between El
Transito and Santa Maria la Blanca, was part of the

Spain

city's two ancient Jewish quarters, where many houses and streets are still much as they were 500 years ago.

Torremolinos

Synagogues

Beth Minzi, Calle Skal La Roca 16   (95) 383952
Calle Skal La Roca is a small street at the seaward end of the San Miguel pedestrian precinct, almost opposite the Police Station. Sephardi and Ashkenazi services are held on Sabbath morning at 9.30am and Friday evening services are held at 6.30pm in winter and 8.30pm in summer.

Tortosa

Museums

The Musem of Santa Domingo Convent
This preserves the sixth-century gravestone of 'Meliosa, daughter of Judah of blessed memory'.

Tudela

Juderia

The remains of the Juderia are near the cathedral. There is memorial stone to the great Jewish traveller, Benjamin of Tudela.

Valencia

Synagogues

Calle Asturias 7-4'   (96) 334-3416
Services: Friday eve. & festivals.
Office, Calle Ingeniero Joaquin Belloch 46006
    (96) 339901

Vitoria

The monument on the Campo de Judimendi commemorates the ancient Jewish cemetery which, following the edict of expulsion in 1492. The town council undertook to take care of, and never to build over it.

Zaragoza

Historic Sites

126 - 132 Calle del Coso
This city was once a very important Jewish centre. A mikva has been discovered in the basement of the modern building found at this address.

Balearic Islands

Majorca

Majorca's Jewish population today numbers about 300, although fewer than 100 are registered with the community. Founded in 1971, it was the first Jewish community in Spain to be officially recognised since 1435. The Jewish cemetery is at Santa Eugenia, some 12 miles from Palma.

Palma Cathedral containes some interesting Jewish relics, including a candelabrum with 365 lights, which was originally in a synagogue. In the 'Tesoro' room are two unique silver maces, over 6 feet long, converted from Torah 'rimonim' brought from Sicily in 1493. The Santa Clara Church stands on the site of another pre-Inquisition synagogue. The Montezion Church was, in the 14th century, the Great Synagogue of this capital. In Calle San Miguel is the Church of San Miguel, which also stands on the site of a former synagogue. It is not far from the Calle de la Plateria, once a part of the Palma Ghetto.

Cemeteries

Santa Eugenia

Community Organisations

Communidad Israelita de Mallorca
Apartado Correos 389   (971) 283799

Synagogues

Orthodox

Communidad Israelita de Mallorca (Jewish Community of Mallorca)
Monsenyor Palmer 3 07014   (971) 283-799
    Email: r_ajkatz@hotmail.com
Web site: www.fortunecity.com/victorian/coldwater/252
This synagogue was dedicated to the community in June 1987. Services are held on Fridays and Holy-days. A communal Seder is also held. The community invites all congregants and guests to kiddush following the services.

Canary Islands

The first Jewish immigrants to the Canary Islands were Conversos from Spain seeking refuge from the Inquisition.

La Palmas De Gran Canaria

Synagogues
Ap. Correos 2142   (928) 248497

Tenerife

Kashrut Information
General Mola 4, Santa Cruz 38006   (922) 274157
Welcomes all Jewish visitors

Organisations
Comunidad Israelita de Tenerife
               (922) 247296, 247246

Synagogues
Ap. De Correos 939 38001

Sri Lanka

Islamic and Samaritan legend relates that Adam came to the island after his expulsion from Eden and that Noah's Ark came to rest there. Solid evidence for Jewish settlement was recorded about 1,000 years ago by Muslim travellers. There was a small Jewish community when the Dutch took the island as a colony. This attracted Jews from southern India to the island because of the possibilities of trade.

There was a plan put forward when the island came under British rule for mass Jewish immigration. The Chief Justice, Sir Alexander Johnston appeared to consider the idea a serious one, but the British government did not act on it. A coffee estate was founded in 1841 near Kandy by Jews from Europe.

There is no communual organisation on the island. The Sri Lankans appear to be supportive of Israel, despite the government's official pro-Arab stance. Diplomatic relations with Israel were resumed in May 2000.

GMT + 5.5 hours   Total Population 18,318,000
Country calling code (94)   Jewish Population Under 100
Emergency Telephone (Police - 433333) (Fire and Ambulance - 422222)
Electricity voltage 230/240

Colombo

Kashrut Information
82 Rosmead Place 7   (1) 695642
                   Fax: (1) 446543

Suriname

Suriname's Jewish community is very old – the first Jews settled in the seventeenth century, escaping from persecution in Brazil. Jews came later from Britain, after the country had passed into British hands. Suriname welcomed more Jewish refugees from the Caribbean and the country became a Dutch colony in 1668, bringing Sephardi Jews from Amsterdam. Eventually, half the white population in the country was Jewish, and there was a 'Jodensavanne' (Jewish savannah), where the Jews owned large sugar plantations. They called the plantations by Hebrew names and built a synagogue in 1685. The community began to decline in the nineteenth century. Recently, many have emigrated to Israel.

Today, there are two synagogues in Paramaribo, the capital. The Ashkenazi synagogue, like the one in Curaçao, has a sandy floor, which is symbolic of the 40 years in the desert and was also supposed to have muffled the footsteps of the Conversos as they carried out their Judaism in secret.

GMT - 3 hours	Total Population 432,000
Country calling code (597)	Jewish Population 200
Electricity voltage 110/220	

Paramaribo

Kashrut Information

Commewijnestr. 21

      (6) 400236
      Fax: (6) 471154

Organisations

Jewish Community
PO Box 1834

      (692) 11998

Synagogues

Ashkenazi

Neveh Shalom, Keizerstr. 82

Services are held every Shabbat in each synagogue alternately.

Sephardi

Sedek Ve Shalom
Herenstr. 20
The entire contents of this 18th century synagogue are currently on 'long term loan' to the Israel Museum in Jerusalem

Tourist Sites

Sights to see include Joden Savanah (Jewish Savanah) one of the oldest Jewish settlements in the Americas.

Sweden was under the influence of the Lutheran church until the late eighteenth century and was opposed to Jewish settlement. Aaron Isaac from Mecklenburg in Germany, a seal engraver, was the first Jew admitted into the country, in 1774. The emancipation of Jews in Sweden was a slow process; Jews had limited rights, as they were designated a 'foreign colony'. After a gradual lifting of restrictions in the nineteenth century, Jews were fully emancipated in 1870, although ministerial office was closed to them until 1951.

The emancipation heralded the growth of the community, and many eastern European Jews found refuge in Sweden at the beginning of the twentieth century. The initial refusal to accept Jews fleeing the Nazis changed to sympathy as evidence for the Holocaust mounted, and in 1942 many Jews and other refugees were allowed into the country, followed, in 1943, by almost all of Danish Jewry. Sweden also accepted Hungarian, Czechoslovakian and Polish Jews after the war.

There is an Offical Council of Jewish Communities in Sweden, and many international Jewish groups, such as WIZO and B'nai B'rith, are represented. There are three synagogues in Stockholm, including the imposing Great Synagogue built in 1870. There are synagogues in other large towns. Although shechita is forbidden, kosher food is imported, and there are some kosher shops.

GMT + 1 hour	Total Population 8,858,000
Country calling code (46)	Jewish Population 18,000
Emergency Telephone (Police, fire and Ambulance - 112)	Electricity voltage 220

Boras

Organisations

Jewish Community of Boras & Synagogue
Varbergsvagen 21, Box 46 50305   (33) 124892
Email: s. rytz@vertextrading.se

Gothenburg

Groceries

Dr. Allards, gata 4   (31) 741-1545

Media

Radio

Thursdays at 9pm on 94.4 MHz.

Organisations

Jewish Community Centre and Community Offices
Ostra Larmgatan 12 S-411 07   (31) 177245
Fax: (31) 7119360
Email: kansli@judforsgot.o.se

Synagogues

Conservative

Ostra Larmgatan 12 S-411 07   (31) 177245
Fax: (31) 711-9360
Email: kansli@judforsgot.o.se

Orthodox

Storgatan 5

Helslingborg

Organisations

Jewish Centre
Springpostgranden 4

Lund

Synagogues

Orthodox

Winstrupsgatan 1   (46) 148052
Services on festivals and High Holy-days only.

Malmo

Mikvaot

Kamrergatan 11   (40) 118860

Organisations

Jewish Community Centre
Kamrergatan 11, Box 4198 20313
(40) 611 6460; 8860; 976043 (Rabbi)
Fax: (40) 234-469
Email: rabeli@alfa.telenordia.se

Synagogues

Orthodox

Foreningsgatan

Stockholm

Embassy

Embassy of Israel
Torstenssongatan 4, 11456, PO Box 14006 S-104 40
(8) 663-1465
Fax: (8) 662-5301
Email: israel.embassy.swipnet.se

Gift Shops

Menorah: Community Centre Shop
Judaica House, Nybrogatan 19, POB 5053 10242
(8) 663-6580

Groceries

Kosherian Blecher & Co
Nybrogatan 19, P O Box 5053, PO Box 5053 10242
(8) 663-6580
Fax: (8) 663-6580
Kosher groceries. Also offers cooked meals such as burgers, sausages, meat sandwiches etc. Delivery to group, hotels etc.

Kashrut Information

Rabbi Meir Horden
Community House, Wahrendorffsgatan 3B, PO Box
7427 10391   (8) 679-2900
Email: info@judiskacentret.a.se
Rabbi Meir Horden supervises kashrut in Stockholm. For the latest and most updated information on kashrut issues, please contact Rabbi Horden's office at the Jewish Community of Stockholm, see Organisations.

Libraries

The Jewish Library
Wahrendorffsgatan 3, PO Box 7427 10391
(8) 679-2934
Fax: (8) 611-2413
Raoul Wallenberg Room also on premises, named after the Swedish diplomat who saved scores of thousands of Hungarian Jews from the Nazis, was arrested by the Russians in Budapest in 1945 and disappeared.

Sweden

Media

Judisk Kronika
P O Box 5053 10242   (8) 660-3872
Fax: (8) 660-3892
Email: judisk.kronika@swipnet.se
Menorah, PO Box 5053 10242   (8) 667-6770
Fax: (8) 663-7676
Email: kh-uia@swipnet.se
Web site: www.menorah-sweden.com

Mikvaot
Community Centre
Judaica House, Nybrogatan 19 10242   (8) 663-2989

Museums
Jewish Museum
Halsingegatan 2   (8) 318 404
Fax: (8) 318404
Email: info@judiska-museet.a.se
Web site: www.judiska-museet.a.se
Arranges exhibitions about the history of Swedish Jewry and is open every day, except Saturday, betweee noon and 4pm

Organisations
Community Centre
Judaica House, Nybrogatan 19, PO Box 5053 10242
(8) 663-6566, 662-6686
Fax: (8) 667-3755
Email: info@judiskacentret.a.se
Jewish Community of Stockholm
Wahrendorffsgatan 3, PO Box 7427 10391
(8) 679-2900
Fax: (8) 679-5042
Open Monday to Thursday 9am-5pm Friday 9am-4pm (closed for lunch noon-1pm)

Restaurants
Community Centre
Nybrogatan 19 10242   (8) 663-6566, 662-6686
Fax: (8) 667-3755
Email: info@judishacentret.a.se
Kosher lunches under Rabbi Meir Horden's supervision at the Community Center are available during the summer. Dinners can be arranged at the Community Centre for groups. Contact Mr Ike Tankus. Tel: 468 647-4475.
Lao Wai
Luntmakargatan 74   (8) 673-7800
Supervision: Rabbi Meir Honden.
Mino's Café
Tegnergatan 36   (8) 30 77 42
Jewish North African Cuisine. All meats kosher but no kosher licence.

The Judaica House
Nybrogatan 19   (8) 663-6566; 662-6686
Offers a meat menu Monday to Friday, 11:30 am to 1:00 pm.

Synagogues

Masorti

Great Synagogue
Wahrendorffsgatan 3, P.O.Box 7427 10391
(8) 679-2900
Fax: (8) 611-2413/679-5042
Email: kansli@jf-stockholm.org
Services: Monday, Thursday morning, Friday evenings & Saturday morning. Open to tourists Mon. - Fri from 10am till 2pm.

Orthodox

Adat Jeshurun
Riddargatan 5PO Box 5053 10242   (8) 679-2900
Fax: (8) 663-6580
Daily services: Weekdays 7.45 am, Shabat 9 am, Sunday 8.30 am.
Adat Jisroel
St. Paulsgatan 13 S11846   (8) 679-2900
Daily Services: weekdays 7.30am, Shabat 9.00am, Sunday 8.15am

Tourist Information
Israeliska Statens Turistbyra
Sveavagen 28-30, 4 tr., Box 7554, 10393 Stockholm 7
(8) 21-3386/7
Fax: (8) 21-7814
Email: info@igto.se
Web site: www.goisrael.nu

Uppsala

Organisations
Jewish Students Club.
Dalgatan 15   (8) 125453

Switzerland

Swiss Jewry originated in medieval times and their history followed the standard course of medieval European Jewry – working as money-lenders and pedlars, attacked by the local population, who accused them of causing the Black Death, then resettling a few years afterwards, only to be subsequently expelled.

By the late eighteenth century, when the Helvetic Confederation was formed, there were three small communities. Freedom of movement was allowed, and full emancipation was granted in 1866. Theodor Herzl held the first World Zionist Conference in Basle in 1897.

Although Switzerland accepted some refugees from Nazism, many were refused, and most of the new refugee Jewish population emigrated soon after the war. The community today has a central body, and is made up of various factions, from ultra-Orthodox to Reform. The major towns have synagogues, and kosher meat is imported. There are several hotels with kosher facilities. Over half of the community live in the German-speaking area, the French-speaking area has the second largest number, and a few are in the southern, Italian-speaking area.

Switzerland had elected its first Jewish (and first woman) president, Ruth Dreifuss.

GMT + 1 hour	Total Population 7,087,000
Country calling code (41)	Jewish Population 18,000
Emergency Telephone (Police - 117) (Fire - 118) (Ambulance - 144)	Electricity voltage 220

Arosa

Hotels
Levin's Hotel Metropol

(81) 377-4444
Fax: (81) 377-2100
Mikva on premises. Own Kosher bakery.

Baden

Catering
Atrium Hotel Blume
Kurplatz 4 5400

(56) 222-5569
Fax: (56) 222-4298
Email: atriumhotel_blume@bluewin.ch
Prepacked kosher meals on request

Synagogues
Israelitische Kultusgemeinde Baden
Parkstrasse 17 5400

(56) 221-5128
Fax: (56) 222-9447
Email: office @bollag
Friday nights: Winter 18.30; Summer 19.30.
Shabbath and Festivals: mornings 8.45am.

Basel

Bakeries
Bakery Schmutz
Austrasse 53   (61) 272-4765
IGB & IRG   (61) 272-6365

Booksellers & Gifts
Victor Goldschmidt
Mostackerstrasse 17 4051   (061) 261 61 91
Fax: (061) 261 61 23

Butchers
Genossenschaftsmetzgerei
Friedrichstrasse 26 CH-4055   (61) 301-3493
Fax: (61) 381-6939
Supervision: Both Basl Rabbinates.
Also sells groceries and wine. Open 7.30am-12.00 noon, 3pm-6.30. Closed Friday afternoon.

Hotels
Hotel Drei Konige
(61) 261-5252
Fax: (61) 261-2153
Offers kosher meals on request.
Hotel Euler
Centralbahnplatz 14 4002   (61) 272-4500
Fax: (61) 271-5000
Offers kosher meals on request.

Media
Newspapers
Judische Rundschau Maccabi
Austr. 25 4009   (61) 206-6060
Fax: (61) 206-6060

Mikvaot
Eulerstr. 10 4051   (61) 301-6831
Thannerstrasse 60   (61) 301-2200

Switzerland

Museums
Jewish Museum of Switzerland
Kornhausgasse 8 4051   (61) 261-9514
Hours: Monday and Wednesday, 2 pm to 5 pm;
Sunday, 11 am to 5 pm. Free entrance.

Restaurants
Restaurant Topas
Leimenstrasse 24 4051   (61) 206-9500
                                    Fax: (61) 206-9501
                            Email: pessach@access.ch
                        Web site: www.restaurant-topas.ch
Supervision: Under the supervision of local rabbinical
authority..
Hours: 11:30 am to 2 pm Sunday to Friday. 6:30 pm
to 9 pm Sunday to Thursday. Friday night, Shabbat
lunch and holidays by reservation before 2 pm of
preceding day.

Synagogues
Israelitische Gemeinde Basel
Leimenstrasse 24 4003   (61) 279-9840
                                    Fax: (61) 279-9851
                                    Email: igb@igb.ch

Israelitische Religionsgemeinschaft
Ahornstrasse 14   (61) 301-4898
Rabbi Telephone: 302-5391

Bern

Embassy
Embassy of Israel
Alpenstrasse 32 3006   (31) 356-3500
                                    Fax: (31) 356-3556
                            Email: info@emb.israel.ch

Synagogues
Synagogue & Community Center
Kapellenstrasse 2   (31) 381-4992
                                    Fax: (31) 382-3861
                                    Email: info@jgb.ch
                                    Web site: www.jgb.ch
Rabbiner Dr Michael Leipziger 41-31 381-7303.

Biel/Bienne

Synagogues
Ruschlistrasse 3   (32) 331-7251

Bremgarten / Aargau

Contact Information
Israelitische Cultusgemeinde
Werner Meyer-Moses, Ringstrasse. 37 CH-5620
                                        (56) 633-6626
                                    Fax: (56) 633-6626

Synagogues
Luzernstr. 1

Davos

Hotels
Etania   (81) 416-5404
                                    Fax: (81) 416-2592
                            Email: etania@bluewin.ch
Supervision: Zurich Rabbinate.

Mikvaot
Etania Rest Home
                                        (81) 416-5404
                                    Fax: (81) 416-2592

Synagogues
Etania Rest Home
Richtsattweg 3, 7270   416-5404

Endingen

Contact Information
J. Bloch, Buckstr. 2 5304   (56) 242-1546
Can arrange visits to the old synagogues and cemetery.

Engelberg

Hotels
Hotel Marguerite
6390 Engelberg   (41) 637-2522
                                    Fax: (41) 637-2926
Supervision: Agudas Achim, Zurich.
Mikva on premises.

Fribourg

Synagogues
9 avenue de Rome   (26) 322-1670

Geneva

Butchers
Boucherie Kosher
Biton 21, rue de Montchoisi   (22) 736-3168

Embassy
Permanent Mission of Israel to the United Nations
9 Chemin Bonvent, Cointrin, Cointrin 1216

Media
Israelitsches Wochenblatt/Revue Juive
Avenue du Mail 5 1205   (22) 800-1026
                                    Fax: (22) 800-1028

Revue Juive/Israelitisches Wochenblatt
10 rue de Beulet, 1211, Geneva 18 1211
(22) 940-2025
Fax: (22) 940-2028

Mikvaot
(22) 346-9732
(22) 736-9632

Restaurant
Restaurant Le Neguev
Rue de la Servette 20 1201 (22) 740-4070
Supervision: Rabbi A Y Schlesinger.
Near to the town centre and 200 yards from the train station.

Restaurants
Le Jardin Rose
10, rue St-Leger (22) 317-8950
Fax: (22) 317-8910
Only open for lunch but arrangements can be made so that lunches and dinners can be delivered to any hotel downtown.

Meat
Heimishe Kitchen
Av Jules Crosnier 4 1206 (22) 346-1741
Fax: (22) 346-0830
Supervision: Machsike Hadas.

Synagogues
Beth Habad
12 rue du Lac (22) 736-3682
The Geneva Synagogue (Ashkenazi)
Place de la Synagogue
Liberal
12 Quai du Seujet (22) 732-3245
Orthodox
Machsike Hadass
2 place des Eaux Vives 1207 (22) 786-2589
Sephardi
Hekhal Haness
54 ter route de Malagnou (22) 736-9632

Kreuzlingen
Contact Information
Louis Hornung
Schulstr. 7 (71) 671-1630

Lausanne
Community Organisations
Communauté Israélite de Lausanne
3 avenue de Georgette, case postale 336 1001
(21) 341-7240
Fax: (21) 341-7241

Groceries
Kolbo Shalom, 7 avenue Juste-Olivier (21) 312-1265

Mikvaot
1 avenue Juste-Olivier (21) 617-5818

Restaurants
Community Centre
3 avenue de Georgette 1003 (21) 341-7242
Serves lunch only, from 12 pm to 2 pm.

Synagogues
Orthodox
1 avenue Juste-Olivier (21) 320-9911
Corner of J. Olivier and av. Florimont

Lengnau
Contact Information
(56) 241-1203
For visits to the old synagogue and cemetery.

Lucerne
Butchers
Judische Metzgerei
Bruchstrasse 26 (41) 240-2560

Mikvaot
Bruchstrasse 51 (41) 320-4750

Switzerland

Synagogues
Bruchstrasse 51   (41) 240-6400

Lugano

Hotels
Hotel Dan
Via Fontana 1 6902   (91) 985-7030

Kashrut Information
via Olgiati 1   (91) 922-9955
Mon.-Thurs. 5.30pm-7pm

Mikvaot
Via Maderno 11

Synagogues
Via Maderno 11   (91) 932-6134

Montreux

Synagogues
Synagogue in Montreux
25 avenue des Alpes

Solothurn

Contact Information
R. Dreyfus, Grenchenstr. 8   (32) 623-2327

St. Moritz

Hotels
Hotel Edelweiss
                                         (81) 833-5533
                                    Fax: (81) 833-5573

St. Gallen

Synagogues
Frongartenstrasse 18   (71) 223-5923

Vevey

Restaurants
Les Bergers du Leman
                                      (21) 923-5355/54
                                    Fax: (21) 922-5923

Synagogues
3 blvd. Plumhof,
                                         (21) 923-5354
                                    Fax: (21) 922-5923

Winterthur

Synagogues
Rosenstrasse 5   (52) 232-8136

Yverdon

Contact Information
Dr Maurice Ellkan
1400 Cheseaux-Noreaz   (24) 425-1851

Zug

Restaurants
Restaurant Glashof
Baarerstr. 41 6301   (42) 221-248
Prepared kosher meals are available.

Zurich

Jews first arrived in Zurich in 1273. Over the following two centuries Jews were repeatedly expelled and allowed to return. There are five stained-glass Chagall windows in the Fraumunster Church (located at Munsterhof Square) of which four are on themes from the Hebrew Bible.

Bakeries
Ruben Bollag
Waffenplatzstrasse 5, (near Bahnhof Enge) 8002
                                         (1) 202-3045

Ruben Bollag
Brauerstrasse 110 8004   (1) 242-8700
                                    Fax: (1) 291-4684

Booksellers
Morasha, Seestrasse 11 8002   (1) 201.11.20
                                    Fax: (1) 201.31.20
                          Email: morascha@bluemail.ch
                         Web site: www.hagalil.com/kolbo
Supervision: Monday, Tuesday and Thursday 9am to 12noon and 2pm to 6.30pm, Wednesday 9am to 6.30pm and Friday 9am to 12 noon..

Butchers
Taam/Metzgerei
                                         (1) 463-9094
Supervision: Judische Gemeinde Agudas Achim.
Zukom, 8 Aemtlerst   (1) 451-8384
                                    Fax: (1) 451-8386
Supervision: Judische Gemeinde Aguda Achim and Israelitsche Religionsgellschaft..

Hotels
Hotel International
                                         (1) 311-4341
Offers kosher meals on request

Media
Israelitisches Wochenblatt/Revue Juive
Rudigerstr 10, Postfach 8027   (1) 206-4200
                                    Fax: (1) 206-4210
                              Email: verlag@iwrj.ch

Jewish City Guide of Switzerland
Spectrum Press International, Im Tannegg 1,
Friesenbergstrasse 221 8055

(1) 462-6411; 462-6412
Fax: (1) 462-6462

Published quarterly in English and German, a guide to
Jewish communities throughout Switzerland.

Mikvaot

(1) 202-0127
Appointment by phone between 9a.m. & 11a.m.
Freigutstrasse 37 (1) 201-7306
Appointment by phone between 9a.m. & 11a.m.

Restaurants
Restaurant Shalom
G. van Dijk Lavaterstrasse 33-37 8002 (1) 201-1476
Fax: (1) 201-1496
Email: catering.schalom@bleuwin.ch

Dairy

Fein & Schein
Schontalstrasse 14, Corner/Ecke Hallwylstrasse
(1) 241-3040
Fax: (1) 241-2112
Supervision: IRGZ Rabbi Daniel Levy.

Meat

Club Savjon, G. van Dijk-Neufeld., Lavaterstr. 33
(1) 201-1476
Supervision: Rabbi Rothschild.

Synagogues
Manessestrasse 198 8045 (1) 202-8784
Freigutstrasse 37 (1) 201-4998
Beth Hamidrash, Chasidei Gur
(1) 242-3899
Chabad Minjan Esra
(1) 386-8403
Israel, Religionsgesellschaft
Freigutstrasse 37 8002 (1) 201-6746
Israelitische Cultusgemeinde
Lavaterstrasse 33 8002 (1) 201-1659
Fax: (1) 202-2287
Email: info@icz.org
Judische Gemeinde Agudas Achim
Erikastrasse 8 8003 (1) 463-5798
Minjan Bels, Weststrasse 151 (1) 463-6598
Minjan Brunau
Mutschellenstrasse 11-15 (1) 202-5167
Minjan Machsikei Hadass
Anwandstrasse 60 (1) 241-3759
Rabbi Schmerler: 01-242-9046
Minjan Wollishofen
Etzelstrasse 6 8038 (1) 289-7050
Email: mmorgen@ivr.unizh.ch
Chabad Lubavitch. Contact person Gabai H
Horgenbesser.

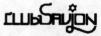

Taiwan

The US Army brought the first Jews to Taiwan in the 1950s, when an American base, now closed, was set up in the country. In the 1970s, some Jewish businessmen began to work on the island, serving two- or three-year contracts with their companies. Most are Americans, although there are some Israelis and other nationalities. Services are held on shabbat in a hotel, and there is a Jewish community centre.

GMT + 8 hours	Total Population 21,463,000
Country calling code (886)	Jewish Population Under 100
Emergency Telephone (Police - 110) (Fire and Ambulance - 119)	Electricity voltage 110

Taipei

Organisations
Taiwan Jewish Community Centre
No 1, Lane 61, Teh Hsing East Road, Shihlin
(2) 396-0159
Fax: (2) 396-4022
Services are held on most Friday evenings at 7.30pm. Visitors to check in advance. All holy-days and major festivals are celebrated.

Restaurants

Meat

Y.Y.'s Steakhouse
Chungshan North Road, Section 3, cnr. The Huei St.
There are no kosher restaurants in Taipei, but this
Steakhouse has a separate kitchen and dining room, where kosher meat meals are served on separate crockery, with separate cutlery. No milk products are available in this section.

Synagogues

Orthodox

Ritz Landis Hotel
41 Min Chuan East Road
(2) 2597-1234
Fax: (2) 2596-9223
Email: ritz@theritz-taipei.com
Shabbat and festival services are held here, also, when Minyan is available, Weekday Services.

One of the former Soviet Republics, Tajikistan has a small Jewish population but, after the fall of the Soviet Union, many Jews emigrated to Israel. The community is a mix of 40 per cent Bokharans and 60 per cent Soviet Jews from other parts of the former USSR who migrated to Tajikistan during the Second World War. The Bokharan Jews are believed to be descendants of Persian Jewish exiles. Dushanbe, the capital, and Shakhrisabz are provided with synagogues, and Dushanbe also has a library.

GMT + 5 hours	Total Population 5,935,000
Country calling code (7)	Jewish Population 1,800
Electricity voltage 220	

Dushanbe

Synagogues

Ashkenazi

Proletarsky Street

Bokharan

Nazyina Khikmeta Street 26

Shakhrisabz

Synagogues
23 Bainal Minal Street

Although the first confirmed presence of Jews in Thailand was in 1890, Thai Jewry really began with Jews escaping Russia and eastern Europe in the 1920s and 1930s, but most of them emigrated after 1945.

The present community arrived in the post-war period of the 1950s and 1960s. They came from Syria and Lebanon, and also Europe and America. Some Israelis also came, and jewellery is an important source of trade with Israel.

Bangkok has Ashkenazi, Sephardi and Lubavitch synagogues. The community centre is based in the Ashkenazi synagogue. The Lubavitch synagogue offers several communual activities, including seders at Passover, which have a large attendance.

GMT + 7 hours
Country calling code (66)
Electricity voltage 220

Total Population 60,003,000
Jewish Population 250

Bangkok

Bakeries
Kosher Store and Bakery
223 Soi Sai, Nam Thip 2 (Soi 22), Sukhumvit (2) 663-8719

Embassy
Embassy of Israel
'Ocean Tower II' 25th floor, 75 Sukhumvit Soi 19, Asoke Road 10110 (2) 204-9200
Fax: (2) 204-9255
Email: consul.bkk@israelfm.org

Kashrut Information
(2) 234-0606
(2) 318-1577
(2) 237-1697

Organisations
Jewish Community of Thailand
Beth Elisheva Building, 121 Soi Sai, Nam Thip 2, Sukhumvit Soi 22 (2) 663-0244
Fax: (2) 663-0245
Email: ykantor@ksc15.th.com
Web site: www.jewishthailand.com
Friday night and Shabbat services with Kiddush & Shabbat meal. Holidays services. Call to confirm.

Restaurants
Ohr Menachem - Chabad House
108/1 Ram Buttri Rd, Kaosarn Road, Banglampoo (2) 282-6388
Fax: (2) 629-1153
Supervision: Rabbi Y. Kantor.
Open 12 noon to 9 pm daily.

Synagogues
Beth Elisheva
121 Soi Sai Nam Thip 2, Sukhumvit Soi 22 (2) 663-0244
Fax: (2) 663-0245
Email: ykantor@ksc15.th.com
Close to Imperial Queens Park, Jade Pavilion, Rembrandt, Landmark and Sheraton Grande Hotels. Friday night service at candle lighting time followed by Shabbat meal & Shabbat services 10.00 am with Kiddush & Shabbat meal. Call to confirm.
Ohr Menachem - Chabad House
108/1 Ram Buttri Road, Kaosarn Road, Banglampoo (2) 282-6388
Fax: (2) 629-1153
Email: chabadbangkok@yahoo.com
Daily services, Friday evenings at sundown with Shabbat meal, attracts young Jewish travellers

Orthodox
Even Chen, The Bossotel Inn, 55/12-14 Soi Charoenkrung, 42/1 New Road (Silom Road area) (2) 630-6120
Fax: (2) 237-3225
Daily morning service. Regular Friday evening and Shabbat morning, afternoon and evening services. Light kosher meal after shabbat service, by advance reservation.

Tunisia

Tunisia

There is written proof of ancient Jewish settlement in Carthage in the year 200, when the region was under Roman control. The community was successful and was left in peace. Under the Byzantine Empire, conditions for the Jews did worsen, but after the Islamic conquest, the 'golden age' of Tunisian Jewry occurred. There was prosperity and many centres of learning were established. This did not continue into the Middle Ages, as successive Arab and Spanish invasions led to discrimination. Emancipation came from the French, but the community suffered under the Nazi-influenced Vichy government. After the war, many emigrated to Israel or to France and the community is shrinking.

There are several synagogues in the country, together with kindergartens and schools. Tunisia is not as extreme in its attitude towards Israel as some Arab states, and there has been communication between the two countries at a high level. An Israeli Interest Bureau in Tunis acts as an unofficial embassy. The Bardo Museum in Tunis has an exhibition of Jewish ritual objects.

GMT + 1 hour

Country calling code (216)

Electricity voltage 220

Total Population 9,057,000

Jewish Population 2,000

Jerba

There are Jews in two villages on this small island off the Tunisian coast. There is also a magnificent synagogue, El Ghriba, many hundreds of years old, in the village of Er-Riadh (Hara Sghira). Jewish silversmiths are prominent in Hournt souk on rue Bizerte.

Sfax

Synagogues
Azriah, 71 rue Habib Mazoun
Near the Town Hall.

Tunis

Kashrut Information
26 rue de Palestine   (1) 282406; 283540

Organisations
Community Offices
15 rue de Cap Vert   (1) 282469, 287153

Synagogues
Beth Yacob
3 rue Eve, Nohelle   (1) 348964
Grande
43 Av. de la Liberte
Lubavitch Yeshiva
73 rue de Palestine   (1) 791429

There have been Jews in Turkey since at least the 4th century B.C.E., making Turkey one of the earliest Jewish communities. The 15th and 16th centuries were periods of major prosperity for the Jews of Turkey.

After the Expulsion of the Jews from Spain in 1492, at a time when Jews were not tolerated in most of the Christian countries of Western Europe, what was then the Ottoman (Turkish) Empire was their principal land of refuge. The Sultan was reported to have said of the Spanish King: 'By expelling the Jews, he has impoverished his country and enriched mine'.

In 1992 they celebrated the 500th anniversary of the establishment of the community. Under the national constitution, their civil rights were reconfirmed. In recent years, many Jews have emigrated to Israel, Western Europe and the United States.

GMT + 2 hours

Country calling code (90)

Emergency Telephone (Police - 155) (Fire - 110) (Ambulance - 112)

Total Population 62,650,000

Jewish Population 25,000

Electricity voltage 220

Ankara

Embassy
Embassy of Israel
Mahatma Gandhi Sok 85
Gaziosmanpasa

Synagogues
Birlik Sokak
Samanpazari   (312) 311-6200
This Synagogue is not easy to find. Off Anafartalar
Caddesi in Samanpazari, there is a stairway down at
the right of the TC Ziraat Bankasi. The synagogue is
several buildings along the street on the left, behind a
wall. Services every morning. Sabbath morning services
begin at 7 or 7.30am depending on the time of year.

Balat

A coastal town about 20 miles west of Istanbul has
a 500-year-old synagogue. Now closed the keys
are with the mosque next door.

Bursa

Synagogues
Gerush Synagogue
Kurucesme Caddesi   (224) 368-636
Services on Friday evening, Shabbat morning and
festivals. This Synagogue is in the old Jewish quarter.
There are 180 Jews in this town.

Istanbul

Community Organisations
Buyuk Hendek
Sokak No 61Galata   (212) 293-7566
Secretary General: Lina Filiba

Embassy
Consul General of Israel
Valikonag Caddesi No 73   (212) 255-1040
                                        Fax: (212) 225-1048
                        Email: isrcon@comnet.com.tr

Hotels
Cartoon Hotel
Tarlabasi Bulvari Carbaci Sokak 3, Taksim
                                             (212) 238-9328
Supervision: Istanbul Rabbinate.
Merit Antique
Ordu Cadessi 226, Lalei, 34470, Lalelil
                                             (212) 513-9300
                                        Fax: (212) 512-6390
With kosher restaurant.

Religious Organisations
Chief Rabbinate
Yemenici Sokak 23, Beyoglu, Tunel 80050
                                             (212) 293-8794/5
                                        Fax: (212) 244-1980

Restaurants
Meat
Robelyu
Omerpasa Cad 38/1   (216) 385-7181
Supervision: Istanbul Rabbinate.

Synagogues
Askenazi Synagogue
Yuksekkaldinm Sok No 37Galata   (212) 243-6909
Saturdays only.
Beth Israel
Efe Sok No 4Sisli   (212) 240-6599
Every day.
Caddesbostan Synagogue
Tasmektep SokGoztepe   (212) 356-5922
Every day.
Etz Ahayim Synagogue
Muallim Naci Cad No 40 & 41Ortakoy(212) 260-1896
Every day.
Hemdat Israel Synagogue
Izettin Sok No 65Kadikoy   (212) 336-5293
Every day.
Hesed Leavraam Synagogue
Pancur Sok No 15Buyukada   (212) 382-5788
June-September including High Holy days.
Italian Synagogue
Sair Ziya Pasa Yokusu No 27, Karakoy, Galata
                                             (212) 293-7784

Neve Shalom Buyuk Hendek Sok
No 61Galata   (212) 293-7566
Saturdays only.

Izmir

Butchers
Kosher Meat   (232) 148-395
Tuesday and Thursday or inquire at the synagogue.

Community Organisations
Jewish Community Council
Azizler Sokak 920/44Guzelyurt   (232) 123-708
                                        Fax: (232) 421-1290

Synagogues
Beth Israel
265 Mithatpasa StreetKaratas
Shaar Ashamayan
1390 Sokak 4/2, Bikur Holim, Esrefpasa Caddesi,
Alsancak

Ukraine

The Ukraine has had a long and complicated history, with areas of the present country being under the rule of a number of other countries, from Austria to Romania. The history of the Jews who live in the modern-day, independent Ukraine is both long and tragic. From settlement in Kiev in the tenth century, before the concept of a Ukrainian national identity had been formed, the Jewish community grew and was joined by many Jews from central Europe. The Chmielnicki massacre of 1648, in which up to 100,000 were killed, was the worst event to befall the Jews before the Holocaust, and much destruction occurred in the west of the country.

Throughout the nineteenth century, the Ukraine was mainly under Russian domination. After 1918, the Ukraine attempted to become independent, and many Jews were killed in the fighting. The Ukraine absorbed some of south-eastern Poland in 1939 and, after the German invasion of the Soviet Union, the Jewish community suffered terrible losses in the Holocaust.

The community today remains fairly large, and is slowly emerging from the atheist Soviet times. Most Jews live in towns, and Kiev (the capital) is a major centre. There are now Jewish schools, and kosher food can be obtained. In a similar way to Belarus, there are many inspiring places to visit – graves of famous Hassidic masters and the monument to the Babi Yar massacre (near Kiev) are frequent destinations. There have been memorials erected (mainly after the fall of Communism) all over the country to events which happened during the Holocaust.

GMT + 2 hours	Total Population 51,273,000
Country calling code (380)	Jewish Population 400,000
Emergency Telephone (Police - 02) (Fire - 01) Ambulance - 03)	Electricity voltage 220

Berdichev

Mikvaot
4 Dzherzhinskaya Street   (4143) 23938 / 20222

Synagogues
4 Dzherzhinskaya Street   (4143) 23938 / 20222
Kosher kitchen on premises.

Beregovo

Synagogues
17 Sverdlov Street

Bershad

Synagogues
25 Narodnaya Street

Chernigov

Synagogues
34 Kommunisticheskaya Street

Chernovtsy

Synagogues
24 Lukyana Kobylitsa Street   54878

Chmelnitsy

Synagogues
58 Komminnestnaya Street

Dnepropetrovsk

Synagogues
Synagogue of Dniepropetrovsk
7 Kotsubinskovo St. 320030   (562) 342-120
Fax: (562) 342-137
Email: dnepr@jewcom.dp.ua
Web site: www.jew.dp.ua

Donetsk

Synagogues
Synagogue of Donetsk
36 Oktabriskaya Street 340000   (622) 357-725
Fax: (622) 938-155

Ivano-Frankivsk

Synagogues
Synagogue of Ivano-Frankivsk
Strachenyh 7 284000   (34) 22- 23029
Fax: (34) 325-367
Rabbi Rolesnik (22-34894) is prepared to assist those doing historical or genealogical research in the Western Ukraine (Galicia)

Kharkov

Synagogues
48 Kryatkovskaya Street
Web site: www.kharkovejewish.com
Synagogue of Kharkov
12 Pushkinskaya Street 310057   (572) 126-526
Fax: (572) 452-140
Email: chabad@kharkov.com

Orthodox
Orthodox Union Project Reunite
Surnskaya 45   (572) 408-378
Fax: (572) 439-209

Kherson

Synagogues
Synagogue of Kherson
27 Gorkovo Street 325025   (552) 223-334
Fax: (552) 325-367

Kiev

Embassy
Embassy of Israel
Lesi Ukrainki 34, GPE-S 252195

Synagogues
Central Synagogue of Kiev
29 Shchekovitzkaya Street   (44) 417-3583

Reform
Reform Congregation
7 Nemanskaya Street   (44) 295-6539

Korosten

Synagogues
8 Shchoksa Street

Kremenchug

Synagogues
50 Sverdlov Street

Lviv

Situated on the edge of shifting imperial boundaries, this city has been under Austrian, Polish and Soviet control. It has had as many names as its number of rulers – among them Lwów in Polish and Lemberg in German. Now called Lviv in Ukrainian, there are 6,000 Jews in the city, once a major Jewish centre in Galicia. A couple of synagogues are still functioning, and a number of monuments have been erected commemorating the Holocaust. Many Jews on 'heritage tours' use the town as a base to explore the region, and guides (generally Yiddish speaking) are available.

Synagogues
4 Brativ Mikhnovskykh Street 290018   (32) 330-524
Fax: (32) 333-536
Email: bald@link.lviv.ua
Kosher kitchen available: 33-35-35. Tour guide and transportation also available.

Nikolayev

Synagogues
Synagogue of Nikolayev
13 Karl Libknechta Street 327001   (512) 358-310
Fax: (512) 353-072

Odessa

Synagogues
Main Synagogue
Corner of ul.Evreiskaya and ul. Richlieu
Synagogue of Odessa
21 Osipovo St. 270011   (482) 218-890
Fax: (482) 247-296

Simferopol

Synagogues
Synagogue of Simferopol
24 Mironovo Street   (652) 276-932

Slavuta

Synagogues
Kuzovskaya Street 2   (447) 925-452
The first edition of Tanya was printed here by the Shapira family whose tombs are in the cemetery.

Zaparozhe

Synagogues
Synagogue of Zaparozhe
22 Turgeneva Street. 330063   (612) 642-961

Zhitomir

Synagogues
59 Lubarskaya Street   (412) 373-468
Reb Ze'ev Wolf, disciple of Dov Baer, is buried in the Smolanka cemetery.
Synagogue of Zhitomire
7 M. Berdishevskaya St. 262001   (412) 226-608
Fax: (412) 373-428

United Kingdom

There were probably individual Jews in England in Roman and (though less likely) in Anglo-Saxon times, but the historical records of any organised settlement start after the Normal Conquest of 1066. Jewish immigrants arrived early in the reign of William the Conqueror and important settlements came to be established in London (at a site still known as Old Jewry), Lincoln and many other centres. In 1190 massacres of Jews occurred in many cities, most notably in York. This medieval settlement was ended by Edward I's expulsion of the Jews in 1290, after which date, with rare and temporary exceptions, only converts to Christianity or secret adherents of Judaism could live in the country.

After the expulsion of the Jews from Spain in 1492 a secret Marrano community became established in London, but the present Anglo-Jewish community dates in practice from the period of the Commonwealth. In 1650 Menasseh ben Israel, of Amsterdam, began to champion the cause of Jewish readmission to England, and in 1655 he led a mission to London for this purpose. A conference was convened at Whitehall and a petition was presented to Oliver Cromwell. Though no formal decision was then recorded, in 1656 the Spanish and Portuguese Congregation in London was organised. It was followed towards the end of the seventeenth century by the establishment of an Ashkenazi community, which increased rapidly inside London as well as throwing out offshoots before long to a number of provincial centres and seaports. The London community has, however, always comprised numerically the preponderant part of British Jewry.

Although Jews in Britain had achieved a virtual economic and social emancipation by the early nineteenth century they had not yet gained 'political emancipation'. Minor Jewish disabilities were progressively removed and Jews were admitted to municipal rights and began to win distinction in the professions.

During the 19th century British Jews spread out from those callings which had hitherto been regarded as characteristic of the Jews.

There has always been a steady stream of immigration into Britain from Jewish communities in Europe, originally from the Iberian Peninsula and Northern Italy, later from Western and Central Europe. The community was radically transformed by the large influx of refugees which occurred between 1881 and 1914, the result of the intensified persecution of Jews in the Russian Empire. The Jewish population rose from about 25,000 in the middle of the 19th century to nearly 350,000 by 1914. It also became far more dispersed geographically.

From 1933 a new emigration of Jews commenced, this time from Nazi persecution, and again many settled in this country. Since the end of the Second World War and notably since 1956, smaller numbers of refugees have come from Iran, Arab countries and Eastern Europe.

LONDON

Well over half the 300,000 (1991) Jews of Britain live in London. Numbering about 210,000, they are spread throughout the metropolis, with the largest concentration in north-western districts like Golders Green, Hendon, Edgware and Hampstead Garden Suburb. There are also large communities in North London (Stamford Hill) and in the East (Redbridge). Once it was in Stepney that the majority of London Jewry lived and, in spite of many changes there, Aldgate and Whitechapel should be visited, not only for the many reminders of their Jewish heyday, but also for the bustling life which is still to be seen there.

The City

There are many historically interesting sites in the City, that square mile of Central London which adjoins the East End. The Bank of England is a useful starting point.

One of the numerous streets which converge on this busy hub is Poultry, leading quickly to Cheapside. The first street on the right is Old Jewry. Here, and in the neighbourhood, the earliest community lived before England expelled all its Jews in 1290. There were synagogues in this street and in Gresham and Coleman Streets, not far from historic Guildhall, which is itself a 'must' for tourists.

Inside the Royal Exchange, situated opposite the Bank of England in Threadneedle Street, there is a series of murals including one, by Solomon J. Solomon, R.A., of 'Charles I Demanding the Five Members', and a portrait of Nathan Mayer Rothschild, who founded the London house of the famous banking firm. There was a time when the south-east corner of the Royal Exchange was known as 'Jews' Walk'.

The Rothschild headquarters is not far away, in St Swithin's Lane. To reach this handsome building (which has in its entrance-hall more Rothschild portraits, as well as a large tapestry of Moses striking the rock), cross carefully from the Royal Exchange to the Lord Mayor's Mansion House and then turn left into King William Street.

Cornhill, which stretches eastwards from the Bank, leads to Leadenhall Street and its shipping offices and, after a short walk, to Creechurch Lane and the Cunard building, on the back of which is an interesting plaque. 'Site of the First Synagogue after the Resettlement 1657–1701. Spanish and Portuguese Jews' Congregation' is the inscription. Here the post-Expulsion Jews whom Oliver Cromwell welcomed to England set up their house of prayer. In 1701 they built a synagogue in Bevis Marks (close by), modelling it on the famous Portuguese Synagogue in Amsterdam. It has been scheduled by the Royal Commission on Ancient Historical Monuments as 'a building of outstanding value', and is considered one of the most beautiful pieces of synagogue architecture extant. In it are some benches from the Creechurch Lane Synagogue.

London's chief Ashkenazi place of worship, the Great Synagogue, stood, until it was bombed during the Second World War, in Duke's Place, which adjoins Bevis Marks. The 'Duke's Place Shool' (as it was called) was the country's best-known synagogue, the scene of many great occasions and a popular choice for weddings. On the wall of International House, which has replaced it, there is a plaque informing the visitor that the synagogue stood there 'from 1690 and served the community continuously until it was destroyed in September, 1941'.

After the Second World War and until the 1970s, the Great Synagogue was in Adler Street, named after the two Chief Rabbis of that name, Rabbi Nathan Marcus Adler and his son, Rabbi Dr Hermann Adler. Duke's Place leads to Aldgate High Street where, on the opposite side, Jewry Street marks another centre of the pre-Expulsion community. At the time of Richard I's coronation many Jews, escaping from rioting mobs, moved here from Old Jewry.

The East End

Further eastwards, along Aldgate High Street, is Middlesex Street, which becomes the crowded Petticoat Lane every Sunday morning. The cheerful and cheeky language of the stall-holders has made 'The Lane' famous throughout the world. On week-days an offshoot, Wentworth Street, continues the market.

Eastwards again, to Whitechapel, which has changed almost out of all recognition since the days before the Second World War, when it had a teeming Jewish population. Just beyond Aldgate East Underground station, two familiar spots remain: Whitechapel Art Gallery and Whitechapel Library.

The library's extensive Yiddish collection has been transferred to the Taylorian Library, Oxford University's modern-language library. The next turning on the left is Osborne Street, which leads to Brick Lane. A large and sombre building in Brick Lane (at the corner of Fournier Street) represents more than anything else the changes that have taken place in the East End over the years. The Huguenots built it as a church, the Jews turned it into a synagogue (the Machzike Hadass), and now the Bengalis, who have replaced the Jews, have converted it into a mosque.

The former synagogue in Princelet Street (No. 19) is being converted into a museum by the Spitalfields Trust, which is collaborating with the Jewish Museum to develop the building to show the history of the different immigrant groups which have inhabited the Spitalfields area during the

United Kingdom

past 300 years. For further information about activities at the Princelet Street Building, contact the Jewish Museum.

In Brune Street, it is possible to see the building of the former Soup Kitchen for the Jewish Poor that was established in 1902. Its work of distributing food to the small, elderly Jewish community still resident in the area is now undertaken by Jewish Care, the largest Jewish social service organisation in Britain.

Further along Whitechapel Road, outside Whitechapel Underground station, stands a drinking fountain. It was erected in 1911 'in Loyal and Grateful Memory of Edward VII Rex et Imperator from subscriptions raised by Jewish inhabitants of East London'.

Brady Street is the site of an old cemetery, opened for the New Synagogue in 1761 and subsequently used also by the Great Synagogue. The cemetery became full in the 1790s, and it was decided to put a four-foot-thick layer of earth over part of the site, using this for further burials. This created a flat-topped mound in the centre of the cemetery. The cemetery is perhaps the only one where, because of the two layers, the headstones are placed back to back. Among those buried here are Solomon Hirschel, who was Chief Rabbi from 1802 to 1842, and Nathan Meyer Rothschild (1777-1836), the banker. To view the cemetery, contact the United Synagogue Burial Society (020-8343 3456).

In Mile End there are three more old cemeteries: two Sephardi and one Ashkenazi. Behind 253 Mile End Rd., where the Sephardi Home for the Aged (Beth Holim) was located before moving to Wembley, is the first Resettlement cemetery, the oldest existing Anglo-Jewish cemetery, opened in 1657. Abraham Fernandez Carvajal, regarded as the founder of the modern Anglo-Jewish community, is buried here, and also Haham David Nieto, one of the greatest of Sephardi spiritual leaders. At 329 Mile End Road, the Nuevo Beth Chaim, opened in 1725, contains the grave of Haham Benjamin Artom. This is among the 2,000 graves remaining on the site. Some 7,500 were transferred to a site in Brentwood, Essex, during the 1970s. The earliest Ashkenazi cemetery, acquired in 1696, is in Alderney Road, and here the founders of the Duke's Place Synagogue, Moses and Aaron Hart and others, and also the 'Baal Shem of London' (the Cabbalist, Haim Samuel Falk) lie buried. In Beaumont Grove, on the south side of Mile End Road, is the Stepney B'nai B'rith Clubs and Settlement, managed in co-operation with Jewish Care, which caters primarily for the needs of the 7,500 Jews still living in the East End.

In Commercial Road, Hessel Street, another Jewish market centre, is now occupied by Bengali traders. Henriques Street is named after Sir Basil Henriques, a leading welfare worker and magistrate, and founder of the Bernhard Baron St George's Jewish Settlement, who died in 1961. On the same side, three turnings along, is Alie Street. At the Jewish Working Men's Club here in July, 1896, Theodor Herzl addressed a meeting which was effectively the launching of the Zionist movement in Britain.

West Central

Chief Rabbi Hermann Adler (1891–1911) is honoured at the Central Court of the Old Bailey (Underground station: St Paul's), where a mural over the entrance to Court No. 1, entitled 'Homage to Justice', includes the figure of Dr Adler. By the City Boundary, High Holborn is the Royal Fusiliers City of London Regiment Memorial. The names of the 38th, 39th and 40th (Jewish Battalions) are inscribed on the monument together with all other battalions which served in the First World War. At the western edge of the City, Chancery Lane Station, Holborn, is a useful centre for several points of interest. To the east, Furnival Street has the *Jewish Chronicle* office. Northward, Gray's Inn Road leads to Theobald's Road. There, at No. 22, a plaque on the wall recalls that it is the birthplace of Benjamin Disraeli. Further to the north is Great Russell Street, which runs along part of the south side of the British Museum. When visiting the Museum, one should certainly see its collection of illuminated haggadot, in particular its copy of the fifteenth-century Ashkenazi Haggadah. No. 77 Great Russell Street was the headquarters of the Zionist organisations from 1919 to 1964.

Westward, in Chancery Lane, the Public Record Office has in its vast collection many documents of Jewish historical value, including the petitions to Cromwell.

Commonwealth House, 1-19 New Oxford Street, is the new centre of British Jewry's communal activities, housing the Board of Deputies and a range of other offices.

B'nai B'rith-Hillel House, the student centre, is at 1-2 Endsleigh Street, in Bloomsbury, at the heart of the University neighbourhood, and the Council of Christians and Jews in Gordon Street is close by. In the building of University College in Gower Street, the Jewish Studies Library houses the Altmann, Mishcon and Mocatta Libraries and the Margulies Yiddish Collection. The School of Oriental and African Studies in the University precinct includes Judaica and Israelitica in its library.

West End

In the Marble Arch district, in the part of Hyde Park known as 'The Dell', a Holocaust Memorial Garden was dedicated in June 1983. The garden plot was given by the British Government to the Board of Deputies, which commissioned Mr Richard Seifert to design the memorial centre-piece of rocks bearing a quotation from the Book of Lamentations. Also in the Marble Arch area, you will find an important associate of the United Synagogue (the amalgamated Western and Marble Arch Synagogues in Great Cumberland Place), the West End Great, as well as the West London (Reform) Synagogue (Upper Berkeley Street) and the magnificent Victorian New West End Synagogue in St Petersburg Place, just off Bayswater Road. The Jewish Memorial Council and Bookshop is in Enford Street.

The British Zionist Federation was inaugurated at the Trocadero Restaurant in Piccadilly Circus in January 1899. At 175 Piccadilly was the London bureau of the Zionist Organisation, set up in August 1917. Here, Dr Chaim Weizmann and other Zionist leaders worked, and here, in November 1917, the Balfour Declaration was delivered by Lord Rothschild. The Westminster Synagogue in Rutland Gardens, Knightsbridge, houses the Czech Memorial Scrolls Centre, where there is a permanent exhibition telling the story of the salvaging from Prague in 1964 of 1,564 Torah Scrolls confiscated by the Nazis during the Second World War, and of their restoration and the donation of many to communities throughout the world. The exhibition is open from 10 am to 4 pm on Tuesdays and Thursdays, and at other times by appointment.

In St John's Wood are three more interesting synagogues: the New London (Abbey Road) and the St John's Wood (Grove End Road), where the Chief Rabbi, who lives in nearby Hamilton Terrace, generally worships. The third synagogue of great interest in St. John's Wood is the Liberal Jewish, opposite Lord's Cricket Ground, recently rebuilt and renovated.

Stamford Hill

Of London's many synagogues, one remarkable group is the series of Chasidic 'shtiblech' in Stamford Hill (and the yeshivot which are attached to some of them). Cazenove Road contains several of these, and it is here and in the vicinity that the long coats and wide hats of chasidim and the curled sidelocks of their children are to be seen. The Lubavitch Foundation headquarters and the Yesodey Hatorah Schools are in Stamford Hill.

AJEX House at East Bank, Stamford Hill houses an interesting military museum. In this district, also, are North African, Adeni, Indian and some Persian Jews and their synagogues.

North-East

The migration of the Jews from the East End took many of them eventually to the London borough of Redbridge where today the greatest density of London's Jews reside. To obtain a flavour of this large Jewish community one should visit the Redbridge Youth and Community Centre, Sinclair House, Woodford Bridge Road, Ilford, Essex. Sinclair House is a large modern, purpose-built Jewish community centre and it is the base for a number of organisations and the focal point of many Israeli and Zionist communal events. It also houses the Clayhall Synagogue, the Redbridge Jewish Programmes Material Project and community representative councils.

United Kingdom

North-West

The Jewish Museum has moved from Woburn House and opened at new premises in Albert Street, Camden Town. It houses Britain's major collection of ritual articles and Anglo-Judaica.

The starting point for visiting North-West London is Golders Green. Jews first settled here during the First World War, and the Golders Green Synagogue (United) in Dunstan Road, was opened in 1922. Walk down Golders Green Road from the Underground station for half a mile or so, and you will come to Broadwalk Lane on the right-hand side, where the Lincoln Institute is. This is the home of Ohel David, a congregation of Indian Jews, many of whom came to England when India was partitioned in 1947. Their forebears went to India from Baghdad.

On the opposite side of the road, at the end of a short turning called The Riding, is the Golders Green Beth Hamedrash – formerly known as 'Munk's' after its founder in the 1930s, Rabbi Dr Eli Munk. This very Orthodox congregation, mainly of German origin, adheres to the religious principles of Rabbi Samson Raphael Hirsch. There are many other strictly Orthodox congregations in Golders Green, including chasidic groups.

Any of the buses travelling along Golders Green Road away from the Underground station will take you to Bell Lane, in Hendon. A few hundred yards down on the left-hand side is Albert Road, where you will find the London School of Jewish Studies (formerly Jews' College) – established in 1855 as an Institute of Higher Education and associated with London University for many years. A group of Persian Jews holds Shabbat morning services there. Its 70,000-volume library is open to the public.

Also in Hendon in Egerton Gardens, a turning opposite Barnet Town Hall in The Burroughs, 10–15 minutes walk from Bell Lane, is Yakar, which provides a wide variety of adult educational and cultural programmes and has a lending library. Several minyanim are held here on Shabbat and festivals. Further information is available on 020-8202 5552.

Return to Golders Green Underground station from Hendon Central, either by Underground or by bus. Once there, take a bus northwards along Finchley Road for two miles or so, getting off at East End Road, which is more or less opposite the bus stop. On the right-hand side is the Sternberg Centre, the largest Jewish community centre in Europe. The Georgian former manor house contains Leo Baeck College, with its library of 18,000 books, which trains Reform and Liberal rabbis; the offices of the Reform Synagogues of Great Britain; and the London Museum of Jewish Life, now the second centre of the Jewish Museum. In addition to permanent displays, the museum also mounts special exhibitions and runs walking tours and educational programmes. There is a Holocaust memorial, as well as a biblical garden, a bookshop and a dairy snack bar.

GMT	Total Population 58,784,000
Country calling code (44)	Jewish Population 300,000
Emergency Telephone (Police, Ambulance, Fire - 999)	

England

Avon

Bristol

Bristol was one of the principal Jewish centres of medieval England. Even after the Expulsion from England in 1290 there were occasional Jewish residents or visitors. A community of Marranos lived here during the Tudor period. The next Jewish settlement in Bristol was around 1754 and its original synagogue opened in 1786. The present building dates from 1871 and incorporates fittings from the earlier building.

Delicatessens
British Hebrew Congregation   (117) 970-6938
Open alternate Sundays at 10 am.

Organisations
Hillel House
45 Oakfield Road, Clifton, BS8 2BA
                                         (117) 946-6589

Restaurants

Vegetarian
Cherries
122 St Michaels Hill , BS2 8BU   (117) 929-3675
Millwards Vegetarian Restaurant
40 Alfred Place, Kingsdown, BS2 8HD
                                         (117) 924-5026

Synagogues
Bristol Hebrew Congregation
9 Park Row BS1 5LP   (117) 927-3334
              Email: simon770@aol.com
Kosher shop at Synagogue alternate Sundays 10 am to 11.45 am. Services: Friday night at 183 Bishop Road BS7 Summer 7.45 pm, Winter 7 pm. Saturday at Synagogue 9.45 am

Progressive
Bristol & West Progressive Jewish Congregation
43 Bannerman Road, Easton, BS5 0RR
                                         (117) 954-1937
        Email: freedman@fishpond.demon.co.uk
Secretary: 968-3524. Chairman: 973-9312

Bedfordshire

Luton

Synagogues
PO Box 215.
LU1 1HW   (1582) 25032
Fri night and Sabbath morn. services. Office open 9.30am to 12.30pm on Sundays.

Berkshire

Maidenhead

Synagogues

Reform

Constituent of Reform Synagogues of Great Britain
9 Boyn Hill Avenue,
SL6 4ET   (1628) 673012
                        Fax: (1628) 625536
              Email: mheadsyn@aol.com
Services; Fri 8.30pm; Sat 10.30am

Reading

Synagogues
Goldsmid Road,
RG1 7YB   (1734) 571018
        Email: secretary@rhc.datanet.co.uk
   Web site: www.datanet.co.uk/enterprise/rhc/
Thames Valley Progressive Jewish Community
6 Church Street, RG   (1628) 781971

Buckinghamshire

Milton Keynes

Butchers
Gilbert's Kosher Foods
Kestrel House
Mount Avenue, MK1 1LJ
                                         (1908) 646-787
                        Fax: (1908) 646-788
Supervision: London Board of Shechita.

Cambridgeshire

Cambridge

Synagogues

Reform

Beth Shalom Reform Synagogue
                                         (1223) 365614

United Kingdom / Cambridgeshire

Community Organisations

Cambridge L'Chaim Society
33 Bridge Street CB2 1UW   (1223) 366335
Fax: (1223) 366338
Email: cambridge@.chaim.org

Cambridge University Jewish Society
33 Thompson's Lane CB5 8AQ   (1223) 354783
Email: soc-cujs@lists.cam.ac.uk
Web site: www.cam.ac.uk/societies.cujs

Kosher Food

Derby Stores
Derby Street   (1223) 354391
Stocks a range of kosher food and wine; fresh bread products each Thursday lunchtime. Can purchase goods to order.

Kosher Meals

(1223) 352145
There is a kosher canteen during term time serving lunch most weekdays and Friday night and Shabbat meals.

Synagogues

Orthodox

Cambridge Synagogue
Syn/Student Centre
3 Thompsons Lane, CB5 8AQ   (1223) 354783
or 368346 answer phone
Web site: www.cam.ac.uk/societies/cujs/h_cmmnty.htm
Daily morning and evening service during term time. Friday evening and Saturday morning during vacations, other services by arrangement.

Cleveland

Middlesbrough

Restaurants

Vegetarian

Filberts
47 Borough Road TS1 4AF   (1642) 245-455

Cumbria

Grasmere

Hotels

Lancrigg Vegetarian Country House Hotel
Easedale LA22 9QN   (1539) 435317

Devon

Exeter

In pre-Expulsion times, Exeter was an important Jewish centre.

Synagogues

Synagogue Place, Mary Arches Street, EX4 3BA
(1392) 251529
Fax: (1392) 01363-772338
Email: exeshul@eclipse.co.uk
The synagogue was built in 1763, while the cemetery in Magdalen Road dates from 1757. The synagogue, a Grade II* listed building, has just had a major refurbishment.

Plymouth

The congregation was founded in 1752 and a synagogue erected ten years later. This is now the oldest Ashkenazi synagogue building in England still used for its original purpose. It is a scheduled historical monument. In 1815 Plymouth was one of the most important provincial centres of Anglo-Jewry.

Libraries

Holcenberg Collection
Plymouth Central Library, Drake Circus, PL4 8AL
(1752) 305907/8
Fax: (1752) 305905
Email: ref@plymouth.gov.uk
Web site: www.plymouth.gov.uk/star/library.htm
A Jewish collection of fiction and non-fiction books, mainly lending copies.

Restaurants

Vegetarian

Plymouth Arts Centre Vegetarian Restaurant
38 Looe Street PL4 0EB   (1752) 202-616
Hours: lunch, Monday to Saturday, 12 pm to 2 pm; dinner, Tuesday to Saturday, 5 pm to 8 or 8.30 pm.

Synagogues

Ashkenazi

Plymouth Hebrew Congregation
Catherine Street PL1 2AD   (1752) 301955
Email: plymshul@ndirect.co.uk
Services: Fri., 6pm; Sat., 9:30am. The congregation offers free use of minister's modern flat as holiday accommodation in return for conducting Orthodox Friday evening and Saturday morning services.

Torquay

Bed & Breakfasts
Brookesby Hall Hotel
Hesketh Road, Meadfoot Beach, TQ1 2LN
(1803) 292-194
Strictly vegetarian/vegan. 14 rooms. Bus stop 200 yards away.

Synagogues
Old Town Hall, Abbey Road, TQ1 1BB
(1803) 607724
Covering also Brixham and Paignton. Services first Sabbath of every month and festivals 10.30am

Dorset

Bournemouth

The Bournemouth Hebrew Congregation was established in 1905, when the Jewish population numbered fewer than 20 families. Today, the town's permanent Jewish residents number 3,500 out of a total population of some 15,000. During the holiday season, however, there are many more Jews in Bournemouth, for it is an extremely popular resort with kosher hotels, guest houses and other holiday accommodation.

Delicatessens
Louise's Butchers & Deli
164 Old Christchurch Road BH1 1NU
(1202) 295-979
Fax: (1202) 295-979
Supervision: Kedassia.

Hotels
Kosher

New Ambassador Hotel
Meyrick Road East Cliff, BH1 3DP (1202) 555-453
Fax: (1202) 311-077
Website: www.newamb.com
Supervision: London Beth Din.
112 rooms, all with bathroom en suite.

Normandie Hotel
Manor Road East Cliff, BH1 3HL (1202) 552-246
Fax: (1202) 291-178
Supervision: Kedassia.
71 rooms.

Mikvaot
Orthodox

Bournemouth Hebrew Congregation
Synagogue Chambers Wootton Gardens, BH1 1PW
(1202) 557-443

Organisations
Bournemouth Jewish Representative Council
(1202) 762101

Synagogues
Orthodox

Bournemouth Hebrew Congregation
Synagogue Chambers Wootton Gardens, BH1 1PW
(1202) 557-433
Fax: (1202) 557-578
Email: bhc.1@virgin.net

Reform

Bournemouth Reform Synagogue
53 Christchurch Road BH1 3PN (1202) 557736

Essex

Basildon

Contact Information
M. Kochmann
3 Furlongs SS16 4BW   (1268) 524947
                              Fax: (1268) 271358
          Email: max.kochmann@btinternet.com

Synagogues

Affiliated

Basildon Hebrew Congregation
3 Furlongs SS16 4BW   (1268) 524947
                              Fax: (1268) 271358
          Email: max.kochmann@btinternet.com

Chigwell

Synagogues
Limes Avenue, Limes Farm Estate, IG7 5NT

Harlow

Synagogues

Reform

Harlow Jewish Community
Harberts Road Essex CM20 4DT   (1279) 432503

Hornchurch

Synagogues

Affiliated

Elm Park Synagogue
Woburn Avenue Elm Park, Essex RM12 4NG
                                    (1708) 449305

Ilford

Grocers
Brownstein's
24a Woodford Avenue, Gants Hill,   (020) 8550-3900
                    Email: deli@brownsteins.co.uk
              Web site: www.brownsteins.co.uk
Under the supervision of the London Beth Din

Loughton

Synagogues
Loughton, Chigwell & District Synagogue
Borders Lane IG10 1TE   (020) 8508-0303
Friday evening. 8pm; Sat Morn. 9.30am

Romford

Synagogues
25 Eastern Road RM1 3NH   (1708) 741690
Inq to: Mr D. Vroobel, 2 Norton Court, Church Road,
Newbury Park IG2 7ES. Tel: 0208-597 2249.

Southend-on-Sea

Jews began settling in the area in the late
nineteenth century, mainly from the East End of
London. The first temporary synagogue was built in
1906. The Jewish population is 4,500.

Booksellers
Dorothy Young
21 Colchester Road SS2 6HW   (1702) 331218
                Email: dorothy@dorothyyoung.co.uk
                    Web site: www.dorothyyoung.co.uk
Religious articles, Israeli giftware, etc., also stocked.
Jewish software ordered. Call for appointment.

Hotels

Kosher

Redstone's Hotel
Pembury Road, Westcliff, SS0 8DS   (1702) 348-441
Supervision: Unsupervised.

Organisations
Southend & District Representative Council
                                    (1702) 343192

Synagogues
Southend and Westcliff Hebrew Congregation
99 Alexandra Road SS0 8AD   (1702) 344900
Southend Reform Synagogue
851 London Road, Westcliff, SS0   (1702) 75809

Westcliff on Sea

Hotels
The Riverside Hotel
4 Cobham Road SS0 8EA   (1702) 346885

Gloucestershire

Cheltenham

The congregation was established in 1824 and the
present synagogue opened in 1839. However,
after two generations, the congregation declined
and the synagogue was closed in 1903. At the
outbreak of the Second World War, the synagogue
was re-opened following the influx of Jewish
newcomers to the town.

Restaurants

Vegetarian

The Orange Tree
317 High Street GL50 3HN
(1242) 234232
Fax: (1242) 234232
Strictly vegan & vegetarian cuisine. Fully licensed with selection of organic wines & beers.

Synagogues
Cheltenham Hebrew Congregation
St James Square GL50 5PU
(1242) 578893
Fax: (1242) 578893

Hampshire
Aldershot
Contact Information
Jewish Committee for H.M. Forces
25 Enford Street W1H 2DD
(020) 7724-7778
Fax: (020) 7706-1710
Email: jmcouncil@btinternet.com
Web site: www.jmcouncil.org
Inquiries to Senior Jewish Chaplain.

Portsmouth & Southsea
The Portsmouth community was founded in 1746. Its first synagogue was in Oyster Row, but the congregation moved to a building in White's Row which it continued to occupy for almost two centuries. A new building was erected in 1936. The cemetery is in a street which was once known as Jews' Lane.

Synagogues
Synagogue Chambers
The Thicket, Southsea, PO5 2AA
(23) 9282 1494

Southampton
Libraries
Hartley Library
University of Southampton SO17 1BJ
Houses both the Parkes Library and the Anglo-Jewish Archives.

Synagogues
Moordaunt Road
The Inner Avenue, SO2 0GP
Services Sat. morn 10am

Southampton & District Jewish Society
Hillel House
5 Brookvale Road, Portswood, SO2 1QN

Hertfordshire
Bushey
Synagogues
Orthodox
Bushey and District
177 Sparrows Herne WD2 1AJ
(020) 8950-7340
Fax: (020) 8421-8267

Hemel Hempstead
Synagogues
Morton House
Midland Road HD1 1RP
(1923) 232007

St Albans
Synagogues
Oswald Road AL1 3AQ
(1727) 825925
St Albans Masorti Synagogue
PO Box 23 AL1 4PH
(1727) 860642
Email: sams@masorti.org.uk

Watford
Synagogues
16 Nascot Road WD1 3RE
(1923) 222755
Covers also Carpenters Park, Croxley Garden, Garston, Kings Langley and Rickmansworth.

Welwyn Garden City
Synagogues
Barn Close
Handside Lane, AL8 6ST
(1707) 890575
Email: floradora@hotmail.com

Humberside
Grimsby
Synagogues
Sir Moses Montefiore Synagogue
Heneage Road DN32 9DZ

Hull
In Hull, as in other English port towns, a Jewish community was formed earlier than in inland areas. The exact date is unknown, but it is thought to be the early 1700s. There were enough Jews in Hull to buy a former Roman Catholic chapel, damaged in the Gordon Riots of 1780, and turn it into a synagogue. Hull was then the principal port of entry from northern Europe, and most Jewish immigrants came through it. Both the Old Hebrew

Synagogue in Osborne Street and the Central Synagogue in Cogan Street were destroyed in air raids during the Second World War.

Museums
Hull Synagogue Museum
Linnaeus Street HU3 2PD   (1482) 217153
Fax: (1482) 216565
Email: jcsc@exobus.org
Correspondence to: Old Synagogue, Linnaeus Street, HU3 2PD.

Synagogues
Orthodox
Hull Hebrew Congregation
30 Pryme Street Anlaby, HU10 6SH   (1482) 653242

Reform
Reform Synagogue
Great Gutter Lane West Willerby, HU10 7JT
(1482) 658312
Fax: (1482) 342836
Email: iansugarman@isa.karoo.co.uk

Kent
Canterbury
Tourist Sites
The Old Synagogue
King Street
The Old Synagogue, an Egyptian-style building of 1847, stands in King Street and is now used by the Kings School for recitals.

Margate
Synagogues
Godwin Road, Cliftonville, CT9 2HA   (1843) 223219

Ramsgate
Synagogues
Montefiore Endowment
Hereson Road
Montefiore Mausoleum & Synagogue
33 Luton Avenue, Broadstairs,   (1843) 862507

Rochester
Synagogues
Magnus Memorial Synagogue
366 High Street ME1 1DJ   (1634) 847665
Grade 2, listed building known as The Chatham Memorial Synagogue.

Lancashire
Blackpool
Delicatessens
The Deli
6 Station Road, Lytham St Annes,   (1253) 735861

Synagogues
Orthodox
United Hebrew Congregation
Synagogue Chambers
Leamington Road, FY1 4HD   (1253) 28164

Reform
Reform Jewish Congregation
40 Raikes Parade FY1 4EX   (1253) 23687

Lancaster
Bed & Breakfasts
Lancaster University Jewish Society
Interfaith Chaplaincy Centre
University of Lancaster, Bailrigg Lane, LA1 4YW
(1524) 594075
Jewish rooms and kosher kitchen. Contact Rev Malcolm Wiseman.

Orthodox
Fairview
32 Hornby Road Caton, LA2 9QS   (1524) 770118

St Annes On Sea
Synagogues
Orchard Road FY8 1PJ   (1253) 721831
Services 7.30am and 8pm

Leicestershire
Leicester
There has been a Jewish presence here since the Middle Ages, but the first record of a 'Jews' Synagogue' dates from 1861 in the Leicester Directory.

Libraries
Jewish Library and Bookshop
Community Hall
Highfield Street, LE2 0NQ   (116) 212-8920

Mikvaot
Synagogue Building
Highfield Street, LE2 0NQ   (116) 270-6622

United Kingdom / London

Restaurants

The Chaat House
108 Belgrave Road LE4 5AT   (116) 266-0513

Vegetarian

Blossoms
17b Cank Street LE1 5YP   (116) 253-9535

The Ark
St Martins Square   (116) 262-0909

The Good Earth
19 Free Lane LE1 1JX   (116) 262-6260

Synagogues

Community Centre
Highfield Street LE2 0NQ   (116) 254-0477
Mikva on premises.

Progressive Jewish Congregation
24 Avenue Road   (116) 271-5584
Fax: (116) 271-7571
Email: jeffrey@kaufmans.co.uk

Lincolnshire
Lincoln

Lincoln was one of the centres of medieval Jewry. One of England's oldest stone houses in the city is known as Aaron the Jew's House. The site of the old Jewry is remembered now at Jews' Court. In the cathedral is a recent token of ecclesiastical apology for the thirteenth-century incident of the blood libel, retold in Chaucer. Jews returned to the area in the nineteenth century. The current community is of very recent date.

Community Organisations
Lincolnshire Jewish Community
3 West End Road, Ulceby, North Lincolnshire,
(1469) 588951

London

There are of course a large number of synagogues of all kinds in London.

The major synagogues in Central London and of possible interest to visitors are the following:
Orthodox
Central (Great Portland Street)
36-40 Hallam Street W1N 6NN
(020) 7580 1355
Fax: (020) 7636 3831

Western Marble Arch
32 Great Cumberland Place W1H 7DJ
(020) 7724 8121
Fax: (020) 7723 4413

New West End
St Petersburg Place W2 4JT

(020) 7229 2631

Fax: (020) 7229 2355
Sephardi
Spanish and Portuguese Synagogue
Bevis Marks EC3A 5DC

(020) 7626 1274
Fax: (020) 7283 8825
Masorti
New London
33 Abbey Road NW8 0AT

(020) 7328 1026
Reform
West London
34 Upper Berkeley Street W1H 6AT
(020) 7723 4404
Fax: (020) 7224 8258
Liberal
West Central Liberal
21 Maple Street W1P 6DS

(020) 7636 7627
Fax: (020) 7436 4184
Visitors wishing to ascertain details of other synagogues in Central London or of synagogues in outlying areas should contact the appropriate central authority as detailed.
Orthodox
Spanish and Portuguese Jews Congregation
Vestry Office
2 Ashworth Road, Maida Vale W9 1JY
(020) 7289 2573
Fax: (020) 7289 2709

Unted Synagogue
Adler House
735 High Road, Finchley N12 0US
(020) 8343 8989
Fax: (020) 8343 6262
Federation of Synagogues
65 Watford Way, Hendon NW4 3AQ
(020) 8202 2263
Fax: (020) 8203 0610
Union of Orthodox Hebrew Congregations
140 Stamford Hill
Stamford Hill N16 6QT
(020) 8802 6226
Fax: (020) 8809 7902
Reform
Reform Synagogues
The Sternberg Centre for Judaism
80 East End Road, Finchley N3 2SY
(020) 8349 5640
Fax: (020) 8343 5699
Email: admin@reformjudaism.org.uk
Website: www.refsyn.org.uk
Union of Liberal and Progressive Synagogues
The Montague Centre
21 Maple Street, W1T 4BE
(020) 7580 1663
Fax: (020) 7436 4184
Email: montgu@ulps.org

United Kingdom / London

Masorti (Conservative in the USA)
Assembly of Masorti Synagogues
1097 Finchley Road
Golders Green NW11 0PU

(020) 8201 8772
Fax: (020) 8201 8917
Email: Masorti@ort.org
Website: www.masorti.org.uk

Bakeries
Carmelli Bakeries Ltd
126-128 Golders Green Road, NW11

(020) 8455-2074
Fax: (020) 8455-2789
Supervision: London Beth Din and Kedassia.

Daniel's Bagel Bakery
12-13 Hallswelle Parade, Finchley Road, NW11 0DL

(020) 8455-5826
Fax: (020) 8455-5826
Supervision: London Beth Din.

David Bagel Bakery
38 Vivian Avenue, Hendon NW4   (020) 8203-9995
Supervision: Kedassia.

Dino'z Bakery
106 Brent Street, Hendon NW4 2HH

(020) 8203-6623
Supervision: London Beth Din and Kedassia.

Dino'z Bakery
11 Edgwarebury Lane, Edgware HA8 8LH

(020) 8958-1554
Fax: (020) 8958-2554
Supervision: Kedassia.

Galillee Bakery
388 Cranbrook Road, Ilford IG2   (020) 8924-5333
Supervision: London Beth Din.

Hendon Bagel Bakery
55-57 Church Road, Hendon NW4

(020) 8203-6919
Fax: (020) 8203-8843
Supervision: Kedassia.

Keene's Patisserie
192 Preston Road, Wembley HA9   (020) 8904-5952
Supervision: London Beth Din.

Keene's Patisserie
Unit 6, Mill Hill Ind. Est., Flower Lane, Mill Hill
NW7 2HU   (020) 806-3729
Supervision: London Beth Din.

M & D Grodzinski Hot Bread Shop
223 Golders Green Road, Golders Green NW119ES

(020) 8458-3654
Fax: (020) 8905-5382
Supervision: London Beth Din and Kedassia.

Mr Bagels Factory
1 Kings Yard, Carpenters Road E15 2HD

(020) 8533-7553
Supervision: Sephardi Kashrut Authority.

Parkway Patisserie Ltd.
30a North End Road, Golders Green NW11

(020) 8455-5026
Supervision: London Beth Din and Kedassia.
Hours: Sunday, 7:30 am to 1:30 pm; Monday to
Thursday, to 5:30 pm; Friday, to 1 hour before
Shabbat.

Parkway Patisserie Ltd.
204 Preston Road, Wembley HA9   (020) 8904-7736
Supervision: London Beth Din and Kedassia.
Hours: Sunday, 7:30 am to 1:30 pm; Monday to
Thursday, to 5:30 pm; Friday, to 1 hour before
Shabbat.

Parkway Patisseries Ltd.
326-328 Regents Park Road, Finchley N3

(020) 8346-0344
Supervision: London Beth Din and Kedassia.
Hours: Sunday, 7:30 am to 1:30 pm; Monday to
Thursday, to 5:30 pm; Friday, to 1 hour before
Shabbat.

Renbake Patisserie Ltd.
Unit a, 8-10 Timber Wharf Road,
Stamford Hill N16 6DB   (020) 8800-2525
Fax: (020) 8880-2023
Supervision: London Beth Din and Kedassia.

Taboon Continental Bakery
204 Preston Road E1 7TD   (020) 7247-7079
Supervision: Sephardi Kashrut Authority.

The Cake Company
2 Sentinel Square, Hendon NW4 2EL

(020) 8202-2327
Fax: (020) 8202-8058
Email: karen@thecakecompany.co.uk
Supervision: London Beth Din & Kedassia.

Woodberry Down Bakery
47 Brent Street, Hendon NW4   (020) 8202-9962
Supervision: London Beth Din.

Bed & Breakfasts
26 Highfield Avenue, Golders Green NW11 9ET

(020) 8455-7136

Harold Godfrey Hillel House
25 Louisa Street, Stepney E1 4NF
Summer accommodation in London at affordable
prices. 20 rooms, kosher, dairy only kitchens, easy
access to London tourist attractions and theatre, across
from Stepney Green Tube station (District line).
Enquiries and bookings to: Evelyn Bacharach,
Kingscliffe, 1a Antrim Grove, London NW3 4XS,
Tel: 020 7722-0420, Fax: 020 8203-8727

Kacenberg's
1 Alba Gardens, Near Alba Court,
Golders Green NW11 9NS   (020) 8455-3780
                    Fax: (020) 8381-4250
Shabbat meals available. Strictly Orthodox.

Booksellers
Hebrew Book and Gift Centre
24 Amhurst Parade,
Amhurst Park N16 5AA   (020) 8802-0609
                    Fax: (020) 8802-0609

J. Aisenthal
11 Ashbourne Parade, Finchley Road,
Temple Fortune NW11 0AD   (020) 8455-0501
Jerusalem the Golden
146a Golders Green Road,
Golders Green NW11 8HE   (020) 8455-4960
                    Fax: (020) 8203-7808

Boreham Wood Judaice
11 Croxdale Road
Boreham Wood
WD6 4QD   (020) 8381 5559

United Kingdom / London

Jewish Memorial Council and Bookshop
25 Enford Street W1H 2DD   (020) 7724-7778
Fax: (020) 7706-1710
Email: jmcbookshop@btinternet.com
Web site: www.jmcouncil.org

Menorah Book and Gift Centre
16 Russell Parade, Golders Green Road NW11 9NN
(020) 8458-8289
Fax: (020) 8731-8403

Torah Treasures
4 Sentinel Square, Brent Street, Hendon NW4 2EL
(020) 8202-3134
Fax: (020) 8202-3161
Email: torahtreasures@btinternet.com
Seforim, Judaica and gifts.

Butchers

A. Perlmutter & Son
1-2 Onslow Parade, Hampden Square,
Southgate N14 5JN   (020) 8361-5441/2
Fax: (020) 8361-5442
Supervision: London Board of Shechita.

Frohwein's
1095 Finchley Road, Temple Fortune NW11
(020) 8455-9848
Supervision: Kedassia.

Golders Green Kosher
132 Golders Green Road
NW11 8H8   (020) 8381 4450
Fax: (020) 8731 6450
Supervision: London Board of Shechita.

Greenspans
9-11 Lyttelton Road N2 0DW
(020) 8455-9921
Fax: (020) 8455-3484
Supervision: London Board of Shechita.

H. Gross & Son
6 Russell Parade, Golders Green Road,
Golders Green NW11   (020) 8455-6662
Fax: (020) 8455-8995
Supervision: London Board of Shechita.

Ilford Kosher Meats
7 Beehive Lane, Ilford IG2   (020) 8554-3238
Supervision: London Board of Shechita.

Ivor Silverman
360 Uxbridge Road,
Hatch End HA4 4HP   (020) 8428-6564
Supervision: London Board of Shechita.

Ivor Silverman
4 Canons Corner, London Road,
Stanmore HA8 8AE   (020) 8958-8682; 958-2692
Fax: (020) 8958-1725
Supervision: London Board of Shechita.

D. Glass & Co
100 High Road, Bushey Heath,
Bushey WD2 3JE   (020) 8420-4443
Supervision: London Board of Shechita.

Jack Schlagman
112 Regents Park Road,
Finchley N3   (020) 8346-3598
Supervision: London Board of Shechita.

La Boucherie
4 Cat Hill, East Barnet EN4 8JB   (020) 8449-9215
Fax: (020) 8441-1848
Supervision: London Board of Shechita.

La Boucherie
145 High Street,
Barkingside IG6 2AJ   (020) 8551-9215
Fax: (020) 8551-9977
Supervision: London Board of Shechita.

Louis Mann
23 Edgwarebury Lane,
Edgware HA8   (020) 8958-3789
Supervision: London Board of Shechita.

M. Lipowicz
9 Royal Parade, Ealing W5   (020) 8997-1722
Fax: (020) 8997-0048
Supervision: London Board of Shechita.

Menachem's
15 Russell Parade, Golders Green Road,
Golders Green NW11   (020) 8201-8629
Fax: (020) 8201-8629
Supervision: London Board of Shechita.

N. Goldberg
12 Claybury Broadway,
Redbridge IG   (020) 8551-2828
Supervision: London Board of Shechita.

R. Wolff
84 Edgware Way,
Edgware HA8 8JS   (020) 8958-8454
Supervision: London Board of Shechita.

Butchers & Delicatessens

Mehadrin Meats
19 Russell Parade,
Golders Green NW11 9NN   (020) 8455-9992
Fax: (020) 8455-3777/599 0984
Supervision: Kedassia.

Mehadrin Meats
25a Belfast Road, Stamford Hill N16
(020) 8880-7686/880-1007
Fax: (020) 8806-9005/880 1112
Supervision: Kedassia.

Communal Organisations

Listings

Board of Deputies of British Jews
Commonwealth House, 5th Floor,
1-19 New Oxford Street WC1A 1NF

(020) 7534-5400
Fax: (020) 7534-0010
Email: info @bod.org.uk
Web site: www.bod.org.uk

Contact Information
Jewish Community Information (JCI)
Commonwealth House,
1-19 New Oxford Street WC1N 1NF

(020) 7543-5421/2
Fax: (020) 7543-0010
Email: jci@bod.org.uk

A comprehensive service of communal information.
For administration please contact 020 7543 5400.

The International Jewish Vegetarianism Society
Bet Teva, 855 Finchley Road NW11 8LX

(20) 8455-0692
Fax: (20) 8455-0692
Email: jvs@ivu.org
Web site: www.vu.org/jvs

The International Jewish Vegetarian Society was formed
35 years ago to promote vegetarianism from a Jewish
perspective.

Delicatessens
Munch Box, 41 Greville Street EC1   (020) 7242-5487
Supervision: London Beth Din.

Embassy
Embassy of Israel
2 Palace Green,
Kensington W8 4QB

(020) 7957-9500
Fax: (020) 7957-9555
Email: isr-info@dircon.co.uk
Web site: www.israel-embassy.org.uk/london/

CENTRAL HOTEL
Private Bathrooms and Parking

35 Hoop Lane, Golders Green
London NW11

Tel: 020 8458 5636 Fax: 020 8455 4792
Credit cards accepted

CROFT COURT HOTEL
UNDER NEW MANAGEMENT
Situated in the heart of Golders Green
44 Ravenscroft Avenue, London NW11 8AY
Telephone: 020 8458 3331 Fax: 020 8455 9175

*Easy access into the West End. All rooms include en suite facilities, direct dial
telephone, colour television and hairdryer.*
Refurbished executive bedrooms with air conditioning, private safes and fridges.
Facilities for Barmitzvahs, private parties, Engagements, Sheva Berachot.

KADIMAH HOTEL
*The only Kosher hotel in East London
Heimishe and Friendly atmosphere*

All rooms with bath/shower, T.V. and Telephone

146 Clapton Common, London, E5 9AG
Tel: 020 8800 5960 020 8800 1716
Fax: 020 8800 6237
Under supervision Beth Din and Kashrus Commission.

United Kingdom / London

Israeli Consulate-General
15a Old Court Place,
Kensington W8 4QB   (020) 7957-9500
Fax: (020) 7957-9577
Web site: www.israel-embassy.org.uk/london
Nearest tube station: High Street Kensington. Consular
office hours: Monday to Thursday, 10 am to 1 pm;
Friday, 10 am to 12 pm. Postal address: Consulate
Section, Embassy of Israel, 2 Palace Green, London W8
4QB

Fishmongers
Leveyuson, 47a Brent Street,
Hendon NW4   (020) 8202-7834
Supervision: London Board of Shechita.

Sam Stoller
28 Temple Fortune Parade, Finchley Road,
Golders Green NW11 0QS
(020) 8455-1957; 458-1429
Fax: (020) 8445-1957
Supervision: Sephardi Kashrut Authority.

Groceries
B Kosher, 91 Bell Lane,
Hendon NW4   (020) 8202-1711
Opposite Vincent Court.

Brownsteins Delicatessen
24a Woodford Avenue IG2 6XG   (020) 8550-3900
Email: deli@brownsteins.freeserve.co.uk
Selection of groceries and delicatessen sold are under
the supervision of various religious authorities. Hours:
Monday to Thursday, 7:30 am to 6 pm; Friday and
Sunday, 7 am to 2 pm. Orders delivered.

Carmel Fruit Shop
40 Vivian Avenue, Hendon NW4   (020) 8202-9587
Fresh fruit and vegetables as well as a good supply of
kosher products, cakes and biscuits.

Kosher King
235 Golders Green Road, Golders Green NW11 9ES
(020) 8455-1429
Fax: (020) 8201-8924
Email: kosherking@compuserve.com

Kosher Paradise
10 Ashbourne Parade, Finchley Road,
Temple Fortune NW11 OAD   (020) 8455-2454
Fax: (020) 8731-6919

Maxine's
20 Russell Parade, Golders Green Road, Golders
Green NW11   (020) 8458-3102
Fax: (020) 8455-3632
Kedassia Deli. Deliveries

Pelter Stores
82 Edgware Way, Edgware HA8   (020) 8958-6910
Supervision: Federation Kashrus Board.

Yarden, 123 Golders Green Road,
Golders Green NW11   (020) 8458-0979
Free delivery on orders over £25. Hours: Sunday,
Wednesday, Thursday, 8 am to 10 pm; Monday,
Tuesday, 8 am to 9 pm; Friday, 8 am.

Guest Houses
Sharon Guest House
7 Woodlands Close, Golders Green   (020) 8458-8531
Email: jlazenga@aol.com
Although not officially supervised it is said to be Shomer
Shabbat Dati.

Hotels
13 Brook Avenue, Edgware HA8 9XF
(020) 8958-4409

Central Hotel
35 Hoop Lane, Golders Green NW11 8BS
(020) 8458-5636
Fax: (020) 8455-4792
Private bathrooms and parking.

Hampstead House Residential Hotel
12 Lyndhurst Gardens, Hampstead NW3 5NR
(020) 7794-6036

King Solomon Hotel
155-183 Golders Green Road NW11 9BX
(020) 8201-9000
Fax: (020) 8201-9853

Kosher

Croft Court Hotel
44 Ravenscroft Avenue, Golders Green NW11 8AY
(020) 8458-3331
Fax: (020) 8455-9175
Twenty rooms.

Golders Green Hotel
147-149 Golders Green Road,
Golders Green NW11 9BN   (020) 8458-7127/9
Fax: (020) 8905-5143
Email: goldersgreenhotel@talk21.com
Supervision: Beth Din of the Federation of Synagogues.

Kadimah Hotel
146 Clapton Common, Clapton E5 9AG
(020) 8800-5960/800-1716
Fax: (020) 8800-6237
Supervision: London Beth Din and Kashrus
Commission.

Menorah Hotel & Caterers
54-54a Clapton Common, Clapton E5
(020) 8806-4925; 6340

Kashrut Information

Federation of Kashrus Board
65 Watford Way, Hendon NW4 3AQ
(020) 8202-2263
Fax: (020) 8203-0610
Email: info@kfkosher.org
Web site: www.kfkosher.org

Joint Kashrus Committee-Kedassia (Union of Orthodox Hebrew Congregations)
140 Stamford Hill, Stamford Hill N16 6QT
(020) 8802-6226
Fax: (020) 8809-7092

London Beth Din
735 High Road, Finchley N12 0US
(020) 8343-6255 (Kashrut hotline: 343-6259)
Fax: (020) 8343-6254
Web site: www.kosher.org.uk
Publishes 'The Really Jewish Food Guide', which
contains a list of all the establishments it certifies as
well as guidance for the shopper in buying general
consumer products.

National Council of Shechita Boards
401 -405 Nether Street, Finchley N3 1YR
(020) 8349-9160
Fax: (020) 8346-2209

Sephardi Kashrut Authority
2 Ashworth Road, Maida Vale W9 1JY
(020) 7289-2573
Fax: (020) 7289-2709
Email: howard@sandpsyn.demon.co.uk

United Kingdom / London

Libraries

British Library, Oriental & India Collections
96 Euston Road NW1 2DB   (020) 7412-7646
Fax: (020) 7412-7641/7870
Email: oioc-enquiries@bl.uk
The Hebrew section contains over 70,000 printed books, ca. 3,000 manuscripts and some 10,000 Genizah fragments. Oriental reading room open to holders of readers' passes: Monday 10.00-17.00; Tuesday-Saturday 09.30-17.00. Hebrew manuscripts on permanent display in the John Ritblat Gallery.

Institute of Contemporary History and Wiener Library
4 Devonshire Street W1N 2BH   (020) 7636-7247
Fax: (020) 7436-6428
Email: lib@wl.u-net.com
The world's oldest institution dedicated to the documentation of Nazi Germay and the Holocaust. The collection includes 60,000 books and pamphlets, periodicals, documents, videos and photographs as well as extensive press cuttings from 1933 onwards. Other subjects include 20th-century Jewish history, anti-semitism, refugees, minorities, fascism, citizenship, etc.

The Jewish Studies Library
University College London Library,
Gower Street WC1E 6BT   (020) 7387-7050
Fax: (020) 7380-7373
In addition to materials purchased for the College's Department of Hebrew Studies it incorporates the Mocatta Library, Altmann Library, William Margulies Yiddish Library and the Library of the Jewish Historical Society of England. Applications to use or view the collections should be made in advance in writing to the Librarian.

Media

Directories

Jewish Year Book
Vallentine Mitchell, Newbury House, 900 Eastern Avenue, Newbury Park, Ilford IG2 7HH
(020) 8599-8866
Fax: (020) 8599-0984
Email: jyb@vmbooks.com
Annual directory of all information relating to the British Jewish Community.

Internet

Brijnet
11 The Lindens, Prospect Hill,
Waltham Forest E17 3EJ   (020) 8520-3531
Email: rafi@brijnet.org
Web site: www.brijnet.org

Listings

The Diary
32 Bell Lane NW4 2AD   (020) 8922-5437
Fax: (020) 8922-8709

Newspapers

Essex Jewish News
900 Eastern Avenue, Newbury Park,
Ilford IG2 7HH   (020) 8599-8866
Fax: (020) 8599-0984
Quarterly publication serving East London and Essex.

Hamodia
149 Kyverdale Road N16 6PS   (020) 8806 7577
Fax: (020) 8806 1222
Email: Post@Hamodia.demon.co.uk

Jewish Chronicle
25 Furnival Street EC4A 1JT   (020) 7415-1500
Fax: (020) 7405-9040
Email: editorial@thejc.com
Established 1841. Weekly publication.

London Jewish News
28 St Albans Lane, Golders Green NW11 7QE
(020) 8731-8031
Fax: (020) 8381-4033

Radio

Jewish Spectrum Radio
558 AM, PO Box 12591 NW2 2ZP   (020) 8905-5533
Fax: (020) 8209-0055

Mikvaot

Adath Yisroel Synagogue Mikvah
40a Queen Elizabeth's Walk, cnr. 28 Gazebrook Rd.,,
Stamford Hill N16 0HH   (020) 8802-2554

Craven Walk Mikvah
72 Lingwood Road, Stamford Hill N16
(020) 8800-8555
Evening Telephone number: 0181-809-6279

Edgware & District Communal Mikvah
Edgware United Synagogue Grounds, 22 Warwick Avenue Drive, Edgware HA8   (020) 8958-3233
Fax: (020) 8958-4004
Email: estrin@clara.co.uk

Ilford Mikvah Federation of Synagogues
463 Cranbrook Road, Ilford IG   (020) 8554-2551
(Evenings: 554-8532)
Correspondence to 367 Cranbrook Road, Ilford.

North West London Communal Mikvah
10a Shirehall Lane, Hendon NW4
(020) 8202-1427 (Evenings: (020) 8517-5706)

Satmar Mikvah
62 Filey Avenue, Stamford Hill N16
(020) 8806-3961

South London Mikvah
42 St Georges Road, Wimbledon SW19 4ED
(020) 8944-7149
Fax: (020) 8944-7563
Stamford Hill and District Mikvah
Margaret Road, Stamford Hill N16   (020) 8806-3880
Other Telephone number: 0181-809-4064 or 0181-
800-5119
The Sternberg Centre for Judaism
80 East End Road, Finchley N3 2SY
(020) 8349-4731
Fax: (020) 8343-0901
Email: admin@refsyn.org.uk
Web site: www.refsyn.org.uk
Hours: 9.30 - 5.30 Monday to Thursday, Friday 9.30 -
3.30 /4.
Union of Orthodox Hebrew Congregations
140 Stamford Hill, Stamford Hill N16 6QT
(020) 8802-6226
Fax: (020) 8809-7097

Museums
Ben Uri Art Society & Gallery
126 Albert Street NW1 7NE   (020) 7482-1234
Fax: (020) 7482-1414
Email: benuri@ort.org
The aim of the Society, which is a registered charity
founded 1915, is to promote Jewish art as part of the
Jewish cultural heritage. The Gallery provides a
showcase for exhibitions of contemporary art as well as
for the Society's own collection of over 800 works by
Jewish artists, including David Bomberg, Mark Gertler,
Jacob Epstein, Reuven Rubin and Leon Kossof. Open
Mon.-Thurs. 10-4, Sunday afternoons during
exhibitions 2-5. Closed Jewish Holy-days and Bank
Holidays.

Jewish Military Museum and Memorial Room
AJEX House, East Bank, Stamford Hill N16 5RT
(020) 8800-2844; 802-7610
Fax: (020) 8800-1117
Memorabilia, artefacts, medals, letters, documents,
pictures and uniforms all illustrating British Jewry's
contribution to the Armed Forces of the Crown from the
Crimea to the present-day. By appointment, Sunday to
present-day Thursday, 11 am to 4 pm.
The Holocaust Exhibition
Imperial War Museum, Lambeth Road SE1 6HZ
(20) 7416-5320
Web site: www.iwm.org.uk
The Jewish Museum
80 East End Road, Finchley N3 2SY   (20) 8349-1143
Fax: (20) 8343-2162
Email: admin@jmus.org.uk
Web site: www.jewmus.ort.org
Permanent exhibitions trace history of London Jewry
with reconstructions of a tailoring and a furniture
workshop. Holocaust education is also a major feature
of the Museum's work and the Museum's displays
include a moving exhibition on London-born Holocaust
survivor, Leon Greenman. Hours: Monday to Thursday,
10:30 am to 5 pm; Sunday (except during August and
Bank Holiday weekends), 10:30 am to 4:30 pm.
Closed Friday, Saturday and Jewish festivals, public
holidays and 25 December to 5 January.

United Kingdom / London

The Jewish Museum

Raymond Burton House, 129-131 Albert Street,
Camden NW1 7NB   (020) 7284-1997
                        Fax: (020) 7267-9008
                        Email: admin@jmus.org.uk
                        Web site: www.jewmusm.ort.org

The Museum explores Jewish history and religious life in Britain and beyond. It has been awarded designated status by the Museums and Galleries Commission in recognition of its outstanding collections of Jewish ceremonial art, which are among the finest in the world. The Museum's attractive premises include a History Gallery, Ceremonial Art Gallery and a Temporary Exhibitions Gallery offering a varied programme of changing exhibitions. Open Sunday to Thursday 10am to 4pm. Closed Jewish Festivals and public holidays. Group visits by prior arrangement. Admission charge.

Organisations

Federation of Synagogues

65 Watford Way, Hendon NW4 3AQ
                        (020) 8202-2263
                        Fax: (020) 8203-0610
                        Email: ingo@kfkosher.org
                        Web site: www.kfkosher.org

Spanish & Portuguese Jews' Congregation

2 Ashworth Road, Maida Vale W9 1JY
                        (020) 7289-2573
                        Fax: (020) 7289-2709
                        Email: howard@sandpsyn.demon.co.uk

The Sephardi Centre

2 Ashworth Road, Maida Vale W9 1JY
                        (020) 7266 3682
                        Fax: (020) 7289 5957
                        Email: sephardbicentre@easynet.co.uk

Union of Liberal and Progressive Synagogues

The Montagu Centre, 21 Maple Street W1T 4BE
                        (020) 7580-1663
                        Fax: (020) 7436-4184
                        Email: montagu@ulps.org
                        Web site: www.ulps.org

Masorti (Conservative in the USA)

Assembly of Masorti Synagogues

1097 Finchley Road, Golders Green NW11 0PU
                        (020) 8201-8772
                        Fax: (020) 8201-8917
                        Email: office@masorti.org.uk
                        Web site: www.masorti.org.uk

Union of Orthodox Hebrew Congregations

140 Stamford Hill, Stamford Hill N16 6QT
                        (020) 8802-6226
                        Fax: (020) 8809-7902

United Synagogue

Adler House, 735 High Road, Finchley N12 0US
                        (020) 8343-8989
                        Fax: (020) 8343-6262
                        Web site: www.unitedsynagogue.org.uk

Reform Synagogues

The Sternberg Centre for Judaism, 80 East End Road,
Finchley N3 2SY   (020) 8349-5640
                        Fax: (020) 8343-5699
                        Email: admin@reformjudaism.org.uk
                        Web site: www.refsyn.org.uk

With more than 200 synagogues in the London area alone, not counting independent synagogues and 'shtieblach', we recommend that you contact one of the above organisations to find the synagogue of your choice nearest you, along with minyan times.

Restaurants

Dairy

Café on the Green

122 Golders Green Road, Golders Green NW11 8HB
                        (020) 8209-0232
Supervision: London Beth Din.
Chalav Yisrael. Open Motzei Shabbat in winter.

Cassit

225 Golders Green Road, Golders Green NW11 9PN
                        (020) 8455-8195
                        Fax: (020) 8458-4837
Supervision: Beth Din of the Federation of Synagogues.

Croft Court

44 Ravenscroft Avenue, Golders Green NW11 8AY
                        (020) 8458-3331
                        Fax: (020) 8455-9175
Supervision: Kedassia.

Folman's Restaurant

134 Brent Street NW4   (020) 8202-5592
Supervision: Beth Din of the Federation of Synagogues.

Macabi King of Falafel

59 Wentworth Street E1   (020) 7247-6660
Supervision: Beth Din of the Federation of Synagogues.

Milk n' Honey

124 Golders Green Road, Golders Green NW11 8HB
                        (020) 8455-0664
Supervision: Kedassia.
Vegetarian/dairy restaurant/coffee shop/airconditioned. Menus in English and Hebrew. Also take-away available.

Tasty Pizza
23 Amhurst Parade, Amhurst Park, Stamford Hill
N16 5AA   (020) 8802-0018; 455-0004
Supervision: London Beth Din and Kedassia.

Meat

Amor, 8 Russell Parade, Golders Green NW11
                           (020) 8458-4221
Supervision: Kedassia.

Aviv Restaurant
87 High Street, Edgware   (020) 8952-2484
Supervision: Beth Din of the Federation of Synagogues.

Blooms World-Famous Kosher Restaurant
130 Golders Green Road, Golders Green NW11 8HB
                    (020) 8455-1338; 3033
                    Fax: (020) 8455-1338
Supervision: London Beth Din.
Free delivery service, air conditioned. Open until

1.00am Sunday to Thursday; Friday lunchtime
and Saturday nights 1 hour after Shabbos until
4.00am.

Catskills
1-4 Belmont Parade, Finchley Road, Temple Fortune
NW11   (020) 8458-1999
                    Fax: (020) 8209-1050
            Email: catskills@hamishe.freeserve.co.uk
                Web site: www.catskills.co.uk
Supervision: London Beth Din.
Kosher deli, diner, restaurant. Open Motzei Shabbat in winter.

Dizengoff
118 Golders Green Road, Golders Green NW11 8HB
(020) 8458-7003; 458-9958
Fax: (020) 8381-4902
Email: s.shurkin@virgin.net
Web site: www.cityscan.co.uk
Supervision: Sephardi Kashrut Authority.
Hours: Sunday to Thursday, 11 am to midnight; Friday, to 4 pm; Saturday night, winter only.

El Gaucho
239 Golders Green Road NW11   (020) 8458-0444
Fax: (020) 8455-2003
Supervision: Sephardi, Kashrut

Kaifeng
51 Church Road, Hendon NW4 4DU
(020) 8203-7888
Fax: (020) 8203-8263
Web site: www.kaifeng.co.uk
Supervision: London Beth Din.
Luxury Chinese restaurant with take-away and delivery service. Free delivery with minimum order of £25.
Hours: Sunday to Thursday, 12:30 pm to 2:30 pm, 6 pm to 11 pm; Open Saturday evening, September to April.

Kinneret
313 Hale Lane, HA8 7AX   (020) 8958 4955
Supervision: Beth Din Federation of Synagogues

Marcus's
5 Hallswelle Parade, Finchley Road, Golders Green
NW11 0DL   (020) 8458-4670
Supervision: London Beth Din.

Reubens
79 Baker Street W1M 1AJ   (020) 7486-0035
Fax: (020) 7486-7079
Supervision: Sephardi Kashrut Authority.
Open daily except for Shabbat; open Friday until two hours before sundown.

Sami's Restaurant
157 Brent Street, Hendon NW4 4DJ
(020) 8203-8088
Fax: (020) 8203-1040
Supervision: Federation of Synagogues Kashrut Board.
Glatt kosher middle eastern cuisine.

Six-13
19 Wigmore Street W1   (020) 7629 6113
Supervision: London Beth Din
Solly's, 148a Golders Green Road, Golders Green
NW11   (020) 8455-0004
Supervision: London Beth Din.

Solly's Exclusive
146-150 Golders Green Road, Golders Green NW11
(020) 8455-2121
Supervision: London Beth Din.

Uncle Shloime's
204 Stamford Hill, Stamford Hill N16
(020) 8802-9355
Supervision: Kedassia.

Restaurants - Take away
Dairy

Tasti Pizza
252 Golders Green Road, Golders Green NW11
(020) 8209-0023
Supervision: London Beth Din and Kedassia.

Snack Bar
Sue Harris Student Centre
B'nai B'rith-Hillel Foundation, 1-2 Endsleigh Street
WC1H 0DS   (020) 7388-0801
Fax: (020) 7916-3973
Email: hillel@ort.org
Supervision: London Beth Din.
Hours: Monday to Thursday, Friday night Shabbat meal available if booked and paid in advance by Thursday 11 am. Please phone for details of summer months opening. Re-opens for students and all other visitors mid-September.

Tourist Information
Israel Government Tourist Office
UK House, 180 Oxford Street W1N 9DJ
(020) 7299-1111
Fax: (020) 7299-1112
Email: igto-uk@dircon.co.uk

Visitorcall – The Phone Guide to London
London Tourist Board, Glen House, Stag Place, Victoria
SW1E 5LT   (9064) 123456
Features over 30 lines of recorded information services
– calls cost 60p per minute at all times.

Travel Agencies

Goodmos Tours
Dunstan House, 14a St Cross Street EC1N 8XA
                                       (020) 7430-2230
                                  Fax: (020) 7405-5049

LestAir Services
80 Highfield Ave, Golders Green NW11 9TT
                                       (020) 8455-9654
                                  Fax: (020) 8455-9654
                        Email: family.schleimer@ukgateway.net
Promoting Jewish Heritage Tours to the Czech Republic,
Poland, Hungary, Byelorus, Latvia and Lithuania and
can be contacted for detailed information and
guidance.

Longwood Travel
182 Longwood Gardens, Ilford IG5 0EW
                                       (020) 8551-4466
                                  Fax: (020) 8551-5588

Magic of Israel
47 Shepherds Bush Green, Shepherds Bush W12 8PS
                                       (020) 8743-9000

Peltours
240 Station Road, Edgware HA8 7AU
                                       (020) 8958-1144
                                  Fax: (020) 8958-5515

Peltours
11-19 Ballards Lane, Finchley N3 1UX
                                       (020) 8346-9144
                                  Fax: (020) 8343-0579
                           Email: sales@peltours.com
                           Web site: www.peltours.com

Sabra Travel Ltd.
9 Edgwarebury Lane, Edgware HA8 8LH
                                       (020) 8958-3244-7

Travelink Group Ltd.
50 Vivian Avenue NW4 3XH   (020) 8931-8000
                                  Fax: (020) 8931-8877
                     Email: general.enq@travelink.uk.com
                        Web site: www.travelink.uk.com

United Kingdom / Manchester

Manchester

The Manchester Jewish community is the second largest in the United Kingdom, numbering about 35,000. There was no organised community until 1780. The present Great Synagogue claims to be the direct descendant of this earliest community. The leaders of Manchester Jewry in those early days had without exception come from the neighbouring relatively important Jewish community of Liverpool. In 1871 a small Sephardi group from North Africa and the Levant drew together and formed a congregation, which extended to fill two handsome synagogues. One has now been turned into a Jewish museum.

Bakeries
Brackman's
43 Leicester Road, Salford M7
(161) 792-1652
Supervision: Manchester Beth Din.
Crusty Corner
24 Bury New Road, Prestwich M25   (161) 773-7997
Supervision: Manchester Beth Din.
Jack Maurer Patisserie
70 St James' Road, Salford M7   (161) 792-3751
Supervision: Manchester Beth Din.
State Fayre Bakeries
Unit 1, Empire Street M3   (161) 832-2911
Supervision: Manchester Beth Din.
Swiss Cottage Patisserie
118 Rectory Lane, Prestwich M25   (161) 798-0897
Fax: (161) 798-8212
Supervision: Manchester Beth Din.

Booksellers
B. Horwitz
20 King Edwards Buildings, Bury Old Road, Prestwich M7 4QJ   (161) 740-5897
Open 9.30am-5.30pm Monday to Friday; 10.00am-1.00pm Sunday; 9.00am-2.00pm Fridays during winter.
B. Horwitz Judaica World
2 Kings Road, Prestwich M25 0LE   (161) 773-4956
Fax: (161) 773-4956
Email: melachim11@aol.com
Hasefer Book Store
18 Merrybower Road, Salford M7   (161) 740-3013
Fax: (161) 721-4649
J. Goldberg
11 Parkside Avenue, Salford M7 0HB   (161) 740-0732
Jewish Book Centre
25 Ashbourne Grove, Salford M7 4DB
(161) 792-1253
Hours: Sunday to Thursday, 9 am to 9 pm; Friday,9.00am-1.00pm.

Butchers
Halberstadt Ltd
55 Leicester Road, Salford M7 4AS   (161) 792-1109
Supervision: Manchester Beth Din.
Open full day Tuesday, Wednesday, and Thursday.
Open half day Sunday, Monday and Friday. Only Glatt Meat-Mehadrin Poultry. Electric doors/disable ramp end year 2000.
Hymark Kosher Meat Ltd
39 Wilmslow Road, Cheadle, Cheshire SK
(161) 428-3400
Supervision: Manchester Beth Din.
Meat department only.
J.A. Hyman (Titanic) Ltd
123/9 Waterloo Road M8   (161) 792-1888
Supervision: Manchester Beth Din.
Suppliers of meat and poultry, cooked meats and delicatessen products.
Kosher Foods
49 Bury New Road, Prestwich M25   (161) 773-1308
Supervision: Manchester Beth Din.
Sells groceries as well.
Kosher Supreme
61 Bury Old Road, Prestwich M25   (161) 773-2020
Supervision: Manchester Beth Din.
Lloyd Grosberg (J. Kreger)
102 Barlow Moor Road M20   (161) 445-4983
Supervision: Manchester Beth Din.
Park Lane Kosher Meats
142 Park Lane, Whitefield M45 7PX   (161) 766-5091
Supervision: Manchester Beth Din.
Hours: Sunday 8.30am - 1.00pm; Monday & Friday 8.00am - 1.00pm; Tuesday, Wednesday & Thursday 8.00am - 6.00pm.
Vidal's Kosher Meats
75 Windsor Road, Prestwich M25   (161) 740-3365
Supervision: Manchester Beth Din.

Delicatessens
Cottage Deli
83 Park Lane, Whitefield M   (161) 766-6216
Supervision: Manchester Beth Din.
Deli King
Kings Road, Prestwich M25 8LQ   (161) 798-7370
Fax: (161) 798-5654
Supervision: Manchester Beth Din.
Hours: Sunday to Friday, 8:30 am to 6 pm.
Haber's
8 Kings Road, Prestwich M25 0LE   (161) 773-2046
Fax: (161) 773-9101
Supervision: Manchester Beth Din.
Hyman's Delicatessen
41 Wilmstow Road, Cheadle   (161) 491-1100
Fax: (161) 491-1100
Supervision: Manchester Beth Din.

Jehu Delis and Take Away
5 Parkhill, Bury Old Road, Prestwich M25
(161) 740-2816
Supervision: Manchester Beth Din.

Groceries
Halperns Kosher Food Store
57-59 Leicester Road, Salford M7
(161) 792-1752 Office 792-2992
Fax: (161) 708-8881
Email: halperns.kosherfood@virgin.net
Supervision: Manchester Beth Din.
State Fayre
77 Middleton Road M8
(161) 740-3435
Supervision: Manchester Beth Din.

Hotels
Fulda's Hotel
144 Old Bury Road, Salford M7 4QY
(161) 740-4748
Fax: (161) 795-5920
Web site: www.here.at/fuldas
Supervision: Manchester Beth Din.
Four star hotel open all year. Glatt kosher. Within easy access of motorways, and uniquely placed in the heart of the Manchester Jewish community in Broughton Park. Within easy walking distance of numerous synagogues and shopping facilities.

Kashrut Information
Manchester Beth Din
435 Cheetham Hill Road M8 0PF   (161) 740-9711
Fax: (161) 721-4249
They certify all the following restaurants, bakeries, butchers, delicatessans, caterers, groceries and hotels. Contact them to ensure that the establishment is still certified.

Libraries
Central Library
St Peter's Square M2 5PD   (161) 234-1983; 1984
Fax: (161) 234-1985
Email: socsci@libraries.manchester.gov.uk
Large collection of Jewish books for reference and loan, including books in Hebrew. Contact the Social Sciences Library.

Media
Newspapers
Jewish Telegraph
Telegraph House, 11 Park Hill, Bury Old Road,
Prestwich M25 0HH   (161) 740-9321
Fax: (161) 740-9325
Email: mail@jewishtelegraph.com
Web site: www.jewishtelegraph.com

Mikvaot
Manchester & District Mikva (Machzikei Hadass)
Sedgley Park Road, Prestwich M25
(161) 773-1537; 773-7403
Manchester Communal Mikvah
Broome Holme, Tetlow Lane, Salford M7 0BU
(161) 792-3970
During opening hours only. For appointments for Friday night and YomTov evenings: 740-4071; 740-5199. For tevilat kelim, 795-2272.
Naomi Greenberg South Manchester Mikvah
Hale Synagogue, Shay Lane, Hale Barns
(161) 904-8296
Use is by appointment only.
Whitefield Mikvah
Park Lane, Whitefield M45 7PB   (161) 796-1054
Ansaphone. Evenings only: 792-0306. Use is by appointment only.

Museums
Manchester Jewish Museum
190 Cheetham Hill Road M8 8LW
(161) 834-9879; 832-7353
Fax: (161) 834-9801
Email: info@manchesterjewishmuseum.com
Web site: www.manchesterjewishmuseum.com
Exhibitions, Heritage trails, Demonstrations & Talks. Calendar of events available on request. Educational visits for schools and adult groups must be booked in advance. Open Mon.-Thurs., 10.30am to 4pm Sundays 10.30am to 5pm Admission charge. Contact Don Rainger, Administrator

Organisations
Machzikei Hadass
17 Northumberland Street, Salford M7 0FE
(161) 792-1313

Restaurants
Antonio's Pizzaria and Restaurant
JCLC, Corner Bury Old Road & Park Road
(161) 795-8911
Supervision: Manchester Beth Din.
Open Monday-Thursday 12.30-3.00 and 5.30-11.0 ; Sunday to 11.00pm. In winter 1 1/2 hours after Shabbat until 2.00 am

Meat

J.S. Kosher Restaurant
7 Kings Road, Prestwich M25 0LE   (161) 798-7776
Supervision: Manchester Beth Din.
Glatt kosher.

United Kingdom / Manchester

Synagogues

Orthodox

Adass Yeshurun
Cheltenham Crescent, Salford M7 0FE
(161) 792-1233
Adath Yisroel Nusach Ari
Upper Park Road, Salford M7 0HL   (161) 740-3905
Central & North Manchester (incorporating Hightown Central and Beth Jacob)
Leicester Road, Salford M7 4GP   (161) 740-4830
Cheetham Hebrew Congregation
453-455 Cheetham Hill Road M8 9PA
(161) 740-7788
Congregation of Spanish and Portuguese
18 Moor Lane, Kersal, Salford M7 0WX
(161) 792-7406
Fax: (161) 792-3471
Hale & District Hebrew Congregation
Shay Lane, Hale Barns, Cheshire WA15 8PA
(161) 980-8846
Fax: (161) 980-1802
Heaton Park Hebrew Congregation
Ashdown, Middleton Road M8 6JX   (161) 740-4766
Higher Crumpsall & Higher Broughton
Bury Old Road, Salford M7 4PX   (161) 740-1210
Higher Prestwich
445 Bury Old Road, Prestwich M25 1QP
(161) 773-4800
Hillock Hebrew Congregation
Beverley Close, Ribble Drive, Whitefield M45
(161) 959-5663
Holy Law South Broughton Congregation
Bury Old Road, Prestwich M25 0EX
(161) 792-6349/721-4705
Fax: (161) 720-6623
Email: office@holylaw.freeserve.co.uk
Kahal Chassidim
62 Singleton Road, Salford M7 4LU   (161) 740-1629
Machzikei Hadass
17 Northumberland Street, Salford M7 0FE
(161) 792-1313
Manchester Great & New Synagogue
Stenecourt, Holden Road, Salford M7 4LN
(161) 792-8399
Fax: (161) 792-1991
North Salford
2 Vine Street, Salford M7 0NX   (161) 792-3278
Ohel Torah
132 Leicester Road, Salford M7 0EA   (161) 740-6678
Prestwich Hebrew Congregation
Bury New Road M25 9WN   (161) 773-1978
Fax: (161) 773-7015
Sale & District Hebrew Congregation
14 Hesketh Road, Sale, Sale M33 5AA
(161) 973-2172

Sedgley Park (Shomrei Hadass)
Park View Road, Prestwich M25 5FA
(161) 773-4828/740-1969
Email: laurencemiller@hotmail.com
South Manchester
Wilbraham Road M14 6JS   (161) 224-1366
Fax: (161) 225-8033
United Synagogue
Meade Hill Road M8 4LR   (161) 740-9586
Whitefield Hebrew Congregation
Park Lane, Whitefield M45 7PB   (161) 766-3732
Fax: (161) 767-9453
Yeshurun Hebrew Congregation
Coniston Road, Gatley- Cheadle, Cheshire SK8 4AP
(161) 428-8242
Fax: (161) 491-5265
Email: yeshurun@btinternet.com

Reform

Cheshire Reform Congregation Menorah Synagogue
Altrincham Road M22 4RZ   (161) 428-7746
Email: menorah@zetnet.co.uk
Manchester Reform Synagogue
Jackson's Row M2 5NH   (161) 834-0415
Fax: (161) 834-0415
Sha'arei Shalom North Manchester Reform Synagogue
Elms Street, Whitefield M45 8GQ   (161) 796-6736
Fax: (161) 796-6736

Travel Agencies
Goodmos Tours (Man) Ltd.
23 Leicester Road, Salford M7 0AS   (161) 792-7333
Fax: (161) 792-7336
Email: goodmos836@aol.com
ITS: Israel Travel Service
427/430 Royal Exchange, Old Bank Street M2 7EP
(161) 839-1111
Fax: (161) 839-0000
Email: all@itstravel.co.uk
Web site: www.itstravel.co.uk
Freephone 0800 0181 839
Peltours Ltd
27-29 Church Street M4 1QA   (161) 834-3721
Fax: (161) 832-9343

Merseyside
Liverpool
There is evidence of an organised community before 1750, believed to have been composed of Sephardi Jews and to have had some connection with the West Indies and with Dublin, although some authorities believe they were mainly German Jews. The largely Ashkenazi Jews, who arrived later, were to some degree intending emigrants for the USA and the West Indies who changed their

minds and stayed in Liverpool. By 1807 the community had a building in Seel Street, the parent of today's synagogue in Princes Road, one of the handsomest in the country.

Booksellers

Liverpool Jewish Bookshop
Harold House
Dunbabin Road, L15 6XL

(151) 475-5671
Fax: (151) 475-5671

Full range of Jewish books, artifacts and gifts. Sundays 11.00am to 1.00pm.

Kashrut Information

Liverpool Kashrut Commission (inc. Liverpool Shechita Board)
c/o Shifrin House
433 Smithdown Road, L15 3JL

(151) 733-2292
Fax: (151) 734-0212

Media

Newspapers

Jewish Telegraph
Harold House
Dunbabin Road, L15 6XL

(151) 475-6666
Fax: (151) 475-2222
Email: mail@jewishtelegraph.com
Web site: www.jewishtelegraph.com

Mikvaot

Childwall Hebrew Congregation
Dunbabin Road L15 6XL

(151) 722-2079

Organisations

Merseyside Jewish Representative Council
433 Smithdown Road L15 3JL   (151) 733-2292
Fax: (151) 734-0212

Restaurants

JLGB Centre   (151) 475-5825; 475-5671
Open Sun, Tues., Thurs. 6.30-11.00pm. Licensed bar.
Out-of-town visitors welcome. Also take-away service.

Kosher

Harold House
Dunbabin Road L15 6XL   (151) 475-5825/5671
Fax: (151) 475-2212
Email: harold.house@ort.org
Web site: www.merseyside-jewish-community.org.uk
Supervision: Liverpool Kashrut Commission.

Vegetarian

Munchies Eating House
Myrtle Parade   (151) 709-7896

Synagogues

Orthodox

Allerton Hebrew Congregation
cnr. Mather & Booker Avenues
Allerton, L18 9TB   (151) 427-6848

Childwall Hebrew Congregation
Dunbabin Road L15 6XL   (151) 722-2079

Greenbank Drive Hebrew Congregation
Greenbank Drive L17 1AN   (151) 733-1417

Old Hebrew Congregation
Princes Road
Merseyside L8 1TG   (151) 709-3431
2* Listed Building. Guided talks available Thursdays 12pm-4pm. Pre-booking essential. Other times by special arrangement.

Progressive

Liverpool Progressive Synagogue
28 Church Road North
Merseyside L15 6TF   (151) 733-5871

Southport

Organisations

Southport Jewish Representative Council
Merseyside PR   (1704) 540704
Fax: (1704) 540704

Synagogues

Orthodox

Southport Hebrew Congregation
Arnside Road
Merseyside PR9 0QX   (1704) 532964
Fax: (1704) 514002
Mikveh on premises.

Reform

New (Reform) Synagogue
Portland Street
Merseyside PR8 1LR   (1704) 535950
Email: snewsyne@aol.com

Middlesex

Ruislip

Synagogues

Shenley Avenue
Ruislip Manor, Middlesex HA4 6BP   (1895) 632934

United Kingdom / Middlesex

Staines

Synagogues
Staines & District Synagogue
Westbrook Road
South Street, Middlesex TW18 4PR   (1784) 254604
                                Fax: (1784) 254604
Includes Slough and Windsor Synagogue.

Stanmore

Delicatessens
Great Food Shop
5 Canons Corner
Middlesex HA8 8AE   (020) 8958-9446
                             Fax: (020) 8905-4700
                        Email: srosenhead@aol.com
Supervision: London Beth Din Supervised.

Norfolk
Norwich

The present community was founded in 1813, Jews having been resident in Norwich during the Middle Ages, and connected with the woollen and worsted trade, for which the city was at that time famous. A resettlement of Jews is believed to have been completed by the middle of the eighteenth century.

Restaurants

Vegetarian

Eat Naturally
11 Wensum Street Norfolk NR3 1LA   (1603) 660-838

The Treehouse
14 Dove Street Norfolk NR2 1DE   (1603) 763-258
Open 10.00am - 5.00pm Monday to Wednesday.
10.00am - 9.30pm Thursday to Saturday. Closed Sunday.

Synagogues
3a Earlham Road
Norfolk NR2 3RA   (1603) 503434

Progressive Jewish Community of East Anglia
c/o Frimette Carr Norfolk   (1603) 714162

Northamptonshire
Northampton

Synagogues
Overstone Road
Northamptonshire BB1 3JW   (1604) 33345
Services on Friday night.

Nottinghamshire
Newark

Holocaust Memorial Centre
Bet Shalom
Laxton, Newark, Notts, NG22 0PA   (1623) 836627
                                Fax: (1623) 836647
Beth Shalom Holocaust Memorial Centre was conceived as a place where some of the implications of the Holocaust can be faced. It is an education centre where Jews and non-Jews work together to forge a united front against the perils of anti-Semitism and racism in society today.

Nottingham

Jews settled in Nottingham as early as medieval times, and centres of learning and worship are known to have existed in that period. The earliest known record of an established community dates from 1822 when a grant of land for burial purposes was made by the Corporation.

Restaurants

Vegetarian

Krisha Restaurant
144 Alfreton Road Redford, NG7 3NS
                                    (115) 970-8608

Maxine's Salad Table
56 Upper Parliament Street NG1 2AG
                                    (115) 947-3622

The Vegetarian Pot
375 Alfreton Road Redford, NG7 5LT
                                    (115) 970-3333

Synagogues
Shakespeare Street NG1 4FQ   (115) 947-2004

Nottingham Progressive Jewish Congregation
Lloyd Street, Sherwood, NG5 4BP   (115) 962-4761

Oxfordshire
Oxford

There was an important medieval community, and the present one dates back to 1842. The Oxford Synagogue and Jewish Centre, opened in 1974, serves both the city and the university. It is available for all forms of Jewish worship.

Community Organisations
L'Chaim Society
Albion House Little Gate, (1865) 794-462
The Synagogue and Jewish Centre
21 Richmond Road OX1 2JL (1865) 553042
Email: information@oxford-synagogue.org.uk
Regular Orthodox, Masorti and Progressive Services.
Wide range of communal activities. A kosher meals
service operates during term time. Phone or email for
information.

Staffordshire
Stoke On Trent
Synagogues
Birch Terrace Hanley, ST1 3JN (1782) 616417

Surrey
Guildford
Synagogues
Guildford & District Synagogue
York Road GU1 4DR (1483) 576470
Email: gould.harry@net.ntl.com
Correspondence: Mr B Gould, Lynwood, Hillier Road,
Guildford, Surrey, GU1 2JG.

Tourist Sites
Surrey GU1
Enquiries about the recent discovery of a medieval
synagogue in the town may be addressed to the
Guildford Museum.

Sussex
Brighton and Hove
The first known Jewish resident of Brighton lived
there in 1767. The earliest synagogue was founded
in Jew Street in 1789. Henry Solomon, vice-
president of the congregation, was the first Chief
Constable of the town. His brother-in-law, Levi
Emanuel Cohen, founded the Brighton Guardian,
and was twice elected president of the Newspaper
Society of Great Britain. The town's Jewish
population today is about 8,000.

Community Organisations
Lubavitch Chabad House
15 The Upper Drive BN3 6GR (1273) 321-919

Delicatessens
Cantor's of Hove
20 Richardson Road Hove, BN3 5BB (1273) 723-669

Media
Newspapers
Sussex Jewish News
PO Box 1623 (1273) 504-455
Mikvaot
Prince Regent Swimming Pool Cmplx.
Church Street, BN1 1YA (1273) 321-919

Organisations
Hillel House
18 Harrington Road BN1 6RE (1273) 503-450
Closed during summer vacation. Friday evening meals
available.

Religious Organisations
Brighton and Hove Joint Kashrus Committee
c/o B.H.H.C.
31 New Church Road, Hove, East Sussex, BN3 4AD
(1273) 888855
Fax: (1273) 888810

Synagogues
Brighton & Hove Hebrew Congregation
Middle Street Synagogue 66 Middle Street, BN1 1AL
(1273) 888855
Fax: (1273) 888810
Hove Hebrew Congregation
79 Holland Road, Hove, Sussex BN3 1JN
(1273) 732035
West Hove Synagogue
31 New Church Road, Hove, Sussex BN3 4AD
(1273) 888855
Fax: (1273) 888810
Email: bhhc@breathemail.net

Progressive
Progressive Synagogue
6 Landsdowne Road BN3 1FF (1273) 737223
9.30am to 1pm

Reform
New (Reform)
Palmeira Avenue BN3 3GE (1273) 735343

Eastbourne
Synagogues
22 Susans Road BN21 3HA (1435) 866928
Fax: (1435) 865783

United Kingdom / Sussex

Hastings

Contact Information
Alfred Ross
PO Box 74, Bexhill on Sea, East Sussex, (1424) 848344

Tyne & Wear

Gateshead
A community with many schools, yeshivot and other training institutions.

Bakeries
Stenhouse
215 Coatsworth Road NE8 1SR   (191) 477-2001

Booksellers
J. Lehmann
28-30 Grasmere Street NE8 1TS   (191) 477-3523
Fax: (191) 430-0555
Email: info@lehmanns.co.uk
Also has wholesale and mail order, Unit E, Viking Industrial Park, Rolling Mill Road, NE32 3DP. Tel: 0191 430-0333

Butchers
K.L. Kosher Butcher
83 Rodsley Avenue NE8   (191) 477-3109
Kosher.

Mikvaot
180 Bewick Road NE8 1UF   (191) 477-3552

Synagogues
138 Whitehall RoadNE8 1TP   (191) 477-3012
180 Bewick Road NE8 1UF   (191) 477-0111
Mikva on premises. For appt: 477-3552

Newcastle
The community was established before 1831, when a cemetery was acquired. Jews have lived in Newcastle since 1775. There are about 1,200 Jews in the city today.

Bed & Breakfasts
Vegetarian
Old School House
Kirkwhelpington NE19 2RT   (1830) 40226

Groceries
Zelda's Delicatessen
Unit 7 Kenton Park Shopping Centre NE3 4RU
(191) 213-0013
Fax: (191) 213-0013
Email: davidsimon1@compuserve.com
Supervision: Newcastle Kashrus Committee, Rabbi Yehuda Black.
Delicatessen, fresh meat, poultry and bread also sold here. Closed Mondays. Buses: 10, 31 from city centre.

Kashrut Information
Kashrus Committee
Lionel Jacobson House
Graham Park Road, Gosforth, NE3 4BH
(191) 284-0959

Media
Newspapers
The North-East Jewish Recorder
28 Montagu Court NE3 4JL   (191) 285-4318
Email: 100410.2647@compuserve.com

Mikvaot
Graham Park Road NE3 4BH   (191) 284-0959

Organisations
Representative Council of North-East Jewry
39 Kenton Road
Gosforth, Newcastle upon Tyne, NE3 4NH
(191) 284-4647
Fax: (191) 01429-274796
Email: martinlev@onet.co.uk
Web site: www.northeastjewish.org.uk

Restaurants
Vegetarian
The Supernatural
2 Princess Square NE1 8ER   (191) 261-2730

Synagogues
United Hebrew Congregation
Graham Park Road NE3 4BH   (191) 284-0959
Mikva on premises.

Newcastle Reform Synagogue
The Croft
off Kenton Road, NE3 4RF   (191) 284-8621

Sunderland

Mikvaot
11 The Oaks East Ryhope Road, SR2 8EX
(191) 565-0224

Organisations
11 The Oaks East Ryhope Road SR2 8EX
(191) 565-0224

Synagogues
Communal Rav.
11 The Oaks East
Ryhope Road, Tyne & Wear SR2 8EX   (191) 565-0224

Sunderland Hebrew Congregation
Ryhope Road SR2 7EQ   (191) 565-8093
This building has been given grade two listed status.

West Midlands

Birmingham

This Jewish community is one of the oldest in the Provinces, dating from at least 1730. Birmingham was a centre from which Jewish pedlars covered the surrounding country week by week, returning home for Shabbat.

The first synagogue of which there is any record was in The Froggery in 1780. There was a Jewish cemetery in the same neighbourhood in 1730. The synagogue of 1780 was extended in 1791, 1809 and 1827. A new and larger synagogue, popularly known as 'Singers Hill', opened in 1856. Today's Jewish population stands at about 2,300.

Booksellers
Lubavitch Bookshop
95 Willows Road B12 9QF   (121) 440-6673
Fax: (121) 446-4199

Contact Information
Lubavitch Centre
95 Willows Road B12 9QF   (121) 440-6673
Fax: (121) 446-4199

Bookshop on premises.

Delicatessens
Gee's Butchers Ltd
75 Pershore Road B5 7NX   (121) 440-2160
Kosher butcher, baker and deli.

Information and Resource Centre
Israel Information Centre & Bookshop
Singers Hill
Blucher Street, B1 1QL   (121) 643-2688
Fax: (121) 643-2688
Email: rjacobs@iicmids.u-net.com
Hours of opening: 10-4pm Monday, Tuesdays, Thursdays or by appointment.

Kashrut Information
Shechita Board
Singers Hill
Ellis Street, B1 1HL   (121) 643-0884

Mikvaot
Birmingham Central Synagogue
133 Pershore Road B5 7PA
(121) 440-4044 - Mobile 07946 642265

Representative Organisations
Representative Council of Birmingham & Midland Jewry
37 Wellington Road Edgbaston, B15 2ES
(121) 236-1801 Evenings: 440-4142
Fax: (121) 236-9906
Email: bjrepco@dircon.co.uk
Web site: www.brijnet.org/birmingham

Synagogues
Bimingham Hebrew Congregation
Singer's Hill
Ellis Street, B1 1HL   (121) 643-0884
Fax: (121) 643-5950

Central Synagogue
133 Pershore Road, Edgbaston, B5 7PA
(121) 440-4044
Fax: (121) 440-4044

Progressive Synagogue
4 Sheepcote Street B16 8AA   (121) 643-5640
Fax: (121) 633-8372
Email: bps@uips.org
Web site: www.bps-pro-syn.co.uk

Coventry

Synagogues
Coventry Hebrew Congregation
Barras Lane CV1 3BW   (24) 7622-0168

Reform
Coventry Jewish Reform Community
(24) 7667-2027
The Jewish presence in Coventry dates back to 1775, if not earlier.

Solihull

Synagogues
Solihull & District Hebrew Congregation
3 Monastery Drive B91 1DW   (121) 707-5199
                              Fax: (121) 706-8736
                Email: rabbiypink@compuserve.com
                     Web site: www.solihullshul.org
Services: Friday evening 6.30 winter, 8.00 pm summer;
Sat 9.45am, Sun 9am

Wolverhampton

Synagogues
Fryer Street WV1 1HT
Est. over 150 years ago. Membership 15 families.
Services Fri. even. & some Sabbath morns.

Yorkshire
Bradford

The Jewish community, although only about 140
years old, has exercised much influence on the
city's staple industry: wool. Jews of German
descent developed the export trade of wool yarns
and fabrics.

Synagogues

Orthodox

Bradford Hebrew Congregation
Springhurst Road Shipley, BD18 3DN (1274) 581189
                         Fax: (1274) 01422-374101
Services 10am monthly on Shabbat Mevorachim , High
holy-days & certain festivals.

Reform

Bradford Synagogue
Bowland Street
Manningham Lane, BD1 3BW   (1274) 728925
Service Sat 11am; Festivals, 6pm & 11am

Harrogate

Guest Houses
Amadeus Vegetarian Hotel
115 Franklin Road HG1 5EN   (1423) 505-151
                              Fax: (1423) 505-151
Totally vegetarian and non-smoking. Meals for resident
guests only. Vegetarian café nearby open Friday
evenings. 10 minutes walk from railway station.

Synagogues
St Mary's Walk HG2 0LW
Friday 6pm in Winter and 7pm in Summer. Sabbath
9.30am

Harrogate Hebrew Congregation
St Mary's Walk   (1423) 871713
                              Fax: (1423) 879143
Services: Saturday 9.30 a.m. 1st Friday evening in
month - Winter 6 p.m. / Summer 7 p.m.

Leeds
The Leeds Jewish community is the second largest
in the provinces, and numbers about 12,000. The
community dates only from 1804, although a few
Jews are known to have lived there in the previous
half-century. The first synagogue was built in 1860.

Bakeries

Orthodox

Chalutz Bakery
378 Harrogate Road LS17 6PY   (113) 269-1350
Supervision: Leeds Kashrut Commission.
Hours: Monday to Thursday, 8 am to 6 pm; Friday, to
1 hour before Shabbat; Saturday, from 1 hour after
Shabbat to 2 pm Sunday.

Butchers
The Kosherie
410 Harrogate Road LS17 6PY   (113) 268-2943
                              Fax: (113) 269-6979
Supervision: Leeds Beth Din.

Community Organisations
Café Martine
Lubavitch Centre
168 Shadwell Lane, LS17 8AD   (113) 266-3311
                              Fax: (113) 237-1130
Supervision: Leeds Kashrut Authority and Leeds Beth
Din.
A community centre which provides educational
activities. Restaurant on premises which is currently not
open. Call to see if it has re-opened. Open Sun 5-9.
Thur 6-10. Direct line to the Café 44-113 237 1130.

Delicatessens
Fisher's Deli
391 Harrogate Road LS17 6DJ   (113) 268-6944
Supervision: Leeds Beth Din.
Butcher and deli.

Gourmet Foods
Sandhill Parade
584 Harrogate Road, LS17 8DP   (113) 268-2726
Supervision: Leeds Beth Din.
Butcher and deli.

United Kingdom / Channel Islands

Hotels

Beegee's Guest House
18 Moor Allerton Drive
off Street Lane, Moortown, LS17 6RZ (113) 293-5469
Fax: (113) 275-3300
Near all synagogues.

Libraries

Jewish Library
Porton Collection; Central Library
Municipal Buildings, LS1 3AB (113) 247-8282
Fax: (113) 247-8426
Web site: www.leeds.gov.uk

Media

Newspapers

Jewish Telegraph
1 Shaftesbury Avenue LS8 1DR (113) 295-6000
Fax: (113) 295-6006
Email: mail@jewishtelegraph.com
Web site: www.jewishtelegraph.com

Mikvaot

411 Harrogate Road LS17 7BY (113) 237-1096
(answerphone)

Religious Organisations

Beth Din
Etz Chaim Synagogue LS17 6BY (113) 269-6902
Fax: (113) 237-0893
Information about kosher food and accommodation
may be obtained here.

Representative Organisation

Leeds Jewish Representative Council
c/o Shadwell Lane Synagogue LS17 (113) 269-7520
Fax: (113) 237-0851
Publishes Year Book.

Restaurant

Hansa's Gujarati Restaurant
72 North Street LS2 7PN (113) 244-4408
Web site: www.hansasrestaurant.co.uk
Indian Vegetarian restaurant

Synagogues

Orthodox

Beth Hamedrash Hagadol
399 Street Lane LS17 6HQ (113) 269-2181
Email: office@bhhs.freeserve.co.uk

Chassidishe
c/o Donisthorpe Hall Shadwell Lane, LS17 6AW

Etz Chaim
411 Harrogate Road LS17 7BY (113) 266-2214

Queenshill Synagogue
26 Queenshill Avenue LS17 6AX (113) 2687364
Email: sabrah2936.aol.com

Shadwell Lane Synagogue (United Hebrew

Congregation)
151 Shadwell Lane LS17 8DW (113) 269-6141
Fax: (113) 269-6165

Shomrei Hadass
368 Harrogate Road LS17 6QB (113) 268-1461

Reform

Sinai
Roman Avenue
off Street Lane, LS8 2AN (113) 266-5256
Fax: (113) 266-1539
Email: synagogue@sinaileeds@freeserve.co.uk

Sheffield

Synagogues

Sheffield Jewish Congregation and Centre
Wilson Road S11 8RN (114) 266-3567
Fax: (114) 266-3567

Reform

Sheffield & District Reform Jewish Congregation
PO Box 675 S11 8TE (114) 230-1054
Fax: (114) 236-2982
Web site: www.shef-ref.co.uk
Service alternate Friday evenings

York

Tours of Jewish Interest

Yorkwalk
3 Fairway
Clifton, YO30 5QA (1904) 622303
Fax: (1904) 656244
Email: barstep.demon.co.uk/homepage.htm
Web site: www.barstep.demon.co.uk/homepage.htm
Introduced new walk called 'The Jewish Heritage Walk',
recalling the Jewish contribution to York's history. The
walk finishes at Clifford's Tower, the site of a dreadful
Jewish massacre in 1190.

Channel Islands

Alderney

Memorials

Corblets Road, Longy
There is a memorial to the victims of the Nazis during
their occupation of the English Channel Islands during
the Second World War. It bears plaques in English,
French, Hebrew and Russian.

Jersey

Contact Information

Armon
3 Clos des Chataigniers, Rue de la Croix, St Ouen, St
Ouen JE3 2HA (1534) 482-429
Honorary secretary of the Jersey Jewish Congregation.

United Kingdom / Channel Islands

Synagogues
Jersey Jewish Congregation
La Petite Route des Mielles
St Brelade, St Brelade JE3 8FY
Shabbat morning service, 10:30 am; Holy days, 7 pm
and 10 am.

Isle of Man
Douglas

Synagogues
Hebrew Congregation   (1624) 24214
There are more than 70 Jews on the island.

Northern Ireland
Belfast

Organisations
Vegetarian & Vegans Charity
66 Ravenhill Gardens
Ulster BT6 8QG   (28) 9028-1640

Restaurants
Jewish Community Centre
49 Somerton Road
Ulster BT15 3LH   (28) 9077-7974
Open Sunday 6.30 pm to 9.30 pm.

Synagogues
49 Somerton Road
Ulster BT15 3LH   (28) 9077-7974
Services: Sat., Sun., Mon., & Thurs.; am.

Scotland
Aberdeen

Restaurants

Vegetarian

Jaws Wholefood Café
5 West North Street AB1 3AT   (1224) 645676
10am to 3pm Mon.-Sat; 10am to 9pm Thurs. & Fri

Synagogues
74 Dee Street AB11 6DS   (1224) 582135

Dundee
Synagogues
St Mary Place DD1 5RB   (1382) 223557

Dunoon
Synagogues
Argyll & Bute Jewish Community
     (1369) 705118

Edinburgh

The Town Council and Burgess Roll minutes of
1691 and 1717 record applications by Jews for
permission to live and trade in Edinburgh.

Butchers
3 Oxgangs Road   (131) 445-3437
Regular meat deliveries from suppliers in Glasgow and
Manchester. Further information from Hon. Sec.
W.Simpson

Kashrut Information
Rabbi D Sedley   (131) 667-9360

Restaurants

Vegetarian

Anna Purna, 45 St Patrick Sq.   (131) 662-1807
Black Bo's, Blackfriars Street   (131) 557-6136
Henderson's
94 Hanover Street EH2 1DR   (131) 225-2131
     Fax: (131) 220-3542
     Email: mail@hendersonsofedinburgh.co.uk
     Web site: www.hendersonsofedinburgh.co.uk
Kalpna Restaurant
2 St Patrick Sq. EH8 9EZ   (131) 667-9890
     Fax: (131) 443-8782
     Web site: www.kalpna.co.uk
Hours: Lunch 1100am to 2.00pm. Dinner 5.30pm to
11.00pm.

Synagogues
4 Salisbury Road EH16 5AB   (131) 667-3144

Glasgow

The Glasgow Jewish community dates back to
1823. The oldest synagogue building is the
Garnethill Synagogue now also the home of the
Scottish Jewish Archives, which opened in 1879.
The community grew rapidly from 1891 with many
Jews settling in the Gorbals. In recent years the
community has gradually spread southwards and
is now mainly situated in the Giffnock and Newton
Mearns areas.

Booksellers
J & E Levingstone
47/55 Sinclair Drive G42 9PT   (141) 649-2962
     Fax: (141) 649-2962

Religious requisites also stocked.
Well of Wisdom
Giffnock Synagogue G46   (141) 577-8260
     Fax: (141) 620-0823

Delicatessens
Hello Deli
200 Fenwick Road G46   (141) 638-8267
     Fax: (141) 621-2290

Marlenes Kosher Deli
2 Burnfield Road G46 7QB   (141) 638-4383
Michael Morrison and Son
52 Sinclair Drive G42 9PY   (141) 632-0998
                                        Fax: (141) 649-2962
Not under official supervision. Stockist of many Glatt
Kosher items.

Hotels
Forres Guest House
10 Forres Avenue G46 6LJ
          (141) 638-5554 (mobile: 07801 666-864)
                                        Fax: (141) 571-9301
                          Email: jtg@junedavies.com
                          Web site: www.junedavies.com
Guest House
26 St Clair Avenue G46 7QE   (141) 638-3924
Kosher, but not supervised.

Media

Newspapers

Jewish Telegraph
43 Queen Square G41 2BD   (141) 423-9200
                                        Fax: (141) 423-9200
                          Email: telegraph@jaytel.demon.co.uk

Mikvaot
Giffnock & Newlands Synagogue
Maryville Avenue, Giffnock G46 7NE   (141) 577-8250
                                        Fax: (141) 577-8252

Organisations
Glasgow Jewish Representative Council
222 Fenwick Road G46 6UE   (141) 577-8200
                                        Fax: (141) 577-8202
                          Email: glasgow@ort.org

Religious Organisations

Orthodox

Lubavitch Foundation of Scotland
8 Orchard Drive, Giffnock G46 7NR   (141) 638-6116
                                        Fax: (141) 638 6478
                          Email: LubOfScot@aol.com
                          Web site: www.lubofscot.com

Restaurants

Meat

Kaye's Restaurant
Maccabi Youth Centre, May Terrace G46
                                        (141) 620-3233
Kosher.

Synagogues

Orthodox

Garnethill
129 Hill Street G3 6UB   (141) 322-4151
Shabbat services 10am. Yomtov services 9.45am

Giffnock & Newlands Hebrew Congregation
Maryville Avenue, Giffnock G46 7NE   (141) 577-8250
                                        Fax: (141) 577-8252
                          Email: giffnock-rabbi@j-scot.org
Langside
125 Niddrie Road G42 8QA   (141) 423-4062
Netherlee & Clarkston
Clarkston Road at Randolph Drive G44
                                  (141) 637-8206/639-7194
                                        Fax: (141) 616-0743
Newton Mearns
14 Larchfield Court G77 5BH   (141) 639-4000
Queen's Park
Falloch Road G42 9QX   (141) 632-1743

Reform

Glasgow New Synagogue
147 Ayr Road, Newton Mearns G77 6RE
                                        (141) 639-4083
                                        Fax: (141) 639-4083
                          Email: shul@gns.org.uk

St Andrews
Contact Information
Jewish Student's Society
c/o Sec., Students' Union
University of St Andrews, Kirkcaldy KY16 9UY

Wales
Cardiff
Mikvaot
Wales Empire Pool Building, Wood Street CF1 1PP
                                        (29) 2038-2296

Restaurants

Vegetarian

Munchies Wholefood Co-op
60 Crwys Road, Cathays CF2 4NN   (29) 2039-9677

Self-catering
Hillel House CF2 5NR   (29) 2022-8845
Self catering for students

Synagogues

Orthodox

Cardiff United Synagogue
Brandreth Road, Penylan
                                  (29) 2047-3728/2048-7377
                                        Fax: (29) 2047-3728
                          Email: rabbi@cardiffunited.org.uk
                          Web site: www.cardiffunited.org.uk

United Kingdom / Wales

Reform

Cardiff New Synagogue
Moira Terrace CF2 1EJ   (29) 2061-4915

Llandudno

Hotels
Plas Madoc Vegetarian Guesthouse
60 Church Walks, Conwy LL30 2HL   (1492) 876514
100% vegetarian. Synagogue 100 yards away.

Synagogues
28 Church Walks LL30 2HL   (1492) 572549
No resident minister, but visiting ministers during
summer months. Friday night services held throughout
year, 6.16pm (winter) and 8pm (summer)

Newport

Synagogues
Newport Mon Hebrew Congregation
Risca Road NP9 5HH   (1633) 262308
                                Fax: (1633) 266362
Communication: 45 St Marks Crescent, Newport, S.
Wales, NP20 5HE

Swansea

Contact Information
Dr Mars
70 Gabalfa Road
Sketty SA2 8NE   (1792) 205263
                   Email: l.mars@swansea.ac.uk
Dr Mars is happy to help and advise students coming
to University of Wales, Swansea.

Restaurants

Vegetarian

Chris's Kitchen
The Market SA1 3PE   (1792) 643455
8.30am to 5.30pm Mon.-Sat

Synagogues
Ffynone
17 Ffynone Drive SA1 6DB   (1792) 473333

GMT -5 to 11 hours
Country calling code (1)
Emergency Telephone (Police, Fire and Ambulance - 911)

Total Population 265,455,000
Jewish Population 5,800,000
Electricity voltage 110/220

Alabama

Birmingham

Community Organisations
Birmingham Jewish Federation
3966 Montclair Road 35213   (205) 803-0416
                                   Fax: (205) 803-1526

Contact Information
Rabbi Avraham Shmidman
3225 Montevallo Road 35223   (205) 879-1664
                                   Fax: (205) 879-5774
                                   Email: kicongreg@aol.com
Visitors requiring information about kashrut, temporary
accommodation, etc., should contact Rabbi
Shmidman..

Delicatessens
Browdy's
2607 Cahaba Road 35223   (205) 879-6411

Libraries
Hess Library
3960 Montclair Road 35213

Mikvaot
Knesseth Israel
3225 Montevallo Rd 35213   (205) 879-1464
Supervision: (O).

Synagogues

Conservative

Beth-El, 2179 Highland Avenue 35205
                                   (205) 933-2740
                                   Fax: (205) 933-2747

Orthodox
Knesseth Israel
3225 Montevallo Road 35223   (205) 879-1464
                                   Fax: (205) 879-5774

Reform
Emanu-El
2100 Highland Avenue 35205   (205) 933-8037

Huntsville

Synagogues

Conservative
Etz Chayim
7705 Bailey Cove Road 35802   (256) 882-2918
                                   Fax: (256) 881-6160

Mobile

Synagogues

Reform

Spring Hill Avenue Temple
1769 Spring Hill Avenue 36607

Montgomery

Community Organisations
Jewish Federation
• PO Box 20058 36120   (334) 277-5820
                                   Fax: (334) 277-8383

Synagogues

Conservative

Agudath Israel
3525 Cloverdale Road 36111
Mikvah attached

Orthodox

Etz Ahayem (Sephardi)
725 Augusta Road 36111   (334) 281-9819

Reform

Beth Or, 2246 Narrow Lane 36106
Maxwell Air Force Base
Building 833, Chaplain's School

Alaska

Anchorage

Groceries
Carr's
Diamond Boulvevard

United States of America / Alaska

Synagogues

Orthodox

Congregation Shomrei Ohr
1210 E. 26th 99508   (907) 279-1200
                              Fax: (907) 279-7890
                      Email: lubavitchofak@gci.net
The Centre offers full Shabbat meals featuring
homemade dishes.

Reform

Beth Sholom
7525 E. Northern Lights Blvd 99504   (907) 338-1836
                              Fax: (907) 337-4013
                      Email: sholom@alaska.net

Denali Park Area

Groceries
PS Kosher Food Services
P.O. Box 240, Mile 248.5 Parks Highway, Healy 99743
                                      (907) 683-1560
                              Fax: (907) 683-4026
                      Email: psfood@juno.com
Kitchens located at Denali North Star Inn. Summer
sales only.

Arizona

Phoenix

Community Organisations
Jewish Federation of Greater Phoenix
32 W. Coolidge, Suite 200 85013   (602) 274-1800
Orthodox Rabbinical Council of Greater Phoenix
515 E. Bethany Home Road 85012   (602) 277-8858
                              Fax: (602) 274-0713

Kashrut Information
Rabbi David Rebibo
Pheonix Vaad Hakashruth, 515 E. Bethany Home Rd.
85012   (602) 277-8858
                              Fax: (602) 274-0713
Visitors requiring kashrut information should contact
Rabbi Rebibo.

Media

Newspapers

Jewish News of Greater Phoenix
1625 E. Northern 106 85020   (602) 870-9470
                              Fax: (602) 870-0426
                      Email: jngphx@aol.com
Shalom Arizona
32 W. Coolidge, Suite 200 85013   (602) 274-1800

Museums
Sylvia Plotkin Judaica Museum
10460 N. 56th St Scottsdale 85253   (480) 951-0323
                              Fax: (480) 951-7150
                      Email: museum@templebethisrael.org
Hours: Most Sundays 12-3 p.m., Tuesday-Friday10-3,
Friday evenings after services. Advanced notice
required for groups of 10 or more.

Restaurants

Meat

Segal's Kosher Foods
4818 North 7th Street 85014   (602) 285-1515
                              Fax: (602) 277-5760
                      Email: segalkosh@aol.com
Supervision: Greater Phoenix Vaad Hakashrut.
Strictly kosher full service restaurant serving lunch and
dinner Monday through Thursday and Shabbat take-out
on Friday. Kosher bakery within premises.

Meat and Dairy

J.J.'s Kosher
1331 E. Northern Av. 85015   (602) 371-0999

Synagogues
Tri-Cities Jewish Community Center
1965 E. Hermosa Temp, AZ 85282   (602) 897-0588

Conservative

Congregation Beth El
1118 W. Glendale 85021   (602) 944-3359
Temple Beth Sholom
3400 N Dobson Road, Chandler 85224
                                      (480) 897-3636
                              Fax: (480) 897-3633
                      Email: templebethsholom@aol.com

Orthodox

Chabad-Lubavitch Center
2110 E. Lincoln Drive 85020   (602) 944-2753
Congregation Beth Joseph
515 E. Bethany Home Road 85012   (602) 277-8858
                              Fax: (602) 274-0713

Congregation Shaarei Tzedek
7608 N. 18th Avenue 85021   (602) 944-1133
Valley of the Sun Jewish Community Center
1718 W. Maryland Avenue 85015   (602) 249-1832
Young Israel of Phoenix
745 E Maryland Avenue, Ste.120 85014
                                      (602) 265-8888
                              Fax: (602) 265-8867
                      Email: cnsil5@home.com

United States of America / Arizona

Reform

Temple Beth Ami
4545 N. 36th Street, No. 211 85018
(302) 956-0805
Temple Chai
4645 E. Marilyn Avenue 85032   (602) 971-1234
Temple Kol Ami
15030 N. 64th Street, 204 85254   (602) 951-9660

Scottsdale

Delicatessens

Cactus Kosher
8005 E. Indian School Road 85251   (602) 970-8441
Supervision: Greater Phoenix Vaad Hakashrut.
Delicatessen which also offers take-out and catering for
area hotel delivery.

Synagogues

Conservative

Beth Emeth of Scottsdale
5406 E. Virginia Avenue 85254   (602) 947-4604
Beth Joshua Congregation
6230 E. Shea Blvd. 85254   (602) 991-5404
Har Zion
5929 E. Lincoln Drive 85253   (602) 991-0720

Reform

Temple Solel
6805 E. MacDonald Drive 85253   (602) 991-7414

Sierra Vista

Synagogues
Temple Kol Hamidbar
228 North Canyon Drive
(520) 458-8637 (Ans. phone only)
Web site: www.uahcweb.org/congs/az/tkh/
Mailing address: P O Box 908, Sierra Vista, Arizona
85636, USA

Sun City and West

Synagogues

Conservative

Beth Emeth of Sun City
13702 Meeker Blvd.,, Sun City West 85373
(602) 584-1957

Reform

Beth Shalom of Sun City
12202 101st Avenue, Sun City 85351
(602) 977-3240

Tempe

Community Organisations
Tri-City Jewish Community Center
1965 E. Hermosa Drive 85282   (602) 897-0588

Synagogues

Orthodox

Chabad-Lubavitch Center
23 W. 9th Street 85281   (602) 966-5163

Reform

Temple Emanuel
5801 Rural Road 85283   (602) 838-1414

Tucson

Butcher shop - Delicatessen
Feig's Kosher Market & Deli
5071 E. 5th Street 85711   (520) 325-2255
Fax: (520) 325-2978
Supervision: Rabbi R. Eisen..
Fresh glatt beef, lamb and veal, full service deli,
groceries. Hours: Monday to Thursday, 8 am to 5:45
pm; Friday, to 3:45 pm; Sunday, to 1:45 pm.

Community Organisations
Jewish Federation of Southern Arizona
3822 E. River Rd. 85718   (520) 577-9393
Fax: (520) 577-0734
Email: stumellan@jon.cjfny.org

Synagogues

Conservative

Congregation Bet Shalom
3881 E. River Road 85718   (520) 577-1171
Fax: (520) 577-8903
Email: cbs3881@juno.com
Supervision: Rabbi Leo M Abrami.
Kosher (dairy kitchen, operated by Sisterhood.

Orthodox

Congregation Chofetz Chayim
5150 E. 5th Street 85711   (520) 747-7780
Fax: (520) 745-6325
Email: ewbecker@flash.net
Young Israel of Tucson
2443 E 4th Street 85710   (520) 326-8362

Reform

Temple Emanuel
225 N. County Club Road 85716

United States of America / Arkansas

Arkansas

El Dorado

Synagogues
Beth Israel
1130 E. Main Street

Helena

Synagogues
Temple Beth-El
406 Perry Street 72342
Founded 1875.

Hot Springs

Synagogues
House of Israel
300 Quapaw Avenue. 71901   (501) 623-5821
                          Fax: (501) 622-3500
            Email: houseofi@direclynx.net
Supervision: (R).
Hot Springs is known for its curative waters. The Leo
Levi Memorial Hospital (for joint disorders, such as
arthritis) was founded by B'nai B'rith, as was the
adjacent Levi Towers, a senior citizen housing project.

Little Rock

Bakeries
Andre's
11121 Rodney Parham Rd 72212

Community Organisations
Jewish Federation of Arkansas
425 N. University Ave., Little Rock, Ak 72205
                          (501) 663-3571
                   Fax: (501) 663-7286
            Email: jfalr@aristotle.net
Monday to Thursday 9.00am to 5.00pm. Friday
9.00am to 4.00pm.

Mikvaot
Agudath Achim
7901 W. 5th St. 72205
Supervision: (O).

Synagogues

Reform

B'nai Israel
3700 Rodney Parham Rd. 72212   (501) 225-9700
                          Fax: (501) 225-6058
            Email: elevy@snider.net

California

As the general population of California continues
to increase, the Jewish community is growing as

well. Places of worship abound, from Eureka in the
north to San Diego in the south, but the major part
of the community lives in the Los Angeles
metropolitan area.

Alameda

Synagogues
Temple Israel
3183 Mecartney Road 94501

Anaheim

Restaurants
Disneyland
Kosher meals are available at the Blue Bayou
restaurant, adjacent to the Pirates of the Caribbean.
Place orders at least one hour in advance.

Synagogues

Conservative

Temple Beth Emet
1770 W. Cerritos Avenue 92804   (714) 772-4720
                          Fax: (714) 772-4710
            Email: tbe-anaheim@tea-house.com

Arcadia

Synagogues
Congregation Shaarei Torah
550 S. 2nd Avenue 91006   (818) 445-0810

Arleta

Synagogues

Reform

Temple Beth Solomon of the Deaf
13580 Osborne Street 91331   (818) 899-2202
                   Fax: (818) (TDD) 896-6721

Bakersfield

Synagogues

Conservative

B'nai Jacob
600 17th Street 93301

Reform

Temple Beth El
2906 Loma Linda Drive 93305   (661) 322-7607
                          Fax: (661) 322-7807
            Email: kernjew@aol.com

Berkeley (See also Oakland)

Mikvaot

Mikvah Taharas Israel
2520 Warring St. 94704-3111   (510) 848-7221
Fax: (510) 849-0536
Email: vaad@flash.net
Available for use by Men. Women by appointment.

Museums

Judah L. Magnes Jewish Museum
2911 Russell St. 94705   (510) 549-6950
Fax: (510) 849-3643
Email: pfpr@magnesmuseum.org
Among the earliest institutions of its kind west of New
York. It includes Judaica and Fine arts collections,
changing and permanent exhibitions, the Western
Jewish History Center, & the Blumenthal Library. Open
Sun-Thurs. 10-4.

Restaurants

Dairy

Noah's Bagels
1883 Solano AvenueSolano   (510) 525-4447
Supervision: The Vaad Kakashrus of Northern
California.

Synagogues

Conservative

Netivot Shalom
1841 Berkeley Way 94708   (510) 549-9447
Fax: (510) 549-9448
Email: ntvt-office@eb.jfed.org
Web site: www.netivotshalom.org
Weekly shabbat/Holiday services at 1414 Walnut
Street.

Egalitarian

Berkeley Hillel Foundation
2736 Bancroft Way 94704   (510) 845-7793
Fax: (510) 845-7753
Traditional egalitarian services on Friday
evening/student programs.

Jewish Renewal

Aquarian Minyan
c/o Goldfarb, 2020 Essex 94703
Kehilla
PO Box 3063 94703

Orthodox

Chabad House
2643 College Avenue 94704

Congregation Beth Israel
1630 Bancroft Way 94703   (510) 843-5246
Fax: (510) 843-5058
Email: office@beth-israel.berkeley.ca.us
Web site: www.beth-israel.berkeley.ca.us

Reform

Temple Beth El
2301 Vine Street 94708

Beverly Hills

Note: Beverly Hills, Hollywood and Los Angeles are
contiguous communities and in many cases have
overlapping bodies.

Synagogues

Orthodox

Beth Jacob
9030 Olympic Boulevard 90211
Young Israel of Beverly Hills
8701 Pico Blvd 90035   (310) 275-3020
Young Israel of North Beverly Hills
9350 Civic Center Drive
North Beverly Hills 90210   (310) 203-0170

Orthodox Sephardi

Magen David
322 N. Foothill 90210

Reform

Temple Emanuel
8844 Burton Way 90211   (310) 274-6388
Fax: (310) 271-7976

Burlingame

Synagogues
Peninsula Temple Sholom
1655 Sebastian Drive 94010   (415) 697-2266
Fax: (415) 697-2544

Carmel

Synagogues
Congregation Beth Israel
5716 Carmel Valley Road 93923   (831) 624-2015
Fax: (831) 624-4786
Email: shalomcbi@aol.com
Services: Friday night 8.00 pm and Saturday 11.00 am

Castro Valley

Synagogues
Shir Ami
4529 Malabar Avenue 94546   (415) 537-1787

United States of America / California

Costa Mesa

Organisations
Jewish Federation of Orange County
250 E. Baker Street 92626   (714) 755-5555
Fax: (714) 755-0307
Email: info@jfoc.org

Daly City

Synagogues

Conservative

B'nai Israel
1575 Annie Street 94015   (415) 756-5430

Davis

Synagogues

Reform

Davis Jewish Fellowship
1821 Oak Avenue 95616

Downey

Synagogues
Temple Ner Tamid
10629 Lakewood Boulevard 90241   (310) 861-9276

Eureka

Synagogues
Beth El, Hodgson & T Streets, PO Box 442 95502
(707) 444-2846

Fairfax

Bakeries
BH International Bakery
7113 Beverly BlvdLa Brea   (213) 939-6497
Supervision: Kehillah of Los Angeles.
Pareve and dairy. Chalav Yisrael.

Fremont

Synagogues

Reform

Temple Beth Torah
42000 Paseo Padre Pkwy 94539   (415) 656-7141

Fresno

Community Organisations
Jewish Federations Office
1340 W. Herndon, Suite 103 93711

Synagogues

Conservative

Beth Jacob
406 W. Shields Avenue 93705

Orthodox

Chabad House
6735 N. ILA 93711

Reform

Temple Beth Israel
6622 N. Maroa Avenue 93704
This temple has its own etrog tree, planted from a sprig brought to the USA from Israel.

Gardena

Synagogues

Conservative

Southwest Temple Beth Torah
14725 S. Gramercy Place 90249

Hancock Park

Synagogues

Orthodox

Young Israel of Hancock Park
225 South LaBrea   (213) 931-4030

Hollywood

Kashrut Information
Kosher Information Bureau
15365 Magnolia Blvd, Sherman Oaks 91403
(818) 762-3197 & 262-5351
Fax: (818) 766-8537
Email: eeidlitz@kosherquest.org
Web site: www.kosherquest.org

La Jolla

Synagogues

Orthodox

Congregation Adat Yeshurun
8950 Villa La Jolla Dr., Ste. 1224 92037
(858) 535-1196
Fax: (858) 535-0037
Web site: www.adatyeshurun.org

Laguna Hills

Delicatessens

The Kosher Bite
23595 Moulton Parkway 92653   (949) 770-1818
Fax: (949) 770-5321
Email: kosherbite.com
Supervision: Rabinical Council of Orange County.
Monday, Tuesday, Thursday 9am to 5pm. Wednesday
9 am to 7 pm. Friday 9am -3pm. .

Lakewood

Synagogues

Conservative

Temple Beth Zion Sinai
6440 Del Amo Blvd. 90713   (562) 429-0715
Fax: (562) 429-0715

Long Beach

Community Organisations

**Jewish Federation of Greater Long Beach & W. Orange
County**
3801 E. Willow St. 90815   (310) 426-7601

Media

Newspapers

Jewish Community Chronicle
3801 E. Willow St. 90815 1791

Mikvaot

3847 Atlantic Avenue 90807

Synagogues

Conservative

Beth Shalom
3635 Elm Avenue 90807
Congregation Shalom of Leisure World
1661 Golden Rain Road
Northwood Clubhouse No. 3, Seal Beach 90740

Orthodox

Congregation Lubavitch
3981 Atlantic Avenue 90807
Young Israel of Long Beach
PO Box 7041 90807-0041   (310) 527-3163

Reform

Temple Beth David
6100 Hefley StreetWestminster
Temple Israel
338 E. 3rd Street 90812

Los Alamitos

Bakeries

Fairfax Kosher Market & Bakery
11196-98 Los Alamitos Blvd 90720   (714) 828-4492

Los Angeles

Los Angeles is America's, and the world's, second
largest Jewish metropolis, with a Jewish population
of around 600,000. Fairfax Avenue and Beverly
Blvd together form the crossroads of traditional
Jewish life while a growing Orthodox enclave
centres around Pico and Robertson Blvds.

Important note: Area telephone codes have
recently been split to 310 and 213 for central Los
Angeles. We have endeavored in all cases to
correct our information, but cannot guarantee the
veracity of those who did not send in updates.

Bakeries

Aviv Bakery
15030 Ventura Blvd   (818) 789-3176
Supervision: RCC.
Back East Bialy Bakery
8562 W. Pico Blvd   (310) 276-1531
Supervision: Kehillah of Los Angeles.
Beverly Hills Patisserie
9100 W. Pico Blvd   (310) 275-6873
Supervision: RCC.
BH International Bakery
7304 1/4 Santa Monica   (213) 874-7456
Supervision: Kehillah of Los Angeles.
Pareve and dairy. Chalav Yisrael.
BH International Bakery
9211 W. Pico Blvd   (310) 859-8927
Supervision: Kehillah of Los Angeles.
Pareve and dairy. Chalav Yisrael.
Eilat Bakery
457 1/2 N. Fairfax Avenue
   (213) 653-5553
Supervision: Kehillah of Los Angeles.
Chalav Yisrael.
Eilat Bakery #2
9233 W. Pico Blvd   (310) 205-8700
Supervision: Kehillah of Los Angeles.
Chalav Yisrael.
Famous Bakery
350 N. Fairfax Avenue   (213) 933-5000
Supervision: Kehillah of Los Angeles.
Chalav Yisrael.
Le Palais
8670 W. Pico Blvd   (310) 659-4809
Supervision: RCC.

United States of America / California

Noah's New York Bagels
1737 Santa Rita Road #400, Pleasanton 94566
(510) 485-1921
Email: noah@noahs.com
Supervision: California Rabbinical Council.
All stores in Southern California are under RCC
supervision; for the location of a store near you, call
the above number.

Renaissance Bakery
22872 Ventura Blvd   (818) 222-0110
Supervision: RCC.

Schwartz Bakery
8616 W. Pico Blvd   (310) 854-0592
Fax: (310) 653-6142
Supervision: RCC.

Schwartz Bakery
441 N. Fairfax Ave 90036   (213) 653-1683
Fax: (213) 653-6142
Supervision: RCC.

Yummy Pita Bakery
1437 S. Robertson Blvd.   (310) 557-2122
Supervision: Kehillah of Los Angeles.
Restaurant as well. Chalav Yisrael.

Booksellers
House of David
9020 W. Olympic Blvd, Beverly Hills 90211
(310) 276-9414
Probably the most complete selection of books of
Jewish interest can be found here.

Butchers
City Glatt
7667 Beverly Blvd   (213) 933-4040
Supervision: Kehillah of Los Angeles.
Sells Kehillah brand meats.

Doheny Kosher Meats
9213 W. Pico   (310) 276-7232
Supervision: RCC.
Non-glatt.

Elat Market, 8730 W. Pico   (310) 659-7070
Supervision: RCC.
Non-glatt meat, deli and fish only.

Kosher Club
4817 W. Pico Blvd   (213) 933-8283
Supervision: RCC.
Market as well.

Royal Palate Foods
960 E. Hyde Park Blvd   (310) 330-7700
Supervision: RCC.

Roz Kosher Meat
12422-24 Burbank Blvd   (818) 760-7694
Supervision: RCC.
Market as well.

Star Meats
12136 Santa Monica Blvd
(310) 447-1612
Supervision: RCC.

Valley Glatt
12450 Burbank Blvd   (818) 766-4530
Supervision: Kehillah of Los Angeles.
Sells Kehillah brand meats.

Community Organisations
Jewish Federation of Greater Los Angeles
6505 Wilshire Blvd 90048   (323) 761-8000
Fax: (323) 761-8123
Web site: www.jewishla.org
Los Angeles West Side Community Center
5870 W. Olympic Blvd. 90036   (323) 938-2531
Fax: (323) 954-9175
Email: westsidejcc@jcc-gla.org

Delicatessens
Micheline's
2627 S. LaCienega Blvd   (310) 204-5334
Supervision: RCC.
Catering and take out.
Pico Kosher Deli
8826 W. Pico Blvd 90035   (310) 273-9381
Fax: (310) 273-8476
Supervision: RCC.
Hours: Sunday to Thursday, 10 am to 9 pm; Friday, 9
am to 3 pm. Glatt

Embassy
Consul General of Israel
Suite 1700, 6380 Wilshire Blvd 90048
(213) 852-5523
Fax: (213) 852-5555
Email: israinfo@primenet.com
Web site: www.israelemb.org/la

Fishmongers
Fairfax Fish
515 N. Fairfax Avenue   (213) 658-8060
Supervision: Kehillah of Los Angeles.

Groceries
Kotlar's Pico Market
8622 W. Pico Blvd   (310) 652-5355
Supervision: RCC.
Market, fish and butcher.
La Brea Kosher Market
410 N. La Brea Avenue   (213) 931-1221
Supervision: Kehillah of Los Angeles.
Little Jerusalem
8917 W. Pico Blvd   (310) 858-8361
Supervision: RCC.
Market, fish and butcher.
Pico Glatt Kosher Mart
9427 W. Pico Blvd   (310) 785-0904
Supervision: Kehillah of Los Angeles.

PS Kosher Food Services
9760 W. Pico Blvd 90035   (310) 553-8804
Fax: (310) 553-8989
Email: psfood@juno.com
Kitchens located at Yeshiva University.
Western Kosher Market
444 N. Fairfax Avenue   (213) 655-8870
Supervision: Kehillah of Los Angeles.

Hospitals
Cedars Sinai Hospital
8700 Beverly Blvd   (310) 855-4797
Supervision: RCC.

Kashrut Information
Board of Rabbis of Southern California
6505 Wilshire Blvd, Suite 415 90036
(323) 761-8600
Fax: (323) 761-8603
Kosher Information Bureau
(818) 792-3197
Fax: (818) 980-6908
Rabbi Bukspan
6407 Orange Street 90048   (310) 653-5083
Rabbinical Council of California
1122 S. Robertson Blvd 90035   (310) 271-4160
Fax: (310) 271-7147

Media

Newspapers
Heritage Southwest Jewish Press
Weekly publication, coming out on Fridays.
Israel Today
Jewish Calendar Magazine

Jewish Journal
Weekly publication, coming out on Fridays.
Jewish News
Yisrael Shelanu

Mikvaot
Los Angeles Mikva
9548 W. Pico Blvd., 90035

Museums
Museum of Tolerance (Beit Hashoah)
9786 West Pico Blvd 90035   (310) 553-8403
Fax: (310) 553-4521
Email: webmaster@wiesenthal.com
Web site: www.wiesenthal.com
High-tech, hands-on museum that focuses on two
themes through interactive exhibits: the dynamics of
racism and prejudice, and the history of the Holocaust
– the ultimate example of man's inhumanity to man.

Organisations
Jewish Social Action Organisation
Simon Wiesenthal Center, 9786 W. Pico Blvd. 90035
(310) 553-9036
Fax: (310) 553-4521
Email: webmaster@wiesenthal.com
Web site: www.wiesenthal.com

Restaurants
Beverly/Fairfax & Downtown
7231 Beverly Blvd   (310) 936-1653

Dairy
Café Elite
7115 Beverly Blvd   (213) 936-2861
Supervision: Kehillah of Los Angeles.
Chalav Yisrael.
Fish Grill
7226 Beverly Blvd   (213) 937-7162
Supervision: Kehillah of Los Angeles.
Chalav Yisrael. Sit down or take out.
Fish Place Restaurant
9340 W. Pico Blv.   (310) 858-8737
Supervision: Kehila Kosher.
Milk N'Honey
8837 W. Pico Blvd   (310) 858-8850
Supervision: RCC.
Milky Way
9108 W. Pico Blvd   (310) 859-0004
Supervision: Kehillah of Los Angeles.
Chalav Yisrael.
Smoothie Queen
8851 W. Pico Blvd   (310) 273-3409
Supervision: Kehillah of Los Angeles.
Chalav Yisrael.

Fish
Tami's Fish House
553 B, Fairfax Avenue   (310) 655-7953
The Fishing Well
W. Pico Blvd   (310) 859-9429
Supervision: RCC.

Meat
Beverly Hills Cuisine
9025 Wilshire Blvd   (310) 247-1239
Supervision: RCC.
Chick'N Chow
9301 W. Pico Blvd 90035   (310) 274-5595
Fax: (310) 274-9693
Supervision: Kehillah of Los Angeles.
Glatt kosher eat in, take out, delivery. Hours: 11:30 am
to 10 pm. Price range: $.
Cohen Restaurant
316 E. Pico Blvd 90015   (213) 742-8888
Fax: (213) 742-0066
Supervision: RCC.

United States of America / California

Dizengoff Restaurant
8103 1/2 Beverly Blvd   (213) 651-4465
Supervision: Kehillah of Los Angeles.
Sit down or take out.

Elat Burger
9340 W. Pico Blvd   (310) 278-4692
Supervision: RCC.

Elite Cuisine
7119 Beverly Blvd   (213) 930-1303
Supervision: Kehillah of Los Angeles.
Sit down or take out.

Glatt Hut
9303 W. Pico Blvd   (310) 246-1900
Supervision: RCC.

Grill at the Beverly Carlton
9400 W. Olympic   (310) 282-0945

Grill Express
501 N. Fairfax Avenue   (213) 655-0649
Supervision: RCC.

Habayit Restaurant
11921 W. Pico Blvd   (310) 488-9877

Haifa Restaurant
8717 W. Pico Blvd   (310) 550-2704
Judy's, 129 N. La Brea Avenue   (213) 934-7667
Supervision: RCC.

Kabob & Chinese Food
11330 Santa Monica   (310) 914-3040
Supervision: Kehillah of Los Angeles.

Kabob & Chinese Food
9180 W. Pico Blvd   (310) 274-4007
Supervision: Kehillah of Los Angeles.

La Gondola Ristorante Italiano
6405 Wilshire Blvd 90048   (213) 852-1915
    Fax: (213) 852-0853
Web site: www.thegondola.com
Supervision: Kehillah of Los Angeles.
  Located next to Beverly Hills, there is a delivery service
to the hotels.

Magic Carpet Restaurant
8566 W. Pico Blvd 90035   (310) 652-8507
    Fax: (310) 652-3568
Supervision: Kehillah of Los Angeles.

Motty's Place
7308 Beverly Blvd   (213) 935-8087
Supervision: Kehillah of Los Angeles.

Museum Cafeteria
9760 W. Pico Blvd, 4th Floor   (310) 553-9036
Supervision: Kehillah of Los Angeles.
Pareve and meat.

Nagila Meating Place
9407 W. Pico Blvd   (310) 788-0119
Supervision: Kehillah of Los Angeles.
Nessim's, 8939 W. Pico Blvd   (310) 204-5334
Supervision: RCC.

Olé
7912 Beverly Blvd   (213) 933-7254
Supervision: Kehillah of Los Angeles.
Hours: 12 pm to 9 pm, five days a week; closed Friday
and Saturday. Price range: $.

Pat's
9233 W. Pico Blvd   (310) 205-8705
Supervision: Kehillah of Los Angeles.
Sit down restaurant and catering.

Rimini Restaurant
9400 W. Olympic Blvd   (310) 552-1056
Supervision: RCC.

Shalom Hunan Restaurant
5651 Wilshire Blvd   (213) 934-0505
Supervision: RCC.
Sharon's II, 306 E. 9th Street   (213) 622-1010
Supervision: RCC.

Shula & Esther
5519 N. Fairfax Ave   (310) 951-9651

Simon's La Glatt
446 N. Fairfax   (213) 658-7730
Supervision: RCC.

Westside Grille
9411 W. Pico Blvd   (310) 843-9829

Yiddishe Mama
9216 W. Pico Blvd   (310) 385-0101
Supervision: Kehillah of Los Angeles.

Pizzerias

Kosher Pizza Nosh
8644 W. Pico Blvd   (310) 276-8708

United States of America / California

Nagila Pizza
9016 W. Pico Blvd (213) 550-7735
Supervision: Kehillah of Los Angeles.
Chalav Yisrael.
Pizza Delight
435 N. Fairfax Avenue 90036 (323) 655-7800
Fax: (323) 655-1142
Supervision: Kehillah of Los Angeles.
Chalav Yisrael.
Pizza Mayven
140 N. La Brea Area (310) 857-0353
Pizza World
365 S. Fairfax Avenue 90036 (213) 653-2896
Supervision: Kehillah of Los Angeles.
An Italian/Mexican dairy restaurant. Chalav Yisrael.
Rami's Pizza
17736 1/2 Sherman Way
(818) 342-0611
Supervision: RCC.
Shalom Pizza, 8715 W. Pico Blvd (310) 271-2255
Supervision: RCC.

Synagogues

Conservative

Adat Shalom
3030 Westwood Blvd. 90034
Sinai Temple
10400 Wilshire Blvd. 90024
Temple Beth Am
1039 S. La Cienega Blvd. 90035 (310) 652-7353
Fax: (310) 652-2384
Email: betham@tbala.org
Web site: www.tbala.org

Orthodox

B'nai David Congregation
8906 W. Pico Blvd. 90035
Breed St. Shule
247 N. Breed St. 90033
This synagogue is of historial interest.
Chabad House
741 Gayley Avenue
West Los Angeles 90025
Etz Jacob Congregation
7659 Beverly Blvd. 90036 (323) 938-2619
Fax: (323) 930-2373
Email: lgbkg@earthlink.net
Ohel David
7967 Beverly Blvd.
Ohev Shalom
525 S. Fairfax Avenue 90036
Young Israel of Century City
9317 West Pico Blvd Century City 90035
(310) 273-6954

Young Israel of Hancock Park
225 South La Brea (323) 931-4030
Fax: (323) 935-3819
Young Israel of Los Angeles
660 N Spaulding Avenue 90036
(213) 655-0300/0322

Orthodox Sephardi

Kahal Joseph
10505 Santa Monica Blvd. 90025
Temple Tifereth Israel
10500 Wilshire Blvd., 90024

Reconstructionist

Kehillat Israel
16019 Sunset Blvd., Pacific Palisades 90272
(310) 459-2328
Fax: (310) 573-2098
Email: kihome@aol.com
Kehillat Israel has a modern sanctuary in the round. It is the largest reconstructionist synagogue in the United States.

Reform

Beth Chayim Chadishim
6000 W. Pico Blvd. 90035
Leo Baeck Temple
1300 N. Sepulveda Blvd. 90049
Stephen S. Wise Temple
15500 Stephen S. Wise DriveBel Air 90024
Temple Akiba
5249 S. Sepulveda Blvd., Culver City 90230
Temple Isaiah
10345 W. Pico Blvd. 90064
University Synagogue
11960 Sunset Blvd. 90049
Wilshire Blvd. Temple
3663 Wilshire Blvd., 90010 (213) 388-2401
Fax: (213) 388-2595

Northridge

Synagogues

Orthodox

Young Israel of Northridge
17511 Devonshire Street 91325 (818) 368-2221
Fax: (818) 360-5754
Email: rebbe@idt.net

Oakland

Delicatessens
Holy Land Restaurant
677 Rand Avenue 94610 (510) 272-0535
Glatt kosher.

JEWISH TRAVEL GUIDE 2001 257

United States of America / California

Oakland Kosher Foods
677 Rand Avenue 94610   (510) 272-0535
Glatt kosher.

Mikvaot

Beth Jacob Synagogue
3778 Park Blvd 94610
    (510) 482-1147
    Fax: (510) 482-2374
    Email: bjc-office@eb.jfed.org

Organisations

Berkeley/Richmond JCC
1414 Walnut St.,, Berkeley 94709   (510) 848-0237
    Fax: (510) 848-0170
    Email: brjcc-office@eb.jfed.org
    Web site: www.brjcc.org

Contra Costa JCC
2071 Tice Valley Blvd., Walnut Creek 94595

Jewish Federation of the Greater East Bay
401 Grand Avenue #500 94610

Synagogues

Conservative

B'nai Shalom
74 Eckley Lane, Walnut Creek 94596

Beth Abraham
327 MacArthur Blvd. 94610

Beth Sholom
642 Dolores, San Leandro 94577

Independent

B'nai Israel of Rossmoor
c/o Fred Rau, 2601 Ptarmigan #3, Walnut Creek 94595

Beth Chaim
PO Box 23632, Pleasant Hill 94523

Orthodox

Beth Jacob Synagogue
3778 Park Blvd 94610
    (510) 482-1147
    Fax: (510) 482-2374
    Email: bjc-office@eb.jfed.org

Reform

B'nai Tikvah
25 Hillcroft Way, Walnut Creek 94596

Beth Emek
PO Box 722, Livermore 94550

Beth Hillel
801 Park Central, Richmond 94803

Temple Isaiah
3800 Mt. Diablo Blvd., Lafayette 94549

Temple Sinai
2808 Summit 94609
    (510) 451-3263
    Fax: (510) 465-0603

Palm Springs

Community Organisations

Jewish Federation of Palm Springs Desert Area
611 S. Palm Canyon Drive 92264   (760) 325-7281

Synagogues

Conservative

Temple Isaiah
332 W. Alejo Road 92262
    (760) 325-2281
    Fax: (760) 325-3235
Jewish community centre at this location .

Orthodox

Chabad of Palm Springs
425 Avenue, Ortega, Palm springs   (619) 325-0774
Daily Services

Desert Synagogue
1068 N. Palm Canyon Drive 92262   (760) 327-4848
Daily minyan: January through Purim (call shul to confirm)

Palo Alto

Community Organisations

Albert L. Schultz Community Center
655 Arastradero Road 94306   (415) 493-9400

Groceries

Garden Fresh
1245 W. El Camino Road, Mount View 94040
    (415) 961-7795

Mollie Stone's Markets
164 South California Avenue   (415) 323-8361
Near Stanford University.

Synagogues

Orthodox

Congregation Chabad
3070 Louis Road 94308   (415) 429-8444

Palo Alto Orthodox Minyan
260 Sheridan Avenue 94306   (415) 948-7498

Pasadena

Synagogues

Conservative

Pasadena Jewish Temple and Center
1434 North Altadena Drive 91107   (626) 798-1161

Poway

Synagogues

Orthodox

Chabad of Poway
16934 Chabad Way, Poway 92064   (619) 451-0455

Sacramento

Community Organisations

Jewish Federation of Sacramento
2351 Wyda Way 95825   (916) 486-0906
Fax: (916) 486-0816
Email: jfed@juno.com
Web site: www.jewishsac.org

Groceries

Bob Butcher Block & Deli
6426 Fair Oaks Blvd, Carmichael 95608

Synagogues

Conservative

Mosaic Law
2300 Sierra Blvd. 95825   (916) 488-1122
Fax: (916) 488-1165
Web site: www.mosaiclaw.org

Orthodox

Kenesset Israel Torah Center
1165 Morse Avenue 95864   (916) 481-1159
Email: ravshlomo@softcom.net

Reform

B'nai Israel
3600 Riverside Blvd. 95818   (916) 446-4861
Beth Shalom
4746 El Camino Avenue 95608   (916) 485-4478

San Bernardino

Synagogues

Emanu El
3512 N. E Street 92405   (909) 886-4818
Fax: (909) 883-5892
Email: cee@emanuelsb.org
This congregation is the oldest in southern California. The 'Home of Eternity' cemetery, 8th St. & Sierra Way, presented by the Mormons, is one of the oldest Jewish cemeteries in western US.

San Carlos

Accommodation Information

Jewish Travel Network
PO Box 283 94070   (650) 368-0880
Fax: (650) 599-9066
Email: info@jewishtravelnetwork.com
Web site: www.jewishtravelnetwork.com/
International hospitality exchange. Bed and breakfast and home exchanges.

San Diego Area

The largest public park in San Diego, includes the house of Pacific Relations, which comprises 30 cottages for various ethnic groups. These include the cottage of Israel, which mounts exhibitions throughout the year, portraying the history and traditions of the Jewish people, biblical and modern Israel. Open Sun. 1:30 pm to 4:30 pm, except on Holy-days and major festivals.

Bakeries

Sheila's Café & Bakery
4577 Clairemont Drive 92117   (858) 270-0251
Fax: (858) 274-5797
Email: sheilascafe@aol.com

Community Organisations

United Jewish Federation of San Diego County
4797 Mercury Street 92111-2101   (858) 571-3444
Fax: (858) 571-0701
Email: outreach@ujfsd.org
Web site: www.jewishinsandiego.org
Hours of opening: 8.30am

Delicatessens

Eva's Fresh & Natural
6717 El Cajon Blvd 92115   (619) 462-5018
Fax: (619) 453-5659
Supervision: Vaad of San Diego.
Dairy and vegetarian food. Meat dinners are available to go only upon request in advance.

Media

Newspapers

Heritage
3443 Camino Del Rio S., Suite 315 92108
(619) 282-7177

San Diego Jewish Times
4731 Palm Avenue, La Mesa 91941   (619) 463-5515

Mikvaot

(858) 546-1563
Call to arrange an appointment.

Restaurants

Aarons Glatt Kosher Market
4488 Convoy Street
92111   (858) 636-7979
Fax: (858) 636-7980
www.kosherfooddelivery.com

Dairy

Lang's, 6165 El Cajon Blvd 92115
(619) 287-7306; 800-60-LANGS
Fax: (619) 582-1545
Email: langsbakery@cari.net
Supervision: Vaad HaRabbanim of San Diego.
Kosher pareve bakery, dairy deli and foods.

United States of America / California

Shmoozers Vegetarian & Pizzeria
6366 El Cajon Blvd 92115   (619) 583-1636
Supervision: Vaad HaRabbanim of San Diego.
Hours: Sunday to Thursday, 11:30am to 9pm; Friday,
to 2pm; Saturday, Motzei Shabbat to 11pm.

Meat

Western Glatt Kosher & N.Y. Deli
7739 Fay Avenue, La Jolla 92037   (619) 454-6328

Synagogues

Conservative

Beth El, 8660 Gilman Drive, La Jolla 92037
                                          (619) 452-1734
Congregation Beth Am
5050 Black Mtn. Road 92130   (858) 481-8454
                                 Fax: (858) 481-6068
                          Email: betham@betham.com
Ner Tamid
16981 Via Tazon, Suite G 92127   (619) 592-9141
Temple Beth Sholom
208 Madrona Street, Chula Vista 91910
                                          (619) 420-6040
Temple Judea
1527 Roma Drive, Vista 92083   (619) 724-8318
Tifereth Israel
6660 Cowles Mountain Blvd 92119   (619) 697-6001

Orthodox

Beth Eliyahu Torah Center
5012 Central Avenue, Bonita 91902   (619) 472-2144
Beth Jacob Congregation
4855 College Avenue 92115   (619) 287-9890
                                 Fax: (619) 287-0578
           Email: bethjacobsandiego@hotmail.com
Chabad at La Costa
1980 La Costa Avenue, Carlsbad 92009
                                          (760) 943-8891
                                 Fax: (760) 943-8892
                  Email: chabad@inetworld.net
Chabad House
6115 Montezuma Road 92115   (619) 265-7700
Supervision: Vaad of San Diego.
Chabad of La Jolla
3232 Governor Drive, Suite N 92122
                                          (619) 455-1670
Congregation of Adat Yeshurun
8950 Villa La Jolla Drive, Suite 1224, La Jolla 92037
                                          (619) 535-1196
                                 Fax: (619) 535-0037

Young Israel of San Diego
7920 Navajo Road, Suite 102 92119
                                          (619) 589-1447

Reconstructionist

Dor Hadash
4858 Ronson Court, Suite A 92111   (619) 268-3674

Reform

Beth Israel
2512 3rd Avenue 92103   (619) 239-0149
Etz Chaim
PO Box 1138, Ramona 92065   (760) 789-7393
Temple Adat Shalom
15905 Pomerado Road, Poway 92064
                                          (619) 451-1200
Temple Emanu-El
6299 Capri Drive 92120   (619) 286-2555
Temple Solel
552 S. El Camino Real, Encinitas 92024
                                          (619) 436-0654
                                 Fax: (619) 436-2748
                          Email: solel@sciti.com

San Fernando Valley

Bakeries
Continental Kosher Bakery
12419 Burbank Blvd   (818) 762-5005
Sam's Kosher Bakery
12450 Burbank Blvd, Suite H   (818) 769-8352
Supervision: RCC.

Catering
Hadar Restaurant and Catering
12514 Burbank Blvd 91607   (818) 762-1155
Supervision: RCC.

Community Organisations
North Valley Center
16601 Rinaldi Street, Granada Hills 91344
Valley Cities Center
13164 Burbank Blvd., Van Nuys 91401
West Valley Center
22622 Vanowen Street
West Hills 91307

Groceries

Ventura Market
18357 Ventura Blvd   (213) 873-1240
Supervision: RCC.
Butcher, market and deli.

Ice Cream Parlors

Carvel's Ice Cream
25948 McBean Parkway, Valencia   (805) 259-1450
Supervision: Kof-K.

Kashrut Information

The Kashrus Information Bureau
12753 Chandler Blvd, N. Hollywood 91607
     (818) 762-3197 & 262-5351
Fax: (818) 766-8537
Email: eeidlitz@kosherquest.org
Web site: www.kosherquest.org

Mikvaot

Teichman Mikvah Society
12800 Chandler Blvd, N. Hollywood 91607
     (818) 506-0996

Restaurants

Apropo Falafel
6800 Reseda Blvd   (818) 881-6608

Dairy

Orly Dairy Restaurant & Pizza
12454 Magnolia Blvd   (818) 508-5570

Meat

Drexler's Kosher Restaurant
12519 Burbank Blvd, N. Hollywood   (818) 984-1160
Falafel Express
5577 Reseda Bl   (818) 345-5660
Falafel Village
16060 Ventura Blvd   (818) 783-1012
Supervision: RCC.
Flora Falafel
12450 Burbank Blvd, N. Hollywood   (818) 766-6567
Supervision: RCC.
Golan
13075 Victory Blvd   (818) 763-5375
Supervision: RCC.
Sharon's
18608 1/2 Ventura Blvd, Tarzana
     (818) 344-7472
Supervision: RCC.
Sportsman Lodge
Sherman Oaks   (818) 984-0202
Tiberias
18046 Ventura BlvdEncino   (818) 343-3705
Supervision: RCC.

Pizzerias

La Pizza
12515 Burbank Blvd   (818) 760-8198
Pacific Kosher Pizza
12460 Oxnard   (818) 760-0087

Synagogues

Conservative

Beth Meier Congregation
11725 Moorpark, Studio City
Ner Maarev Temple
5180 Yarmouth Avenue, Encino 91316
Shomrei Torah
Valley CircleWest Hills   (818) 346-0811
Temple Aliyah
24400 Aliyah Way Woodland Hills 91367
Temple B'nai Hayim
4302 Van Nuys Blvd, Sherman Oaks
Temple Emanu-El
1302 N. Glenoaks Avenue, Burbank 91504
Temple Ramat Zion
17655 Devonshire Avenue, Northridge
Valley Beth Shalom
15739 Ventura Blvd, Encino 91316

Orthodox

Adat Ari El Synagogue
5540 Laurel Canyon Blvd, N. Hollywood 91607
There are eleven beautiful stained-glass windows,
designed by Mischa Kallis, depicting significant dates in
the religious calendar.
Chabad House
4915 Hayvenhurst, Encino 91346
Shaarey Zedek
12800 Chandler Blvd, N. Hollywood 91607
     (818) 763-0560
Fax: (818) 763-8215

Reform

Beth Emet
320 E. Magnolia Blvd, Burbank 91502
Shir Chadash
17000 Ventura Blvd, Encino
Temple Ahavat Shalom
11261 Chimineas Avenue, Northridge
Temple Judea
5429 Lindley Avenue, Tarzana

San Francisco

Embassy

Consul General of Israel
Suite 2100, 456 Montgomery Street 94104

Groceries

Gourmet Kosher Meals
Cong. Adath Israel, 1851 Noriega St., 94122
Supervision: Orthodox Rabbinical Council.
Grill Middle Eastern Cuisine
430 Geary Street   (415) 749-0201
Jacob's Kosher Meats
2435 Noriega Street 94122   (415) 564-7482

United States of America / California

Jerusalem
420 Geary (at Mason) 94108   (415) 776-2683
Supervision: Cong. Thilim.
Kosher Meats Israel & Cohen Kosher Meats
5621 Geary Blvd 94121   (415) 752-3064
Kosher Nutrition Kitchen
Montefiore Senior Center, 3200 California Av.,
Supervision: Orthodox Rabbinical Council.
Tel Aviv Strictly Kosher Meats
2495 Irving Street 84122   (415) 661-7588
Supervision: Orthodox Rabbinical Council.

Libraries
Holocaust Library & Research Center
601 14th Avenue 94118   (415) 751-6040

Mikvaot
Mikva, 3355 Sacramento Street 94118
(415) 921-4070

Museums
The Jewish Museum San Francisco
121 Steuart St 94105   (415) 543-8880
Fax: (415) 788-9050
Email: info@jewishmuseumsf.org
Web site: www.jewishmuseumsf.org
Administrative offices 166 Geary St. Suite 1500, San
Fransisco, CA 94108. Ph. 415-788-9990. Contact:
Victoria Shelton

Organisations
**Jewish Com. Fed. of San Francisco, the Peninsula,
Marin & Sonoma Counties**
121 Steuart St. 94105   (415) 777-0411
Fax: (415) 495-6635
Email: info@sfjcf.org
Publishes 'Resource guide to the Bay Area' and
'Resource guide to Jewish life in Northern California'.

Restaurants

Dairy
Red Ox, 1271 South Carolina Blvd, Walnut Creek
(925) 256-6500
Supervision: Glatt Kosher.

Meat
Sabra
419 Grant AvenueChinatown   (415) 982-3656
Fax: (415) 982-3650
Supervision: Vaad Hakashrus of Northern CA.
Bishul Yisrael, Pat Yisrael and Mashgiach Temidi. Israeli
mediterranean cuisine. Catering available.
This Is It
430 Geary Street 94210   (415) 749-0201
Middle Eastern cuisine.

Vegetarian
Lotus Garden
532 Grant Avenue 94108   (415) 397-0130

Synagogues

Conservative
B'nai Emunah
3595 Taraval Street 94116   (415) 664-7373
Fax: (415) 664-4209
Email: emuna@jps.net
Web site: www.uscj.org/ncalif/sanfranbe
Beth Israel-Judea
625 Brotherhood Way 94132   (415) 586-8833
Beth Sholom
14th Avenue & Clement Street 94118
(415) 221-8736
Fax: (415) 221-3944
Email: cbsholom@aol.com
Ner Tamid
1250 Quintara Street 94116   (415) 661-3383

Orthodox
Adath Israel
1851 Noriega Street 94122   (415) 564-5565
Anshey Sfard
1500 Clement Street 94118   (415) 752-4979
Chabad House
11 Tillman Place 94108   (415) 956-8644
Chevra Thilim
751 25th Avenue 94121   (415) 752-2866
Keneseth Israel
873 Sutter Street, Suite 203 94102   (415) 771-3420
A downtown synagogue offering meals over Shabbat.
Torat Emeth
768 27th Avenue 94121   (415) 386-1830
Young Israel of San Francisco
1806 A Noriega Street 94122   (415) 387-1774

Reform
Emanu-El
Arguello Blvd. & Lake Street 94118
(415) 751-2535
Fax: (415) 751-2511
Email: mail@emanuelsf.org
Sha'ar Zahav
290 Dolores Street 94103   (415) 861-6932
Fax: (415) 841-6081
Email: office@shaarzahav.org
Sherith Israel
2266 California Street 94118   (415) 346-1720

Sephardi
Magain David
351 4th Avenue 94118   (415) 752-9095

Tourist Information

Jewish Com. Information & Referral
121 Steuart St 94105
(415) 777-4545
Fax: (415) 495-6635
Email: jewishnfo@aol.com
Web site: www.sfjcf.org

San Jose

Booksellers

Alef Bet Judaica
14103-0 Winchester Blvd, Los Gatos 95032
(408) 370-1818
Fax: (408) 725-8269
Email: nurit@best.com

Community Organisations

Jewish Federation of Greater San Jose
14855 Oka Road, Los Gatos 95030   (408) 358-3033
Fax: (408) 356-0733

Delicatessens

Willow Glen Kosher Deli
1185 Lincoln Avenue 95125
(408) 297-6604
Fax: (408) 297-0122
Under Orthodox Rabbinical supervision. Glatt kosher.
Catering & meals for travelers available.

Restaurants

White Lotus, 80 North Market Street   (408) 977-0540

Synagogues

Conservative

Congregation Beth David
19700 Prospect Road, Saratoga 95070
(408) 257-3333
Congregation Emeth
PO Box 1430, Gilroy 95021   (408) 847-4111

Orthodox

Ahavas Torah
1537-A Meridian Avenue 95125   (408) 266-2342
Fax: (408) 264-3139
Web site: www.ahava.org
Almaden Valley Torah Center
1281 Juli Lynn Drive 95120   (408) 997-9117
Congregation Am Echad
1504 Meridian Avenue 95125   (408) 267-2591

Reform

Congregation Shir Hadash
16555 Shannon Road, Los Gatos 95032
(408) 358-1751
Fax: (408) 358-1753
Web site: www.shirhadash.org

Temple Beth Sholom
2270 Unit D, Canoas Garden Avenue 95153
(408) 978-5566
Temple Emanu-El
1010 University Avenue 95126   (408) 292-0939

Traditional

Congregation Sinai
1532 Willowbrae Avenue 95125-4450
(408) 264-8542
Fax: (408) 264-4316
Email: eitanj@cs.com

San Rafael (Marin County)

Synagogues

Reform

Rodef Sholom
170 N. San Pedro Rd 94903

Santa Barbara

Synagogues

Orthodox

Chabad Synagogue
6047 Stow Canyon, Fairview
Young Israel of Santa Barbara
1826 C Cliff Drive 93109   (805) 966-4565

Reform

Congregation B'nai B'rith
1000 San Antonio Creek Road 93111
(805) 964-7869
Fax: (805) 683-6473
Email: cbbrav@aol.com

Santa Monica

Synagogues

Orthodox

Chabad House
1428 17th Street 90404
Young Israel of Santa Monica
21 Hampton Avenue   (213) 399-8514
Mailing address is: PO Box 5725, 90405. Shul is
actually located at 21 Hampton Avenue

Reform

Beth Sholom
1827 California Avenue 90403

United States of America / California

Santa Rosa

Synagogues

Conservative

Beth Ami
4676 Mayette Avenue 95405   (707) 545-4334
Dairy kitchen on premises.

Reform

Congregation Shomrei Torah
1717 Yulupa Avenue, . 95405   (707) 578-5519
Fax: (707) 578-3967
Email: shomrei@pacbell.net

Saratoga

Synagogues

Conservative

Congregation Beth David
19700 Prospect Road at Scully 95070-3352
(408) 257-3333

Stockton

Stockton is one of the oldest communities west of the Mississippi River, founded in the days of the California Gold Rush. Temple Israel was founded as Congregation Ryhim Ahoovim in 1850 and erected its first building in 1855.

Synagogues

Reform

Temple Israel
5105 N. El Dorado St 95207

Thousand Oaks

Synagogues

Conservative

Temple Etz Chaim
1080 E. Janss Rd 91360   (805) 497-6891
Fax: (805) 497-0086
Kosher catering. Synagogue contains unique artistic Aron Kodesh and Holocaust memorial.

Tiburon

Synagogues
Congregation Kol Shafar
215 Blackfield Dr 94920   (415) 388-1818

Tustin

Synagogues
Congregation B'nai Israel
655 S. "B" St 92680   (714) 259-0655

Vallejo

Synagogues

Unaffiliated

Congregation B'nai Israel
1256 Nebraska St. 94590   (707) 642-6526

Venice

Organisations

Orthodox

National Council of Young Israel West Coast Regional Office
1050 Indiana Avenue 90291   (310) 396-3935
Fax: (310) 581-0904
Email: ncyi.west@youngisrael.org

Synagogue

Kosher

Pacific Jewish Center
505 Ocean Front Walk 90291   (310) 392-8749
Fax: (310) 392-8740
Email: office@pjcenter.com
Web site: www.pjcenter.com
Mailing address: 2633 Lincoln Blvd., 516 Santa Monica, CA 90405

Synagogues

Orthodox

Jewish Pacific Center
505 Ocean Front Walk & 720 Rosa Avenue 90291
(310) 392-8749
Mikva and an elementary day school with summer camp facilities for visitors. It also offers a full range of kosher food, bakery products and meat, as well as accommodation.
Young Israel Torah Learning Center of Venice
949 Sunset Avenue 90021   (310) 450-7541

Ventura

Community Organisations
Jewish Community Centre
259 Callens Road   (805) 658-7441

Synagogues

Reform

Temple Beth Torah
7620 Foothill Road 93004   (805) 647-4181

Walnut Creek

Synagogues

Conservative

Congregation B'nai Shalom
74 Eckley Lane 94595   (925) 934-9446
                          Fax: (925) 934-9450
Contra Costa Jewish Community Center
2071 Tice Valley Blvd 94595

Reform

Congregation B'nai Tikvah
25 Hillcroft Way 94595

Whittier

Synagogues

Conservative

Beth Shalom Synagogues Center
14564 E. Hawes Street 90604   (310) 914-8744

Colorado

Boulder

Organisations
Lubavitch of Boulder County
4900 Sioux Drive 80303   (303) 494-1638
                          Fax: (303) 938-8350
          Web site: www.lubavitchofboulder.org
Offering home hospitality

Synagogues
Hillel Foundation
2795 Colorado Avenue, University of Colorado
                          (303) 442-6571

Conservative

Congregation Bonai Shalom
1527 Cherryvale Rd, 80303   (303) 442-6605
                          Fax: (303) 442-7545
          Email: bonaishalom@aol.com
          Web site: www.bonaishalom.org
Offering home hospitality

Reform

Congregation Har Hashem
3950 Baseline Road 80303   (303) 499-7077
Jewish Renewal Community of Boulder
5001 Pennsylvania 80303   (303) 271-3541
Meets third Friday of each month.

Colorado Springs

Synagogues

Conservative & Reform

Temple Shalom
1523 E. Monument Street 80909   (719) 634-5311
Reform services are held on Fri. evening & Conservative
services on Sat. morning

Orthodox

Chabad House
3465 Nonchalant Circle 80909   (719) 596-7330

Denver

Bakeries
New York Bagel Boys
6449 E Hampden Avenue 80231   (303) 759-2212
Supervision: Vaad Hakashrus of Denver.
The Bagel Store
942 South Monaco 80224   (303) 388-2648
Supervision: Vaad Hakashrus of Denver.
A bakery serving bagels, challah, rye bread, wheat
bread, pumpernickel bread, donuts, rugelach,
mandelbrot, honey cakes, poppyseed rolls, etc.

Groceries
Cub Foods
1985 Sheridan Blvd, Edgewater

                          (303) 232-8972
With Kosher section.
King Soopers
6470 East Hampden Avenue

                          (303) 758-1210
With kosher section.
King Soopers
890 S.Monaco Parway   (303) 333-1535
With Kosher section.
Safeway
6460 E. Yale (& Monaco)   (303) 691-8870
With Kosher section.
Safeway
7150 Leetsdale drive (& Quebec)

                          (303) 377-6939
With Kosher section.

United States of America / Colorado

Kashrut Information

Rabbi Mordecai Twerski
295 South Locust Avenue 80224   (303) 377-1200
    Fax: (303) 355-6010
    Email: ravtwerski@aol.com

Scoll K Vaad Hakashrus of Denver
1350 Vrain 80204   (303) 595-9349
    Fax: (303) 629-5159

Media

Newspapers

Intermountain Jewish News
1275 Sherman Avenue, Suite 214 80203
    (303) 861-2234
Weekly American Jewish newspaper of the
intermountain region

Mikvaot

1404 Quitan 80204   (303) 893-5315
Mikvah of Denver
1404 Quitan 80204   (303) 893-5315
    Fax: (303) 825-5810

Organisations

Allied Jewish Federation of Colorado
300 S. Dahlia Street 80222   (303) 321-3399
    Fax: (303) 322-8328

Com. Center
4800 E. Alameda Avenue 80222
Com. Ctr Kosher Childrens Camp
4800 E. Alameda Avenue 80222
Jewish Family & Children's Service
1335 S. Colorado Blvd, Building C-800 80222
    (303) 759-4890

Rocky Mountain Rabbinic Council
6445 East Ohio Avenue 80224   (303) 388-4441
Synagogue Council of Greater Denver
PO Box 102732 80250   (303) 759-8484

Restaurants

East Side Kosher Deli
5475 Leetsdale Drive 80246   (303) 322-9862
    Fax: (303) 331-3290
    Email: eskd1@aol.com
Supervision: Vaad Hakashrus of Denver.
Glatt Kosher. Deli, restaurant, grocer, butcher shop and
caterer. Closed on Saturday and Friday afternoon.

Dairy

Mediterranean Health Cafe
2817 East 3rd Avenue 80206   (303) 399-2940
Supervision: Vaad Hakashrus of Denver.
Kosher/dairy/vegetarian food. Chalav Yisrael and Pat
Yisrael available. Hours: Sunday, 12 pm to 8 pm;
Monday to Thursday, 11 am to 8 pm; Friday, to 2 pm.

Meat

East Side Kosher Deli
5475 Leetsdale Drive   (303) 322-9862
    Fax: (303) 321-3290
Supervision: Supervised.

Synagogues

Beth Shalom
2280 East Noble Place, Littleton 80121
    (303) 794-6643
A congregation serving the southern metropolitan area.
Provides religious services religious school (weekend
and after-noon) social and educational activities, and
rabbinic services.

Conservative

Hebrew Educational Alliance (HEA)
3600 South Ivanhoe St. 80237   (303) 758-9400
    Fax: (303) 758-9500
    Email: headenver@aol.com
Rodef Shalom
450 S. Kearney 80224   (303) 399-0035

Orthodox

**Ahavas Yisroel - Aish HaTorah Center for Jewish
Discovery**
9550 E Belleview Ave, Greenwood Village 80111
    (303) 220-7200
    Fax: (303) 290-9191
    Email: ymeyer@aish.com

Bais Medrash Kehillas Yaakov
295 S. Locust Street 80222   (303) 377-1200
    Fax: (303) 355-6010
    Email: tai@jewishpeople.com
Congregation Zera Abraham
1560 Winona Court 80204   (303) 825-7517
100 + year old Orthodox Congregation, 2 morning
Minyanim, Mincha and Maariv every day. Call for
Davening times. Mikvah, Eruv, nationally recognized
Vaad HaKashrus. "We are a very warm, welcoming
community that looks forward to every opportunity to
welcome guests and assist visitors."

Reconstructionist

B'Nai Havurah
6445 East Ohio Avenue 80224   (303) 388-4441

Reform

Congregation Emanuel
51 Grape Street 80220   (303) 388-4013
     Fax: (303) 388-6328
     Email: shalomcongregationemanual.com

Temple Micah
2600 Leyden Street 80207   (303) 388-4239
     Fax: (303) 773-0321
A small but long established Reform Jewish
congregation, style is warm and traditional though
progressive. Encourages members participation
welcomes visitors.

Temple Sinai
3509 South Glencoe Street 80237   (303) 759-1827
     Fax: (303) 759-2519
     Web site: www.americanct.com/sinai

Traditional

B.M.H.-BJ Congregation
560 S. Monaco Pkwy., CO 80224   (303) 388-4203
     Fax: (303) 388-4210

Evergreen

Synagogues

Liberal

Congregation Beth Evergreen
2931 Evergreen Parkway 80439   (303) 670-4294
     Fax: (303) 836-6470
     Email: cyberrebbe@aol.com

Littleton

Synagogues

Reform

Beth Shalom
2280 E. Noble Place 80121   (303) 794-6643

Pueblo

Synagogues

Conservative

United Hebrew Congregation
106 W. 15th Street 81003

Reform

Temple Emanuel
1325 Grand Avenue 81003

Connecticut

Bridgeport

Delicatessens
Chai Café at the JCCS
4200 Park Avenue   (203) 374-5556
Supervision: Vaad Hakashrus of Fairfield County.
Glatt kosher deli serves a wide variety of eat in and
take out products. Some grocery items are sold. Dairy
items are packaged. Weekly and Shabbat take out
specials. Large selection of fresh meat and poultry.

Media

Radio

WVOF Radio
c/o Fairfield University, Fairfield 6430
     (203) 254-4111
Jewish public affairs show on Sundays at 7pm on
88.5FM

Mikvaot
Mikveh Israel
1326 Stratfield Road, Fairfield 6432

Organisations
**Jewish Center for Community Services of Eastern
Fairfield County**
4200 Park Avenue 6604   (203) 372-6567
     Fax: (203) 374-0770
     Email: info@jccs.org
Serving Bridgeport, Easton, Fairfield, Monroe, Shelton,
Stratford, Trumbull and Westport

Religious Organisations
Va'ad of Fairfield County
1571 Stratfield Road, Fairfield 6432   (203) 372-6529
     Fax: (203) 373-0467
     Email: rbaun64732@aol.com

Restaurants
Cafe Shalom, c/o Abel, Community Center
     (203) 372-6567

Synagogues

Conservative

B'nai Torah
5700 Main St.,, Trumbull 6611
Congregation Beth El
1200 Fairfield Woods Rd, Fairfield 6430
Rodeph Sholom
2385 Park Avenue 6604

Orthodox

Agudas Achim
85 Arlington Street 6606

United States of America / Connecticut

Bikur Cholim
Park & Capitol Avenues 6604
Shaare Torah Adath Israel
3050 Main Street 6606

Reconstructionist

Congregation Shirei Shalom
PO Box 372, Monroe 6468

Reform

Temple B'nai Israel
2710 Park Avenue 6604

Danbury

Organisations
Jewish Federation
105 Newtown Road 6810   (203) 792-6353
                               Fax: (203) 748-5099
Issuing monthly publication.

Synagogues

Conservative

Congregation B'nai Israel
193 Clapboard Ridge Road 6811   (203) 792-6161
                                   Fax: (203) 792-8315
                           Email: cbi193clab@juno.com

Reform

United Jewish Center
141 Deer Hill Avenue 6810   (203) 748-3355

Fairfield

Bakeries
Carvel Ice Cream Bakery
1838 Black Rock Turnpike   (203) 384-2253
Supervision: Vaad Hakashrus of Fairfield County.
Ice cream, cakes & novelties. All products in the store
are under supervision, except for those Snapple drinks
not marked with an OK.
The Original Bagel King of Fairfield
22670 Black Rock Turnpike   (203) 368-3365
Supervision: Vaad Hakashrus of Fairfield County.
Wide variety of bagels and challah. The uncut bagels
and uncut challah are supervised.

Synagogues

Orthodox

Congregation Ahavath Achim
1571 Stratfield Road, Fairfield 6432   (203) 372-6529
                                   Fax: (203) 373-0647
                           Email: rbaum64732@aol.com
                           Web site: 222.ahavathachim.org
Home hospitality, mikveh, youth programs, adult
education

Hartford

Kashrut Information
Kashrut Commission
162 Brewster Road 6117   (860) 563-4017

Media

Guides

All Things Jewish
333 Bloomfield Avenue 6117   (860) 232-4483

Mikvaot
Mikva
61 Main Street 6119

Organisations
Jewish Federation of Hartford
333 Bloomfield Avenue 6117   (860) 232-4483
Publishes 'All Things Jewish'.

Synagogues

Conservative

Beth El
2626 Albany Avenue, West Hartford 6117
Beth Tefilah
465 Oak St, East Hartford 6118
Congregation B'nai Sholom
26 Church St, Newington 6111   (860) 667-0826
                                   Fax: (860) 667-0827
                         Email: cbsnewington@aol.com
Emanuel Synagogue
160 Mohegan Dr, West Hartford 6117
                                   (860) 236-1275
                                   Fax: (860) 231-8890
                         Email: emansyn@ziplink.net

Orthodox

1137 Troutbrook Drive 6119   (860) 523-7804
Agudas Achim
1244 N. Main St, West Hartford 6117
Beth David Synagogue
20 Dover Road, West Hartford 6119   (860) 236-1241
                                   Fax: (860) 232-8272
                         Email: rabbi@bethdavidwh.org
Chabad House of Greater Hartford
798 Farmington Avenue 6119
Contact for kosher meal & Shabbat arrangements.
Teferes Israel
27 Brown St, Bloomfield 6002
United Synagogue of Greater Hartford
840 N. Main St, West Hartford 6117
Young Israel of West Hartford
2240 Albany Avenue, West Hartford 6117
                                   (860) 233-3084
                                   Fax: (860) 232-6417
                         Email: yiwhrac@ao.com

Reform

Beth Israel
701 Farmington Avenue, West Hartford 6119
Temple Sinai
41 W. Hartford Road, Newington 6011

Manchester

Synagogues

Conservative

Temple Beth Sholom
400 Middle Turnpike E 6040   (860) 643-9563
                                    Fax: (860) 643-9565
                          Email: riplavin@prodigy.net
          Web site: www.uscj.org/ctvalley/manchestertbs
Services 7 days a week. Call for times.

Meriden

Synagogues
B'nai Abraham
127 E. Main St 6450

Middletown

Synagogues
Adath Israel
48 Church St 6457

New Britain

Synagogues
B'nai Israel
265 W. Main St 6051

Orthodox

Tephereth Israel
76 Winter Street 6051

New Haven

Contact Information
Young Israel House at Yale University

          Web site: www.yale.edu/hillel/orgs/yihy.html

Delicatessens
The Westville
1460 Whalley Avenue 6515   (203) 397-0839
                                  Fax: (203) 387-4129
                          Email: pweinb@aol.com

Zackey's
1304 Whalley Avenue 6515

                                  (203) 387-2454

Groceries
Westville Kosher Meat Market
95 Amity Road 6525   (203) 389-1723

Mikvaot
86 Hubinger Street 6511   (203) 387-2184

Organisations
Jewish Federation of Greater New Haven
360 Amity Road, Woodbridge Ct., 6525
                                 (203) 387-2424

Restaurants

Vegetarian

Claire's Gourmet Vegetarian Restaurant & Caterer
1000 Chapel Street 6510   (203) 562-3888
Supervision: Young Israel of New Haven.

Synagogues

Conservative
Beth-El Keser Israel
85 Harrison Street 6515   (203) 389-2108

Orthodox

Beth Hamedrosh Westville
74 West Prospect Street 6515   (203) 389-9513
Congregation Bikur Cholim Sheveth Achim
112 Marvel Road 6515   (203) 387-4699
Young Israel of New Haven
292 Norton Street 6511   (203) 776-4212
                  Web site: www.youngisrael.org/yinh

New London

Organisations
Jewish Federation of Eastern Connecticut
28 Channing Street 6320   (203) 442-8062

Norwalk

Bakeries
The Original Bagel King of Norwalk
250 Westport Avenue   (203) 846-2633
Supervision: Vaad Hakashrus of Fairfield County.
Wide variety of bagels and challah. The uncut bagels
and uncut challah are supervised.

Organisations
Jewish Federation of Greater Norwalk
Shorehaven Road 6855   (203) 853-3440

Norwich

Synagogues

Orthodox

Brothers of Joseph
Broad & Washington Avs., 6360   (203) 887-3777
Mikva attached.

United States of America / Connecticut

Stamford

Bakeries
Carvel Ice Cream Bakery
810 East Main Street   (203) 324-0944
Supervision: Vaad Hakashrus of Fairfield County.
All products in the store are under supervision, except
for those Snapple drinks not marked with an OK.
Cerbone Bakery
605 Newfield Avenue   (203) 348-9029
Supervision: Vaad Hakashrus of Fairfield County.

Delicatessens
Delicate-Essen at the JCC
1035 Newfield Avenue 6902   (203) 322-0944
    Fax: (203) 322-5160
Supervision: Vaad Hakashrus of Fairfield County.
Glatt kosher sit down café serving hot and cold
sandwiches, soups and grilled items.
Nosherye
JCC Building, 1035 Newfield Av., 6905
    (203) 321-1373

Kosher Food
Delicate-Essen
111 High Ridge Road 6905   (203) 316-5570
    Fax: (203) 316-5573
    Email: bhert2b111@aol.com
Supervision: Vaad Hakashrus of Fairfield County.
Full selection of grocery items. Glatt kosher butcher and
take-out products available. Open six days a week.

Media

Magazines
United Jewish Federation
39 Regent Court 6907   (203) 322-2840

Organisations
United Jewish Federation
1035 Newfield Avenue 6905   (203) 321-1373

Synagogues

Orthodox
Young Israel of Stamford
69 Oak Lawn Avenue 6905   (203) 348-3955

Waterbury

Bakeries
Ami's Hot Bagels
111 Tomaston Avenue   (203) 596-9020
Supervision: Vaad Hakashrus of Fairfield County.
Bagels, sandwiches and spreads are all supervised. All
products are dairy.

Organisations
Jewish Federation of Greater Waterbury
73 Main Street, South Woodbury 6798
    (203) 263-5121

West Hartford

Booksellers
The Judaica Store
31 Crossroads Plaza 6117   (860) 236-9956

Synagogues

Orthodox
Young Israel of West Hartford
2240 Albany Avenue 6117   (860) 233-3084
    Fax: (860) 232-6417
    Email: yiwhrdc@aol.com

Westport

Synagogues
215 Post Road West 6880   (203) 226-6901

Woodbridge

Libraries
Center Cafe & Jewish Library
360 Amity Road 6525   (203) 387-2424

Restaurants

Dairy
Center Cafe & Jewish Library
JCC of Greater New Haven, 360 Amity Road 6525
    (203) 387-2424
Kosher dairy café offering breakfast, lunch and light
snacks.

Delaware

Dover

Synagogues

Conservative
Congregation Beth Sholom of Dover
PO Box 223 19903

Newark

Synagogues

Reconstructionist
Temple Beth El
101 Possum Park Rd 19711

Wilmington

Community Organisations

Jewish Community Center
101 Garden of Eden Road 19803   (302) 478-5660
                                    Fax: (302) 478-6068

Synagogues

Conservative

Beth Shalom
18th St. and Baynard Blvd 19802

Orthodox

Adas Kodesh Shel Emeth
Washington Blvd & Torah Drive 19802
                                       (302) 762-2705
                                  Fax: (302) 762-3236
                            Web site: www.akse.org

Reform

Beth Emeth
300 W. Lea Blvd. 19802

District of Columbia

Washington

Delicatessens

Hunan Deli, "H" Street   (202) 833-1018
Posins Bakery & Deli
5756 Georgia Avenue   (202) 726-4424
Bakery is under Conservative hashgacha.

Embassy

Embassy of Israel   (202) 364-5500
3514 International Drive 20008   Fax: (202) 364-5423

Eruv Information

Eruv in Georgetown
                                       (202) 338-ERUV

Galleries

The National Portrait Gallery
"F" Street between 7th & 8th Sts.,
Houses more than 100,000 portraits including Albert
Einstein, Golda Meir and George Gershwin

Kashrut Information

Rabbinical Council of Greater Washington
7826 Eastern Avenue 20012   (202) 291-6052
                                  Fax: (202) 291-5377
                            Web site: www.capitolk.org

Media

Directories

Jewish Com. Council of Greater Washington
American Israel Public Affairs Com., 500 N. Capitol St.,
N.W.,, Suite 412 20001

Newspapers

The Jewish Week
1910 "K" Street 20006

Museums

B'nai B'rith Klutznick National Jewish Museum
1640 Rhode Island Av. 20036   (202) 857-6583
                                  Fax: (202) 857-1099
                         Email: eberman@bnaibrith.org
Hours 10 am to 5 pm Sunday through Friday and 10
am to 3 pm, Fridays in Winter. Shop telephone
numbe: 202-857-6608. Shop email:
sguggenhe@bnaibrith.org
John F. Kennedy Center
2700 "F" Street
Israeli lounge donated by the people of Israel
Lillian & Albert Small Museum
3rd & "G" Sts. N.W. 20008
Housed in Washington's oldest synagogue building,
Adas Israel, built in 1876
National Museum of American Jewish Military History
1811 R. Street N.W. 20009   (202) 265-6280
                                  Fax: (202) 462-3192
                          Email: nmajmh@nmajmh.org
                            Web site: www.nmajmh.org
The National Museum of American Jewish Military
History, under the auspices of the Jewish War Veterans
of the USA., documents and preserves the contributions
of Jewish Americans to the peace and freedom of the
United States, educates the public concerning the
courage, heroism and sacrifices made by Jewish
Americans who served in the armed forces, and works
to combat anti-Semitism. The Museum includes
exhibitions, a library, a chapel and a Study Centre.
Hours: 9 am to 5 pm Monday to Friday and 1 pm to
5pm on Sundays.
Smithsonian Institute
The Natural History Building, 10th & Constitution Avs.
N.W. 20001
Contains a collection of Jewish ritual articles.

United States of America / District of Columbia

The Isaac Polack Building
2109 Pennsylvania Av. N.W.
Built in 1796, The Isaac Polack Building was the home
of the first Jew to settle in Washington

South West

United States Holocaust Memorial Museum
100 Raoul Wallenberg Place 20024-2150
(202) 488-0400
Fax: (202) 488-2606
Email: group_visit@ushmm.org
Web site: www.ushmm.org
Hours: 10.00am to 5.30pm. The Museum is accessible
to people with disabilities

The permanent exhibition recommended for visitors 11
years and older presents a comprehensive history of the
Holocaust through artefacts photographs films and
eyewitness testimonies. There are other changing
special exhibitions and an exhibition designed for
children 8 years and older.
Jewish Community Centre
16th Street at Q
Supervision: Va'ad Hakashrut of Washington.
Kosher restaurant on site (dairy and fish) with Hechser.
Jewish Historical Society of Greater Washington
701 3rd Street N. W. 20001-2624   (202) 789-0900
Fax: (202) 789-0485
Also the Lillian & Albert Small Jewish Museum. Hours:
Sunday-Thursday 12-4pm.

Religious Organisations
Young Israel Washington DC Office
1101 Penn Avenue, Suite 1050 20004
(202) 347-4111
Fax: (202) 347-8341

Restaurants

Meat
Letoile
1310 New Hampshire Avenue NW   (202) 835-3030
Fax: (202) 466-1988
Supervision: Supervised.

Pizzerias
Nuthouse Pizza   (301) 942-5900
Synagogues
Reform
Temple Micah
2829 Wisconsin Avenue N.W. 20007 (202) 342-9175

Florida

Aventura

Synagogues

Orthodox

Young Israel of Aventura
2956 Aventura Blvd, 2nd Floor 33180
(305) 931-5188

Belle Glade

Synagogues

Conservative

Temple Beth Sholom
224 N.W. Avenue, "G" 33430   (202) 996-3886

Boca Raton

Bakeries
Colette French Pastry
21000 Boca Rio Road 33433   (561) 451-4840
Supervision: South Palm Beach Vaad.
Dushan's Bakery
5994 S W 18th Street 33433   (561) 395-4080

Mikvaot
Boca Raton Synagogue
7900 Montoya Circle 33433   (561) 394-5854

Organisations
Jewish Federation of South Palm Beach County
9901 Donna Klein Blvd 33428-1788 (407) 852-3100

Restaurants
Strathmore Deli Restaurant
22191 Powerline Road, Palm Plaza   (561) 395-0337
Fax: (561) 395-6849
Supervision: South Palm Beach Vaad.

Dairy
JCC Café
Cultural Arts Building, 9801 Donna Klein Blvd
33428-1788   (561) 852-4103
Breakfast - dairy; Lunch - meat.

Meat
Eliat Cafe
Delmar Shopping Village, 7158 N. Beracasa Way
33434   (561) 368-9550
Falafel Armon
22767 State Road 7 33428   (407) 477-0633
Orchids Garden
9045 La Fontana Blvd, Boca Raton 33434
(561) 482-3831
Fax: (561) 482-5951
Supervision: So Palm Beach County. Vaad Hakasrut.
Hours: Monday to Thursday, 11:30 am to 9 pm;
Sunday, 3 pm to 9 pm..

Synagogues

Conservative

Beth Ami Congregation
1401 N.W. 4th Avenue 33432   (561) 347-0031

Orthodox

Boca Raton
7900 Montoya Circle 33433   (561) 394-5732
Young Israel of Boca Raton
7200 Palmetto Circle Blvd 33433   (561) 391-5509

Reform

Congregation B'Nai Israel
2200 Yamato Road 33431   (561) 241-8118

Clearwater

Organisations

Jewish Federation of Pinellas County
13191 Starkey Road, Suite 8, Largo 33773-1438
     (727) 530-3223
     Fax: (727) 531-0221
     Email: pinellas@jfedpinellas.org

Synagogues

Conservative

Beth Shalom
1325 S. Belcher Road 33764   (727) 531-1418
     Fax: (727) 531-0798

Orthodox

Young Israel of Clearwater
2385 Tampa Road
Suite 1, Palm Harbor 34684   (727) 789-0408

Reform

B'nai Israel
1685 S. Belcher Road 34624   (727) 531-5829
Temple Ahavat Shalom
1575 Curlew Road, Palm Harbor 34683
     (727) 785-8811
     Fax: (727) 785-8822
     Email: rabgar@tampabay.rr.com

Daytona Beach

Organisations

Jewish Federation of Volusia & Flagler Counties
733 S. Nova Road, Ormond Beach 32174
     (904) 672-0294
     Fax: (904) 673-1316

Synagogues

Conservative

Temple Israel
1400 S. Peninsula Drive 32118   (904) 252-3097

Deerfield Beach

Synagogues

Orthodox

Young Israel of Deerfield Beach
1880 H West Hillsboro Blvd 33442   (954) 421-1367

Delray Beach

Groceries

Meat Market
Oriole Kosher Market, 7345 West Atlantic Ave., 33446

Synagogues

Conservative

Temple Anshei Shalom of West Delray
Oriole Jewish Center, 7099 W. Atlantic Avenue 33446
     (561) 495-1300

Temple Emeth
5780 W. Atlantic Avenue 33446   (561) 498-3536

Orthodox

Anshei Emuna
16189 Carter Road 33445   (561) 499-9229

Reform

Temple Sinai
2475 W. Atlantic Avenue 33445   (561) 276-6161
     Fax: (561) 276-3485
     Email: sinai1@juno.com

Fort Lauderdale

Delicatessens

East Side Kosher Restaurant & Deli
6846 W. Atlantic Blvd, Margate 33063

Organisations

Jewish Federation of Greater Fort Lauderdale
8358 W. Oakland Park Blvd 33321   (305) 748-8400
     Fax: (305) 748-6332

Restaurants

Meat

Amore' Ristorante
8067 West Oakland Park Blvd., Sunrise(954) 749-6888
Supervision: Glatt Kosher.

United States of America / Florida

Fort Meyers

Synagogues

Reform

Temple Beth El
16225 Winkler Road Ext 33908   (941) 433-0018

Fort Pierce

Synagogues
Temple Beth-El Israel
4600 Oleander Drive 34982   (407) 461-7428

Hollywood & Vicinity

Media

Newspapers

The Jewish Community Advocate of South Broward
2719 Hollywood Blvd 33020   (305) 922-8603

Mikvaot
Mikveh/Young Israel of Hollywood - Ft. Lauderdale
3291 Stirling Road
Fort Lauderdale, Ft Lauderdale 33312
                                        (954) 963-3952
                                   Fax: (954) 962-5566

Organisations
Jewish Federation of South Broward
2719 Hollywood Blvd 33020   (305) 921-8810

Restaurants

Meat

Pita Plus
5650 Stirling Road 33021   (305) 985-8028

Pizzerias

Jerusalem Pizza II
5650 Stirling Road 33021   (954) 964-6811
                                   Fax: (954) 964-2911

Synagogues

Conservative

B'nai Aviv
200 Bonaventure Blvd.Weston
Century Pines Jewish Center
13400 S.W. 10 St, Pembroke Pines
Hallandale Jewish Center
416 N.E. 8 Av, Hallandale
Temple Beth Ahm Israel
9730 Stirling Rd   (954) 431-5100
Temple Beth Shalom
1400 N. 46 Avenue, Hollywood

Temple Judea of Carriage Hills
6734 Stirling Rd, Hollywood
Temple Sinai
1201 Johnson St, Hollywood
                                        (954) 987-0026

Orthodox

Chabad Ocean Synagogue
4000 S. Ocean Drive, Hallandale   (954) 458-7999
Chabad of Southwest Broward
11251 Taft St, Pembroke Pines
Congregation Ahavat Shalom
315 Madison St, Hollywood   (954) 922-4544
Congregation Levi Yitzchok-Lubavitch
1295 E. Hallandale Beach Blvd, Hallandale
                                        (954) 458-1877
                                   Fax: (954) 458-1651
                            Email: chai@dialisdn.com
Young Israel of Hollywood/Ft. Lauderdale
3291 Stirling Road, Ft. Lauderdale 33312
                                        (954) 966-7877
                                   Fax: (954) 962-5566
                            Email: rred@gate.net
Young Israel of Pembroke Pines
13400 S.W. 10 St, Pembroke Pines

Reform

Temple Beth El
1351 S. 14 Av, Hollywood
Temple Beth Emet
4807 South Flamingo Road, Cooper City,
Pembroke Pines   (954) 680-1882
                            Email: bethemet@aol.com
Temple Solel, 5100 Sheridan St, Hollywood
                                        (954) 989-0205

Sephardi

B'nai Sephardim
3670 Stirling Rd, Ft. Lauderdale

Jacksonville

Mikvaot
Etz Chaim
10167 San Jose Blvd 32257   (904) 262-3565

Organisations
Jacksonville Jewish Federation
8505 San Jose Blvd 32217   (904) 448-5000
Kosher Nutrition Center
5846 Mt. Carmel Terrace. 32216   (904) 737-9075

United States of America / Florida

Kendall

Synagogues

Orthodox

Young Israel of Kendall
7880 SW 112th Street 33156   (305) 232-6833

Key West

Synagogues

Conservative

B'nai Zion
750 United Street 33040-3251   (305) 294-3437

Lakeland

Synagogues
Temple Emanuel
600 Lake Hollingsworth Drive 33803   (813) 682-8616

Melbourne

Groceries
Breyard Kosher Zone
416N Harbor City Blvd., 1/4 mile south of Eau Gallie
    (407) 752-8000
    Fax: (407) 752-8000
    Email: bkz1@mindspring.com

Miami/Miami Beach

Booksellers
Jerusalem Judaica
459 41st Street 33140   (305) 535-8888

Community Organisations
Greater Miami Jewish Federation
4200 Biscayne Blvd 33137   (305) 576-4000
    Fax: (305) 573-8115
Has information and referral service, ext. 283.

Embassy
Consul General of Israel
Suite 1800, 100N Biscayne Blvd 33132

Hotels
The Saxony
3201 Collins Avenue, Miami Beach 33140
    (305) 538-6811
    Fax: (305) 672-3721
Supervision: National Kashruth.

Media

Directories

Jewish Life in Dade County
4200 Biscayne Blvd 33137   (305) 576-4000
    Fax: (305) 573-8115

Mikvaot
B'nai Israel & Greater Miami Youth Synagogue Mikveh
16260 S. W. 288th Street, Naranja 33033
    (305) 264-6488
Boca Raton Synagogue Mikveh
7900 Montoya Circle South, Boca Raton 33433
    (305) 538-0070
Congregation and Mikvah Adas Dej
225 37th Street 33140   (305) 538-0070
Daughters of Israel
2530 Pinetree Drive 33140   (305) 672-3500
Miami Beach Mikveh
2530 Pinetree Drive 33140   (305) 672-3500
Mikveh Blima of North Dade, Inc.,
1054 N.E. Miami Gardens Drive 33179
    (305) 949-9650
Rabbi Meisel's Mikveh
Washington Av. & 2nd Street 33139   (305) 673-4641
For men only
Shul of Bal Harbour Mikvah
9500 Collins Avenue, Surfside 33154
    (305) 868-1411

Museums
Jewish Museum of Florida
301 Washington Avenue, Miami Beach 33139-6965
    (305) 672-5044
    Fax: (305) 672-5933
    Email: mzerivitz@aol.com
    Web site: www.jewishmuseum.com
Open Tuesday to Sunday 10.00am to 5.00pm. Closed
Mondays and Jewish holidays.

Organisations

Orthodox

**National Council of Young Israel Southern Regional
Office**
1035 NE 170th Terrace 33162   (305) 770-3993
    Email: ncyi.south@youngisrael.org

Religious Organisations
Young Israel Southern Regional Office
173575 NE 7th Avenue 33162   (305) 770-3993
    Fax: (305) 770-3993
    Email: ncyi.south@youngisrael.org

Restaurants
Aviva's Kitchen
16355 W. Dixie Hwy., 33160   (305) 944-7313
Pinati Restaurant
2520 Miami Gardens Drive 33180   (305) 931-8086
Shalom Haifa
1330 N.E. 163 Street 33162   (305) 945-2884

United States of America / Florida

Dairy

Bagel Time
3915 Alton Road 33140   (305) 538-0300
Supervision: Star-K.
Eat in or take out. Hours: Sunday to Friday, 6:30 am to
4 pm.

Gitty's Hungarian Kitchen
6565 Collins Avenue, Sherry Frontenac Hotel 33141
(305) 865-4893

Ocean Terrace Restaurant & Grille
4041 Collins Avenue 33140   (305) 531-5771

Shemtov's Pizza
514 41st Street 33140   (305) 538-2123
                                    Fax: (305) 534-4213
Supervision: Star-K.
Cholov Yisroel. Sun-Thurs 11am-10pm, Fri 11am-3pm,
Sat - Motzei Shabbos - 1am

The Noshery (Seasonal dairy)
Saxony Hotel, 3201 Collins Ave., 33140
                                         (305) 538-6811

Meat

China Kikor Tel Aviv
5005 Collins Avenue 33140   (305) 866-3316

Embassy Peking Tower Suite
4101 Pine tree Drive, Tower 41 33140
                                         (305) 538-7550
                                    Fax: (305) 538-7570
Supervision: NK.

Jerusalem Peking
4299 Collins Avenue 33140   (305) 532-2263

Pita Plus
20103 Biscayne Blvd 33180   (305) 935-0761

Tani Guchi's Place
2224 N.E. 123rd St, North Miami   (305) 892-6744
                                    Fax: (305) 892-1035
Supervision: Glatt Kosher.

Wing Wan II
1640 N.E, 164 Street 33162   (305) 945-3585

Pizzerias

Jerusalem Pizza
761 N.E. 167th Street 33162   (305) 653-6662

Sarah's Kosher Pizza
2214 N.E. 123 Street 33181   (305) 891-3312

Sarah's Kosher Pizza
1127 N. E. 163 Street 33162   (305) 948-7777

Yonnie's Kosher Pizza
19802 W. Dixie Hwy. 33180   (305) 932-1961

Synagogues

Conservative

Beth Raphael
1545 Jefferson Avenue 33139   (305) 538-4112
This synagogue is dedicated to the six million martyrs of
the Holocaust. On an outside marble wall, a large six-
light menorah burns every night in their memory. Six
hundred names, representing each city, have been
inscribed on the marble. There is also a notable
Holocaust Memorial at Dade Av., and Meridian Av.;

Orthodox

Young Israel of Greater Miami
990 NE 171st Street, North Miami Beach 33162
                                         (305) 651-3591

Young Israel of Miami Beach
4221 Pine Tree Drive 33140   (305) 538-9462

Young Israel of Sky Lake
1850 NE 183rd Street, North Miami Beach 33179
                                    (305) 945-8712/8715

Tours of Jewish Interest
Jewish Travel and Education Network - JTEN
                                         (305) 931-1782
Offers organised tours of Miami and Miami Beach.

Orlando

Delicatessens
Market Place Deli, Hyatt Orlando
6375 W. Irlo Bronson Highway   (407) 396-1234
Has frozen kosher food only.

Groceries
Amira's Catering and Specialty
1351 E. Altamonte, Altamonte Springs
                                         (407) 767-7577
Cold cuts, side dishes, frozen meals, groceries.

Kosher Korner
8464 Palm Parkway, Vista Center 32836
                                         (407) 238-9968
                                    Fax: (407) 238-2008
Supervision: Florida Kosher Services.
Complete kosher grocery and takeout. Packaged frozen
glatt meat. Will deliver to hotels. Two minutes from
downtown Disney

Hotels
Catalina Inn – Lower East Side Restaurant
3401 MacLeod Road 32805   (407) 648-4830
Supervision: OU.

Mikvaot
Mikvah Yisrael
8 Lake Howell Road 32751   (407) 644-2362

Organisations
Jewish Federation of Greater Orlando
851 N. Maitland Avenue, Maitland 32751
                                  (407) 645 5933
                            Fax: (407) 645 1172
Email: postmaster@orlandojewishfed.org

Restaurants
Kinneret Kitchens
517 South Delany   (407) 422-7205
Senior Citizens dining room. Meals: d, Mon.-Fri at 5pm. Call at least 24 hours in advance to reserve a meal.

Meat

Kosher Korner
Vista Center, 8464 Palm Pkwy. 32836
                                  (407) 238-9968
                            Fax: (407) 238-2008
Glatt kosher.Dine in take out and delivery
The Lower East Side Restaurant
8548 Palm Parkway 32836   (407) 425-8292
                            Fax: (407) 425-2325
Supervision: Florida Kosher Services.
There is a Shul at the back of the restaurant

Synagogues

Conservative

Congregation Beth Shalom
13th & Center Streets, Leesburg 32748
                                  (407) 742-0238

Congregation Ohev Shalom
5015 Goddard Avenue 32804   (407) 298-4650
Congregation Shalom (Williamsburg)
c/o Sydney Ansell, 11821 Soccer Lane 32821-7952
Congregation Shalom Aleichem
PO Box 424211, Kissimmee 34742-4211
Southwest Orlando Jewish Congregation
11200 S. Apopka-Vineland Road 32836
                    Web site: www.sojc-orlando.org
The closest Synagogue to Walt Disney world (one mile away).
Temple Israel
4917 Eli Street 32804   (407) 647-3055

Orthodox

Cong. Ahavas Yisrael/Chabad
708 Lake Howell Road, Maitland 32751
                                  (407) 644-2500
                            Fax: (407) 644-7763

Reform

Congregation of Liberal Judaism
928 Malone Drive 32810   (407) 645-0444

Ormond Beach

Synagogues
Temple Beth El
579 N. Nova Road, Ormond Beach 32174
                                  (904) 677-2484

Palm Beach

Synagogues

Conservative
Temple Emanu-el
190 N. County Road 33480   (561) 832-0804

Orthodox
Palm Beach Orthodox Synagogue
120 North County Road, PO Box 3225 33480
                                  (561) 838-9002
                            Fax: (561) 838-5356

Palm Beach West

Synagogues
Congregation Aitz Chaim
2518 N. Haverhill Road 33417   (561) 686-5055

Palm City

Synagogues

Conservative
Treasure Coast Jewish Center-Congregation Beth Abraham
3998 S.W. Leighton Farms Avenue. 34990
                                  (407) 287-8833

Palm Coast

Synagogues
Temple Beth Shalom
40 Wellington Drive, POB 350557 32135-0557
                                  (904) 445-3006

United States of America / Florida

Pembroke Pines

Synagogues

Orthodox

Young Israel of Pembroke Pines
13400 SW 10th Street 33027   (954) 433-8666

Pensacola

Synagogues

Conservative

B'nai Israel
1829 N. 9th Avenue, P O Box 9002 32513
                                   (805) 433-7311
                              Fax: (805) 435-9597

Reform

Beth El, 800 N. Palafox Street 32501

Rockledge

Organisations
Jewish Federation of Brevard
108A Barton Avenue   (321) 636-1824
                              Fax: (321) 636-0614
                         Email: jfbrevard@aol.com

Sarasota

Organisations
Sarasota-Manatee Jewish Federation
580 S. McIntosh Road 34232-1959   (941) 371-4546
                              Fax: (941) 378-2947
                          Email: smjf@jon.cjfny.org

Sky Lake

Synagogues

Orthodox

Young Israel of Sky Lake
1850 NE 183rd Street, North Miami Beach 33179
                              (305) 945-8712/8715

St Augustine

Synagogues
The First Congregation Sons Of Israel
161 Cordova Street 43084

St Petersburg

Groceries
Jo-El's Specialty Foods
2619 23rd Avenue N. 33713   (727) 321-3847
                              Fax: (727) 327-0682
Also has delicatessen and butcher shop. Hours:
Monday to Thursday, 9 am to 5 pm; Friday, to 4 pm;
Sunday, to 1 pm.

Synagogues

Conservative

B'nai Israel
301 59th Street N. 33710   (813) 381-4900
Beth Shalom
1844 54th Street S. 33707   (813) 321-3380

Reform

Beth-El, 400 Pasadena Avenue S. 33707
                                   (813) 347-6136

Sunny Isles

Synagogues

Orthodox

Young Israel of Sunny Isles
17395 North Bay Road, North Miami Beach 33160
                                   (305) 935-9095

Sunrise

Restaurants
Amore Ristorante
8067 W.Oakland Park Blvd. 33351   (954) 749-6888
Supervision: O.R.B..

Surfside

Synagogues

Orthodox

The Shul of Bal Harbor, Bay Harbor & Surfside
9540 Collins Avenue 33154   (305) 868-1411

Tamarac

Synagogues
Young Israel of Taramac
8565 W McNab Road 33321   (954) 726-3586

Tampa

Delicatessen
Jo-El's, 11727 N Dale Mabry 33618
                                   (813) 964-9299
Also has bakery and groceries. Hours Monday to
Thursday 10 am to 7.30 pm; Friday 10 am to 3.30 pm
and Sunday 9 am to 2.30 pm

United States of America / Georgia

Mikvaot
Bais Tefilah
14908 Pennington Road 33624   (813) 963-2317
Mikva, Orthodox pre-school on premises.

Organisations
Tampa Jewish Federation
13009 Community Campus Drive 33625-4000
        (813) 264-9000
        Fax: (813) 265-8450
        Email: tjfjcc@aol.com

Synagogues
Conservative
Kol Ami, 3919 Moran Road 33618   (813) 962-6338
Rodeph Shalom
2713 Bayshore Blvd. 33629   (813) 837-1911
Temple David
2001 Swann Avenue 33606   (813) 254-1771

Orthodox
Hebrew Academy
14908 Pennington Road 33624   (813) 963-0706
Young Israel of Tampa
3721W Tacon Street 33629   (813) 832-3018

Reform
Schaarai Zedek
3303 Swann Avenue 33609   (813) 876-2377

Vero Beach

Synagogues
Temple Beth Shalom
365 43rd Street   (407) 569-4700
        Fax: (407) 617-864-0507
        Email: tbs-of-camb@juno.com

West Palm Beach

Community Organisations
Chabad House
4800 23rd St. N 33407   (561) 640-8111

Delicatessens
Glatt Mart
4869 Okeechobee Blvd 33417   (561) 689-6267
        Fax: (561) 689-2595

Organisations
Jewish Federation of Palm Beach County
4601 Community Drive 33417   (561) 478-0700
        Fax: (561) 478-9696

Georgia

Athens

Synagogues
Reform
Congregation Children Of Israel
Dudley Drive 30606   (404) 549-4192

Atlanta

Bed & Breakfasts
Bed & Breakfast Atlanta
1608 Briarcliff Road, Suite 5 30306   (404) 875-0525
        Fax: (404) 875-8198
        Web site: www.bedandbreakfast.com
Kosher and Shomer Shabbat accommodation.

Community Organisations
Jewish Federation
1753 Peachtree Road, NE 30309   (404) 873-1661
        Fax: (404) 874-7043
Publishes an annual community guide.

Delicatessens
Chai Peking
2205 La Vista Road, N.E. 30329   (404) 327-7810
        Fax: (404) 327-7811
Supervision: Atlanta Kashruth Commission.
Inside Kroger Supermarket. Authentic Glatt Kosher
Chinese Cuisine.
Harris Teeter
1799 Briarcliff Road, 2nd level 30329
        (404) 607-1189
Supervision: Atlanta Kashrut Commission.
Kosher fish, meat and deli.
Kroger
2205 La Vista Road, N.E. 30329
        (404) 633-8694
        Fax: (404) 315-4411
Supervision: Atlanta Kashrut Commission.
Select departments only. Glatt meat, Glatt deli & full
line of Cholov Yisroel products.
Quality Kosher
2153 Briarcliff Road 30329
        (404) 636-1114 or 1-800-305-6328
        Fax: (404) 636-8675
Supervision: Atlanta Kashrut Commission.
Glatt and take out foods butcher, deli and grocery.
Open 7.30am-6pm Monday to Thursday. 7.30am-3pm
Friday and Sunday.

United States of America / Georgia

Embassy
Consul General of Israel
Suite 440, 1100 Spring Street, NW 30309-2823

Kashrut Information
Atlanta Kashrut Commission
1855 La Vista Road, N.E. 30329   (404) 634-4063
Fax: (404) 634-4254
Email: akc613@usa.com
A non-profit organisation dedicated to promoting
kashrut through education, research and supervision.
Publishes a monthly kashrut newsletter.

Mikvaot
Beth Jacob
1855 La Vista Road 30329   (404) 633-0551

Restaurant

Dairy

CJ's Café
5825 Glenridge Drive, Bldg 2, Suite 115 30342
(404) 705-9100

Restaurants
Broadway Café
2166 Briarcliff Road 30329   (404) 329-0888
Fax: (404) 329-9888
Supervision: Atlanta Kashrut Commission.
Seafood, vegetarian, and vegan foods.

Wall Street Pizza
2470 Briarcliff Road, 30329   (404) 633-2111
Supervision: Atlanta Kashrut Commission.
Delivery available.

Meat

Quality Kosher
2153 Briarcliff Road 30329   (404) 636-1114
Fax: (404) 636-8675
Supervision: Atlanta Kashrut Commission.

Synagogues

Conservative

Ahavath Achim
(404) 355-5222

Orthodox

Anshe S'Fard
1324 North Highland Avenue, N.E. 30306
(404) 874-4513

Congregation Beth Jacob
1855 La Vista Road NE 30329   (404) 633-0551
Fax: (404) 320-7912
Email: cbj@mindspring.com
Web site: www.toll-free.com/bethjacob
Mikveh on premises

Young Israel of Toco Hills
2074 La Vista Road
Toco Hills 30329   (404) 315-1417
Fax: (404) 315-1417
Email: youngisrael@toll-free.com

Reform

Temple Sinai
5645 Dupree Drive, N.W. 30327   (404) 252-3073
The Temple, 1589 Peachtree Road   (404) 873-1731

Sephardic

Ner Hamizrach
1858 La Vista Road, N.E. 30329   (404) 315-9020

Augusta

Bakeries
Sunshine Bakery
1209 Broad Street 30902

Delicatessens
Parti-Pal
Daniel Village 30904
Strauss, 965 Broad Street 30902

Synagogues

Orthodox

Adas Yeshuron
935 Johns Road, Walton Way 30904
(706) 733-9491

Columbus

Synagogues

Conservative

Shearith Israel
2550 Wynnton Road 31906   (706) 323-1443

Reform

Temple Israel
1617 Wildwood Avenue 31906   (706) 323-1617

Decatur

Tours
Kosher Expeditions
2932 Westbury Drive, Suite 100   (770) 441-2545
Fax: (770) 234-5170
Email: dl@kosherexpeditions.com
Web site: www.kosherexpeditions.com
World wide kosher travel organisers.

Macon

Synagogues

Conservative
Sha'arey Israel
611 First Street 31201   (912) 745-4571
Fax: (912) 745-5892
Web site: www.csimacon.org

Reform
Beth Israel
892 Cherry Street 31201   (912) 745-6727

Savannah

Community Centre
Savannah Jewish Federation
5111 Abercorn Street 31405   (912) 355-8111
Fax: (912) 355-8116
Email: sharon@sauj.org

Contact Information
Rabbi Avigdor Slatus
5444 Abercorn Street 31405   (912) 354-2359
Fax: (912) 354-5272
Visitors requiring information about kashrut, temporary accommodation, etc., should contact Rabbi Slatus.

Guest apartments
Buckingham South
5450 Abercorn Street 31405   (912) 355-5550
Fax: (912) 353-9393
Email: information@buckinghamsouth.com
Supervision: Rabbi Avigdor Slatus.
Glatt kosher meals available on request. Next door to Orthodox Synagogue, minyan available.

Synagogues
Mickve Israel
Bull & Gordon Sts. 31401
The oldest synagogue in Georgia, having been founded before 1790

Conservative
Agudath Achim
9 Lee Blvd. 31405

Orthodox
B'nai B'rith Jacob
5444 Abercorn Street 31405   (912) 354-7721
Fax: (912) 354-9923

Hawaii

Hilo

Synagogues

Unaffiliated
Temple Beth Aloha
PO Box 96720   (808) 969-4153

Honolulu

Bed & Breakfasts
Bed & Breakfast Honolulu (Statewide)
3242 Kaohinani Drive 96817
(808) 595-7533; 800-288-4666
Fax: (808) 595-2030
Email: rainbow@hawaiibnb.com
Web site: www.hawaiibnb.com
Not specifically kosher, but within walking distance of Orthodox services for the High Holy Days.

Groceries
Down To Earth
King's Street, Near University Av.,
Foodland Supermarket Beretania
1460 S. Beretania St.

Organisations
Jewish Federation of Hawaii
44 Hora Lane 96813   (808) 941-2424

Synagogues

Conservative
Congregation Sof Ma'arav
2500 Pali Highway 96817   (808) 595-3678

Orthodox
Chabad of Hawaii
2nd floor conference room, 1777 Ala Moana Blvd.,
96822   (808) 735-8161
Fax: (808) 735-4130

Kihei

Synagogues
Jewish Congregation of Maui
PO Box 6101, Maui 96732   (808) 243-2499

Reform
Congregation Gan Eden
P.O. Box 555, Kihei Road 96753   (808) 879-9221
Fax: (808) 874-8570

United States of America / Hawaii

Kona

Synagogues
Kona Beth Shalom Kailua-Kona
                              (808) 322-4192 or 322-6004

Waikiki

Synagogues

Orthodox

Chabad, Alana Hotel, Park Plaza,
1956 Ala Moana Blvd.   (808) 735-8161

Idaho

Boise

Synagogues

Conservative

Ahavath-Beth Israel
1102 State Street 83702
The oldest continually functioning synagogue in the
western USA

Illinois

Champaign-Urbana

Community Organisations
Champaign-Urbana Jewish Federation
503 E. John St, Champaign 61820   (217) 367-9872
                              Fax: (217) 367-0077
                              Email: cujf@shalomcu.org
                              Web site: www.shalomcu.org

Synagogues

Reform

Sinai Temple
3104 Windsor Road, Champaign 61821
                              (217) 352-8140

Chicago

Chicagoland (Greater Chicago) consists of the City
of Chicago and the collar counties of Cook,
Dupage, Kane, Lake and McHenry Counties. The
Jewish community is spread throughout
Chicagoland, with the main concentrations being
in West Rogers Park (City of Chicago), Skokie
(Cook County), Buffalo Grove and Highland Park
(Lake County).

Greater Chicago has a Jewish population of
about 260,000. For a history of the Jews of
Chicago see: I. Cutter: The Jews of Chicago: from
Shtetl to Suburbs.

Entries in this section are arranged in the
sequence that Chicagoland residents think of the
area. There are three basic divisions in
Chicagoland:
a. City of Chicago (telephone area code 312 and
773) includes West Rogers Park and the
California/Dempster Avenue areas
b. North and Northwest Suburbs (includes Cook
Lake and McHenry counties; telephone area code
773, 815 and 847) includes Buffalo Grove
Deerfield, Evanston, Highland Park, Northbrook
and Skokie.
c. South and West Suburbs (includes DuPage and
Kane counties' telephone area codes 630 or 708
includes Flossmoor and Olympia Fields.

For more information see the Jewish Chicago
website at www.jewishchicago.com

Bakeries
Gitel's Bakery
2745 W. Devon City of Chicago 60659
                              (773) 262-3701
Supervision: Chicago Rabbinical Council.

North Shore Bakery
2919 W. Touhy City of Chicago 60645
                              (773) 262-0600
Supervision: Chicago Rabbinical Council.

Tel Aviv Bakery
2944 W. Devon City of Chicago 60659
                              (773) 764-8877
Supervision: Chicago Rabbinical Council.

Booksellers
Chicago Hebrew Book Store
2942 W. Devon City of Chicago 60659
                              (733) 973-6636
                              Fax: (733) 973-6465

Rosenblum's World of Judaica, Inc.
2906 W. Devon Ave City of Chicago 60659
                              (773) 262-1700
                              Fax: (773) 262-1930
                              Email: afox@rosenblums.com
                              Web site: www.rosenblums.com

The Barriff Shop at the Spertus Museum
618 S. Michigan Avenue City of Chicago 60605
                              (312) 322-1740
                              Fax: (312) 922-640
                              Email: bariff_shop@spertus.ed
                              Web site: www.bariff.org
Hours: Sunday to Wednesday 10am to 5pm. Thursday
10am to 8pm. Friday 10am to 3pm. Closed Saturday

Butchers
Jacob Miller & Sons
2727 W. Devon City of Chicago 60659
                              (773) 761-420
Supervision: Chicago Rabbinical Council.

United States of America / Illinois

Community Organisations
Jewish Federation of Metropolitan Chicago
1 S. Franklin Street City of Chicago 60606
(312) 346-6700
Chicago Board of Rabbis (multi-denominational) is
located here as well.

Delicatessens
Good Morgan Fish
2948 W. Devon City of Chicago 60645
(773) 764-8115
Supervision: Chicago Rabbinical Council.

Kosher Karry
2828 W. Devon City of Chicago 60659
(773) 973-4355
Fax: (773) 973-7913
Supervision: Chicago Rabbinical Council.
Sells groceries as well. Prepared good and carry out.

Moshe's New York Kosher
2900 W. Devon City of Chicago 60659
(773) 338-3354
Supervision: Chicago Rabbinical Council.
Sells groceries as well.

Romanian Kosher Sausage
7200 N. Clark City of Chicago 60625
(773) 761-4141
Supervision: Orthodox Union.

Embassy
Consul General of Israel
Suite 1308
111 East Wacker Drive, City of Chicago 60601

Groceries
Kol Tuv
2938 W. Devon, City of Chicago 60659
(773) 764-1800
Supervision: Chicago Rabbinical Council.

Media
Newspapers
Chicago Jewish News
5301 W Dempster St
City of Chicago 60077
(847) 966-0606
Fax: (847) 966-1656
Email: chijewnes@aol.com

JUF News
1 S. Franklin Street
City of Chicago 60606
(312) 346-6700

Museums
Spertus Museum
Spertus Institute of Jewish Studies
618 S. Michigan Avenue,
City of Chicago 60605
(312) 322-1747
Fax: (312) 922-3934
Email: musm@spertus.edu
Web site: www.spertus.edu
Hours: 10-5.00pm Sunday to Wednesday. 10-8
Thursday. 10-3.00pm Friday. Closed Saturday.

Religious Organisations
Chicago Mikva Association
3110 W. Touhy Avenue
City of Chicago 60645

Chicago Rabbinical Council
3525 W. Peterson Avenue
Suite 315, City of Chicago 60659   (312) 588-1600
Fax: (312) 588-2141
Information about kashrut and related matters may be
obtained from the Council, which issues an annual
directory.

Restaurants
Shallots
2324 N. Clark St.
City of Chicago 60614   (773) 755-5205
Web site: www.shallots-chicago.com

Dairy
Jerusalem Kosher Restaurant
3014 W. Devon
City of Chicago 60659   (773) 262-0515
Supervision: OK.

Tel Aviv Kosher Pizza & Dairy Restaurant
6349 N. California
City of Chicago 60659   (773) 764-3776
Supervision: Chicago Rabbinical Council.

Meat
Great Chicago Food & Beverage Co.
3149 W. Devon
City of Chicago 60659   (773) 465-9030
Fax: (773) 465-9011
Email: gcfbken@aoi.com
Supervision: Chicago Rabbinical Council.

Mi Tsu Yun Kosher Chinese Rest.
3010 W. Devon
City of Chicago 60659   (773) 262-4630
Fax: (773) 262-4835
Supervision: Chicago Rabbinical Council.
Sunday-Thursday 12.00pm-9.00pm.

United States of America / Illinois

Synagogues

Orthodox

K.I.N.S of West Rogers Park
2800 W. North Shore Avenue
City of Chicago 60645   (773) 761-4000
Fax: (773) 761-4959
Email: congkins@cs.com

Lake Shore Drive Synagogue
70 E. Elm street
City of Chicago 60611

Loop synagogue
16 S Clark street
City of Chicago 60603

Young Israel of Chicago
4931 North Kimball Street
City of Chicago 60625

Evanston

Bakeries
King David's Bakery
1731 W. Howard St.
North and Northwest 60202   (847) 475-0270
Supervision: Chicago Rabbinical Council.

Glenview

Bakeries
The Glenview Breadsmith
2771 Pfingsten
North and Northwest 60025   (847) 509-9955
Supervision: Chicago Rabbinical Council.

Highland Park

Delicatessens
Best's Kosher Outlet Store
1630 Deerfield Rd.
North and Northwest 60035   (847) 831-9435
Fax: (847) 831-9440

Now we're cooking grill
710 Central
North and Northwest 60035   (847) 432-7310
Fax: (847) 432-8352
Supervision: Chicago Kashrut Association Inc.
Eat in and take out.

Synagogues

Conservative

North Surburban Synagogue Beth El
1175 Sheriden Road
North and Northwest 60035   (847) 432-8900

Lincolnwood

Delicatessens

Dairy

Wally's Milk Pail
3320 W. Devon
City of Chicago 60645   (773) 673-3459
Supervision: Chicago Rabbinical Council.
Sells groceries as well.

Northbrook

Synagogues

Orthodox

Young Israel of Northbrook
3545 West Walters Road
North and Northwest Suburbs 60062   (708) 480-9462

Peoria

Community Organisations
Jewish Federation
Town Hall Building, 5901 N. Prospect Road 61604
(309) 689-0063

Synagogues

Orthodox

Agudas Achim
5614 N. University 61614   (309) 692-4848
Fax: (309) 692-7255

Reform

Anshai Emeth   (309) 691-3323

Rock Island

Community Organisations
Jewish Federation of the Quad Cities
209 18th Street 61201   (309) 793-1300
Fax: (309) 793-1345

Rockford

Community Organisations
Jewish Federation
1500 Parkview Avenue 61107   (815) 399-5497

Synagogues

Conversative

Ohave Sholom
3730 Guildford Road 61107

Reform

Temple Beth El
1203 Comanche Drive 61107   (815) 398-5020

Skokie

Delicatessens

Chaim's Kosher Deli & Supermarket
4954 Dempster
North and Northwest 60077   (847) 675-1005
                                   Fax: (847) 675-0028
Supervision: Chicago Rabbinical Council.
Bakery and grocery shop as well.

Hungarian Kosher Foods
4020 W. Oakton St.
North and Northwest 60076   (847) 674-8008
Supervision: Chicago Rabbinical Council.
Butcher shop and sells groceries as well.

Judaica

Hamakor Gallery Ltd.
4150 Dempster
North and Northwest 60076   (847) 677-4150
                                   Fax: (847) 677-4160
                                   Email: gallery@jewishsource.com
                                   Web site: www.jewishsource.com

Media

Newspapers

Chicago Jewish Star
PO Box 268
North and Northwest 60076   (847) 674-7827
                                   Fax: (847) 674-0014
                                   Email: chicago-jewish-star@mcimail.com

Restaurants

Dairy

Bagel Country
9306 Skokie Blvd
Skokie, IL, North and Northwest 60077
                                   (847) 673-3030
                                   Fax: (847) 673-4040
Supervision: Chicago Rabbinical Council.

Da'Nali's
4032 W. Oakton
North and Northwest 60076   (847) 677-2782
Supervision: Chicago Rabbinical Council.

Slice of Life
4120 W. Dempster
North and Northwest 60076   (847) 674-2021
Supervision: Chicago Rabbinical Council.

Meat

Bugsy's Charhouse
3355 W. Dempster
North and Northwest 60076   (847) 679-4030
                                   Fax: (847) 835-3354
                                   Email: gcfbken@aol.com
Supervision: Chicago Rabbinical Council.

Hy Life, 4120 W. Dempster, Skokie 60076
                                   (847) 674-2021
Supervision: Chicago Rabbinical Council.

Ken's Diner
3353 W. Dempster
North and Northwest 60076   (847) 679-4030
                  Fax: (847) 835-3354; 3835- Deli
                                   Email: gcfbken@aoi.com
Supervision: Chicago Rabbinical Council.

Vegetarian

Mysore Woodlands
2548 Devon Avenue
North and Northwest 60659   (773) 338-8160
                                   Fax: (773) 338-8162
Supervision: CKA.

Synagogues

Orthodox

Young Israel of Skokie
P O Box 3572
3740 W Dempster, North and Northwest Suburbs
60076   (847) 329-0990
Shul is located in the Timber Ridge School, Samoset
and Davis

West Rogers Park

Synagogues
Young Israel of West Rogers Park
2716 West Touhy Avenue
City of Chicago 60645   (773) 743-9400

Indiana
Bloomington

Synagogues
Chabad House
516 E. 17th Street 47408   (812) 332-6784

Reform

Congregation Beth Shalom
3750 E. Third 47401   (812) 334-2440

United States of America / Indiana

East Chicago

Synagogues

Orthodox

B'nai Israel
3517 Hemlock Street 46312

Evansville

Synagogues

Conservative

Adath Israel
3600 E. Washington Avenue 47715   (812) 477-1577

Reform

Tempe, Washington Avenue Temple, 100 Washington
Avenue 47714

Fort Wayne

Synagogues

Conservative

B'nai Jacob
7227 Bittersweet Moors Drive 46814   (219) 672-8459
Fax: (219) 672-8928

Reform

Achduth Vesholom
5200 Old Mill Road 46807   (219) 744-4245

Gary

Synagogues
Temple Israel
601 N. Montgomery Street 46403   (219) 938-5232

Hammond

Synagogues

Conservative

Beth Israel
7105 Hohman Avenue 46324

Reform

Temple Beth-El
6947 Hohman Avenue 46324

Highland

Organisations
Jewish Federation of North West Indiana
2939 Jewett Street, Highland 46322   (219) 972-2251
Fax: (219) 972-4779
Serving Lake Porter and LaPorte Counties

Indianapolis

Organisations
Bureau of Jewish Education
6711 Hoover Road 46260   (317) 255-3124
Anglo-Jewish visitors are invited to get in touch with the
Executive Vice President.
Jewish Federation of Greater Indianapolis
6705 Hoover Road 46260   (317) 726-5450
Fax: (317) 205-0307
Email: hnadler@jewishinindy.org

Synagogues

Conservative

Shaarey Tefilla Congregation
5879 Central Avenue 46220-2509   (317) 253-4591
Fax: (317) 253-8529

Conservative/Reconstructionist

Beth-El Zedeck
600 W. 70th Street 46260   (317) 253-3441
Fax: (317) 259-6849
Email: bez613@bez613.com

Orthodox

B'nai Torah
6510 Hoover Road 46260   (317) 253-5253
Etz Chaim (Sephardi)
826 64th Street 46260   (317) 251-6220

Reform

Indianapolis Hebrew Congregation
6501 N. Meridian Street 46260   (317) 255-6647

Lafayette

Synagogues

Orthodox

Sons of Abraham
661 N. 7th Street 47906   (765) 742-2113
Email: retrovir@bragg.bio.purdue.edu

Reform

Temple Israel
620 Cumberland Street 47901   (765) 463-3455
Fax: (765) 463-9309
Email: rsw@nlci.com

Michigan City

Synagogues
Sinai Temple
2800 S. Franklin Street 46360   (219) 874-4477

Muncie

Synagogues
Temple Beth El
525 W. Jackson Street, cnr. Council Street 47305
(317) 288-4662

South Bend

Contact Information
Rabbi Y. Gettinger
Hebrew Orthodox Congregation, 3207 S. High Street
46614   (219) 291-4239
Fax: (219) 291-9490
Visitors requiring information about kashrut, temporary
accommodation, etc., should contact Rabbi Gettinger.
Or contact Michael Lerman, 1-800-348-2529. Ext.
137.

Kashrut Information
Hebrew Orthodox Congregation
3207 S. High Street 46614   (219) 291-4239
Fax: (219) 291-6100

Mikvaot
(219) 291-6240

Organisations
Jewish Federation of St. Joseph Valley
105 Jefferson Center, Suite 804 46601
(219) 233-1164
Fax: (219) 288-4103
Email: mgardner@jon.cjfny.org
With effect from August 2000 the address will be 3202
Shalom Drive, South Bend, IN 46615.

Synagogues

Conservative

Sinai
1102 E. Laselle Street 46617   (219) 234-8584
Fax: (219) 234-6856
Email: sinai@michiana.org
Web site: www.uscj.org/midwest/southbend

Orthodox

Hebrew Orthodox Congregation
3207 S. High Street 46614   (219) 291-4239
Fax: (219) 291-9490

Reform

Beth-El, 305 W. Madison Street 46601
(219) 234-4402

Terre Haute

Delicatessens
Kosher Meat & Sandwiches
410 W. Western Avenue 47807

Valparaiso

Synagogues

Conservative

Temple Israel
PO Box 2051 46383

Whiting

Synagogues

Orthodox

B'nai Judah
116th Street & Davis Avenue 46394   (219) 659-0797

Iowa
Cedar Rapids

Synagogues

Reform

Temple Judah
3221 Lindsay Lane S.E. 52403   (319) 362-1261

Davenport

Synagogues
Temple Emanuel
12th Street & Mississippi Avenue 52803
Davenport is part of the Rock Island, Illinois area, which
is divided by the Mississippi River. See the Rock Island
entry.

Des Moines

Delicatessens
The Nosh
800 First Street 50265

Organisations
Jewish Community Relations Commission
910 Polk Blvd, Des Moines, IA 50312
(515) 277-6321
Fax: (515) 277-4061
Email: jcrc@jon.cjfny.org
Jewish Federation of Greater Des Moines
910 Polk Blvd 50312   (515) 277-6321

Synagogues

Conservative

Tifereth Israel
924 Polk Blvd. 50312   (515) 255-1137

United States of America / Iowa

Orthodox

Beth El Jacob
954 Cummins Parkway 50312   (515) 274-1551
Fax: (515) 274-1552
Email: rav613@hotmail.com
Web site: www.cyberconnect.com/bej
Vaad Hakashrut of Des Moines offer information on
Kosher establishment & home hospitality. Contact
Rabbi. Mikvah available by appointment.

Reform

Temple B'nai Jeshurun
5101 Grand Avenue 50312   (515) 274-4679
Fax: (515) 274-2072
Email: rabbifink@aol.com

Dubuque

Synagogues
Beth El, 475 W. Locust Street 52001   (319) 583-3483

Fort Dodge

Synagogues

Conservative

Beth El, 501 N. 12th Street 50501   (515) 572-8925

Iowa City

Synagogues

Conservative & Reform

Agudas Achim
602 E. Washington Street 52240   (319) 337-3813
Fax: (319) 337-6764

Postville

Contact Information
Aaron Koschitsky
P.O. Box 126   (319) 864 7140
Postville 52162   Fax: (319) 864 7890

Synagogue
Orthodox
440 South Lawlor Street   (319) 863-3013

Sioux City

Groceries
Sam's Food Market
1911 Grandview 51104

Organisations
Jewish Federation
525 14th Street 51105   (712) 258-0618

Synagogues

Conservative

Congregation Beth Shalom
815 38th Street 51104   (712) 255-1990
Fax: (712) 258-0619
Email: drosen4005@aol.com
Hours 8-5 Monday-Thursday. 8-4 Fridays.

Orthodox

United Orthodox
14th & Nebraska Streets 51105

Kansas

Lawrence

Synagogues
Lawrence Jewish Community Center
917 Highland Drive 66046   (785) 841-7636
Email: ljcc@grapevine.net

Overland Park

Media

Newspapers

Kansas City Jewish Chronicle
7375 W. 107th Street 66204
Weekly publication.

Synagogues

Orthodox

Congregation Beth Israel Abraham & Voliner
9900 Antioch 66212   (913) 341-2444
Fax: (913) 341-2467

Kehilath Israel Synagogue
10501 Conser 66212   (913) 642-1880
Fax: (913) 642-7332

Reform

Congregation Beth Torah
6100 W 127th Street 66209   (913) 498-2212
Fax: (913) 498-1071

Prairie Village

Butchers
Jacobsons Strictly Kosher Foods
5200 W95th Street 66207

Synagogues

Conservative

Ohev Sholom
5311 W. 75th Street 66208   (913) 642-6460
Fax: (913) 642-6461
Email: rabbidanny@aol.com
Orthodox rite but mixed seating.

Topeka

Organisations
Topeka Lawrence Jewish Federation
4200 Munson Street 66604

Synagogues

Reform

Beth Sholom
4200 Munson Street 66604   (785) 272-6040

Wichita

Groceries
Dillon's
Foodbarn Woodlawn & Central Sts., 67208
Dillon's
13th Street & Woodlawn Street 67208
Dillon's
21st Street & Rock Road 67208
The Bread Lady
20205 Rock Road, #80 2607

Synagogues

Orthodox

Hebrew Congregation
1850 N. Woodlawn 67208   (316) 685-1139

Reform

Congregation Emanu-El
7011 E. Central Street 67206   (316) 685-5148

Kentucky

Lexington

Organisations
Central Kentucky Jewish Federation
340 Romany Road 40502   (606) 268-0672
                                Fax: (606) 268-0775
                  Email: ckjf@jewishlexington.org

Synagogues

Conservative

Lexington Havurah
PO Box 54958 40551
Ohavay Zion
2048 Edgewater Ct. 40502   (606) 266-8050

Reform

Adath Israel
124 N. Ashland Avenue 40502   (859) 269-2979
                                Fax: (859) 269-7347

Louisville

Organisations
Jewish Community Federation
3630 Dutchman's Lane 40205   (502) 451-8840
                                Fax: (502) 458-0702
                          Email: jfed@iglou.com

Synagogues

Conservative

Adath Jeshurun
2401 Woodbourne Avenue 40205   (502) 458-5359
Knesseth Israel
2531 Taylorsville Road 40205   (502) 459-2780

Orthodox

Anshei Sfard
3700 Dutchman's Lane 40205   (502) 451-3122
Mikvah attached.

Reform

Temple Shalom
4615 Lowe Road 40220   (502) 458-4739
                          Fax: (502) 451-9750
                  Email: rsmiles@pipeline.com
The Temple
5101 Brownsboro Road 40241   (502) 423-1818

Paducah

Synagogues
Temple Israel
330 Joe Clifton Drive 42001

Louisiana

Alexandria

Contact Information
Jewish Welfare Federation
71301   (318) 445-4785

Groceries
Dr & Mrs B Kaplan
100 Park Place 71301   (318) 445-9367
                          Fax: (318) 445-9369
Kosher food by arrangement.

Libraries
Meyer Kaplan Memorial Library (Judiaca)
c/o B'nai Israel, 1908 Vance Street 71301

Synagogues

Conservative

B'nai Israel
1907 Vance Street 71301   (318) 455-9367

United States of America / Louisiana

Reform

Gemiluth Chassodim
2021 Turner Street 71301   (318) 455-3655

Baton Rouge

Organisations
Jewish Federation of Greater Baton Rouge
P.O.B. 80827 70898   (504) 291-5895

Synagogues

Reform

B'nai Israel
3354 Kleinert Avenue 70806   (504) 343-0111
Beth Shalom
9111 Jefferson Highway 70809   (504) 924-6773

Lafayette

Synagogues
Temple Sholom
603 Lee Avenue, P.O.Box 53711 70505
                                       (318) 234-3760
There is a fine Judaica library at the University of
Southwestern Louisiana.

New Orleans

Delicatessens
Kosher Cajun Deli & Grocery
3250 N. Hullen Street, Metairie 70002
                                       (504) 888-2010
                                 Fax: (504) 888-2014
Glatt N.Y. Deli - Dine in or takeout. Challah, wine,
large selection of kosher grocery items -
refrigerated/frozen/dry. Under strict rabbinical
supervision. Hours: Monday to Thursday, 10 am to 7
pm; Friday and Sunday, 10am to 3 pm. We also
deliver to Hotels.

Groceries
Casablanca
3030 Seven Avenue, Metrairie 70002-4826
                                       (504) 888-2209
Touro Infirmary
1401 Foucher Street 70115   (504) 897-8246
Glatt kosher meals available

Hotels
The Pontchartrain Grand Heritage Hotel
2031 St Charles Avenue 70140   (800) 777-6193
                                 Fax: (800) 529-1165
Kosher food available on request.

Media

Newspapers
The Jewish News
3500 N. Causeway Blvd, #1240, Metairie 70002
                                       (504) 828-2125
                                 Fax: (504) 828-2827
                     Email: jewishnews@jewishnola.com

Mikvaot
Beth Israel
7000 Canal Blvd 70124   (504) 283-4366

Organisations
Jewish Federation of Greater New Orleans
3500 N. Causeway Blvd., #1240, Metairie 70002
                                       (504) 828-2125
                                 Fax: (504) 828-2827

Restaurants

Meat
Casablanca, 3030 Severn Avenue, Metair
                                       (504) 888-2209
                                 Fax: (504) 888-5605
Supervision: Lubavitch Shechita & Chabad Sup..

Synagogues

Orthodox
Anshe Sfard
2230 Carondelet Street 70130   (504) 422-4714

Shreveport

Community Organisations
Jewish Federation
2032 Line Avenue 71104   (318) 221-4129

Synagogues

Conservative
Agudath Achim
9401 Village Green Drive 71115   (318) 797-6401
                                 Fax: (318) 797-6402

Reform
B'nai Zion
245 Southfield Road 71105   (318) 861-2122

Maine

Auburn

Synagogues

Conservative

Congregation Beth Abraham
Main Street & Laurel Avenue 4210   (207) 783-1302
Temple Shalom
74 Bradman Street 4210   (207) 786-4201
Fax: (207) 786-4202
Email: temple6359@aol.com

Bangor

Restaurants

Bagel Central
33 Central Street 4401   (207) 947-1654
Supervision: Beth Abraham Rabbi Boaz Tomsky.

Synagogues

Conservative

Congregation Beth Israel
144 York Street 4401   (207) 945-3433
Fax: (207) 945-3840

Orthodox

Beth Abraham
145 York Street 4401   (207) 947-0876

Lewiston

Community Organisations

Lewiston-Auburn Jewish Federation
74 Bradman Street 4210   (207) 786-4201
Fax: (207) 786-4202
Email: temple6359@aol.com

Old Orchard Beach

Kashrut Information

Eber Weinstein
187 E. Grand Avenue 4064   (207) 934-7522
Eddie Hakim   (207) 934-7223
Harold Goodkovski

(207) 934-4210

Synagogues

Orthodox

Beth Israel
49 E. Grand Avenue 4064   (207) 934-2973
Fax: (207) 934-5800
Daily minyan, May 28 to Yom Kippur, Shabbat & Yom Tov minyan all year round.

Portland

Butchers

Penny Wise Super Market
182 Ocean Avenue 4130
Take-out counter at a local supermarket.

Mikvaot

Shaarey Tphiloh
76 Noyes Street 4103

Organisations

Jewish Fed.-Com. Council of Southern Maine
57 Ashmont Street 4103   (207) 773-7254

Synagogues

Conservative

Temple Beth El
400 Deering Avenue 4103   (207) 774-2649
Fax: (207) 774-7518
Email: office@templebethel-maine.org
U.S.C.J.

Orthodox

Etz Chaim
267 Congress Street 4101
Shaarey Tphiloh
76 Noyes Street 4103
Mikvah & Hebrew Day School on premises.

Maryland

Bethesda, Bowie, Chevy Chase, Gaithersburg, Greenbelt, Hyattsville, Kensington, Laurel, Lexington Park, Olney, Potomac, Rockville, Silver Spring & Wheaton and Temple Hills are all part of Greater Washington, DC.

Annapolis

Synagogues

Conservative

Congregation Kol Ami
1909 Hidden Meadow Lane 21401   (410) 266-6006
Email: kolami2@toadmail.toad.net

Reform

Temple Beth Shalom
1461 Baltimore-Anaapolis Blvd., 21012

Baltimore

There are more than 50 synagogues in the Baltimore metropolitan area. Visitors are advised to contact one of the community organisations in the area to find the synagogue nearest them.

United States of America / Maryland

Bakeries

Dunkin Donuts
1508 Reisterstown Road 21208   (410) 653-8182
Supervision: Rabbi Salfer.

Goldman's Kosher Bakery
6848 Reistertown Road, Farstaff Shopping Center
21215   (410) 358-9625
Fax: (410) 358-5859
Email: mcohn@home.com
Star-K Certified.

Pariser's Kosher Bakery
6711 Reistertown Road 21215   (410) 764-1700

Schmell & Azman Kosher Bakery
21215   (410) 484-7343

Schmell-Azman
7006 Reisterstown Road 21215   (410) 484-7373
Supervision: Star K.

Butchers

Seven Mile Market
4000 Seven Mile Lane 20208   (410) 653-2000

Wasserman & Lemberger
7006-D Reisterstown Road 20208   (410) 486-4191

Communal Information

Jewish Information Service
5750 Park Heights Avenue 21215   (410) 466-4636
Fax: (410) 664-0551
Email: jfs@jfs.org
Open daily from 9am to 2.0pm for help on almost anything.

Community Organisations

Associated Jewish Community Federation of Baltimore
101 W. Mount Royal Avenue 21201   (410) 727-4828

Delicatessens

Knish Shop
508 Reisterstown Road 21208   (410) 484-5850
Conservative supervision

Liebes Kosher Deli Carry Out
607 Reistertown Road 21208   (410) 653-1977
Only glatt kosher meats. Hours: Sunday to Wednesday, 8:30am to 6pm; Thursday, late night Friday, to 1 hour before sundown. Specializing in party trays.

Groceries

Seven Mile Market
4000 Seven Mile Lane, Pikesville 21208
(410) 653-2000

Shlomo Meat & Fish
506 Reisterstown Road 21208   (410) 602-7888

Wasserman & Lemberger
7006-D Reistertown Road 21208   (410) 486-4191

Kashrut Information

Star-K Kosher Certification
11 Warren Road 21208   (410) 484-4110
Fax: (410) 653-9294
Email: stark11@aol.com
Web site: www.star-k.org
Also issues Worldwide Kashrut Certification

Mikvaot

Mikva of Baltimore Inc.,
3207 Clarks Lane 21215   (410) 764-1448
Fax: (410) 578-0018

Museums

The Jewish Museum of Maryland
15 Lloyd Street 21202   (410) 732-6400
Fax: (410) 732-6451
Email: info@jewishmuseummd.org
This newly-enlarged complex of museum buildings is unlike anything else in the United States, comprising two historic synagogues (Lloyd Street Synagogue, built in 1845, and B'nai Israel, built in 1876) and an adjoining research center and museum featuring changing exhibits and regional Judaica.Opening hours: Tuesday, Wednesday, Thursday and Sunday 12-4 pm.

Organisations

The Baltimore Jewish Council
Gay & Water Sts.,

The Jewish Museum of Maryland
15 Lloyd Street 21202   (410) 732-6400
Fax: (410) 732-6451
Email: info@jhsm.org
Open: Tuesday, Wednesday, Thursday and Sunday 12-4.00pm

Restaurant

Brasserie
Pomona Square Shopping Centre
1700 Reisterstown Road

Caramel's Pizza & Ice Cream
700 Reisterstown Road   (410) 486-2365
Star-K supervision

Goldberg's Bagels
708 Reisterstown Road   (410) 415-7001
Star-K supervision

Krispy Kremes
10021 Reisterstown Road (nr. Painters Mill Rd).
(410) 356-2655
Star-KD supervision

Mama Leah's Pizza
604 Reisterstown Road   (410) 653-7600
Star-K supervision

Dairy

Milk and Honey Bistro
Commercecentre, 1777 Reisterstown Road
(410) 484-3544
Supervision: Star K.

I Can't Believe It's Yogurt
1430 Reisterstown Road   (410) 484-4411
Supervision: Rabbi Salfer.

Meat

Kosher Bite
6309 Reistertown Road 21215   (410) 358-6349
Supervision: Star K.
Royal Restaurant
7006 Reistertown Road 21208   (410) 484-3544
Supervision: Star K.
The Brasserie
Pomona Square Shopping Center,
1700 Reistertown Rd., 21208   (410) 484-0476
Supervision: Star K.

Pizzerias

Tov Pizza
6313 Reistertown Road 21215   (301) 358-5238
Supervision: Kof-K.

Supermarket

Seven Mile Market
4000 Seven Mile Lane 21208
(410) 653-2000; 2002
Supervision: Star K.
Items sold in the Fresh Meat, Fresh Fish, Fresh Bakery, Fresh Deli, Fresh Dairy, Hot Prepared Foods & Salad Departments are approved by the Vaad Hakashrus Of Baltimore, when so stated on sign or label.

Tours of Jewish Interest

Holocaust Memorial
Gay & Lombard Sts.   (410) 542-4850
Fax: (410) 542-4834
Email: mtishler@aea-bal.tjc.org

Bethesda

Organisations

United Jewish Appeal Federation of Greater Washington
7900 Wisconsin Avenue 20814   (301) 652-6480

Bowie

Synagogues

Conservative

Nevey Shalom
12218 Torah Lane 20715   (301) 262-4020

Reform

Temple Solel
2901 Mitchelville Road 20716   (301) 249-2424

Chevy Chase

Synagogues

Conservative

Ohr Kodesh
8402 Freyman Drive 20815   (301) 589-3880
Fax: (301) 495-4801
Email: okcjmm@erols.com

Reform

Temple Shalom
8401 Grubb Road 20815   (301) 587-2273

College Park

Libraries
The National Archives
8601 Adelphi Road 20740
Containing historical Jewish documentation

Cumberland

Synagogues

Conservative

Beth Jacob
1 Columbia Street 21502   (301) 777-3717

Reform

B'Er Chayim
107 Union Street 21502   (301) 722-5688

Gaithersburg

Synagogues

Conservative

Kehilat Shalom
9915 Apple Ridge Road 20886   (301) 869-7699
Fax: (301) 977-7870
Email: mail@kehilatshalom.org
Web site: www.kehilatshalom.org

Greenbelt

Synagogues
Mishkan Torah
Westway and Ridge Road 20770   (301) 474-4223

Hagerstown

Delicatessens
Celebrity Deli
6700 Adelphi Road 20782   (301) 927-5525

United States of America / Maryland

Synagogues

Reform

B'nai Abraham
53 E. Baltimore Street 21740   (301) 733-5039

Hyattsville

Synagogues

Conservative

Beth Torah Congregation
6700 Adelphi Road 20782   (301) 927-5525

Kensington

Synagogues

Reform

Temple Emanuel
10101 Connecticut Avenue 20895   (301) 942-2000
     Fax: (301) 942-9488

Laurel

Synagogues

Reconstructionist

Oseh Shalom
8604 Briarwood Drive 20708   (301) 498-5151

Lexington Park

Synagogues

Conservative

Beth Israel
Bunker Hill Drive 20650   (301) 862-2021

Olney

Synagogues
B'nai Shalom
18401 Burtfield Drive 20832   (301) 774-0879

Pocomoke

Synagogues
Temple Israel
3rd Street 21851

Potomac

Restaurants

Meat

Hunan Gourmet
350 Fortune Terrace   (301) 424-0191

Synagogues

Conservative

Har Shalom
11510 Falls Road 20854   (301) 299-7087

Orthodox

Beth Sholom of Potomac
11825 Seven Locks Road 20854   (301) 279-7010
Young Israel of Ezras Israel of Potomac
11618 Seven Locks Road 20854   (301) 299-2827

Rockville

Groceries
Katz Supermarket
4860 Boiling Brook Parkway   (301) 468-0400

Restaurants

Meat

Moshe Dragon Glatt Kosher Chinese Restaurant
4840 Boiling Brook Parkway   (301) 468-1922
Royal Dragon, 4840 Boiling Brook Parkway
     (301) 468-1922

Meat and Dairy

Kat'z Kafe, 4860 Boiling Brook Parkway
     (301) 468-0400

Synagogues

Conservative

B'nai Israel
6301 Montrose Road 20852   (301) 881-6550
Tikvat Israel
2200 Baltimore Road 20853   (301) 762-7338
     Fax: (301) 424-4399

Orthodox

Magen David Sephardic Congregation
11215 Woodglen Drive, Rockville, MD 20852
     (301) 770-6818
     Fax: (301) 881-0498

Reform

Temple Beth Ami
800 Hurley Avenue 20850   (301) 340-6818

Salisbury

Synagogues

Conservative

Beth Israel
Camden Avenue & Wicomico Street 21801
     (410) 742-2564

Silver Spring

Groceries

Shalom Meat Market
2307 University Blvd West   (301) 946-6500

Synagogues

Orthodox

Woodside Synagogue Ahavas Torah
9001 Georgia Avenue 20910   (301) 587-8252
    Web site: www.wsat.org
Hospitality - (301) 585-8080

Silver Spring & Wheaton

Bakeries

The Wooden Shoe Pastry Shop
11301 Georgia Avenue 20902
Virtuoso
11230a Lockwood Avenue 50901   (301) 593-6034
Wooden Shoe Bakery
    (301) 942-9330

Booksellers

Lisbon's Hebrew Books & Gifts
2305 University Blvd West 20902   (301) 933-1800
    Fax: (301) 933-7466
    Email: slisbon@idsonline.com
The Jewish Bookstore
11252 Georgia Avenue 20902   (301) 942-2237
    Fax: (301) 933-5464

Delicatessens

Shalom
2307 University Blvd 20902

Groceries

Shaul & Hershel Meat Market
    (301) 949-8477

Guest Houses

Hebrew Sheltering Society
11524 Daffodil Lane 20902
    (301) 649-3141; 649-4425; 649-2799
For people unable to afford accommodation, will get 3
free nights stay at the shelter.

Mikvaot

Mikva
8901 Georgia Avenue 20910
    (301) 565-3737

Restaurants

Dairy

The Nut House
11419 Georgia Avenue 20902   (301) 942-5900

Synagogues

Conservative

Har Tzeon-Agudath Achim
1840 University Blvd. W 20902
Shaare Tefila
11120 Lockwood Drive 20901   (301) 593-3410
    Fax: (301) 593-3860
    Email: stefila@capaccess.org
Temple Israel
420 University Blvd. E 20901   (301) 439-3600

Orthodox

Silver Spring Jewish Center
1401 Arcola Avenue 20902   (301) 649-4425
    Fax: (301) 649-1274
South-East Hebrew Congregation
10900 Lockwood Drive 20902
Young Israel of White Oak
PO Box 10613
White Oak 20914   (301) 369-1531
Young Israel Shomrai Emunah of Greater Washington
1132 Arcola Avenue 20902   (301) 593-4465

Temple Hills

Synagogues

Conservative

Shaare Tikva
5405 Old Temple Hills Road 20748   (301) 894-4303

Massachusetts

Acton

Synagogues

Independent

Beth Elohim
10 Hennessy Drive 7120   (978) 263-8610

Amherst

Synagogues

Jewish Community
742 Main Street 1002   (413) 256-0160
    Fax: (413) 256-1588
    Web site: www.j-c-a.org

Andover

Synagogues

Reform

Temple Emanuel
7 Haggett's Pond Road 1810   (978) 470-1563

United States of America / Massachusetts

Arlington

Bakeries
Dough-C-Donuts
1460 Massachusetts Avenue 2174   (617) 643-4550
Supervision: Vaad Harabonim of Massachusetts.

Athol

Synagogues

Conservative

Temple Israel
107 Walnut Street 1331   (978) 249-9481

Attleboro

Synagogues

Reconstructionist

Agudas Achim Congregation
901 N. Main Street 2703   (508) 222-2243
                  Email: agudasachim@netzero.net
             Web site: www.shamash.org/jrf/agudasma

Ayer

Synagogues

Independent

Congregation Anshey Sholom
Cambridge Street 1432   (508) 772-0896

Belmont

Synagogues

Reform

Beth El Temple Center
2 Concord Avenue 2478   (617) 484-6668
                             Fax: (617) 484-6020
                  Web site: www.uahc.org/ma/betc

Beverly

Synagogues

Conservative

B'nai Abraham
200 E. Lothrop Street 1915   (978) 927-3211

Boston (Greater Boston)

Embassy
Consul General of Israel
1020 Statler Office Blvd 2116

Kashrut Information
Synagogue Council of Massachusetts
1320 Centre Street, Newton Centre 02459-2400
                                    (617) 244-6506
                             Fax: (617) 964-7055
                  Email: syncouncil@aol.com.

The Kashruth Commission
177 Tremont Street 2111   (617) 426-2139
                             Fax: (617) 426-6268
                  Email: kvh613@aol.com

Vaad Harabonim of Massachusetts
177 Tremont Street 2111   (617) 426-2139
                             Fax: (617) 426-6268

Media

Directories

Synagogue Council of Massachusetts
1320 Centre Street, Newton Centre 02459-2400
                                    (617) 244-6506
                             Fax: (617) 964-7055
                  Email: syncouncil@aol.com.

Guides

Jewish Guide to Boston and New England
15 School Street 2108   (617) 267-9100
                             Fax: (617) 267-9310

Newspapers

Boston Jewish Times
15 School Street 2108   (617) 267-9100
                             Fax: (617) 367-9310

The Jewish Advocate
15 School Street 2108   (617) 367-9100
                             Fax: (617) 367-9310
                  Email: thejewadv@aol.com
             Web site: www.thejewishadvocate.com

Mikvaot
Daughters of Israel
101 Washington Street, Brighton 2135
                                    (617) 782-9433

Organisations
Jewish Community Relations Council of Greater Boston
1 Lincoln Plaza, Suite 308 2111   (617) 330-9600
Represents 34 community organisations in the area.

Religious Organisations
Rabbinical Council of New England
177 Tremont Street 2111   (617) 426-2139
                             Fax: (617) 426-6268

Rabbinical Court
177 Tremont Street 2111   (617) 426-2139
                             Fax: (617) 426-6268

Restaurants

Dairy

Milk Street Cafe
The Park at Post Office Square, Zero Post Office Square
(617) 350-PARK
Supervision: Orthodox Rabbinic Council of Greater
Boston.
Dairy foods and sealed meat sandwiches from meat
corporate catering kitchens. In the summer, 4 carts in
the park with hot dogs and BBQ beef; deli wraps and
sandwiches; Italian specialties – pizza and calzone; and
ice cream and frozen desserts.
Milk Street Cafe
50 Milk Street
(617) 542-FOOD
Fax: (617) 451-5FAX
Supervision: Orthodox Rabbinic Council of Greater
Boston.
Hours: Monday to Friday, 7 am to 3 pm.

Meat

B.U. Hillel
233 Bay State Road 2215   (617) 353-3663
Supervision: Vaad Harabonim of Massachusetts.
Hillel Foundation
Boston University, 233 Bay State Road 02215-1499
(617) 353-7200
Fax: (617) 353-7660
Supervision: Rabbi Joseph Polak and Vaad HaRabonim
of Massachusetts.
Hours: 11:30 am to 1:15 pm; 5 to 7 pm. Shabbat
meals need to be pre-paid. For information: 353-2947.
Rubin's Kosher Deli and Restaurant
500 Harvard Street, Brookline 2146   (617) 731-8787

Synagogues

Conservative

Hillel B'nai Torah
120 Corey St, W. Roxbury 2132   (617) 323-0486
Temple B'nai Moshe
1845 Commonwealth Avenue, Brighton 2135
(617) 254-3620

Orthodox

Chabad House
491 Commonwealth Avenue 2215   (617) 424-1190
Fax: (617) 266-5997
Congregation Kadimah-Toras Moshe
113 Washington Street, Brighton 2135
(617) 254-1333
Lubavitch Shul of Brighton
239 Chestnut Hill Avenue, Brighton 2135
(617) 782-8340

The Boston Synagogue
(at Charles River Park), 55 Martha Road 2114
(617) 523-0453
Fax: (617) 723-2863
Administrator: Rebecca Sussman. Services: Fri evening
Sat 9.15am.
Zvhil-Mezbuz Beis Medrash
15 School Street 2108
(617) 227-8200
Fax: (617) 227-8420
Web site: www.rebbe.org

Reform

Temple Israel
Longwood Ave & Plymouth Street 2215
(617) 566-3960
Fax: (617) 731-3711
Web site: www.tisrael.org

Tours of Jewish Interest
BostonWalks and The Jewish Friendship Trail
(617) 489-5020
Email: rossocp@gis.net

Braintree

Bakeries
Sara's Kitchen
South Shore Plaza 1501   (617) 843-8803
Supervision: Vaad Harabonim of Massachusetts.

Synagogues

Conservative

Temple Bnai Shalom
41 Storrs Avenue 2184   (781) 843-3687

Bridgewater

Bakeries
J & E Baking Company
10 Bedford Park, Unit #5 2324   (508) 279-0990
Supervision: Vaad Harabonim of Massachusetts.
Shomer Shabbat.

Brighton

Restaurants
B-B-N J.C.C. Dining Hall
50 Sutherland Road 2146   (617) 278-2950
Supervision: Vaad Harabonim of Massachusetts.
J.C.H.E. Dining Hall
30 Wallingford Road 2146   (617) 254-9001
Supervision: Vaad Harabonim of Massachusetts.

Brockton

Synagogues

Conservative

Temple, 479 Torres Street 2401   (508) 583-5810

Orthodox

Agudath Achim
144 Belmont Avenue 2401   (508) 583-0717

Reform

Temple Israel
184 W. Elm Street 2401   (508) 587-4130

Brookline

Bakeries

Catering by Andrew
402 Harvard Street 2446   (617) 731-6585
   Fax: (617) 232-3788
   Email: cbandrew@aol.com
Supervision: Vaad Harabonim of Massachusetts.
Shomer Shabbat.

Taam Tov Bakery
305A Harvard Street 2146   (617) 566-8136
Supervision: Vaad Harabonim of Massachusetts.
Shomer Shabbat. Pareve.

Kashrut Information

Jewish Commercial Center
Harvard Street
Harvard Street is the Jewish commercial Center, with
art & bookshops, as well as many kosher butcher's
shops and bakeries.

Restaurants

Meat

Cafe Shiraz
1030 Commonwealth Avenue 2215
   (617) 566-8888
New private function rooms for group parties. Glatt
kosher Persian and Middle Eastern cuisine. Wheelchair
accessible. Hours: Monday to Thursday, 5 pm to 10
pm; Saturday, 45 minutes after sundown to midnight;
Sunday, 4 pm to 10 pm.

Rami's
324 Harvard Street 2146   (617) 738-3577
Supervision: Vaad Harabonim of Massachusetts.
Glatt kosher.

Rubin's
500 Harvard Street 2146   (617) 566-8761
Supervision: Vaad Harabonim of Massachusetts.
Glatt kosher.

Ruth's Kitchen
401 Harvard Street   (617) 734-9810

Shalom Hunan
92 Harvard Street 2146   (617) 731-9760
Supervision: Vaad Harabonim of Massachusetts.
Glatt kosher.

Pizzerias

Victor's Pizza
1364 Beacon Street 2146   (617) 730-9903

Synagogues

Conservative

Kehillath Israel
384 Harvard St 2146   (617) 277-9155

Orthodox

Beth David
64 Corey Road 2146   (617) 232-2349

Beth Pinchas (Bostoner Rebbe)
1710 Beacon Street 2146   (617) 734-5100
   Fax: (617) 739-0163
   Email: rofeh@world.std.com

Chai Odom
77 Englewood Av 2146   (617) 734-5359

Congregation Lubavitch
100 Woodcliff Road 2167   (617) 469-0088
   Fax: (617) 469-0089

Young Israel of Brookline
62 Green Street 2446   (617) 734-0276
   Fax: (617) 734-8475
   Email: yibrookline@juno.com
   Web site: www.yibrookline.org

Reform

Ohabei Shalom
1187 Beacon St 2146   (617) 277-6610

Temple Sinai
50 Sewall Av, Coolidge Corner 2146
   (617) 277-5888

Sephardic

Sephardic Congregation
1566 Beacon St 2146   (617) 566-8171

Burlington

Synagogues

Reform

Temple Shalom Emeth
14-16 Lexington Street 1803   (781) 272-2351

Cambridge

Kashrut Information
Hillel House
Harvard University, 52 Mt. Auburn St 2138
(617) 495-4696
Fax: (617) 864-1637
Email: imulliga@camailz.harvard.edu
Kosher meals are obtainable, by previous arrangement.

Restaurants
Harvard Hillel Dining Hall
52 Mt. Auburn Street 2138
(617) 495-4695; 495-4696
Supervision: Vaad Harabonim of Massachusetts.
Dining Hall: 876-3535

Meat

M.I.T. Hillel
40 Massachusetts Avenue 2139
(617) 253-2982
Fax: (617) 253-3260
Email: hillel@mit.edu
Supervision: Vaad Harabonim of Massachusetts.

Synagogues

Conservative

Temple Beth Shalom of Cambridge
8 Tremont Street 2139
(617) 864-6388

Canton

Synagogues
Beth Abraham
1301 Washington Street 2021
(781) 828-5250

Reform

Temple Beth David of the South Shore
1060 Randolph Street 2021
(781) 828-2275
Fax: (781) 821-3997
Web site: www.templebethdavid.org

Cape Cod

Synagogues

Orthodox

Beth Israel
cnr. of Onset Avenue & Locust Street, PO Box 24,
Onset 2558
(508) 295-9185
Email: capeshul@att.net
Web site: www.home.att.net/capeshul
Services 3 times daily from last Sat. in June to Labour
Day. Services are also held on the Holy days.
Apartments available near synagogue. Further
information from Burt Parker.

Chelmsford

Synagogues

Reform

Congregation Shalom
Richardson Road 1824
(978) 251-8090

Chestnut Hill

Bakeries
Cheryl Ann's Bakery
1010 West Roxbury Parkway 2167
(617) 469-9241
Supervision: Vaad Harabonim of Massachusetts.

Clinton

Synagogues

Independent

Shaarei Zedeck
Water Street 1510
(978) 365-3320

East Dedham

Bakeries
Cookies Express
252 Bussey Street 2026
(617) 461-0044
Supervision: Vaad Harabonim of Massachusetts.
Shomer Shabbat.

East Falmouth

Synagogues

Reform

Falmouth Jewish Congregation
7 Hatchville Road 2536
(508) 540-5081

Easton

Synagogues

Traditional

Temple Chayai Shalom
238 Depot Street 2334
(508) 238-6385
Mail address: P.O.Box 404, N. Easton 02356

Everett

Synagogues
Tifereth Israel
34 Malden Street 2149
(617) 387-0200

Fall River

Organisations
Fall River Jewish Community Council
Room 327, 56 N. Main St., 2720
(508) 673-7791
Fax: (508) 673-7791

United States of America / Massachusetts

Synagogues

Conservative

Beth El, 385 High Street 2720   (508) 674-9761

Orthodox

Adas Israel
1647 Robeson Street 2720   (508) 674-9761
                         Fax: (508) 678-3195

Fitchburg

Synagogues

Independent

Agudas Achim
40 Boutelle Street 1420   (978) 342-7704

Framingham

Bakeries

Boston Cookie
Framingham Mall, Route 30 1701   (508) 872-1052
Supervision: Vaad Harabonim of Massachusetts.
Bread Basket Bakery
151 Cochituate Road 1701   (508) 875-9441
Supervision: Vaad Harabonim of Massachusetts.

Synagogues

Conservative

Beth Sholom
50 Pamela Road 1701   (508) 877-2540
                         Fax: (508) 877-8278

Orthodox

Chabad House
74 Joseph Road 1701   (508) 877-5313
                         Fax: (508) 877 5313

Reform

Beth Am, 300 Pleasant Street 1701   (508) 872-8300
                         Fax: (508) 872-9773
             Email: tempbetham@aol.com

Gloucester

Synagogues

Conservative

Ahavat Achim
86 Middle Street 1930   (978) 281-0739
                         Fax: (978) 281-0739

Greenfield

Synagogues
Temple Israel
27 Pierce Street 1301   (413) 773-5884

Haverhill

Synagogues

Orthodox

Anshe Sholom
427 Main Street 1830   (508) 372-2276

Reform

Temple Emanu-El
514 Main Street 1830   (508) 373-3861

Hingham

Synagogues
Congregation Sha'aray Shalom
112 Main Street 2043   (781) 749-8103

Holbrook

Synagogues

Conservative

Temple Beth Shalom
95 Plymouth Street 2343   (617) 767-4922

Holliston

Synagogues
Temple Beth Torah
2162 Washington Street 1746   (508) 429-6268

Holyoke

Synagogues
Sons of Zion
378 Maple Street 1040   (413) 534-3369

Orthodox

Rodphey Sholom
1800 Northampton Street 1040   (413) 534-5262

Hull

Synagogues

Conservative

Temple Beth Sholom
600 Nantasket Avenue 2045   (781) 925-0091
                         Fax: (781) 925-9053

Temple Israel of Nantasket
9 Hadassah Way 2045   (617) 925-0289
Summer only.

Hyannis

Synagogues

Reform

Cape Cod Synagogue
145 Winter Street 2601   (508) 775-2988

Hyde Park

Synagogues

Conservative

Temple Adas Hadrath Israel
28 Arlington Street 2136   (617) 364-2661

Lawrence

Organisations

Jewish Com. Council of Greater Lawrence
580 Haverhill Street 1841   (617) 686-4157

Synagogues

Orthodox

Anshai Sholum
411 Hampshire Street 1843   (508) 683-4544

Leominster

Synagogues

Conservative

Congregation Agudat Achim
268 Washington Street 1453   (508) 534-6121

Lexington

Synagogues

Temple Emunah
9 Piper Road 2421   (781) 861-0300
                               Fax: (781) 861-7141
                  Email: rholmes@emunahlex.org
                  Web site: www.templeemunah.org

Orthodox

Chabad Center
9 Burlington Street 2173   (781) 863-8656

Reform

Temple Isaiah
55 Lincoln Street 2173   (781) 862-7160

Lowell

Bakeries

Donut Shak, 487 Westford Street   (508) 937-0178
Supervision: Vaad Harabonim of Massachusetts.

Bed & Breakfasts

The Very Victorian Sherman-Berry House
c/o Montefiore Synagogue, 48 Academy Drive
                                           (508) 970-2008

Mikvaot

Mikvah
48 Academy Drive   (508) 970-2008

Synagogues

Conservative

Temple Beth El
105 Princeton Blvd. 1851   (508) 453-7744

Orthodox

Montefiore Synagogue
460 Westford Street 1851   (978) 459-9400

Reform

Temple Emanuel of Merrimack Valley
101 W. Forest Street 1851   (508) 454-1372

Lynn

Synagogues

Orthodox

Ahabat Shalom
151 Ocean Street 1902   (617) 593-9255
Houses the Eliot Feuerstein Library.
Anshai Sfard
150 S. Common Street 1905   (617) 599-7131
Chevra Tehilim
12 Breed Street 1902   (617) 598-2964

Malden

Bakeries

Brick Oven Bakery
237 Ferry Street 2148   (781) 322-3269
Supervision: Vaad Harabonim of Massachusetts.

Synagogues

Conservative

Ezrath Israel
245 Bryant Street 2148   (617) 322-7205

Orthodox

Congregation Beth Israel
10 Dexter Street 2148
                                           (781) 322-5686
                               Fax: (781) 322-6678
                  Email: congbi@aol.com

Young Israel of Malden
45 Holyoke Street 2148   (617) 961-9817

United States of America / Massachusetts

Reform

Tifereth Israel
539 Salem Street 2148   (617) 322-2794

Traditional

Agudas Achim
160 Harvard Street 2148   (781) 322-9380

Marblehead

Community Organisations
Jewish Federation of the North Shore
4 Community Road 1945   (781)-598-1810
                                      Fax: (978)-745-4222
                                      Email: mail@jfns.org

Synagogues

Conservative/Masorti

Temple Sinai
1 Community Road 1945   (781) 631-2244
                                      Fax: (781) 631-2244
                                      Email: rbyona@mediaone.net

Orthodox

Orthodox Congregation of the North Shore
4 Community Road 1945   (617) 598-1810

Reform

Temple Emanu-El
393 Atlantic Avenue 1945   (617) 631-9300

Marlboro

Synagogues

Conservative

Temple Emanuel
150 Berlin Road 1752
                         (508) 485-7565; 508-562-5105

Medford

Bakeries
Donuts with a Difference
35 Riverside Avenue 2155   (781) 396-1021
Supervision: Vaad Harabonim of Massachusetts.

Restaurants
Tufts Hillel
474 Boston Avenue 2155   (781) 627-3242
Supervision: Vaad Harabonim of Massachusetts.

Synagogues

Conservative

Temple Shalom
475 Winthrop Street 2155   (781) 396-3262

Melrose

Synagogues

Reform

Temple Beth Shalom
21 E. Foster Street 2176   (617) 665-4520

Milford

Synagogues

Conservative

Beth Shalom
55 Pine Street 1757   (508) 473-1590

Millis

Synagogues
Ael Chunon
334 Village Street 2054   (508) 376-5984

Milton

Synagogues
Temple Shalom
180 Blue Hill Avenue 2186   (617) 698-3394

Orthodox

B'nai Jacob
100 Blue Hill Parkway 2187   (617) 698-0698

Natick

Synagogues

Conservative

Temple Israel
145 Hartford Street 1760   (508) 650-3521
                                      Fax: (508) 655-3440
                                Email: tiofnatick@aol.com

Orthodox

Chabad Lubavitch Center
2 East Mill Street 1760   (508) 650-1499

Needham

Synagogues

Conservative

Temple Aliyah
1664 Central Avenue 2492   (781) 444-8522
                                      Fax: (781) 449-7066

Reform

Temple Beth Shalom
670 Highland Avenue 2494   (781) 444-0077
                                      Fax: (781) 449-3274
                                Email: tbshalom@fcl-us.net

New Bedford

Organisations

Jewish Federation of Greater New Bedford
467 Hawthorn Street, N. Dartmouth 2747
(508) 997-7471

Synagogues

Conservative

Tifereth Israel
145 Brownell Avenue 2740
(508) 997-3171
Fax: (508) 997-3173

Orthodox

Ahavath Achim
385 County Street 2740
(508) 994-1760
Fax: (508) 994-8186
Email: rabbibarry@aol.com
Web site: www.members.aol.com/rabbibarry

Newburyport

Synagogues
Congregation Ahavas Achim
Washington & Olive Streets 9150
(508) 462-2461

Newton

Bakeries
Lederman's Bakery
1223 Centre Street 2159
(617) 527-7896
Supervision: Vaad Harabonim of Massachusetts.
Tuler's Bakery
551 Commonwealth Avenue 2159
(617) 964-5653
Supervision: Vaad Harabonim of Massachusetts.
Pareve. Shomer Shabbat.

Cafeterias
Orthodox Rabbinical Council of Massachusetts
(617) 558-6475
Provides snack bar for Jewish Community Center of
Greater Boston.

Organisations
Jewish Community Center of Greater Boston
333 Nahanton Street 2159
(617) 558-6522
Kosher snack bar provided. See below.
Synagogue Council of Massachusetts
1320 Centre Street, Suite 306 Newton Center 2459
(617) 244-6506
Fax: (617) 964-7055
Email: syncouncil@aol.com

Restaurants
Golda Meir House
160 Stanton Avenue, Dining Hall 2166
(617) 969-1764
Supervision: Vaad Harabonim of Massachusetts.
Kitchen: 965-0770

Dairy
J.C.C. Campus Snack Bar
333 Nahanton Street 2159
(617) 965-7410
Supervision: Vaad Harabonim of Massachusetts.

Synagogues

Orthodox
Congregation B'nai Jacob (Zvhil-Mezbuz Rebbe)
955 Beacon Street
(617) 227-8200
Fax: (617) 227-8420
Web site: www.rebbe.org

North Adams

Synagogues

Conservative

Congregation Beth Israel
265 Church Street 1247
(413) 663-5830
Fax: (413) 663-5830
Email: cbi@bcn.net

Northampton

Synagogues
B'nai Israel
253 Prospect Road 1060
(413) 584-3593

Norwood

Synagogues
Temple Shaare Tefilah
556 Nichols Street 2062
(781) 762-8670
Fax: (781) 762-8670

Onset

Hotels
Bridge View Hotel
12 S. Water Street 2558
(508) 295-9820
Welcomes Jewish guests. Self-catering flatlets available.
Kosher meat and other products available.

Peabody

Bakeries
Anthony's Bakery
4 Lake Street 1906
(508) 535-5335
Supervision: Vaad Harabonim of Massachusetts.

United States of America / Massachusetts

Synagogues

Conservative

Temple Ner Tamid
368 Lowell Street 1960   (978) 532-1293
        Fax: (978) 532-0101
Conservative (United Synagogue)

Independent

Congregation Tifereth Israel
Pierpont Street 1960   (508) 531-8135

Reform

Beth Shalom
489 Lowell Street 1960   (978) 535-2100
        Fax: (978) 536-3115

Traditional

Congregation Sons of Israel
Park & Spring Streets 1960   (508) 531-7576

Pittsfield (Berkshires)

Organisations
Jewish Federation of the Berkshires
235 East Street 1201   (413) 442-4360

Plymouth

Synagogues

Reform

Congregation Beth Jacob
Synagogue on Pleasant Street, Community Center on
Court Street, P O Box 3284 2361
        (508) 746-1575
     Email: cbethjacob@juno.com

Quincy

Synagogues

Conservative

Adas Shalom
435 Adams Street 2169   (617) 471-1818
     Email: adasshalom@aol.com

Temple Beth El
1001 Hancock Street 2169   (617) 479-4309

Orthodox

Beth Israel
33 Grafton Street 2169   (617) 472-6796

Randolph

Bakeries
Zeppy's Bakery
937 North Main Street 2368   (617) 963-9837
Supervision: Vaad Harabonim of Massachusetts.

Booksellers
Davidson's Hebrew Book Store
1106 Main Street 2368   (781) 961-4929

Synagogues

Conservative

Temple Beth Am
871 N. Main Street 2368   (617) 963-0440

Orthodox

Young Israel - Kehillath Jacob of Mattapan & Randolph
374 N. Main Street 02368-6461
        (781) 986-6461
     Email: yikjrand@juno.com

Revere

Delicatessens
Myer's Kosher Kitchen
168 Shirley Avenue 2151

Restaurants
Chelsea-Revere J.C.C.
65 Nahant Avenue 2151   (617) 584-8395
Supervision: Vaad Harabonim of Massachusetts.

Synagogues

Independent

Temple B'nai Israel
1 Wave Avenue 2151   (781) 284-8388

Orthodox

Ahavas Achim Anshei Sfard
89 Walnut Way 2151   (617) 289-1026
Tifereth Israel
43 Nahant Avenue 2151   (617) 284-9255

Salem

Synagogues

Conservative

Temple Shalom
287 Lafayette Street 1970   (508) 741-4880

Sharon

Bed & Breakfasts
Sharon Woods Inn
80 Brook Road 2067   (781) 784-9401
        Fax: (781) 784-5162
     Email: kctova@yahoo.com

Mikvaot

Young Israel of Sharon
9 Dunbar Street 2067   (781) 784-6112
Operated by the Mikvah Organisation of the South
Shore, Chevrat Nashim Mikvah

Religious Organisations

Eruv Society   (614) 784-6112
Eruv maintained by Sharon County Eruv Society

Synagogues

Conservative

Adath Sharon
18 Harding Street 2067   (617) 784-2517
Temple Israel
125 Pond Street 2067   (781) 784-3986
                              Fax: (781) 784-0719

Orthodox

Chabad Center
101 Worcester Road 2067   (617) 784-8167
Young Israel of Sharon
9 Dunbar Street 2067   (617) 784-6112/5391

Reform

Temple Sinai
100 Ames Street 2067   (617) 784-6081

Somerville

Bakeries
La Ronga
599 Somerville Avenue 2143
                              (617) 625-8600
Supervision: Vaad Harabonim of Massachusetts.
Pareve. Bread and rolls with KVH emblem only.

Synagogues

Independent

B'nai B'rith of Somerville
201 Central Street 2145   (617) 625-0333

Springfield

Synagogues

Conservative

Temple Beth El
979 Dickinson Street 1108   (413) 733-4149
                              Fax: (413) 739-3415
                        Email: russ979@aol.com
Daily a.m. and p.m. services.

Springfield & Longmeadow

Groceries
Waldbaum's Food Mart
355 Belmont Avenue 1108   (413) 732-3866

Mikvaot
Mikveh Association
1104 Converse, Long. MA 1106   (413) 567-1607

Organisations
Jewish Community Center
1160 Dickinson Street 1108   (413) 739-4715
                              Fax: (413) 739-4747
Kosher Coffee Corner.
Jewish Federation of Greater Springfield
1160 Dickinson Street 1108   (413) 737-4313

Synagogues

Conservative

B'nai Jacob
2 Eunice Dr, Longmeadow 1106   (413) 567-3163

Orthodox

Beth Israel
1280 Williams St, Longmeadow 1106
                              (413) 567-3210
Congregation Kodimoh
124 Summer Avenue 1108   (413) 781-0171
The largest Orthodox congregation in New England.
Kesser Israel
19 Oakland Street 1108   (413) 732-8492
Lubavitcher Yeshiva Synagogue
1148 Converse St, Longmeadow 1106
                              (413) 567-8665

Reform

Temple Sinai
1100 Dickinson Street 1108   (413) 736-3619

Stoughton

Bakeries
Green Manor
31 Tosca Drive 2072   (617) 828-3018
Supervision: Vaad Harabonim of Massachusetts.
Shomer Shabbat.
Ruth's Bake Shop
987 Central Street 2072   (781) 344-8993
Supervision: Vaad Harabonim of Massachusetts.

Restaurants

Dairy

Café Choopar Striar J.C.C.
445 Central Street 2072   (413) 341-2016
Supervision: Vaad Harabonim of Massachusetts.

United States of America / Massachusetts

Synagogues

Conservative

Adhavath Torah Congregation
1179 Central Street 2072   (781) 344-8733
         Fax: (781) 344-4315

Dairy

Striar Jewish Community Center on the Fireman Campus
445 Central Street 2072   (617) 341-2016

Sudbury

Synagogues

Independent

Congregation B'nai Torah
Woodside Road 1776   (508) 443-2082

Reform

Congregation Beth El
105 Hudson Road 1776   (978) 443-9622
         Fax: (978) 443-9629
Email: secretary@bethelsudbury.org
Web site: www.bethelsudbury.org

Swampscott

Bakeries
Newman's,
252 Humphrey Street 1901   (617) 592-1550
Supervision: Vaad Harabonim of Massachusetts.

Synagogues

Conservative

Beth El,
55 Atlantic Avenue 1907   (617) 599-8005
         Fax: (617) 599-1860

Temple Israel
837 Humphrey Street 1907   (781) 595-6635
         Fax: (781) 595-0033

Vineyard Haven

Synagogues
Martha's Vineyard Hebrew Center
Center Street 2568   (508) 693-0745

Wakefield

Synagogues

Conservative

Temple Emmanuel
120 Chestnut Street 1880   (781) 245-1886
     Web site: www.geocities.com/temple_emanuel

Waltham

Synagogues
American Jewish Historical Society
(Brandeis University campus)
2 Thornton Road 2154   (617) 891-8110
         Fax: (617) 899-9208

Conservative
Beth Israel
25 Harvard Street 2154   (617) 894-5146

Watertown

Bakeries
Tabrizi Bakery
56A Mt. Auburn Street 2172   (617) 926-0880
Supervision: Vaad Harabonim of Massachusetts.

Wayland

Synagogues

Reform
Templr Shir Tikva
141 Boston Post Road 1778   (508) 358-5312

Wellesley Hills

Synagogues
Beth Elohim
10 Bethel Road 2181   (617) 235-8419

Westboro

Synagogues
B'nai Shalom
117 E. Main Street, PO Box 1019 01581-6019
         (508) 366-7191

Westwood

Synagogues
Beth David
40 Pond Street 2090   (617) 769-5270

Winchester

Synagogues
Temple Shir Tikvah
PO Box 373 1890   (617) 792-1188

Winthrop

Bakeries
Fabiano Bakery
7 Somerset Avenue 2152   (617) 846-5946
Supervision: Vaad Harabonim of Massachusetts.

Synagogues

Orthodox

Tifereth Abraham
283 Shirley Street 2152   (617) 846-5063
Tifereth Israel
93 Veteran's Road 2152   (617) 846-1390

Worcester

Contact Information

Agudath Israel of America Hachnosas Orchim
Committee
69 S. Flagg Street 1602   (508) 754-3681
Contact Rabbi Reuven Fischer.
Rabbi Hershel Fogelman
22 Newton Avenue   (617) 752-5791
Visitors requiring information about kashrut, temporary
accommodation, etc., should contact Rabbi Fogelman.

Mikvaot

Mikva
Huntley Street 1602   (508) 755-1257

Organisations

Jewish Federation
633 Salisbury Street 1609   (508) 756-1543

Synagogues

Orthodox

Young Israel of Worcester
889 Pleasant Street 1602   (508) 754-3681

Michigan
Ann Arbor

Mikvaot

Chabad House Mikva
715 Hill Street 48104

Organisations

Jewish Federation/UJA
2939 Birch Hollow Drive 48108   (734) 679-0100
                                  Fax: (734) 679-0109
                                  Email: jccfed@aol.com

Synagogues

Orthodox

Ann Arbor Orthodox Minyan
1429 Hill Street 48104   (734) 994-5822

Benton Harbour (St Joseph)

Synagogues

Conservative

Temple B'nai Shalom
2050 Broadway 49022

Detroit

With tens of synagogues in the Bloomfield, Oak
Park and Southfield areas, visitors are
recommmended to contact one of the local
religious organisations listed for the nearest
synagogue.

Delicatessens

Sarah's Glatt Kosher Deli
15600 W. Ten Mile Road, Southfield 48075
                                  (313) 443-2425

Groceries

Sperber's Kosher Karry-Out
25250 W. Ten Mile Road, Oak Park 48237
                                  (313) 443-2425

Kashrut Information

Council of Orthodox Rabbis of Greater Detroit
16947 W. Ten Mile Road, Southfield 48075
                                  (248) 559-5005/6
                                  Fax: (248) 559-5202

Media

Newspapers

Jewish News
Franklin Road, Southfield 48034

Organisations

B'nai B'rith Hillel Foundations
Wayne State University, 667 Charles Grosberg
Religious Ctr. 48202
Hot lunch, sandwiches, salads, soups served during
academic year (Sept. - April).
Council of Orthodox Rabbis of Detroit (Vaad
Harabonim)
16947 W. Ten Mile Road, Southfield 48075
                                  (248) 559-5005/06
                                  Fax: (248) 559-5202
Jewish Community Center of Metr. Detroit
6600 W. Maple Road, W. Bloomfield 48322
                                  (810) 661-1000
                                  Fax: (810) 661-3680
Jewish Federation of Metr. Detroit
Telegraph Road, Bloomfield Hills 48303
Machon L'Torah (The Jewish Network of Michigan)
W. 10 Mile Road 48237

Restaurants

Center Branch
Jimmy Prentis Morris Building, 15110 W. Ten Mile
Road, Oak Park 48237   (810) 967-4030

United States of America / Michigan

Dairy
La Difference
7295 Orchard Lake Road   (248) 932-8934
                                Fax: (248) 932-8942
Supervision: Orth. Rabbis of Greater Detroit.

East Lansing
Organisations
B'nai B'rith Hillel Foundation
Michigan State University, 402 Linden St., 48823
                                (517) 332-1916
                                Fax: (517) 332-4142
Kosher meals available during academic year.

Synagogues

Conservative & Reform
Shaarey Zedek
1924 Coolidge Road 48823

Flint
Organisations
Flint Jewish Federation
619 Wallenberg Street 48502   (810) 767-5922

Synagogues

Conservative
Congregation Beth Israel
5240 Calkins Road 48532   (810) 732-6310
                                Fax: (810) 732-6314
                                Email: cbiflint@tir.com
                    Web site: www.uscj.org/michigan/flint/

Orthodox
Chabad House
5385 Calkins 48532   (810) 230-0770

Reform
Temple Beth El
501 S. Ballenger Highway 48532   (810) 232-3138

Grand Rapids
Synagogues

Conservative
Congregation Ahavas Israel
2727 Michigan Street N.E. 49506   (616) 949-2840
                                Fax: (616) 949-6929
                                Email: davkrishef@aol.com

Orthodox
Chabad House of Western Michigan
2615 Michigan Street N.E. 49506

Reform
Temple Emanuel
1715 E. Fulton Street 49503

Jackson
Synagogues
Temple Beth Israel
801 W. Michigan Avenue 49202

Kalamazoo
Synagogues

Conservative
Sons of Moses
2501 Stadium Drive 49008   (616) 342-5463

Lansing
Synagogues

Reconstructionist
Kehillat Israel
2014 Forest Road 48910   (517) 882-0049

Oak Park
Synagogues

Orthodox
Young Israel of Oak Park
15140 West Ten Mile Road 48237   (810) 967-3655

Saginaw
Synagogues

Conservative
Temple B'nai Israel
1424 S. Washington Avenue 48601   (517) 753-5230

Reform
Congregation Beth El
100 S. Washington Avenue 48607   (517) 754-5171

South Haven
Synagogues

Orthodox
First Hebrew Congregation
249 Broadway 49090   (616) 637-1603

Southfield

Synagogues
Young Israel of Southfield
27705 Lahser Road 48034   (248) 358-0154
                                 Fax: (248) 358-0154
                                 Email: rabg@aol.com

West Bloomfield

Museums
Holocaust Memorial Center
6602 W. Maple Road 48322-3005   (248) 661-0840
                                 Fax: (248) 661-4204
                                 Email: info@holocaustcenter.org
                                 Web site: www.holocaustcenter.org
First free-standing holocaust museum in U.S. Consists
of museum, library-archive, garden. Services include
tours, lectures, oral history program, exhibits, speakers'
bureau. No admission fee.

Synagogues

Orthodox

Young Israel of West Bloomfield
6111 West Maple Road 48322
                  (810) 661-4183/855-8722/626-7651

Minnesota
Duluth

Organisations
Jewish Federation & Com. Council
1602 E. 2nd Street 55812   (218) 724-8857

Synagogues

Conservative & Reform

Temple Israel
1602 E. 2nd Street 55812   (218) 724-8857

Orthodox

Adas Israel
302 E. Third Street 55802   (218) 722-6459

Minneapolis

Butchers
Fishman's Kosher
4000 Minnetonka Blvd 55416   (612) 926-5611
Glatt butcher and take-out certified by the local
Orthodox vaad.

Contact Information
Rabbi Perez
55416   (612) 926-3185
Contact for kosher establishments in the area and for
eruv information.

Mikvaot
Knesseth Israel
4330 W. 28th Street, St Louis Park 55416
                                 (612) 926-3829
                                 Fax: (612) 920-2184

Organisations
Jewish Com. Center of Greater Minneapolis
4330 Cedar Lake Rd. S., 55416

Synagogues

Orthodox

Congregation Bais Yisroel
4221 Sunset Blvd 55416   (952) 926-7867
Kenesseth Israel
4330 W. 28th Street 55416   (952) 920-2183
                                 Fax: (952) 920-2184
                                 Email: rabbiki@mtn.org
                                 Web site: www.kenessethisrael.org

Rochester

Home Hospitality
Lubavitch Bais Chaya Moussia Hospitality Center
730 2nd Street S.W. 55902   (507) 288-7500
                                 Fax: (507) 286-9329
                                 Email: rstrav@rconnect.com
Also provides Shabbat dinners and hospital visitations.
Mikva on premises.

St Paul

Groceries
L'chaim, 655 Snelling Avenue 55116

Restaurants

Dairy

Old City Cafe
1571 Grand Avenue   (612) 699-5347
Supervision: Upper Midwest Kashrus.
Dairy/vegetarian. Hours: Sunday, 10 am to 9 pm;
Monday to Thursday, 11 am to 9 pm; Friday, to 2 pm.
Corner of Grand and Snelling Avenues, both of which
are buslines.

Mississippi
Greenville

Synagogues

Reform

Hebrew Union Congregation
504 Main Street 38701   (601) 332-4153

United States of America / Mississippi

Greenwood

Synagogues

Orthodox

Ahavath Rayim
Market & George Streets, PO Box 1235 38935-1235
(601) 453-7537
Only services on the first Friday of each month.

Natchez

Synagogues

Reform

B'nai Israel
Washington & S. Commerce Streets,
PO Box 2081 39120
Oldest synagogue in Mississippi

Tupelo

Synagogues

Conservative

B'nai Israel
Marshall & Hamlin Streets 38801

Missouri
Ft. Leavenworth

Synagogues

Reform

Ft. Leavenworth Jewish congregation
Main Post Chapel, Pope Avenue 64114
(816) 523-5757

Kansas City

Media

Newspapers

Kansas City Jewish Chroncicle
7375 W. 107th Street, Overland Park 66204
Note: Please consult under Kansas, Overland Park and
Prairie Village, since Kansas City spans both Missouri
and Kansas.

Organisations

Jewish Federation of Greater Kansas City
5801 W. 115th Street, Suite 201,
Overland Park 66211

Restaurants

Sensations

1148 W. 103 Street 64114

Synagogues

Conservative

Congregation Beth Shalom
9400 Wornall road 64114
361-2990
Fax: 361-4495

Reform

Temple B'nai Jehudah
712 E. 69th Street 64131
(816) 363-1050
Fax: (816) 363-8610

The New Reform Temple
7100 Main 64114
(816) 523-7809
Fax: (816) 523-2454
Email: nrt7100@aol.com

St Louis

Bakeries

Schnuck's Nancy Ann Bakery
Olive & Mason
(314) 434-7323

Butchers

Diamant's Kosher Meat Market
618 North & South Road
(314) 721-9624
S. Kohn's
10405 Old Olive St. Road 63141
(314) 569-0727
Fax: (314) 569-1723
Sol's, 8627 Olive
(314) 993-9977

Groceries

Lazy Suzan Imaginative Cartering
110 Millwell Drive
(314) 291-6050
Simon Kohn's Kosher Meat & Deli
10405 Old Olive Street
(314) 569-0727
Fax: (314) 569-1723
Complete kosher deli & meat market. Seating
available. Fresh cold & hot selections available daily.
Pizza available for carryout.
Sol's Kosher Meat Market
8627 Olive
(314) 993-9977

Libraries

The Brodsky Jewish Community Library
12 Millstone Campus Drive 63146

Mikvaot

Mikva
4 Millstone Campus 63146
(314) 569-2770

Organisations
Jewish Federation of St. Louis
12 Millstone Campus Drive 63146   (314) 432-0020
Fax: (314) 432-1277
Email: stljf@jon.cjfny.org
The Vaad Hoeir (United Orthodox Jewish Community of St. Louis)
4 Millstone Campus 63141   (314) 569-2770
Fax: (314) 569-2774
Recognised Orthodox religious authority for the city.

Restaurants

Dairy
NoBull Cafe, 10477 Old Olive   (314) 991-9533

Meat
Diamant's
618 North & South Rd.   (314) 712-9624
Simon Kohn's
10424 Old Olive   (314) 569-0727

Synagogues

Orthodox
Young Israel of St Louis
8101 Delmar Blvd 63130   (314) 727-1880
Fax: (314) 727-2177
Email: yi-stl@juno.com

Tours of Jewish Interest
Jewish Tercentenary
Forest Park
Home to the Monument & Flagpole

St. Joseph
Synagogues

Conservative
Temple B'Nai Sholem
615 S. 10th Street 64501   (816) 279-2378
Fax: (816) 361-4495

Montana
Billings
Synagogues

Reform
Congregation Beth Aaron
1148 N. Broadway 59101   (406) 248-6412

Great Falls
Synagogues
Aitz Chaim
PO Box 6192 59406-6192   (406) 452-9521
Email: aaron@weissman.com

Missoula
Synagogues
Har Shalom
PO Box 7581 59807   (406) 523-5671

Nebraska
Lincoln
Synagogues

Conservative
Tifereth Israel
3219 Sheridan Blvd. 68502   (402) 423-8569

Reform
South Street Temple B'nai Jeshurun
20th & South Streets 68502   (402) 435-8004

Omaha
Mikvaot
Com. Mikva
323 S. 132nd Street 68154   (402) 334-8200

Organisations
Jewish Federation of Omaha
333 S. 132nd Street   (402) 334-8200
Fax: (402) 334-1330
Email: pmonsk@top.net
Web site: www.jewishomaha.org

Synagogues
B'nai Israel
PO Box 24161 68124

Conservative
Beth El, 14506 California Street 68154

Orthodox
Beth Israel
1502 N. 52nd Street 68104   (402) 556-6288

Reform
Temple Israel
7023 Cass Street 68132   (402) 556-6536

United States of America / Nevada

Nevada

Las Vegas

Delicatessens

Casba Glatt Kosher
2845 Las Vegas Blvd   (702) 791-3344
Jerusalem Kosher Restaurant & Deli
1305 Vegas Valley 89109   (702) 791-3668
Rafi's Place
6135 West Sahara 89102   (702) 253-0033
Sara's Place, 4972 S. Maryland

Kashrut Information

Community Relations
     (702) 732-0556

Restaurants

Meat

Jerusalem Glatt Kosher Restaurant
1305 Vegas Valley Dr., 89109   (702) 696-1644
     Fax: (702) 696-0919
Shalom Hunan, 4850 W Flamingo Road
     (702) 871-3262

Supervision: R.C.C..

Synagogues

Conservative

Midbar Kodesh Temple
33 Cactus Garden, Henderson   (702) 454-4848
     Fax: (702) 454-4847
Shabbat Services: weekly, Fri. 7:30pm, Sat. 9:00am
and all holidays. Special Services.
Temple Beth Shalom
1600 E. Oakley Blvd.   (702) 384-5070
     Fax: (702) 383-3246
Shabbat Service: Fri. 7:30pm (at the Hebrew Academy);
Sat. 9:30am; Daily minyon Mon-Fri. 7:30am; Sat, Sun
& holidays 9:00am (at the synagogue).
Temple Emanu-El
     (702) (Wally Klein) 248-6515 or
     (Mae Futterman) 255-1666
Shabbat Service: Fri. 7:30pm. Organizations:
Sisterhood, Chavurah.

Orthodox

Congregation Or-Bamidbar
2959 Emerson Ave.   (702) 369-1175
Shabbat Service: Mon-Fri. 7:00am; Sat. 8:30am; Sun.
9:00am; Mincha & Ma'ariv daily at sunset. Education:
Hebrew School, Sun. 12-2pm; Judaism Class, Wed.
8pm.

Young Israel of Las Vegas
9510 West Sahara 89117   (702) 360-8909
Shabbat Service: Sat. 9am, Sun. 9am. Beginners
minyon for ages 10-15. Radio-talk show: 1230AM,
Tues. at 8pm.

Reconstructionist

Valley Outreach Synagogue
Luthern Church, 2 S. Pecos Rd.,
Henderson   (702) 436-4900
     Fax: (702) 436-4901
Shabbat Service: 1st Fri. of month 8pm.

Reform

Adat Ari El, 3310 S. Jones Blvd.   (702) 221-1230
     Fax: (702) 221-1385
     Email: info@adatariel.com
AAE Event Hotline: (702) 390-8142. Shabbat Service:
Fri. 7:30pm.
Bet Knesset Bamidbar
Desert Vista Community Center, 10360 Sun City Blvd.,
Sun City   (702) 391-2750
Shabbat Service: 2nd & 4th Fri. 7:30pm.
Congregation Ner Tamid
2761 Emerson Ave.   (702) 733-6292
     Fax: (702) 733-8553
CNT Event Hotline: (702) 263-5960. Shabbat Service:
Fri. 7:30pm.
Temple Adat Chavarim
Bonner School, 765 Crestdale Lane   (702) 647-7254
Shabbat Service: Fri. 7:30pm.
Temple Bet Emet
Presbyterian Church, 8601 Del Webb Blvd., Sun City
     (702) 255-2348
Shabbat Service: 1st & 3rd Fri. 7:30pm.
Temple Beth Am
9001 Hillpointe Road   (702) 254-5110
     Fax: (702) 254-0997
Shabbat Service: Fri. 7:30pm; Sat. 10:30am; Sat.
Torah Study 9:30am.

Traditional

Chabad of Southern Nevada
1261 So. Arville   (702) 259-0770
     Fax: (702) 877-4700
     Email: chabadlv@aol.com
     Web site: www.chabadlv.org
Daily services. Mikvah on premises (call (702) 224-
0184).
Chabad of Summerlin
2620 Regatta Dr. #117   (702) 259-0770
Shabbat Service: Fri. 6:00pm; Sat. 10:00am. Special
children's service, 11:00am; Sun. 8:30am is the B-L-T
service (Bagels, Lox, Tefillah).

Reno

Synagogues

Conservative

Temple Emanu-El
1031 Manzanita Lane at Lakeside Dr. 89509
(702) 825-5600
This is the oldest active congregation in Nevada.

Reform

Temple Sinai
3405 Gulling Road 89503
(775) 747-5508
Fax: (775) 747-1911
Email: myrabbi@aol.com

New Hampshire
Bethlehem

Hotel
New Arlington Kosher Hotel
Main Street and Lewis Hill Road 3574
(603) 869-3353
Summer only

Mikvaot

Orthodox

Machzikei Hadas
Lewis Hill Road 3574
(603) 869-3336

Synagogues

Conservative

Bethlehem Hebrew Congregation
Strawberry Hill 3574
(603) 869-5465
Temple Israel
66 Salmon Street 3104
(603) 622-6171

Orthodox

Machzikei Hadas
Lewis Hill Road 3574
(603) 869-3336

Manchester

Media

Newspapers

The Reporter
698 Beech Street 3104
(603) 627-7679
Fax: (603) 627-7963
Lists further communities in Amherst, Concord, Derry,
Dover, Durham, Hanover, Keene, Laconia and Nashua.

Organisations
Jewish Federation of Greater Manchester
698 Beech Street 3104
(603) 627-7679
Fax: (603) 627-7963

Synagogues

Conservative

Temple Israel
66 Salmon St 3104
(603) 622-6171

Orthodox

Lubavitch
7 Camelot Drive 3104
(603) 647-0204

Reform

Adath Yeshurun
152 Prospect Street 3104
(603) 669-5650

Portsmouth

Synagogues

Conservative

Temple Israel
200 State Street 3801
(603) 436-5301

New Jersey
Aberdeen

Synagogues

Orthodox

Bet Tefilah
479 Lloyd Road 7747
(908) 583-6262

Atlantic City

Restaurants

Meat

Jerusalem
6410 Ventnor Ave, Ventnor 8406
(609) 822-2266
Supervision: Rabbi Abraham Spacirer.

United States of America / New Jersey

Synagogues

Conservative

Beth El, 500 N. Jerome Ave, Margate 8402
Fax: (609) 823-1810

Beth Judah
6725 Ventnor Av, Ventnor 8406 (609) 822-7116
Chelsea Hebrew Congregation
4001 Atlantic Av 8401 (609) 345-0825
Community Synagogue
Maryland & Pacific Avs 8401 (609) 345-3282

Orthodox

Rodef Shalom
3833 Atlantic Av 8401 (609) 345-4580

Reform

Beth Israel
2501 Shore Rd, Northfield 8225 (609) 641-3600
Temple Emeth Synagogue
8501 Ventnor Av, Margate 8402 (609) 822-4343

Bayonne

Community Organisations
Jewish Community Centre
1050 Kennedy Blvd 7002 (201) 436-6900

Synagogues

Conservative

Temple Emanuel
735 Kennedy Blvd 7002 (201) 436-4499

Orthodox

Ohab Sholom
1016-1022 Ave. C 7002
Ohav Zedek
912 Ave. C 7002 (201) 437-1488
Uptown Synagogue
49th St. & Ave C 7002

Reform

Temple Beth Am
111 Avenue B 7002 (201) 858-9052

Belmar

Synagogues

Orthodox

Sons of Israel Congregation
PO Box 298 7719 (973) 681-3200

Bergenfield

Butchers
Glatt World, 89 Newbridge Road (201) 439-9675
Fax: (201) 439-0342
Supervision: RCBC.

Delicatessen

Meat
Foster Village Kosher Delicatessen & Catering
469 S. Washington Avenue 7621 (201) 384-7100
Fax: (201) 384-0303
Supervision: Quality Kashrut Supervisory Service.

Synagogues

Conservative
Congregation Beth Israel of Northern Valley
169 N. Washington Avenue 7621 (201) 384-3911
Fax: (201) 384-3738
Email: cbitemple@juno.com
Web site: www.uscj.org/njersey/bergenfield

Bordentown

Synagogues

Non-affiliated
Congregation B'nai Abraham
59 Crosswicks Street 8505
Founded in 1918.

Bradley Beach

Synagogues

Orthodox
Congregation Agudath Achim
301 McCabe Avenue 7720 (973) 774-2495

Bridgeton

Organisations
Jewish Federation of Cumberland County

Synagogues

Conservative
Congregation Beth Abraham
330 Fayette Street 8302

Burlington

Synagogues
B'nai Israel
212 High Street 8332

Cherry Hill

Bakeries
Pastry Palace Kosher Bakery
State Highway 70 8034   (609) 429-3606

Butchers
Cherry Hill Kosher Market
907 W. Marlton Pike 8002   (609) 428-6663
                                   Fax: (609) 216-0752

Delicatessen
Leo's Deli, J.C.C. 1301 Springdale Road
                    (856) 424-4444 Ext 158
Supervision: Tri-County Vaad.

Media

Newspapers
The Jewish Community Voice
2393 W. Marlton Pike 8002

Mikvaot
Sons of Israel
720 Cooper Landing Road 8002   (856) 667-9700
                                 Fax: (856) 667-9765
                                 Email: congsoi@aol.com

Organisations
Jewish Federation of Southern New Jersey
2393 W. Marlton Pike 8002   (609) 665-6100

Restaurants

Meat

Maxim's
404 Route 70 East 8034   (609) 428-5045
Supervision: Tri-County Vaad.
Glatt kosher middle eastern cuisine.

Synagogue

Orthodox

Congregation Sons of Israel
720 Cooper Landing Road 8002   (856) 667-9700
                                 Fax: (856) 667-9765
                                 Email: congsoi@aol.com
Daily Minyan

Synagogues

Conservative

Beth El, 2901 W. Chapel Avenue 8002
                                  (609) 667-1300
Beth Shalom
901 Kresson Road 8003   (609) 751-6663
Congregation Beth Tikva
115 Evesboro-Medford Road, Marlton

Reform

Congregation M'kor Shalom
850 Evesham Road   (609) 424-4220
                            Fax: (609) 424-2890
Temple Emmanuel
1101 Springdale Road

Cinnaminson

Synagogues

Conservative
Temple Sinai
New Albany Road, & Route 130 8077
                                (609) 829-0658

Clark

Synagogues
Temple Beth O'r
111 Valley Road 7066   (609) 381-8403

Clifton

Media

Newspapers

Jewish Community News
199 Scoles Avenue 7012

Organisations
Jewish Federation of Greater Clifton-Passaic
199 Scoles Avenue 7012   (973) 777-7031
                            Fax: (973) 777-6701
                    Email: yymuskin@jon.cjfny.org

Restaurants
Jerusalem II Pizza
224 Brook Avenue 7055   (201) 778-0960
Kosher Konnection
200 Main Avenue 7055   (201) 777-1120

Synagogues

Conservative

Clifton Jewish Center
18 Delaware Street 7011   (973) 772-3131

Reform

Beth Shalom
733 Passaic Avenue 7012   (973) 773-0355

United States of America / New Jersey

Colonia

Synagogues

Conservative

Ohev Shalom
220 Temple Way 7067   (908) 388-7222

Cranbury

Synagogues

Jewish Congregation of Concordia
c/o Club House 8512   (609) 655-8136

Cranford

Contact Information

Rabbi Hoffberg
     (201) 276-9231

Contact for kosher hospitality.

Synagogues

Conservative

Temple Beth El Mekor Chayim
338 Walnut Avenue 7016   (908) 276-9231
Fax: (908) 276-6570
Web site: www.uscj.org/njersey/cranfotb

Deal

Restaurants

Deal Gardens   (908) 531-4887
Lhangmao, 214 Roosevelt Avenue, Oakhurst 7755

Pizzerias

Jerusalem II Pizza
106 Norwood Avenue 7723   (908) 531-7936

Synagogues

Orthodox

128 Norwood Avenue 7723   (908) 531-3200
Ohel Yaacob Congregation
6 Ocean Avenue, P.O. Box 225 7723
(732) 531-0217/531-2405

East Brunswick

Butchers

East Brunswick Kosher Meats
1020 State Highway 18 8816   (908) 257-0007

Synagogues

Conservative

E. Brunswick Jewish Center
511 Ryders Lane 8816   (908) 257-7070

Orthodox

Young Israel of East Brunswick
195 E Dunhams Corner Road 8816   (908) 254-1860

Reform

Temple B'nai Shalom
Old Stage Road & Fern Road 8816   (908) 251-4300

Edison

Butchers

Edison Kosher Meats
State Highway 27, and Evergreen Rd
(201) 549-3707

Community Organisations

Jewish Community Center of Middlesex County
1775 Oak Tree Road 8820   (732) 494-3232
Fax: (732) 548-2850

Synagogues

Conservative

Beth El, 91 Jefferson Blvd 8817   (732) 985-7272

Elizabeth

Contact Information

Mikva Tomor Deborah
330 Elmora Avenue 7208   (908) 355-4850
Fax: (908) 289-5245
Email: remt@juno.com

Contact for information about kosher rooms, temporar
accommodation, etc.

Groceries

Kosher Express
155 Elmora Avenue 7202

Mikvaot

Mikva
35 North Avenue 7208   (908) 352-5048

Restaurants

Dairy

Dunkin' Donuts
186 Elmora Avenue 7202

Meat

New Kosher Special
163 Elmora Avenue 7202   (908) 353-181

Pizzerias

Jerusalem Restaurant
150 Elmora Avenue 7202

Elmwood Park

Organisations
Elmwood Park Jewish Center
100 Gilbert Ave., (201) 797-7320/797-9749

Englewood

Delicatessen

Meat

Sol & Sol
54 E Palisade Avenue 7631 (201) 541-6880
Fax: (201) 541-6883
Supervision: Kashrut Committee of Bergen County.

Groceries
The Menageries
41 East Palisade Avenue 7631 (201) 569-2704
Supervision: RCBC.
Dairy and meat.

Groceries and meats
Kosher By the Case & Less
255 Van Nostrand Avenue 7631 (201) 568-2281
Fax: (201) 568-5681
Supervision: RCBC.

Mikvaot
Mikva
89 Huguenot Avenue (201) 567-1143

Restaurants

Dairy

J.C. Pizza at Jerusalem V
24 W. Palisade Avenue 7631 (201) 569-5546
Supervision: RCBC.
The Fish Grill
16 W. Palisade Avenue (201) 227-6182
Supervision: RCBC.

Synagogues

Conservative

Temple Emanu-El
147 Tenafly Road 7631 (201) 567-1300
Fax: (201) 569-7580

Orthodox

Ahavath Torah
240 Broad Avenue 7631 (201) 568-1315
Fax: (201) 568-2991
Web site: www.ahavathtorah.org
Shomrei Emunah
89 Huguenot Avenue 7631 (201) 567-9420
Daily morning services, and mikva.

Fair Lawn

Bakeries
New Royal Bakery
19-09 Fair Lawn Avenue 7410 (201) 796-6565
Fax: (201) 796-8501
Supervision: RCBC.
Pat Yisrael.

Butchers
Food Showcase
24-28 Fair Lawn Avenue 7410 (201) 475-0077
Fax: (201) 794-6728
Supervision: RCBC.
Sells food provisions as well.

Groceries
Kosher Express
22-16 Morlot Avenue 7410 (201) 791-8818
Supervision: RCBC.
Petak's Glatt Kosher Fine Foods
19-03 Fair Lawn Avenue 7410 (201) 797-5010
Supervision: RCBC.
Glatt kosher caterers as well.

Restaurants

Dairy

J.C. Pizza of Fairlawn
14-20 Plaza Road 7410 (201) 703-0801
Supervision: RCBC.

Synagogues
Bris Arushon, 2204 Fairlawn Ave., (201) 791-7200

Fort Lee

Butchers
Blue Ribbon Self-Service Kosher Meat Market
1363 Inwood Terr. 7024 (201) 224-3220
Fax: (201) 224-7281
Email: koshercomida@msn.com

Delicatessen

Meat

Al's Kosher Deli
209 Main Street 7024 (201) 461-3044
Fax: (201) 461-7188
Supervision: Quality Kashrut Supervisory Service.

Synagogues

Conservative

Jewish Community Center of Fort Lee
1449 Anderson Avenue 7024 (201) 947-1735
Fax: (201) 947-1530
Email: aschafer@jcc.org

United States of America / New Jersey

Orthodox

Young Israel of Fort Lee
1610 Parker Avenue 7024   (201) 592-1518
Fax: (201) 592-8414

Freehold

Restaurants

Fred and Murry's
Pond Road Shopping Center, Route 9 7728
(732) 462-3343
Web site: www.fredandmurrys.com
Not glatt kosher or shomer Shabbat, but has
Conservative supervision.

Synagogues

Orthodox

Agudath Achim/Freehold Jewish Center
Broad & Stokes Streets 7728   (732) 462-0254
Fax: (732) 462-0217
Traditional congregation with daily minyans

Hackensack

Organisations

Jewish Federation of Community Services of Bergen County
170 State Street 7601

Synagogues

Conservative

Temple Beth El
280 Summit Avenue 7601   (201) 342-2045

Haddonfield

Butchers

Sarah's Kosher Kitchen
63 Ellis Road

Hasbrouck Heights

Synagogues

Reform

Temple Beth Elohim
Bourlevard & Charlton Aves.,   (201) 393-7707

Highland Park

Groceries

B&E Kosher Meat Market
76 Raritan Avenue   (908) 846-3444

Berkley Bakery
405 Raritan Avenue 8904
Dan's Deli & Meat Market
515 Raritan Avenue 8904
Kosher Catch
239 Raritan Avenue   (908) 572-9052
Mystic Gourmet
229 Raritan Avenue 8904

Mikvaot

Park Mikva
112 S. 1st Avenue 8904   (732) 249-2411

Synagogues

Conservative

Highland Park Conservative Temple & Center
201 S. 3rd Av 8904   (908) 545-6482

Orthodox

Congregation Ahavas Achim
(732) 247-0532
Fax: (732) 247-6739
Email: aa613@juno.com
Congregation Etz Ahaim (Sephardi)
230 Denison St 8904   (732) 247-3839
Fax: (732) 545-3191
Email: etzahaim@earthlink.net
Web site: www.home.earthlink.net/netzahaim
Congregation Ohav Emeth
415 Raritan Avenue 8904   (908) 247-3038

Hillside

Synagogues

Conservative

Shomrei Torah Ohel Yosef Yitzchok
910 Salem Avenue 7205   (908) 289-0770

Orthodox

Congregation Sinai Torath Chaim
1531 Maple Avenue 7205   (908) 923-9500

Hoboken

Synagogues

Conservative

United Synagogue of Hoboken
830 Hudson Street & 115 Park Avenue 7030
(201) 659-2614
Fax: (201) 659-7944

James Burg

Synagogues
Rossmoor Jewish Congregation Meeting Room
8831   (609) 655-0439

Lakewood

Bakeries
Gelbsteins Bakery
415 Clifton Avenue 8701   (732) 363-3636
Supervision: Orthodox supervision.
Lakewood Heimishe Bakeshop
225-2nd St 8701   (732) 905-9057
Supervision: Orthodox supervision.

Booksellers
Torah Treasures
254-2nd St 8701   (732) 901-1911

Butchers
Shloimy's Kosher World
23 E. County Line Road 8701   (732) 363-3066

Kashrut Information

Orthodox
KCC - Cashrus Council of Lakewood
                                        (732) 901-1888

Mikvaot
Mikvah Tahara
1101 Madison Avenue 8701   (732) 370-1666
Call to schedule appointment

Organisations
Ocean County Jewish Federation
301 Madison Avenue 8701   (201) 363-0530

Restaurants
Pizza Plus
241-4th St 8701   (732) 367-0711
Supervision: Orthodox supervision.
Yum Mee Glatt
116 Clifton Avenue 8701   (732) 886-9688
Chinese and American.

Dairy
Bagel Nosh
380 Clifton Avenue 8701   (732) 363-1115

Meat

Kosher Experience
Kennedy Blvd., 8701
Supervision: Rabbi Chumsky.

R. & S. Kosher Restaurant and Deli
416 Clifton Avenue 8701   (732) 363-6688
Glatt kosher meat only. Hours: Sunday to Thursday,
12:30 pm to 9 pm; Friday, 8 am to 2:30 pm. On
Friday, take-out only.

Synagogues

Conservative
Ahavat Shalom
Forest Avenue & 11th Street 8701   (732) 363-5190
                                    Fax: (732) 363-5225
            Email: ahavat_shalom_nj@netzero.com
            Web site: www.uscj.org/njersey/lakewood

Orthodox
Kol Shimshon
323 Squamkum Road 8701   (732) 901-6680
Lakewood Yeshiva
Private Way & 6th Street 8701   (732) 367-1060
Sons of Israel
Madison Avenue & 6th Street 8701   (732) 364-2230

Reform

Beth Am, Madison Avenue & Carey Street 8701
                                        (732) 363-2800

Lawrenceville

Synagogues

Orthodox
Young Israel of Lawrenceville
2556 Princeton Pike 8648   (609) 883-8833
                                Web site: www.yiol.com

Linden

Synagogues

Conservative
Mekor Chayim Suburban Jewish Center
Deerfield Road & Academy Terrace 7036
                                        (908) 925-2283

Orthodox
Congregation Anshe Chesed
100 Orchard Terrace at St George Av 7036
                                        (908) 486-8616

Livingston

Delicatessens
Super Duper Bagels
498 S. Livingston Avenue 7052   (201) 533-1703
Supervision: Vaad Hakashrus of the Council of
Orthodox Rabbis Metrowest.

United States of America / New Jersey

Restaurants

Jerusalem West
16 E. Mt. Pleasant Avenue 7039   (973) 533-1424
Metro Glatt/Delancy Street
515 Livingston Avenue 7039   (973) 992-9189
Fax: (973) 992-6430
Fax number for take-out orders
Moshavi, 515 S. Livingston Avenue 7039
(201) 740-8777
Supervision: Vaad Hakashrus of the Council of
Orthodox Rabbis Metrowest.

Pizzerias

Jerusalem Pizza
99-101 West Mt. Pleasant Avenue 7039
(973) 533-1424
Fax: (973) 533-9275
Supervision: Vaad Hakashrus of the Council of
Orthodox Rabbis Metrowest.

Synagogues

Orthodox

Etz Chaim Synagogue
Mt Pleasant Avenue
Synagogue of the Suburban Torah Center
85 W. Mount Pleasant Avenue 7039
(973) 994-0122; 994-2620
Fax: (973) 535-3898

Makwah

Synagogues
Temple Beth Haverim
280 Remjo Valley Road   (201) 512-1983

Manalapan

Restaurants

Meat
Kosher Chinese Express
335 Route 9 South 7726   (908) 866-1677
Fax: (908) 866-1621
Glatt kosher and Shomer Shabbat.

Maplewood

Booksellers
Rabbi L. Sky Hebrew Book Store
1923 Springfield Avenue, Maplewood, NJ 7040
(973) 763-4244/5
Fax: (973) 763-1412

David and Feigie Sky

Metuchen

Synagogues

Conservative
Neve Shalom
250 Grove Avenue 8840   (732) 548-2238
Fax: (732) 603-7976
Email: neveshal@webspan.net

Millville

Synagogues
Beth Hillel
3rd Avenue & Oak Street 8332   (609) 825-8672

Morris Plains

Restaurants

Kosher Delicatessan
Jonathan's Deli Restaurant
2900 Route 10 West 7950   (973) 539-6010
Fax: (973) 539-6011

Morristown

Kashrut Information
Congregation of Ahavath Yisrael
9 Cutler Street 7960   (973) 267-4184
Fax: (973) 898-1711
Email: sofernj@aol.com
This synagogue operates a kosher food buying service
for the community, dealing only in strictly kosher
products.
Rabbinical College of America
226 Sussex Avenue 7960   (973) 267-9404
Fax: (973) 267-5208
Email: rca226@aol.com

Mikvaot
Sarah Esther Rosenhaus Mikvah Institutue
93 Lake Road 7960

Synagogues

Conservative
Morristown Jewish Center
177 Speedwell Avenue 7960   (973) 538-9292

Reform
Temple B'nai Or
60 Overlook Road 7960   (973) 539-4539

Mount Freedom

Synagogues

Orthodox

Mount Freedom Jewish Center
1209 Sussex Turnpike 7970   (973) 895-2100

New Brunswick

Synagogues

Chabad House Friends of Lubavitch
8 Sicard St 8901   (908) 828-9191

Reform

Anshe Emeth Memorial Temple
222 Livingston Av 8901   (732) 545-6484
                              Fax: (732) 745-7448
                    Email: anshe.emeth@rcn.com
                 Web site: www.uahc.org/hj/aemt

Unaffiliated

Congregation Poile Zedek
145 Neilson St 8901   (908) 545-6123

North Brunswick

Synagogues

Conservative

Congregation B'nai tikvah
1001 Finnegans Lane 8902   (732) 297-0696
                              Fax: (732) 297-2673
                      Email: bnaitik@aol.com
                 Web site: www.bnaitikvah.org

Paramus

Butchers
Harold's Self Service Kosher Meat
67-A E. Ridgewood Avenue 7652   (201) 262-0030

Organisations
Jewish Center of Paramus
304 Midland Ave.,   (201) 262-7691

Synagogues

Conservative

Jewish Community Center of Paramus
E-304 Midland Ave., 7652   (201) 262-7691
                              Fax: (201) 262-6516
                    Email: jccparam@mail.idt.net
              Web site: www.uscj.org/njersey/paramus

Parlin

Synagogues
Ohav Shalom
3018 Bordertown Avenue 8859   (201) 727-4334

Parsipanny

Delicatessens
Arlington Kosher Deli, Restaurant & Caterers
Arlington Shopping Center, 744 Route 46W 7054
                                   (973) 335-9400

Passaic

Delicatessens
B&Y Kosher Korner Inc.,
200 Main Avenue 7055   (201) 777-1120

Restaurants
Main-Ly Chow
227 Main Avenue 7055   (201) 777-4900

Pizzerias

Jerusalem II Pizza of Passaic
224 Brook Avenue 7055

Synagogues

Orthodox

Young Israel of Passaic-Clifton
200 Brook Avenue 7055   (201) 778-7117

Paterson

Synagogues

Conservative

Temple Emanuel
151 E. 33rd Street 7514   (973) 684-5565

Perth Amboy

Synagogues
Beth Mordechai
224 High Street 8861   (732) 442-2431

Orthodox

Shaarey Teflioh
15 Market Street 8861   (732) 826-2977

United States of America / New Jersey

Piscataway

Synagogues

Reform

B'nai Shalom
25 Netherwood Avenue 8854   (908) 885-9444

Plainfield

Synagogues

Orthodox

United Orthodox Synagogue
526 W. 7th Street 7060   (908) 755-0043

Reform

Temple Sholom
815 W. 7th Street 7063   (201) 756-6447

Princeton

Synagogues

Traditional

Jewish Center
435 Nassau Street 8540   (609) 921-0100
                               Fax: (609) 921-7531

Rahway

Synagogues

Conservative

Temple Beth Torah
1389 Bryant Street 7065   (609) 576-8432

Ridgewood

Synagogues
Temple Israel
475 Grove Street   (201) 444-9320

River Edge

Synagogues

Reform

Temple Sholom
385 Howland Avenue 7661   (201) 489-2463
                               Fax: (201) 489-0775
          Web site: www.uahcweb.org/nj/tsholomre/

Roselle

Media

Guides

Shalom Book
843 St Georges Avenue 7203   (908) 298-8200
                               Fax: (908) 298-8220

Organisations
Jewish Federation of Central New Jersey
843 St Georges Avenue 7203   (908) 298-8200
                               Fax: (908) 298-8220

Rumson

Synagogues

Conservative

Congregation B'nai Israel
Hance & Ridge Roads 7760   (908) 842-1800

Scotch Plains

Organisations
Jewish Community Center of Central New Jersey
1391 Martine Avenue 7076   (908) 889-1830

Synagogues

Conservative

Congregation Beth Israel
1920 Cliffwood Street 7076   (908) 889-1830
                               Fax: (908) 889-5523

Somerset

Synagogues
Temple Beth El
1945 Amwell Road 8873   (201) 873-2325

South Orange

Groceries
Zayda's Super Value Meat Market & Deli
309 Irvington Avenue 7079   (973) 762-1812

South River

Community Organisations
Jewish Federation of Greater Middlesex County
230 Old Bridge Turnpike
South River, NJ, Middlesex County 8882
                               (732) 432-7711
                               Fax: (732) 432-0292
                               Email: jfednj@aol.com

Synagogues

Traditional

Congregation Anshe Emeth of South River
88 Main Street 8882   (732) 257-4190
                              Fax: (732) 254-8819
        Web site: www.members.home.net/ebweiss
See also Edison

Sportswood

Synagogues

Reform

Monroe Township Jewish Center
11 Cornell Avenue 8884   (201) 251-1119

Teaneck

Bakeries

Butterflake Bake Shop
448 Cedar Lane 7666   (201) 836-3516
                              Fax: (201) 836-3056
Supervision: RCBC.
Pat Yisrael.

Royal Too Bakery
172 West Englewood Avenue 7666   (201) 833-0114
Supervision: RCBC.
Pat Yisrael.

Sammy's New York Bagels
1443 Queen Anne Road 7666   (201) 837-0515
                              Fax: (201) 837-9733
Supervision: Kof-K.
Pat Yisrael.

Bagels

Hot Bagels
976 Teaneck Road 7666   (201) 833-0410
Supervision: RCBC.
Dairy. Only the bagels are under supervision.

Booksellers

The Judaica House
478 Cedar Lane 07666   (210) 801-9001
                              Fax: (201) 801-9004

Zoldan's Judaica Center
406 Cedar Lane 7666   (201) 907-0034

Butchers

Glatt Express
1400 Queen Anne Road 7666   (201) 837-8110
                              Fax: (201) 837-0084
Supervision: RCBC.
Sells food provisions as well.

Delicatessens

Chopstix
172 West Englewood Avenue 7666
                                       (201) 833-0200
                              Fax: (201) 833-8326
Supervision: RCBC.

Glatt kosher Chinese take-out. Hours: Sunday to
Thursday, 11:30 am to 10 pm; Friday, closing times
vary – please call.
Ma'adan, 446 Cedar Lane 7666   (201) 692-0192
Supervision: RCBC.
Take-out.

Groceries

Dovid's Fresh Fish Market
736 Chestnut Avenue 7666   (201) 928-0888
Supervision: RCBC.

Mikvaot

Mikveh
1726 Windsor Road 7666   (201) 837-8220

Restaurant

Meat

Grill Street
184 West Englewood Avenue 7666   (201) 833-0001
                              Fax: (201) 833-8030
Supervision: RCBC.

Restaurants

Dairy

Jerusalem Pizza
496 Cedar Lane 7666   (201) 836-2120
                              Fax: (201) 836-2261
Supervision: RCBC.

Plaza Pizza & Restaurant
1431 Queen Anne Road 7666   (201) 837-9500
                              Fax: (201) 836-2261
Supervision: RCBC.

Shelly's
482 Cedar Lane 7666   (201) 692-0001
                              Fax: (201) 692-1890
                       Email: shellys@noahsark.net
Supervision: RCBC.
Cholov Yisrael. Hours: Monday to Thursday, 10:30 am
to 9:30 pm; Sunday, 9 am to 9 pm. Ten minutes from
the George Washington Bridge.

Meat

Hunan Teaneck
515 Cedar Lane 7666   (201) 692-0099
                              Fax: (201) 692-1907
Supervision: RCBC.
Glatt kosher Chinese and American cuisine. Eat in or
take out. Mashgiach temidi. Hours: Sunday to
Thursday, 11:30 am to 9:45 pm; Friday, to 3 pm;
Saturday night, after Shabbat until midnight.

United States of America / New Jersey

Noah's Ark
493 Cedar Lane 7666 (201) 692-1200
Fax: (201) 692-1890
Email: info@noahsark.net
Supervision: RCBC.
Chassidishe shechita meats. Hours: Monday to
Thursday, 10:30 am to 10:30 pm; Friday, 8 am to 4
pm; Sunday, 9:30 am to 10:30 pm; Saturday during
winter, after Shabbat to midnight. Ten minutes from the
George Washington Bridge.

Synagogues

Conservative

Beth Sholom
354 Maitland Avenue 7666 (201) 833-2620
Fax: (201) 833-2323
Email: bsteaneck@aol.com
Web site: www.uscj.org/njersey/teaneckcbs
Jewish Center of Teaneck
70 Sterling Place 7666 (201) 833-0515
Fax: (201) 833-0511
Email: execdir@aol.com

Orthodox

Congregation Beth Aaron
950 Queen Anne Rd 7666 (201) 836-6210
Fax: (201) 836-0005
Email: mail@bethaaron.org
Web site: www.bethaaron.org
Congregation Bnai Yeshurun
641 W. Englewood Avenue 7666 (201) 836-8916
Fax: (201) 836-1888
Rinat Yisrael
389 W. Englewood Av 7666 (201) 837-2795
Fax: (201) 837-2091
Email: office@rinat.org
Roemer Synagogue
Whittier School, W. Englewood Av., 7666
Young Israel of Teaneck
868 Perry Lane 7666 (201) 833-4419

Reform

Beth Am
510 Claremont Av 7666 (201) 833-2620
Temple Emeth
1666 Windsor Rd 7666 (201) 833-1322
Fax: (201) 833-4831
Email: temple@emeth.org
Web site: www.emeth.org

Tenafly

Restaurants

Dairy

P.K. Café & Pizza at the JCC
411 East Clinton Avenue (201) 894-0801
Supervision: RCBC.

Synagogues

Reform

Temple Sinai of Bergen County
1 Engle Street 7670 (201) 568-3035
Fax: (201) 568-6095
Email: temsinai@idt.net
Web site: www.uahc.org/congs.nj/nj009

Trenton

Organisations

Jewish Federation of Mercer & Bucks Counties
999 Lower Ferry Road 8628 (609) 883-5000

Union

Organisations

Jewish Federation of Central New Jersey
Green Lane 7083 (201) 351-5060

Synagogues

Conservative

Beth Shalom
2046 Vauxhall Road 7083 (908) 686-6773
Temple Israel
2372 Morris Avenue 7083 (201) 686-2120

Vineland

Organisations

Jewish Federation of Cumberland County
1063 East Landis Avenue, Suite B 08360-3785
(856) 696-4445
Fax: (856) 696-3428
Email: jfedcc@aol.com
Also serves the Bridgeton & Cumberland County areas

Synagogues

Conservative

Beth Israel
1015 E. Park Avenue 8630 (609) 691-0852

Orthodox

Ahavas Achim
618 Plum Street 8360 (609) 691-2218

United States of America / New Jersey

Sons of Jacob Congregation
321 Grape Street 8360   (609) 692-4232
Fax: (609) 691-4985
Monday to Friday 6.45 a.m. Saturday 9.00 a.m.
Sunday 7.30 a.m. For evening service, please call
synagogue.

Warren

Organisations
Jewish Federation of Central New Jersey
Suburban Services Office, 150 Mt. Bethel Rd., 7059
(908) 647-0232
Fax: (908) 647-3115

Synagogues

Reform

Mountain Jewish Community Center
104 Mount Horeb Road 7060   (908) 356-8777

Washington Township

Synagogues
Temple Beth Or
56 Ridgewood Rd.,   (201) 664-7422

Wayne

Organisations
Jewish Federation of New Jersey
1 Pike Drive 7470   (973) 595-0555

Synagogues

Conservative

Shomrei Torah
30 Hinchman Avenue 7470   (973) 694-6274

Reform

Temple Beth Tikvah
950 Preakness Avenue 7470   (973) 595-6565

West Caldwell

Delicatessens
David's Deco-Tessen
555 Passaic Avenue 7006   (973) 808-3354
Fax: (973) 808-5806

West New York

Synagogues

Orthodox

Congregation Shaare Zedek
5308 Palisade Avenue 7093   (201) 867-6859

West Orange

Groceries
Gourmet Galaxy
659 Eagle Rock Avenue 7052   (201) 736-0060
Supervision: Vaad Hakashrus of the Council of
Orthodox Rabbis Metrowest.
Dairy and meat available.

Judaica
Lubavitch Center of Essex County
456 Pleasant Valley Way 7052   (973) 731-0770
Fax: (973) 731-6821
Books, gifts, Judaica and all Chabad Outreach
activities.

Mikvaot
Essex County Ritualarim
717 Pleasant Valley Way 7052
(201) 731-1427; 669-0462

Restaurants

Meat

Eden Wok
478 Pleasant Valley Way 7052
(973) 243-0115
Fax: (973) 243-1332
Supervision: Vaad Hakashrus of the Council of
Orthodox Rabbis Metrowest.
Chinese food, also a sushi bar.
Pleasantdale Kosher Meat
470 Pleasant Valley Way 7052   (973) 731-3216

Synagogues

Orthodox

Congregation Ahawas Achim B'nai Jacob and David
700 Pleasant Valley Way 7052   (201) 736-1407

Westfield

Synagogues

Reform

Temple Emanu-El
756 E. Broad Street 7090   (908) 232-6770
Fax: (908) 233-3959

United States of America / New Jersey

Whippany

Media

Newspapers

The New Jersey Jewish News
901 Route 10 7981   (973) 887-3900
Weekly publication owned by United Jewish Fed. of
Metrowest; also publishes a weekly edition in
arrangement with the Jewish Federation of Central New
Jersey.

Organisations
United Jewish Federation of Metrowest
901 Route 10 7981   (973) 884-4800
                                Fax: (973) 884-7361

Willingboro

Synagogues

Reform

Adath Emanu-El
299 John F. Kennedy Way 8046   (609) 871-1736

Woodbridge

Synagogues

Conservative

Adath Israel
424 Amboy Avenue 7095   (732) 634-9601
                                Fax: (732) 634-1593

Wykoff

Synagogues

Reform

Temple Beth Rishon
585 Russell Ave.,   (201) 891-4466

New Mexico

Alberquerque

Kashrut Information
JFGA   (505) 821-3214

Media

Newspapers

The Link
5520 Wyoming Blvd 87109   (505) 821-3214
                                Fax: (505) 821-3351

Organisations
Jewish Federation of Greater Alberquerque
5520 Wyoming Blvd N.E. 87109   (505) 821-3214
                                Fax: (505) 821-3351
                        Email: andrewl@jon.cjfny.org

Las Cruces

Synagogues

Reform

Temple Beth El
702 Parker Road, at Melendres 88004
                                     (505) 524-3380
                                Fax: (505) 521-3737
                        Email: rabbikane@cs.nmsu.edu
                    Web site: www.uahc.org/nm/nm002/

Los Alamos

Synagogues
Jewish Center
2400 Canyon Road 87544   (505) 662-2440

Rio Rancho

Synagogues

Reform

Rio Rancho Jewish Center
2009 Grande Blvd. 87124   (505) 892-8511

Santa Fe

Contact Information
                                     (505) 986-2091
For information about home hospitality, Shabbat and
Mikva

Synagogues
Chabad Jewish Center
1428 Don Gaspar Avenue 87505   (505) 983-2000
                                Fax: (505) 983-2055
                    Email: chabadsantafe@aol.com
            Web site: www.chabad-centers.com/santafe
Friday night Kabbalat Shabbat and community dinner
every second Friday. Kosher Catering for small or
large events, including conferences in hotels. (please
call in advance to order meals).

Conservative & Reform

Temple Beth Shalom
205 E. Barcelona Road 87501   (505) 982-1376
Rabbi Bentley Tel 505-983-7446

Orthodox

Pardes Yisroel
1307 Don Diego Avenue 87505   (505) 989-7711
Email: shammes@pardes-yisroel.org
Web site: www.pardes-yisroel.org/py/
Mailing address: 1307 Don Diego Ave, Santa Fe, NM,
USA 87505. Shabbat home hospitality. Kosher meals.

Reform

Congregation Beit Tikvah
PO Box 2112 87504   (505) 820-2991
Fax: (505) 820-2991
Email: rap1818@aol.com
Web site: www.beittikva.org

Temple Beth Shalom
205 E. Barcelona Road 87501   (505) 982-1376
Also Conservative service Shabbat morning. Religious
pre-school on premises.

New York

New York City encompasses so much territory and so much activity that it can sometimes be easy to forget that there is also a whole state named New York. The Empire State stretches from New York City in the south to the Canadian border at Quebec and Ontario provinces in the north; from the New England border with Connecticut, Massachusetts and Vermont in the east to Pennsylvania and the Great Lakes of Erie and Ontario in the southwest and west.

Within this 50,000 square mile expanse lie metropolis, suburb, small town, large city, village, vast state parks and preserves, seashores, islands, high mountains and rolling foothills, and abundant natural wilderness.

To New York City residents, anything outside the five boroughs (Manhattan, Queens, Brooklyn, the Bronx, and Staten Island) is either upstate or Long Island. But within those areas are numerous large and thriving Jewish communities. The cities of Buffalo, Rochester, Binghamton, Syracuse, and Schenectady, the suburban counties of Westchester and Rockland, and the Long Island counties of Nassau and Suffolk count hundreds of thousands of Jews among their residents.

Jewish settlement began in New York in early September 1654 when twenty-three Sephardic and Ashkenazi Jews disembarked at the harbour of New Amsterdam from the French ship St Catherine. They had escaped the Spanish Inquisition in Recife, Brazil to settle in the Dutch colony. Though Governor Peter Stuyvesant forbade their admission to his jurisdiction, the travellers' protests to his bosses at the Dutch West India Company were accepted and the Jews were allowed to settle. Ten years later, in 1664, four British men-of-war appropriated New Amsterdam in the name of King Charles II of England, who, in turn, made a gift of it to his brother, James, Duke of York. Hence the name, New York.

Jewish immigration was sparse for the next 150 years, but it increased dramatically, especially in New York City between 1880 and 1924, as more than two million Jews made their way to 'der goldene medinah' (the golden door) from eastern and central Europe.

From that original group of 23 Jews in 1654, some made their way up the Hudson river as far as Albany (now the state capital). Two of them, Asser Levy and Jacob de Lucena, became Hudson river traders and also dealt in real estate in the Albany and Kingston areas. South of Albany, in nearby Newburgh, Jewish merchants established a trading post in 1777, but no Jewish community existed there until 1848.

New York's first Jewish community outside of New York City was the town of Sholom in the Catskill mountains in Ulster county. Founded by twelve families, it no longer exists. The oldest existing community is Congregation Beth El, founded in 1838 in Albany and later merged with Congregation Beth Emeth.

Westchester (just north of New York City) county's present Jewish population of close to 150,000 dates from 1860.

Rockland

Southeast of the Catskills, in Rockland county just north of New York City, are a number of communities with large Hasidic and orthodox populations. New Square, a corruption of the name Skvir, was founded by the Skvirer Hasidim and is incorporated as a separate village within the town of Ramapo. With such an administrative and legal designation, New Square has its own zoning rules, its own village council, its own mayor, etc., and is run on strictly orthodox precepts. Monroe, Monsey and Spring Valley have very large orthodox and Hasidic communities. Though observant Jews are predominant, these communities are also home to non-Jews and less observant Jews. There are a number of villages in the area which have been incorporated with the express purpose of keeping orthodox and Hasidim out, through regulations such as zoning to prevent synagogues from being built too close to residences and through the prohibition of having a synagogue in one's house.

United States of America / New York

Albany

Groceries
Price Chopper Market
1892 Central Avenue 12205   (518) 456-2970
Supervision: Vaad Hakashruth.
Full service kosher department.

Home Hospitality
Shabbos House
State University of New York, 316 Fuller Road
(518) 438-4227
Email: shabbos@albany.net

Mikvaot
Bnos Israel of the Capital District
190 Elm Street 12202

Restaurants

Meat

Goldberg's Café
Located at Howard Johnson Hotel   (518) 465-1335
Supervision: Vaad Hakashruth of the Capital District.

Synagogues

Conservative

Ohav Shalom
New Krumkill Rd 12208   (518) 489-4706
Temple Israel
600 New Scotland Av 12208   (518) 438-7858

Orthodox

Beth Abraham-Jacob
380 Whitehall Rd 12208
(518) 489-5819; 489-5179
Fax: (518) 489-5179
Email: mbomzer@aol.com
Chabad-Lubavitch Center of the Capital District
122 S. Main Av 12208   (518) 482-5781
Fax: (518) 482-3684
Email: albanychabad@knick.net
Web site: www.chabadonline.com/albany
Shomray Torah
463 New Scotland Av 12208   (518) 438-8981

Reform

B'nai Sholom
420 Whitehall Rd 12208   (518) 482-5283
Beth Emeth
100 Academy Rd 12208   (518) 436-9761
At this 160-year-old congregation, Rabbi Isaac Mayer
Wise, founder of American Reform Judaism, served
when he first arrived in the United States.

Daughters of Sarah Nursing Center
Washington Av. Extension 15103   (518) 456-7831
Fax: (518) 456-1563
Email: info@daughtersofsarah.org
Web site: www.daughtersofsarah.org
Traditional service, Sat. 9:15 am. Reform service, Fri. 3
pm.

Amsterdam

Synagogues

Conservative

Congregation of Sons of Israel
355 Guy Park Avenue 12010   (518) 842-8691

Beacon

Synagogues
Hebrew Alliance
55 Fishkill Avenue 12508   (914) 831-2012

Binghamton

Mikvaot
Beth David Synagogue
39 Riverside Drive 13905   (607) 722-1793
Fax: (607) 722-7121
Email: bethdavidrabbi@aol.com

Synagogues
Community Center
500 Clubhouse Road 13903   (607) 724-2417
Fax: (607) 824-2311
Email: JCC13850@AOL.com

Conservative

Temple Israel
Deerfield Place, Vestal 13850   (607) 723-7461

Reform

Temple Concord
9 Riverside Drive 13905   (607) 723-7355

Buffalo

Media

Guides

Shalom Buffalo
787 Delaware Av,. 14209   (716) 886-7750
Fax: (716) 886-1367

Newspapers

Buffalo Jewish Review
15 Mohawk Street 14203   (716) 854-2192

Mikvaot
Mikva, 1248 Kenmore Avenue 14216
(716) 875-8451

United States of America / New York

Organisations

Jewish Federation of Greater Buffalo
787 Delaware Avenue 14209   (716) 886-7750
Fax: (716) 886-1367

Synagogues

Conservative

Beth El, 2360 Eggert Road, Tonawanda 14223
(716) 836-3762
Hillel of Buffalo
Campus Center for Jewish Life, 520 Lee Entrance, The Commons/Suite #204, Amherst, NY 14228
(716) 639-8361
Fax: (716) 639-7817
Shaarey Zedek
621 Getzville Rd 14226   (716) 838-3232

Orthodox

B'nai Shalom
1675 N. Forest Rd 14221   (716) 689-8203
Beth Abraham
1073 Elmwood Av 14222   (716) 874-4786
Chabad House
3292 Main St., & N. Forest Rd 14214 &14068
(716) 688-1642
Saranac Synagogue
85 Saranac Avenue 14216   (716) 876-1284
Fax: (716) 833-7178
Daily Minyan.
Young Israel of Greater Buffalo
105 Maple Rd, Williamsville 14221   (716) 634-0212

Reconstructionist

Temple Sinai
50 Alberta Dr. 14226   (716) 834-0708

Reform

Beth Am
4660 Sheridan Dr 14221   (716) 633-8877
Fax: (716) 633-8952
Email: rabbif@aol.com
Beth Shalom
Union & Center Sts., Hamburg
Congregation Havurah
6320 Main St. 14221   (716) 874-3517
Judaic Museum of Temple Beth Zion
700 Sweet Home Road 14209-2095
(716) 836-6565
Fax: (716) 831-1126
Email: zbt@webt.com
Web site: www.tbz.org

Traditional

Kehilat Shalom
700 Sweet Home Rd 14226   (716) 885-6650

Catskills

Ellenville

Mikvaot

Congregation Ezrath Israel
Rabbi Herman Eisner Square 12428
(914) 647-4450/72
Fax: (914) 647-4472
Email: ezrathisrael@cs.com
Mikvah - call for hours.

Fleischmanns

Hotels

Kosher

Oppenheimer's Regis
P O Box 700, Fleischmanns 12430
(845) 254-5080
Fax: (845) 254-4399
Email: kurtopp@aol.com
Supervision: Rabbinate of K'hal Adas Jeshurun, NYC.
Open from Pesach to Succos. Off- season fax 1-732-367-5917

Loch Sheldrake

Synagogues

Orthodox

Young Israel of Vacation Village
PO Box 650 12759   (914) 436-8359

Monticello

Hotels

Kutsher's Country Club
12701   (845) 794-6000
Fax: (845) 794-0157
Email: kutshers@warwick.net
Daily services.

Mikvaot

Mikva, 16 North Street 12701   (914) 794-6757
Summer: Opens at sunset for two hours. Winter: By appointment only.

Synagogues

Orthodox

Tifereth Israel
18 Landfield Avenue 12701   (914) 794-8470
Fax: (914) 794-8478
Daily services.

United States of America / New York

Reform

Temple Sholom
Port Jervis & Dillon Roads 12701   (914) 794-8731
Daily services.

Sharon Springs

Hotels
Yarkony's Adler Spa Hotel
PO Box 328 13459
                    (518) 284-2285 or 1 800 448-4314
                              Fax: (518) 284-2215
Supervision: OU.

Woodbourne

Hotels
Chalet Vim   (914) 434-5124
Glatt kosher.

Woodridge

Hotels
The Lake House Hotel
12789   (914) 434-7800
Glatt kosher. Chalav Yisrael products only. Open
Pesach to Succot.

Clifton Park

Synagogues

Conservative

Beth Shalom
Clifton Park, Center Road 12065   (716) 371-0608

Delmar

Synagogues

Orthodox

Delmar Chabad Center
109 Elsmere Avenue 12054   (716) 439-8280

Elmira

Synagogues

Orthodox

Shomray Hadath
Cobbles Park 14905   (607) 732-7410

Reform

B'nai Israel
Water & Guinnip Streets 14905   (607) 734-7735

Geneva

Synagogues
Temple Beth El
755 South Main Street 14456   (315) 789-9710
                         Email: rosenfield@hws.edu

Glens Falls

Synagogues

Conservative

Shaaray Tefila
68 Bay Street 12801   (518) 792-4945
                              Fax: (518) 792-4945

Reform

Temple Beth El
3 Marion Avenue 12801   (518) 792-4364

Gloversville

Synagogues
Community Center
28 E. Fulton Street 12078

Conservative

Knesseth Israel
34 E. Fulton Street 12078   (518) 725-0649

Harrison

Synagogues

Orthodox

Young Israel of Harrison
207 Union Avenue 10528   (914) 777-1236

Reconstructionist

Reconstructionist Havurah of the Capital District
98 Meadowland Street 12054   (716) 439-5870

Haverstraw

Synagogues
Congregation Sons of Jacob
37 Clove Avenue 10927

Hudson

Synagogues

Conservative
Anshe Emeth
240 Jolsen Blvd. 12534   (518) 828-9040

Ithaca

Synagogues
Temple Beth El
402 N. Tioga Street 14850   (607) 273-5775
                                Email: tbe18@aol.com

Orthodox
Young Israel of Cornell
106 West Avenue 14850   (607) 272-5810

Lake Placid

Synagogues

Traditional
20 Saranac Avenue, PO Box 521 12946-0521
                                (518) 523-3876
                           Fax: (518) 891-3458

Long Island

By 1760 Jews had settled on Long Island, whose present day Jewish population is around 500,000 with some 150 synagogues. Though two of New York City's five boroughs, Brooklyn and Queens, are geographically part of Long Island, when New Yorkers say Long Island they mean the counties of Nassau and Suffolk. Large concentrations of Jews are in the communities of West Hempstead, Plainview, Great Neck, Long Beach, Cedarhurst, Lawrence, Hewlett and Woodmere. The latter four are part of what is known as the Five Towns.

Nassau County
Baldwin

Restaurants
Ben's Kosher Delicatessen
933 Atlantic Avenue   (516) 868-2072
                          Email: info@bensdeli.net
                     Web site: www.bensdeli.net
Supervision: Supervised.

Cedarhurst

Restaurants

Meat
Burger Express
140 Washington Ave   (516) 295-2040
Supervision: Supervised.
K.D.'s El Passo BBQ
546 Central Avenue, Cedarhurst   (516) 569-2920
Supervision: Supervised.

Elmont

Bakeries
Sapienza
1376 Hempstead Turnpike
Nassau County 11003   (516) 352-5232
Supervision: Kof-K.

Five Towns

Incorporates the towns of Cedarhurst, Hewlett, Inwood, Lawrence and Woodmere.

Bakeries
Hungry Harbor Bakery
311 Central Avenue
Lawrence, Nassau County 11559   (516) 374-1131
Supervision: Vaad HaKashrus of the Five Towns.

Moish's Bake Shop
536 Central Avenue
Cedarhurst, Nassau County   (516) 374-2525
Supervision: Vaad HaKashrus of the Five Towns.

Zomick's Bake Shop
444 Central Avenue
Cedarhurst, Nassau County   (516) 569-5520
Supervision: Vaad HaKashrus of the Five Towns.

Bagels
Gotta Getta Bagel
1033 Broadway
Woodmere, Nassau County 11598   (516) 374-5245
Supervision: Vaad HaKashrus of the Five Towns.

Donuts
Donut Delite
125 Cedarhurst Avenue
Cedarhurst, Nassau County   (516) 295-5005
Supervision: Vaad HaKashrus of the Five Towns.
Dunkin' Donuts
299 Burnside Avenue
Lawrence, Nassau County 11559   (516) 239-2052
Supervision: Vaad HaKashrus of the Five Towns.

United States of America / New York

Delicatessens

Mauzone
341 Central Avenue
Lawrence, Nassau County 11559   (516) 569-6411
Supervision: Vaad HaKashrus of the Five Towns.
Take-away.

Groceries

Gourmet Glatt Emporium
137 Spruce Street
Cedarhurst, Nassau County   (516) 569-2662
Supervision: Vaad HaKashrus of the Five Towns.

Supersol
330 Central Avenue
Lawrence, Nassau County 11559   (516) 295-3300
Supervision: Vaad HaKashrus of the Five Towns.

Kashrut Information

Vaad HaKashrus of the Five Towns
859 Peninsula Blvd.
Woodmere, Nassau County 11598   (516) 569-4536
Fax: (516) 295 4212

Mikvaot

Peninsula Blvd.
Hewlett, Nassau County 11557   (516) 569-5514

Restaurants

Wok Tov
594 Central Avenue
Cedarhurst, Nassau County   (516) 295-3843
Fax: (516) 295-3865
Supervision: Vaad HaKashrus of the Five Towns.

Dairy

Primavera
357 Central Avenue
Lawrence, Nassau County   (516) 374-5504
Fax: (516) 374-5589
Supervision: Supervised.

Meat

Cho-Sen Island
367 Central Avenue
Lawrence, Nassau County 11559   (516) 374-1199
Fax: (516) 374-1459
Supervision: Vaad HaKashrus of the Five Towns.

King David
550 Central Avenue
Cedarhurst, Nassau County   (516) 569-2920
Supervision: Vaad HaKashrus of the Five Towns.

King David Delicatessen and Caterers
550 Central Avenue
Cedarhurst, Nassau County   (516) 569-2920
Supervision: Vaad HaKashrus of the Five Towns.
Glatt kosher, shomer shabbat. 20 minutes from JFK
International Airport

Synagogues

Orthodox

Shaarey Tefila
25 Central Avenue
Lawrence, Nassau County 11559

Young Israel of North Woodmere
634 Hungry Harbor Road
North Woodmere, Nassau County 11581
(516) 791-5099
Email: info@yinw.org

Great Neck

Bakeries

Strauss Bake Shop
607 Middle Neck Road
Nassau County 11023   (516) 487-6853
Supervision: Vaad Harabonim of Queens.

Butchers

Great Neck Glatt
501 Middle Neck Road
Nassau County 11023   (516) 773-6328
Fax: (516) 773-4699
Supervision: Vaad Harabonim of Queens.

Media

Newspapers

Long Island Jewish Week
98 Cutter Mill Road
Nassau County 11020   (516) 773-3679

Long Island Jewish World
115 Middle Neck Road
Nassau County 11021   (516) 829-4000

Mikvaot

26 Old Mill Road
Nassau County 11023   (516) 487-2726

Restaurants

Meat

Colbeh
75 N. Station Plaza
Nassau County 11021   (516) 466-8181
Supervision: Kof-K.
Glatt kosher.

United States of America / New York

Hunan Restaurant
505/07 Middle Neck Road
Nassau County 11023   (516) 482-7912
Supervision: Vaad Harabonim of Queens.
Chinese food.

Shish Kabob Palace
90 Middle Neck Road
Nassau County 11021   (516) 487-2228
Supervision: Vaad Harabonim of Queens.

Pizzerias

Great Neck Kosher Pizza
770 Middle Neck Road
Nassau County 11024   (516) 829-2660
Supervision: Kof-K.

La Pizzeria
114 Middle Neck Road
Nassau County 11021   (718) 466-5114
Supervision: Vaad Harabonim of Queens.

Greenvale

Restaurants
Ben's Kosher Delicatessen
140 Wheatley Plaza
Nassau County   (516) 621-3340
Email: info@bensdeli.net
Web site: www.bensdeli.net
Supervision: Supervised.

Jericho

Restaurant
Ben's Kosher Delicatessen
437 No. Broadway   (516) 939-2367
Email: info@bensdeli.net
Web site: www.bensdeli.net
Supervision: Supervised.

Long Beach

Mikvaot
Sharf Manor
274 W. Broadway, Nassau County 11561
          (516) 431-7758

Merrick

Restaurants

Meat
Kosher Food Emporium
1984 Merrick Road   (516) 378-6463
          Fax: (516) 377-1456
Supervision: Rabbi Gershon Kreuser.

New Hyde Park

Kashrut Information
Long Island Commission of Rabbis
1300 Jericho Turnpike
Nassau County 11040   (718) 343-5993

Oceanside

Mikvaot
3397 Park Avenue Oceanside, 11572
          (516) 766-3242

Plainview

Restaurants
Te'Avone
64 Manetto Hall Road
Plainview, 11803   (516) 822-4545

Syosset

Representative Organisations
Conference of Jewish Organisations of Nassau County
North Shore Atrium
6900 Jericho Turnpike, Nassau County 11791
          (516) 364-4477
          Fax: (516) 921-5092

UJA Federation
6900 Jericho Turnpike
Nassau County 11791   (516) 677-1800
          Fax: (516) 921-5092

Wantagh

Bakeries
B & B Bakery Bagels
2845 Jerusalem Avenue
Nassau County 11793
Supervision: Kof-K.
Pat Yisrael.

West Hempstead

Bakeries
The Bagel Gallery
540 Hempstead Turnpike
Nassau County 11552   (516) 483-7311
Supervision: Vaad Harabonim of Queens.

Butchers
J & M Glatt
177 Hempstead Avenue
Nassau County 11552   (516) 489-6926
Supervision: Vaad Harabonim of Queens.

United States of America / New York

Mikvaot
775 Hempstead Avenue
Nassau County 11552   (516) 489-9358

Restaurants

Pizzerias

Hunki's Kosher Pizza & Felafel
338 Hempstead Avenue
Nassau County 11552   (516) 538-6655
Supervision: Vaad Harabonim of Queens.

Woodbury

Restaurants
Ben's Kosher Delicatessen
7971 Jericho Turnpike   (516) 496-4236
                         Email: info@bensdeli.net
                      Web site: www.bensdeli.net
Supervision: Supervised.

Suffolk County

Commack

Community Organisations
Suffolk Jewish Communal Planning Council
74 Hauppauge Road
Suffolk County 11725   (631) 462-5826
                         Email: sjcpc@att.net
                 Web site: www.lijewishlinks.org
Publishes "Suffolk Jewish Directory"

Restaurants

Meat

Pastrami 'N Friends
110a Commack Road
Suffolk County 11725   (516) 499-9537

Dix Hills

Tourist Information
Jewish Genealogy Society of Long Island
37 Westcliff Drive
Suffolk County 11746-5627   (631) 549-9532
                      Email: jgsli@suffolk.lib.ny.us
                 Web site: www.jewishgen.org/jgsli
Offers assistance to Jewish travellers about their New
York or US roots.

Lake Grove

Restaurants
Ben's
135 Alexander Avenue
Suffolk County   (516) 979-8770
                                  Fax: (516) 979-8774
Supervision: Rabbi Buchler, Conservative.
Hours: 9 am to 10 pm.

Monroe

Synagogues

Conservative

Congregation Eitz Chaim
County Route 105 10950   (914) 783-7424

Reform

Monroe Temple of Liberal Judaism
314 N. Main Street 10950

Monsey

Bakeries
Bubba's Bagels
Wesley Hills Plaza, Wesley Hills 10952
                                       (914) 362-1019
                                  Fax: (914) 362-0549
Supervision: Va'ad Harabonim of Greater Monsey.

Delicatessens
Sammy's Bagels
421 Route 59 10952

Restaurants
Al di La
455 Route 306, Wesley Hills 10952   (914) 354-2672
Supervision: Va'ad Harabonim of Greater Monsey.
Italian/Dairy. Cholov Yisrael.
Chai Pizza
94 Route 59 10952
Jerusalem Pizza & Restaurant
190 Route 59 10952
New York Café
Cot Route 59 & 306 10952

Meat

Fleigals Restaurant
43 Route 59 10952
Glatt kosher.
Pulkies, 455 Route 306, Wesley Hills 10952
Glatt kosher.

Synagogues

Orthodox

Young Israel of Monsey and Wesley Hills Inc
58 Parker Blvd 10952   (914) 362-1838

Mount Vernon

Synagogues
Brothers of Israel
116 Crary Avenue 10550
Fleetwood
11 E. Broad Street 10552

New City

Delicatessens
Steve's Deli-Bake
179 South Main Street 10956   (914) 634-8749

Groceries
M&S Kosher Meats
191a South Main Street 10956   (914) 638-9494

Synagogues

Conservative

New City Jewish Center
47 Old Schoolhouse Road 10956   (914) 634-3619
                                   Fax: (914) 634-3481
                                   Email: ncjc@js1.com

Reform

Temple Beth Sholom
228 New Hempstead Road 10956

New Rochelle

Restaurant
Eden Wok
1327 North Avenue 10804   (914) 637-9363
                                   Fax: (914) 637-9371
Supervision: Vaad of Westchester.

Synagogues

Conservative

Bethel, Northfield Road

Orthodox

Cong. Anshe Sholom
50 North Avenue, New Rochelle, NY 10805
                                   (914) 632-9220
                                   Fax: (914) 632-8182
                                   Email: ashewroch@aol.com
Young Israel
1228 North Avenue 10804
Young Israel of New Rochelle
1228 North Avenue 10804   (914) 777-1236
Contact Rabbi on 835-5581

Reform

Temple Israel
1000 Pine Brook Blvd. 10804

New York City

Nowhere in the United States is there a city richer in Jewish heritage than New York. From the city's beginnings as a Dutch trading post in the seventeenth century up to the present day, Jews have flocked to New York, made it their home, and left an indelible mark on the city's heritage, language, culture, physical structure, and day to day life. There are more Jews in the New York metropolitan area than in any other city in the world, and more than in any country except Israel. So, without a great deal of effort, just being in this largest urban Jewish community in history affords you the opportunity to be a tourist without concern about the ease of observing kashrut and Shabbat.

The estimated Jewish population of New York City proper is just over one million. Another million or so live in the immediate suburbs which include not only New York, but New Jersey and Connecticut as well. Roughly one-third of American Jews live in and around New York City and virtually every national Jewish organisation has its headquarters here.

New York City neighbourhoods with large Jewish populations are the upper west and upper east sides of Manhattan (modern orthodox and secular Jewish), Borough Park, Williamsburg (orthodox and Hasidic) and Brighton Beach (Russian) in Brooklyn, Forest Hills (Israelis and Russians), Kew Gardens, Kew Garden Hills (orthodox) in Queens, Riverdale in the Bronx, and Staten Island.

In this largest urban Jewish community in history, the Jewish traveller is overwhelmed with choices of where to eat, where to find a minyan, what to see of Jewish interest and so on. And the variety of kosher restaurants makes choosing a pleasure: Chinese, Moroccan, Italian (both meat and dairy), traditional European, Indian, Japanese and seafood.

Though Jews from numerous countries of origin live together throughout New York's Jewish communities, many

United States of America / New York

groups tend to congregate in their own neighbour-hoods or sections of neighbourhoods.

Ever since the fateful year of 1654 Jews have been coming to New York City. Sometimes a few, sometimes more, and sometimes by the boatload, as was the case between 1880 and 1924 when some two million Jews entered the United States. And though one might argue cause and effect, New York City is still the commercial, intellectual and financial centre of the country.

Synagogues

Hundreds if not thousands of synagogues, chavurot and shtiblech lie within the city, representing the myriad expressions of Judaism: Orthodox, Hasidic, Conservative, Reform and Reconstructionist.

Complete lists of synagogues in all five boroughs can be obtained from the various umbrella organisations listed in the beginning of the section on the USA .

The 1,300-seat, Moorish-style Central Synagogue (Reform) at 652 Lexington Avenue in Manhattan is the city's oldest synagogue on an original site and is an official New York City landmark; the oldest Ashkenazi congregation, founded in 1825, is B'nai Jeshrun (Conservative) at 270 West 89th Street; Shearith Israel, the Spanish and Portuguese synagogue on Central Park West at 70th Street, is one of the oldest congregations in the United States and originated with those 23 refugees from the Spanish Inquisition in Brazil in 1654. The present building still has religious items from the earliest days of the congregation and its small chapel is representative of the American colonial period; Temple Emanu-El (Reform) at Fifth Avenue and 65th Street is not only the city's largest, but the world's largest synagogue. The congregation was founded in 1848 and the building, built in 1929, can seat over 2,000 people; the Fifth Avenue synagogue at 5 East 62nd Street was, until early 1967, presided over by the then Rabbi Dr Immanuel Jakobovits, who later became the Chief Rabbi of Great Britain and the Commonwealth; the Park East synagogue at 163 East 67th Street on the very fashionable Upper East Side was founded in 1890 and is an historic landmark. Kehilath Jeshurun (Orthodox), 125 E. 85th Street, is a popular option if you are on the Upper East Side. Also among Synagogues worth visiting is the Park Avenue Synagogue (Conservative) at 50 E. 87th Street. On the Upper West Side, Lincoln Square Synagogue (Orthodox), 200 Amsterdam Avenue at 69th Street, and Ohab Zedek (Orthodox), 118 West 95th Street, are both very popular options.

Visitors may be interested in a 9 am minyan on the Upper West Side at 303 W.91st East between West End Avenue and Riverside Drive.

Libraries, Museums, and Institutes of Learning

One of New York's living museums is the Eldridge Street Synagogue (14 Eldridge Street, 212-219-0888). At 108 years old, the Eldridge Street synagogue is a ghost of its former splendour. But, in its heyday at the turn of the century, it was among the busiest synagogues on the Lower East Side, and the first built for that purpose by New York's eastern European Jews. An official New York City landmark, and listed on the National Register of Historic Places, the synagogue is an ongoing restoration project. The synagogue functions as a museum and has a whole host of programmes.

In the same neighbourhood and sociologically related is the Lower East Side Tenement Museum (97 Orchard Street, 212-431-0233). Contrary to popular opinion, the word tenement does not mean slum housing, but a particular building design devised to house the masses of immigrants who came to New York in the latter part of the nineteenth century. Tenements are five- or six-storey walk up buildings distinguished by narrow entry halls and a central air shaft. Each floor contained four apartments. Toilet facilities, located in the hallway, were shared by all the residents. Baths were taken at numerous local public bath houses. The museum, located in a restored tenement built in 1863, shows visitors what tenement life was like via a model apartment. In addition, actors in period dress present 90-minute shows in a small theatre. This is how the vast majority of Jews lived when they first came to New York City.

Ellis Island National Monument (212-269-5755) was once the point of entry for Jews and other immigrants. Some five million Jews came to the United States between 1850 and 1948 and most were processed through immigration at Castle Garden (the present ferry ticket office) or, after 1890, Ellis Island.

The Jewish Museum (Fifth Avenue and 92nd Street, 212-423-3200) has been in existence since 1904. Under the auspices of the Conservative Jewish Theological Seminary, the museum has permanent and changing exhibits and programmes and an excellent collection of Jewish ritual and ceremonial objects.

The library at the Jewish Theological Seminary (3080 Broadway at 122nd Street, 212-678-8000), houses one of the greatest collections of Judaica and Hebraica in the world. Its holdings include a rare manuscript by Maimonides (the Rambam).

The YIVO Institute for Jewish Research (555 West 57th Street, 212-246-6080) houses a large collection of books, documents, photographs and recordings pertaining to Jewish life in Europe before the Holocaust.

Other libraries with large Judaica collections are at Yeshiva University (212-960-5400), the Judaica Collection a the New York Public Library (212-340-0849), New York University (212-998-1212), Columbia University (212-854-1754), the House of Living Judaism at Temple Emanu-El (212-744-1400) and the Leo Baeck Institute (212-744-6400) Inquire at each one individually as to availability of the collections.

The main Jewish universities and seminaries are Yeshiva University which offers undergraduate and graduate degrees in the arts, sciences and humanities, rabbinical study and professional degrees such as medicine and social work, including the renowned Albert Einstein College of Medicine in the Bronx; Hebrew Union College; Touro College and the Jewish Theological Seminary.

Neighbourhoods and areas of historical interest

Manhattan

The Lower East Side has physically changed very little in over a century. Cramped tenements and crowded, dirty streets have always characterised the area. But for the absence of vendors calling out 'I cash clothes' one can get a pretty good idea of what life looked like for Jews newly arrived in New York City from eastern European countries, although it is difficult to imagine the strangeness of a new language or being away from home for the first time.

Although the Lower East Side is not as Jewish as it once was and many Jewish shops have closed, it is appropriate that historical jaunts in New York begin in its tangle of streets and alleys. For the ancestors of some 80 per cent of American Jews, this was the first piece of America they saw. Now other immigrant groups call the Lower East Side home. Settlement houses such as the Henry Street Settlement and the Educational Alliance on East Broadway once served the Jewish immigrant population in their need to learn English and become Americanised. Still in existence, they provide services to current residents, Jewish and non-Jewish alike.

Many Jews still do business in the neighbourhood and the area is full of historic buildings, Jewish shops, foodstores and stores selling all manner of ritual items (kipot, taliltot, tefilin, siddurim, etc). Look along Essex, Orchard, Grand, Rivington, Hester and Canal streets.

One of the best guidebooks for this area (as well as the rest of New York City) is the AIA [American Institute of Architects] Guide to New York City by Elliot Willensky and Norval White. An organisation called Big Onion Walking Tours gives Lower East Side tours and they are worth a telephone call (212-439-1090).

You may notice that a number of churches on the Lower East Side used to be synagogues. They were re-consecrated as churches when the Jewish community dwindled. But in many cases you still can tell which were synagogues. Look for things like Stars of David on building cornerstones, darkened mezuzah shaped areas on doorposts, and shadows of Stars of David on building façades. They are quite evident if you look.

Synagogues of note in the area are the Bialystoker synagogue (7 Wilet Street); Beth Midrash HaGadol (60 Norfolk Street); First Roumanian American Congregation (89 Rivington Street); and the Eldridge Street Synagogue (14 Eldridge Street).

The only kosher winery in Manhattan is Schapiro's Kosher Winery (126 Rivington Street, 674-4404), founded in 1899. Call for tour information.

Along Second Avenue below 14th Street you can still see the remnants of the scores of Yiddish theatres that once lined the street. Note particularly the movie theatre on Second Avenue at 12th Street, currently the City Cinemas Village East. In the upper level auditorium you can get an idea of what the place looked like when stars like Molly Picon and Boris Tomeshevsky held forth on the stage.

Forty-seventh Street between Fifth Avenue and Avenue of the Americas is the diamond centre. Some 75 per cent of all the diamonds which enter the United States pass through here. As this is overwhelmingly a Jewish and Hasidic business, the street is bustling with diamond dealers concluding deals in the open market atmosphere that is pervasive. Most deals are made with a handshake. There are a number of small kosher restaurants up and down the block.

Historical Cemeteries

Manhattan

Shearith Israel Cemeteries

Vestiges of early Jewish settlement in New York can be gleaned from the remnants of the community's first cemeteries. The following three are owned by New York's oldest congregation, Shearith Israel, the Spanish Portuguese Synagogue.

First Shearith Israel Graveyard: 55 St. James Place (between Oliver and James St), the first Jewish cemetery in New Amsterdam, was consecrated in 1656 and was located near the present Chatham Square. Its remains were moved to this location. It contains the remains of Sephardic Jews who emigrated from Brazil.

Second Cemetery of the Spanish and Portuguese Synagogue (1805–1829): 72-76 West 11th Street, just east of Sixth Avenue on the south side of the street.

Third Cemetery of the Spanish and Portuguese Synagogue (1829-1851): 98-110 west 21st Street, just west of Sixth Avenue on the south side of the street.

Brooklyn

Green-Wood Cemetery (Fifth Avenue and Fort Hamilton Parkway, Brooklyn) contains the graves of many prominent Jewish figures.

Queens

Fourth Cemetery of the Spanish and Portuguese Synagogue: Cypress Hills Street and Cypress Avenue, Queens. The beautiful chapel and gate were built in 1885.

Arts and Entertainment

As American entertainment is largely a secular Jewish enterprise, one need not look very far for Jewish references in plays and musicals. However, there are some dedicated Jewish theatrical companies and venues: the Jewish Repertory Company (212-831-2000); the American Jewish Theater (212-633-1588); the YM & YWHA (212-427-6000) has

United States of America / New York

several outstanding lecture series, some with specific Jewish themes. For other events of Jewish interest consult one of the weekly listings magazines such as Time Out New York or New York Magazine, or the Sunday Arts & Leisure section of the New York Times. Jewish newspapers with events listings are Jewish Week, Forward, and Jewish Press, all available at most newsstands.

Jewish Neighbourhoods of Interest outside Manhattan
Brooklyn
Williamsburg was for many years the centre of Hasidic life in New York City. But in the last decade many rebbes and their followers have moved to the suburbs, particularly Rockland county. However, a trip to Williamsburg is still worthwhile.

Boro Park is almost completely orthodox and is almost a world apart from the rest of the city.

Crown Heights is populated by Hasidim of many sects, but particularly the Lubavitch, whose world headquarters is at 770 Eastern Parkway. The neighbourhood is not totally Jewish and there are often clashes (sometimes violent) between the Caribbean residents and Jewish residents.

New Jersey
Many towns in northern and central New Jersey are less than 40 minutes travel time by either car or public transport from Manhattan, and as such are part of metropolitan New York. They are: Bayonne, Clifton, Elizabeth, Englewood, Fairlawn, Hackensack, Hoboken, Jersey City, Newark, Passaic, Teaneck, Union and West New York.

Restaurants
By law in New York State, the selling of non-kosher food as kosher is a punishable fraud. Administered by the Kosher Law Enforcement Section of the New York State Department of Agriculture, heavy penalties are imposed on violators. An orthodox rabbi oversees the operation. Businesses selling kosher food must display proper signage, indicating under whose hashgacha they operate, and establishments which sell both kosher and non-kosher food must display that as well, with a sign in block letters no smaller than four inches high.

In August 2000 a Federal Judge ruled that this law violated the First Ammendment. An appeal is however expected.

The Kosher Directory, issued by the Union of Orthodox Jewish Congregations, lists foods and services which bear the symbol. It is available for a charge by calling 212-563-4000. Other reliable kashruth insignias are Circle K and the Hebrew letter KOF-K.

Note that kosher packaged foods, including bread, meat, fish, cake, biscuits and virtually anything you can think of, are widely available in supermarkets throughout the New York metropolitan area. Many foodstores, especially on the Upper West Side of Manhattan and in Jewish neighbourhoods in Brooklyn and Queens, sell fresh kosher prepared meals as well.

Bronx

Bakeries
Gruenebaum Bakery
3530 Johnson Avenue 10463   (718) 884-5656
Supervision: Rabbi Jonathan Rosenblatt, Riverdale Jewish Center.

Heisler's Pastry Shop
3601 Riverdale Avenue, at 236th Street, Riverdale 10463   (718) 549-0770
Supervision: Westchester Vaad.

Mr Bagel of Broadway
5672 Broadway, Riverdale 10463   (718) 549-0408
Supervision: Rabbi Jonathan Rosenblatt, Riverdale Jewish Center.

Booksellers
Judaica Book Store
3706 Riverdale Avenue 10463   (718) 601-7563

Butchers
Glatt Emporium
3711 Riverdale Avenue, Riverdale 10463
        (718) 884-1200
Supervision: Rabbi Jonathan Rosenblatt, Riverdale Jewish Center.

Glatt Shop
3540 Johnson Avenue 10463   (718) 548-4855
Supervision: Rabbi Jonathan Rosenblatt, Riverdale Jewish Center.
Stock groceries as well.

Restaurants
Second Helping
3532 Johnson Avenue 10463   (718) 548-1818
Supervision: Vaad Harabonim of Riverdale.
Take out food only, Glatt kosher.

Yeshiva University: Bronx Center
Eastchester Rd. & Morris Park Avenue 10461
        (718) 430-2131

Dairy
Corner Café and Bakery
3552 Johnson Avenue, Riverdale 10463
        (718) 601-2861
Supervision: Rabbi Jonathan Rosenblatt, Riverdale Jewish Center.

Main Event
3708 Riverdale Avenue, Riverdale 10463
(718) 601-6246
Fax: (718) 601-0008
Email: maineventc@aol.com
Supervision: Rabbi Jonathan Rosenblatt, Riverdale
Jewish Center.

Meat

Riverdelight
3543 Riverdale Ave., Flushing
(718) 543-4270
Fax: (718) 543-7475
Supervision: Va'ad Riverdale.
Glatt Kosher. Grill, Deli and Middle-Eastern Cuisine.
Take-out and catering.

Szechuan Garden Chinese Restaurant
3717 Riverdale Avenue, Riverdale 10463
(718) 884-4242
Supervision: Rabbi Jonathan Rosenblatt, Riverdale
Jewish Center.

Brooklyn

Bakeries

Donuts

Dunkin' Donuts
2630 86th Street 11223
(718) 372-0650
Supervision: Kof-K.
Pat Yisrael.
Dunkin' Donuts
1410 Avenue J 11230
Supervision: Kof-K.
Pat Yisrael.
Dunkin' Donuts
1611 Avenue M 11230
(718) 336-2641
Supervision: Kof-K.
Pat Yisrael.

Delicatessens

Eden Delicatessen and Steak House
5928 Glenwood Road 11236
(718) 209-4244
Fax: (718) 209-3268
Supervision: Kehilah (Flatbush).
Essex on Coney
1359 Coney Island Avenue 11230
(718) 253-1002
Fax: (718) 253-8322
Supervision: Kehilah (Flatbush).
Gourmet on J
1412 Avenue J 11230
(718) 338-9181
Supervision: Kehilah (Flatbush).
Meat. Take out only.

Kenereth
1920 Avenue U 11229
(718) 743-2473
Supervision: Kehilah (Flatbush).
Take out only.
Kings Glatt Deli
924 Kings Highway 11223
(718) 336-7500
Supervision: Kehilah (Flatbush).
Take out only.

Groceries

Mountain Fruit
1520 Avenue M 11230
(718) 998-3333
Fax: (718) 998-0726
Supervision: Kehilah (Flatbush).
Hashgacha is limited to bakery, store packaged dry
fruits and nuts, and candies.
Shop Smart
2640 Nostrand Avenue 11210
(718) 377-4166
Fax: (718) 252-2363
Supervision: Kehilah (Flatbush).

Hotels

Avenue Plaza Hotel
4624 13th Avenue 11219
Midwood Suites
1078 East 15 St. 11230
(718) 253-9535
Fax: (718) 253-3269
Email: shalom@midwoodsuites.com
Scharf's Ateret of Midwood
1410 East 10th Street 11230
(718) 998-5400
Fax: (718) 645-8600
Daily Minyon. Under strict Hashgocha. Cholov
Yisroel/Glatt Kosher
The Crown Palace Hotel
570-600 Crown Street
(718) 604-1777
Glatt kosher.
The Park House Hotel
1206 48th Street 11219
(718) 871-8100

Libraries
Levi Yitzhak Library
305 Kingston Avenue 11213

Museums
The Chasidic Art Institute
375 Kingston Avenue

Organisations

Orthodox

Lubavitch Movement
770 Eastern Parkway 11213
(718) 221-0500
Fax: (718) 221-0985

United States of America / New York

Restaurants

Dairy

Bernies Place
1287 Ave. J.   (718) 677-1515
Supervision: Rabbi Gornish.
Chapp-u-Ccino
4815 12th Avenue   (718) 633-4377
Supervision: Rabbi Amrom Roth.
Fontana Bella
2086 Coney Island Avenue   (718) 627-3904
Supervision: Rabbi Gornish.
Garden of Eat-In
1416 Avenue J 11230   (718) 252-5289
                                        Fax: (718) 252-1856
Supervision: Kehilah (Flatbush).
Sunflower Café
1223 Kings Highway, cor. E. 13th St.
                                              (718) 336-1340
Supervision: Rabbi Gornish.
Tea For Two Café
547 Kings Highway   (718) 998-0020/0990
Supervision: Rabbi Gornish.

Meat

Bamboo Garden
904 Kings Highway   (718) 375-8501
Supervision: Rabbi Yisroel P. Gornish.
Dougies, 4310 18th Ave, Bet. McDonald Ave. & E. 2nd
St., Off Ocean Parkway   (718) 686-8080
Supervision: Udvar Kashruth of America.
Edna's Restaurant & Deli
125 Church Avenue 11202   (718) 438-8207
Fuji Hana, 512 Av.U   (718) 336-3888
Supervision: Vaad Harabonim of Flatbush.
Glatt Kosher Family
4305 18th Ave., Bet. McDonald & E. 2nd St.
                                              (718) 972-8085/6
Supervision: Vaad of Flatbush.
Glatt-a-la-Carte
5502 18th Ave   (718) 621-3697
Supervision: R'Yechiel Babad.
Gottlieb's Glatt Kosher
352 Roebling Street   (718) 384-9037
Jerusalem Steak House
533 Kings Highway 11223   (718) 336-5115
Kineret Steak House
521 Kings Highway, Bet. E. 2nd - E. 3rd Sts.
                                              (718) 336-8888
Supervision: Kehilah Kashruth.
Kosher Delight Glatt Kosher
1223 Avenue J (E. 13th Street), Flatbush 11230
                                              (718) 377-6873
                                        Fax: (718) 677-0831
Supervision: Rav S.D. Beck and Vaad Rabonim of
Flatbush.

Mama's Restaurant
906 Kings Highway 11223   (718) 382-7200
Supervision: Rabbi Gornish.
McFleishig's
5508 16th Avenue   (718) 435-2779
Supervision: Rabbi Babad, Tartikover.
Nathan's Famous
825 Kings Highway, cor. E. 9   (718) 627-5252
Supervision: Kehilah Kashrus.
Olympic Pita
1419 Coney Island Avenue, Bet. J & K
                                              (718) 258-6222
Supervision: Kehilah Kashrus.
Shalom Hunan
1619 Avenue M   (718) 382-6000
Shang-Chai Glatt Kosher
2189 Flatbush Avenue 11234   (212) 377-6100
Sushi Kosher
1626 Coney Island Avenue 11230   (718) 338-6363
                                        Fax: (718) 338-2922
Supervision: Kehilah (Flatbush).
Tokyo of Brooklyn
2954 Ave U, off Nostrand Ave.   (718) 891-6221
Supervision: Kehilah Kashrus.
Yun-Kee Glatt Kosher
1424 Elm Avenue, cnr. E.15th Street & Avenue M
                                              (718) 627-0072
Supervision: ARK.

Pizzerias

Chadash Pizza
1919 Avenue M 11230   (718) 253-4793
Supervision: Kehilah (Flatbush).

Manhattan

There are of course a large number of synagogues
of all kinds in New York.
The major synagogues in Manhattan and of
possible interest to visitors are the following.
Orthodox
Fifth Avenue Synagogue
5 East 62nd Street, NY, 10021   (212) 838 2122
Kehilath Jeshurun
125 East 85th Street, NY, 10028   (212) 427 1000
Lincoln Square
220 Amsterdam Avenue at 69th Street,
NY, 10023
                                              (212)874 6100
Ohab Zedeck
118 West 95th Street, NY,
10025   (212) 749 5150
Park East
163 East 67th Street, NY, 10021
                                              (212) 737 6900
                                        Fax: (212) 570 648

Sephardi
Shearith Israel
2 West 70th Street, NY, 10023   (212) 873-0300
Reform
Central Synagogue
652 Lexington Avenue, NY, 10022

(212) 838 5122

Temple Emanuel-El
1 East 65th Street, NY, 10023
(212) 744 1400
Conservative
B'nai Jeshrun
270 West 89th Street, NY, 10010
(212) 787 7600
Park Avenue Synagogue
50 East 87th Street, NY, 10128
(212) 369 2600
Fax: (212) 410 7879
Visitors wishing to ascertain details of other synagogues in Manhattan or of synagogues in outlying areas should contact the appropriate central authority as detailed below.
Orthodox
Agudat Israel World Organization
84 William Street, NY, 10038
(212) 797 9600
Fax: (212) 269 2843
Lubavitch Movement
770 Eastern Parkway,
Brooklyn, NY, 11213
(718) 221 0500
Fax: (718) 221 0985
National Council of Young Israel National Office
3 West 16th Street, NY, 10011
(212) 929 1525
Fax: (212) 727 9526
Email: nyci@youngisrael.org
www.youngisrael.org
Union of Orthodox Jewish Congregations of America
333 Seventh Avenue, NY, 10001
(212) 563 4000
Fax: (212) 613 8333
Conservative
United Synagogue of America
155 Fifth Avenue, NY, 10010
(212) 533 7800
World Council of Synagogues can be found at the same location.

Reform
Union of America Hebrew Congregations
838 Fifth Avenue, NY, 10021
(212) 650 4085
Fax: (212) 650 4169
Progessive
World Union for Progressive Judaism
838 Fifth Avenue, NY, 10021
(212) 650 4090
Fax: (212) 650 4090
Email: 5448032@mcimail.com
Sephardi
Union of Sephardi Congregations
8 West 70th Street, NY, 10023
(212) 873 0300

Bakeries
H & H / The Excellent Bagel
2239 Broadway 10024   (212) 692-2435
Supervision: Kof-K.

Delicatessens
Essen West
226 West 72nd Street 10023   (212) 362-1234
Supervision: OU.
Meat take out and caterers.
L'Chaim Caterers
4464 Broadway 10040   (212) 304-4852
Supervision: Kof-K.
Take out food store.
Lou G. Siegel
240 West 14th Street   (212) 921-4433
Supervision: OU.
Meat, take out only.
Second Avenue Delicatessan-Restaurant
156 2nd Avenue cnr. 10th Street   (212) 677-0606
Fax: (212) 477-5327
Email: 2ndavedeli@quicklink.com
Hours - Sunday-Thursday 7.30am-12.00am. Friday & Saturday 7.30am-3.00am.

Embassy
Consul General of Israel
800 Second Avenue 10017   (212) 499-5400
Fax: (212) 499 5555
Permanent Mission of Israel to the United Nations
800 Second Avenue 10017

Kashrut Information
Agudath Israel World Organisation
84 William Street 10273   (212) 797-9600
The organisation will provide free of charge, a list of people in most major US cities who can provide kashrut information.

United States of America / New York

Libraries

Butler Library of Colombia University
Broadway at 116th Street 10027
Has some 6,000 Hebrew books and pamphlets, plus
1,000 manuscripts and a Hebrew psalter printed at
Cambridge University in 1685 and used by Samuel
Johnson at the graduation of the first candidates for
bachelor's degrees.
New York University of Judaica and Hebraica
Housing a stunning collection of priceless items.
The Jewish Division of the New York Public Library
Fifth Avenue at 42nd Street 10017
Has 125,000 volumes of Judaica and Hebraica, along
with extensive microfilm and bound files of Jewish
publications, one of the finest collections in existence.

Museums

Jewish Museum
1109 Fifth Avenue 10028
This is one of the outstanding museums in the city and
a 'must' not just for Jewish visitors but for all interested
in art. The permanent display consists of one of the
finest collection of Jewish ritual and ceremonial art in
the world, along with notable paintings and sculptures.
Jewish Theological Seminary of America
3080 Broadway at 122nd Street 10027
Housing rare manuscripts, including a work in the hand
of Maimonides, as well as Cairo Geniza fragments (on
application to the librarian only). Has what is believed
to be the greatest collection of Judaica and Hebraica in
the world.
Leo Baeck Institute
129 E. 73rd Street 10021
Has a vast collection of books, manuscripts, letters and
photographs of German Jewish authors, scientists,
rabbis and communal leaders, as well as an art
collection of the Jews of Germany.
Lower East Side Tenement Museum
90 Orchard Street 10002   (212) 431-0233
                                 Fax: (212) 431-0402
                      Web site: www.tenement.org
Housed in a 1863 structure the Museum presents and
interprets the variety of immigrant experience on
Manhattan's Lower East side , a gateway to America.
The House of Living Judaism
5th Avenue and 65th Street
Frequently shows paintings and ritual objects. Twelve
marble pillars symbolise the Twelve Tribes.
The Museum of Jewish Heritage
18 First Place 10004   (212) 509-6130
The Museum's core exhibition combines archival
material with modern media as a living memorial to
the Holocaust

Theological Seminary of America
Fifth Avenue & 92nd Street 10028
An outstanding museum, with permanent displays of
Jewish ritual and ceremonial art, along with notable
paintings and sculptures.
Yeshiva University
Amsterdam Avenue, 185th Street 10033
The museum's salient feature is a permanent display o
scale-model synagogues.
Yivo Institute for Jewish Research
555 West 57th Street 10019   (212) 246-608▮
                                 Fax: (212) 292-189▮
This Museum has a large collection of original
documents on Jewish life, along with some 300,000
volumes, and thousands of photographs, music sheets
gramophone records, etc.

Organisations
UJA-Federation Resource Line
130 E. 59th Street 10022   (212) 753-228▮
                                 Fax: (212) 888-753▮
                      Email: resourceline@ujafedny.or▮

Conservative
United Synagogue of America
155 Fifth Avenue 10010   (212) 533-780▮

Orthodox
Agudat Israel World Organization
84 William Street 10038   (212) 797-960▮
Union of Orthodox Jewish Congregations of America
333 Seventh Avenue 10001   (212) 563-400▮
                                 Fax: (212) 613-833▮

Progressive
World Union for Progressive Judaism
838 Fifth Avenue 10021   (212) 249-0100 ext. 50▮
                                 Fax: (212) 517-394▮

Reform
Union of American Hebrew Congregations
633 Third Avenue 10017-6778   (212) 650-400▮
                                 Email: uahc@uahc.o▮

Sephardic
Union of Sephardic Congregations
8 West 70th Street 10023   (212) 873-030▮

Religious Organisations
Young Israel National Office
3 West 16th Street 10011   (212) 929-152▮
                                 Fax: (212) 727-952▮
                      Email: ncyi@youngisrael.o▮
                      Web site: www.youngisrael.o▮
Contact the Department of Synagogue Services at this
number for information regarding the Young Israel sh▮
nearest you.

United States of America / New York

Restaurant

Mom's Bagels of NY
15 West 45th Street 10036   (212) 764-1566
                                            Fax: (212) 764-1566
                                    Email: info@momsnyc.com
Supervision: Kof-K.
Chulov Yisruel
Ben's Kosher Delicatessen
209 West 38th Street   (212) 398-2367
                                       Fax: (212) 398-3354
                               Email: info@bensdeli.net
                               Web site: www.bensdeli.net
Supervision: Supervised.
Hours: 11am to 9.30 pm.
Deniz
400 East 57th 10022   (212) 486-2255
Eden Wok
127 W. 72 Street 10023   (212) 787-8700
                                          Fax: (212) 787-9801
Supervision: OU.
Pita Express, 1470 2nd Avenue (77th Street)
                                       (212) 249-1300
Glatt kosher.
Sammy's Restaurants
157 Chrystie Street   (212) 673-0330
Yeshiva University: Main Center
500 W. 185th Street 10033-3201   (212) 960-5248
                                          Fax: (212) 960-0070
Yeshiva University: Mid-town Center
245 Lexington Avenue at 35th Street 10016
                                       (212) 340-7712

Dairy

All-American Health Bar
24 E. 42nd Street   (212) 370-4525
American Cafe Health Bar and Pizza
160 Broadway 10038   (212) 732-1426
Supervision: Kof-K.
Chalav Yisrael.
Bagels & Co.
1428 York Ave., cor. E. 76th St.
                                       (212) 717-0505
Supervision: New York Kosher.
Broadway's Jerusalem 2
1375 Broadway, at 38th Street 10018
                                       (212) 398-1475
                                    Fax: (212) 212-398-6797
                               Email: n.y.pies@.com
Supervision: OU.
Chalav Yisrael, Prs Yisruel. Home of the N.Y. Flying
Pizza Pies. Visit the 'Jewish Wall of Fame'. 7.00am to
12.00pm. Saturday nights to 2.00am.
Café 18
8 East 18th Street, Bet. 5th and Broadway
                                       (212) 620-4182
Cafe 123
2 Park Avenue   (212) 685-7117

Cafe Roma Pizzeria
175 W. 90th Street   (212) 875-8972
Diamond Dairy Kosher Lunchonette
4 W. 47th Street 10036   (212) 719-2694
On the gallery overlooking the diamond & jewelry
exchange. Hours: Monday to Thursday, 7:30 am to 5
pm; Friday, to 2 pm.
Great American Health Bar
35 W. 57th Street   (212) 355-5177
Gusto va Mare
237 E. 53rd St.   (212) 583-9300
Supervision: Organised Kashrut.
Joseph's Cafe
50 West 72 St   (212) 721-1943
My Most Favorite Desert
120 West 45th Street   (212) 997-5130
Supervision: OU.
Chalav Yisrael.
Provi, Provi, 228 W, 72nd St.,
Bet. B'way and West End Ave.   (212) 875-9020
Supervision: Organised Kashrut.
Va Bene, 1589 Second Avenue 10028
                                       (212) 517-4448
                                    Fax: (212) 517-2258
Supervision: OU.
Chalav Yisrael Italian restaurant.
Vege-Vege II
544 3rd Avenue   (212) 679-4710
Vegetable Garden
15 East 40th Street 10016   (212) 545-7444
Supervision: Kof-K.
Village Crown Italian Dairy Cuisine
94 Third Avenue 10003   (212) 777-8816; 388-9639
                               Email: info@villagecrown.com
                               Web site: www.villagecrown.com
Supervision: Kof-/Cholev Israel.

Meat

Abigael's Grill and Caterers
9 East 37th Street 10016   (212) 725-0130
                                          Fax: (212) 725-3577
Supervision: Kof-K.
Glatt kosher.
Abigael's on Broadway
1407 Broadway, at 39th Street 10016
                                       (212) 575-1407
                                    Fax: (212) 866-0666
Supervision: Kof-K.
Glatt kosher. Lunch Mon-Friday 12pm-3pm. Dinner
Sun-Thursday 5pm-10pm.
Alexi 56
25 West 56th Street 10019   (212) 767-1234
                                          Fax: (212) 767-8254
Supervision: OU.
Continental cuisine. Open for lunch and dinner. Near
public transportation.

United States of America / New York

Cafe Classico
35 West 57th Street   (212) 355-5411
Glatt kosher.

Chick Chack Chicken
121 University Place   (212) 228-3100
Supervision: OU.

China Shalom II
686 Columbus Avenue 10025   (212) 662-9676
Supervision: Kof-K.
Glatt kosher.

Colbeh, 43 West 39th Street 10018   (212) 354-8181
Supervision: Kof-K.
Glatt kosher.

Deli Glatt
150 Fulton Street   (212) 349-3622

Deli Kasbah
2553 Amsterdam Avenue
                                       (212) 568-4600

Deli Kasbah
251 W. 85th Street   (212) 496-1500
                                  Fax: (212) 496-2273
Supervision: Circle K.
Hours: Sunday to Thursday, 12 pm to 11 pm.
Mediterranean food.

Domani Ristorante
1590 First Ave, Bet. 82nd-83rd St.
                                 (212) 717-7575/7557
Supervision: Organised Kashrut.

Dougie's BBQ
222 West 72nd Street 10023   (212) 724-2222
Supervision: OU.
Glatt kosher.

Galil, 1252 Lexington Avenue 10028
                                       (212) 439-9886
Supervision: Kof-K.

Glatt Dynasty
1049 Second Avenue, East 55th & East 56th Street
10022   (212) 888-9119
                                  Fax: (212) 888-9163
Supervision: Kof-K.
Glatt kosher.

Haikara, 1016 2nd Avenue   (212) 355-7000
Supervision: OU.

Il Patrizio
206 East 63rd St., Bet. 2nd and 3rd Aves.
                                       (212) 980-4007
Supervision: OU.

Jasmine
11 East 30 Street,
between Madison and 5th Avenues   (212) 251-8884
Supervision: Vaad l'Kashrut Badatz Sepharadic.
Glatt kosher Persian and Middle Eastern cuisine. Open
Sunday to Friday, for lunch and dinner.

Jerusalem Pita Glatt Kosher
212 E. 45th Street   (212) 922-0009
                                  Fax: (212) 922-0018
Under Rabbinical Supervision

Jewish Theological Seminary of America cafeteria
3080 Broadway at 122nd Street 10027
                                       (212) 678-8000

Kosher Delight
1359 Broadway (37th Street)   (212) 563-3366

La Fontana
309 East 83rd Street 10028   (212) 734-6343
Supervision: Kof-K.
Glatt kosher.

La Marais 2
15 John St @ B'way   (212) 285-8585
Supervision: Organised Kashrut.

Le Marais
150 W. 46th Street 10036   (212) 869-0900
                                  Fax: (212) 869-1016
Supervision: Circle K.
Glatt kosher. Hours: Sunday to Thursday, 12 pm to 12
am; Friday, to 3 pm; Saturday, October to May, one
hour after sundown to 1 am.

Levana
141 West 69th Street 10023   (212) 877-8457
                                  Fax: (212) 595-7522
                             Email: info@levana.com
                         Web site: www.levana.com
Supervision: Orthodox Union..
Glatt kosher.

Mendy's Restaurant
61 East 34th Street 10016   (212) 576-1010
Supervision: OU.

Mendy's West
208 West 70th Street 10023   (212) 877-6787
Supervision: OU.

Mr. Broadway
1372 Broadway   (212) 921-215
Supervision: OU.

Penguin
258 W. 15th St., Bet. 7-8 Av.
                                       (212) 255-360
Supervision: Vaad Hakashrus.

Pita Express
261 1st Avenue (15th Street)
                                       (212) 533-195
Glatt kosher.

Siegel's Kosher Deli & Restaurant
1646 2nd Avenue   (212) 288-363

Tevere '84'
155 E. 84th Street 10028   (212) 744-021
Supervision: OU.
Glatt kosher Italian restaurant. Private party available.
Open for lunch, brunch and dinner.

Village Crown
96 Third Avenue 10003   (212) 674-206
Supervision: Kof-K.
Glatt kosher.

What's Cooking, Manhattan
18 E. 41st Street   (212) 725-6096
Breakfast and lunch are dairy. Dinner is meat.

Wolf & Lamb Steakhouse
10 E. 48th St., Nr Rockerfeller Ctr.   (212) 317-1950
Supervision: Organised Kashrut.

Organic

Caravan of Dreams
405 East 6th Street, Bet. 1st Ave. & Ave. A
      (212) 254-1613
Supervision: Orthodox Rabbinical Assoc..

Vegetarian

Madras Mahal, 104 Lexington Avenue
      (212) 684-4010

Saffron (Indian Vegetarian Cuisine)
81 Lexington Avenue 10016   (212) 696-5130
      Fax: (212) 696-5146

Theatres

Dramatics

Jewish Repertory Theatre
c/o Midtown YMHA, 344 E. 14th Street
     (212) 505-2667; 674-7200

Winery

Shapiro's Wine Company
124 Rivington Street   (212) 475-7383
In business since 1899. Providing free tours on
telephone call.

Queens

Bakeries

Aron's Bake Shop
71-71 Yellowstone Blvd, Forest Hills 11375
     (718) 263-5045
Supervision: Vaad Harabonim of Queens.

Bagel King
116-26 Metropolitan Avenue, Kew Gardens 11418
     (718) 847-3623
Supervision: Vaad Harabonim of Queens.

Beigel's Bakery
189-09 Union Turnpike, Flushing 11366
     (718) 468-1243
Supervision: Vaad Harabonim of Queens.

G & I Bakeries
72-22 Main Street, Flushing 11367 (718) 544-8736
Supervision: Vaad Harabonim of Queens.

G & I Bakeries
69-49 Main Street, Flushing 11367 (718) 261-1155
Supervision: Vaad Harabonim of Queens.

Hot Bagels and Bialys
67-11 Main Street, Flushing 11367 (718) 575-1071
Supervision: Vaad Harabonim of Queens.

King David Bakery
77-51 Vleigh Place, Flushing 11367 (718) 969-6165
Supervision: Vaad Harabonim of Queens.

L & L Bakery
64-17 108th Street, Forest Hills 11375
     (718) 997-1088
Supervision: Vaad Harabonim of Queens.

Queens Kosher Pita
68-36 Main Street, Flushing 11367 (718) 263-8000
Supervision: Vaad Harabonim of Queens.

Donuts

Dunkin' Donuts
83-47 Parsons Blvd, Jamaica 11432
     (718) 738-0465
Supervision: Vaad Harabonim of Queens.

Butchers

Abe's Glatt Kosher Meats
98-106 Queens Blvd, Forest Hills 11375
     (718) 459-5820
Supervision: Vaad Harabonim of Queens.

Herman Glick's Sons
101-15 Queens Blvd, Forest Hills 11375
     (718) 896-7736
Supervision: Vaad Harabonim of Queens.

Herskowitz Glatt Meat Market
164-08 69th Avenue, Hillcrest 11365
     (718) 591-0750
     Fax: (718) 591-0750
Supervision: Vaad Harabonim of Queens.

S & L Glatt Kosher Meats
75-37 Main Street, Flushing 11367
     (718) 459-4888
Supervision: Vaad Harabonim of Queens.

Super Glatt Meat
189-23 Union Turnpike, Flushing 11367
     (718) 776-7727
Supervision: Vaad Harabonim of Queens.

Tov Hamativ
69-38 Main Street, Flushing 11367 (718) 263-7009
Supervision: Vaad Harabonim of Queens.

Delicatessens

Asian Glatt
67-21 Main Street, Flushing 11367 (718) 793-3061
Supervision: Vaad Harabonim of Queens.
Take out only.

Berso Foods
64-20 108th Street, Forest Hills 11375
     (718) 275-9793
Supervision: Vaad Harabonim of Queens.
Take out only.

Mauzone Home Foods of Queens
69-60 Main Street, Flushing 11367 (718) 261-7723
Supervision: Vaad Harabonim of Queens.
Take out only.

United States of America / New York

Mauzone Take Home Foods
61-36 Springfield Blvd, Bayside 11364
(718) 225-1188
Supervision: Vaad Harabonim of Queens.
Take out only.

Maven Kosher Foods
188-09 Union Turnpike, Fresh Meadows 11366
(718) 479-5504
Supervision: Vaad Harabonim of Queens.
Take out only.

Meal Mart
72-10 Main Street, Flushing 11367   (718) 261-3300
Fax: (718) 261-3435
Supervision: Vaad Harabonim of Queens.
Catering and take out.

The Wok
100-19 Queens Blvd, Forest Hills 11375
(718) 896-0310
Supervision: Vaad Harabonim of Queens.
Chinese. Take out only.

Tov Caterers
97-22 63 Road, Rego Park 11374   (718) 896-7788
Supervision: Vaad Harabonim of Queens.
Take out only.

Groceries

Supersol
68-18 Main Street, Flushing 11367   (718) 268-6469
Supervision: Vaad Harabonim of Queens.

Wasserman Supermarket
72-68 Main Street, Flushing 11367   (718) 544-7413
Supervision: Vaad Harabonim of Queens.

Hotels

Washington Hotel
124-19 Rockaway Beach Blvd, Rockaway Park 11694
(718) 474-9671
Supervision: OU.

Ice Cream Parlors

Yogurt Planet
71-26 Main Street, Flushing 11367   (718) 793-8629
Supervision: Vaad Harabonim of Queens.

Restaruants

Meat

Colbeh
68-34 Main Street, Flushing   (718) 268-8181
Supervision: Kof-K.

Dougie's
73-27 Main Street, Kew Gardens Hills
(718) 793-4600
Fax: (718) 793-9003
Supervision: Vaad Harabonim of Queens.

Pita House
98-102 Queens Blvd., Bet. 66-67th Ave.   (718) 897-4829
Supervision: Rabbi David Katz.

Restaurants

Ben's Best Deli Restaurant
96-40 Queens Blvd, Rego Park 11374
(718) 897-1700
Fax: (718) 997-6503
Email: bensbest@worldnet.att.net
Supervision: Vaad Harabonim.

Knish-Knosh
101-02 Queens Blvd, Forest Hills 11375
(718) 897-5554

Dairy

Chef's Market
30-00 47th Avenue 11101   (718) 706-8070
Supervision: Vaad Harabonim of Queens.

Jerusalem Café
72-02 Main Street, Flushing 11367   (718) 520-8940
Supervision: Vaad Harabonim of Queens.

Main Street Kosher Corner
73-01 Main Street, Flushing 11367   (718) 263-1177
Supervision: Vaad Harabonim of Queens.

Meat

Annie's Kitchen
72-24 Main Street, Flushing 11367   (718) 268-0960
Supervision: Vaad Harabonim of Queens.
Chinese food.

Burger Nosh
69-48 Main Street, Flushing 11367   (718) 520-1933
Supervision: Vaad Harabonim of Queens.

Cho-Sen Garden
64-43 108th Street, Forest Hills 11375
(718) 275-1300
Supervision: Vaad Harabonim of Queens.
Chinese food.

Empire Kosher Roasters #2
180-30 Union Turnpike, Flushing 11365
(718) 591-4220
Supervision: Vaad Harabonim of Queens.

Glatt Wok Express
190-11 Union Turnpike, Flushing 11366
(718) 740-1675
Supervision: Vaad Harabonim of Queens.
Chinese food. Take away service available.

Hapina
69-54 Main Street, Flushing 11367
(718) 544-6262
Supervision: Vaad Harabonim of Queens.

Hapisgah
147-25 Union Turnpike, Flushing 11367
(718) 380-4449
Supervision: Vaad Harabonim of Queens.

Kosher Haven
65-30 Kissena Blvd, Flushing 11367   (718) 261-0149
Supervision: Vaad Harabonim of Queens.
Located at Queens College.

United States of America / New York

Kosher International Restaurant
JFK Airport, Arrivals Bldg   (718) 656-1757
Kosher King
72-30 Main Street, Flushing 11367   (718) 793-5464
Supervision: Vaad Harabonim of Queens.
Pastrami King
124-24 Queens Blvd, Kew Gardens   (718) 263-1717
Pninat Hamizrach
178-07 Union Turnpike, Fresh Meadows 11365
                                          (718) 591-3367
Supervision: Vaad Harabonim of Queens.
Stargate
73-27 Main Street, Flushing 11367   (718) 793-1199
Supervision: Vaad Harabonim of Queens.
Steakiat Mabat
68-36 Main Street, Flushing 11367   (718) 793-2926
Supervision: Vaad Harabonim of Queens.
Surf Deli
101-05 Queens Blvd, Forest Hills 11375
                                          (718) 459-7875
Supervision: Vaad Harabonim of Queens.
Tashkent Glatt Kosher Restaurant
149-15 Union Turnpike, Flushing 11367
                                          (718) 969-9810
Supervision: Vaad Harabonim of Queens.

Pizzerias

Benjy Kosher Pizza and Falafel
72-72 Main Street, Flushing 11367   (718) 268-0791
Supervision: Vaad Harabonim of Queens.
Dan Carmel Ice Cream and Pizza
98 Queens Blvd, Forest Hills 11375   (718) 544-8530
Supervision: Vaad Harabonim of Queens.
Hamakom Pizza
101-11 Queens Blvd, Forest Hills 11375
                                          (718) 275-3992
Supervision: Vaad Harabonim of Queens.
King Solomon Pizza
75-43 Main Street, Flushing 11367   (718) 793-0710
Supervision: Vaad Harabonim of Queens.
Manna Kosher Pizza
68-28 Main Street, Flushing 11367   (718) 520-8754
Supervision: Vaad Harabonim of Queens.
Moshe's Kosher Pizza
181-30 Union Turnpike, Flushing 11366
                                          (718) 969-1928
Supervision: Vaad Harabonim of Queens.
Shimon's Kosher Pizza
71-24 Main Street, Flushing 11367   (718) 793-1491
Supervision: Vaad Harabonim of Queens.
Spencer's Pizza
248-06 Union Turnpike, Bellerose 11426
                                          (718) 347-5862
Supervision: Vaad Harabonim of Queens.

Vegetarian

Budda Bodai, 42-96 Main Street, Flushing
                                          (718) 939-1188
Supervision: Rabbi Mayer Steinberg.

Staten Island
Kashrut Information

Directories

Organised Kashrus Laboratories
PO Box 218, Brooklyn   (718) 851-6428
Including the Circle K trademark.
The Dining Guide of the Jewish Press
                                          (718) 330-1100
Providing information on where to get kosher Won-Ton
soup, couscous, hot pastrami and corned (salt) beef
sandwiches, gefilte fish, hummus, tehina and much,
much more.
UOJC
333 7th Avenue 10001   (212) 563-4000

Newburgh
Kashrut Information
Agudas Israel
290 North Street 12550   (914) 562-5604

Museums
Gomez Mill House
Millhouse Road, Marlboro 12542   (845) 236-3126
                                     Fax: (845) 236-3365
                          Email: gomezmillhouse@juno.com
                               Web site: www.gomez.org
Oldest Jewish residence maintained as a museum.

Niagara Falls

Organisations
Jewish Federation of Niagara Falls
c/o of Beth Israel   (716) 284-4575

Synagogues

Conservative
Beth Israel
College & Madison Avenues 14305   (716) 285-9894
Reform
Beth El, 720 Ashland Avenue 14301   (716) 282-2717

Orangeburg
Synagogues

Conservative
Orangetown Jewish Center
Independence Avenue 10962

Peekskill
Synagogues
First Hebrew Congregation
1821 E. Main Street 10566   (914) 739-0500
                                     Fax: (914) 739-0684

Port Chester

Synagogues

Conservative

Kneses Tifereth Israel
575 King Street 10573   (914) 939-1004
Fax: (914) 939-1086

Poughkeepsie

Organisations
Jewish Community Center of Dutchess County
110 Grand Avenue 12603   (914) 471-0430

Synagogues

Conservative

Temple Beth El
118 Grand Avenue 12603   (914) 454-0570
Fax: (914) 454-7257
Web site: www.uscj.org/empire/poughktb

Orthodox

Shomre Israel
18 Park Avenue 12603   (914) 454-2890

Reform

Vassar Temple
140 Hooker Avenue 12601   (914) 454-2570

Rochester

Bakeries
Brighton Donuts
Monroe Avenue   (716) 271-6940

Delicatessens
Brownstein's Deli and Bakery
1862 Monroe Avenue 14618
Fox's Kosher Restaurant and Deli
3450 Winton Place 14623

Media

Newspapers

Jewish Ledger
2525 Brighton-Henrietta Town Line R 14623

Organisations
Jewish Community Federation
441 E. Avenue 14607   (716) 461-0490

Restaurants

Meat

Jewish Home of Rochester Cafeteria
2021 S. Winton Road 14618

Saratoga Springs

Synagogues

Conservative

Shaare Tfille
260 Broadway 12866   (518) 584-2370

Orthodox

Congregation Mikveh Israel
26 Lafayette Street 12866   (518) 584-6338
Services in July & August. Kosher food available.
Orthodox Minyan
510 1/2 Broadway 12866
(518) 437-1738; 584-3091

Reform

Temple Sinai
509 Broadway 12866   (518) 584-8730

Scarsdale

Synagogues
Magen David Sephardie Congregation
1225 Weaver Street, P O B 129H 10583
(914) 633-3728
Fax: (914) 636-0608
Email: mitchser@aol.com

Orthodox

Young Israel of Scarsdale
1313 Weaver Street 10583   (914) 636-8686
Fax: (914) 636-1209

Schenectady

Synagogues

Conservative

Agudat Achim
2117 Union Street 12309   (518) 393-9211

Orthodox

Beth Israel
2195 Eastern Parkway 12309   (518) 377-3700

Reform

Gates of Heaven
852 Ashmore Avenue 12309   (518) 374-8173

Spring Valley

Delicatessens
GPG Deli
Main Street 10977

Home Hospitality

Mendel & Margalit Zuber
32 Blauvelt Road, Monsey 10952   (914) 425-6213
The Zuber's write 'Anyone wishing to spend a Shabbat
or Yom Tov with us is more than welcome. We are
Lubavitch Chasidim, glatt kosher.'

Hotels

Gartner's Inn
Hungry Hollow Road 10977   (914) 356-0875

Restaurants

Eli's Bagel Shop
58 N. Myrtle Avenue 10977   (845) 425-6166
Hours: Sunday - Thursday 6.30am-5.00pm. Friday
6.30am-2.00pm. Open Motzei Shabbos from after
Succos until Pesach. Catering and Platters for all
occasions. Under the Hashgocha of Rabbi B.
Gruber/Yoshen.

Mehadrin Restaurant
32 Route 59, Monsey 10952

Dairy

Sheli's Café and Pizza
26 Maple Avenue 10977   (914) 426-0105
                               Fax: (914) 362-5004
                               Email: shely@ucs.net
Supervision: Rabbi Breslaver.

Synagogues

Orthodox

Young Israel of Spring Valley
23 Union Road 10977   (914) 356-3363

Suffern

Synagogues

Bais Torah
9 West Carlton Road 10901   (914) 352-1343
                                   Fax: (914) 352-0841
                                   Email: yhaber@ou.org

Syracuse

Synagogues

Young Israel Shaarei Torah of Syracuse
313 E Genesee Street 13214   (315) 446-6194
                                    Fax: (315) 446-7936

Troy

Mikvaot

Troy Chabad Center
306 15th Street 12180   (518) 274-5572

Synagogues

Conservative

Temple Beth El
411 Hoosick Street 12180   (518) 272-6113

Reform

Congregation Berith Shalom
167 3rd Street 12180   (518) 272-8872
                              Fax: (518) 272-8984

Utica

Synagogues

Orthodox

Congregation Zvi Jacob
112 Memorial Parkway 13501   (315) 724-8357

Reform

Temple Emanu-El
2710 Genesee Street 13502   (315) 724-4177

Vestal

Media

Newspapers

The Reporter
500 Clubhouse Road 13850   (607) 724-2360
                                  Fax: (607) 724-2311
                                  Email: treporter@aol.com

Organisations

Jewish Federation of Broome County
500 Clubhouse Road 13850   (607) 724-2332
                                  Fax: (607) 724-2311

West Point

Synagogues

United States Military Academy Jewish Chapel
Building 750 10096   (914) 938-2766
                            Fax: (914) 446-7706
With a local community of over 200 the Chapel was
designed by the firm responsible for the United Nations
building and the Lincoln Center.

White Plains

Restaurants

Meat

Lexington Glatt Kosher Restaurant
166 Mamaroneck Avenue 10601   (914) 682-7400
Glatt kosher.

United States of America / New York

Synagogues

Conservative

Temple Israel Center
280 Old Mamaroneck Road, at Miles Avenue 10605
(914) 948-2800
Fax: (914) 948-4755

Orthodox

Hebrew Institute of White Plains
20 Greenridge Avenue 10605
(914) 948-3095
Fax: (914) 949-4676
Email: hebinst@tdt.com

Reconstructionist

Bet Am Shalom
295 Soundview Avenue 10606
(914) 946-8851

Reform

Jewish Community Center
252 Soundview Avenue 10606

Williamsville

Synagogues

Orthodox

Young Israel of Greater Buffalo
105 Maple Road 14221
(716) 634-0212

Yonkers

Synagogues

Conservative

Agudas Achim
21 Hudson Street 10701
Lincoln Park Center
323 Central Park Avenue 10704
(914) 965-7119

Orthodox

Rosh Pinah
Riverdale Avenue 10705
Sons of Israel
105 Radford Avenue 10705

Reform

Temple Emanu-El
306 Rumsey Road 10705
(914) 963-0575

North Carolina

Asheville

Synagogues

Conservative

Congregation Beth Israel
229 Murdock Avenue 28804
(828) 252-843
Fax: (828) 252-388
Email: bethisrael@buncombe.main.nc.u

Reform

Beth Ha-Tephila
43 N. Liberty Street 28801

Charlotte

Delicatessens
Shalom Park Sandwich Shoppe
5007 Providence Rd,
(704) 366-500
The Kosher Mart & Delicatessen
Amity Gardens Shopping Center, 3840 E.
Independence Blvd 28205
(704) 563-828
Fax: (704) 532-91
Email: koshermartusa@mindspring.co
Web site: www.koshermartusa.co
Sandwiches and deli department are glatt kosher.
Groceries also sold here. Hours: Monday to
Wednesday, 10 am to 6 pm; Thursday, to 7 pm; Frid
to 3 pm; Sunday, to 3:30 pm; Shabbat, closed.

Libraries
Speizman Jewish Library
5007 Providence Road 28226

Media

Newspapers

Charlotte Jewish News
(704) 366-50

Mikvaot
Chabad House
6619 Sardis Road 28270
(704) 366-39
Fax: (704) 362-14

Organisations
Jewish Federation
5007 Providence Road 28226
(704) 366-50
The Hebrew Academy & Social Services
5007 Providence Rd 28226

Synagogues

Conservative

Temple Israel
4901 Providence Road (704) 362-2796

Orthodox

Chabad House
6619 Sardis Road 28270 (704) 366-3984
Fax: (704) 362-1423
Email: sardis@earthlink.net

Reform

Temple Beth El
5101 Providence Road 28207 (704) 366-1948

Durham

Kashrut Information

Leon Dworsky
1100 Leon Street, Apt. 28 27705

Organisations

Durham-Chapel Hill Jewish Federation and Community Council
205 Mt. Bolus Road, Chapel Hill 27514
(919) 967-6916

Synagogues

Conservative

Beth El, 1004 Watts Street 27701 (919) 682-1238

Reform

Judea Reform Congregation
1955 Cornwallis Road 27705 (919) 489-7062
Fax: (919) 489-0611
Email: infobox@judeareform.org

Fayetteville

Synagogues

Conservative

Beth Israel Congregation
2204 Morganton Road 28303 (910) 484-6462

Greensboro

Organisations

Greensboro Jewish Federation
5509 C West Friendly Avenue 27410-4211
(336) 852-5433
Fax: (336) 852-4346
Email: mfcgsonc@jon.cjfny.org

Synagogues

Conservative

Beth David
804 Winview Drive 27410 (336) 294-0006

Hendersonville

Synagogues

Agudas Israel Congregation
328 N. King Street, PO Box 668 28793

Raleigh

Groceries

Congregation of Sha'arei Israel
7400 Falls of the Neuse Road 27615
(919) 847-8986

Mikvaot

Congregation of Sha'arei Israel
7400 Falls of the Neuse Road 27615
(919) 847-8986

Organisations

Wake County Jewish Federation
3900 Merton Drive 27609 (919) 751-5459

Synagogues

Conservative

Beth Meyer
504 Newton Road 27615 (919) 848-1420

Orthodox

Congregation of Sha'arei Israel - Lubavitch
7400 Falls of the Neuse Road 27615
(919) 847-8986
Fax: (919) 847-3142

Reform

Temple Beth Or
5315 Creedmoor Road 27612 (919) 781-4895
Pre-school.

Wilmington

Synagogues

Conservative

Beth Jacob
1833 Academy Street 27101

Reform

Temple Emanuel
201 Oakwood Drive 27103 (919) 722-6640

United States of America / North Dakota

North Dakota

Fargo

Synagogues

Orthodox

Fargo Hebrew Congregation
901 S. 9th Street 58103   (701) 237-5629

Reform

Temple Beth El
809 11th Avenue S. 58103   (701) 232-0441

Ohio

Akron

Mikvaot
(330) 867-6798

Organisations
Jewish Community Board of Akron
750 White Pond Drive 44320   (330) 869-2424
Fax: (330) 867-8498
Web site: www.jewishakron.org

Synagogues

Conservative

Beth El, 464 S. Hawkins Avenue 44320
(330) 864-2105

Orthodox

Anshe Sfard Synagogue
646 N.Revere Road 44333   (330) 867-7292
Fax: (330) 867-7719

Reform

Temple Israel
133 Merriman Road 44303   (330) 762-8617
Fax: (330) 762-8619
Email: rabbi@neo.rr.com

Beachwood

Synagogues

Orthodox

Young Israel of Beachwood
2463 South Green Road 44122   (216) 691-9007

Canton

Organisations
Jewish Community Federation
2631 Harvard Avenue 44709   (216) 452-6444

Synagogues

Conservative

Shaaray Torah
423 30th Street N.W. 44709   (216) 492-0310

Orthodox

Agudas Achim
2508 Market Street N. 44704   (216) 456-8781

Reform

Temple Israel
333 25th Street N.W. 44709   (216) 455-5197

Cincinnati

Bakeries
Golf Manor
2200 Losantiville Avenue
All pareve. Closed Shabbat.
Hot Bagels Factory
7617 Reading Road 45237
Supervision: Vaad Ho-ir of Cincinnati.
DBA Marx Hot Bagels also at 316 Northland Blvd,
9701 Kenwood Road, 2327 Buttermilk Crossings and I-
75 Cres. Spgs, Kentucky. Open daily, 6 am to 9 pm.
40 varieties of bagels, 26 spreads.
Hot Bagels Factory
477 E. Kemper Road 45246

Delicatessens
Bilkers, 7648 Reading Road 45237

Groceries
Pilder's Kosher Foods
7601 Reading Road 45237

Libraries
The Hebrew Union College-Jewish Institute of Religion
3101 Clifton Avenue 45220   (513) 221-1875
Fax: (513) 221-0519
Email: klau@cn.huc.edu
One of the largest Jewish libraries in the world. It is
also has an art gallery of artefacts, houses a collection
Jewish 'objets d'art' and religious and ceremonial
appurtenances as well as rare books and manuscripts.

Media

Newspapers

American Israelite
906 Main Street 45202
Oldest Anglo-Jewish weekly in the US.

Mikvaot
Kehelath B'nai Israel
1546 Beaverton Avenue 45237   (513) 761-5260

Organisations

Community Center
1580 Summit Road 45237   (513) 761-7500
Fax: (513) 761-0084

Jewish Federation
1811 Losantiville, Suite 320 45237   (513) 351-3800

Synagogues

Conservative

Northern Hills Synagogue - Congregation B'nai Avraham
715 Fleming Road 45231   (513) 931-6038
Fax: (513) 931-6147
Email: berniceu@fuse.net
Web site: www.uscj.org/ohio/cincincb/index.htm

Cleveland

Libraries
The Temple Museum of Religious Art Library.
University Circle, Silver Park 44106
Housing Abba Hillel Silver Archives (Jewish art objects, religious & ceremonial treasures, rare books and manuscripts.)

Media

Newspapers

Cleveland Jewish News
3645 Warrensville Center Road, Suite 230 44122

Mikvaot
1774 Lee Road 44118

Museums
Park Synagogue
3300 Mayfield Road 44118
Holding a collection of Jewish art and sculpture.

Organisations
Jewish Community Federation of Cleveland
1750 Euclid Avenue 44115   (216) 566-9200
Fax: (216) 861-1230
Email: info@jcfcleve.org
Web site: www.jewishcleveland.org
With literally dozens of synagogues of each demonination, it is advisable to contact the local religious organisation for specific details.

Restaurants

Dairy

Kinneret Kosher Restaurant
1869 S. Taylor Road 44118
Yacov's Restaurant
13969 Cedar Road 44118

Meat

Empire Kosher Kitchen
2234 Warrensville Center Road   (216) 691-0006

Columbus

Bakeries
Block's Hot Bagels
6800 E. Broad Street 43068   (614) 575-9690
Supervision: Vaad Ho-ir of Columbus.
Baked goods only are kosher.
Block's Hot Bagels
2847 Festival Lane   (614) 798-1550
Supervision: Vaad Ho-ir of Columbus.
Baked goods only are kosher. Also, all 5 Block's Hot Bagels located inside the Kroger grocery stores at the Chambers, Gahanna, Pickerington, Reynoldsburg and Bethel Roads have supervised baked goods.
Block's Hot Bagels
6115 McNaughten Center   (614) 863-0470
Supervision: Vaad Ho-ir of Columbus.
Baked goods only are kosher.
Block's Hot Bagels
3415 E. Broad Street   (614) 235-2551
Supervision: Vaad Ho-ir of Columbus.
Baked goods only are kosher.

Delicatessens
Kosher Buckeye
2942 E. Broad Street 43209   (614) 235-8070
Supervision: Vaad Ho-ir of Columbus.

Groceries
Bexley Kosher Market
3012 E. Broad Street 43209   (614) 231-3653
Supervision: Vaad Ho-ir of Columbus.
Butcher as well.

Ice Cream Parlors
Graeters Ice Cream
1534 Lane Avenue   (614) 488-3222
Supervision: Vaad Ho-ir of Columbus.
Graeters Ice Cream
6255 Franz Road   (614) 799-2663
Supervision: Vaad Ho-ir of Columbus.
Graeters Ice Cream
2282 E. Main Street   (614) 236-2663
Supervision: Vaad Ho-ir of Columbus.

Mikvaot
Beth Jacob
1223 College Avenue 43209   (614) 237-8641

Representative Organisations
Jewish Federation
1175 College Avenue 43209   (614) 237-7686

United States of America / Ohio

Restaurants

Dairy

Sammy's New York Bagels
40 N. James Road 43213   (614) 237-2444
Fax: (614) 235-4177
Supervision: Vaad Ho-ir of Columbus.
Deli as well.

Meat

Yitzi's Kosher Dogs
207 E. 15th Avenue 43214   (614) 294-3296
Supervision: Vaad Ho-ir of Columbus.

Synagogues

Orthodox

Agudas Achim Synagogue
2767 E. Broad Street 43209   (614) 237-2747
Beth Jacob Congregation
1223 College Avenue 43209   (614) 237-8641
Nusach sefard; daily and Shabbat minyan.
Congregation Ahavas Sholom
2568 E. Broad Street 43209   (614) 252-4815
Fax: (614) 252-1316
Email: ahavas@beol.net
Web site: www.yi-ahavas-sholom.org
Nusach sefard; daily and Shabbat minyan.

Dayton

Accommodation Information

Home Hospitality

Shomrei Emunah
1706 Salem Avenue 45406   (937) 274-6941
Fax: (937) 274-7511
Email: shomrei@earthlink.net
Please contact the synagogue to arrange for
accommodations.

Bakeries

Rinaldo's Bakery
910 West Fairview Avenue 45406   (513) 274-1311
Supervision: Rabbi Hillel Fox, Beth Jacob
Congregation..
Certain products only, please ask for certification
certidicate.

Media

Newspapers

Dayton Jewish Observer
4501 Denlinger Road 45426   (937) 854-4150
Fax: (937) 854-2850
Email: dayjobs@aol.com

The Dayton Jewish Advocate
(937) 854-4150 ext. 118
Published by the Jewish Federation of Greater Dayton
by Marshall Weiss, editor.

Mikvaot

556 Kenwood Avenue 45406

Organisations

Jewish Federation of Greater Dayton
4501 Denlinger Road 45426   (937) 854-4150
Old Age Home
Covenant House, 4911 Covenant House Drive 45426
(937) 837-2651

Kollel

Dayton Community Kollel
1706 Salem Avenue 45406   (937) 274-6941
Email: KollelDayton@Juno.com
The Kollel offers classes in a variety of Judaic topics in
addition to schedule of Torah study. Visitors are warmly
welcomed. Please call for details. There are no kosher
restaurants, hotels or butchers in Dayton or in the area.
However, the Kollel families will be kosher hospitality.

Synagogues

Orthodox

7020 North Main Street 45415   (937) 274-2149
Fax: (937) 274-9556
Email: bethjacob1@aol.com
Web site: www.bethjacobcong.org
Supervision: Rabbi Hillel Fox, Beth Jacob
Congregation..

Supervision: Rabbi Hillel Fox, Beth Jacob
Congregation..
Shomrei Emunah/Young Israel of Dayton
1706 Salem Avenue 45406   (937) 274-6941
Fax: (937) 274-6941
Rabbi's study: (937)-277-4626. Shachris daily: 6:45am.
Sundays and National holidays 8:30am. Shabbos and
Yom Tov 9:15am. Mincha and Maariv at sunset, call
for details.
Young Israel of Dayton
1706 Salem Avenue 45406   (937) 274-6941

Traditional

Beth Jacob Synagogue
Supervision: Rabbi Hillel Fox, Beth Jacob
Congregation..
Runs a kosher restaurant approximately every sixth
Sunday.

Lorain

Synagogues

Conservative

Agudath B'nai Israel
1715 Meister Road 44053   (216) 282-3307

Toledo

Synagogues
B'nai Israel
2727 Kenwood Blvd. 43606   (419) 531-1677

Orthodox

Congregation Etz Chayim
3852 Woodley Road 43606   (419) 473-2401

Reform

The Temple-Congregation Shomer Emunium
6453 Sylvania Avenue 43560   (419) 883-3341

Westerville

Ice Cream Parlors
Graeters Ice Cream
1 State Street   (614) 895-0553
Supervision: Vaad Ho-ir of Columbus.

Worthington

Ice Cream Parlors
Graeters Ice Cream
654 Hight Street   (614) 848-5151
Supervision: Vaad Ho-ir of Columbus.

Youngstown

Mikvaot
Children of Israel
3970 1/3 Logan Way 44505   (216) 759-8692

Organisations
Youngstown Area Jewish Federation
505 Gypsy Lane 44501   (216) 746-3251

Synagogues

Conservative

Beth Israel Temple Center
2138 E. Market Street, Warren 44483-6104
(330) 395-3877
Fax: (330) 394-5918
Email: bethisrael1@juno.com
Ohev Tzedek-Shaarei Torah
5245 Glenwood Avenue 44512   (216) 758-2321
Temple El Emeth
3970 Logan Way 44505   (216) 759-1429

Reform

Rodef Sholom
Elm Street & Woodbine Avenue 44505

Oklahoma
Oklahoma City

Bakeries
Ingrid's Kitchen
2309 N.W. 36th Street 73112

Kashrut Information

Orthodox

Chabad House
6401 Lenox Avenue, Oklahoma City 73116
(405) 810-1770
Fax: (405) 810-1772

Organisations
Jewish Federation of Greater Oklahoma City
3022 N.W. Expressway, Suite 116 73112
(405) 949-0111

Synagogues

Conservative

Emanuel Synagogue
900 N.W. 47th Street 73106   (405) 528-2113

Reform

Temple B'nai Israel
4901 N. Pennsylvania Avenue 73112
(405) 848-0965

Tulsa

Kashrut Information
Chabad House
6622 S. Utica Avenue 74136
(918) 492-4499; 493-7006
Fax: (918) 492-4499
Hospitality for travellers. Services: Shabbat and Sunday
9/00 am and by arrangement (Kaddish, Yarziet, etc).

Orthodox

Beth Torah - Chabad
66225 St. Utica Ave. 74136   (918) 496-4555

Media

Newspapers

Tulsa Jewish Review
2021 E. 71st Street 74136   (918) 495-1100

Mikvaot
Mikva Shoshana - Chabad
6622 So. Utica Avenue 74136   (918) 493-7006

United States of America / Oklahoma

Museums

The Gershon & Rebecca Fenster Museum of Jewish Art
Box 52188 74152 (918) 294-1366
Email: fenstermuseum@ibm.net
Only Jewish Museum in the South-West.

Organisations

Jewish Federation
2021 E. 71st Street 74136 (918) 495-1100
Fax: (918) 495-1220
Email: federation@jewishtulsa.org

Synagogues

Chabad House
6622 S Utica Avenue 74136
(918) 492-4499; 493-7006
Fax: (918) 492-4499
Services: Shabbat and Sunday 9.00 am and by
arrangement (Kaddish, Yarziet, etc).

Conservative

B'nai Emunah
1719 S. Owasso Avenue 74120 (918) 583-7121

Reform

Temple Israel
2004 E. 22nd Place 74114 (918) 747-1309
Fax: (918) 747-3564
Email: templeis@ionet.net

Oregon
Ashland

Synagogues

Temple Emek Shalom-Rogue Valley Jewish Community
1081 E. Main St 97520 (541) 488-2909
Fax: (541) 488-2814
Email: teshalom@mind.net
Office hours only 10-3 Tu-F. Street address: 1081 E.
Main St. Call for schedule of services.

Eugene

Synagogues

Conservative

Temple Beth Israel
42 W. 25th Avenue 97405 (541) 485-7218

Portland

Groceries

Albertson's
5415 SW Beaverton Hillsdale Highway 97221
(503) 246-1713

Mikvaot

Ritualarium
1425 S.W. Harrison Street 97219 (503) 224-3409

Organisations

Jewish Federation of Portland
6651 S.W. Capitol Highway 97219 (503) 245-6219

Restaurants

Mittleman Jewish Community Center (Kosher restaurant)
6651 S. W. Capitol Highway 97219 (503) 244-0111

Synagogues

Reform

Neveh Shalom Synagogue
2900 SW Peaceful Lane 97201 (503) 246-8831
Fax: (503) 246-7553
Web site: www.nevehshalom.org

Temple Beth Israel
1972 NW Flanders 97209 (503) 222-1069

Salem

Synagogues

Reconstructionist

Beth Shalom
1795 Broadway NE 97303 (503) 362-5004

Pennsylvania
Allentown

Mikvaot

1834 Whitehall Street 18104 (610) 776-7948

Organisations

Jewish Federation
702 22nd Street 18104 (610) 821-5500

Restaurants

Meat

Glatt Kosher Community Center
702 N. 22nd Street 18104 (610) 435-3571
Since opening hours vary according to season, it is
advisable to call before visiting.

Altoona

Synagogues

Conservative

Agudath Achim
1306 17th Street 16601 (814) 944-5317

Reform

Temple Beth Israel
3004 Union Avenue 16602   (814) 942-0057

Bala Cynwyd

Synagogues

Orthodox

Young Israel of the Main Line
PO Box 117 19004   (215) 667-3255

Bethlehem

Synagogues

Conservative

Congregation Brith Sholom
Macada & Jacksonville Roads 18017   (215) 866-8009

Orthodox

Agudath Achim
1555 Linwood Street 18017   (610) 866-8891
Contact person: Gerald Wekberger. 1-610-838-0767.

Blue Bell

Synagogues

Conservative

Tiferet Bet Israel
1920 Skippack Pike 19422   (610) 275-8797

Easton

Synagogues
B'nai Abraham
16th & Bushkill Streets 18042   (610) 258-5343
Established 1888.

Reform

Temple Covenant of Peace
1451 Northampton Street 18042   (610) 253-2031
                                       Fax: (610) 253-7973
                                       Email: tcp@ fast.net
Established 1839.

Elkins Park

Synagogues

Orthodox

Young Israel of Elkins Park
7715 Montgomery Avenue 19027   (215) 635-3152
Web site: www.philly-direct.com/frum/brisman.html

Erie

Organisations
Jewish Community Council
Suite 405, Professional Building, 161 Peach St., 16501
                                       (814) 455-4474
                                       Fax: (814) 455-4475

Synagogues

Conservative

Brith Sholom Jewish Center
3207 State Street 16508   (814) 454-2431

Reform

Anshe Hesed
10th & Liberty Streets 16502   (814) 454-2426

Harrisburg

Caterers
Norman Gras Catering
3000 Green Street 17110-1234   (717) 234-2196
                                      Fax: (717) 234-3943
                                      Email: normangras@aol.com
Glatt kosher. Offers catering for groups. Stocks kosher
vending machines at the JCC, 3301 N Front St. Tel:
717-236-9555 ext 3105.

Groceries
Bakeries Giant Food Store and Weis Market
Linglestown Road
Quality Kosher
7th Division Street 17110

Organisations
United Jewish Community of Greater Harrisburg
100 Vaughn Street 17110   (717) 236-9555

Synagogues

Conservative

Beth El, 2637 N. Front Street 17110   (717) 232-0556
Chisuk Emuna
5th & Division Streets 17110   (717) 232-4851
                                      Fax: (717) 232-7950
                                      Email: muroff@juno.com

Orthodox
Kesher Israel
2945 N. Front Street 17110   (717) 238-0763

Reform
Ohev Sholom
2345 N. Front Street 17110   (717) 233-6459
                                    Fax: (717) 236-7844

United States of America / Pennsylvania

Hazleton

Synagogues

Conservative

Agudas Israel
77 N. Pine Street 18201   (717) 455-2851

Reform

Beth Israel
98 N. Church Street 18201   (717) 455-3971

Johnstown

Organisations

United Jewish Federation of Johnstown
700 Indiana Street 15905   (814) 536-0647

Synagogues

Conservative

Beth Sholom Congregation
700 Indiana Street 15905   (814) 536-0647

Lancaster

Organisations

Jewish Federation
2120 Oregon Pike 17601   (717) 597-7354

Synagogues

Jewish Community Center
2120 Oregon Pike 17601

Conservative

Beth El, 25 N. Lime Street 17602   (717) 392-1379

Orthodox

Degel Israel
1120 Columbia Avenue 17603   (717) 397-0183

Reform

Temple Shaarei Shomayim
N. Duke & James Streets 17602   (717) 397-5575

Levittown

Synagogues

Conservative

Congregation Beth El
21 Penn Valley Road, Fallsington 19054
     (215) 945-9500

Reform

Temple Shalom
Edgley Road, off Mill Creek Pkwy. 19057
     (215) 945-4154

McKeesport

Synagogues

Conservative

Tree of Life-Sfard
Cypress Avenue 15131   (412) 673-0938

Orthodox

Gemilas Chesed
1400 Summit Street, White Oak 15131
     (412) 678-9859

Reform

B'nai Israel
536 Shaw Avenue 15132   (412) 678-6181
     Fax: (412) 678-6908
     Email: tbi536@juno.com or tbi536@aol.com

Melrose Park

Libraries

Tuttleman Library
Gratz College, Mandell Education Campus, 7605 Old
York Road 19027   (215) 635-7300 ext. 169
     Fax: (215) 635-7320
     Email: rlandau@gratz.edu
Specialised library of Judaic and Hebraic studies.
Multilingual collection of approximately 100,000
books, periodicals, music and audio-visual materials.
Special collections include a rare book room, a music
library, and a Holocaust oral history archive. Open to
the public.

Philadelphia

Bakeries

Arthur's Bakery
Academy Plaza, Red Lion and Academy Roads 19114
     (215) 637-9146
Supervision: Rabbinical Assembly.
An additional location in the Northeast.

Bestcake Bakery
7594 Haverford Avenue 19151   (215) 878-1127
     Email: rugalah@aol.com
Supervision: Orthodox Vaad of Philadelphia.
Closed Shabbat and holidays. Intersection Route 1 and
Haverford Avenue (close to Route 3).

Buy the Dozen
219 Haverford Avenue
Narberth 19072   (610) 667-9440
Supervision: Orthodox Vaad of Philadelphia.
Wholesale croissant bakery open to the public.

Dante's Bakery
Richboro Centre, Bustleton and Second Street Pikes,
Richboro 18954   (215) 357-9599
Supervision: Rabbinical Assembly.

Hesh's Eclair Bake Shoppe
7721 Castor Avenue 19152   (215) 742-8575
Supervision: Vaad Hakashruth.
Closed on Shabbat.

Hutchinson's Classic Bakery
13023 Bustleton Pike 19116   (215) 676-8612
Supervision: Rabbinical Assembly.

Kaplan's New Model Bakery
901 Norht 3rd Street 19123   (215) 627-5288
Supervision: Rabbi Solomon Isaacson.

Lipkin and Sons Bakery
8013 Castor Avenue 19152   (215) 342-3005
Supervision: Rabbi Abraham Novitsky.

Masi-Schaber Wedding Cakes
1848 South 15th Street 19145   (215) 336-4557
Supervision: Rabbinical Council.

Michael's
6635 Castor Avenue 19149   (215) 745-1423
Supervision: Rabbi Dov Brisman.

Moish's Addison Bakery
10865 Bustleton Avenue 19116   (215) 469-8054
Supervision: Rabbinical Assembly.

Rilling's Bakery
2990 Southampton Road 19154   (215) 698-6171
Supervision: Rabbinical Assembly.

The Village Baker
2801 South Eagle Road, Newton 18940
          (215) 579-1235
Supervision: Rabbinical Assembly.

Viking Bakery
39 Cricket Avenue, Ardmore 19003   (215) 642-9227
Supervision: Rabbi Joshua Toledano.

Weiss Bakery
6635 Castor Avenue 19149   (215) 722-4506
Supervision: Rabbi Dov Brisman.
Closed on Shabbat.

Zach's Bakery
6419 Rising Sun Avenue 19111   (215) 722-1688
Supervision: Rabbinical Assembly.

Booksellers

Because We Care
Mandell Education Campus
7603 Old York Raod, Melrose Park 19027
          (215) 635-4774
Sends baskets of homemade cookies, candy and food all over the Philadelphia area and out of town. You can order by telephone. All proceeds go to the Federation Allied Jewish Appeal.

Gratz College
Old York Road and Melrose Avenue, Melrose Park
19027   (215) 635-7300
          Fax: (215) 635-7320
          Email: gratzinfo@aol.com

Jerusalem Israeli Gift Shop
7818 Castor Avenue 19152   (215) 342-1452

Rosenberg Hebrew Book Store
409 Old York Road
Jenkintown, Jenkintown 19046
          (215) 884-1728; 800-301-8608
          Fax: (215) 884-6648

Rosenberg Hebrew Book Store
6408 Castor Avenue 19149

Butchers

Aries Kosher Meats
6530 Castor Avenue 19149   (215) 533-3222
Supervision: Vaad Hakashruth.

Best Value Kosher Meat Center
8564 Bustleton Avenue 19152   (215) 342-1902
          Fax: (215) 342-5775
Supervision: Rabbi Dov Brisman.

Bustleton Kosher Meat Market
6834 Bustlton Avenue 19149   (215) 332-0100
Supervision: Rabbi Shalom Novoseller.

Glendale Meats
7730 Bustleton Avenue 19152   (215) 725-4100
Supervision: Vaad Hakashruth.

Main Line Kosher Meats
75621 Haverford Avenue 19151   (215) 877-3222
Supervision: Vaad Hakashruth.

Simons Kosher Meats and Poultry
6926 Bustleton Avenue 19149   (215) 624-5695
Supervision: Vaad Hakashruth.

Wallace's Krewstown Kosher Meat Market
8919 Krewstown Road 19115   (215) 464-7800
Supervision: Vaad Hakashruth.

Contact Information

Jewish Information and Referral Service
2100 Arch Street, 7th Floor 19103   (215) 832-0821
          Fax: (215) 832-0833
          Email: lyouman@philafederation.org
A free confidential service that provides answers to questions about Jewish organisations, institutions, community services and various subjects of Jewish interest in the five-county Greater Philadelphia area. JIRS is the connection to the Jewish community. It is open to callers during regular working hours.

United States of America / Pennsylvania

Embassy

Consul General of Israel
230 South 15th Street 19102   (215) 546-5556
                                     Fax: (215) 545-3986
                                     Email: info.ph@israelfm.org
                                     Web site: www.israelemb.org/pa

Groceries

Best Value Losher Meat Center
8564 Bustleton Avenue 19152   (215) 342-1902
Supervision: Rabbi Dov Brisman.

Milk and Honey
7618 Castor Avenue 19152   (215) 342-3224
Supervision: Vaad Hakashruth.

R & R Produce and Fish
7551 Haverford Avenue 19151   (215) 878-6264
Supervision: Orthodox Vaad of Philadelphia.

Judaica

Bala Judaica Center
222 Bala Avenue
Bala Cynwyd, Bala Cynwyd 19004   (610) 664-1303
                                     Fax: (610) 664-4319
                                     Email: jewishwedding@erols.com

Kashrut Information

Board of Rabbis of Greater Philadelphia
2100 Arch Street - 3rd Floor 19103   (215) 832-0675
                                     Fax: (215) 832-0689
                                     Email: info@brdavphila.com

Ko Kosher Service
5871 Drexel Road 19131   (610) 696 0408
                                     Fax: (610) 696-9249
                                     Email: ko_kosher_service@msm.com
                                     Web site: www.ko-kosher-service.org

Orthodox Vaad of Philadelphia
7505 Brookhaven Road 19151   (215) 473-0951
                                     Fax: (215) 473-6220
Rabbi Shlomo Caplan (610) 658-1967 Rabbi Aaron
Felder (215) 745-2968 Rabbi Yehoshua Kaganoff
(215) 742-8421

Rabbinical Assembly
United Synagogue of Conservative, Judaism, 1510
Chestnut Street 19102   (215) 563-8814

Rabbinical Council of Greater Philadelphia
44 North 4th Street, Philadelphia 19106
                                     (215) 922-5446
                                     Fax: (215) 922-1550
Supervision: (O).

Vaad Hakashruth and Beth Din of Philadelphia
1147 Gilham Street, Philadelphia 19111
                                     (215) 725-5181
                                     Fax: (215) 725-5182
Supervision: (O).

Landmarks

Beth Sholom Congregation
8231 Old York Road, Elkins Park 19027
                                     (215) 887-1342
                                     Fax: (215) 887-6605
                                     Web site: www.bethsholomcongregation.org
Conservative synagogue whose building is the only
synagogue ever designed by renowned architect Frank
Lloyd Wright.

Congregation Beth T'fillah of Overbrook Park
7630 Woodbine Avenue 19151   (215) 477-2415
Conservative synagogue with a 10-foot high replica of
the Western Wall in its lobby.

Mikveh Israel Cemetery
8th and Spruce Streets 19107   (215) 922-5446
One of the oldest Jewish cemeteries in the United
States, with graves dating from 1740. Interred here are
Haym Solomon, Rebecca Gratz and 21 veterans of the
American Revolution.

Monument to the Six Million Jewish Martyrs
16th Street and the Benjamin, Franklin Parkway 19103
This memorial sculpture was the first public Holocaust
monument in the United States.

The Frank Synagogue
Albert Einstein Medical Center, Old York and Tabor
Roads 19141   (215) 456-7890
Modelled after first - and second - century synagogues
discovered in the Galilee region of north central Israel,
this small, historically certified synagogue was originally
dedicated in 1901

Libraries

Philadelphia Jewish Archives Center
Balch Institute for Ethnic Studies,
18 South 7th Street 19106   (215) 925-8090
Jewish community archives containing records of
agencies synagogues and community organisations
personal and family papers autobiographies and
memoirs and a photograph collection Open to the
public

Reconstructionist Rabbinical College Library
Church Road and Greenwood Avenue, Wyncote 19095
                                     (215) 576-0800
The Kaplan Library serves rabbinical students and the
general public 33,000 books and periodicals in English
Hebrew and other languages The Kaplan Archives
house documents of the Reconstructionist movement.

Talmudical Yeshivah Library
6063 Dexel Road 19131   (215) 477-1000
Library of Sefarim (Hebrew books on the Bible the
Talmud Responsa etc.) among the finest of its kind in
the city. Open for in-library work to the general public
by appointment.

Temple University
Paley Library, 13th Street and Berks Mall 19122
(215) 787-8231
Large collection of Judaica Hebraica and Talmudic
studies and literature in Hebrew and in translation.
Main stacks are open Borrowing can be arranged
through inter library loan

The Free Library of Philadelphia
Central Library, Logan Square 19103
(215) 686-5392
Fax: (215) 563-3628
Web site: www.library.phila.gov
3,000-volume Moses Marx Collection of Judaica and
Hebraica in the Central Library, covers history liturgy,
printing and bibliography with some books on
philosophy, religion, the Bible, the Talmud, and
Passover haggadahs. Open to the public. Russian-
language collection available at the Northeast Regional
Library.

University of Pennsylvania
Van Pelt Library, 3420 Walnut Street 19104
(215) 898-7556
Large collection of biblical studies rabbinics Jewish
history and medieval and modern Hebrew language
and literature. Stacks and seminar rooms open to the
public.

Media

Magazines

Inside Magazine
Jewish Publishing Group, 226 South 16th Street 19102
(215) 893-5797
Fax: (215) 546-3957
Email: expent@netaxs.com
Quarterly magazine of Jewish life and style Sold at
news-stands and sent to all Jewish Exponent and Jewish
Times subscribers

Jewish Quarterly Review
420 Walnut Street 19106
(215) 238-1290
Email: jqroffice@sas.upenn.edu
Scholarly Journal of the Annenberg Research Institute
published four times a year.

Shofar Magazine
P.O. Box 51591 19115
(215) 676-8304
Russian-language monthly magazine

Newspapers

Jewish Exponent
Jewish Publishing Group, 2100 Arch Street,
Philadelphia 19103
(215) 832-0700
Fax: (215) 832-0786
Email: dalpher@jewishexponent.com
Weekly newspaper covering world news of Jewish
interest and detailed information on local activities
including Jewish Federation of Greater Philadelphia
meetings and events. Special sections include
community and health calendars singles and campus
activities a Russian-language column and synagogue
activities.

Jewish Post
P.O.Box 442, Yardley 19067
(215) 321-3443
Monthly newspaper serving Bucks County Pa and
Mercer County N.J.

Jewish Times
Jewish Publishing Group, 103A Tomlinson Road,
Huntingdon Valley 19006
(215) 938-1177
Weekly newspaper covering issues and programs of
interest to area Jewish residents of the greater
Northeast and Bucks County including Jewish
Federation of Greater Philadelphia meetings and
events. Special sections include synagogue senior adult
singles and campus activities.

Mir
P.O. Box 6162, Philadelphia 19115
(215) 934-5512
Local weekly Russian-language newspaper

Radio & TV

Barry Reisman Show
(609) 365-5600
WSSJ (1310AM) Jewish music in Yiddish Hebrew and
English and Jewish news. Mondays through Fridays
3.30 to 5.30pm Sundays 9.30 am to 1 p.m..

Bucks County Jewish Life
(215) 949-1490
WBCB (1490AM) Rabbi Allan Tuffs hosts this weekly
Sunday morning radio program at 10 am

Comcast Cablevision of Philadelphia
4400 Wayne Avenue 19140
(215) 673-6600
Channel 66 (Cable Television) Half-hour program on
Jewish culture shown twice a week in the evening
usually midweek and Sundays See local listings for
exact time

Dialogue
(215) 878-9700
WPVI - TV (channel 6) Discussion Program on religious
issues sponsored by Delaware Valley Media Ministry
Sundays 6.30 to 7.30am

United States of America / Pennsylvania

Keneseth Israel Sabbath Services
(215) 581-2100
Hour of Jewish worship for shut-ins the elderly and
people unable to attend Sabbath services Saturdays
11am to noon
Pulse, WSSJ, Camden   (609) 365-5600
WSSJ (1310AM) Russian-language news and music
program Sundays 9.30 to 10.30am

Meridian   (609) 962-8000
Russian language program Saturdays 10 to 10.30 am

Mikvaot
Mikveh Association of Philadelphia (Ardmore)
Torah Academy, Wynnewood and Argyle Roads,
Ardmore 19003   (610) 642-8679
Mikveh association of Philadelphia (Northern)
7525 Loretto Avenue, Philadelphia 19111
(215) 745-3334

Museums
Balch Institute for Ethnic Studies
18 South 7th Street 19106   (215) 925-8090
Documents and interprets American multi-culturalism
Research library has a Yiddish collection. Houses the
Jewish Archives Center.
Borowsky Gallery
Jewish Community Centers of Greater, Philadelphia,
401 South Broad Street 19147   (215) 545-4400
Continuing exhibits of special interest to the Jewish
community.
Fred Wolf Jr Gallery
Jewish Community Centers of Greater, Philadelphia,
10100Jamison Avenue 19116   (215) 698-7300
Continuing exhibits of special interest to the Jewish
community
Holocaust Awareness Museum
Gratz College, Mandell Education Campus, 7601 Old
York Road, Melrose Park 19027 (215) 635-6480
Previously known as the Jewish Identity Center the
Holocaust Awareness Museum contains donations form
Holocaust survivors and concentration camp liberators.
The collection documents and teaches the facts of
genocide and dangers of ethnic hatred and bigotry.
National Museum of American Jewish History
55 North 5th Street, Independence Mall East
19106-2197   (215) 923-3811
Fax: (215) 923-0763
Email: nmajh@nmajh.org
Web site: www.nmajh.or
Presents programs and experiences that preserve,
explore and celebrate the history of Jews in America.
Award-winning gift shop.

Philadelphia Congregation Rodeph Shalom
615 North Broad Street 19123   (215) 627-6747
Nationally recognised for exhibits of contemporary
Jewish art and history. Permanent collection of 20th-
century Jewish are and photographs.
Rosenbach Museum & Library
2010 Delancey Place 19103   (215) 732-1600
Fax: (215) 545-7529
Email: info@rosenbach.org
The collection includes the first Haggadah printed in
America and letters, portraits and furniture of the Gratz
family of Philadelphia. Access to books is by
appointment only. Also home to the earliest printing of
the Pentateuch in Hebrew of which complete copies are
known.
Temple Judea Museum of Keneseth Israel
8339 Old York Road, Elkins Park, PA 19027
215) 887-8700
Fax: (215) 887-1070
Email: tjmuseum@aol.com
This synagogue museum has four changing exhibitions
of Judaica and Jewish art each year.

Organisations
Annenberg Research Institute
420 Walnut Street 19106   (215) 238-1290
Approximately 180,000 books and thousands of
periodicals with emphasis on Judaic and Near Eastern
studies. Rare book collection Archives of American
Judaica particularly that of Philadelphia

Pizzeria
Shalom Pizza, 7598a Haverford Avenue
(215) 878-1500
Email: shalom2u@rcn.com
Supervision: Orthodox Vaad of Philadelphia.
Vegetarian, middle-eastern. Open 11.00 am to 9.00
pm daily. Friday closed at 4.00 pm (winter at 2.00pm).
Closed Shabbat. Cholov Israel and Pas Israel.

Restaurants
Gratz College Cafeteria
Mandell Education Campus, Old York Road and
Melrose Avenue, Melrose Park 19027
(215) 635-7300
Supervision: Rabbinical Council.
Hillel Dining Room
University of Pennsylvania, 202 South 36th Street
19104   (215) 989-7391
Fax: (215) 898-8259
Supervision: Orthodox Vaad of Philadelphia.
Hours of operation are for lunch and dinner during the
school year.

Dairy

Cherry Street Chinese vegetarian
1010 Cherry Street 19107   (215) 923-3663
Supervision: Rabbinical Assembly.

Meat

Dragon Inn
7628 Castor Avenue 19152   (215) 742-2575
Supervision: Rabbi Dov Brisman.
Maccabeam
128 South 12th Street 19107   (215) 922-5922
Supervision: Rabbinical Council.
Zenya Snack Bar
Jewish Community Centers of Greater, Philadelphia,
Red lion Road and Jamison Avenue 19116
                                  (215) 677-0280
Supervision: Ko Kosher Service.

Synagogues
Congregation Mikveh Israel
44 North 4th Street 19106   (215) 922-5446
                            Fax: (215) 922-1550
                  Web site: www.mikvehisrael.org
Spanish-Portuguese synagogue founded in 1740
Located on Independence Mall. Entrance is shared with
the National Museum of American Jewish History. All
Shabbat and holiday and Monday and Thursday
services are still conducted using historic artifacts and
tradition.

Orthodox
Young Israel of Oxford Circle
6427 Large Street 19149   (215) 725-7087
With dozens of synagogues of the various
demoninations in the area, travellers are advised to
contact a local religious organisation for specific
details.

Theatres
Theatre Ariel/Habima Ariel
P.O. Box 0334, Merion Station 19066
                                  (215) 567-0670
Theatre productions, readings workshops mini-
performances and speakers all dedicated to exploring
he Jewish theatrical experience.

Tours of Jewish Interest
American Jewish Committee Historic Tour
117 South Seventeenth Street, Suite 1010
                                  (215) 665-2300
                            Fax: (215) 665-8737
Tours, run by Simmi Hurwitz, may be arranged to suit
personal or group interests or needs.

Pittsburgh

Bakeries
Pastries Unlimited
4743 Liberty Avenue
Pastries Unlimited
2119 Murray Avenue 15217

Books and Judaica
Pinskers Judaica Center
2028 Murray Avenue 15217
    (412) 421-3033;1- 800-JUDAISM (1-800-583-2476)
                            Fax: (412) 421-6103
                         Email: info@judaism.com
                      Web site: www.judaism.com

Groceries
Brauner's Emporium
2023 Murray Avenue 15217
Koshermart
2121 Murray Avenue 15217

Media

Newspapers
Pittsburgh Jewish Chronicle
5600 Baum Blvd   (412) 687-1000
                            Fax: (412) 687-5119
                      Email: pittjewchr@aol.com

Mikvaot
2326 Shady Avenue 15217   (412) 422-8010

Museums
**Holocaust Center of the United Jewish Federation of
Greater Pittsburgh**
5738 Darlington Road 15217   (412) 421-1500
                            Fax: (412) 422-1996
                         Email: lhurwitz@ujf.net
Serves as a living memorial by providing educational
resources, sponsoring community activities, housing
archives and cultural materials related to the Holocaust.

Organisations
**Jewish Federation of Greater Wilkes-Barre and
Community Center**
60 S. River Street   (712) 822-4646
                            Fax: (712) 824-5966
United Jewish Federation of Greater Pittsburgh
234 McKee Place 15213   (412) 681-8000
                            Fax: (412) 681-8804
                         Web site: www.ujf.net
Houses all administrative offices of the Federation and
Community Relations Committee.

Restaurants
Prime Kosher
1916 Murray Avenue 15217

United States of America / Pennsylvania

Dairy

Yaacov's
2109 Murray Av, 15217   (412) 421-7208

Meat

Greenberg's Kosher Poultry
2223 Murray Avenue 15217
King David's
2020 Murray Avenue 15217   (412) 422-3370

Synagogues

Conservative

Ahavath Achim
Lydia & Chestnut Sts., Carnegie 15106
           (412) 279-1566
B'nai Israel
327 N. Negley Av. 15206
Beth El of South Hills
1900 Cochran Rd. 15220   (412) 561-1168
Beth Shalom
Beacon & Shady Avs. 15217   (412) 421-2288
          Fax: (412) 421-5923
       Web site: www.bethshalom-pgh-org
New Light
1700 Beechwood Blvd. 15217   (412) 421-1017
Parkway Jewish Center
300 Princeton Dr. 15235   (412) 823-4338
          Fax: (412) 823-4338
Tree of Life
Wilkins & Shady Avs. 15217   (412) 521-6788

Orthodox

B'nai Emunoh
4315 Murray Av. 15217
B'nai Zion
6404 Forbes Av. 15217   (412) 521-1440
Beth Hamedrash Hagodol
1230 Colwell St. 15219   (412) 471-4443
          Fax: (412) 281-1965
Bohnei Yisroel
6401 Forbes Av. 15217   (412) 521-6407
Kether Torah
5706 Bartlett St. 15217   (412) 521-9992
Poale Zedeck
6318 Phillips Avenue 15217   (412) 421-9786
          Fax: (412) 421-3383
       Email: mil313@aol.com
       Web site: www.pzonline.com
Shaare Tefillah
5741 Bartlett St. 15217   (412) 521-9911
Shaare Torah
2319 Murray Av. 15217   (412) 421-8855
Shaare Zedeck
5751 Bartlett St. 15217

Torath Chaim
728 N. Negley Av. 15206
       (412) 362-7736; 362-0036
       Email: joeberger1@juno.com
Contact person is Arnie Schwartz at 362-0036.
President Joe Berger at 521-4060.
Young Israel of Greater Pittsburgh
5831 Bartlett Street 15217-1636   (412) 421-7224

Reconstructionist

Dor Hadash
6401 Forbes Av. 15217

Reform

Rodef Shalom
4905 5th Av. 15213   (412) 621-6566
          Fax: (412) 621-5475
       Email: rshalom@pgh.net
Temple David
4415 Northern Pike, Monroeville 15146
Temple Emanuel of South Hills
1250 Bower Hill Rd. 15243   (412) 279-2600
          Fax: (412) 279-7628
Hours: M-Th 9.00 to 5.00. Friday 9.00 to 4.00.
Temple Sinai
5505 Forbes Av. 15217   (412) 421-9715

Pottstown

Synagogues

Conservative

Congregation Mercy & Truth
575 N. Keim Street 19464   (610) 326-1717

Reading

Organisations
Jewish Federation
1700 City Line St,. 19604   (610) 921-2766
          Fax: (610) 921-2766
       Email: sramati@epix.net

Synagogues

Conservative

Kesher Zion
Eckert & Perkiomen Streets 19602   374-1763

Orthodox

Shomrei Habrith
2320 Hampden Blvd. 19604   (610) 921-0881

Reform

Congregation Oheb Sholom
555 Warwick Drive, Wyomissing Hill 19610
(610) 375-6034
Fax: (610) 375-6036
Web site: www.ohebsholom.org

Scranton

Butchers

Blatt's Butcher Block
420 Prescott Avenue 18510
(570) 342-3886
Fax: (570) 342-9711
Supervision: Rabbi Fine and Rabbi Herman of Scranton Rabbinate.
Glatt kosher meat, poultry, delicatessen and groceries. Also meat restaurant.

Museums

Houdini Museum
1433 N.Main 18508
(570) 342-5555
The only museum totally devoted to Harry Houdini (Eric Weiss born in Budapest, the son of Rabbi Mayer Samuel Weiss).

Organisations

Scranton-Lackawanna Jewish Federation
601 Jefferson Avenue 18510
(570) 961-2300
Fax: (570) 346-6147

Synagogues

Conservative

Temple Israel
Gibson Street & Monroe Avenue 18510
(570) 342-0350
Fax: (570) 342-7250
Email: tiscron@epix.net
Web site: www.ncx.com.wwi/tis

Orthodox

Beth Shalom
Clay Avenue at Vine Street 18510
(570) 346-0502
Fax: (570) 346-8800
Daily service. Close to motels & hotels.

Congregation Machzikeh Hadas
cnr. Monroe & Olive 18510
(570) 342-6271

Ohev Zedek
1432 Mulberry Street 18510
(717) 343-2717

Reform

Temple Hesed
Lake Scranton 18505
(717) 344-7201

Sharon

Synagogues

Temple Beth Israel
840 Highland Avenue 16146
(412) 346-4754

Wallingford

Synagogues

Conservative

Ohev Shalom
2 Chester Road 19086
(610) 874-1465
Web site: www.uscj.org/delvlly/wallingford
The synagogue vestibule contains 12 stained glass panes (designed and executed by Rose Isaacson) each depicting a Jewish holiday.

Wilkes-Barre

Organisations

Jewish Federation of Greater Wilkes-Barre & Community Center
60 S. River Street
(717) 822-4146
Fax: (717) 824-5966

Synagogues

Conservative

Temple Israel
236 S. River Street 18702

Orthodox

Ohav Zedek
242 S. Franklin Street 18701
(570) 825-6619
Fax: (570) 825-6634

Reform

B'nai B'rith
408 Wyoming Street, Kingston 18704

Williamsport

Synagogues

Conservative

Ohev Sholom
Cherry & Belmont Streets 17701
(717) 322-4209

Reform

Beth Ha-Sholom
425 Center Street 17701
(717) 323-7751

Yardley

Bakeries

Cramer Bakery
18 E. Afton Avenue 19067
(215) 493-2760

United States of America / Pennsylvania

Contact Information
Rabbi Budow   (215) 493-1800

Rhode Island

Barrington

Synagogues

Reform

Temple Habonim
165 New Meadow Road 2806   (401) 245-6536

Bristol

Synagogues

Conservative

United Brothers
215 High Street 2809

Cranston

Synagogues
Temple Torat Yisrael
330 Park Avenue 2905   (401) 785-1800

Reform

Temple Sinai
30 Hagan Avenue 2920   (401) 942-8350

Middletown

Synagogues

Conservative

Temple Shalom
223 Valley Road 2842   (401) 846-9002
                                      Fax: (401) 682-2417

Narragansett

Synagogues
Congregation Beth David
Kingstown Road 2882   (401) 846-9002

Newport

Tours of Jewish Interest
Touro Synagogue
85 Touro Street 2840   (401) 847-4794
                                      Fax: (401) 847-8121
The synagogue, designed by Peter Harrison and
dedicated in 1763, is one of the finest examples of
18th-century Colonial architecture. It has been declared
a national site by the US government. The Jewish
cemetery, the second oldest in the US, dates back to
1677 and was immortalised in Longfellow's poem 'The
Jewish Cemetery of Newport'. Judah Touro is buried
here.

Pawtucket

Synagogues

Orthodox

Ohawe Sholam/Young Israel of Pawtucket
671 East Avenue 2860   (401) 722-3146
                                 Email: rijewish@aol.com
                   Web site: www.members.tripod.com/~ohave
Mailing address: 77 Blodgett St.

Providence

Bakeries
Kaplan's Bakery
                                      (401) 621-8107
Supervision: Rabbi Ephraim Berlinski, Vaad of Rhode
Island.

Butchers
Marty Weissman's Butcher Shop
                                      (401) 467-8903
Supervision: Rabbi Ephraim Berlinski, Vaad of Rhode
Island.
Butcher shop only; 'Deli Counter' meat and hot dogs
not under supervision.

Documentation Centres
Rhode Island Jewish Historical Association
                                      (401) 863-2805
Has a vast amount of material regarding Colonial
Jewry.

Kashrut Information
Brown University-RISD Hillel
80 Brown Street 2906   (401) 863-2805
                                 Fax: (401) 863-1591
                                 Email: spf@brown.edu

Vaad Hakashrut
                                      (401) 621-9393
                                 Fax: (401) 331-9393
                        Email: bethshalom1@juno.com

Media

Magazines

L'Chaim, 130 Sessions Street 2906   (401) 421-4111

Mikvaot
401 Elmgrove Avenue 2906

Museums
Rhode Island Holocaust Memorial Museum
401 Elmgrove Avenue 2906   (401) 861-8800
The state memorial to the victims of the Holocaust.
Many survivors now living in Rhode Island have
donated memorabilia and personal mementoes. There
is also a garden of remembrance.

Organisations
Jewish Federation of Rhode Island
130 Sessions Street 2906   (401) 421-4111

Synagogues

Conservative

Temple Emanu-El
99 Taft Avenue 2906

Orthodox

Beth Shalom
275 Camp Avenue 2906   (401) 621-9393
Fax: (401) 331-9393
Email: bethshalom1@juno.com
Congregation Sons of Jacob
24 Douglas Avenue 2908   (401) 274-5260
Mishkon Tfiloh
203 Summit Avenue 2906   (401) 521-1616
Shaare Zedek
688 Broad Street 2907   (401) 751-4936

Reform

Beth El, 70 Orchard Avenue 2906   (401) 331-6070

Warwick

Synagogues

Conservative

Temple Am David
40 Gardiner Street 2888   (401) 463-7944

Westerly

Synagogues

Orthodox

Congregation Shaare Zedek
Union Street 2891

Woonsocket

Synagogues

Conservative

Congregation B'nai Israel
224 Prospect Street 2895   (401) 762-3651
Fax: (401) 762-3651

South Carolina
Charleston

Bakeries
Ashley Bakery
1662 Savannah Highway 29407   (803) 763-4125
Great Harvest Bread Company
975 Savannah Highway 29407   (803) 763-2055

Delicatessens
Nathan's Deli
1836 Ashley River Road 29407   (803) 556-3354
West Side Market and Deli
1300 Savannah Highway 29407   (803) 763-9988
Fax: (803) 763-4476
Kosher market, restaurant and catering. Open Sunday
to Friday.

Organisations
Jewish Federation and Community Center
1645 Raoul Wallenberg Blvd, PO Box 31298 29416
(803) 571-6565
Fax: (803) 556-6206

Synagogues

Reform

Beth Elohim
90 Hasell Street 29401   (843) 723-1090
Fax: (843) 723-0537
Email: office@kkbe.org
Web site: www.kkbe.org

Tours of Jewish Interest
Beth Elohim
86 Hasell Street 29401   (843) 723-1090
Fax: (843) 723-0537
Email: kkbe@awod.com
Dating from 1749, it is the birthplace of Reform
Judaism in the United States, the Second oldest
synagogue building in the country, and the oldest
surviving Reform synagogue in the world. It has
designated a national historic landmark. A museum is
housed in the administration building next door.

United States of America / South Carolina

Columbia

Delicatessens
Groucho's
Five Points 29205

Organisations
Columbia Jewish Federation
4540 Trenholm Road, Cola 29206   (803) 787-2023

Synagogues

Conservative

Beth Shalom
5827 N. Trenholm Road 29206   (803) 782-2500

Reform

Tree of Life
6719 Trenholm Road, Cola 29206   (803) 787-0580

Georgetown

Cemeteries
Although there are now very few Jews in Georgetown,
and there is no synagogue, there is a very old Jewish
cemetery, which is maintained by the city.

Myrtle Beach

Synagogues

Orthodox

Beth El, 401 Highway 17 N., 56th Avenue 29577
                                (803) 449-3140

Chabad Lubavitch
2803 N. Oak Street   (843) 448-0035
                    Fax: (843) 626-6403

Services every day.

South Dakota

Aberdeen

Synagogues

Conservative

B'nai Isaac
202 N. Kline Street 57401   (605) 225-3404 or 7360

Rapid City

Synagogues

Reform

Synagogue of the Hills
417 N. 40th Street 57702   (605) 348-0805
                    Email: bhshul@rapidnet.com
Affiliated with UAHC. Services Friday evenings at 7.30

Tennessee

Chattanooga

Museums
Siskin Museum of Religious Artifacts
1 Siskin Plaza 37403   (423) 634-1700
                    Fax: (423) 634-1717

Organisations
Jewish Community Federation
5326 Lynnland Terrace 47311   (423) 894-1317
                    Fax: (423) 894-1319

Synagogues

Conservative

B'nai Zion
114 McBrien Road 37411   (423) 894-8900

Orthodox

Beth Sholom
20 Pisgah Avenue 37411   (423) 894-0801

Reform

Mizpah Congregation
923 McCallie Avenue 37403   (423) 264-9771
                    Fax: (423) 267-9773
                    Email: admmizpahcong@juno.com

Memphis

Bakeries
Carl's Bakery
1688 Jackson Avenue 38107   (901) 276-2304
Supervision: Vaad Hakehilloth of Memphis.
Open daily except Shabbat and Monday.

Delicatessens
Rubenstein's
4965 Summer Avenue 38122
Closed Shabbat.

Kashrut Information
Vaad Hakehilloth of Memphis
Memphis Orthodox Jewish Community Council,
PO Box 41133 38104   (901) 767-2263
                    Fax: (901) 761-3788

Mikvaot
Baron Hirsch Congregation
369 Winter Oak Lane 38119   (901) 683-7485

Organisations
Jewish Federation and Community Center
6560 Poplar Avenue 38138   (901) 767-7100

Restaurants

Dairy

Jon's Place
764 Mt. Moriah Road 38117   (901) 374-0600
Supervision: Vaad Hakehilloth of Memphis.
Open daily except Shabbat for dairy and fish lunch and dinner.

Meat

M.I. Gottlieb's
5062 Park Avenue 38120   (901) 763-3663
Supervision: Vaad Hakehilloth of Memphis.
Hours: Sunday to Thursday, 9 am to 7 pm; Friday, 7 am to 2:30 pm.

Synagogues

Conservative

Beth Sholom
482 S. Mendenhall Ave 38117   (901) 683-3591

Orthodox

Anshei Sephard-Beth El Emeth
120 E.Yates Road N. 38117   (901) 682-1611

Reform

Temple Israel
1376 E. Massey Road   (901) 761-3130

Nashville

Mikvaot

Sherith Israel
3600 West End Avenue 37205   (615) 292-6614
                                    Fax: (615) 463-8260

Organisations

Jewish Federation of Nashville and Middle Tennessee
801 Percy Warner Blvd. 37205   (615) 356-3242
                                    Fax: (615) 352-0056

Synagogues

Conservative

West End Synagogue
3814 West End Avenue 37205   (615) 269-4592
                                    Fax: (615) 269-4695
                    Email: office@westendsyn.org or
kec@westendsyn.org

Reform

The Temple
5015 Harding Road 37205   (615) 352-7620

Oak Ridge

Synagogues

Jewish Congregation of Oak Ridge
101 W. Madison Lane 37830   (615) 482-3581

Texas

Amarillo

Synagogues

Reform

Temple B'nai Israel
4316 Albert Street 79106   (806) 352-7191

Austin

Organisations

Jewish Federation and Community Center of Austin
7300 Hart Lane 78731   (512) 331-1144
                            Fax: (512) 331-7059

Synagogues

Conservative

Agudas Achim
4300 Bull Creek Road 78731
Congregation Beth El
8902 Mesa Drive 78759   (512) 346-1776

Orthodox

Chabad House
2101 Neuces Street 78705   (512) 499-8202
Mikvah on premises.

Reform

Temple Beth Israel
3901 Shoal Creek Blvd. 78756   (512) 454-6806

Baytown

Synagogues

Unaffiliated

K'nesseth Israel
100 W. Sterling, P.O.Box 702 77522
                              (281) 428-2666

Beaumont

Synagogues

Reform

Temple Emanuel
1120 Broadway 7740   (409) 832-6131

United States of America / Texas

Bellaire

Bakeries
Ashcraft
1301 N. First 77401

Corpus Christi

Synagogues

Conservative

B'nai Israel
3434 Fort Worth Street 78411   (512) 855-7308
                                      Fax: (512) 855-7309

Reform

Temple Beth El
4402 Saratoga Street 78413   (512) 857-8181

Dallas

The Dallas Jewish community was founded in the decade following the Civil War by predominantly German Jews. The social importance of German Jewish ancestry can still be seen in the Temple Emanu-El cemetery which is home to scores of 19th-century headstones bearing German regional names for eastern European birth-places.

The JCC sponsors a prestigious Jewish Arts Festival each August along with concerts and gallery exhibitions. A Holocaust Museum has served as a regional focal point for preserving the memory of the Shoah. For more information, see the Dallas Virtual Jewish Community website at www.dvjc.org.

Bakeries
Cakes of Elegance
9205 Skillman 75243   (214) 343-2253
Supervision: Vaad Hakashrus of Greater Dallas.
Minyards Kosher Bakery & Deli
714 Preston Forest Shopping Center 75230
Supervision: Vaad Hakashrus of Greater Dallas.
Neiman-Marcus Bakery
North Park   (214) 363-8311
Supervision: Vaad Hakashrus of Greater Dallas.
Location only. Closed Sats.
Strictly Cheesecake
8139 Forest Lane, Suite 117,
Forest Central Village 75243   (972) 783-6545
Supervision: Vaad Hakashrus of Greater Dallas.
Tom Thumb Bakery & Kosher Deli
11920 Preston Road 75230   (972) 392-2501
Supervision: Vaad Hakashrus of Greater Dallas.
Forest Lane only open 24 hours. Most Tom Thumb and Albertson grocery stores in North Dallas have a small kosher section for dried goods.

Caterers
Simcha Kosher Caterers
75230   (972) 620-729
Supervision: Vaad Hakashrus of Greater Dallas.
Prepares and delivers meals to order.

Community Organisations
Jewish Federation of Greater Dallas and Community Center
7800 Northaven Road 75230   (214) 369-331
                                     Fax: (214) 369-894
                                     Email: contact@jfgd.o
                                     Web site: www.jewishdallas.o
The Campus houses the Dallas Holocaust Center and the Dallas Jewish Historical Society. There is a kosher café on Sundays and lunch service on some weekday during the fall and winter months (under the supervision of the Vaad Hakashrus of Greater Dallas)

Hotels
Sheraton Park Central
12720 Merit Drive 75240   (972) 385-300
The Westin Galleria, Dallas
13340 Dallas Parkway   (972) 934-949
                                    Fax: (972) 851-286
                                    Email: galas@westin.co
Supervision: Vaad Hakashrus of Dallas.
Lock-up kosher kitchens under the supervision of the Vaad Hakashrus of Dallas.

Media

Newspapers

Texas Jewish Post
11333 N. Central Expressway 75230
Weekly publication. Includes weekly listing of synagogue services and times in the Greater Dallas area. Includes addresses and phone numbers.

Mikvaot
Congregation Tiferet Israel
                                     (214) 397-34
Call for appointment.
Mikvah Association
5640 McShan 75230   (972) 776-00

Religious Organisations
Dallas Area Torah Association (Kollel)
5840 Forest Lane 75230   (214) 987-32
                                    Fax: (214) 987-17
                                    Email: data@datanet.c
                                    Web site: www.datanet.e
Mikvah Association
5640 McShann 75230   (972) 776-00
Beeper: (972) 397-3428.
Rabbinic Association of Greater Dallas
6930 Alpha Road   (972) 661-18

aad Hakashrus of Greater Dallas
'900 Northaven Road 75230
(214) 739-OKDK (6535)
Iso known as 'Dallas Kosher', they can be contacted
or all kashrut information.

ites

aide Reuven's Esrog Farm
(972) 931-5596
Fax: (972) 931-5476
Email: zrsesrog@aol.com
Web site: www.members.aol.com/arsesrog
allas' only Esrog tree farm is open by appointment.

ynagogues

onservative

ongregation Anshai Emet
220 Village Creek Drive Plano   (972) 735-9818
ongregation Beth Emunah
"5230   (972) 416-8016
ongregation Beth Torah
20 Lookout Richardson   (972) 234-1542
ongregation Shearith Israel
401 Douglas 75230   (214) 361-6606

Orthodox

habad of Plano
5230   (972) 596-8270
ongregation Ohev Shalom
321 McCallum Blvd 75230   (972) 380-1292
orest Lane Shul
008 Forest Lane 75230   (214) 361-8600
                                  Fax: (214) 361-8680
                         Email: shull@airmail.net
Web site: www.chabadcenters.com/dallas
hr HaTorah,
2800 Preston Road   (972) 404-8980
aare Tefilla
31 Churchill Way, off Preston Road 75230
(972) 661-0127
Fax: (972) 661-0150
Email: shaaretefilla@juno.com
oung Israel of Dallas
504 Dykes Way 75230   (972) 386-7162

eform

ongregation Beth-El Binah
ay and Lesbian Center, 2701 Regan 75219
(214) 497-1591
ongregation Kol Ami
887 TimbercreekFlower Mound   (972) 539-1938
ongregation Ner Tamid
12 Trinity Mills Road, Suites 160A and B, Carrollton
(972) 416-9738

Temple Emanu-El
8500 Hillcrest Road 75230   (214) 706-0000
                                  Fax: (214) 706-0025
                         Web site: www.tedallas.org
Temple Shalom
6930 Alpha Road 75230   (972) 661-1810

Traditional

Tiferet Israel Congregation
10909 Hillcrest Road 75230   (214) 691-3611

El Paso

Bakeries

Kahn's Bakery and Sweet Shop
918 N. Oregon Street 79901
Under rabbinical supervision.

Community Organisations

Chabad House
6515 Westwind 79912   (915) 584-8218
                    Web site: www.chabadelpaso.com
Have a mikva as well.
Jewish Federation
405 Wallenberg Drive 79912   (915) 584-4437

Museums

El Paso Holocaust Museum and Study Center
401 Wallenberg Drive 79912   (915) 833-5656
                                  Fax: (915) 833-9523
                         Email: epholo@flash.net
Web site: www.flash.net/~epholo.com
The museum features an impressive collection of
artifacts, dramatic displays, pictures and posters
depicting the chronological history of Europe during the
Nazi era. Open Sunday and Tuesday 1-4pm or by
appointment.

Synagogues

Conservative

B'nai Zion
805 Cherry Hill Lane 79912   (915) 833-2222
Have a mikva as well.

Reform

Sinai, 4408 N. Stanton Street 79902   (915) 532-5959

Fort Worth/Arlington

Synagogues

Conservative

Ahavath Shalom
4050 South Hulen 76109   (817) 731-4721
Beth Shalom, 1211 Thannisch Drive (817) 860-5448

United States of America / Texas

Orthodox
Chabad-Lubavitch
6804 Del Prado   (817) 346-7700

Reform
Beth-El Congregation
207 W. Broadway 76104   (817) 332-7141
                                          Fax: (817) 332-7157
Just south of downtown Fort Worth, offers a full range
of Shabbat and holiday worship services and other
programs for children and adults. Call for service times
and other information.

Houston

Bakeries
Kroger's
S. Post Oak @ W. Bellfort 77096   (713) 721-7691
Supervision: Houston Kashruth Association.
LeMoulin European Bakery
5645 Beechnut 77096   (713) 779-1618
Supervision: Houston Kashruth Association.
New York Bagel Shop
9724 Hillcroft 77096   (713) 723-5879
Supervision: Houston Kashruth Association.
Randall's Bakery

Supervision: Houston Kashruth Association.
Can be found at eight locations including : Clear Lake,
Sugar Land, Highway 6 & Memorial, Fondren &
Bissonnet, W. Bellfort & S. Post Oak, Gessner & W.
Bellfort, and Holcombe & Kirby.
Three Brothers Bakery
4036 S. Braeswood 77025   (713) 666-2551
Supervision: Houston Kashruth Association.

Butchers
Albertson's
S. Braeswood@Fondren   (713) 271-1180
Supervision: Houston Kashruth Association.
Kroger's
S. Post Oak @ W. Bellfort 77096   (713) 721-7691
Supervision: Houston Kashruth Association.

Embassy
Consul General of Israel
Suite 1500, 24 Greenway Plaza 77046

Grocers
Albertson's
S. Braeswood@Fondren   (713) 271-1180
Supervision: Houston Kashruth Association.

Kashrut Information
Houston Kashrut Association
9001 Greenwillow 77096   (713) 723-3850
                                   Fax: (713) 723-3852

Mikvaot
Chabad Lubavitch Center
10900 Fondren Road 77096   (713) 777-200(
United Orthodox Synagogues
4221 S. Braeswood Blvd., 77096   (713) 723-385(

Organisations
Jewish Federation of Greater Houston
5603 S. Braeswood Blvd. 77096   (713) 729-70C
                                   Fax: (713) 721-623(
                          Email: ujchouston@jon.cjfny.o(

Restaurants

Dairy
Saba's Mediterranean
9704 Fondren   (713) 270-722(
Supervision: Houston Kashruth Association.
Pizza, Felafel Fish

Meat
Nosher's at the Jewish Community Centre
5601 S. Braeswood 77096   (713) 729-32(
Supervision: Houston Kashruth Association.

Vegetarian
Madras Pavilion
3910 Kirby Drive 77098   (713) 521-26(
Supervision: Houston Kashruth Association.
Wonderful Vegetarian Restaurant
7549 Westheimer 77063   (713) 977-31:
Supervision: Houston Kashruth Association.

Synagogues

Conservative
B'rith Shalom
4610 Bellaire Blvd. 77401
Beth Am, 1431 Brittmore Rd. 77043   (713) 461-77:
                                   Fax: (713) 461-77
                          Email: ebbe@earthlink.(
                          Web site: www.bethamtx.o(
One room and board is available to anyone attendin(
Services.
Beth Yeshurun
4525 Beechnut St. 77096   (713) 666-18
                                   Fax: (713) 666-77(
                       Email: arthur@bethyeshurun.c(
                       Web site: www.bethyeshurun.c(
Congregation Shaar Hashalom
16020 El Camino Real 77062   (281) 488-58(
                                   Fax: (281) 488-35
                       Email: Ferderow@blkbox.c(
                  Web site: www.uscj.org.sowest/houstc

Orthodox

Congregation Beth Rambam
11333 Braesridge Blvd. 77071   (713) 723-3030
Fax: (713) 726-8737
Email: gez@flash.net
Web site: www.flash.net/~bentzion/br.htm
Home hospitality available. Office hours Mon - Fri
9am to 2 pm

United Orthodox Synogogues
9001 Greenwillow 77096   (713) 723-3850
Web site: www.uosh.org
Mikva on premises. Daily minyan and Shabat services.

Young Israel of Houston
7510 Apache Plume 77071   (713) 729-0719
Web site: www.flash.net~bentzion/yi.htm

Reform

Beth Israel
5600 N. Braeswood Blvd. 77096   (713) 771-6221
Fax: (713) 771-5705
Web site: www.Beth-Israel.org

Congregation for Reform Judaism
801 Bering Dr. 77057   (713) 782-4162
Fax: (713) 782-4167

Emanu-El
1500 Sunset Blvd. 77005   (713) 529-5771
Fax: (713) 529-0703
Email: emanuelhouston.org
Web site: www.emanuel.org

Jewish Community North
5400 Fellowship Lane 77379   (281) 376-0016
Fax: (281) 251-1033
Email: jcn@wt.net

Temple Sinai
783 Country Place Dr. 77079   (281) 496-5950
Fax: (281) 496-1537

Lubbock

Groceries

Albertson's   (806) 794-6761

Lowe's Supermarket
82nd & Slide Rd

United   (906) 791-0220
Good selection for Passover.

Synagogues

Congregation Shaareth Israel
6928 3rd Street 79424   (806) 794-7517
Mailing address: PO Box 93594, 79493-3594

San Antonio

Delicatessens

Delicious Food
7460 Callaghan Road 78229   (512) 366-1844

Museums

Holocaust Memorial
12500 N W Military Highway 78231
(210) 302-6807
Fax: (210) 408-2332
Email: cohenm@jfstx.org

Institute of Texan Cultures
Hemisphere Plaza, Downtown Riverfront

Organisations

Jewish Federation
8434 Ahern Drive 78216   (512) 341-8234

Synagogues

Conservative

Agudas Achim
1201 Donaldson Avenue 78228

Orthodox

Rodfei Sholom
3003 Sholom Drive 78230   (210) 493 3558
Fax: (210) 492 0629
Email: rodfei@world-net.net
Web site: www.ou.org
Mikvah on premises.

Reform

Beth El, 211 Belknap Place 78212

Waco

Synagogues

Conservative

Agudath Jacob
4925 Hillcrest Drive 76710

Reform

Rodef Sholom
1717 N. New Road 76707   (254) 754-3703
Fax: (254) 754-5538

Utah

Salt Lake City

Organisations

United Jewish Federation of Utah
2416 East, 1700 South 84108   (801) 581-0102
Fax: (801) 581-1334

Synagogues

Chabad Lubavitch of Utah
1433 South 1100 East 84105   (801) 467-7777
Web site: www.chabadutah.com

United States of America / Utah

Reconstructionist

Chavurah B'yachad
P.O. Box 9115 84109   (801) 325-4539
                    Email: byachad@aol.com

Reform

Congregation Kol Ami
2425 E. Heritage Way 84109   (801) 484-1501
                    Fax: (801) 484-1162
                    Email: clyon@conkolami.org
                    Web site: www.conkolami.org

Vermont
Burlington

Synagogues

Conservative

Ohavi Zedek
188 N. Prospect Street 5401   (802) 864-0218

Orthodox

Ahavath Gerim
cnr. Archibald & Hyde Streets 5401   (802) 862-3001

Reform

Temple Sinai
500 Swift Street 5401   (802) 862-5125

Virginia
Alexandria

Synagogues

Conservative

Agudas Achim
2908 Valley Drive 22302   (703) 998-6460

Reform

Beth El Hebrew Congregation
3830 Seminary Road 22304   (703) 370-9400
                    Fax: (703) 370-7730
                    Email: bethelhc@erols.com

Arlington

Synagogues

Conservative

Arlington-Fairfax Jewish Congregation
2920 Arlington Blvd. 22204   (703) 979-4466
                    Fax: (703) 979-4468
                    Email: office@arfax.net
                    Web site: www.arfax.org
Daily Minyan and Shabbat services. Includes areas
known as Crystal City, Rosslyn and Skyline.

Charlottesville

Synagogues

The Hillel Jewish Center
The University of Virginia, 1824 University Circle 22903
                    (804) 295-4963

Reform

Congregation Beth Israel
301 E. Jefferson Street 22902   (804) 295-6382
                    Fax: (804) 296-6491
                    Email: barbcbi@aol.com

Danville

Synagogues

Temple Beth Sholom
Sutherlin Avenue   (804) 792-3489
This building is 95 years old, one of oldest synagogues
in the South. Friday evening and holiday services.

Fairfax

Synagogues

Conservative

Congregation Olam Tikvah
3800 Glenbrook Road 22031   (703) 425-1880
                    Fax: (703) 425-0835
2 miles from Beltway Exit 6W.

Falls Church

Synagogues

Reform

Temple Rodef Shalom
2100 Westmoreland Street 22043   (703) 532-2217
                    Email: trsfcva@erols.com

Norfolk

Groceries

Meat

The Kosher Place
738 W. 22nd Street   (757) 623-1770
Supervision: Vaad Hakashrus of Tidewater.
Meats, deli, prepared foods. Hours: Monday to
Thursday, 9 am to 6 pm; Friday, to 3 pm; Sunday, 10
am to 4 pm. Close to colonial Williamsburg and
Virginia Beach.

Hotels

Sheraton Norfolk Waterside Hotel
777 Waterside Drive 23510   (757) 622-6664
Supervision: Va'ad.

United States of America / Virginia

Kashrut Information
Va'ad Hakashrut
c/o B'nai Israel   (757) 627-7358
Fax: (757) 627-8544
Email: rebyosef@hotmail.com

Mikvaot
B'nai Israel Congregation
420 Spotswood Avenue 23517   (757) 627-7358
Fax: (757) 627-8544
Email: bnaioffice@juno.com

Va'ad Hakashrut

Organisations
United Jewish Federation of Tidewater
5029 Corporate Woods Drive, Suite 225,
Virginia Beach 23462   (757) 671-1600
Fax: (757) 671-7613

Synagogues

Conservative

Beth El, 422 Shirley Av. 23517   (757) 625-7821
Fax: (757) 627-4905
Email: bethelc@erols.com

Temple Israel
7255 Granby St. 23505   (804) 489-4550

Reform

Ohef Sholom
Stockley Gdns. at Raleigh Av. 23507
(804) 625-4295

The Commodore Levy Chapel
Frazier Hall, Building C-7 (inside Gate 2), Norfolk US
Navy Station   (757) 444-7361
Fax: (757) 444-7362
Email: sphillips@nsn.cmar.navy.mil
The US Navy's oldest synagogue. Visitors welcome for
tour or Erev Shabbat services. Contact Jewish chaplain
(Lt. S.D. Phillips) for Base Pass first.

Richmond

Bakeries
Chesapeake Bagel Bakery
Willow Lawn Shopping Center,
5100 Monument Avenue 23226
Supervision: Vaad of Richmond.
Kosher bagels, challah and rolls.

Groceries
Hannafords
Willow Lawn Shopping Center,
5100 Monument Avenue 23226
Supervision: Vaad of Richmond.
Newly opened supermarket with a kosher deli.

Hotels
The Farbreng-Inn Kosher Retreat Center
1800 SEE Virginia 23233
(804) 740-2000/800-733-8474
Fax: (804) 750-1341
Email: info@chabadofva.org
Kosher retreat center open year round. Under the
Hashgacht of Lubavitch of Virginia

Mikvaot
Young Israel
4811 Patterson Avenue 23226   (804) 353-3831
Fax: (804) 288-4381
Email: adere@juno.com

Museums
Beth Ahabah
1117 W. Franklin Street 23220
Also housing Jewish archives which are of great
historical interest.

Organisations
Jewish Community Federation
5403 Monument Avenue 23226   (804) 288-0045

Synagogues

Conservative

Or Atid, 501 Parham Road 23229   (804) 740-4747

Orthodox

Keneseth Beth Israel
6300 Patterson Avenue 23226   (804) 288-7953
Fax: (804) 673-9558
Email: kbi6300@erols.com
Young Israel of Richmond
4811 Patterson Avenue 23226   (804) 353-5831
Email: yosefb@juno.com

Reform

Or Ami, 9400 N. Huguenot Road 23235

Virginia Beach

Media

Magazines

Renewal Magazine
5029 Corporate Woods, Suite 225 23462
(757) 671-1600
Fax: (757) 671-7613
Published 3 times per year.

United States of America / Virginia

Newspapers

Southeastern Virginia Jewish News
5029 Corporate Woods Drive, Suite 225 23462
(757) 671-1600
Fax: (757) 671-7613
Email: news@ujft.org
Published every 2 weeks.

Synagogues

Conservative

Kempsville Conservative
952 Indian Lakes Blvd. 23464   (757) 495-8510
Web site: www.uscj.org/seabd/virginiabeach/
Temple Emanuel
25th Street 23451

Orthodox

Chabad Lubavitch
533 Gleneagle Drive 23462   (804) 499-0507

Reform

Beth Chaverim
3820 Stoneshore Road 23452-7965   (757) 463-3226
Fax: (757) 463-1134
Email: bethchaverim@ddaccess.com

Virginia Peninsula

Bakeries

Brenner's Warwick Bakery
240 31st Street, Newport News 23607
Supervision: Va'ad Hakashrut.

Mikvaot

Adath Jeshurun
12646 Nettles Drive, Newport News 23606

Organisations

United Jewish Community of the Virginia Peninsula
2700 Spring Road, Newport News 23606
(804) 930-1422

Synagogues

Conservative

Rodef Shalom
318 Whealton Road, Hampton 23666

Reform

Temple Sinai
11620 Warwick Blvd., Newport News 23601

Traditional

B'nai Israel
3116 Kecoughtan Road, Hampton 23661

Washington

Aberdeen

Synagogues

Conservative

Temple Beth Israel
1219 Spur Street 98520   (360) 533-3784

Seattle

Bakeries

Bagel Deli, 340 15th Avenue E.   (206) 322-2471
Supervision: Va'ad HaRabanim of Greater Seattle.
All bagels, bialys and fragels are pareve; brownies are
dairy. Pat Yisrael. No other food products are under
kosher supervision. Hours: Monday to Friday, 6:30 am
to 6 pm; Saturday, to 5 pm; Sunday, 7 am to 4 pm.
Price range: $.
International Biscuit
5028 Wilson Avenue   (206) 722-5595
Supervision: Va'ad HaRabanim of Greater Seattle.
All bakery goods on site are under supervision and Pat
Yisrael. Available at various grocery stores.

Jewish Student/Young Adult Center

**Hillel, Foundation for Jewish Campus Life at the
University of Washington**
4745 17th Av. N.E. 98105   (206) 527-1997
Fax: (206) 527-1999
Email: mail@hilleluw.org
Programs, Services, occasional kosher meals for
students & young adults, 18-30.

Kashrut Information

Va'ad HaRabanim
6500 52nd Avenue St 98118   (206) 760-0805
Fax: (206) 725-0347
Email: seavaad@aol.com
The Va'ad HaRabanim was organised in 1993 to
replace the former Seattle Kashruth Board which had
been organised in the early 1900s to provide kosher
meat for the community. In addition to providing
kosher meat, the new board provides kosher
supervision for many restaurants, bakeries, retail outlets
and catering facilities in the Seattle area. For further
questions and information, please contact David
Grashin at the number above.

Media

Transcripts

The Jewish Transcript
2031 3rd Avenue 98121

Museums

Community Center
3801 E. Mercer Way, Mercer Island 98040
(206) 232-7115
A Holocaust memorial with a bronze sculpture by Gizel Berman has been dedicated here.

Organisations

Jewish Federation of Greater Seattle
2031 3rd Avenue 98121 (206) 443-5400

Stroum Jewish Community Center, Northend Facility
8606 35th Avenue NE 98115 (206) 526-8073
Fax: (206) 526-9958
Email: cherie@sjcc.org

Washington Association of Jewish Communities
2031 3rd Avenue 98121

Restaurants

Chinese Vegetarian

Bamboo Garden
364 Roy Street, near Seattle Center (206) 282-6616
Fax: (206) 284-2775
Email: bamboogarden@aol.com
Supervision: Va'ad HaRabanim of Greater Seattle.

Spokane

Organisations

Jewish Community Council
North 221 Wall, Suite 500, Spokane 99201
(509) 838-4261

Synagogues

Conservative

Temple Beth Shalom
1322 E. 30th Street 99203 (509) 747-3304

West Virginia

Huntingdon

Synagogues

Conservative & Reform

B'nai Sholom
949 10th Avenue 25701 (304) 522-2980

Wisconsin

Madison

Organisations

Madison Jewish Community Council
6434 Enterprise Lane 53179 (608) 278-1808
Fax: (608) 278-7814
Email: mjcc@mjcc.net
Web site: www.jewishmadison.org

Synagogues

Hillel Foundation
611 Langdon Street 53703 (608) 256-8361

Conservative

Beth Israel Center
1406 Mound Street 53711 (608) 256-7763

Orthodox

Chabad House
1722 Regent Street 53705 (608) 231-3450
Fax: (608) 231-3790

Reform

Beth El, 2702 Arbor Drive 53711

Milwaukee

Community Organisations

Coalition for Jewish Learning
6401 North Santa Monica Boulevard 53217
(414) 962-8860
Fax: (414) 962-8852

Media

Directories

Milkwaukee Jewish Federation
1360 N. Prospect Avenue 53202 (414) 271-2992

Newspapers

Wisconsin Jewish Chronicle
1360 N. Prospect Avenue 53202 (414) 390-5888
Fax: (414) 271-0487
Email: milwaukeej@aol.com

Organisations

Milkwaukee Jewish Federation
1360 N. Prospect Avenue 53202 (414) 271-8338
Fax: (414) 271-7081
With more than a dozen synagogues in the area, travellers are advised to contact a local religious organisation for specific details.

United States of America / Wisconsin

Restaurants

Meat

Kosher Meat Klub
4731 West Burleigh 53210   (414) 449-5980
Fax: (414) 449-5985
Meat sandwiches, delicatessen and kosher groceries
are available.

Shelley's Deliworks
4311 West Bradley Road 53223   (414) 365-8560
Fax: (414) 365-8526

Regular meals

Synagogues

Beth Jehudah
3100 North 52nd Street 53216   (414) 442-5730
Fax: (414) 442-6171
Email: bethjehudah@juno.com
Web site: www.bethjehudah.org

Congregation Agudas Achim
2233 West Mequon Road 53092   (262) 242-2235
Fax: (262) 242-2268
Email: chabadmequon@aol.com
Web site: www.chabad-mequon.org

Congregation Anshai Leibowitz
2415 West Mequon Road 53092   (414) 873-7704

Sheboygan

Synagogues

Traditional

Temple Beth El
1007 North Avenue 53083

Wyoming

Casper

Synagogues

Reform

Temple Beth El
4105 S. Poplar, PO Box 3534 82602
(307) 237-233(

Cheyenne

Synagogues

Conservative

Mount Sinai
2610 Pioneer Avenue 82001   (307) 634-305
Gift shop and Mikvah by appointment.

Green River

Synagogues
Congregation of Beth Israel
PO Box 648 Green River Way 82935
(307) 875-419

Laramie

Synagogues

Reform

Laramie JCC
PO Box 202 82070   (307) 745-881

In Search of Refuge
Jews and US Consuls in Nazi Germany
Bat-Ami Zucker

US consuls played a distinctive and crucial role in control of Jewish
refugee entry into the United States in 1933–1941. The consuls decided
individual cases and in doing so had discretion to grant immigration
visas. This extended to interpreting aspects of the immigration laws and
regulations which were not fully defined, notably the 'likely to become
a public charge' clause.

The book examines how the consuls perceived, interpreted and administered immigration
policy towards the refugees.

224 pages 2001
0 85303 400 1 cloth £37.50/$57.50   0 85303 399 4 paper £18.50/26.50
Parker-Wiener Series on Jewish Studies

VALLENTINE MITCHELL
**Newbury House, 900 Eastern Avenue, Ilford, Essex, IG2 7HH, England
Tel: +44 020 8599 8866   Fax: +44 020 8599 0984**

Uruguay

After the Conversos in the sixteenth century, there was no known Jewish community in Uruguay until the late nineteenth century, when the country served as a stop-over on the way to Argentina. The Jewish population rose in the twentieth century, with immigration from the Middle East and eastern Europe. A synagogue was opened by 1917. Despite restrictive immigration laws imposed against European Jews fleeing Nazism, 2,500 Jews managed to enter the country between 1939 and 1940. Further Jewish immigration followed, from Hungary and the Middle East, in the post-war period.

There are many Jewish organisations functioning in Uruguay, including Zionist and women's organisations. Kosher restaurants exist in Jewish institutions, and there are a number of synagogues.

GMT - 3 hours	Total Population 3,140,000
Country calling code (598)	Jewish Population 30,000
Emergency Telephone 999	Electricity voltage 220

Montevideo

With approximately 10,000 families in the capital of Uruguay, Montevideo contains almost all of the country's Jewish community. There is a Museum of the Holocaust in Montevideo, and near the Teatro Solis opera house stands a Golda Meir monument. An Albert Einstein monument can be found in Rodo Park.

Communal organisation

Centro Recordatoria del Holocausto
Canalones 1084 11100   (902-5750) 902-5740
is the home for several Jewish institutions and events are frequently held here.

Community Organisations

Centro Lubavitch
Av. Brasil 2704, CP 11300   (2) 709-3444; 708-5169
Fax: (2) 711-3696
Email: shemtov@chasque.apc.org

Embassy

Embassy of Israel
Bulevar Artigas 1585-89   (2) 400-4164
Fax: (2) 409-5821
Email: emisuyur@adlnet.com.uy

Groceries

avne, Cavia 2800   (2) 908-7869
Fax: (2) 707-0866

Media

Newspapers

Semanario Hebreo
Soriano 875/201   (442) 925-311
Spanish-language weekly. Editor also directs daily Yiddish radio programme.

Mikvaot

Adat Yiereim, Durazno 1183   (2) 711-1686
Fax: (2) 711-7736

Restaurants

Kasherissimo, Camacua 623   (2) 915-0128
Fax: (2) 208-1536
Supervision: Chief Rabbi Yosef Bitton.
The restaurant is situated in the Hebraica Macabi building.

Synagogues

Anshei Jeshurun
Durazno 972   (2) 900-8456
Fax: (2) 900-8456

Asociacion Israelita Ortodoxa y Sinagoga
Canelones 828, CP
Bet Aharon, Harishona, Inca 2287
Comunidad Israelita Hungara
Durazno 972   (2) 900-8456
Fax: (2) 900-8456

Nueva Congregacion Israelita (Central European)
Wilson F Aldunete 1168   (442) 926-620
Social Isralite Adat Yeshurun
Alarcon 1396
Vaad Ha'ir
Canelones 828   (2) 900-6106
Fax: (2) 711-7736
Email: marebis@com.uy

Ashekenazi

Comunidad Israelita de Uruguay
Canelones 1084, Piso 1   (2) 902-5750
Fax: (2) 902-5740
Email: kehila@adinet.com.uy

Uruguay

Sephardi
Comunidad Israelita Sefardi
Buenos Aires 234, 21 de Setiembre 3111
(442) 710-179
Templo Sefardi
de Pocitos L. Franzini 888

Tourist Sites
Memorial a Golda Meir
Reconquista y Ciudadela

Uzbekistan

The ancient Jewish community in this central Asian republic is believed to have originated from Persian exiles in the fifth century. The Jews were subject to harsh treatment under the various rulers of the region, but still managed to become important traders in this area, which straddled the route between Europe and China and the far east. In the late Middle Ages Jewish weavers and dyers were asked to help in the local cloth industry, and Bukhara became a key Jewish city after it became the capital of the country in the 1500s. Once the area had been incorporated into the Russian Empire in 1868, many Jews from the west of the Empire moved into Uzbekistan, and a further influx occurred when Uzbekistan was used to shelter Jews during the Nazi invasion of the Soviet Union; many subsequently set up home there.

The original Bukharan Jews are generally more religious than the Ashkenazim who entered the area in the nineteenth and twentieth centuries. There are Jewish schools in the area, and although there is no central Jewish organisation, there are many Jewish bodies operating on separate levels for the Ashkenazim and the Bukharans.

GMT + 5 to 6 hours
Country calling code (998)
Emergency Telephone (Police, Fire, Ambulance - 03)

Total Population 23,206,0
Jewish Population 35,00
Electricity voltage 22

Andizhan

Synagogues
7 Sovetskaya Street

Bukhara

Synagogues
20 Tsentralnaya Street

Katta-Kurgan

Synagogues
1 Karl Marx Alley

Kermine

Synagogues
36 Narimanov Street

Kokand

Synagogues
Dekabristov Street, Fergan Oblast

Margelan

Synagogues
Turtkilskaya Street, Fergan Oblast

Navoy

Synagogues
36 Narimanov Street

Samarkand

Synagogues
45 Respublikanskaya Street
5 Denauskaya Street
34 Khudzumskaya Street

Tashkent

Embassy
Embassy of Israel
16A Shakhrisabz Street, 5th floor   (71) 152911
                                   Fax: (71) 1521378
                      Email: isremb@online.ru

Synagogues
9 Chkalov Street

Gorbunova Street 62

Ashkenazi
77 Chempianov Street

Sephardi
3 Sagban Street

Venezuela

                      (71) 1525978
               Fax: (71) 1525978
        Email: jewish@bcc.com.uz
          Web site: www.jewish.uz

                      (71) 40-0768

Venezuela

Settlement in Venezuela began in the early nineteenth century from the Caribbean. The Jews were granted freedom early (between 1819 and 1821), which encouraged more settlement. The community at that time was not religious. At the beginning of the twentieth century, some Middle Eastern Jewish immigrants organised a central committee for the first time. The powerful influence of the Catholic Church meant few Jews were accepted as immigrants in the pre-war rush to escape Nazi Europe.

After the war, however, the community began to expand, with arrivals from Hungary and the Middle East. The successful oil industry and the excellent Jewish education system attracted immigrants from other South American countries.

Today most Jews live in Caracas, the capital. Fifteen synagogues serve the country. The Lubavitch movement is present and maintains a yeshivah. Caracas has a Jewish bookshop and a weekly Jewish newspaper. Venezuela has an expanding Jewish community, in contrast to many of its South American neighbours. The oldest Jewish cemetery in South America, in Coro, with tombstones dating from 1832, is still in use today.

GMT - 4 hours   Total Population 22,315,000
Country calling code (58)   Jewish Population 35,000
Emergency Telephone (Ambulance - 545 4545) (Dr. - 483 7021)   Electricity voltage 110

Caracas

Bakeries
Le Notre
Avenida Andres Bello   (2) 782-4448
Pasteleria Kasher
Avenida Los Proceres   (2) 515-086

Booksellers
Libreria Cultural Maimonides
Av Altamira Edif. Carlitos PB
(near Av. Galapen), San Bernardino   (2) 551-6356
                                   Fax: (2) 552-9127
                       Email: judaico@tecel.net.ve

Contact Information
Chabad-Lubavitch Centre
Apartado 5454 1010A   (2) 523-887

Delicatessens
La Belle Delicatesses
Av. Bogotá, Edif Santa María, Local 2, Los Caobos
                      (2) 781-7204
                 Fax: (2) 781-7182
Kosher delicatessen and mini-market, restaurant and take-out.

Embassy
Embassy of Israel
Avenida Francisco de Miranda, Centro Empresarial
Miranda, 4 Piso Oficina 4-D, Apartado Postal Los
Ruices 70081   (2) 239-4511; 239-4921
                 Fax: (2) 239-4320

Groceries
Mini Market, Avenida Los Caobos   (2) 781-7204
Take away.

Venezuela

Hotels

Hotel Aventura

A short walk away from the Union Synagogue, convenient for Shabbat observers.

Hotel Avila
Next door to the Union Synagogue, convenient for Shabbat observers.

Media

Newspaper

Nuevo Mundo Israelita
Av Marques del Toro 9Los Caobos

Mikvaot

Shomrei Shabbat Association Synagogue
Av Anauco
San Bernardino   (2) 517-197

Union Israelita de Caracas Synagogue & Community Centre
Av Marques del Toro 9
San Bernardino   (2) 552-8222
                              Fax: (2) 552-7628
          Email: rabino@brener@eldish.net

Restaurants

Dairy

Eilat, Av. Roraima con Cajigal   (517) 763-7880

Meat

La Belle Delicatesses
Avenida Bogota   (517) 781-7204

Synagogues

Ashkenazi

Great Synagogue of Caracas
Av Francisco Javier Ustariz
San Bernardino   (2) 511-869

Shomrei Shabbat Assoc. Synagogue
Av Anauco
San Bernardino   (2) 517-197

Union Israelita de Caracas Synagogue & Community Centre
Av Marques del Toro 9
San Bernardino   (2) 552-8222
                              Fax: (2) 552-7628
          Email: rabino@brener@eldish.net
If notified in advance, they can arrange kosher lunches. There is also a meat snack bar open in the evening.

Sephardi

Bet El
Av Cajigal
San Bernardino   (2) 522-008

Keter Tora
Av Lopez Mendez
San Bernardino

Shaare Shalom
Av Bogota, Quinta Julieta, Los Caobos
Tiferet Yisrael
Av MariperezLos Caobos   (2) 781-1942

Maracaibo

Community Organisations
Associación Israelita de Maracaibo
Calle 74 No 13-26   (61) 70333

Porlamar

Synagogues
Or Meir
Margarita Island
Mikva on premises.

Virgin Islands

Jews first began to settle on the island in 1655, taking advantage of liberal Danish rule. They were mainly traders in sugarcane, rum and molasses, and by 1796 a synagogue had been founded. The Jewish population of 400 in 1850 made up half of the islands' white community. There have been three Jewish governors; one being the first, Gabriel Milan appointed by King Christian of Denmark.

The community began to shrink after the Panama Canal was opened in 1914, and by 1942 only 50 Jews remained. Since 1945, the community has expanded again, with families arriving from the US mainland.

Jewish Population 400GMT - 4 hours
Country calling code (1)

Total Population 106,000
Jewish Population 400

St Thomas

Synagogues
St Thomas Synagogue
PO Box 266
Charlotte Amalie 00804   (340) 774-4312
                              Fax: (340) 774-3249
                   Email: hebrewcong@islands.vi
This synagogue was built in 1833.

Orthodox
Khal Hakodesh

(809) 779-2000

Yugoslavia

(Yugoslavia at present comprises Serbia and Montenegro.) The history of Serbian Jewry is both long and comparatively happy, with initial settlement in Roman times. After Turkish domination in 1389, the community continued to thrive and also prospered under Austrian rule in the eighteenth century. The nineteenth century saw some measures being taken against the Jews after Serbia became independent, but these were quickly redressed in 1889, following the Treaty of Berlin.

After 1918, Serbia was united with Croatia, Slovenia and the other south Slavic states into one country, known as Yugoslavia. The community suffered heavily under Nazi domination. The Jews were active in the Yugoslav partisans and, after liberation, many who had hidden or fought with the partisans began to return to their homes. Before the break-up of Yugoslavia, the Jews were allowed contact with other communities, including Israel. Since the civil war, some Jews still remain in the country, and there is a synagogue and a Talmud Torah school in Belgrade.

GMT + 1 hour	Total Population 10,473,000
Country calling code (260)	Jewish Population 2,5000
Emergency Telephone (Police - 92) (Fire - 93) (Ambulance - 94)	Electricity voltage 220

Belgrade

Some 2,000 Jews now live in the capital of Serbia, compared with hardly any during the latter stages of World War Two. There is an Ashkenazi synagogue which follows Sephardi tradition (or nusach), and there is a community centre, although kosher food is not available.

Cemeteries
Jewish Cemetery
There are monuments to fallen fighters and martyrs of fascism, fallen Jewish soldiers in the Serbian army in the First World War here. In 1990 a new monument to Jews killed in Serbia was erected by the Danube, in the pre-war Jewish quarter Dorcol.

Community Organisations
Local Community
7 Kralja Petra Street 71a/11 11001
                              (11) 624-289

Museums
Jewish Museum
7 Kralja Petra Street 71a/1 11001
                              (11) 622-634
                         Fax: (11) 626-674
It is open daily from 10 am to 12 pm except Mondays.

Representative Organisations
Federation of Jewish Communities
7 Kralja Petra Street 71a/111,
PO Box 841 11001   (11) 624-359/621-837
                              Fax: (11) 626-674

Synagogues
Birjuzova Street 19
Services are held Friday evenings and Jewish holidays.

Novi Sad

Cemeteries
Jewish Cemetery
There is a monument to the Jews who fell in the war and the victims of fascism. The synagogue here is no longer open but it's reported to be extremely beautiful, and is currently being converted to a concert hall.

Community Organisations
Community Offices
Jevrejska 11   (21) 613-882

Subotica

Community Organisations
Community Offices
Dimitrija Tucovica Street 13   28483

Zambia

The Jewish community began in the early twentieth century, with cattle ranching being the main attraction for Jewish immigrants. The community grew, and the copper industry was developed largely by Jewish entrepreneurs. With refugees from Nazism and a post-war economic boom, the Jewish community in the mid-1950s totalled 1,200. The community declined after independence in 1964.

Today, the Council for Zambian Jewry (founded in 1978) fulfils the role of the community's central body.

GMT + 2 hours	Total Population 9,715,000
Country calling code (260)	Jewish Population Under 100
Emergency Telephone (Police, Fire and Ambulance - 999)	Electricity voltage 220

Lusaka

Communal Organisation
Council for Zambian Jewry
P O Box 30089 10101   (1) 229-556
                                   Fax: (1) 223-798

Synagogues
Lusaka Hebrew Congregation
Chachacha Road, POB 30020   (1) 229-190
                                   Fax: (1) 221-428
                                   Email: galaun@zamnet.zm

Jews were among the earliest pioneers of Zimbabwe, in fact the first white child born there (Apri 1894) was Jewish.

The first synagogue in Zimbabwe (formerly Rhodesia) was set up in 1894, in a tent in Bulawayo In 1897 a Jew was elected as the first mayor of Bulawayo.The first Jews came from Europe (especially Lithuania), and they became involved in trade and managing hotels. They were joine in the 1920s and 1930s by Sephardis from Rhodes. Some senior politicians in the country wer Jewish, including one prime minister.

The 1970s saw the turbulent transition to Zimbabwe and many Jews emigrated to escape th unrest. The community is now mainly Ashkenazi, with an important Sephardi component. Harar has both an Ashkenazi and a Sephardi synagogue; Bulawayo has a Ashkenazi synagogue. Ther are community centres in both the towns, and schools, although the latter have many local, non Jewish pupils. There are also Zionist youth organisations.

GMT + 2 hours	Total Population 11,515,00(
Country calling code (263)	Jewish Population 90(
Emergency Telephone (Police, Fire and Ambulance - 999)	Electricity voltage 220/24(

Bulawayo

Synagogues
Bulawayo Hebrew Congregation
Jason Moyo Street, PO Box 337   (9) 60829

Harare

Representative Organisations

Zimbabwe Jewish Board of Deputies
P.O. Box 1954   (4) 702506/7
                                   Fax: (4) 70250(

Hours of opening 8.30 a.m. to 12 noon

Synagogues
Harare Hebrew Congregation
Milton Park Jewish Centre, Lezard Avenue, POB 342
                                   (4) 727-57(

Sephardi Congregation
54 Josiah Chinamano Avenue, POB 1051 (4) 722-89(

KOSHER FISH THROUGHOUT THE WORLD
(Courtesy of Kashrut Division, The London Beth din)

AUSTRALIA

Anchovy
Baramundi
Barracouta
Barracuda
Blue Eye
Blue Grenadier
Bream
Butterfly-fish
Cod
Coral Perch
Duckfish
Flathead
Flounder
Garfish
Groper
Gurnard
Haddock
Hake
Harpuka
Herring
Jewfish
John Dory
Lemon Sole
Mackerel
Morwong
Mullet
Murray Cod
Murray Perch
Orange Roughy
Perch
Pike
Pilchard
Red Emperor
Redfin
Salmon
Sardines
Sea Perch
Shad
Sild
Snapper

Tailor
Tasmanian
Trumpeter
Terakiji
Trevally
Trout
Tuna:
  Albacore,
Bluefin
  North bluefin
  South bluefin
  Skipjack
  (striped)
  Yellowfin
Whiting
Yellowtail

CANADA

Albacore
Anchovies
Bass
Boston Bluefish
Carp
Cisco
Cod
Flounder
Goldeye
Haddock
Hake
Halibut
Herring
Mackerel
Orange Roughy
Perch
Pickerel
Pike
Pollock
Pompano
Salmon
Sardines
Silversides

Smelts
Snapper
Sole
Sunfish
Tarpon
Trout
Tuna

CARIBBEAN

Bonito
Grouper
Kingsish
Mullets
Muttonfish
Pompano
Roballo
Smelts
Snapper
Red/Yellow
Spanish Mackerel
Trout
Tuna

CYPRUS

Antzouva
Bacceliaos
Barbouni
Cephalos
Glossa
Lavraki
Sardella
Scoumbri
Tonos
Tsipoura

**CZECH
REPUBLIC**

Ancovicka
Belicka
Kambala

Kapr
Lin
Lipan
Losos
Makrela
Okoun
Parmice
Platejs
Platyz
Plotice
Prazama
Pstruh
Sardinka
Sled
Sprota
Stika
Treska
Tunak

DENMARK

Aborre
Ansjos
Bars
Brasen
Brisling
Gedde
Helleyflynder
Hvilling
Ising
Karpe
Knurhane
Kuller
Kulmule
Laks
Lange
Lubbe
Makrel
Multe
Orred
Rodspaette
Sardin

Sild
Skalle
Skrubbe
Slethvarre
Suder
Torsk
Tun fisk
Tunge

FRANCE

Aiglefin
Anchois
Bar Commun
Barbue
Breme
Brochet
Cabillaud
Carpe
Carrelet
Flet
Fletan
Gardon
Grondin
Hareng
Lieu Jaune
Limande
Lingue
Maquereau
Merlan
Merlu
Mulet
Ombre
Perche
Pilchard
Plie
Sardine
Saumon
Sole
Sprat
Tanche
Thon
Truite

GERMANY

Asche

Barsch
Brasse
Flunder
Forelle
Glattbutt
Hecht
Heilbutt
Hering
Kabeljau
Knurrhahn
Lachs
Leng
Makrele
Meerasche
Pilchard
Plotze
Pollack
Sardelle
Sardine
Scharbe
Schellfisch
Schlei
Scholle
Seebarsch
Seehecht
Seezunge
Sprotte
Thun
Weissfisch
Wittling

GREECE

Antjuga
Bakaliaros
Chematida
Chromatida
Gados
Giavros
Glinia
Glossa
Glossaki
Hippoglossa
Kaponi
Kephalos
Kyprinos

Lavraki
Lestia
Papalina
Pentiki
Perca chani
Pestropha
Pissi
Regha
Romvos
Sardella
Sardine
Scoumbri
Solomos
Tonnos
Tourna
Tsironi

HONG KONG

Anchovies
Bigeyes
Carp
Crevalles
Croakers
Giant Perch
Grey Mullet
Groupers
Japanese Sea
Perch
Leopard Coral
Trout
Pampano
Pilchards
Red Sea Bream
Round Herring
Sardines
Scads
Whitefish

ITALY

Acciuga
Aringa
Asinello
Brama
Carpa
Cefalo

Halibut
Limanda
Luccio
Maccerello
Merlano
Merluzzo Bianco
Merluzzo Giallo
Molva
Nasello
Passera
Passera Pianuzza
Pesce
Pesce Capone
Rombo Liscio
Salmone
Sardina
Sogliola
Spigola
Spratto
Tinca
Tonno
Triotto
Trota

JAPAN

Bora
Hirasaba
Hobo
Iwashi
Kadoiwashi
Kanagashira
Karei
Katakuchiiwashi
Kawakamasu
Koi
Maguro-rui
Maiwashi
Masu
Nishin
Ohyo
Saba
Sake masu-rui
Shitabirame
Tara

386

NETHERLANDS

Aaldoe
Ansjovis
Baars
Blankvoorn
Bot
Brasem
Forel
Griet
Harder
Haring
Heek
Helibot
Kabeljauw
Karper
Leng
Makree
Pelser
Poon
Salm
Sardien
Schar
Schelvis
Schol
Snoek
Sprot
Tong
Tonijn
Wijting
Witte koolvis
Zeebaars
Zeelt

NEW ZEALAND

Hoki
John Dory
Kingfish
Mackerel
Mullet
Orange Roughy
Perch
Piper
Salmon
Smooth Black
Snapper
Sole
Southern Whiting
Terakihi
Trevally
Trout

PORTUGAL

Alabote
Anchova
Arenque
Arinca
Atum
Bacalhau
Badejo
Biqueirao
Carpa
Donzela
Espadilha
Linguado
Lucio
Perca
Pescada
Petruca
Robalo
Rodovalho
Ruivaca
Ruivo
Salmao
Sarda
Sardinha
Sargo
Solha
Solhao
Tainha
Tenca
Truta

SOUTH AFRICA

Albacore Tuna
Anchovies
Butterfish
Carp
Euthynnus Tuna
Haddock
Hake
Herring
Kabeljou
Kingklip
Maas Banker
Mackerel
Pilchards
Red Roman
Salmon
Sardines
Seventy Four
Skipjack Tuna
Snoek
Sole
Steembras
Stock Fish
Stump Nose
Tongol Tuna
Trout
Yellowfin Tuna

SPAIN

Albadejo
Anchoa
Arenque
Atun
Bacalao
Bermejuela
Boqueron
Caballa
Carpa
Eglefino
Espadin
Halibut
Lenguado
Limanda
Lisa
Lubina
Lucio
Maruca
Merlan
Merluza
Perca
Platija
Remol
Rubios
Salmon
Sardina
Solla
Tenca
Trucha

TURKEY

Alabalik
Bakalyaro
Berlam
Caca
Civisiz kalkan
Derepissi
Dil baligi
Gelincik
Hamsi
Kadife baligi
Kefal
Kirlangic
Kizilgoz
Levrek
Morina
Palatika
Pisi baligi
Ringa
Sardalya
Sazan
Som baligi
Tahta baligi
Tatlisu levregi
Ton baligi
Turna baligi
Uskumru

UNITED KINGDOM

Anchovy
Barbel
Bass
Bloater
Bonito
Bream
Brill
Brisling

Buckling
Carp
Coalfish
Cod
Coley
Dab
Dace
Flounder
Fluke
Grayling
Gurnard
Haddock
Hake
Halibut
Herring
Hoki
John Dory
Keta Salmon
Kipper
Ling
Mackerel
Megrim
Mock Halibut
Mullet Grey
Mullet Red
Norway Haddock
Parrot Fish
Perch
Pike
Pilchard
Plaice

Pole
Pollack
Redfish
Roach
Saithe
Salmon
Sardine
Shad
Sild
Smelt
Snapper
Snoek
Sole Dover
Sole Lemon
Sprat
Tench
Tilapia
Trout
Tuna (Tunny)
Whitebait
Whiting
Witch

**UNITED STATES
OF AMERICA**

Albacore
Alewife
Amberjack
Anchovies
Barb
Barracouta

Barracuda
Bass
Bigeyes
Black Cod
Blackfish
Blueback
Bluefish
Bluegill
Bonito
Bream
Brill
Capelin
Carp
Cero
Char
Chub
Cisco
Coalfish
Cod
Crevalle
Dab
Flounders
Fluke
Gag
Grayling
Grouper
Haddock
Hake
Halibut
Herrings
John Dory

Kingfish
Mackerel
Mahi Mahi
Merluccio
Mullet
Orange Roughy
Perch
Pike
Pilchard
Plaice
Pollock
Pomfrets
Red Snapper
Roach
Saithe
Salmon
Sardine
Shad
Sierra
Skipjack
Snapper
Sole
Sprat
Tench
Tilapia
Trout
Tuna
Wahoo
Whiting
Yellowtail

Abridged Jewish Calendar

2001 (5761-5762)

Fast of Esther	Thursday	March 8th
Purim	Friday	March 9th
First Day Pesach	Sunday	April 8th
Second Day Pesach	Monday	April 9th
Seventh Day Pesach	Saturday	April 14th
Eighth Day Pesach (Yizkor)	Sunday	April 15th
Holocaust Memorial Day	Thursday	April 19th
Israel Independence Day	Thursday	April 26th
Lag B'Omer	Friday	May 11th
First Day Shavout	Monday	May 28th
Second Day Shavout (Yizkor)	Tuesday	May 29th
Fast of Tammuz	Sunday	July 8th
Fast of Av	Sunday	July 29th
First Day Rosh Hashanah	Tuesday	September 18th
Second Day Rosh Hashanah	Wednesday	September 19th
Fast of Gedaliah	Thursday	September 20th
Yom Kippur (Yizkor)	Thursday	September 27th
First Day Succot	Tuesday	October 2nd
Second Day Succot	Wednesday	October 3rd
Shemini Atseret (Yizkor)	Tuesday	October 9th
Simchat Torah	Wednesday	October 10th
First Day Chanucah	Monday	December 10th

2002 (5762-5763)

Fast of Esther	Monday	February 25th
Purim	Tuesday	February 26th
First Day Pesach	Thursday	March 28th
Second Day Pesach	Friday	March 29th
Seventh Day Pesach	Wednesday	April 3rd
Eighth Day Pesach (Yizkor)	Thursday	April 4th
Holocaust Memorial Day	Tuesday	April 9th
Israel Independence Day	Wednesday	April 17th
Lag B'Omer	Tuesday	April 30th
First Day Shavout	Friday	May 17th
Second Day Shavout (Yizkor)	Saturday	May 18th
Fast of Tammuz	Thursday	June 27th
Fast of Av	Thursday	July 18th
First Day Rosh Hashanah	Saturday	September 7th
Second Day Rosh Hashanah	Sunday	September 8th
Fast of Gedaliah	Monday	September 9th
Yom Kippur (Yizkor)	Monday	September 16th
First Day Succot	Saturday	September 21st
Second Day Succot	Sunday	September 22nd
Shemini Atseret (Yizkor)	Saturday	September 28th
Simchat Torah	Sunday	September 29th
First Day Chanucah	Friday	November 30th

Index

Index

Index

Index

Index

Index

Index

Index

Index

Index

Index

ADVERTISEMENT ORDER FORM 2002

Please complete and return Jewish Travel Guide form to us by 1 September 2001

Please reserve the following advertising space in
Jewish Travel Guide 2002:

☐ Full Page   £475   181 x 115 mm
☐ Half Page   £245   91 x 115 mm
☐ Quarter Page   £145   45.5 x 115 mm

(UK advertisers please note that the above rates are subject to VAT)
Special positions by arrangement

☐ **Please insert the attached copy (If setting is required a 10% setting charge will be made.)**

☐ **Copy will be forwarded from our Advertising Agents (*see below*)**

Contact Name: _____

Advertisers Name:_____

Address for invoicing: _____

_____

Tel: _____   Fax: _____

Signed: _____   Title: _____

VAT No:_____

Date:_____

Agency Name (if applicable): _____

Address: _____

_____

Tel: _____   Fax: _____

All advertisements set by the publisher will only be included if they have been signed and approved by the advertiser.

To the Advertising Department
Jewish Travel Guide
Vallentine Mitchell & Co. Ltd.
Newbury House, 890–900 Eastern Avenue,
Newbury Park, Ilford, Essex IG2 7HH
Fax: + 44(0)20-8599 0984. E-mail: jtg@vmbooks.com

Update for Jewish Travel Guide 2002

Readers are asked kindly to draw attention to any errors or omissions. If errors are discovered, it would be appreciated if you could give up-to-date information, referring to page, place, etc., and return this form to the Editor at the address given below.

With reference to the following entry:

Page:

Country:

Entry should read:

Kindly list on separate sheet if preferred.

Signed:_____ Date:_____

Name (BLOCK CAPITALS) _____

Address: _____

_____

Telephone: _____

The Editor
Jewish Travel Guide
Vallentine Mitchell & Co. Ltd.
Newbury House, 890–900 Eastern Avenue,
Newbury Park, Ilford, Essex IG2 7HH
Fax: + 44(0)20-8599 0984. E-mail: jtg@vmbooks.com